# THE LOCKHEED P-38

# LIGHTNING

"It Goes Like Hell".... Kelsey

Milo Burcham bends the
P-38J-20-LO " YIPPEE" into
a roll in springtime 1944.

# THE LOCKHEED P-38
# LIGHTNING

*"It Goes Like Hell".... Kelsey*

## By WARREN M. BODIE

Published in the United States of America in 1991 by:
**Widewing Publications**
Post Office Box 238
Hiawassee, Georgia 30546-0238

Registered Office:
Rt 1, Box 255 C
Hayesville, NC 28904

ISBN 0-9629359-0-5
Library Of Congress Card Number: 91-65419

Book design by Anthony Enyedy
Line drawings by Robert Pike

Printed by Bookbuilders Ltd., Hong Kong

Widewing Publications holds exclusive worldwide distribution rights.

# CONTENTS

# DEDICATION

TO:

My beautiful, faithful, loving, compassionate wife
of nearly a half century, the late, lamented Catherine
Cecelia Larson Bodie . . . .

She was my best friend,
She was the wind beneath my wings.

Only the Good Lord knows how much I miss her.

# FOREWORD

Mr. Warren Bodie's book on the history of the Lockheed P-38 fighter airplane of World War II is the most thoroughly researched and well written book on such a subject that I have ever read. In spite of my close association with most aspects of the P-38 program throughout the life of the type, I learned a great deal about its operational successes and problems encountered in the worldwide use of the aircraft and its pilots. General Ben Kelsey's role as the Army Air Corps project manager and the first pilot to fly the P-38 is well told and completely accurate. The many modifications developed for the P-38 both at the factory in Burbank, California, and in the field, are well documented and clearly shown by excellent photographs. I am proud to have played a part in such a vitally impressive program.

*Clarence L. "Kelly" Johnson*

Clarence L. "Kelly" Johnson*
Lockheed Aircraft Corporation

*\* The ultimately remarkable Kelly Johnson passed away after a long illness on December 21, 1990.*

*The maestro, C.L. "Kelly" Johnson (left) leans on his pride and joy, the XP-80A "Gray Ghost" as test pilot Anthony "Tony" LeVier talks to test pilot James White. The first XP-80 prototype flight had taken place 5 years to the month after the original XP-38 flight. In June 1944, LeVier, just returned from the ETO, checked out on the XP-80 and was then assigned to make the first flights in the improved XP-80A. "Gray Ghost" made its first takeoff on June 10, 1944, at Muroc, California. The 5,000th P-38 had made its flight just three months earlier. Kelly Johnson's other triumphs include the F-104, T-33, U-2, TR-1 and SR-71. (Lockheed)*

# ACKNOWLEDGEMENTS

There is some validity to the general belief that writing a book is much like creating an oil painting or a lithograph. If one only thinks in terms of fiction, that is probably the absolute truth. Even in writing about ancient history, the tone is set by the author's personal feelings and by the reference material that he chooses to employ as his base material; it is always listed in the "Bibliography," if one is provided.

But writing modern history is quite a different thing. The investigative author soon finds that every trail leads to another, many of which can be considered as "hot" trails. If new ground is plowed, people who were absolutely unknown a few years earlier can suddenly take on hero status or be found to deserve tremendous personal or philosophical kinds of respect. The writer soon finds that even small errors in judgment or interpretation can hurt an innocent person. However, the same writer can do a great deal of good in setting the record straight where erroneous stories - even falsehoods - have distorted the real truth. Such distortions are often picked up as bibliographical material, being repeated over the years when some writer finds that it is easier to draw on existing material than to get involved in investigative research.

It may seem odd that my own personal research on the history of the P-38 Lightning, when it became something more than a research project for the *American Aviation Historical Society Journal*, did not have its origins with the airplane designer, Mr. Clarence L. "Kelly" Johnson. Perhaps it was because I was an employee of Lockheed, at that time in middle management at Lockheed Missiles and Space Co. in Sunnyvale, and I was more than a little bit in awe of the obviously brilliant top-level executive, Mr. Johnson.

Eventually, it seemed more logical to contact the man who started the ball rolling in 1936, although he lived nearly 3,000 miles away, and we were unacquainted. Fate intervened, and I left the Trident program to become involved in the new L-1011 commercial venture. Within a short time, I was in contact with a special Lockheed employee, retired Lt. Gen. L. C. Craigie. I told Bill Craigie of my interest in the P-38, and especially about my admiration for a largely unpublicized officer, Benjamin S. Kelsey, since age 15. While I admired Charles Lindbergh in my youth, my respect for Kelsey was closer to a "hero" status because of all that I learned about him. For a man who had received so little recognition, he appealed to me because he was a real "mover and shaker" in the true sense of the term. In my opinion, the man had been instrumental in saving America from some decisive defeats in history by his earlier actions.

Well, General Craigie was the right man to put me in touch with retired Brig. Gen. Ben Kelsey. Not many months later, nearly 20 years ago, I was on my way across America to the Kelsey farm in beautiful Virginia. Mrs. Kelsey and Ben were gracious hosts, and my intensive interviews with the general led to a lasting friendship.

From there, the trails fanned out like wildfire. They led me to Cass Hough, a brilliant scientific man with the aeronautical heart of a fighter ace. The total recall capabilities of such men were overwhelming. They were still very close to Lt. Gen. James Doolittle, so it was not long before I was taping his memories. The inherent warmth of Doolittle, Kelsey, Hough, Craigie, Lt. Gen. John Gerhart, and a dozen or more of the same genre was a pleasant surprise. These men had all enjoyed remarkable careers, often gaining a great deal of fame. As soon as they learned that this was a serious "crusade" of sorts, not aimed at eking out "a penny a word" (a thing that annoyed Kelsey, no end), they all gave generously of their time and knowledge.

Having written the true story of the final flight of the late Ralph Virden, one of Lockheed's most talented test pilots, in order to counter all of the totally erroneous tales of his demise, I proceeded to contact Kelly Johnson about the possibilities of an interview. He granted my request promptly. In the course of a busy working day as he neared retirement from the daily activities in his Advanced Development Projects (ADP) organization, he spent several hours of his valuable time discussing the P-38 and his other projects. It was a shock to learn that no other history writer had ever interviewed him on this specific subject. And yet, as things were in the 1930s, he was the man who had designed the airplane. Oh, it was a complex machine and he had specifications in specific areas of design, but Lt. Ben Kelsey's specifications and Kelly Johnson's design talent made the airplane a reality.

The Clarence Johnson that I know is a remarkably astute, meticulous dresser, kindly and ever-encouraging man. Our interview was not just one of accommodation and politeness; it was enlightening, enjoyable and, above all, friendly.

Of course I am biased. After doing several P-38 articles in a lengthy series, plus articles on the Lockheed XP-49, XP-58, and XP-90 – all of which really surprised Mr. Johnson – I was most fortunate to have him spark my P-38 Symposium panel in 1977 with his presence. The symposium served as a reunion for Johnson and Kelsey. About a year later, I transferred to Mr. Johnson's ADP organization after an interview with his long-time associate, Ben Rich, who succeeded him. The ADP "Skunk Works" had always been the most coveted place of employment in Lockheed.

The list of those who gave so freely of their time, knowledge, remembrances, photographs, drawings, and encouragement reads like an Aviation Who's Who. The people have not been listed in order of rank, volume of material provided or even alphabetically, and that is not accidental. Perhaps most of them realize that if there was to be great accuracy in presenting a definitive history of the P-38, it was a "now or never" proposition. As matters have turned out, the 1980s saw a great change in big corporations. The old core people have either retired or have been lost to us forever. A wave of corporate raiding had changed organizational structures in a dramatic manner: "junk bonds" and aircraft history do not intermingle at all. History is something to be dredged up now and then to use in advertising. Facts have little to do with what is used in the ads. So original records are often destroyed or stored in obscure warehouses. To retrieve even portions of the material becomes expensive; usually it is not "cost effective" to locate them. The fate of Republic Aviation and its history files is but one sad reminder.

Attempting to trace military history in the mammoth file system at Norton AFB after past presidents disbanded the useful Audio-Visual center in Arlington, Virginia, has become ridiculously time consuming and expensive. And Norton AFB is now in danger of being closed. The fate of file access hangs in the balance.

That is just one reason why the assistance of the following people and organizations became so important. My interviews with the late Maj. Gen. James "Buster" Briggs and the late, great Jimmy Mattern provided material that could come from no other source.

My appreciation for the help provided by those listed is boundless: (An asterisk [*] indicates that the person is deceased): Maj. Gen. James Briggs*, William H. Caughlin, Cass Hough, Col. Jack S. Jenkins, James Kunkle, Harvey Christen, Lt. Gen. James H. Doolittle, Col. Ralph Garman, Col. John W. Weltman, Col. Harold Rau*, Col. Chet Patterson, Gayle O. Glenn, Col. Stanley A. Long*, James Mattern*, Thomas E. Lanphier, Jr.*, Jack Ilfrey, W.A. "Dick" Pulver, Col. Harry Dayhuff, Raymond Crawford, Anthony LeVier, Col. James W. Harris III, Arthur Heiden, George McCutcheon, Col. Sammy Pierce, Col. Robert A. Vrilakas, Kenneth Pittman, A. Kevin Grantham, Dustin Carter*, Maj. Gen. Marshall Roth, Col. Frederick G. Hoffman, Joseph Onesty, Col. Raymond Toliver, G. H. "Bert" Estabrook, Col. Joseph Kuhn, Denise Henry, Lt. Gen. L. C. "Bill" Craigie, Robert DeHaven, "Stumpy" Hollinger, Walter Boyne, Louis Casey, Roger A. Freeman, Bernard W. Crandell, Lt. Gen. John K. Gerhart, James McM. Gerschler, Cy Homer*, Maj. Gen. Frank O'D. Hunter*, James D. Hawkins, Mrs. Robert Shafer, Col. Oliver B. "Obie" Taylor, Ralph Virden, Jr., David Tallichet, Neil Harrison*, Russ Rajani and James "Jimmy" Haizlip.*

Joseph Mizrahi, Editor/Publisher of Sentry Magazines, deserves a special salute. How many publishers or editors would commit to a 150,000-word series with 1,000 photographs in a non-contiguous series of 13 articles in their magazines? Most book publishers recoil at the suggestion of more than 90,000 words and 200 or 300 photographs in a book. Our association extends back to 1973. I guess Joe has published about a half million of my written words. He continues to be more than just a little supportive.

The following men were the sources of some outstanding photographs over a period of years; without their contribu-

tions, a tremendous slice of history would never have come to light: Eric Miller, Robert Ferguson, Glen Sunderland, Eric Schulzinger (all with Lockheed), Stephen Hudek, Al Meryman, Kenneth Sumney and Ray Bowers.

Robert Pike has long put up with my unflinching demands for detail accuracy to turn out some remarkably authentic illustrations over a period of 15 years. Without his good work for me, it is most unlikely that anybody would ever have published accurate drawings on the XP-58, XP-38, and the P-38E seaplane proposal. Only Bob and I ever uncovered the proposed P-38 that was to have a 75-mm cannon installed. He was always good natured about every bit of the relationship, despite his time-consuming liaisons with very attractive women. Bob was cursed with good looks and a friendly manner.

Alan Bedford, a quiet and unassuming fighter pilot who was equally good at the controls of an F8F Bearcat or an F3H-2M jet fighter, has been like a brother since we crossed paths in connection with the Radioplane XKD4R-1 rocket drone. We have done a couple of lengthy articles together. Al flew Panthers (F9Fs) off carriers to bomb bridges (as in the movies) during the Korean conflict. He has been a supreme enthusiast who knows his airplanes.

Gayle O. Glenn and I are a generation apart, but we have shared automotive and aviation interests for years. He is like a proximate son who wants to take the helm. It was Gayle who lit the fuse to launch us on the course to a successful P-38 Anniversary Symposium in 1977. We created the Split-S Society to organize and conduct the symposium and to extend the life of some historical materials by at least 100 years. The symposium was so successful that it almost overwhelmed us. It is easy to trace the origins of the present P-38 National Association to that September 1977 meeting.

Naturally there are governmental agencies, companies, and many military organizations to which we are indebted for photographs and historical/technical data. They include:

Lockheed-California Co.
    (now Lockheed Aeronautical Systems Co.)
United States Air Force Audio-Visual Service (MAC)
USAF Historical Research Center (USAFHRC)
United States Army Office of Information
USAF Office of History (Pentagon)
United States Air Force Museum
    (Charles Worman and his staff)
National Air and Space Museum - Smithsonian Institution
National Archives
Imperial War Museum (London, England)
*Flight* magazine (Great Britain)
Pursuits Unlimited (Russ Rajani, Fayetteville, GA)

*"Great cause to give thanks"* - Shakespeare.

# PROLOGUE

Two unsung heroes of World War II were Col. Cass Hough (Deputy Chief) and Col. Benjamin S. Kelsey (Chief) at the Technical Operations Unit in Bovingdon, not far from Eighth Fighter Command Headquarters (AJAX) and London. The picture was taken about June 21, 1944. For various reasons, the organization had no less than five different names within two years. It appears that they had just inherited a new P-38 to add to the stable of test aircraft. Colonel Hough had commanded the unit's predecessor organizations throughout most of 1943 under Gen. Hunter. When Lt. Gen. Doolittle reorganized the Eighth Air Force, he requested that Kelsey take command and expand the scope of operations with Hough as his DCO. (As originally created under Doolittle, the organization name was Operational Engineering.)

One cold, crisp day in January 1942, less than a month after the Imperial Japanese Navy had attacked our key base at Pearl Harbor, I found myself standing in front of Gen. Henry H. Arnold's cluttered desk in Army Air Force Headquarters in Washington. We had just ended an intensive meeting, and he punctuated it with "Kelsey, what makes you think this P-38 fighter will really be any good?" To make his point, he said, "The Me 110 (really Bf 110) is a two-engine fighter, but it's no good."

I responded with, "General, to begin with the P-38 is a very different kind of airplane. It isn't a two seater, it is much more advanced in design, it's faster and it's right."

Content that I had made my point, he came back impatiently with something like, "Oh, all right Kelsey, all right. Get going and get on with it."

(The rapidly growing Army Air Corps had been reorganized on June 22, 1941, with all commands being unified under the direction of Maj. Gen. H. H. Arnold. Less than six months later, he was faced with commanding a war machine with the greatest growth rate of any organization in history.)

That meeting had, in effect, emphasized just how different the P-38 was from any prior concept. The primary subject of that assembly was concerned with the possibility that we might have to ferry fighters across the Atlantic to England. A year or two earlier, that would have been unthinkable, let alone possible. I had been called to Washington from Wright Field by my boss, Maj. Gen. Oliver P. Echols. He took me in to see Gen. Arnold. Brig. Gen. Carl Spaatz was in the office with him. I knew that all my commitments had come home to roost.

The first few minutes of that meeting had gone something like this:

Q. "Kelsey, what can we do to get enough range out of the P-38s to fly them to England?"

A. "Well, General, it can't be done without drop tanks. But it just happens that Lockheed's thirteenth drop tank design has satisfactorily completed tests, including a demonstration flight of more than 2,200 miles."

Q. "Kelsey, where in hell did you get the authority for this?"

A. "There wasn't any, General."

Q. "Okay! Okay!" The General took a long breath. "How long will it take to get the tanks that we need?"

A. "If we cycle the planes already delivered back through the factory, we should be able to start in about 90 days."

Q. "Why in heaven's name will it take so long?"

A. "Well, General, you know that we have been forbidden by directive for several years to put external tanks on fighters, so . . . "

The General ended that meeting with a terse, direct order to "get this thing moving."

Although the idea of flying a single-seat fighter for 2,200 miles seemed pretty startling at that time, a slightly later version of the P-38 drop tank provided a 3,300-mile range. Furthermore, a proposed raised tail modification of the airplane was part of a program to get a 5,000-mile range by using floats in place of drop tanks in order to fly the planes as far as Australia if necessary. Events in the Pacific War overtook that requirement, so the experiment was dropped. But the cooperation between the development agencies in the USAAF and the main contractor was, in itself, unique in making available a capability at the time it was needed. This was even more notable when you consider that it went beyond the limitations of specific authorization and any contractual provisions.

In fact, all of the performance parameters to which the P-38 was designed and built were, at the time, staggering advances. The fighter was specifically required to have a 360-mph top speed, whereas its immediate predecessors had been obligated to attain 300 mph, a speed that none of the prototypes could even approach. The P-38 was to operate successfully at altitudes exceeding 20,000 feet, where our new generation of bombers would be flying. Not even the newest foreign fighters of 1936-37 were intended to fight above 20,000 feet. Our new fighter was to employ armament providing firepower that was three or four times that of warplanes then in service. The armament included a cannon, something that had never even been seriously considered for an American fighter plane in the single-seat category.

Using a devious approach to avoid the policy roadblocks, we even referred to it as an "Interceptor." That was actually a semantic dodge in working with the Military Requirement and the Type Specifications for the design competition in order to deviate widely from conventional design and operational philosophy dictated by Congress, the Executive Branch appointees and the War Department. At a later date, there was an attempt by an unsophisticated aviation media to read into that terminology some mission significance. However, between the Air Corps Board and the Experimental Engineering Branch of General Echols' Materiel Division, there was absolutely no confusion. From the outset, the P-38 was to do anything that any fighter had to do, yet not be constrained by preconceived limitations imposed by some hypothetical mission.

The procurement system under which the airplane was obtained was different, too. This particular system applied to only a very few aircraft, such as the Boeing XB-15, the Douglas XB-19, and the Bell XP-39, for instance. The Type Specification – which established the basis for the design competition – included extremely ambitious goals. It set minimums which expressly precluded any simple extension of existing designs or service articles. A selected group of contractors, limited to about four in number for each competition, were invited to bid in this classified competition. These contractors were, in each case, selected on the basis of demonstrated capability arising from previous construction experience using advanced techniques, design studies or related activities. Lockheed and Bell had been included because of the technologically advanced designs they had submitted for the Multiplace Fighter competition, which Bell produced as the XFM-1. Lockheed's XFM-2 design was not as radical in concept as the Bell design, but its real potential for ultimate success was greater.

Any well-researched history will reveal the chronological and statistical milestones as well as the roles played by the various personalities and organizations in the drama of the P-38. But the significance of these can only be appreciated with a feeling for the environment in which the specifications were created and the actions taken. Isolationism was the preponderant guiding principle in politics and in foreign affairs in 1936. Defense of our shores was the governing military philosophy in line with isolationist policy. Economically, the nation was just emerging from the devastating Great Depression, so there was little money available for weapons development or procurement. The aeronautical industry could only expect orders for about 200 aircraft of one operational type in a single year. At Wright Field, just outside of Dayton, the action center for engineering and procurement for the Air Corps employed fewer than 100 military and 1,000 civilian personnel. It was not an area in which anybody had trouble finding a parking space.

This was an era – the mid-thirties – in which the bombing plane was in the ascendancy and the fighter (still categorized as the pursuit, a holdover from World War I) was the poor-as-a-churchmouse relative. Emphasis was placed on observation (for the ground army), attack and bombardment. The pursuit was tolerated, not considered to be of much military importance, but it had good public relations value.

But even the bombardment element suffered from a penny-pinching mentality. The thirteen Y1B-17 Flying Fortress service test articles ordered came close to being the end of the line. Under the circumstances, it is not inconceivable that small policy changes would have wound up forcing Boeing to sell Model 299 prototypes to Japan or Russia. Seversky sold close cousins of the P-35 to Russia and to Japan, and Vought sold its 1936 pursuit plane from the Wright Field competition to a Japanese buyer. It was even a greatly improved version of the fighter we had evaluated; all of the best Northrop and Vought design data went with it, and it was all sold at a financial loss. So few people were involved in or interested in national defense – and the obstacles were so overwhelming – that the XB-15, XB-19, XP-39 and XP-38 were procured and manufactured under the tightest security we could muster. Of course this also tended to obscure from any potential enemies that our very restricted activity was really well advanced technologically.

Austerity approaching poverty influenced all facets of aircraft development and procurement. Design studies for projected fighter performance requirements indicated a demand for powerplant outputs that did not even exist and, with the resources available, could not possibly be developed in the critical time frame. The only viable alternative was to use a multiple-engine configuration, which led directly to our Type Specification to which the four contenders for a P-38 contract had to adhere. Thus the configuration was as much born from compelling necessity as from any conceptual desires. Frankly, there was a strong antipathy, if not downright hostility, toward a two-engined fighter as revealed by Gen. Arnold's lingering doubts as late as 1942. It meant venturing into untested waters. However, the remarkable excellence of the design did much to minimize characteristics and maximize some of the inherent benefits.

In 1936, even the liquid-cooled inline engine was suspect and belittled. Air-cooled radial engines were firmly entrenched in military and naval circles to the virtual exclusion of a type we had pioneered with so successfully in the late 1920s and early 1930s, the monoblock inline engine cooled with an ethylene-glycol solution. Thanks to the efforts of Gen. Malin Craig, absolutely no funds were available for years to develop two-stage, two-speed mechanical superchargers for any of our aero engines. Therefore, the Air Corps was committed to the turbo-supercharger that had been under development for well over a decade.

While the Navy avoided the liquid-cooled engine like the plague as the carrier-based airplane came into its own, the Air Corps applied great effort to development of the Allison V-12 after being beset with a plethora of engine failures in a wide selection of air-cooled engines during the 1935-36 pursuit competition. With intensive development the General Motors-backed Allison became one of the best liquid-cooled engines of all time. Progress by 1941 had been so good that a special demonstration flight of several P-38s was quietly arranged to demonstrate just how good the airplane and the engine were. Only the Japanese attack on Pearl Harbor caused cancellation of the trans-continental speed dash, totally unknown to the general public, that would have publicly corroborated the claims made for the combination of airplane and engine. By the fall of 1941, the P-38 had become an operational reality. It was only a few short months earlier that the first XP-51 Mustang was delivered to the Air Corps and the first XP-47B Thunderbolt took to the air for the first time.

New to the realm of service fighters, and in many cases of all aircraft, were characteristics such as heavy weight, high wing loading, great increases in speed, low drag, all-metal control surfaces, flush riveting and butt-joint skins, tricycle landing gear, self-sealing fuel tanks, armor plate, high-lift flaps and tremendous increases in firepower. What was accepted as normal wing loading for the P-38 had been, up to that time, in the exclusive realm of the most advanced racing and record-breaking aircraft. All of these characteristics had appeared in the P-38. In one detail for instance, the combination of heavy weight, high landing speed and (frequently) short runways expedited the development of alloy wheels, high-pressure tires and disc brakes. Initial flights in the XP-38 revealed that development in these areas had lagged behind the demands of modern aircraft performance capabilities.

Because of its low-drag aerodynamic shape and relatively heavy weight, the P-38 fighter accelerated to high speeds faster than any previous airplane. Coupled with its ability to reach very high altitudes, it was the P-38 that introduced us to compressibility, the frontier of transonic problems. The precise speeds reached in dives from altitude is immaterial. Pilots involved in testing, exploring the phenomena of absolute control loss due to compressibility and in operational situations, were frequently engaged in dives to terminal velocity. The dives revealed extraordinarily fast accelerations, and pilots experienced all of the startling control and recovery difficulties attendant upon the changes in airflow as the vehicle approached the speed of sound. Our current ability to fly safely at these speeds and to penetrate to supersonic speeds was facilitated by the pioneering exploits of the Lockheed Lightning.

In many ways . . . in operations, design, manufacturing and progressive development . . . the P-38 was the trailblazer for an entire new generation of aircraft. For the era in which it was designed and built, it was a quantum leap forward in the field of aeronautics, just as the Lockheed SR-71 was about a quarter of a century later.

Author Warren Bodie has demonstrated in numerous previous writings that he is obviously in the front rank of popular press aviation writers. His determination to delve deeply into the underlying causes, effects, decisions, capabilities and reasons leading to the conception of an aircraft which advanced the state of the art so rapidly in the aeronautical field is reflected in his product. His desire to maximize technical accuracy without compromising a story in a popular medium is refreshingly unique. He has accurately reached independent conclusions about P-38 episodes, advances and successes that I had long believed would never be acknowledged in historical records. This manuscript, I have no doubt, will be expanded significantly by the time it is published. I have no reason to believe that Warren's continuing research will by any less exacting. The ultimate publication will, therefore, become a reliable historical benchmark for those seeking knowledge about a great airplane.

s/Benjamin S. Kelsey
Brigadier General, USAF (Ret)
Sherwood Farm
Stevensburg, Virginia

(After a brilliant career, this self-effacing prince
of a man died at his home in Stevensburg on March 3, 1981.
His brilliance *is not diminished in death.)*

# FROM PROTOTYPE TEST

## TO TRAINING

## TO COMBAT

ABOVE: Lt. Ben Kelsey and Lockheed XP-38 at Wright Field.

LEFT ABOVE: Lt. Col. Frank B. James, C.O. of the 55FG at McChord Field, Washington, with P-38G-15-LO.

LEFT: At Nuthampstead, Lt. Col. Jack S. Jenkins demonstrates a tactic to Lt. Russell Gustke. "Texas Ranger" was a P-38H.

# INTRODUCTION

It was beautiful to see in flight. It had a distinctive, almost melodic sound that was pleasant to the senses. As viewed by almost any prospective pilots in the setting of the 1940-45 era, it was awesome. Although it tended to intimidate some who saw it as a fearsome machine that was beyond the capability of even the most advanced flying school pilots to control, it was remarkably easy to operate and docile to fly. The destructive firepower and blazing speed characteristics exhibited by the aircraft could hardly have been comprehended just five years before Pearl Harbor became the target of the Japanese. That was true even for military pilots flying first-line fighters in 1936. What was this multi-personality aircraft that was so awe inspiring? It was, of course, the Lockheed P-38 Lightning.

To tell the story of the P-38 without telling the full story of the twin-engine, single-seat, propeller-driven fighter would be all but impossible. While the Lightning ultimately proved to be the only fighter in all of World War II that was mass produced and could meet all of those other criteria, there were more than a dozen other serious attempts by a half-dozen nations to develop a viable fighter with those specific qualities. That they all failed is a matter of record.

One perverse element of the P-38's great success was that the fighter was ultimately penalized for that success by the very nation it was serving with distinction. Designer C. L. "Kelly" Johnson's early proposals to install Rolls-Royce/Packard Merlin engines featuring mechanical two-stage supercharging instead of turbosupercharging offered significant performance and reliability advantages. Weight and complexity would have been reduced, fuels would have become almost no problem at all and all-round performance showed important gains. Having failed to provide a second production source for the complicated Lightning at a critical stage in the war – while

having second-sourced the P-51, P-47, B-24, B-17 and the Corsair – the War Production Board (WPB) was naturally opposed to any change that would seriously reduce production for even a short time. What was needed was divine intervention on the part of someone having real political influence, and nobody was available to play that role.

Few people realize how truly remarkable it was for numerous engineering developments to reach production status at the precise moment of greatest need. Brig. Gen. Benjamin Kelsey, who at one time was the ENTIRE Fighter Projects Office staff in the old Army Air Corps, made the following statement in 1965, about 10 years after his retirement:

"If there is a good story in the early developments of World War I, there is an even more exciting one in the evolution of the World War II fighter which came into existence in the mid-1930s. Everything had to happen at once for success."

And happen it did. The General Electric turbosupercharger, under development for a decade and a half, suddenly moved from an experimental device of dubious value to mass production. Tiny Allison Engineering came up with one of the four best liquid-cooled engines in the world. Both England and America were roused from a fitful sleep and overcame strong anti-war and isolationist sentiments to select a new French-developed automatic cannon as a standard weapon, swallowing a lot of pride in the process. The British were first to recognize their basic shortcomings in weaponry. They put the cannon into production as the clouds of war loomed ominously. A bit later, as the United States became the "Arsenal of Democracy," that weapon was converted to American standards and rushed into mass production. These were but a few of the nearly simultaneous developments that were combined in the Lockheed Model 22 aircraft design that became the potent P-38.

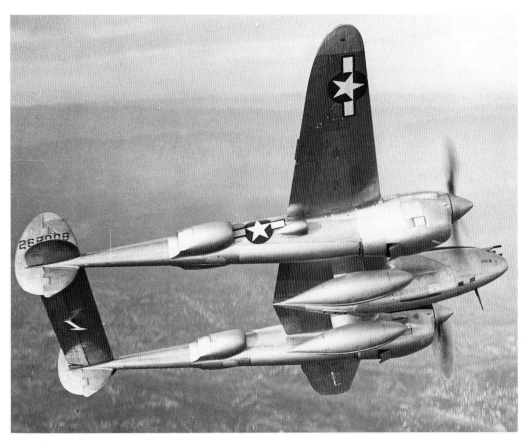

*LEFT: The ultimate Lockheed Lightning fighter, a P-38L-1-LO, demonstrates flight on one engine as it flies near its training base at Van Nuys, California, late in 1944. That San Fernando Valley base was a key component of the Fourth Air Force. (USAAF)*

*RIGHT: Noble holder of title of being the greatest weight-carrying fighter of World War II, a Lockheed Lightning shows its underside as it banks away. This P-38J-10-LO did not enjoy the benefits of boosted aileron controls and compressibility dive flaps; nevertheless, America's top aces gained their victories in this and earlier models. (Lockheed)*

*BOTTOM: With the California sun reflecting on its flush-skin structure, the first P-38J-15-LO was photographed by Eric Miller in December 1943, just two short years after America's Pacific air power was all but wiped out by the Japanese. A mere handful of earlier model Lightnings had an enormous effect in deterring a major Japanese success against New Guinea and Australia. The Yamamoto Mission was not among the least of those deterrent actions in far away places. (Eric Miller, Lockheed)*

Before anyone can really evaluate the aeronautical contribution of the Lockheed P-38 Lightning in its various developed forms and contents, that person must understand what America and, indeed, the world was all about in the 1930s. It is easy to forget or be unaware of the fact that the P-38 was first conceived, constructed and flown in that much disturbed, yet ironically lethargic, decade.

Most of the world suffered from the Great Depression that engulfed it as the decade of the 1930s unfolded. Anyone who has suffered through significant economic deprivation may come close to having the "feel" of the Depression decade. Until Europe plunged into war in 1939, open political dissent or strife surfaced only sporadically in the United States. In almost every

case, what dissent appeared was centered on economic factors. While we are now deeply involved in foreign affairs everywhere on the globe and are sometimes virtually overwhelmed by the impact of instantaneous worldwide communications, such was hardly the case in the 1930s. Today, vast numbers of people are almost totally aware of world conditions and tensions within minutes of their actual occurrence. It was a very different world before 1939.

There was a time – a long, drawn-out time between 1930 and 1940 – when prolonged poverty was a way of life. Unemployment in the United States affected over 25 percent of the workforce. The actual figures will never be known for certain because the government was small at the time and lacked effective systems and procedures for accumulation of such data. One out of every four employable persons was without hope of finding work, and that situation persisted for several years. State and federal funds for social aid simply did not exist. Eventually the U.S. banking system collapsed, just as the stock and bond markets had at an earlier date.

The mood of the nation was bleak. Tarpaper shack enclaves sprang up in the shadows of skyscrapers in most of the big cities. Breadlines, soup kitchens and the pitiful apple sellers on downtown street corners were commonplace. "Buddy, can you spare a dime?" was a national password, and the now nearly extinct hobo might, in those days, have been your former employer.

Franklin Delano Roosevelt was elected to replace a largely hide-bound and ineffective Herbert Hoover in the presidency and took immediate and radical steps aimed at putting the people back to work or on the road to recovery. The National Recovery Act (NRA) was to become a household word within months. Eventually, hundreds of thousands of men worked on federal programs, with the WPA (Works Progress Administration) being the largest of these under Roosevelt's New Deal.

Recovery from that astoundingly deep depression was slow, agonizingly slow. Mistakes were unavoidable. Factory managements often engaged in lengthy but mostly futile struggles to reopen; some never returned to productive activities. It is ironic that F.D.R. rode in an aristocratic Pierce-Arrow limousine at his inaugural procession in 1933, only to see that manufacturer's business founder in the same year. More than 5000 banks closed their doors, and the United States Steel Corporation's net worth was only 8 percent of what it had been in 1930. The population of the U.S. at the time Roosevelt became president was about 125 million, with an active labor force of about 45 to 50 million. By the best estimates, as many as 17 million people were unemployed at the time, or possibly a third of the labor force.

It is nothing short of remarkable that a small, barely surviving aircraft company, which had never even attempted to produce any purely military aircraft, should conceive and construct an outstanding advanced fighting machine that has to be looked upon as one of the most underrated aircraft of all time. That was the Detroit-Lockheed YP-24, first flown in the late summer of 1931. Potential success was effectively blocked when Detroit Aircraft skidded into bankruptcy, dragging the California-based Lockheed with it.

Even more remarkable is the fact that Lockheed rose from an early grave to enjoy modest success in commercial aircraft production and then win a hard-fought competition for development and production of the most advanced fighting aircraft built in America before the outbreak of World War II. When it was designed, the Lockheed Aircraft Corporation was again going against the grain - the completely restructured firm had never produced a single military combat-type aircraft. Although it could not be said that 1936 or 1937 were inspirational years in the U.S.A., the minuscule design staff at Burbank managed to conceive and design the most totally radical and advanced fighting aircraft built anywhere in the 1930s. That was Lockheed's Model 22, far more widely recognized as the XP-38. The format adopted was brazenly radical in a world that all but ignored single-seat, twin-engine fighters. That alone set the XP-38 apart. But that was only a tiny part of its advanced concept.

In a worldwide industry still addicted to metal tube (and, yes, even wood frame) structures covered with fabric, the Lockheed design featured butt-jointed metal skins with flush riveting throughout. External bracing had been avoided like a plague; it was the first fighter anywhere to feature a tricycle landing gear that was fully retractable, and every wheel opening was also totally faired in with tight-fitting covers. Extremely heavy armament was fully concentrated in the central nacelle. All control surfaces were metal covered at a time when fabric-covered control surfaces dominated the scene. The list of other advanced features would be extremely long.

All of this came about in a nation overwhelmingly isolationist and, therefore, bitterly opposed to war in any form. That such a combat machine should even survive in the prevailing political and financial environment is truly another remarkable happening. To have it go on to become one of the world's great combat aircraft of all time nearly boggles the senses. Later versions of the XP-38 may not have been as pleasing to the visual senses, but the demands of warfare are not as well served by beauty as they are by efficiency.

In the eyes of one special aviation great, Gen. James Doolittle, a man with tremendous knowledge relating to the necessities best suited to the conduct of effective warfare, the P-38 Lightning may not have been the best fighter of World War II, but he does concede that this can probably be attributed to factors unrelated to the aircraft's capabilities. Strategic and tactical doctrine proved to be a severe handicap to utilization of the type at the time the first groups were deployed in northern Europe (the ETO), first in the fall of 1942 and again in 1943. The mode of operation left much to be desired. Early P-47Ds and P-51Bs would have fared poorly under the rules prevailing, but it is necessary to recognize that neither type was developed or mass produced until later.

Pilots with little more than advanced flying training, little if any gunnery training and not even a scintilla of pseudo combat training were pitted against some of the most competent and aggressive *Luftwaffe* pilots in combat-proven aircraft. Allison's newly developed V-1710 engine, heavily boosted with turbosupercharging, was frankly prone to indigestion on a diet of British aviation fuel. (The reliable Merlin engine responded poorly to any attempts to boost it with turbosupercharging.)

General Doolittle expressed the opinion that the P-38 was surely at its very best when operating in the various Pacific theaters of operation and in the lower combat altitudes and warmer climes of the Mediterranean Theater (MTO). On balance, the Lightning - in his personal opinion - was far ahead of all but one or two of the most outstanding fighters of World War II. It was certainly the most versatile, outstripping even its contemporaries of the war years because it served widely and effectively in combat as an air-to-air combat fighter, long-range escort fighter, dive bomber/skip bomber, strategic (pinpoint and saturation) bomber (with bombardier), tactical (ground attack) fighter-bomber, photographic reconnaissance aircraft and radar-equipped night fighter.

Lockheed P-38s have been credited with many "firsts," often at the expense of credibility. As an example, public relations officials and some media members stated that it was the only U.S. military aircraft in production on December 7, 1941, that was continuing in production on VJ Day, 1945. However, it can lay claim to being the only AAF fighter actually in volume production status for first-line squadron service on that infamous date and was continuously in production when hostilities ceased in the Far East.

No other fighter anywhere on the globe was flown with a tricycle landing gear before the P-38 demonstrated that feature.

It was the first aircraft known to have encountered the phenomenon of compressibility. The airplane's high-flying capability coupled with a predisposition to accelerate rapidly in a dive caused it to reach a limiting "Mach's number" long before any other type encountered that almost unknown phenomenon.

Taken individually or collectively, the P-38 Lightning was the first fighter-type aircraft to demonstrate the capability of flying across the North Atlantic Ocean for delivery to Europe (accomplished "in spades" as part of Operation BOLERO in the summer of 1942.)

No other fighter (or any other known aircraft for that matter) was ever equipped with irreversible power-boosted flight controls before late-series P-38s adopted them as standard (all modern high-performance aircraft are now equipped with power-boosted controls).

A P-38 was the first fighter anywhere to fly with two full-size aerial torpedoes . . . in fact, no other fighter ever demonstrated such a capability; it was evidently the first fighter aircraft ever to carry and launch such a weapon.

Early in the war, a production P-38 was the first – if not only – fighter type able to demonstrate a nonstop, unrefueled range capability of more than 3,000 miles, and within months of that demonstration, any production P-38 had the inherent ability to challenge that mileage.

No other fighter, including the Mustang or Thunderbolt, ever toted a 4,000-pound bomb load in combat in the war – Lightnings demonstrated that feat on numerous missions.

Most importantly, it was *exclusively* the only mass-produced twin-engine, single-seat, propeller-driven fighter of World War II.

While the P-38 possessed superb fighting capabilities, the F-5 versions that were developed from the pre-war F-4 for photographic work were, without any doubt, the finest photo-reconnaissance aircraft of the war years. Attributes included range, speed, altitude capability and a pod capable of housing several cameras.

Critics of the Lightning seem to have been concentrated in the ETO and in the AAF training centers; therefore, any responsible rebuttal has to be directed at those sectors. First of all we must recall that the Eighth Air Force Bomber Command was desperately attempting to prove the doctrine of daylight bombing. The Royal Air Force was convinced by earlier attempts that the results would be unacceptable. Germany's *Luftwaffe* had encountered even less success with daylight bombing.

When USAAF Boeing B-17s in large numbers struck at targets deep inside the Continent without escorts in the summer of 1943, the daylight bombing doctrine was tested to the breaking point. VIIIth Fighter Command had long since been stripped of its P-38 groups for North African operations, and external fuel tanks for P-47s were mostly in the unpopular planning stage. Rolls-Royce Merlins and North American Mustangs were only being mated at Hucknall by the fall of 1942; a few energetic British engineers and pilots shotgunned the marriage of high-altitude Merlins to Mustang I airframes and reported the marriage to Maj. Thomas Hitchcock. His "pipeline" to the White House lit a fuse in Washington and at Inglewood, but even then the first Merlin-powered P-51s were not ready for combat until more than 12 months later.

What is evident here is that some luck, a few aggressive engineers and potent political connections played a massive part in the ultimate success of the P-51 fighter. Had the RAF taken delivery of half a dozen or more Lightning I fighters in 1941, had even one aircraft been sent to Rolls-Royce Hucknall and had a couple of high-altitude Merlins been available for installation then, P-38s might well have been given an injection of new life. All models of the P-38 from the F model on had range capabilities that could not even have been foreseen in the P-47 and P-51 in late 1941. Had there been a P-38 liaison like Tommy Hitchcock, the course of history would surely have been altered significantly.

In the meantime, where were the P-38s? They were where the P-47s and P-51s weren't! They were successfully combating the Nazis in North Africa, Sicily and ultimately in Italy. Defense of Alaska and the Aleutians was almost entirely in the hands of P-38 and P-40 pilots. A thin line of defense in Australia and New Guinea consisted entirely of P-38s and the outclassed P-40s. Oh, there were some P-39s and P-40s, but any success the Allies may have enjoyed would have been far more difficult to attain if at least a handful of P-38s was not available.

Maj. Gen. George C. Kenney, formerly a dynamo with the Materiel Command and then commander of the Fourth Air Force, was placed in command of the Southwest Pacific Allied Air Forces under General MacArthur in mid-1942. Allied forces were in peril of losing control of the entire area, including Australia, and the air force was virtually inept in combating Imperial Japanese airpower.

Before leaving for Australia, (then) Maj. Gen. Kenney – knowing that Gen. Hap Arnold, a proponent of lightweight fighters and bombers with long range, was no real admirer of the P-38 Lightning – got Arnold to commit 50 new P-38s and an appropriate number of Fourth Air Force pilots to his new command. Suffice it to say, Kenney became a great advocate of the P-38, demanding delivery of more and more throughout the war. After all, you don't argue with success.

War in the Aleutians was no picnic. While there was not a great deal of raucous air combat of the type more indigenous to the ETO, flying conditions and operations over great distances of largely unmapped territory made the P-38 a more than welcome addition to the Alaskan Command. Lt. Stanley Long (later Col. Long), one of the first to fight way out there at the end of the Aleutian chain, loved the P-38 and continued to love it long after he was assigned to fly more modern types.

Thousands of miles away in North Africa, Lt. Jack Ilfrey became an ace while flying the P-38 as 1942 came to an end. He did tours in Lightnings and Mustangs throughout the war, and he has great admiration for the performance of the twin-engine battler. By way of contrast, Lt. Leonard "Kit" Carson (later Colonel), with more than 600 hours of good training under his belt, was with the second P-51B group to go operational in the Eighth Air Force, but that was not until the end of 1943. Carson became a multiple ace on the P-51, developing a high regard for the type. He has few good things to say about the P-38; however, since he did not fly one in combat, his comparisons may be somewhat biased. Both Long and Ilfrey did go operational on the later Mustangs. To be objective, much as in choosing cars or political candidates, each person defends that choice. So it is with fighter aircraft.

Harking back to Army Air Force's expansion days in the early 1940s it is necessary to recall that there were few pilots qualified to fly high-performance multiengined aircraft. Quite logically, when young inexperienced pilots were assigned to fly a 400-mph twin-engine fighter, not a few of them quickly discovered that they were overmatched. As if that was not bad enough, training command personnel were frequently not up to the job. If pilots were assigned to war zones with as few as 10 to 15 hours logged in a P-38, or had never fired the guns or been through an OTU (Operational Training Unit), it is easy to imagine what might happen if a prop was to run away on take-off. Many youngsters were killed as a result of panic before Gen. Barney Giles commissioned a senior Lockheed test pilot, Jimmy Mattern, to demonstrate P-38 flight capabilities before students throughout the United States. With a concerted training syllabus approved and placed in effect, accident rates dropped appreciably even as the number of trainees increased rapidly.

Despite a dearth of long-range escort fighters in the United Kingdom in the summer of 1943, Bomber Command made the great decision to attack targets in Schweinfurt and Regensburg, deep inside the Third Reich. Massed bomber formations had to perform perfectly if losses were to be kept within acceptable limits. Timing errors, weather and a host of other "Gremlins" conspired to sabotage perfection, so fierce and relentless attacks by home defense fighters and flak took a terrible toll of B-17 bombers and crewmen; the daylight bombing doctrine was severely wounded. It was time to either abandon the doctrine or to provide some effective fighter protection . . . a thing that had not been foreseen when the concept of precision daylight bombing was developing in the latter half of the 1930s.

At least three command decisions were made with respect to the escort fighter. New long-range fighters would be designed and produced. From the outset it had to be obvious that such an approach, at best, would mean long delays in carrying out the mission of destroying German production facilities. Nevertheless, the effort was initiated. The second decision was aimed specifically at fighter range extension, which meant reversal of a long-standing attitude that had existed for years. Air Technical Service Command, affected manufacturers and Col. Cass Hough's Technical Operations Section in VIIIth Fighter Command were virtually given *carte blanche* authorization to proceed apace to develop and produce viable range extension systems. (One scheme involved towing P-47s to combat areas behind bombers, then releasing the fighters to defend the bombers.) As an interim measure, every P-38 group that had adequate training was pulled out of the Continental Air Defense Command and sent to the United Kingdom for escort duties, beginning in late summer 1943. (It was long overdue.)

Few, if any, of the critics have ever looked objectively at the fight-at-odds into which the Lightnings were catapulted in 1943. Thrown into the breech at a time when the bomber force was reeling from unacceptable losses and when no other fighter – American or British – could penetrate continental air space by more than 100 miles, more or less, the Lightnings carried the full load. Facilities were not prepared, the new pilots were neither combat wise nor familiar with operating in the area, and they arrived to face one of the worst winters in European history. AAF depots were soon faced with supporting no less than three main types of fighters for the Eighth AF, and every one of those had a different type engine. Talk about your logistics nightmares!

For several interminable months, the *only* escort fighters that could penetrate deep into European air space to escort bombers were the P-38 Lightnings with their dual 165-gallon external tanks. The airplane came through in the face of tremendous adversity.

Neither the P-38 pilots, mechanics nor facilities were prepared to operate efficiently in that bitter winter, and no other Allison-powered aircraft had ever operated at altitudes above 20,000 feet over Europe for even an hour. No test data had been gathered to reveal how turbosupercharged V-1710s would perform with the low-quality fuels that were to be provided in Great Britain, so the Allisons suddenly encountered some severe digestive problems. How was anyone to know that the engine type would not be happy under the command of pilots who had never before been asked to fly for hours at 25,000 feet or more, who had never even released a drop tank, who knew little if anything about long-range cruise control and who were being ordered to fly twice as far into enemy-dominated territory as the combat-hardened Thunderbolt pilots had ever been able to venture? Any suggestions that fewer than 150 of the twin-engined fighters would be delegated to protect up to 600 or 700 heavy bombers and medium bombers in the face of attack by hundreds of home defense fighters over periods of hours at a time would be scoffed at if described in a fiction narrative. But this was not fiction.

Until satisfactory expendable drop tanks could be developed for the many Thunderbolts and forthcoming P-51B and D Mustangs, it was up to the Lightnings to carry the load. That they did the job is history.

Weren't we fortunate to have a man like Gen. Jimmy Doolittle for a crucial change in management when it was sorely needed? And isn't it remarkable that the man-of-the-hour needed to get the VIIIth Fighter Command up to "raging bull" status, Maj. Gen. William Kepner, was there to support Doolittle? The latter was absolutely correct in focusing on one main fighter type, the P-51D, for his inventory. But the pragmatic Jimmy Doolittle did the best job possible with what he had until those new Mustangs could be melded with both experienced and new pilots in great numbers.

Gen. George Kenney had done essentially the same thing about a year earlier in the Southwest Pacific, concentrating on Lockheed P-38s for the job to the exclusion of all other types when possible. When civilian P-47 specialist Charles Lindbergh demonstrated the full capabilities of P-38J and L models, Kenney's judgment proved to be of the highest order.

One highly respected author pretty well summed up the situation in Europe when he wrote: "Probably the greatest single contribution of the Eighth Air Force to victory in Europe was the star part its fighters played in attaining combat superiority in continental air space. Originally furnished for bomber protection, the U.S. fighters came to be a potent offensive weapon."

Lightnings were an effective part of the Eighth Air Force, and they were often the only competent game in town at other wide-spread combat zones around the globe. The tale of the development and employment of the Lockheed Lightning is an exciting, nearly overwhelming story. To tell all of that story is not within our capabilities, but many of the most significant aspects are to be revealed as truthfully as our detailed research can make it within these pages.

First Lieut. Ernest
Fiebelkorn, ace.
A (not so) little friend
to the 8AF bombers.

1

# CHAPTER 1

## Prelude to an Air Force: Depression, Isolationism, Service Rivalry and Politics

A Considering the state of the union in the disastrous days that followed the Wall Street stock market debacle of October 1929, who would imagine that officials of the struggling four-year-old United States Army Air Corps would appear at the door of an unpretentious, dingy red brick factory on Campeau Avenue at the Detroit River hoping to buy a new pursuit plane. What made it preposterous was the fact that the company had never built a military airplane before and it had not even been designed. It had merely been proposed by Lockheed Aircraft's chief engineer way out west in California. Gerard "Gerry" Vultee had talked about such an airplane at Wright Field as commercial airplane orders continued to diminish under pressure of the Great Depression.

Members of the plebeian Army Air Corps certainly could not approach a manufacturer with promises of near-term wealth or success. They, themselves, were struggling just to exist in the face of parsimonious budget allocations from President Herbert Hoover, intraservice rivalries with Army line officers at General Staff levels, and jarringly ferocious opposition from Navy officialdom. Not only that, they knew that this particular corporation – Detroit-Lockheed – had only been in existence for about a year, had never built any sort of military combat aircraft, and at that particular place in time it could hardly write a check that would not "bounce."

A critical observer might have asked, "Is that place really an aircraft factory?" To be factual, it looked more like a minor facility for small-scale production of automobiles or large industrial motors. What passed for an assembly hall was a clearspan area dominated by an overhead crane, with floor space that would have been overtaxed in trying to hold even one Fokker or Ford trimotor.

Air Corps fliers had cast envious glances from their biplane Curtiss A-3 attack planes or Boeing P-12 pursuits as Lockheed Vega and Sirius monoplanes cruised past without undue effort. Those snappy looking Lockheed commercial models couldn't be caught by anything in the first-line service inventories of America, Great Britain, France or any other significant power. The truth be known, even stripped down, cleaned-up racing versions of the best military fighters (pursuits) could barely attain 200 miles per hour in 1930.

Inside that "General Motors of Aviation" facility, perfunctorily named Detroit Aircraft, the military representatives wanted to know if engineer Robert S. Woods – later to become known for design of the Bell XFM-1 Airacuda, XP-39, XP-63 and a host of others – could team with Gerry Vultee to design a fast monoplane pursuit for bomber escort or interception. Their idea was to get a fast Lockheed-style monoplane fighter, preferably rendered in aluminum, and powered by the new Curtiss V-1570C Conqueror engine. It was a Prestone-cooled V-12 that could churn out a nominal 600 horsepower in ungeared form. The Conqueror was really a larger displacement version of the earlier D-12, a standard Air Corps engine. Several new airplanes, including the Curtiss P-6E and Berliner-Joyce P-16 biplane fighters soon to be procured in moderate numbers for the Air Corps, featured Conqueror power. (Technology relating to the monoblock Conqueror V-12 served as the conceptual basis for the Rolls-Royce Kestrel and Goshawk engines that were the progenitors of the famed Merlin.)

*Yes, America was a financially sick nation in 1930, but inventiveness was not comatose. While some builders of large military and commercial aircraft toyed with semi-retractable landing gears, Marshall Headle, Dick Palmer and a few others borrowed a page from Alfred Verville's V-S R-3 racer of a decade earlier. Result: the Lockheed Sirius-Altair was born with the first flush-retracting commercially successful and viable landing gear. Executive Carl Squier (left) had backed it and Headle (in plus fours) did the flight testing. It was soon to become the Air Corps' first Lockheed airplane with retracting landing gear. (Harvey Christen)*

The Office of the Chief of the Air Corps wanted an advanced bomber-escort fighter designed to a concept then in worldwide favor because France – considered *the* air power of the day – had embraced that format with open arms. This new fighter would be a two-seater of metal construction, featuring the monoplane wing and those brand new Lockheed-developed assets, a fully retractable landing gear and a cockpit enclosure. The dream was too logical and too good to come true. Here was America's chance to make a substantial leap forward of every air power in the world. Evidence that the U.S. was on the threshold of a major breakthrough in the field of medium and heavy bombers was already in the hands of the visiting Air Corps officers. Within a matter of months, the Air Corps was to have a choice of two very advanced twin-engine bombers that could outrun virtually every fighter airplane anywhere in the world. These would later be identified as the Boeing XB-901 and the Martin XB-907.

Project engineer Bob Woods had the opportunity to bring a very substantial order to a business-starved company, producing a product that would have raised American prestige throughout the world.

Detroit Aircraft was the newly formed holding corporation that had acquired all California-based Lockheed Aircraft Company stock in a boom-time exchange of "paper" valuations. Woods was a visionary designer, but he lacked some of the pragmatism of Jack Northrop or Gerry Vultee. Starting with minimal specifications, Detroit Aircraft had a fine opportunity to develop the most advanced-concept fighter since World War I. It seized the opportunity with vigor; the specter of unemployment was all around. For political expediency, the airplane was designated XP-900.

All of the pieces were essentially there. A slightly revised Lockheed Sirius-Altair wooden wing was well suited to visions of the Verville-Sperry R-3 racer of 1924 that were seen by Woods as he worked with Vultee's proposals. He quickly drafted up a streamlined two-seat pursuit airplane of extremely advanced concept featuring a retractable landing gear. Lockheed was a pioneer in that field, having probably been inspired by Col. Charles Lindbergh's suggestions about providing one for his Sirius. Most of the geometry, if not the mechanism, appears to have evolved from the arrangement used by Alfred Verville on the Verville-Sperry as early as 1922. In the XP-900 design, that landing gear was absolutely duplicated, even to the shape of the coverplates provided.

The attitudes and actions of President Hoover and his

ABOVE: *Aerial view of Lockheed's Burbank factory (hangars at right, ranch house office at left and about half of the Mission Glass building between them) revealed a bustling business for Vega monoplanes prior to the stock market crash (or at least soon thereafter). Big factory (upper left) was Empire China; Mission Glass was within the square building adjacent to Lockheed hangars. Both companies failed in early 1930. LAC had evidently leased part of the glass factory in 1929 or perhaps earlier.*
(J. H. Washburn)

BELOW: *Lockheed designed it; Detroit Aircraft manufactured the duralumin fuselage to mount on a Burbank-manufactured wing. Shell Oil Co. pilot James Doolittle was soon streaking around the United States in the Orion 9C Special to market his products on a grand scale. The U.S. oil industry developed 100-octane (+) fuels. Building behind tailplane was, incredibly, the company's first expansion after rescue from bankruptcy.*
(Lockheed)

LEFT: More than 15 years later, the 9C "Shellightning" was still in reasonably good condition (flying status) and for sale. The salesman, in cockpit, offered N12222 to the author for $2,500 that September 1950. That was the price of a new Oldsmobile 88 convertible. (Warren Bodie photo)

BOTTOM: Built atop a real modified Sirius-Altair wing, the wooden mockup of the projected Detroit-Lockheed XP-900 was hardly overdone. A government-furnished Curtiss V-1570C Conqueror engine reposes in nose section; it eventually wound up in the actual prototype as completed in Detroit. (Lockheed Aircraft Company)

Secretary of War, Patrick J. Hurley, ensured that the Air Corps was in a financial quandary. Those Wright Field officers visiting Detroit Aircraft did not actually have any funding available for the new pursuit airplane project. But, starved for orders in 1930, the company agreed to develop a prototype privately, with the exception of being reimbursed at the time of delivery. A cheap XP-900 mockup was prepared for military board review by March 1931. It received approval, and construction of a prototype metal monocoque fuselage began at Detroit. The Lockheed subsidiary contributed a wooden Altair-type wing, complete with retracting landing gear. But Detroit Aircraft was also getting more than that: it was taking excessive overhead charges from Lockheed to help fight its own red ink.

Pre-delivery trials of the XP-900 were conducted at the Grosse Isle Naval Reserve Air Station in the Detroit area. The sleek blue and chrome yellow monoplane departed for Wright Field, Ohio, on September 29, 1931, with Bob Woods in the aft cockpit. Woods recalled some years ago, "All 12 of us in the engineering department put in almost unbelievable overtime for five months at half our regular pay. When the XP-900 was delivered to Dayton, I rode in the back seat to save the train fare."

As promised, the Air Corps purchased the product and designated it YP-24, a subterfuge intended to avoid alerting Congress and others to the fact that a new fighter had been procured. Suddenly the Army had a spirited 235-mph fighter in its grasp, joining such aircraft as the 139-mph Curtiss A-3Bs and the 195-mph Boeing P-12 types. The newest standard Air Corps pursuit – the pretty Curtiss P-6E biplane – was lucky to be only about 35 mph slower. Detroit-Lockheed appeared to have a stunning winner of unprecedented value. Its plane had the lowest drag coefficient of any military aircraft of that period, and with the two forward machine guns that included a Browning .50-caliber weapon, it was reasonably armed. As a reward, the Air Corps Procurement Branch of the War Department awarded a combination contract calling for five Y1P-24 service test pursuits and five Y1A-9 attack airplanes – the latter probably as a sop for the line Army types who had become enamored of the new ground attack or assault aircraft. The contractual price for the 10 airplanes was $276,000, with the Air Corps furnishing engines and other GFE.

Fate was not on the side of Detroit-Lockheed in 1931. That, coupled with tightwad budgets which did nothing to inspire component testing, led to Lt. Harrison Crocker encountering landing gear extension problems on October 19 at Wright Field when the manual handcrank extension shaft sheared. Lt. Crocker did everything possible to get the gear fully extended or up and locked (he was successful in the latter) so that he could make an emergency landing and save the aircraft. Simply because officers in charge had no experience with retractable-gear aircraft, they concurred when Brig. Gen. H. Conger Pratt ordered Crocker to "hit the silk."

After some exciting attempts to successfully bail out, the lieutenant cleared the airplane several thousand feet above Fairborn, a nearby town. The YP-24 seemed almost determined to embarrass the general. It spiraled down and nearly made a reasonable belly landing, but a wing dropped. It cartwheeled and tore off the wings and sent the engine spinning off to destruction. The cockpit area remained nearly intact.

Young Assistant Secretary of the Navy David Ingalls was keeping abreast of Detroit-Lockheed progress and managed to arrange for procurement of one Detroit Aircraft-built Altair metal fuselage constructed on the basic Altair wing. With accommodation for three or four people, it became a high-performance command transport for Secretary Ingalls. Designated XRO-1, it was the first operational (as opposed to racing) naval aircraft to have a retractable landing gear. Featuring a big 625-horsepower Wright Cyclone up front, it was possibly the fastest naval airplane.

With the Depression driving the economy ever deeper, Detroit Aircraft found itself on the brink of catastrophe in October. The corporation's stock, originally offered at $15 per share in 1929, had slipped to $1.63 per share in 1930, then plummeted to $0.12 at about the same time the XRO-1 and YP-24 were delivered. With hardly a whimper, the organization went into receivership (bankruptcy), dragging Lockheed Aircraft with it. Air Corps contracts were, of course, automatically canceled, but some fast negotiating with Maj. Reuben Fleet at Consolidated Aircraft over in Buffalo saved the day for the Air Corps. Robert Woods, the design drawings and some tooling all went to Buffalo, New York. The Air Corps was then able to supply geared Conquerors, so the Consolidated Model 25 was born as a somewhat improved version of the YP-24/XP-900.

Equipped with the newest geared and turbosupercharged Conqueror engine and an all-metal wing in place of the wooden affair, it received the military designation Y1P-25 as well as the default contracts that had been awarded to Detroit Aircraft. Two Y1P-25s were built. One was to become the Y1A-11 in unsupercharged form, but history became very cloudy with regard to the two sleek aircraft. Both evidently were involved in fatal crashes, but a later corporate history fails to shed light on the matter. However, the Air Corps was convinced that it had an outstandingly advanced fighter (two-seater or otherwise), and it was needed. It is likely that Maj. Gen. Benjamin Foulois personally had something to do with it. As Chief of the Air Corps, advocate of two-seater fighters and former com-

*ABOVE: Bomber/observation-oriented Army Air Corps somehow sprang the Martin XB-907 on an amazed world very early in the new decade. It could actually cruise at nearly twice the speed of the world's contemporary biplane bombers. It was soon to be greatly improved to become the backbone of the Air Corps' heavy bomber force. (Wright Field/Air Corps)*

*BELOW: Detroit Aircraft Corporation's dingy factory, next to the Detroit River, looked more like a transformer plant than an aircraft factory. The metal and wood XP-900 was nearly ready to be moved to Grosse Isle's exclusive airport farther downriver. Three-blade metal propellers were a distinct rarity in 1931. If the XP-900 had been scaled down to the same dimensions as the V-S R-3 racer of 1924 and limited to a single seat, the airplane might have been the Spitfire of its time. It would surely have been the first 250-mph fighter in the world. (Lockheed Aircraft Company)*

ABOVE: *Three or four years after the XP-900 was abandoned in flight because a belly landing was feared, this is what first-line pursuit planes looked like (a Boeing P-12E). The much advanced Martin B-10 heavy bomber alongside was somewhat faster. (15th Photo Section - AAC)*

BELOW: *Boeing's B-9A lost out to the Martin XB-907/B-10, but it was still a magnificent improvement over every foreign and Air Corps bomber with its metal structure, retractable landing gear and absence of struts. (Bodie Archives)*

rade-in-arms with Fleet, it is logical to assume that "Benny" Foulois played a part in the contract transfer.

Just about a year after the Detroit YP-24 was abandoned in flight, the Y1P-25 was ready for test on November 22, 1932. Test results (and other factors) led to a small production contract for four improved pursuit models to be designated P-30, plus four unsupercharged A-11 attack planes. The first P-30 and the first A-11 flew in the early months of 1934, and it would be expected that deliveries would have continued apace. If the more complicated and larger Martin B-10 bombers were being delivered to squadrons in 1934 after a later start, all P-30/A-11 types should have been delivered by the end of 1935.

However, Consolidated had leased a former Curtiss plant for 10 years back in 1924. It was the World War I Curtiss factory on North Elmwood Avenue, more or less abandoned by that company right after World War I ended. Maj. Reuben Fleet was doing quite well with flying boat deliveries to the U.S. Navy and some commercial customers, but the bitter winters in Buffalo were hardly conducive to flight testing of the big boats. As Consolidated completed negotiations for a new West Coast factory, production of the P-30s lagged.

In the meantime, having observed a then phenomenal speed of 247 mph demonstrated, not to mention a capability of fighting at 25,000 feet, the Air Corps placed a further

order for no less than 50 of the P-30A version equipped with the Curtiss Electric controllable-pitch propeller. (That model was eventually redesignated PB-2A as replacement for the biplane Berliner-Joyce PB-1, formerly P-16)

Support for the procurement was received in the form of a report by Capt. Victor Herbert Strahm, World War I ace and Chief of the Air Corps flying branch. In August, he reported that "the P-30 is an exceptional performing airplane and is considered by pilots of the Test Branch as extremely good in all respects." High praise.

Although the P-30A should have been in squadron service by 1935, the vicissitudes of the ever deepening Depression, politics and Maj. Fleet's desires led to the decision to move out of the leased factory and into a newly constructed plant in San Diego, California, some 3,000 miles diagonally across America. That was the most complicated and largest move ever attempted by any major aircraft manufacturer. The actual move was completed in September 1935. It wasn't until January 1936 that the new PB-2As (ex-P-30A) began to roll off the assembly lines at the new plant adjacent to Highway 101, Lindbergh Field and San Diego Bay.

Six long years had evaporated the true impact of a design that could have revolutionized fighter design. But by early 1936, the combat wing of the Air Corps was the formally authorized GHQ Air Force, major changes in command had occurred, and 1st Lt. Benjamin Kelsey, Fighter Projects Officer, recognized the deadly flaws in the two-seat fighter concept. His boss, Brig. Gen. H. H. Arnold, shared Kelsey's views and went one better in advocating development of the multiseat bomber destroyer. Kelsey, in company with Captains Claire Chennault and Ross Hoyt among others, was strongly opposed to the idea of hauling around an aft-facing gunner who was really nothing better than ballast. Curtiss's Conqueror engine was not likely to generate a more powerful successor. America had literally wasted its advances in technology of the early 1930s.

C How the amazing Lt. Kelsey managed to avoid the fate that befell the bombardment people is unknown, but avoid it he did. Military and civilian politics, the illogical Harry Woodring (Secretary of War), an inflexible Chief of Staff, Gen. Malin Craig, and other factors all led to Air Corps procurement of hundreds of comfortable but defenseless Douglas B-18/B-18A bombers in lieu of far more capable but expensive Boeing Flying Fortress bombers. (The "dead end" Douglas neocommercial B-18 wasn't "worth a farthing" as a bomber in World War II.)

In fact, under the direction of Harry Woodring, orders came down from the War Department in 1939 to end procurement of any more B-17 Flying Fortress bombers that had been bought in very small numbers. Had Woodring's intentions prevailed, a disaster of inestimable magnitude would have befallen the U.S. within a matter of months. Only the outbreak of war in Europe turned that tide.

One tiny happening of 1939 might have gone unnoticed except for the impact it probably had on the success of the subject of this book. A single Consolidated A-11 managed to

provide a connecting link between the Detroit-Lockheed YP-24 and the Lockheed Lightning. An experimental Allison V-1710 engine of the type dear to the hearts of the Air Corps leadership and eventually used in all Lockheed P-38s was subjected to lengthy accelerated flight testing at Wright Field in a modified Y1A-11. (Retired Gen. Mark Bradley recalls having spent hour after hour in the cockpit of that airplane with its big propeller and normal landing gear. His prime recollection was the trouble they had with turbosupercharger control mechanisms.)

It is clear that America's Army Air Corps entered into the decade of the thirties with a technological lead in world aviation. Retractable landing gears, metal monocoque fuselages, controllable-pitch propellers, NACA low-drag cowlings, Prestone cooling, high-octane aviation fuels, cantilever monoplane wings and turbosuperchargers all began to come into widespread use early in the decade.

But effects of the Depression, isolationism of intense proportions, intraservice and interservice rivalry and the widespread recognition of the rapidly growing importance of air power on the part of Britons and Europeans conspired to strip America of its initial favorable status. By the end of 1938, the United States was a third-rate air power in numbers of firstline aircraft in service or on order. Most of the Air Corps' new B-18 bombers could not keep up with domestic airline DC-3s, and the very thought of a Curtiss P-36 or a Seversky P-35 taking on a Spitfire, Hurricane or Bf 109D with any chance of success is, in retrospect, laughable. Certain politicians and militarists who were respected and sometimes even revered were responsible for squandering America's technical advantages. Major segments of the population had little but contempt for men in uniform, based on isolationistic views.

Events conspired to overcome retardant forces and atti-

*ABOVE: Fast enough to contend with the new Martin and Boeing bombers - and they were still a year or two away from first flights - was the prototype Detroit-Lockheed XP-900. Shown here during engine runup at Grosse Isle Airport in 1931, it was to be test flown by Vance Breese. The site was chosen because the fighter was (logically) transported to the island by barge. The Woods-Vultee-Palmer design team never acknowledged how much the XP-900 design owed to Alfred Verville's 1922-24 race-winning Verville-Sperry R-3 and to John Northrop's wooden wing. (Lockheed Aircraft Corp.)*

*BELOW: Fourteen months later, the prototype Y1P-25 rolled out of Consolidated's aircraft plant at Buffalo, New York, proudly displaying a new General Electric turbosupercharger. It was 1933! It obviously was not "Secret" in 1933, and it surely was not classified in 1940 when the new Lockheed 322-Bs were ordered en masse. They were about as secret as the relatively new Prestone anti-freeze/coolant. The production version became the P-30 (A-11 without the supercharger) and, subsequently, the PB-2A. (Consolidated Aircraft)*

tudes. Few things did more to awaken "the sleeping giant" than receipt of immense orders for weapons from the United Kingdom and France. America was virtually dragged or kicked into the role of the "Arsenal of Democracy." Massive orders for the militarized Lockheed 14 Super Electra (produced for the RAF as the Hudson) forced tiny Lockheed to expand at an astronomical rate. In the process it proved to its competition that the impossible was possible.

Not to be ignored in the overall structure of history was the rise to positions of power of "a few great captains" (and more), including "Hap" Arnold, Ira Eaker, Carl Spaatz (originally Spatz), Oscar Westover, Frank Andrews and Delos Emmons as advocates of air power. They were assisted in no small way by no less than "a few good men" like Lts. Ben Kelsey and Cass Hough and no small numbers of regulars and reservists.

One great boost for the Air Corps was the selection of Gen. George C. Marshall as Army Chief of Staff in 1939. Almost immediately, Col. Frank Andrews was brought back from virtual obscurity, promoted and placed in a position of great responsibility on the Army staff. With reorganization, Henry Arnold became the new Chief of the Air Corps.

Americans began, in a small way, to shake off the effects of isolationism. However, until the attack on Pearl Harbor, the isolationists could hardly be ignored. The long-standing and determined resistance to being involved in "foreign entanglements" had divided the nation for years, but it virtually disappeared overnight with Japan's attack.

On the plus side of a ledger, if we compiled one for the thirties, would be the ascendancy of three determined airmen to positions of power in 1935. They were crucial to the birth of American air power at a critical time. Maj. Gen. Oscar Westover became Chief of the Air Corps. His assistant was Brig. Gen. Henry H. Arnold. As Commanding General of the GHQ Air Force – the branch with combat capability – Maj. Gen. (temp.) Frank M. Andrews was given the helm.

On the negative side, Gen. Malin Craig had become Chief of Staff in 1935. Neither he nor Secretary of the Army Harry H. Woodring were advocates of air power. Funds were not allocated for power plant development, weapons research, or systems components to keep up with progress. Eventually, for speaking out, Andrews had been demoted.

D Procurement of 77 Seversky P-35 pursuit airplanes, developed from the Sev 1XP in 1936, was a mistake (admitted by Brig. Gen. Ben Kelsey in 1973). When a competition for a new pursuit airplane contract was initiated in 1935, Kelsey was already aware of the brand new British Hawker Hurricane, but U.S. manufacturers were doing virtually nothing to advance the state of the art in aviation (they had little financial incentive to do so). As examples, Consolidated Aircraft entered a single-seat version of the P-30 with a faired-over rear cockpit. Power was not increased, weight was not reduced, the thick 1928 wing was not replaced; virtually nothing was changed. Suddenly, in 1935/36, it was 1930 again.

Seversky's initial entry for the 1935 competition displayed either an unconscionable disregard of the Air Corps' needs or a terribly ill-conceived idea that a 1933 executive/commercial airplane, the basic Sev-3, could be transformed like a pumpkin into a modern pursuit aircraft. Even a reading of some contemporary British aviation magazines would have revealed the folly of Seversky's concept. Whatever transpired, the entry from Farmingdale, NY, was proudly revealed as the Sev-2XP. Powered by an underdeveloped, unproven engine, it had *two* seats, a *fixed* spatted landing gear, an overly large exposed tailwheel and several hundred pounds of useless aft gunner system weight. Even if you believed Seversky's figures, its top speed would barely exceed that of the 1930 Detroit-Lockheed XP-900.

Fortunately for all concerned, the airplane's engine failed during the delivery flight to Wright Field, terminating the flight in a forced landing. Once Alex de Seversky learned the facts about his competition, the rush was on to totally rebuild the aircraft as a single-seat pursuit with a retractable landing gear of retrograde design. An old axiom comes to mind: there is never time to do it right the first time, but there is always time to do it over! Redesignated Sev-1XP, the airplane still had to go through three different powerplant selections before it became a reasonably viable pursuit. It was a good counterpart of Douglas's B-18 bomber of the same era. The only thing to be proud of was the excellent-quality all metal monocoque structure. It was superb.

Designer Don Berlin's Curtiss Model 75 design for the competition went through a quartet of engine types in 1935-36 in an effort to attain a speed of 300 mph. Even then it failed. By that time, everybody must have been aware that the Supermarine Spitfire and Hawker Hurricane had flown. Since the British were notorious for understating performance figures, American designers involved in the competition at Wright Field must have been more than a bit embarrassed.

Project Officer Lt. Kelsey and his superiors should have rejected all entries, canceled the competition and started over with new and more demanding specifications, but the young lieutenant had only been in that job for about a year, and more than one aspiring officer had learned that you didn't stir up too many waves around the Old Guard. Curtiss management had alluded to probable lawsuits over the contract award process, and Seversky was in such straits that he soon wound up selling a version of the Sev-2XP to Russia to help pay the bills.

In later years, Ben Kelsey confirmed that he regretted not limiting the P-35 contract to a small service test quantity of 13. At least there was the definite likelihood that any production version would have had a flush landing gear and refined canopy similar to those that were soon applied to the XP-41. If nothing else, the new (and only) Pursuit Projects Officer quickly became a proponent of advanced fighter concepts and gained confidence to battle ardently in support of those beliefs. Far-reaching changes in the Air Corps hierarchy were already being formulated. Kelsey was the right man in the right place at the right time.

One vigorous advocate of a "superior" interceptor airplane was Air Corps Tactical School instructor Capt. Claire L. Chennault. His outspoken opposition to the multiseat fighter concept, exemplified by the then forthcoming Bell XFM-1 Airacuda, eventually led the captain to retire on disability in 1937. He immediately departed for China, a move that would ultimately benefit America to a great extent. On the other hand, Capt. Ross G. Hoyt, long with the 1st Pursuit Group at Selfridge Field, advocated adoption of an "Interceptor Pursuit" and a long-range multiplace fighter. While the interceptor concept seemed to be suited to the needs of Europe, it was totally unsuited for Western Hemisphere defense. Proof that multiseat fighters were a throwback to conditions prevailing in the 1920s was soon to be widely perceived.

With all of this and a dozen other things in mind, and considering the sorry state of the economy and the American aircraft and engine industries in particular at mid-decade, advances that can be attributed directly to Lt. Kelsey were generated against what must have appeared to be overwhelming odds. The innovative Kelsey created and gained approval for a new generation of fighter aircraft specifications that only months earlier would have been unthinkable. A quantum leap forward was needed as it had never been needed before. America, in 1936, was about to benefit from just such a giant step.

# CHAPTER 2

# A Profound Conception

A The story of the Lockheed P-38 Lightning really began in 1916 when the brothers Loughead (pronounced Lockheed) built a reasonably successful hydroaeroplane for carrying paying passengers. It is also the saga of several talented men whose ideas blended eventually with the concepts of a brilliant young military flyer to inspire, in 1936, the design of what was to become one of the world's greatest fighter aircraft.

While Allan Loughead failed in his early attempt to keep his fledgling company solvent in 1921, his tenacity eventually paid off. By 1926, with a revised spelling of his name and some capital, he had joined forces with former associate John (Jack) Northrop to develop the design for the first of many outstandingly successful and popular Lockheed monoplanes. During the next few years of boom times and soaring aviation popularity, the resurrected Lockheed Aircraft Company prospered. The Los Angeles-based company basked in the limelight and notoriety of many pilots who established a fabulous string of record-breaking flights in a family of Lockheed products: Vegas, Sirius, Air Expresses, Altairs and Orions. The clean-lined molded plywood "Wooden Wonders" were the envy the designers the world over. In an era of wooden frame or metal tube and fabric aircraft everywhere, the full monocoque fuselage, cantilever wing monoplanes designed by Jack Northrop were aerodynamic gems.

*More's the pity that nobody realized the importance of photographing the XP-38 in its element when it flew in 1939. Only this painting reveals the beauty of the prototype in flight. Possibly planned for a Lockheed ad campaign, it was suppressed when the XP-38 crashed in New York.*

But the cycle of flamboyant boom and cataclysmic bust was to prove to be almost fatal for the fast-rising Lockheed star. With the worldwide financial collapse at the start of the century's fourth decade, the Detroit Aircraft Corporation – which relished being called the "General Motors of Aviation" – foundered and went into receivership. The owners had gained a controlling interest in Lockheed (by then located in Burbank) in July 1929, mostly by exchanging overvalued stock. While the California company was itself viable, management eventually was unable to resist the burdens imposed by the parent corporation's failure. On October 27, 1931, Lockheed succumbed to the demands of its creditors.

When the Detroit people assumed command in 1929, they had chosen veteran aviator Carl B. Squier as general manager of their new West Coast entity. The plant he was to manage consisted of a red brick ranch house, about half of the failing Mission Glass Works building and two parallel hangar-like assembly buildings. Scattered metal sheds and a small flight service building, barely large enough to hold one Vega, were located behind the bankrupt Empire China Company. This motley collection of disassociated buildings was located at the intersection of San Fernando Road/Victory Place and Empire Avenue, a mile or so north of downtown Burbank. A company-built airstrip paralleled the Southern Pacific Railroad tracks that slanted to the west. Even in sunny Southern California there was a certain dinginess about the whole place; on overcast days it was downright depressing. About a mile west, the relatively new United Airport gleamed like an oasis in a valley. A large public park located at the southeast quadrant of the east-west and north-south runways was adjacent to the terminal building and two steel and masonry hangars. Within a decade, the park was destined to be the site of a huge new Vega Aircraft Corporation plant. (Vega was originally a subsidiary of Lockheed and later became Lockheed Plant A-1).

However, in the austere 1930s, Lockheed's lean and hungry engineering staff was housed in what had been the ranch house kitchen. Chief Engineer Gerard "Gerry" Vultee was assisted by two draftsmen/engineers - Richard von Hake and James M. Gerschler. Vultee had become engineering boss upon the departure of Jack Northrop in 1928. Ultimately, Vultee resigned to pursue personal interests and von Hake became the top man in engineering.

By 1932, the Great Depression had clamped a lid on business in the U.S.A. General Motors stock was selling for about 2 dollars a share. Other famous automotive companies like Reo, Auburn, Duesenberg, Hupp and Pierce-Arrow had either disappeared from the scene or were soon to fail. Lockheed, then in the throes of receivership, had struggled along at a production rate of about one monoplane a month in 1931. As the Depression deepened in the twelfth month, employment was below 100. Carl Squier even mortgaged all of his personal assets to meet the tiny payroll at year end. Americans were emotionally drained by New Year's Day, 1932, but there was a brief flurry of activity when three of the last four Orion monoplanes built were sold to Varney Air Lines as the New Year dawned.

Unrecognized in the mists of time was the purchase by a Japanese firm of what evidently was the last airplane manufactured at Lockheed Burbank before Squier padlocked the doors. Mainichi Shimbun, an Osaka-based newspaper, purchased a Model 8E Altair that was manufactured in January 1932. Other orders had evaporated. Finally, the super salesman and ever dapper Carl Squier offered all company assets – valued by the bankruptcy receiver at $129,961 – for sale. There weren't any buyers. It appeared to be the death knell for Lockheed.

**B**On the morning of June 6, 1932, three slightly nervous young businessmen entered the federal courthouse in downtown Los Angeles to appear in the U.S. District Court. The spokesman for this group was Robert E. Gross, a 35-year-old aviation entrepreneur who had successively been financially involved with Stearman Aircraft, Viking Flying Boat Co. and Varney Speed Lines. At age 39, Carl Squier was the eldest in this group. The junior member in the trio, but already having gained a national reputation for designing excellent aircraft, was Lloyd C. Stearman, age 33.

Gross had used every means at his command to scrape up $40,000, an amount the group believed would allow them to purchase all of the assets of Lockheed. Airline magnate and flamboyant investor Walter Varney had contributed 50 percent of the money. District Court Judge Hollyer asked if Gross had the required $10,000 – 25 percent of the purchase price – with him as mandated by U.S. law. After inquiring in court if there were any other bids, the judge could not resist saying what was on his mind. "I hope you know what you are doing." Little could he or disappointed Allan Lockheed or anybody else in court that day know what a profound conception it was. As of June 21, the Lockheed Aircraft Corp. was in business.

By July, the somewhat revitalized manufacturer had re-hired von Hake as Chief Engineer under Stearman, brought 29-year-old Hall Hibbard on board as Assistant Chief Engineer, and everybody set about trying to figure out what the new corporation would build. Money was extremely tight in the

final months of 1932, but they completed one Orion for sale to TWA. Slightly more than one airplane a month was completed and sold in 1933. Most of their sales for the first year consisted of orders for an airplane that was still on the drawing boards, Lockheed's first all-metal and first twin-engine airplane, the Model 10. They filled only a half-dozen orders for the wooden Lockheeds in 1934, essentially bringing an end to that effort. Incredibly, a bit of *deja vu* crept into the final transaction in 1934 when the Japanese firm Mainichi Shimbun purchased an Altair 9F as a mate to their first one. (Ten years later, that Altair 9F was destroyed by a USAAF air raid on Tokyo.)

Good Southern California weather had prevailed back in 1932 when Bob Gross made a momentous decision. Most of the airliners operating on the airlines of the U.S. were trimotors and a small number of single-engine Lockheeds. At least three larger single-engine airliners were being developed, inspiration coming from airmail contracts and some Bureau of Air Commerce requirements. Included were Northrop's Delta, the General Aviation GA-43 and the Vultee V-1. All were metal low-wing monoplanes having about the same passenger-carrying capacity as the new Boeing 247, an advanced two-engine airliner. Gross, speaking to Stearman, von Hake, Hibbard and Gerschler said, "Let's junk what we are doing (a Stearman-Varney design) and put two engines on it." What resulted was a fast version of the Boeing 247 concept, the Model 10 Electra. As things turned out, it was a brilliant decision at the right time.

General Aviation, in poor financial condition, was soon absorbed into North American Aviation and the GA-43 was abandoned. Possibilities of success for the Northrop Delta and the Vultee V-1A dissolved in the wake of a government decision against single-engine airliners. Only the Model 10 Electra went on to full acceptance and a prosperous future. However, even that did not come about easily. Lockheed had made an 18-month financial commitment to develop the Model 10, and at times the new corporation came frightfully close to financial disaster. But the great energies of Bob Gross and his associates prevailed.

Determination to do the job right soon led to a major

*Fabrication of the first Model 10 Electra forced Lockheed to expand its facilities in 1934. The round top shop between the two assembly hangars was completed in September. The buildings all looked shabby, but at least there was a lot of activity by April 1935, when this aerial view was recorded on film. Disturbingly, there was not an airplane in sight, and only one person is to be seen. Mission Glass (left center) either had rigor mortis or Lockheed had taken over the entire plant. There were absolutely no signs of life at the big Empire China works. (J. H. Washburn)*

building block being added to the Lockheed pyramid – Hall Hibbard insisted on complete wind tunnel testing to avoid expensive errors. With only a few options to choose from, they went to the excellent facility at the University of Michigan. Starting in March 1933, a young graduate engineer, Clarence L. Johnson, began to test a scale model of the Model 10. He quickly reported a low-speed directional control problem associated with the single vertical stabilizer and rudder. With one engine disabled, control could not be maintained.

Telephone conversations with Burbank led young "Kelly" Johnson to leave Ann Arbor, Michigan, and join the Lockheed staff in California. Within a matter of days, Johnson redesigned the empennage to incorporate twin vertical surfaces. At the same time, he put his own brand on Lockheed products, one that would last for decades. By August 1934, the Model 10 Electra had completed flight tests and received the government Approved Type Certificate (ATC). Sales of that fast airliner made Lockheed a viable manufacturer, even it if wasn't in the same league as giants Douglas, Martin, Curtiss and Boeing.

More than a few people now realize the close relationship that exists between the Electra and the XP-38, but – strange as it may seem – the Buffalo-built Bell XFM-1 Airacuda played an almost equally important role in the development of the XP-38. It had absolutely nothing to do with any decision made by anybody even remotely associated with Lockheed at the time. In retrospect, it tends to make anybody a true believer in predestination.

In the mid-1930s period when Maj. Reuben Fleet relocated Consolidated Aircraft from Buffalo, New York, more than 3,000 miles to San Diego, California, at least one of his prime executives elected to remain. Larry Bell decided to form his own business, the Bell Aircraft Corporation. Robert Woods, the former Detroit Aircraft engineer, stayed on as his chief designer. When Great Lakes Aircraft failed, the initial Bell product on the assembly line was the GLA-designed BG-1 biplane dive bomber for the Navy.

Bell and Woods recognized the need to do something spectacular in aviation if the corporation was to survive. Working on a military non-requirement that had low-level official sanction, they designed what was close to a "Buck Rogers" concept (for 1935) for a multi-seat bomber-interceptor, or bomber-destroyer as some preferred. The basic undercurrent for a "dream" aircraft in that category was only then meandering through the backwaters of the Air Corps planning. At that moment, there was no formal requirement for such an aircraft, and in any other era it most likely would have stayed that way. It is possible that long-time associates of Capt. Ross Hoyt supported his advocacy of such an airplane, leading to a firm contract. Perhaps that action, more than any other, led to the resignation of Capt. Claire Chennault, a pilot vehemently opposed to such a project. It is a fair supposition.

Enter a youthful MIT graduate with a burning passion for flying, a fervent love for exceptional aircraft and a great faith

A Seversky P-35, one of 77 ordered by the AAC for the 1st Pursuit Group, was beautifully built, but certain high-drag components were attributable to cutting corners in research in order to protect profits. The canopy was ridiculously large, and the retractable landing gear was a throwback to the Boeing Monomail and that company's XF7B-1 Navy fighter. As late as 1936, many engineers and executives were acting like they had never heard of the Lockheed Orion or the XP-900 retractable landing gears. In order to avoid any payment of tiny royalties, Curtiss made its Curtiss P-36 Hawk landing gear excessively complicated. As if to exhibit some sort of contempt for the AAC, Consolidated had the gall to fair over the rear cockpit of a PB-2A (essentially an XP-900) and try to win the 1936 (!) pursuit competition. Lt. Kelsey and his superiors would have been justified in giving everybody a failing grade. (The dark hand of politics probably controlled the situation.) (GHQ AF)

in himself. Lt. Benjamin Kelsey had been appointed officer-in-charge of the Fighter Projects Office at Wright Field just a year earlier. He was, in fact, *the* project officer. The "Bomber Mentality" led the way in the 1930s Air Corps, closely trailed by support of observation and then attack aircraft categories. Incredibly, politicians and the military hierarchy looked upon pursuit (read that as a fighter) airplanes as the tool for stirring up public interest in the Air Corps at air shows. After all, with the Navy offshore and the American continent so far from any possible aggressor, pursuit aircraft would never be a viable requirement. They were expensive (?) toys.

Ben Kelsey had formed some personal opinions about fighter aircraft that were Wellsian in their foresight. He was strongly opposed to the two-seat fighter concept that had gained a foot-hold in this country over a 10-year period. While the Detroit-Lockheed YP-24 was extremely advanced for its time, without obstructionist pressures and the need for political expediency it could have appeared in a smaller-size single-seat pursuit guise. It would have been a world beater.

France's *Armee de l'Air*, probably by far the most powerful and recognizable air power on earth in the 1920s and early 1930s by shear force of numbers, was the leading advocate of the multiseat bomber-destroyer format. The French were irrevocably enmeshed in an *affair de coeur* with these so-called "aerial destroyers" that never could seem to decide if they wanted to be bombers or pursuits. Favored designs ran the gamut from twin-engine, slab-sided flying greenhouses, as exemplified by the gigantic and ugly Bleriot 127, to the single-engine, two-seater sesquiplane or the tandem-wing, twin-tail monstrosity identified as the Arsenal Delanne Type 10. With Gallic grandiloquence, it was claimed that this strut-braced staggered biplane with one single 860 horse-power engine could attain the supernatural speed of 346 mph. Even the Hawker Hurricane I was slower than that on 1030 reliable horsepower. Obviously the French succeeded in misleading only themselves.

*Luftwaffe* authorities, strangely enough, also believed in the two-seater fighter concept, albeit more or less along the lines of America's Curtiss A-18 attack aircraft utilizing a pair of engines. The Germans did not change their ideas to any extent until late in World War II when they got the message that two engines and one crewman were far superior to one or two engines and two crewmen.

British militarists, not unmindful of the success of the Bristol F.2B in the First World War, were at least partially beholden to the single-engine, two-seat idea approximating the Army Air Corps Berliner-Joyce P-16/P-1B pursuits. In fact, the turreted fighter configuration exemplified by the World War II Boulton Paul Defiant and Blackburn Roc – both of which came along with one of the expansion schemes of the late 1930 – carried the concept almost to the brink of disaster. These fighters, somewhat akin to Royal Navy monitors in operational tactics, were "sitting ducks" against attacks by contemporary single-seat fighters. As if the induced drag and extra weight of the Roc were not already a severe handicap, somebody decided to mount one version on twin floats. (It was probably then renamed Rock.)

Stateside, Lt. Kelsey was appalled by such thinking. As he viewed it, the aft gunner in even the best of two-seat fighters had an initial handicap merely in flying backwards. The gunner was usually armed with a light-caliber weapon, often had a severely restricted field of fire and there was absolutely no way in which he could anticipate changes of direction or attitude on a par with the pilot. Every multiseat fighter was larger and slower than a single-seater with the latest engines available for installation. As for the turret fighters, the application was all wrong. Gunners in bomber aircraft had a reasonably stable platform for firing, but in any fighter melee the gunner would always be zigging as the pilot was zagging.

As Fighter Projects Officer, Kelsey did consider the possibility that a reasonably fast bomber-destroyer, featuring shell-firing armament with a fairly high muzzle velocity (for range), was a fascinating theory. Thus, the lieutenant was quite in tune with the proposal put forth by Woods of the Bell organization. A circular proposal soon emanated from Kelsey's office calling for a heavily armed fighter with the mission of

*Developed directly from the Northrop 3-A pursuit, the Vought V-143 looked like this at the time Lockheed won the contest for a single XP-38. Failing to even get close to winning Air Corps or production contracts from foreign countries, United Aircraft Corp. sold the prototype, drawings, etc., to the Japanese government through an export-import firm. In spite of denials from key Japanese personnel, the V-143 was absolutely instrumental in forcing design redirection of the Mitsubishi A6M (Zero) and the Nakajima Army Type 1 Fighter Hayabusa, later to be known as Oscar. All timing, changes in design concepts, and the IJ government's orders provide substantial evidence to refute their stance. (Harvey Lippincott - UAC)*

destroying high-flying bombers and having an attainable top speed exceeding that of any known or proposed bomber. The original designation was XPB-3, in keeping with existing practice, but this was soon revised to XFM-1 to reflect a new mission not previously recognized by the Air Corps.

The Bell-Woods team, having a flair for the theatrical, called their brainchild the Airacuda. In a happy coincidence, Woods's design appeared concurrently with what seemed to be the beginning of a recovery for American industry from the ravages of the Great Depression. Circumstances and timing conspired to make the XFM-1 the first aircraft designed from the start around the new Allison V-1710 engine, the General Electric turbosupercharger and the Browning M4 cannon with the 37-mm bore. Not only that, the design epitomized the airborne gun platform that seemed to have eluded the French aircraft designers completely. Bell's Airacuda was extremely sleek in design for the period, featured a virtually unlimited and overlapping field of fire in the frontal aspect, had a superior altitude capability at a time when only the Boeing B-17 could operate at altitudes of four or five miles, enjoyed a relatively good turn of speed and could (at least on paper) unleash a torrent of firepower.

If the various versions of the Airacuda had ever lived up to their appearances, the design most certainly could have been adapted to perform the mission of bomber formation defensive fighter. Nearly a half-dozen years later, the USAAF adapted B-17s to that role (as the XB-40). That experiment failed completely because the defense system could not even keep up with the bomber formations. In a target defense role, frontal assaults on enemy bombers could have been made while presenting the smallest possible target to the bombers' defensive gunners at extreme range.

Since Lt. Kelsey was serving as project officer and primary test pilot for the prototype XFM-1 (Bell had no qualified test pilot), he was soon aware that the Airacuda design had failed to achieve its goal. Every incident tended to convince him that any multi-engine fighter must be a single-seater of smaller dimensions and be capable of exceptional performance. He would have preferred, at that particular time, to have a 2,000-horsepower single-engine type with two 25-mm cannons and four .50-caliber heavy machine guns, but no such engine was even projected for the Air Corps at that time (1936). As for

*ABOVE: In essence, it was a Dolphin on a tricycle. Douglas Aircraft modified one AAC amphibian to this OA-4C configuration, contributing something good to tricycle landing gear progress in the late 1930s. That company used the experience in developing its DC-4X, DC-5, 7B and XB-19 concepts. After conducting his own test, Lt. Kelsey enthusiastically included the requirement in "interceptor" specifications X-608 and X-609. (USAAF)*

*Bell's radical-looking XFM-1 Airacuda was not all that it seemed to be. Many advanced features were coupled to an obsolete wing design that appears to be right off the Curtiss XA-14/A-18. The first aircraft to be designed around the new Allison had radically advanced armament (at least for the American scene), but it was all based on a World War I 37-mm cannon design and .30-caliber machine guns. Earlier style B-17 side "turrets" added drag, weight and complexity, but little else. In essence, Bell's first original design was ahead of its ability to produce it. (USAAF)*

fighter armament on any single-seater, AAC planners were only thinking in terms of .50-caliber machine guns at most.

In the meantime, the circular proposal that led to procurement of a single XFM-1 had been transmitted to Lockheed. There it became the initiating document for C. L. Johnson's first military aircraft design. His proposal drawings featured some of the characteristics of the Model 12 feederliner then in the drawing boards. Initial inputs for the newly projected Model 14 high-speed 14-passenger airliner were thrown in for good measure. Lockheed's fuselage for its XFM-1 proposal was no wider than the maximum diameter of the cannon-equipped turret. Responding to the AAC preferences, Johnson incorporated Allison V-1710 engines, and these were to be boosted by turbosuperchargers. But its most novel feature – requested, not required, in the circular – was the incorporation of a tricycle landing gear, a concept almost totally ignored in that and previous eras. There can be no doubt that the Lockheed design was the first modern military aircraft to feature the arrangement from the outset.

Johnson's design offered so many practical, yet advanced, features that the Wright Field project office was impressed to the point of requesting co-equal contracts – as prescribed by law – for the Bell XFM-1 and the Lockheed fighter, by then redesignated as XFM-2.

Unfortunately for Lockheed (and the American public) inflexible rules of the merit point contest prevailed, with the XFM-2 losing out to the Bell proposal by a mere four-tenths of a point on a scale of 100! Dual procurement was not authorized, so Bob Woods's radical pusher design was awarded an experimental development contract for a single prototype. Although the XFM-1 did not live up to expectations, other contracts were eventually awarded for a total of 13 Service Test fighters bearing the designations YFM-1, YFM-1A and YFM-1B. None of the versions ever overcame some basic problems, so attainment of specified performance figures always managed to elude the Airacuda. It was one case of an aircraft that looked right but was not right. On the other hand, a clinical analysis of Kelly Johnson's design and his ultimate design track record would have convinced even the most determined skeptic that the XFM-2 would have attained or even exceeded the specifications.

Young Ben Kelsey was thoroughly impressed with the Lockheed design, and he instinctively knew that Johnson's talent was worth tapping eventually. The seeds of that impression soon began to sprout.

C Years later, a retired Brig. Gen. Benjamin Kelsey recalled numerous conditions that affected fighter aircraft design as a result of Depression-decade thinking, related and unrelated pressures and numerous financial impingements. Never having been asked before for an objective view of the factors that affected fighter procurement in that turbulent decade, Kelsey spoke with what has to be seen as total recall.

"American fighters were geared to a peacetime concept. Armament was limited to about 500 pounds (arbitrarily consisting of one .30-caliber and one .50-caliber machine guns and the ammunition for them. A large baggage compartment was required, and a reasonable range was mandatory for (consideration of) this country's geography. We could see the need for a fighter having 1500 horsepower and at least 1,000 pounds of armament. But no such engine was in our inventory and a twin-engine fighter was not really wanted for 'safety' reasons." (Army Air Corps and much foreign thinking decreed that pilots could not fly, operate the radio and navigate alone in a twin-engine aircraft.)

"There were simply no research and development funds available for development of the required aircraft, at least as a

'pursuit-type' airplane. Lt. (later Gen.) Gordon Saville was on the Army Board involved with aircraft procurement. Gordon, based at Maxwell Field (in Alabama), and I were in total agreement that some special gimmick was needed if we ever hoped to launch our joint pet project." Their solution was not really innovative. Audacious? Yes. "We merely 'invented' the Interceptor category, at least in the American vernacular.

"This (category) had absolutely nothing to do with the European term pertaining to fast-climbing, short-range bomber interceptors. Our nomenclature was aimed at getting 1,000 pounds of armament on board versus the standard 500 pounds," Kelsey said without equivocation.

The law of the land mandating issuance of circular proposals to avoid single-source procurement was watched over with paternal vigilance by Senator Carl Vinson and his Armed Services committee. It took extremely careful planning and full knowledge of the laws to avoid rejection, but Kelsey and Saville were equal to the task.

One unorthodox component desired by Kelsey was a tricycle landing gear. Old line Air Corps officers, including some who had opposed enclosed cockpits among other innovations, were generally opposed to the landing gear development pioneered by Glenn Curtiss as early as 1906. Halfway through the decade, Lt. Millard "Jake" Harmon (later Gen.) and Ben Kelsey were associated with Carl Green, then Chief of the Project Offices at Wright Field. Green had initiated research on modern stressed-skin pressure cabins – as exemplified by the Lockheed XC-35 version of the Model 10 Electra – and tricycle landing gear applications to large bombers. While the GHQ Air Force, the combat component of the Air Corps, was not ready for that innovation, some Air Corps development people had the foresight to recognize the oncoming need for such improvements.

Not entirely coincidentally, one lone Douglas OA-4C Dolphin amphibian was ordered, for test, (from the Santa Monica, California, plant) with a rudimentary tricycle landing gear installation. Col. Oliver P. Echols (later, Lt. Gen.) was induced to order Kelsey and Jake Harmon (Bomber Projects Officer) to investigate performance of the three-wheeler configuration for possible application to airplanes within their project responsibilities. Off they went on a 10-day TDY assignment to Santa Monica. Douglas test pilot/salesman Carl Cover demonstrated the modified Dolphin amphibian to the two lieutenants at Clover Field, home of the main Douglas factory. Both officers were elated at the prospects of applying the concept to military fighters and bombers.

Mr. Cover, who was Donald Douglas's veritable "right hand man," let them take it over to the much larger Mines Field (eventually to become Los Angeles International Airport), where their testing would be less inhibited. Each flyer took a turn at trying to outdo the other while conducting a series of high-speed taxi tests. That included some wild highspeed dashes in the direction of the spectator stands that had been erected for the Los Angeles National Air Races. As if that was not bad enough, the Dolphin was not equipped with brakes or nosewheel steering. Local observers of such antics probably anticipated a crash at any time.

Back at Wright Field, Kelsey promptly began to prepare preliminary requirements for two new experimental fighters – one for a single-engine interceptor and one for a twin-engine interceptor. Although the leisurely pace at peacetime Wright Field raised little dust, young Ben Kelsey attacked these ideas with a vengeance. He was motivated. Of course both new designs were to be constructed around the most powerful engine that was expected to be ready for production on 1938; that was the Allison V-1710C. High-altitude performance requirements dictated installation of turbosuperchargers built by General Electric. Extremely heavy armament (overwhelm-

ing by 1936 standards) was mandatory, and the contractor could derive several extra merit points by utilizing a tricycle landing gear that had to be fully retractable. A high rate of climb was specified, and it was necessary to incorporate long-range internal fuel tankage – primarily because of a silly Air Corps edict against the use of external tanks on monoplanes!

All of this was summed up in a circularized proposal design competition/invitation to bid. Lockheed in Burbank – a manufacturer which had never produced a combat-type military aircraft in California – was invited to bid as a consolation prize for not having won a contract for its XFM-2. Bell

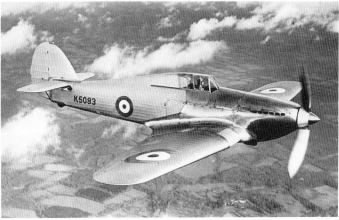

Project Officer Kelsey may have learned about the Hawker Hurricane F.36/34 too late to modify his thinking about the 1935 Pursuit Competition because it did not fly until November 6. By the start of 1936 activity on the "fly-offs" in the springtime, his decision making was evidently affected by Curtiss-Wright (and other) political pressures. (Flight)

Aircraft was on the mailing list, although they had never built one aircraft of any type that was designed by the new company. Two other companies that eventually responded with designs were Curtiss and little Vultee. Lt. Kelsey had two major building blocks on tap that would materially affect the P-38 prospects more than any other American aircraft. One of these was the acceleration of engine development at the tiny Allison Division of General Motors Corporation; the other was a spark from a small clique of Air Corps officers that finally ignited some activity at General Electric to produce long-awaited turbosuperchargers. The big corporation had been dabbling with development of the units since immediately after World War I, with the primary idea of developing some sort of gas turbine engine.

D James A. Allison had died in 1928, and the Allison Experimental Company was acquired by GM in 1929 when Allison was in dire need of fresh capital. By taking advantage of the benefits of ethylene-glycol (Prestone) cooling, developed almost entirely by the Air Corps Materiel Division in cooperation with Union Carbide, Allison engineers began full development of the V-1710 inline engine about 1931. Other contractors working to achieve the same end were minor manufacturers such as Lycoming and Continental Motors.

Quite unexpectedly, the A series and B series V-1710 Allisons were built to Navy requirement, with the latter type

intended for use in dirigibles of the *Akron* class. Army Air Corps development centered on the C series, featuring a long, smooth gear case containing epicyclic reduction gears. By 1937, the V-1710-7 (C-4 series) was being subjected to intensive flight testing in a Consolidated A-11A (an airplane design that had its beginnings with a branch of Lockheed; that was the XP-900 or YP-24) at Wright Field. All A-11s were a spinoff of the P-30/PB-2A fighter. While the PB-2As were the first fighters in the world to enter service in quantity with turbosuperchargers, the small batch of A-11s went unsupercharged.

Lt. Mark Bradley (later, Gen.) was one pilot involved in the "fly, refuel, fly" program that involved the single A-11A. Bradley stated that the airplane was "not at all pleasant to fly because it had a large-diameter propeller, forcing the pilot to land and take off from the 3-point position every time or pay the price." Bradley and other test pilots logging hours on this development engine had a boring job. They could not stray too far from the airfield because an engine failure would make any emergency landing pretty difficult with that large windmilling prop up front.

Although Lockheed had entered into some tentative design study effort prior to issuance of the circular proposals in 1936, largely on the basis of some informal conferences, the formal design inception date for its Model 22 was March 1936. It was also identified as Project M-12-36 in some circles. For security reasons, more than three years elapsed before a patent application was filed on June 27, 1939.

Several miles southeast of Burbank, in a hot and uninteresting part of the Los Angeles Basin that was largely agricultural, Gerry Vultee had established his own company near the little town of Downey. Everything being considered, he was doing reasonably well building a few V-1A transports and a greater number of light bomber-attack versions for export.

The former Lockheed chief engineer gathered together a small team of expert designers and very youthful draftsmen to generate a completely new fighter design to compete with Curtiss and Lockheed for a twin-engine interceptor contract. Vultee's final design was identified as the XP1015. At least 6,000 miles to the east, an equally small British firm, Westland Aircraft – with no more experience in designing fighters than Vultee – was designing a twin-engine interceptor. Amazingly, the two aircraft shared a great number of basic characteristics, although the procurement specifications dictated that the XP1015 would, of necessity, be about 25 percent larger and heavier than Westland's P.9. The latter aircraft was produced and became known as the Whirlwind.

Clarence Johnson's preliminary design was remarkably unlike the Vultee design in almost every way, except for the specified engines. Conventional in most ways, as if it was the next generation up from the Curtiss Y1A-18, the Vultee (and, of course, the P.9) was not going to be any trendsetter. Kelly Johnson's XFM-2 design had been far less radical than Bell's XFM-1, but at least it featured a tricycle landing gear. His Model 22 design was a coalescence of everything that Lt. Kelsey dreamed of. You can almost feel it; when Kelsey spoke, Johnson paid attention. Every great designer probably dreams of such an opportunity.

Curtiss management, for whatever reasons, evidently went on a spree of feeding tranquilizers to most of their designers – except for a slightly non-conformist engineer by the name of Walter Tydon. After the P-36A/Hawk H-75 had become an American standard, designs emanating from Buffalo's large engineering force seemed to be aimed hell-bent-for-leather toward using last year's technology and modifications of 1935 tooling jigs and fixtures. Although we have never managed to find even a sketch of the Curtiss interceptor design entry, it was probably a version of the A-18 with a single seat and two Allisons. Other examples, their much later XP-46, and XP-55 designs with single unsupercharged V-1710 engines offered absolutely nothing over the Bell XP-39 of far earlier vintage. Even then, the XP-55 design came out of St. Louis, not Buffalo. The Curtiss Airplane Division, by 1937, had become an overly fat, flabby, and pompous organization intent only on making big profits. Lockheed, Bell and Vultee were all young contenders intent on beating the competition at their own game.

Quite coincidentally with the initiation of work on the Model 22, the inception date for work on the experimental XC-35 high-altitude pressure-cabin research airplane was May 1936. Carl Green, one of Ben Kelsey's superiors at Wright Field, made it his pet project. Based on a modified Model 10A Electra airframe, the XC-35 made many remarkable contributions to the science of substratospheric and stratospheric flight. General Electric turbosuperchargers boosted the normal engine types for high-altitude flight, while cabin pressurization and control equipment was developed. Just one year later, on May 7, 1937, the XC-35 made its initial flight. Experiments led directly to the development of the Boeing 307, the North American XB-28 and the Boeing B-29.

In the meantime, Air Corps requirements for the interceptor design were finalized and defined with issuance of Specification X-608 in February 1937. Throughout the 12 months preceding issuance of those final requirements, the entire preliminary design section at Lockheed had been hard at work on Project M-12-36 in the old ranch house design office. That "design section" was composed of new Chief Engineer Hall

Hibbard and young Kelly Johnson with some periodic help from Willis Hawkins and much stress analysis work by James Gerschler. Everybody else was busy with the design of the XC-35, the new Model 12 and improvement of the Electra. Work was also moving ahead on an airplane that was to play a tremendous role in the fortunes of Lockheed. It was the Model 14 Super Electra. That sleek airliner flew for the first time in July.

These were not exactly "salad" days for Lockheed. The company had been in poor financial shape during development of the Model 10; in fact, it was (in 1934) in debt to the then awesome tune of $139,404. Total assets hardly exceeded the debt. As of the date on which Model 22 work formally started there were only 50 engineering employees on board, but overall employment had grown to some 1,200. Plant area had expanded to more than 100,000 square feet, but everybody in the industry was aware that the company had only sold five military aircraft (total) since 1928, and most of those were commercial types with military markings. It was a bit like the Old West. If you didn't experience it, it is nearly impossible to conceive of what it was like.

Six extremely radical design layouts for the Model 22 were drawn and had been analyzed by Hibbard and Johnson late in 1936. One rejected concept was very close to the design that ultimately became the De Havilland Mosquito. Another layout was comparable to what must have been the Merlin-powered version of the Fokker D.XXIII. The Netherlands-Fokker design featured a central nacelle with engines fore and aft, with the pilot sandwiched between them, but that did not come along until a couple of years later. Another design featured an asymmetrical layout with the pilot located in one of two booms. The original North American XP-82 design that appeared toward the end of the war was of similar concept.

Johnson studied the idea of burying the engines within the fuselage with extended shafts driving wing-mounted propellers. While the drag numbers were, of course, very low, complexity, weight and reliability were strong factors to be reckoned with. The concept was rejected by Johnson. (A near contemporary Vultee design, the XP-46-2 – Vultee's number – followed the same line of thinking.)

The now-familiar twin-boom arrangement favored by Johnson and Hibbard was not the configuration most designers would have employed to enhance their reputations. One entirely original Fokker design, the G-1, was adopted in small numbers by the Netherlands military in the later 1930s. Well armed, it might have become a decent attack airplane, but various details of design defeated it. The G-1 was cumbersome, and it proved to be hardly faster or more maneuverable than a Lockheed Model 10 airliner.

Lockheed's team, knowing that they faced some very tough competition from Curtiss, Vultee, probably Bell and perhaps Douglas, had confidence that they could use innovations that none of the others was likely to attempt. They had to endure a long, wet winter with rainwater leaking through the old roof to increase their discomfort. Young Johnson's calculations covered reams of paper, while his K&E slide rule worked overtime. With the full support of an enlightened management, Johnson made a gutwrenching decision in midstream to revamp the wing design, resulting in a major change in the chord/thickness ratio. He had looked with envy at the thin wing picked for the brand new Supermarine Spitfire, but he was handicapped by the internal space needs dictated by the specifications requiring that all fuel be carried internally.

To give some idea of the problem facing Johnson, it is necessary to know that early Spitfires had a total internal tankage of 85 Imperial gallons of fuel, and the contemporary Westland Whirlwind only carried 134 (Imp.) gallons. It would be necessary for the Model 22 to carry no less than 400 gallons (U.S.) of fuel internally. Lockheed's interceptor would also have to carry nearly four times as much oil as the Spitfire because of longer range and two engines. Consequently, a near symmetrical airfoil of relatively thick section was adopted, namely the NACA 23016 section at the root. At the tip attachment point, it had changed to NACA 4412. In planform, the wing virtually duplicated that used on the Model 14.

James McMinn Gerschler, a name not large in history records, was involved in the structural design, which resulted in the Model 22 being the first aircraft in which the substructure was joggled for a butt-jointed, flush-surface skin. It was also the first production fighter to use metal-covered control surfaces all around.

In an era of 5,000-pound fighters and 13,000-pound bombers, the new Model 22 was to tip the scales at 11,400 pounds with the 400-gallon fuel load. For direct comparison, the 10-place Electra airliner only grossed 10,500 pounds. While light wing loadings were still the rule, Lockheed's new offspring was shattering the rules. Problems encountered with the XC-35 superchargers were transmitted to Johnson from Dayton, Ohio, without delay. Considering the number of turbosuperchargers built by General Electric and licensed manufacturers during World War II, it seems incredible that fewer than one hundred production exhaust-driven superchargers had been manufactured in the entire world at the time Lockheed was getting ready to build the prototype XP-38 in 1937. Even early Boeing B-17 Flying Fortresses flew without turbosupercharging in those days.

Soon after AAC Design Competition requirements appeared in Spec. X-608, Clarence Johnson completed his classic, visionary LAC Report No. 1152 bearing the title "Aerodynamics and Performance Study, Lockheed Model 22 Pursuit Airplane." Notice that the "interceptor" title had already disappeared from the scene. Dated April 13, 1937, the report was signed by Johnson and approved by his boss, Hall Hibbard. It proved to be an extremely farsighted report, even if there was some optimism mixed in. This was the leading edge of an era in which the customer began to demand equipment changes almost immediately after a contract was awarded.

Air Corps optimism was not absent either. Allison promised to deliver 1150 horsepower from each engine, and with the alternate 260-gallon fuel carried in integral tanks the design gross weight was to be 10,500 pounds. Reflecting peacetime thinking of the era, the report went on to say that the "airplane is to be not only flush riveted, but painted and polished as well." It was, in the vernacular of its creator, "designed to operate at a critical altitude of 20,000 feet and at speeds up to 400 mph." With the power-to-weight ratio based on AAC engine performance figures, the company came out with very conservative and realistic calculated figures showing a top speed at 20,000 feet of 417 mph! In 1937, such figures were astronomical. Just for comparison, the World's Absolute Speed Record established by the pure racing type Macchi-Castoldi MC.72 was just a bit over 440 miles per hour.

Of very special interest is the fact that Lockheed's proposal Aircraft Specification No. 221 dated April 12 did *not* call for counter-rotating propellers. Lt. Ben Kelsey's hand showed clearly in the armament area. A 25-mm shell-firing cannon was specified, in spite of the fact that America had no such weapon and the only weapon of that caliber anywhere in the world was an undeveloped and unavailable Hotchkiss weapon to be produced in France. (Small-bore cannon development in the United States was best described as pitiful. Money for work on such objects in an isolationist atmosphere was as scarce as chicken lips.)

Young Johnson's formal report (No. 1152) contained a quiet block-buster of infinite importance, in spite of the fact

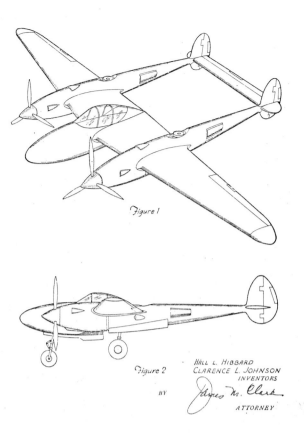

Figure 1

Figure 2

HALL L. HIBBARD
CLARENCE L. JOHNSON
INVENTORS

BY

ATTORNEY

*For a dozen valid reasons, patent drawings for Lockheed's Model 22 prototype were not filed until the XP-38 had actually flown. Hall Hibbard and Clarence L. Johnson were (logically) listed as co-inventors. Johnson was still in his twenties.*

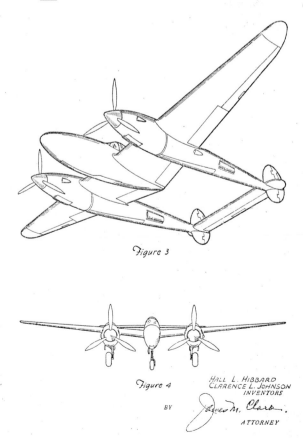

Figure 3

Figure 4

HALL L. HIBBARD
CLARENCE L. JOHNSON
INVENTORS

BY

ATTORNEY

that hardly anybody knew anything about the specific subject. It was 1937, when only the rarest of aircraft could climb above 30,000 feet and the world's formal landplane speed record over a short course was below 360 miles per hour. No matter, Johnson's study report devoted six pages of that document to a subject entitled "Compressibility Effects," and that ethereal subject was covered in great detail. Before finalizing the report, Johnson had contacted Drs. Theodore von Karman and Clark B. Milliken to solicit their comments on the validity of the designer's calculations and conclusions relative to the effects of Mach's Number. (In those days, the few who had delved into the subject at all referred to it as Dr. Mach's number.)

Surprisingly, neither von Karman – who was a top authority on compressibility of fluids (and air is a fluid) – nor Milliken could provide any formula for calculating the increase in profile drag of an airfoil. Neither scientist nor anybody else at respected Caltech could help Johnson with several other penetrating questions. Some valuable support and suggestions did, however, prompt Johnson to make that decision about revising the airfoil, mentioned earlier. The implications of the report were not lost on Lt. Kelsey, an MIT graduate. Compressibility was waiting – like the dark at the top of the stairs – for those brash enough and fast enough to venture into the realm.

Lockheed President Robert Gross, replacing the departed Lloyd Stearman, boarded an airliner for Dayton with Report No. 1152 and an armful of drawings which he delivered to Ben Kelsey at Wright Field. He was confident that Lockheed would win over any competition because every performance figure exceeded every requirement of what most people viewed as the toughest set of specifications ever devised by the Air Corps. Whereas a top speed of 360 mph was required, the Model 22 was likely to exceed 400 miles per hour by a significant margin. Kelly Johnson's brainchild was not just a giant step forward in aircraft design; it was a magnificent leap forward in an era of careful evolution. Now it was time for the design team to sit down and fret over the things they had not thought of while awaiting the outcome of proposal evaluations.

Although some Air Corps evaluators were openly skeptical of Lockheed's claims of speeds in excess of 400 mph at critical altitude, Kelsey was highly elated. Hibbard and Johnson had, in effect, incorporated everything that Kelsey had ever wanted to see in a design. There had been a complete meeting of the minds.

As for the concurrent single-engine interceptor competition, Kelsey's boss, Col. Oliver Echols, was approached by the youngish aviation/motion picture mogul Howard Hughes, shortly after issuance of the Project X-609 Circular Proposal. Hughes wanted the Air Corps to purchase his record-setting H-1 racer that had been designed by Richard Palmer. Not one to adhere to convention, Hughes may have been attempting to upset the 1936 Pursuit Competition with an exciting design, or he may have been trying to pressure his way into the "interceptor" competition with what came to be know as an "off-the-shelf" sale.

Colonel Echols assured Hughes that there were no funds available anywhere for procurement of a composite (wood and metal) racing airplane that met none of the requirements for a military pursuit or any other military classification.

"Howard," Echols said in a fatherly tone, "you submit a design proposal that meets the official requirements and it will get full consideration. Or, build a plane that meets our requirements; then we can buy it. But we can't pay you a dime for your beautiful wooden racer." You can almost see Hughes turning on his heel and leaving without the usual courtesies. He evidently learned nothing from that because the situation was nearly duplicated when he built the Hughes D-2 a few years later.

Bob Woods and his leader, Larry Bell, had submitted their

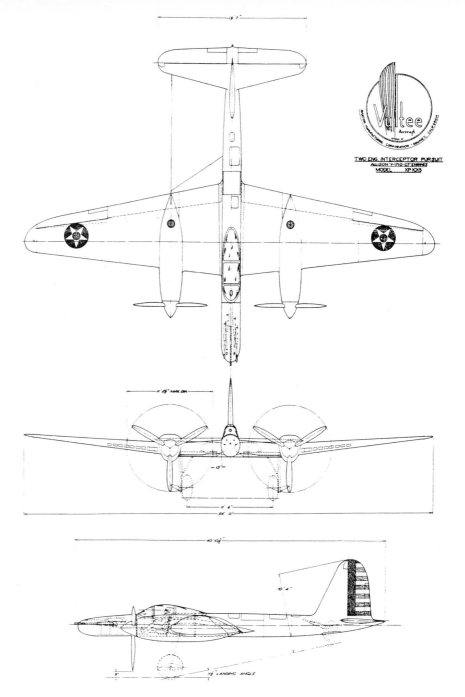

*OPPOSITE LEFT: Lockheed XP-38 central fuselage (gondola) mockup shared tight shop space with actual prototype airplane. Automotive-style steering wheel was a specific solution to the control of such a large fighter in the mid-1930s. That odd drum affair in nose section was the rotary magazine for the .90 T1 Army Ordnance .90-caliber cannon as a replacement for the non-existent 25-mm cannon originally proposed. The Browning (Colt) 37-mm cannon was eventually adopted. (Lockheed)*

*RIGHT: Former Lockheed Chief Engineer Gerard "Gerry" Vultee (or Jerry) gathered a young group of engineers at the Aircraft Development Corporation to submit this XP1015 design as his entry to Circular Proposal X-608. In many respects, it was not terribly advanced over the Curtiss Y1A-18, already in production at the time except for the Allison engines and early bubble-type canopy. It did not feature contrarotating propellers. (Dustin Carter)*

*OPPOSITE BOTTOM LEFT: Where did it go wrong? Bell's XP-39 (AC38-326) in its original configuration puts lie to all statements that it was designed for low-level operation from the outset. Seen at Wright Field in April 1939, it had a B-5 turbosupercharger for high-altitude operation. The critical altitude specified was 20,000 feet, well above that of any European contemporary at that date. While no verified figures have been seen, the XP-39 is supposed to have attained just under 400 mph at altitude in the early flights. When Kelsey was preoccupied with the suddenly urgent YP-38 project, NACA and Fighter Branch conspired to strip XP-39 of its turbo. After that, performance of the Airacobra declined steadily. For the record, Bell P-39s never employed American Armament Corporation 37-mm cannon, a ripoff of the unsuccessful Baldwin cannon. No long-barrel AAC guns were ever built; the guns actually used in most P-39s were the Browning (Colt) M4 model. Remainder had 20-mm shell guns.*

second radical design under Circular Proposal Spec. X-609 that – on paper at least – appeared to be another world beater like the Lockheed. Woods packed every specification item into an airframe that was nearly as pretty as the Spitfire. It featured very heavy armament, including the Browning (Colt) 37-mm cannon; a rather simple tricycle landing gear was fitted; the required Allison V-1710 was included, but in this unusual case it was behind the pilot; and it was going to be a high flyer because a Type B-5 turbosupercharger was included. No doubt about it, the airplane was handsome, cleanlined and featured the radical mid-engine concept that was tried by Koolhoven in Holland (with inadequate resources). Their FK-55 fighter had an unreliable engine and the airframe was lagging in modern technology. The only thing really shared by the two designs was placement of the engine aft of the pilot. But it was one of those rare instances where a single design philosophy emerges at two entirely unrelated locations in the same time frame.

Contract awards were made to Lockheed and Bell for their individualistic designs for "interceptors" in 1937. The Project Office at Wright Field declared that Lockheed was winner of the twin-engine competition on June 23, assigning the military designation XP-38 under Contract AC-9974. The monetary value was $163,000. Bell won the other competition, receiving Contract AC-10341 for an aircraft to be designated XP-39. No official identifying names were assigned because it was definitely not Army policy in those days, but it was not long before Bell applied the name Airacobra to its vehicle.

Contrary to reports of many "authorities" over a multidecade timespan, the Bell XP-39 was not a low-level fighter from the outset any more than the XP-38 was an unadulterated bomber-interceptor. Any aircraft equipped with a turbosupercharger was specifically intended to fly at altitudes well above a more commonplace 20,000 feet in the thin air generally referred to as the stratosphere. Having flown virtually every service type and experimental aircraft in the Air Corps' inventory by 1937, Ben Kelsey was convinced that America's standard pursuit planes – intended to intercept bombers and tackle an enemy's fighters in the classic dogfight style – were incapable of performing either task satisfactorily. To him, Projects X-608 and X-609 were contrived methods to overcome long-standing political constraints that came from inter-service rivalries, punitive actions against people like Gen. Billy Mitchell and, sometimes, laws that were enacted almost entirely as reactions to World War I.

No matter what Kelsey may have suggested with terms such as "interceptor" or that longstanding holdover from our participation in the Great War, the "Pursuit," he had great vision in recognizing that these aircraft were fighters, pure and simple. If ever there were two combat aircraft that were commissioned from the start to intercept bombers as their prime responsibility, the RAF Spitfire and Hurricane were those aircraft. Like the Bulldog and Fury biplanes before them, they were intended to be home-defense fighters. Fast, maneuverable and rapid in climb, the ability to defend themselves against other fighters was an indigenous asset.

But for a series of unfortunate decisions on the part of the Bell design team, the new Project Officer assigned to relieve Kelsey of full responsibility for two major fighter projects and some well-meaning NACA engineers, the P-39 might well have remained a high-altitude type that would go on to greater success. However, the turbosupercharger was an early victim of a misguided drag reduction effort. Something was gained by a reduced canopy height and some inlet changes, but it is a highly unlikely that the mid-ship scoop for the turbo created any really serious drag. If anything proved to be really wrong, it was the directional stability provided by the tiny empennage and a poor choice of airfoil sections for the wing.

Designer Woods, lacking some of the skills with which Kelly Johnson had been blessed, committed his basic design to some subtle but serious design errors that tended to plague the P-39 as similar errors had plagued the XFM-1 and YFM-1 series of multiseat fighters. Streamlined as it appeared to be, the FM-1 design was retarded by an unfortunate choice of airfoil section, wing-fuselage intersection, overweight structure and engine overheating on the ground (the pusher propellers provided no engine cooling while the aircraft was taxiing). Much larger and heavier than the older Curtiss Y1A-18, but with little more horsepower and probably the same airfoil, the XFM-1 Airacuda was doomed to failure from the start. Ben Kelsey provided a number of designers with the greatest opportunity of their lives by giving them specifications that were clear roadsigns to success. He could not, in his procurement role, help them design the airplanes.

Meanwhile, James McMinn Gerschler took over as XP-38 project engineer for Lockheed in July when Johnson moved into a more responsible position with a company that was heading off on the road to triumph at a full gallop. Preliminary design ventures were numerous. One of Gerschler's first documents out of the Ozalid machine was LR-1160, issued on September 23, 1937, calling for installation V-1710-C7 and -C9 opposite-rotation engines and either the .90-caliber T1 cannon or the 23-mm Madsen cannon produced in Europe. Other changes recommended by Johnson were included in the report.

Quite coincidentally, the Bell XFM-1 took off on its maiden flight in September with Lt. Ben Kelsey at the controls. Not unexpectedly, Bell had no test pilot qualified to fly high-performance twin-engine aircraft, so it was logical for Kelsey to do the initial flight work and then take the aircraft to Wright Field for further trials. The ravages of the Great Depression impacted America's military aircraft industry in many ways from 1935 to 1939. As exemplified by the XFM-1, Grumman's XF4F-2 Navy fighter, Vought's V-143 and at least a dozen other types, gestation periods seemed to bring on an avalanche of change requirements. There was great upheaval in the major engine manufacturing companies because they were trying to produce too many different engines to meet too many requirements. Complete failures of new models were so frequent, the public hardly got to know many existed. When the Air Corps finally got its requirements in focus and industry began to get back on track, the threat of war, followed by actual combat, forced periodic revisions of virtually every major plan.

As France wallowed around without defined direction, England and Germany were surging ahead with new, efficient fighter airplanes based on some reliable high-performance engines. Both nations literally catapulted ahead of the U.S. between 1935 and 1939 with Hawker, Supermarine and Messerschmitt designs. Seversky fell on hard times after the P-35 contract was filled and survived primarily by exporting; Boeing had abdicated from the fighter business and came perilously close to ending activity on B-17s; Vought gave up all hope of building anything for the Air Corps and, after the V-143 fiasco, was struggling to come up with any truly modern aircraft.

Douglas was in real trouble. The OA-5 giant amphibian was a dead end; the prototype DC-4X had gone off in the wrong direction; the DF boat was outmoded before it left the drawing board; B-18s were numerous, but if ever committed to combat they would have fared as badly as Fairey Battles eventually did. Vultee struggled, then appeared to sit down to build trainers and to contemplate its navel. Only Lockheed and Bell seemed to have the spirit, while Grumman continued to up the power in its cute, fat little biplane fighters well into 1939!

Any detailed analysis of the Lockheed P-38 naturally leads to some unrecognized – or at least previously unstated – coincidences that occurred virtually simultaneously in democracies and in a nation ruled by a dictator. In one democracy, the British Air Ministry established technical requirements, in 1935, for a powerfully armed twin-engine single-seat fighter – primarily a killer-type interceptor with very short range, but capable of air-to-air combat in any situation. An initial development contract expanded into a production contract as the pressures of a war mounted, overtaxing tiny Westland Aircraft's abilities. Under less pressure, the P.9 Whirlwind might have developed into a fighter of merit. At about the same time, but under the peculiar constraints of a dictatorship, Dipl.-Ing. Kurt Tank concluded – quite independently of official *Luftwaffe* thinking – that a well-designed fighter with two powerful engines and concentrated firepower must, of a certainty, be faster and more potent than standard single-engine fighter types. Prototypes were constructed, but without full sponsorships in the right places, it never really had the chance to develop into a viable weapon.

Such coincidental appearance of previously ignored two-engine single-seat fighter aircraft was rather remarkable in that era. Even if some evidence should appear to reveal that Germany and/or Great Britain had gained knowledge about each other's developments though espionage, there can be no thought that Lt. Kelsey was ever privy to that information. His (profound) conception was an immaculate one. But for the brilliant teamwork achieved by Benjamin Kelsey and C. L. Johnson, it is a 99-percent certainty that America would not have produced a viable twin-engine fighter with performance approaching that of the P-38 during the war. Imagination, design genius, determination and leadership were all on the American side. At least a majority of those traits did not come together to support the British and German projects, so neither the Westland Whirlwind nor the Kurt Tank-designed Focke-Wulf Fw 187 achieved mass deployment status or a modicum of success.

A minimum of 15 completely different two-engine, single-seat fighter aircraft attained at least prototype status in no fewer than five nations during the war. Only one, the P-38 Lightning, was ever given the production status of a true first-line combat fighter, i.e., ordered into and committed to mass production.

# CHAPTER 3

# Spectacular Growth and Potential Competitors

A Nobody at Lockheed Aircraft, except possibly Robert Gross and Clarence Johnson, had the slightest conception that the corporation's near-term destiny would be categorized as incredible. And that was true even after the interceptor proposal had won them a prototype contract for one XP-38. But there were some telltale signs. A fast feedliner transport design by Hall Hibbard and Johnson, the Model 12, had been moderately successful in winning a Bureau of Air Commerce competition, and design of the Model 14 Super Electra had more or less paralleled preliminary design work on the Model 22 (XP-38).

On the other hand, this inspired group, working in a totally uninspiring hodgepodge of leased buildings on leased land, had delivered no more than 98 aircraft between late 1932 and the end of 1936. Whatever motivated Gross, it prompted him to purchase all of the land and buildings – 43 acres and 108,000 square feet of old, nonintegrated (and shabby) plant – in 1936. Expecting great things of the Model 14, he also decided (not unilaterally) to double plant floor space and to get modernized equipment. The new additions were all in place within days of notification that Lockheed had won the XP-38 competition.

California's motion picture industry, in 1937, was coming into its glory days from a good 1935 start. Lockheed's "star" seemed to be following in close formation. Another warm and sunny day embraced Los Angeles County on July 29, the light reflecting brightly off the polished aluminum surfaces of the new prototype Model 14 Super Electra. It bore simple Northwest Airlines markings because it was the first customer for Lockheed's latest product. In the cockpit were Marshall Headle, the chief test pilot, and Kelly Johnson. As designer, he insisted on being on board for the initial flight.

The newest in airliners lifted off the dirt strip paralleling the Southern Pacific tracks behind the expanding factory. The Model 14, on this first flight, had to be the world's fastest airliner, outpacing the rapid Model 10 by nearly 50 mph. Circling easily to the left, they landed just minutes later at Union Air Terminal located about one mile west. Not a single person aboard could have guessed that hundreds of near duplicates would one day help to bring down a powerful dictatorship. During the next eight years after the short 1937 flight, Lockheed would produce more than 3,000 of that basic airframe type, bringing in $263 million in sales.

Two distinctive Kelly Johnson features were embodied in the Model 14 design; twin tails were carried over from the Models 10 and 12, and an unusually high wing loading was adopted to get maximum performance. Johnson compensated for that by incorporating the new Fowler flap, combining drag for landing with greatly increased lift. The sleek Super Electra was the world's first production aircraft to feature the Lockheed-Fowler flap system, and probably the P-38 was the only type to use it more successfully.

While Britain's Prime Minister Neville Chamberlain was possibly 110 percent sincere in believing that his paper agreement with Adolph Hitler was valid and would not be abrogated, more pragmatic officials in government were certain

*One almost precisely accurate and well-executed painting of the XP-38 in flight appeared on the back cover of a magazine, but the original artwork disappeared. Nobody at March Field ever made any arrangements for air-to-air photographs of the XP-38, although the base photographers probably would have been delighted to have the opportunity.*

that their "tight little isle" would soon come under attack by the Nazis. Thanks to the foresight of such men, a determined British Purchasing Commission hurriedly departed for the United States with the aim of buying combat airplanes and trainers. Too small to have a Washington staff, Lockheed knew nothing of the impending visit until five days before they were scheduled to arrive. Only with the arrival of a Western Union telegram at Burbank from the British Air Attache did anyone become aware of a great potential sale. The Purchasing Commission was planning to visit Consolidated, Douglas, Vultee and Boeing, and possibly, the newly formed Northrop Aircraft and perhaps Lockheed. Here was a "dream come true" situation for the company. But it didn't have one military product that could be sold to the British, not even a training plane.

Clarence Johnson's mind didn't skip a beat. Borrowing heavily on his XFM-2 concept, he quickly adapted a warplane nose and top turret to the Model 14 fuselage and figured out how to incorporate a useful bomb bay to create a light bomber. Few, if any, Lockheed people knew that the RAF was sorely in need of a coastal reconnaissance aircraft to either supplement or replace their slightly smaller but decidedly obsolete Avro Ansons. Those contemporaries of a "militarized" Model 12 had fabric-covered fuselages and wooden wings; they were at least 60 mph slower than any Super Electra and had less than one-half the range capability. As engineers worked rapidly on two versions of proposed armament arrangements (both adapted from alternative XFM-2 designs), a spare corner of the factory was cleared. Working around the clock, a small team fabricated a wooden-fabric mockup of a B14 (Model 14 bomber). It was finished in just five days.

Purchasing Commission members were greatly impressed by the enthusiasm and skill shown by Lockheed's team. Some crew and armament changes desired by the British were incorporated in the mockup overnight. This effort, in April 1938, soon brought forth a remarkable contract for an over-whelming $25 million to procure at least 200 Model B14L coastal reconnaissance aircraft. They were to be the submarine hunters of that era. The contract was signed on June 23, and the 215,000-square-foot factory was obligated to deliver all aircraft by the end of 1939! An additional plum offering: LAC was authorized to deliver up to 250 of the B14Ls within the same time frame.

Was luck instrumental in all of this? The British had not a clue that the only orders for aircraft remaining on the books at Lockheed (other than one XP-38) were a few orders from Japan for some Model 14 airliners. Without that order from the Japanese, the Purchasing Commission would have see an empty factory . . . a sight that would not have been very encouraging. And based largely on their own experiences, management people at Consolidated, Boeing, Douglas, and Curtiss – the "Big Four" – were somewhere between hysterical laughter and cries of anguish. "Lockheed," they said almost in unison, "can never build that many airplanes." They were bitter that the upstart company had beaten them at their own game. On Lockheed's books, the new aircraft that would eventually be called Hudson was recorded as the Model 214-40-01.

With British and French orders flowing into American industry, aircraft production and aviation activity in general began to accelerate early in 1938, although there was little sign that Army Air Corps procurement had awakened from its Rip van Winkle-like slumber. But by 1939, there was acceler-ating activity because of sudden awareness that expansion of Air Corps and Navy aviation was long overdue. With most of the world teetering on the brink of war, the expansion was being funded and contracts were, at long last, being awarded. It had become obvious that the British and French procurement

Lockheed's Burbank factory looked like this on July 29, 1937, when the first flight of a Super Electra took place. Mission Glass facility had been absorbed, integrated. AiRover, a Lockheed subsidiary (soon to become Vega Aircraft), had taken over the Empire China facility (upper left). Ranch house was embedded in new two-story office building. (LAC)

efforts could not for long be limited to "training plane" buys in the face of Nazi aggression.

As is so often the case when subterfuge is employed in international dealings, something went awry. All of the press services on the West Coast reported on January 23 that a "secret" new airplane flying over the Douglas El Segundo plant at Mines Field had crashed. When it was revealed that a previously unmentionable and security-classified Douglas 7B attack-bomber – the linear progenitor of the 1940s RAF Boston and U.S. Army A-20 – had slammed into the nearby North American Aviation employees' parking lot, it became a news item that would not soon fade away. Newsmen then learned that a representative of the French Air Ministry had accompanied the test pilot on the flight of this previously unannounced military aircraft, and it was unheard of for an official of any foreign nation to fly in one of the most advanced aircraft supposedly intended for the Air Corps. (Martin's Model 167, North American's NA-40-2 and Stearman's X-100 were other challengers for government contracts.) The crash triggered a Senate Military Affairs Committee investigation. Ultimately it was revealed that President Roosevelt – in his continuing battle with the ultra-isolationist congressional bloc – had provided the authority for such activities.

Less than a month later, the first Supermarine Spitfire Mk. Is began to move off the production lines in England. In the new age of Hydromatic constant-speed and the other adjust-able or controllable-pitch metal propellers, the big wooden fixed-pitch propellers fitted to the new and sleek Spitfires provided an anachronistic touch as the fighters took to the air at Eastleigh. Concurrently, new Hawker Hurricanes were be-ing posted to squadron service at Debden, a military airfield later to become the home of the USAAF's Fourth Fighter Group.

Unnoticed by any but the most avid and observant re-searcher, a small reference to a new Westland twin-engine "435-mph" fighter appeared in the French aviation journal *Les Ailes* (Wings). It was the first public reference to the Whirl-wind fighter, and it predated any official British revelation about Westland's P.9 by three years. The speed mentioned turned out to be optimistic by almost 100 mph (not at all unusual in those years), but what is far more interesting is

that the "rumor" item was published within days or weeks of the far more flamboyant entry of the radical and burnished Lockheed XP-38 into the public eye.

Previously sleepy and dull Burbank at the northeastern fringes of the San Fernando Valley must have been "popping" in 1939. The nearby motion picture studios were doing very well, air traffic into Union Air Terminal was way up and Lockheed was bursting at the seams. Even with the huge British contract, the corporation entered 1939 with a small staff of only about 2,500 employees. The initial Model 214-40-01 Hudson made its first takeoff from the Lockheed Airstrip on December 10, 1938, a flight witnessed by most of the employees. Bob Gross had every right to be proud of his organization. Less than six months had elapsed since the contract for 200 RAF Coastal Command aircraft had been signed; and it was every bit as remarkable to learn, if the fact was overlooked, that not even one and a half years had elapsed since the very first Model 14 had taken off from that same strip.

These were momentous times for the Burbank company. In the following month, three more Hudsons were delivered – yes, delivered – to the Royal Air Force and the prototype XP-38 was being groomed for flight at March Field, about 82 air miles to the southeast of the plant. Risen like the phoenix from the ashes of bankruptcy (in just a half-dozen years), Lockheed was performing so brilliantly in 1939 that no less than 287 of those

Hudson reconnaissance-bombers were delivered by December 31, 1939!

Out in a walled-off remote corner of one building the XP-38 was being fabricated in absolute secrecy. In some ways, that might be considered the real beginning of Kelly Johnson's fabled "Skunk Works" because some of the same people were involved in the later XP-80 project, routinely viewed as the initial project for that organization. Subassembly construction got under way on the XP-38 in July 1938, just about a month after Lockheed got the "go ahead" on building Hudsons. Fabrication of the XP-38 posed some serious problems for the experimental crew. Perhaps the most difficult process was in joggling, fitting and flush-riveting of skin panels to obtain a smooth surface of butt-jointed aluminum sheets.[1] Engineers worked closely with assembly workers to solve problems as they arose.

During this same period, the company was, of course, experimenting with one system that was a truly pioneering effort and, in this case, it was rather complex. We address the retractable tricycle landing hear. Lockheed had really pioneered retractable landing gear systems with its Altair/Orion civil types, but even the most advanced types in Europe or Japan had obsolete or unsophisticated systems as late as 1935. Tricycle landing gears were unheard of outside of the United States. With the introduction of the Model 12, the Air Corps and Navy each ordered one to be fitted with a non-retracting tricycle landing gear for experimentation. The Army type was called the C-40B and the Navy version was the XJO-3. Before the two test planes were built, the company constructed a large structural steel beam affair fitted with a tricycle landing gear (main wheels from a Vega Starliner) plus a seat and a "fifth wheel" for speed recording and anti-tipover purposes. It

1. One of the things that made the XP-38 a "quantum leap forward" in aviation was its advanced structure. Hall Aluminum Aircraft was formed only a decade earlier to fabricate experimental flying boats with metal hulls, while John Northrop pioneered in smooth-skin aluminum aircraft structures from 1929-30. Detroit-Lockheed Aircraft and (later on) Consolidated Aircraft followed suit, as did Boeing (with the Monomail and XB-9) and Martin (XB-907). However, the Lockheed team led the way in producing flush-riveted, butt-jointed aluminum-skinned airplanes with its Model 22. That was something that even Lt. Kelsey had not put into his specifications.

was actually the fourth wheel on the rig, but in automotive parlance it was a fifth wheel. This entire brutish affair was meant to be towed down the runway by a dinosaur of a Cadillac roadster that had seen more opulent days. With this unit, they could determine what angles and damping would be needed to avoid dreaded wheel shimmy.

Lt. Kelsey was sent on TDY to California after Thanksgiving Day to track manufacturing progress and, eventually, to do all of the test flying. The lieutenant had flown just about every type the Air Corps had in inventory, but Marshall Headle had never flown a fighter aircraft. A company photographer made a few detail photos of the XP-38, but it remained for Kelsey to sneak a partial overall view prior to movement to another location (evidently the GGG Distillery which Lockheed had just purchased for development and subassembly work).

Partially dismantled, the prototype was loaded on to a flatbed truck on December 31, 1938, for transport to March Field. The wings and other items were wrapped in white cloth, appearing to be a huge loaf of French bread from Fisherman's Wharf at San Francisco. With 14 Lockheed plant protection men and a consignment of Army MPs, the caravan set off on a trek over mostly two-lane roads in pre-freeway California. They had to cover at least 120 miles to reach the Army airfield about 8 miles south of Riverside, then a charming town in desert-like country. The road trip involved about 14 hours of nonstop travel in the dark of night, because they encountered low-hanging power lines, trees and hanging traffic signals. Kelsey "bootlegged" one more picture from the back of an Army 4x4 in which he was riding. (The negatives evidently were not processed for years.)

Guard Chief P. M. Scott said, "It turned out to be an illegal move. Our highway travel permit expired at midnight, but we didn't arrive (at March) until early morning. The trip took 14 hours." By evening the XP-38 was offloaded into a hangar set aside for the purpose, the Lockheed flight test and experimental technicians assigned had settled in for at least six weeks of intensive activity. There was an air of anticipation that a full decade of Air Corps lethargy regarding fighter planes was about to be jolted as never before. Instead of being on the threshold of being embalmed, the pursuit/fighter in America was about to be shown as a thriving, vibrant entity.

**B**Although the basic theme of this story is the development and operational history of the Lockheed P-38 Lightning, there is a closely related secondary aspect which relates to the entire species of twin-engine, single-seat, propeller-driven fighter aircraft developed before and during World War II. Fortunately for the Allied nations, the most successful and outstanding example of the strain was the P-38 – by a significant, even outstanding, margin. Nevertheless, capable design teams the world over tackled the demanding and challenging problem between 1935 and 1945 and several of the world's most eminent design teams came close to success, but combinations of technical failures, political interference and military trend changes conspired to defeat them.

From a design appearance standpoint, the various aircraft involved ranged from sleek and graceful to downright ugly. W. E. W. Petter's low-altitude P.9 Whirlwind was one of the most pleasant to gaze upon, but his later high-level Welkin variation of the theme inherited none of the good looks of its progenitor. Despite being several years newer than the Lightning, the Welkin's performance fell short in virtually every category. In no respect could it be envisioned as a "dogfighter" in the true sense, while time and the constructor seemed determined to prove that it was not a mass-producible aircraft.

As the path of the war reached its zenith, American's Grumman Aircraft turned out the "airplane that should have been" (three years earlier), a Double Wasp-powered F7F-1 Tigercat. With two of the powerful, reliable R-2800 engines, a slim, curvaceous fuselage and low-aspect-ratio wings, the F7F would have been ideal for the island-hopping campaign in the Pacific and, in an AAF version, could have been a superb bomber escort fighter over Europe. Great Britain produced the startlingly beautiful De Havilland Hornet, a perfectly sculpted aircraft with blazing speed. Yet it could not match the P-38 for strength, range or load-carrying capacity in spite of its late appearance on the scene.

Nazi Germany attempted something that matched and even outdid a group of U.S. designs (mostly single-engine types) that were best remembered for their extreme radicalism of concept. Their Dornier Do 335A, though not a pretty aircraft, managed a bit of "one upmanship" over the Fokker D-XXIII in the push-pull category avoided by most designers. Had it been possible to mass produce the Dornier a year earlier, it might have had a profound effect on the progress of the air war over Europe.

For those unbelievers and for those who have been unable to view the P-38 objectively, it is necessary to provide a sort of "road test" as done by automotive publications. Therefore, this section of the chapter is devoted to briefly detailing the history of the three earliest contestants (and XP-38 contemporaries) in the "twin-engine fighter design tournament," a figurative contest in which success or failure may have proven crucial in the conduct of the war.

A German penchant for aeronautical innovation surfaced in 1936, when designer Kurt Tank – an inappropriate name – displayed drawings of a comparatively long-range fighter with a single crewman and twin engines. It was shown in connection with a highly classified military exhibition at the Henschel Aircraft Co. near Berlin. Virtually every *Luftwaffe* official involved in the unauthorized rebirth of German air power attended the multiday exhibit. That was especially true of the procurement authorities in the German Air Ministry equivalent of the British Air Ministry and the U.S. Army Air Corps Procurement Board.

Engineer Tank, the key designer for Focke-Wulf, was "marching to a different drum beat" with his then radical concept, but officialdom in the *Reichluftfahrtministerium* (RLM) equated the two-engine fighter with long-range escort duties and, more importantly, a two-man crew. Therefore, Dipl.-Ing. Tank was faced with two major problems:

(1) Developing a new design concept for which there was precious little empirical data, and

(2) Overcoming the inflexible opinions established in the minds of those who controlled the issuance of contracts.

From his point of view, the actual design problems were the easiest things to solve; in fact, he had already resolved them. He did have many staunch supporters in the Technical Bureau, and eventually he was successful in getting the chief of the Development Section to allocate funds for three Fw 187 fighter prototypes.[2]

All specifications for the two-engine interceptor, including

2. *Criticism of the performance of entries in the Army Air Corps pursuit competition at Wright Field in 1936 was warranted, especially when the designs of the RAF's Hurricane and Spitfire were evaluated. However, the newest Luftwaffe fighters were not doing any better at that time. It is true that the American types were having serious engine problems, but the main issue was their uninspired airframe designs. The Germans had much more advanced airplanes, but they were handicapped by their weak 610 horsepower Junkers Jumo 210A engines pending development of the far superior inverted Daimler-Benz DB series engines. Messerschmitt's Bf 109B and Heinkel's He 112, in head-to-head competition at Travemunde, were unable to attain speeds of 280 mph in the autumn of 1936.*

a rather realistic top speed expectation of 348 mph, were predicated on availability on Daimler-Benz DB600 engines having a maximum output rating of 960 horsepower (very close to what the Allison V-1710 was actually producing at the beginning of 1939). The fact that Kurt Tank was displaying layouts of his radical fighter in mid-1936 confirms that he was, indeed, a designer of great talent.

About 550 miles to the east, across the narrow English Channel, the Air Ministry was probably ecstatic about the early performances of the Hurricane and Spitfire prototypes, since both fighters (truly interceptor types at that time) were demonstrating speeds exceeding 325 mph with relative ease.

Willy Messerschmitt's eventual success with the Bf 109 and Bf 110 types, plus Germany's involvement in the Spanish Civil War by 1937, impeded development of the Focke-Wulf Fw 187 Falke (Falcon) when it was completed in prototype form in the summer of 1937, just after Lockheed was given a contract for one XP-38. Tank and his Project Engineer (Blaser) were restricted by a low priority. Denied access to DB600-series engines, they had to settle for Jumo 210D units of 610-675 horsepower.

Even in the face of low priorities, the Focke-Wulf team forged ahead and completed the Fw 187 V1 in less than 12 months. Half a world away and with no convincing mandate to hurry construction of the XP-38, it took the Lockheed team about 18 months to complete their airplane of similar dimensions. In all fairness, however, the higher-flying, turbosupercharged XP-38 with its more complex systems and flush skin construction was far more difficult to build. American in 1937 and 1938 had economically backslid into a recession that was nearly as painful as the Great Depression. In fact, it was an "aftershock" of that financial disaster. Concern about the worsening world political situation was limited to the few souls who were so anti-fascist in their thinking that siding with the communists (as in joining up to battle Franco) was acceptable thinking. All of this seemed to increase isolationist power. Fortunately for America, Lt. Kelsey supplied whatever impetus might have been necessary to keep his project moving apace.

America's espionage corps must have been "out to lunch" with respect to German military expansion and technical progress. Even with the unguarded warnings from people like Col. Charles Lindbergh, Maj. Alford Williams and the blaring editorials in *Aviation* and *Aero Digest* magazines, few military

*ABOVE & BELOW: Rarely seen first prototype of the Focke-Wulf Fw 187 V1 was Germany's concept of a twin-engine, single-seat fighter. Luftwaffe executives showed no real interest. The Messerschmitt Bf 110 three-seater was preferred. A developed Fw 187 would have been the scourge of B-17s. (Hans Redemann)*

*ABOVE: Landing gear engineers designed a dynamic test rig for the XP-38 tricycle landing gear nose wheel. It was towed on runways by an aged Cadillac roadster. (LAC)*

*LEFT: One Lockheed Electra Jr. (Model 12) was tested with the XP-38 style nose gear after XP-38 was lost. It was designated C-40B. The Navy tested nearly identical XJO-3 version on a carrier. Main wheels were nonretractable. (LAC)*

or political people – and only a tiny segment of the civilian population – paid the slightest heed to what was said about the expansion of German air power. (Ultimately, Charles Lindbergh was denounced so vociferously by the President that he felt compelled to resign his commission in the Air Corps. His warnings about the *Luftwaffe* went unheeded.)

While the Air Corps was awarding the XP-38 contract to Lockheed, the Nazi counterpart was preparing to fly. Britain's Westland P.9 Whirlwind also remained more than a year away from its premier flight date – largely due to the manufacturer's almost total lack of experience in construction of all-metal aircraft plus nagging development problems associated with the Rolls-Royce Peregrine engines. Every hour of effort that went into that program wasted manpower that could have aided Merlin or other R-R engine efforts. It would, in retrospect, seem to have made far more sense to merely derate Merlins or beef up the aircraft structure. The Merlin II was only about 15 percent stronger than a Peregrine. The P-38 structure did not seem to object to a 60-70 percent increase in power, even without structural changes.

Nobody, at least in print, has ever commented about the remarkable similarity of design configuration among three aircraft that must have been conceived within one year. Those designs were the Fw 187, the P.9 Whirlwind, and Vultee's Model XP1015 design that lost out to the Lockheed Model 22 in the bidding for Project X-608. All three airplanes had high-aspect-ratio wings, versions of (then) rare bubble-type canopy cockpits located well forward, conventional tailwheel undercarriage, and rather long-moment-arm aft fuselages. A single fin and rudder were predominant in every case (although the P.9 was originally designed with twin fins and rudders). Design top speeds on all three were probably within 5 percent, often considered as a nominal margin of error. Of the three, the XP1015 was the largest dimensionally and in weight. The P.9 was the smallest. At least in power, the Fw 187 V1 was the weakest. Original design specifications for the XP-38 were generally within the same range, but the weight of that aircraft increased dramatically before it made its first flight. Speed, altitude and range requirements were 5 to 15 percent higher, thanks to Lt. Kelsey's foresight.

Focke-Wulf's chief test pilot, Captain Hans Sander, was a man with a graduate engineering degree. He flew the Fw 187 V1 for the first time in that unsettled summer of 1937, promptly demonstrating the substantial top speed of 326 mph on a total of only 1260 horsepower. Just as some Air Corps skeptics in Dayton scoffed at Kelly Johnson's projections of superior performance for the Model 22, RLM staff members refused to believe that any fighter weighing in at more than twice as much as their favored Bf 109B – even if it did boast twice as much power – could be almost 40 mph faster. However, it didn't take Project Engineer Blaser very long to substantiate his figures.

No real armament was carried by the Fw 187 V1, but with everybody's sudden awareness about the reasons for fighters being created, the V2 (second) prototype carried six rifle-caliber machine guns (7.6 mm) in the nose section beneath the cockpit. Four Rheinmetall-Borsig MG17 machine guns and two Mauser 20-mm MG FF or MG151 cannons were used in the No. 3 prototype.

One common thread employed by the designers of the Fw 187 Falke, P.9 Whirlwind and Vultee's XP1015 was the concept of keeping the fuselage cross-section to a minimum to accommodate a pilot. While those airframes and that of the XP-38 all featured what amounted to early "bubble canopy" enclosures, the pilot's accommodation in the Lockheed was the only one that can be described as commodious. The slimmer fuselages evaluated by Johnson and Hibbard and used by the others were certain to inhibit design growth,

particularly in the areas of armament, photographic equipment and auxiliary systems. In retrospect, it must be acknowledged that the Lockheed designers' methods for keeping drag to a minimum were far and way more sophisticated and ultimately effective.

All three Fw 187V prototypes proved to be very maneuverable, but Development Section Chief Ernst Udet – the very same Udet who scored 62 aerial victories in World War I and was an aerobatics competitor in the 1936 National Air races in Los Angeles – refused to believe that a twin-engine fighter could turn or roll with the smaller fighters. He dismissed the fact that the high-aspect-ratio wing of the Fw 187 also gave it outstanding climb characteristics. (Viewed objectively, it seems that a great number of officials in the world who make some of the most important decisions cannot overcome a tendency toward pomposity. By contrast, Benjamin Kelsey was blessed with one of the most pragmatic, yet brilliant, minds in the business. His decisions went a long way toward making the P-38 the one success of its genre.) Udet's viewpoint went a long way toward defeating the Falke as a potential interceptor.

Crashes of prototypes in the first 50 years of aviation were almost accepted as a fact of life. It was more likely for one to suffer a crash landing or total destruction than to survive the first year of testing. Focke-Wulf's Fw 187 V1 was no exception. Test pilot Bauer was killed in an accident on May 14, 1938, that closely paralleled the loss of the first YP-38 about three years later. Bauer made a very fast, low-level pass over the airfield, ending it with an abrupt pull-up maneuver. The airplane began to lose parts, either because fabric on the control surfaces ballooned and ripped or possibly something related to the little understood "Q" factor.

While testing of the two remaining prototypes continued, demonstrating good performance, Ernst Udet and his staff became disenchanted with progress of the Messerschmitt Bf 110 program. As a hedge, the Technical Bureau placed an order for three additional Fw 187s, but they were to be two-seat fighters with a radio operation/navigator as the second crew member in each. Prototypes V4 and V5 were equipped with slightly updated engines to compensate for the increased weight. Adolph Hitler's intensive nationalistic pride programs were to affect the V6 airplane.

It was 1939 and pilot Hans Dieterle had established a new Landplane Speed Record and a new Absolute World's Speed Record in what was then propagandized as a Heinkel He 112U fighter. In actuality, it was an entirely different prototype know as the He 100 V8. Using a special short-life speed record engine, Dieterle piloted the small aircraft over an approved course at Oranienburg on March 30 at an average speed of 463.92 mph to smash the long-standing absolute speed record by about 23 mph. In the process, he overwhelmed the landplane speed record established by Howard Hughes in 1935, exceeding that record speed by more than 110 mph! It was terrific propaganda.

As part of the Nazi program aimed at "psyching out the opposition," the sixth and last Focke-Wulf Fw 187 was fitted with two special Daimler-Benz DB600A high-performance (record) engines, each said to produce more than 1000 horsepower. Skin-surface radiators – a derivation of the system used by Curtiss on its racers starting in 1922 – were employed on the Fw 187 V6 (as they had been on the He 100 V8). A top speed of 394.5 mph was recorded during a speed run in October 1939. It was wasted effort.

Six months earlier, on April 26, 1939, *Flugkapitan* Fritz Wendel had flown a specially constructed Messerschmitt Me 209 V1 at a record speed of 469.22 mph to provide the Third Reich Propaganda Ministry with yet one more exhibition of "super achievement" with which to haunt their detractors. In keeping with their plan, the Ministry eulogized the record flight and stated that it was accomplished with a special version of the Bf 109 fighter, listed as the Bf 109R. The Me 209 V1 was no more a military airplane than was the Hughes H-1. All thoughts of using the Fw 187 V6 for any record attempt were abandoned, of course, with the outbreak of war. Obviously it was the smart thing to do. More than six months earlier, the overweight and militarized XP-38 had far overshadowed the Falke's best possible speed, and that was in the course of a 2,700-mile cross-country flight.

Whatever the reasons might have been, the Fw 187 as a single-seat fighter had really been put on the shelf months before the flight of the specialized V6 version. By direction of the RLM or the Technical Bureau itself, the third prototype (the V3) was revamped as a two-seat *Zerstorer* (destroyer/heavy fighter), and the V4 through V6 aircraft were completed as two-seaters. Following the six initial aircraft, a small service test batch of three Fw 187A-O two-seat versions was ordered. Although their delivery coincided with the end of Kurt Tank's uphill battle to produce a viable multi-engine single-seat fighter, the Falke still had one or two important roles to play in the war.

Nazi propagandists convinced British Intelligence that the Fw 187A was a force to be reckoned with. They issued a baseless "Most Secret" document pertaining to the type. A reading of the counter-espionage data gives the reader the impression that most of the data were derived from reading contemporary foreign aviation magazines. Since incompetence is not limited to any one group, the Army Air Force promptly issued a document entitled "Foreign Aircraft, Evaluation of Characteristics and Estimate of Performance – Focke-Wulf Fw 187" in December 1941. Compiled by the Experimental Engineering Section of the Materiel Division at Wright Field, it was completely erroneous. It gave the (Nazi) desired impression that the type was in production and service with the *Luftwaffe*. Any thorough reading of RAF Bomber Command or other encounter reports would have revealed a total lack of contact with the type. Actually, the three surviving Fw 187As spent most of their remaining days as Focke-Wulf factory defense fighters; in other words, they became part of the plant protection staff.

And then there was Westland's Whirlwind.

Either British Intelligence (MI) was far more effective than we have any right to believe or the Air Ministry had its own equivalent of the U.S. Army's Lt. Benjamin Kelsey. By amazing coincidence, the year 1935 brought forth the first of several specifications for bidding on a new Royal Air Force single-place, two-engine fighter. It all culminated in Spec. F.37/35. Responses from Bristol, Hawker, and Westland varied from uninspired to exceptional. Westland Aircraft's design offering by well-known W. E. W. Petter was extremely attractive and extraordinarily clean lined by any standard. As originally proposed in the tender submittal in April 1936, the aircraft featured smallish

twin tails. Petter, at variance with the findings of Kelly Johnson and the University of Michigan wind tunnel data, abandoned the undersized twin tails and substituted an oversized single fin and rudder. Quite independently, too, Petter adopted the Fowler flap for his fighter, designated the P.9 at that time. The flaps were quite small and did not capitalize on the effectiveness they could provide, but the P.9 also featured a set of Handley Page slots.

Westland Aircraft, with one or two unsuccessful exceptions, had never built a modern fighter. Its greatest success had been in the field of army cooperation (observation) types, and even its latest production machine for 1936 and later was one that featured tube and fabric construction. They were hardly conversant with retractable landing gears, and had produced nothing at all featuring stressed-skin metal construction. Not many would contend that the P.9 (Whirlwind) was not aerodynamically sound in design. But almost from the beginning, the fighter was hamstrung by the same sort of deficiencies that plagued the Bell XFM-1 and the Focke-Wulf Fw 187. The design team managed to conjure up a number of its own shortcomings. So it went with any and all who believed that developing a good twin-engine, single-seat fighter would be an easy task.

Because the Whirlwind was cloaked in such great secrecy, few have ever really known that the Westland fighter was designed and built in direct parallel with Lockheed's Model 22 (XP-38) and that its first flight – also conducted in secrecy – was on October 11, 1938, a bit more than three months before Lockheed's fighter took to the air for the first time. And like the Fw 187, the P.9 type was never able to lay claim to anything really near a 400-mph maximum speed. Physical size, several design considerations and severely limited growth potential of the German and British types were factors that inhibited any possibilities of real success. There was one more extremely serious defect in all the multi-engine fighters built prior to the beginning of World War II, with only the P-38 being an exception: all were designed to operate effectively at critical altitudes of less than 16,000 feet. (Critical altitude is the maximum level at which the engines are capable of producing rated power and at which the airframe can achieve its optimum speed.)

From the outset (established by Kelsey) the XP-38 was designed for a critical altitude of 20,000 feet. Four years later the Battle of Britain had the effect of almost instantaneously elevating the combat level far beyond any altitude envisioned by most pre-war strategists and planners, thereby dooming the P-38's contemporaries to short lives. Early in its career, the Whirlwind's combat capabilities were found to closely emulate those of the Allison-powered Mustang I, although the Whirlwind could not carry a greater bomb load and was not as fast. If the RAF declined to match the low-level Mustang against Messerschmitts and Focke-Wulf Fw 190s on a continuing, deliberate basis, they would have been foolish to commit Whirlwinds to that assignment. Even with the drastic impetus of the "Fight at Odds" in 1940, the Whirlwind was not put on operations until January 1941 for a variety of reasons. Lessons learned during that Battle of Britain summer led members of the Air Staff to re-evaluate that entire program. Ultimately a major contract was canceled and the total number of Whirlwinds procured fell to almost exactly 1 percent of all P-38s procured during the war, or 114 airplanes.

In early tests, some of the design limitations came home to haunt the manufacturers and the RAF. With a total internal fuel capacity of 134 gallons (Imp.) and no provision at all for external tanks, the P.9 Whirlwind had an endurance of about two hours, but if it was flown at high boost or if it carried an external bomb load, the endurance fell off sharply. (When you learn that the aircraft burned 114 gph at high cruise power, it taxes credibility to accept the two-hour endurance figure.) Time to climb to 15,000 feet was almost exactly the same as the time required for the XP-38 to climb to 20,000 feet; namely 6 minutes or a fraction less.

One huge design oversight was the lack of any provision for fuel transfer. If one engine was lost after climb to altitude, for example, it would be necessary to apply high boost to the other engine for return and landing approach. Since no fuel could be transferred from the other tank, fuel consumption would be critical. Not only that, but fuel (weight) remained on the side of the aircraft having the "dead" engine. Propellers were not contrarotating, giving the aircraft a tendency to

"swing" on normal landings. Landings with one propeller feathered must have been exciting. As noted earlier, the airframe overall design was good. Westland's lack of experience with advanced aircraft really showed up in the unskillful handling of systems design. Whatever possessed the designers to ignore certain advantages of crossfeed systems will probably never be determined, but as it was designed it created numerous potentially bad situations for combat pilots. Consider the pilot who, after about one hour of patrol or low-level attack, loses one engine. Even with no other "situations" rising, he has a poor chance of making it back to his station. Increasing power on the good engine to stay in the air would increase fuel consumption, and he could not transfer any fuel from the opposite tank. The Peregrine was not a "happy" engine at best, so the increased chance of failure was of a high order while flying with high boost.

Several advantages accrued from the decision to terminate production of additional Whirlwinds: development and production of Peregrines would stop, permitting an increase in production of the much needed Merlins. An early decision to produce the Peregrine was terribly flawed, and the idea of fitting that underdeveloped engine to a totally new class of fighter merely compounded the disaster.

Another dismal piece of design work showed up in the landing gear which, in a slightly different form, was employed in the Fw 187 V prototypes. Each landing gear had a double shock strut arrangement of the type that was originally seen on the Douglas DC-1/-2/-3 commercial aircraft, the Fokker G-1 and the earliest form of the Martin B-10 bomber, all dating back to the early 1930s. That old-fashioned Dowty landing gear on the Whirlwind made the relatively simple maintenance job of changing tires and brakes a veritable nightmare. And speaking of tires, both of these fighter types were equipped with small-diameter, low-pressure (balloon) tires. If you have never witnessed similarly equipped Martin 187 Baltimores landing on a paved runway, you have missed excitement. Earlier in the decade, Curtiss had experimented with low-pressure tires on its Navy F11C carrier-based fighter. After at least one wound up flat on its back while an attempted arrested landing was under way, low-pressure tires found little acceptance in America. It is conceded that versions were used on early twin Beech Model 18 types and in less radical form on the Super Electra and Hudson, but most U.S. military types were produced with more conventional tires fitted.

It seems appropriate to relate a couple of incidents that tied the Whirlwind type at least remotely to the XP-38. When the first prototype (L6844) was moved on to the tiny grass airfield at Yeovil for engine runup tests and preparation for its first flight over southwestern England on October 11, 1938, Chief Test Pilot Harald Penrose had few problems, which proved to be misleading. After a series of builder's tests, he delivered the P.9 to Farnborough on December 31, 1938 – the very same day that Lockheed's XP-38 was being trucked down the highways to Southern California's remote March Field. The initial P.9 production contract for 200 airplanes was awarded shortly thereafter.

That is when some real troubles began. Both the airframe manufacturer and the engine maker, Rolls-Royce, were bedeviled with production snags and engine reliability problems from an early date. Not until May 30, 1940, was the first production Whirlwind delivered to a Royal Air Force squadron. That delivery of a "production" airplane, which was in reality the second prototype disguised in operational service colors, proved to be premature. Those production delays had cost the RAF some 17 months, closely matching the delays incurred in America because of the XP-38 single prototype loss. However, the Army Air Corps followed a path quite different from that of the Air Ministry. A great deal of production design was

*RIGHT: Fokker's unique and interesting D.XXIII push-pull fighter arrived at the wrong time and without benefit of modern construction techniques. Donated Czechoslovakian engines overheated badly. Hitler's Wehrmacht quietly took over that country a bit later. It was unlikely that the D.XXIII was ever going into production anyway. (Bodie Archives)*

*BELOW: Almost unbelievably, Gloster's F.9/37 was the absolute contemporary of the XP-38. It first flew in April 1939. Not only ugly, it was a dismal performer. (Bodie Archives)*

cranked into the YP-38 design, and no less than 13 of those Service Test airplanes were delivered – the first one coming off the line less than three months after that first Whirlwind was delivered. Like it or not, the RAF wound up with what amounted to a batch of service test airplanes, too. The earlier start (circa 1935) achieved by the RAF had evaporated.

Why did the Whirlwind fail to achieve renown as the world's second-best mass-produced twin-engine, single-seat fighter? Any answer is bound to be complex (and probably subjective), but here are some of the most profound flaws that seriously inhibited any chance for success?

Second-rate, unproven and really undeveloped engines were selected.

Endurance was so limited that it appeared to reflect specifications for a target-defense interceptor. But rate of climb was indifferent.

There were no provisions at all for carrying external fuel tanks, but even if there had been, each of the two external tanks would have been limited to about 60 Imperial gallons. With the maximum bomb load of 1,000 pounds, climb and top or cruise speed decayed precipitously.

A cramped cockpit guaranteed pilot misery if endurance could have been doubled or tripled.

Prestone coolant and oil cooling exit air flow was limited, especially during taxiing. The Whirlwind would have been a "teakettle" in any semi-tropical region.

Even with slots and Fowler flaps, the stalling speed was about 98 mph (landing gear and flaps down) so "over the fence" speed was in excess of 100 mph. With both propellers turning in the same direction (torque effect) and those balloon tires, landings were "interesting."

With a critical altitude of 15,000 feet, it quickly became outmoded for contemporary bomber and fighter interception. The Battle of Britain had strongly indicated that fighters must be able to combat at much higher altitudes if they were to cope with the enemy.

What is terribly obvious, even with this greatly abridged listing of faults, is that the Air Ministry understated what was needed and the designers were out of their class. When the first Lockheed Lightning I fighters were tested at Boscombe Down many months after the initial Whirlwinds were committed to operations, there was no chance at all that they could perform to meet completely changed requirements. While they did not suffer many of the faults of the Westland airplanes, the absence of turbosuperchargers cast them in the mold of low-altitude creatures, a role no longer acceptable to the RAF. Lockheed had not yet, in mid-1941, developed its long-range external tankage system; the lack of contrarotating propellers created a special set of problems. Performance was, in a word, lackluster. And the British were of a mind that tricycle landing gears had not (as of 1942) shown themselves to be well adapted to rolling, grassy airfields. Having been emasculated at conception, the Lightning I was stillborn. Deprived of virility by some overzealous logistics people (most likely), the 322-B fighter was a dud!

The first Lightning I (AE978) supposedly went to the U.K. for flight testing, followed by AF105 and AF 106 – all in 1942, long after any Whirlwind controversy had been resolved. No real evidence has ever been revealed to prove that AE978 was evaluated in England at all, but official USAAF records confirm that all of the Lightnings served in the AAF Training Command, some as P-322-Is and some as P-322-IIs. The latter series were modified to use V-1710F series engines when virtually all C series engines were withdrawn from service. (Later discussion will show that 1941 test results in California were used by the Ministry of Aircraft Production as a basis for refusing acceptance of Lightning I fighters. Robert Gross challenged, proving that the airplanes met all requirements of contract specifications established before the Battle of Britain.)

One final comment about the Whirlwind is necessary to support the negative attitude toward that fighter. Production versions had been committed to combat on January 12, 1941; a review of the first six months in action is most revealing. By July, No. 263 Squadron (one of two operating the type) had managed to shoot down some 58 assorted aircraft – including at least one Arado Ar 196 twin-float scout (observation) aircraft – for the loss of no less than 50 Whirlwind pilots and the writeoff of even a greater number of aircraft. Few of the victories had been against enemy fighters of any type. No. 263 Squadron flew the last significant combat missions in October 1943.

The Air Ministry had made at least one additional early attempt to produce a useful fighter of this species. An official requirement was generated as a "spinoff" of the original competition that had been won by Westland Aircraft. Responding to Spec. F.9/37, Gloster Aircraft submitted a substantially revised version of its earlier unsuccessful design, and this was rewarded with a contract for two experimental prototypes (L7999 and L8002). With graceful Gloster Gladiators still in production and one experimental radial-engine monoplane fighter having lost out to the Spitfire and Hurricane, the appearance of the new but nameless F.9/37 twin-engine, single-seat fighter did not elicit many compliments. It had all of the grace and sleekness of a rhinoceros. While everything about the Whirlwind was pleasant to the eye, the Gloster vehicle was more like sand in the eye. One of the few aircraft designs that might be considered comparable in ugliness was Vultee's Vengeance.

The Gloster began life much later than the Whirlwind, but construction proceeded more quickly. (It had the appearance of a group of unrelated parts riveted together.) Shortly after Lockheed's XP-38 made its first flight, the Gloster F.9/37 took off from Hucclecote for the first time, but an accident at Martlesham in July severely damaged the new fighter. When the second prototype was completed, the powerplants had been changed from 1,050 horsepower Bristol Taurus TE/1 radial engines to a pair of the troublesome Rolls-Royce Peregrines (895 horsepower). Results were predictable. Almost beyond belief, the first prototype (RAF L7999) with the small-diameter Tauruses supposedly attained a top speed of 360 miles per hour, but the sleeve-valve engines were proving to be absolutely unreliable. When crash damage was repaired on L7999, it was repowered with Taurus III engines derated to 900 horsepower each. (The point has been made that derated Rolls-Royce Merlins installed in the Whirlwind would have made a lot more sense than using the unproved Peregrines. Gloster could hardly have done more to prove the point.)

Flight trials with L7999 did not resume until spring 1940, when it was ascertained that the loss of 300 horsepower had reduced top speed to a mere 332 mph at critical altitude - again only 15,000 feet. Whatever good flight characteristics the Gloster exhibited, they were not sufficient to defeat the widely encountered versions of the Messerschmitt Bf 110C. As if the non-production status of the airplane and its mediocre perfor-

mance were not enough, adding on the distinct unreliability associated with the Taurus engines and lessons derived from the Battle of Britain had the effect of furnishing the *coup de grace* to F.9/37 aspirations.

Thus ended contemporary British efforts to produce a successful co-equal of the Lockheed P-38. In overall performance, reliability, airframe strength, adaptability, and maneuverability – just to name the most obvious advantages of the Lockheed type – the Westland and Gloster products fell far short. Even with a head start, the top talent in the military-industrial complexes of the two most advanced air powers of the world in 1940 had been unable to produce viable twin-engine, single-seat fighters let alone fighters of advanced concept and outstanding performance. The United States may have deserved its status as a third-rate (or worse) air power as the new decade dawned, but with both the P-38 and B-17 bases to build on, all of that was about to change.

E Created only in prototype form in the closing years of the Great Depression decade, at least one additional fighter of this genus deserves mention if for no other reasons than (1) its extremely novel solution to a perplexing set of problems generated by the intrinsic specification and (2) the fact that C. L. Johnson had

given serious consideration to the basic configuration during initial design work on the Model 22 (XP-38). The Janus-faced fighter built by Fokker (Holland), identified as the D.XXIII, appeared in semi-mockup form at the 1938 *Salon de l'Aeronautique* within the Paris Grand Palais in November of that year. It was a twin-engine, single-thrust-line layout that had stymied many earlier designers because of certain complexities. Fokker (Holland) wished to produce a fighter powered by a 1000-1200 horsepower engine, but Chief Engineer Beeling and his staff were handicapped by a paucity of powerplant choices, and the choices were declining almost daily. As has been noted to some extent, even the major European powers were hard-pressed to obtain all of the powerful engines they needed.

Drawing on what might be available, Beeling created a group of design layouts for a "push-pull" fighter, each based on a different pair of engines. Their effort began in December 1937, months after Johnson's XP-38 had won the Air Corps design competition and perhaps 18 months after Johnson rejected the tandem-engine layout. The initial Fokker project was based on Czechoslovakian-manufactured Walter Sagitta inverted V-12 aircooled engines – being roughly equal to the contemporary Ranger IV-440 in concept and output. Beeling found that the Walter product was readily available (until the Nazi takeover) and inexpensive. In fact Fokker obtained them free, "on approval."

Proliferation in design layouts at Fokker was amazing, and as work progressed with an assortment of engines being considered, wing spans varied accordingly. The Walter Sagitta version had a span of 37 $^3/_4$ feet, while a projected Rolls-Royce Merlin-powered version had a span of 47 $^1/_2$ feet. Gross weights ranged from a low of 6,614 pounds to a high of 9,480 pounds. Range, equipment, structural strength and performance requirements were nowhere near equal to what was required of the U.S.-built aircraft. At least Design Leader Beeling was not looking for ultra-high speed out of his machine, predicting 326 mph at critical altitude. Once again the XP-38 was the only projected fighter of the five pre-war types discussed to this point that had a critical altitude rating above 16,000 feet. Therefore, it was the only one that reflected an anticipation of the air combat requirements that would be encountered in the 1940s.

If it has not been recognized previously, the exceptional importance of having a visionary with outstanding technical capability at the helm when a firm requirement is established must certainly be acknowledged now. And, once that project has been initiated, it becomes imperative that project control must be maintained by the military project office that established the requirements. If control passes to others with less foresight, the product invariably suffers (as witness the fate that befell the Bell P-39 when another person assumed responsibility).

Fokker designated its 9,480-pound version that was to be propelled by approximately 2050 total horsepower from the Merlin II engines as Design 156. That projected design weight was not too far below the projections made for the Model 22/XP-38, an estimate that proved to be pretty optimistic but not ridiculous when you take into consideration that Lockheed was making a radical step forward in aircraft structures. Considering the fact that Design 156 called for a 621-mile range as opposed to the Model 22's 1,000-mile range on internal fuel, comparable range figures would have dictated a substantial increase in weight for the Fokker airplane. Beeling projected that the Merlin-powered version would have a top speed of 373 mph at a critical altitude of 16,000 feet. It must be seen as frustrating to increase weight by almost 3,000 pounds, double the horsepower available, add to complexity and yet only see a speed increase of about 50 miles per hour.

Flamboyant Tony Fokker, a power to be reckoned with at the Netherlands factory, exhibited an early interest in the Walter Sagitta 1-SR version, designated as Design No. 155. With his intervention, a decision was made to display it as the D.23 at the Paris Salon in 1938. A superbly finished wooden/metal replica, containing numerous components of the eventual prototype, was displayed in such a manner than only the most technically qualified observers could argue that it was not a "real" airplane. With its unique (for Europe) tricycle landing gear extended, it created a sensation. Unfortunately, its fate was already sealed.

Fokker had seriously overstepped its capabilities by not upgrading equipment and personnel to maintain equality with a rapidly changing industry. In an era of 400-mph aircraft, they were forced to install a typical Fokker wooden wing; therefore, they were saddled with a wing having a root chord thickness ratio and tip ratio of 22 percent and 11 percent, respectively. Comparable figures for the sleek Spitfire were 13 percent and 6 percent. Most of the remaining structure employed on the D.23 was a melange of steel tube and "button-down" shaped plates *a la* North American's BT-9 trainers. So, in the early months of 1939, Fokker was building an advanced technology fighter with structural techniques abandoned (even for new commercial aircraft) in America as early as 1930. Every performance figure released by Fokker was based on a version that would feature a definitive metal wing with a 25 percent reduction in thickness and Walter engines that would be producing rated power without undue difficulty.

Dutch engineers knowingly or unknowingly emulated Lockheed by using the Paris Salon mockup for tow testing of the tricycle landing gear that was an absolute necessity for the D.23. Unlike the system devised by Lockheed and the Air Corps, Fokker's system lacked nosewheel damping. It would pay dearly for the oversight.

Test pilot Gerben Sonderman flew the D.23 (D.XXIII) on May 30 and was immediately beset with cooling problems. It was a bit disconcerting to see the aft engine cylinder head temperatures move into the redline area during takeoff and climb. Almost simultaneously, the supply of spares, replacement engines, or technical help from the Czechs evaporated with the Nazi subjugation of that country. As a direct result of those factors, the prototype made only eleven test flights in 1939, logging an insignificant four hours in the air! When the *Wermacht* and *Luftwaffe* terminated the so-called "phoney war" rather abruptly in May 1940, the Fokker plant at Shiphol was a primary target. But probably by plan, the Germans inflicted only superficial damage on the structures. Rather unexpectedly and not publicized to any extent, Fokker executives offered to complete additional flight testing of the single D.23 if the Nazis would provide the necessary financial and material aid. The *Reichluftfahrtministerium* and others evinced little or no interest in the airplane, and did not seriously consider the self-serving, even traitorous Fokker offer.

In every classic race there is a winner; some entrants look very good at first but fade or crash in the event, and others would have been well advised to forget the whole thing. Lattermost entries in the competition really are out of their element and have no reason to even be considered as competitors. Nobody likes to see accolades heaped on those latecomers that materialize after the heat of the battle has cooled to ambient. Only the victorious combatants involved in turning the tide of battle really deserve the commendations - and most certainly not the postbellum types that were never really subjected to the true test of worth. With this in mind, we turn to the tale of the Lockheed Lightning, which, when viewed objectively in a retrospective environment, has to be acknowledged as the most outstanding twin-engine, propeller-driven, single-seat fighter of all time.

# CHAPTER 4

# A Quantum Leap Forward — The Prototype Flies

Only a handful of people knew about the visual beauty of the Lockheed XP-38 as it appeared in January 1939. Even in the face of rotten weather, it displayed a spectacular advancement in aviation. (J. H. Washburn)

A Few people have entered this world who were, perhaps, never in awe of the heavenly constellations. Most of us relate to the more or less ethereal feeling that comes over us when we do any star gazing. Halley's Comet has always enraptured a large segment of the earthly population. Lockheed adopted the star symbology as its trademark early in its history, although circumstances sometimes conspired to prevent an absolute tie-in to its aircraft. But Halley's Comet and the unnamed Lockheed XP-38 did have much in common. Both made a tremendous impression when they first appeared in the skies, they were in view for only a short time, and then they disappeared from the scene with little fanfare.

As is often the case, fate and one insignificant decision had a tremendous effect on history. When a nervous military test pilot took off in Boeing's B-299 (XB-17) with the flight controls locked, the aircraft crashed and burned. Opinions were changed, decisions were affected and the course of history was redirected for a time. Fate and a bad decision were soon to have a profound effect on the beautiful new XP-38.

Lockheed's one and only $761,000 (actual cost) prototype of the Model 22, almost always referred to as the XP-38, arrived at March Field – then under command of Col. Carlyle H. Wash – on New Year's Day 1939. It was accompanied by a bone-tired and thoroughly chilled crew after a long 14-hour night trip over highways that would now be considered back roads. With Christmas and New Year holidays in effect, activity at the old Air Corps base was minimal.

March Field was then a major component of the GHQ Air Force and was home to the 17th Attack Group and an outfit that would later gain fame for its exploits in the Western Pacific in B-17s, the 19th Bombardment Group. The base's bright metal A-17As and B-18s were among the newest military aircraft in service anywhere, but their brightness only reflected the sun, not a state of readiness. Not one airplane type on the field, other than the XP-38, would have any significant role in the forthcoming war. In keeping with isolationist attitudes, all were lined up in neat, close order ranks. With ramp activity registering zero, about the only real movement was at the hangar designated as a temporary home for the new fighter. Only hours after the convoy had arrived, company mechanics began the precise process of reassembling the sleek prototype under the ever critical gaze of Jimmy Gerschler and Benjamin Kelsey.

In two weeks time, the fighter was readied for initial taxi

testing. It was immediately evident that the machine had a lot of "go" power, but test pilot Kelsey soon encountered a major problem in the stopping power. Warner brakes on the main landing wheels failed to meet the specification requirements. Kelsey scattered a crew of civilian construction workers at the end of one runway after a high-speed run down the new concrete strip. With wheels smoking and inadequate deceleration, the XP-38 eliminated a wooden comfort station that had been provided for those workers and the lieutenant bent a brake pedal support that had been tested under a loading of 500 pounds. Back in the hangar, they installed an additional brake on

the nosewheel, gaining virtually nothing in the process. That continuing brake problem delayed flight testing for at least two weeks, but they finally provided an interim solution in switching to brakes supplied by another manufacturer and doubling the brake contact area.

By January 27, Gerschler felt that the airplane was ready for its first flight. It was towed out to the flight line, fueled and warmed up. An old, venerable Ford trimotor – the same "chase" aircraft that had been utilized to photograph the prototype Electra on its first flight in 1935 – was readied for flight, too, in case the XP-38 ran into trouble. (Mission support equipment was really quite elementary in the 1930s.) Lt. Kelsey slipped into his parachute, climbed up to the cockpit and prepared to fly. Seldom, if ever, in history has the man who established the specifications for any airplane been the first person to fly it. He fired up the engines, appreciating the melodic sound. Many curious eyes followed his progress to the end of the runway. The flaps were positioned for takeoff and Kelsey opened the throttles all the way. The grin on Ben's face was not to last long.

As the wheels left the runway, both sets of flaps began to vibrate violently during the straight ahead climb over the desert. Unknown to Kelsey, all but one of four aluminum support rods had failed, allowing the flaps to run out to the stops. The flaps flailed up and down rather violently as they tried to tear loose. Ben did not like to leave troubled airplanes, as he had proven a few years earlier when he landed a burning Martin B-10, even though much of the fabric had burned off the wing.

He throttled back on the Allisons to stop the vibration and get a better appraisal of the situation. If any of the four separate flap units tore off on final approach, the fighter might become unmanageable. After all, the XP-38 had the highest wing loading of any airplane in America . . . probably in the entire world. The fuel tanks were full, and that surely could not have made any pilot feel good. Kelsey felt ill. Was he going to have to abandon the airplane that he had focused on almost to a fault during the past 30 months or so? He must have been aware that Bob Gross's team had invested about four and a half times as much money in the prototype as they would receive in payment. The pressure was intense.

That old Ford was loaded with engineers and technicians in a hurry, and it headed out for a rendezvous with the XP. As it chugged slowly into the sky with everybody pressing faces against the windows, Kelsey had managed to get things

*ABOVE: Detail parts, such as exhaust manifold shrouds and the nose landing gear door, were still missing. But, like viewing a breathtakingly beautiful woman, who even noticed? Young Kelly Johnson had obviously been inspired. (J. H. Washburn)*

*BELOW: Lt. Kelsey must have felt like an excited schoolboy on a date with the annual Queen of Something-or-Other as he gazed upon the product of his 1936 wish list. Even the Hughes H-1 racer looked like a farm tractor by comparison. (J. H. Washburn)*

settled down. He would minimize vibration by maintaining a low angle of attack during the approach, but the critical point would come during flareout, when he would need a very high angle. Engineers would supply the pilot with a hand-operated pump to increase brake pressure for future flights, but as they looked on this day, their plan had little value. Those brakes might not get the aircraft stopped in time, even if Kelsey managed to get it safely on the runway. The normal approach angle of attack for most modern fighters in 1939 was about 12 degrees. Ben made a long, flat approach at about 120 to 130 mph, crossed the threshold, pulled back on the automobile-type wheel and held it there. The prototype glued itself to the ground, nose up over 18 degrees as sparks flew from the twin tail bumpers mounted on the bottoms of the twin vertical fins. Unintentionally, the XP had become a "taildragger." In typical Kelsey style, he later pointed out that they had proved that the aircraft was not stalled out an angle of attack as high as 18 1/2 degrees. The airplane had been in the air for 34

*Exposed to the Dayton (Ohio) newspaper reporters for the first time at Wright Field during the refueling stop, the XP-38 was about to burst like a bomb on an unsuspecting public in that winter of 1939. Best story of all was one in the popular* Model Airplane News. *(WADC)*

minutes, but they never did try to retract the landing gear that day and few of the planned flight objectives were attained.

The effects of an inefficient flap seal and the aluminum support link rods had been the culprits behind the failure on the 27th. The gap problem was fixed easily, and temporary steel link rods were made almost overnight. That proposed handpump for the brakes was installed for Flight 2, and new Rusco brake linings were fitted. Kelsey took the airplane up for 36 minutes on February 5, but they soon found out that extra brake pressure did little to correct the marginal braking effect. But at least they got the landing gear up and down.

The third test flight revealed that there was some longitudinal instability, or at least it was marginal under some conditions. Kelly Johnson calculated that an increase of 7 square feet in horizontal stabilizer area, entirely outboard of the fins, would solve the problem. That explains why the XP-38 was the only aircraft in the series that had a short-span stabilizer.

At about the same time, the aerodynamicists concluded that elevator buffeting at high speed was more than likely the result of high-activity "prop wash" from the inboard wing area. A change from inboard propeller rotation (at the top) to outboard rotation would solve that problem, so they interchanged the right and left engines. Problem solved. Tests conducted in the wind tunnel, together with flight testing, proved that the Prestone radiator scoops and ducts provided adequate cooling but at the cost of some rather high drag counts. Calculations showed that elimination of the two retractable outlets and redesign of the four side scoops could increase top speed by as much as 8 miles per hour. The flight had lasted just seven minutes under one hour.

All in all, everything was going along quite well for any new aircraft, let alone one that was exceptionally radical for the period. No engine problems had been encountered; rare indeed for a turbosupercharged fighter, especially one with Allison C-series powerplants. To get three flight tests out of a new prototype in three days was virtually unheard of. Did they dare try for Flight No. 4 the next day, February 7? Of course.

Kelsey slipped away in the XP for one hour 36 minutes to check on engine cooling and aerodynamic stability. He would have stayed up a bit longer except for a minor problem with the propellers. They changed the pitch; changed it to 49.5 degrees in the high range. Finally, a common hobgoblin made its appearance: the menace of turbo regulation had at last

surfaced. That was during Flight No. 5 on February 9, but it wasn't really serious because Kelsey managed to log another 45 minutes on the airplane.

Throughout the 1930s, record-breaking flights had become almost routine, except for the newspaper space they commanded. By February 10, Ben Kelsey was convinced that the XP-38 was ready to show its good breeding and head off for Wright Field. He managed to get his boss's approval for a speed record attempt, at least as far as his home base. The Boeing 299X had done it, establishing a good precedent. That was four years ago, and the Air Corps could stand a bit of good publicity. Gen. Henry Arnold assured him that if all was going well when he landed at Dayton, the fighter would be refueled quickly and he would then decide whether or not to have Kelsey continue on to New York in an assault of the standing Howard Hughes official record. Young Hughes had done a fine job of flying his "airborne gas tank" racer across America in record time almost exactly two years earlier (January 19, 1937).[1]

Flight testing on the 10th was limited to about 25 minutes, just long enough to check out the performance of a wastegate spring on a turbosupercharger. Kelsey did not even bother to

_____

1. *Designer Richard Palmer was responsible for the Hughes H-1 racer and he prepared it with sets of interchangeable wings. The short set was meant for high-speed runs and pylon racing (which never happened) while the long-span set was purely for long-distance record attempts and cross-country racing. On January 19, 1937, Hughes flew nonstop from Burbank to New York in 7 hours, 28 minutes, 25 seconds, breaking his own record established with his Northrop Gamma (also a nonstop flight).*

*With the Twin Wasp Jr. throttled well back, Hughes burned only about 200 gallons of his 280-gallon fuel load. A friendly tailwing helped him post an average speed of 327.5 mph for the distance of approximately 2,700 miles. For comparison, the XP-38 carried an overload of 400 gallons of fuel, but Lt. Kelsey had two military engines to feed, there were no fuel consumption tables that were validated and nobody wanted to press their luck anymore than they were already. If the XP-38 was going to break the record, it would have to do so with the two refueling stops.*

retract the landing gear that day. As the day ended, the XP-38 log registered only 4 hours and 49 minutes of actual flight time, but with the airplane performing in a relatively troublefree manner there was little reason to stay at March Field.

Quite candidly, anyone at Burbank who was associated with the XP-38 program was 100 percent behind Lt. Kelsey in the desire to make a speed dash across America. It was an aggressive body of men. Since nobody could come up with a valid reason to delay the effort, preparations were completed for Maj. Gen. H. H. Arnold, the new Chief of the Army Air Corps, to arrive at Wright Field in time to greet Lt. Kelsey.

There were some remarkably interesting circumstances here. It seems that the popular Chief of the Air Corps in the summer of 1938, Maj. Gen. Oscar Westover, was killed at Burbank when his Northrop A-17AS Special crashed on September 21, 1938. His friend and associate Hap Arnold was then promoted and put in charge of the Air Corps. In another coincidence, Gerry Vultee – whose Vultee XP1015 design was second to the Lockheed Model 22 in the XP-38 competition – was killed on January 29, 1938, in a crash in Arizona. It should be remembered that Vultee had been the chief of design at Lockheed just a few years earlier.

While Ben Kelsey may have rated highly with Westover, he was most likely appreciated even more by Hap Arnold. The general was acutely aware of the part Kelsey had played in advancing Air Corps technology since the days when the lieutenant was involved with Jimmy Doolittle in developing the science of blind flight. If Kelsey believed that the XP-38 flight could be pulled off with success, Arnold was certainly unlikely to object.

At the time Howard Hughes shattered the transcontinental speed record there had been meticulous preparations. As he flashed past the control tower and the attendant FAI records official at Newark Airport, the timing went off like clockwork. Unfortunately, nothing was really worked out in advance for Kelsey's speed dash to Dayton and points east. If the transcon record had really been the immediate target in the planning, the XP-38 had adequate range to cross the United States with only one fueling stop at Wichita or Kansas City. With a single 7- to 10-minute stop, elapsed time would have been below the Hughes record time.

Knowing that he had to land at Wright Field to comply with his orders, Kelsey was forced into making one interim stop to ensure that he could make it all the way to Dayton. Therefore, he flew at much higher power settings than Hughes had used. At least that helped to make up for some of the lost time. Possibly more detrimental was the fact that nobody had time to arrange for and train special refueling crews at the two intermediate stops. Communications oversights were unforgivable, and at least one of them caused a lot of grief.

Military and company personnel serviced the fighter for its upcoming delivery flight on the night of February 10 in preparation for the planned 6 a.m. PST (Pacific Standard Time) departure. Lt. Ben Kelsey was every bit as competitive in spirit as Howard Hughes; in fact, he had closely observed Howard's activities and his intense motivation, tenaciousness and competitiveness for something like five years. As he prepared to get several hours of sleep at the BOQ, he was well aware of his own great potential for establishing a new record – stops or no stops. It really did not matter to him whether it was official or not. Only serious technical problems en route were going to deter him from making the dash all the way to Mitchel Field (which was not, by the way, named for Gen. William "Billy" Mitchell or his brother.)

Raw, cold winds met the Air Corps and Lockheed people on the morning of February 11, 1939. The dry desert air was bone-chilling as they moved around in the darkness. It had not

been one of California's highly publicized winters. But at least they weren't being pelted by the heavy rains that had been so common during the winter of 1938-39. At the base alongside Highway 395, activity in the pre-dawn hours was concentrated on completing all final preparations for the speedy delivery of the new Lockheed Model 22-64-01, company serial number 2201. The XP-38 also carried military serial AC37-457. Its dural skin had been buffed to a high gloss, cowl panels were rechecked for security and the newest of the world's fighting planes was made ready for the most important venture of its short existence. No pilot other than the 33-year-old Army test pilot had logged even a minute at the controls.

There was a certain amount of apprehension intermingled with an abundance of enthusiasm among the bystanders at 6 a.m. because most of them were engineers and crewmen who had lived with the XP-38 since construction had been initiated. One of those on the sidelines was a man destined to become one of the most notable field service representatives in P-38 history, big Dorsey Kammerer. An added boost was the knowledge that National Aeronautics Association timers would be on the job as a result of some last-minute negotiations.

Ben Kelsey climbed onto the wing and then into the cockpit, adjusted his parachute and goggles and prepared to fly about 2,500 miles with the idea of being on the East Coast before the evening meal, after crossing four time zones. Following completion of the cockpit check, Kelsey started the engines, set the propeller controls to AUTOMATIC after checking out the switches and circuit breakers, and then called the tower operator for takeoff instructions. Ground crew members cleared the aircraft and the XP-38 began to move out to the end of the runway. The stilletto-like fighter drifted past the rows of obese Douglas B-18s of the 30th, 32nd and 34th Bombardment Squadrons, then past a scattering of Northrop A-17A attack planes. As he turned onto the runway, the yellow and black checkerboard roofs of the hangars were visible in the early half light of dawn.

At an overload weight of 15,550 pounds, the XP-38 was about one-third over the design gross weight of the airplane Kelly Johnson had proposed. Of course there was alternate fuel on board, but most of the extra weight was attributable to the beefy Jim Gerschler structure and the fact that Lockheed did not employ any weight control engineers. That prototype was supported by less than half the wing area of a fully loaded Martin B-10 bomber, but the gross weights of the bomber and the fighter were within just a few hundred pounds.

As the fighter attained takeoff speed, Kelsey eased it off the long runway and turned east toward Flagstaff, Arizona. Takeoff time was recorded as 6:12 a.m. (PST). Climbing easily at 3,000 feet per minute, he picked up a fair tailwind at 18,000 feet before setting his new course direct for Amarillo, Texas. Although the weather couldn't be viewed as outstanding, it was at least being cooperative.

(After half a century has elapsed, it is difficult for those not intimately familiar with the status of aviation in the 1930s to realize that probably fewer than a half-dozen pilots in the entire world had made even one flight in a twin-engine single-seat high-performance fighter. Lt. Kelsey had already logged more hours than any of the others – including those who had flown the Whirlwind – and none of the pilots had come within 50 mph of the speeds he was not attaining. In fact there were only three pilots in the entire world who had flown faster!)

Approximately 2 hours after the XP-38 turned away from March Field, an Air Corps medium bomber took off from Wichita, Kansas, with Maj. Gen. Henry Arnold on board. It took a heading for Dayton, destined to arrive at Wright Field just 20 minutes before the new fighter touched down there. Although Arnold was designated as Chief of the Air Corps, he was not – either in 1939 or 1941 – the highest ranking general in that branch of the service.

After a very fast but uneventful flight of 3 hours 10 minutes, the XP-38 touched the runway at 9:22 a.m. (PST) in Amarillo, located on the flat plains of the Texas Panhandle. It was there that the first anomaly was encountered, one of the few that had an impact on the flight. Refueling of the airplane was accomplished by a military crew in the very leisurely time of 23 minutes, although the total amount transferred was only between 240 and 300 gallons. With two refueling rigs, the entire process should not have taken over 12 minutes. Nobody even recorded the exact gallonage. Kelsey was not on his way again until 9:45. He climbed to 18,000 feet and then drifted up to 21,000 to pick up a cooperative tailwind. The recorded ground speed from Enid, Oklahoma, to St. Louis, Missouri, was in excess of 400 mph, even with the engines throttled back to deliver 755 horsepower each.

Winter days (and nights) at Wright Field in February can be bitterly cold, but when the lieutenant made a routine approach to his very familiar home base and turned onto "final" from the base leg, there was no snow in evidence and the sun was shining. Kelsey taxied into place on the new parking ramp as Lockheed and Allison personnel moved in and Air Corps mechanics prepared to refuel the XP-38. Gen. Arnold and Brig. Gen. A. Warner Robins, Chief of the Materiel Division, personally greeted the pilot to congratulate him on his performance and to discuss their decision relating to a dash for New York. Both officers were attired in mufti, which was quite common in those peacetime years.

Parked in front of a blunt blue and yellow Douglas O-46A and a similarly painted North American BT-9B, the silvery, stiletto-like fuselages of the XP-38 were almost totally incongruous. It didn't even reveal a sign of labor, no matter that it had already streaked across 1,920 miles of American soil. No exhaust stains smeared the red, white and blue tail strips on the twin rudders. The overall appearance must have impressed Gen. Arnold. His decision: Head for Mitchel Field "and don't spare the horses."

While refueling proceeded (seemingly at a snail's pace), the two generals and the pilot carried on a serious conversation; then there was a round of congratulations again, a brief conference with the Allison representative, a flurry of activity. Kelsey started the two engines, taxied out and took off after 18 minutes on the ground. This time there was no effort to conserve fuel. A high continuous power setting was selected as the fighter climbed, heading east over Columbus and on toward Pittsburgh. In reporting his position to the tower operator at Pittsburgh Airport, he inadvertently gave the impression that he was a humorist because the message that he was cruising at a true airspeed of 380 miles per hour at 21,000 feet brought an argument from the operator. Just as the conversation was beginning to make sense to those at Pittsburgh, the XP-38 had flown out of radio range.

Lt. Kelsey began his letdown procedure a few minutes later, descending to about 6,000 feet before contacting the tower at Mitchel Field on Long Island to request landing instructions. At this point, the entire foundation for the "record flight" started to crumble. If the refueling teams had seemed nonchalant about their efforts, Arnold's subordinates at Wright Field must have been "out to lunch."

Nobody even bothered to telephone or radio those in command at Mitchel Field to inform them that something very special was coming their way in a matter of minutes. If the FAI official was at the base, nobody else seemed to be aware of it. Any proper climax to that flight was being sabotaged as if by some foreign agent. The unassuming character of Ben Kelsey did him no favors at that point. He did not advise the tower of his desire to make a fast flyby or ask for a specific time notation. When he was instructed to "land No. 4 behind three Consolidated PB-2As" that were in the pattern after having flown up from Langley Field, Virginia, on a routine cross-country exercise, he did not insist on a priority of any kind. That certainly would have been appropriate under the circumstances. As a result, Kelsey was forced to fly an extremely long base leg before turning onto final at about 6,000 feet.

Many years later, a long-retired Brig. Gen. Ben Kelsey gave a very personalized description of what happened in the ensuing minutes (after he was asked a series of questions by this writer). With almost total recall, Kelsey related the full experience of the February 11 episode.

"When we decided to make the transcontinental delivery dash, or whatever you want to call it, we still had some fairly serious, unresolved problems with the XP-38. The brake system was one of the most perplexing. We knew how to fix it later, but there wasn't time to do it then. You couldn't expect to get more than three landings out of the (hydraulic) lines because of the extra pressure, and you never knew when they just wouldn't work.

"The Fowler flap setup really only had a temporary fix. We knew that it was necessary to slow (the airplane) way down in order to avoid severe flap buffeting as they were extended. The stabilizer area had not been increased, so there was still a slight longitudinal instability problem."

"Back to the brakes. There was a great deal of change taking place with regard to landing in 1939. Concrete runways were coming in big (but only in the U.S.A) and we were now pioneering in landing with tricycle landing gears. It is one thing to land an airplane with a wing loading of 25 to 27 pounds per square foot at an approach speed of 65 mph and touch down on grass with a tailwheel landing gear. But when you are at 90 mph at touchdown, sporting a 45- to 47-pound wing loading and landing on concrete with a 14,000 pound airplane, everything is much different. You don't stop right away and the brakes really get a workout.

"I really didn't give it a second thought when the tower instructed me to take a position behind the PB-2A because I had to get the plane slowed down for flap extension anyway. I put the gear down and throttled way back; I did not even think of icing because we had none of it before. The turbos slowed way down and power went down with that to about 15 percent. The nose was up and the flaps came out without difficulty. Oh, of course the descent rate was quite high, but I planned to drop it in near the end of the runway with power on to keep the nose up and let the plane act as its own brake. The runway was plenty long, but I didn't want to have to count on those brakes stopping me. You just had to drag it – only the XP-38 – in at around 90 and the nosewheel well off. It was a peculiar landing technique. Of course it was.

"I really wasn't prepared, at least mentally, for what actually happened. When I started to add power, I was really surprised to see those damned engines just sit there and idle at around 1,500 rpm. Of course everything was happening in a second, but I just knew . . . in my own mind . . . that this was a temporary thing and that the power would surge on at any minute. The gauges didn't give a clue that anything was wrong, but it (they) just sat there. If the engines had just quit, I thought at the moment and have often thought later, while I was going down . . if they had just stopped altogether, I would have kicked it off to the right and would have landed in an open field. It would have been a reasonably good landing and we would have had minimal damage. But the damn things just continued to sit there and tick over at idle rpm. There was simply nothing I could do to make them speed up, you know. In just another second or two, if they had quit, I would probably have been all right.

"I would think that the gear was about halfway up by the

time I went into the treetops, and . . . as you noted . . . the flaps were almost fully retracted. If I had left them out, it wouldn't have helped a bit at that time, and I knew that the busy highway was in front of me anyway. It was a pretty rough ride from there on in, but quite frankly I don't remember much about that aspect of it."

Gen. Kelsey was clearly aware that this writer had experienced strong feelings that the failure of the Allisons to respond was the result of carburetor icing. Hardly anybody shared that view because it was believed that it could not happen with turbosupercharged engines. The general was then presented with a clearcut question about his own viewpoint on that subject.

"Tom McCrea, one of Allison's top field representatives, sat down and made out a list of nine things that would cause the engines to lose power like that, e.g. with no indications on the instruments. After we went through the list of everything I did on the approach, we eliminated four or five of those things. Of the remaining items, the only ones we could not positively pin down were vapor lock and icing. With the fuel cross-suction and cross-pressure system of the XP, a system specifically designed to make sure that you didn't wind up with a lot of unusable fuel if you lost one engine – a critical failing of the Westland Whirlwind – some funny things could happen. Those were, therefore, the two most likely causes.

"When we came into the YP series, we went down the list and changed everything that had not been eliminated (in that analysis). So we never did find out the true cause of the failure. It never showed up in just that way again. However, we had similar problems with icing on early supercharged Boeing B-17 Flying Fortresses, the Y1B-17A and B-17B. If things slowed down too much, an engine would develop icing and you couldn't get the turbine speed up to generate enough heat to melt the ice. You simply came in with one engine that was iced up enough to cut off the power." (Note: Later on, all P-38 training and flight manuals warned of possible carburetor icing, and provided information on how to deal with it.)

After some of the attributes of the XP-38 were discussed, the retired general was pointedly asked why he had not really been allowed to make every effort to go after the official transcontinental speed record as if they meant it.

"Ha," Kelsey bellowed, "we didn't dare . . . no, we didn't dare. Arnold knew precisely what he wanted; in fact, I had talked to Carl Squier about it. He got ahold of (in touch with) Arnold, who was under intense pressure all the time because of the performance of the Messerschmitts and the English planes - the fighters that were so much better than our service fighters. Arnold, who was certainly not an engineer, did not have much patience with test flights in which hours were spent to evaluate performance. All he wanted to know was, 'Did it go or didn't it go?' If it did the job, he didn't want to be bothered with the detailed circumstances.

"We told him that the chances of bettering Howard Hughes's elapsed time were pretty slim . . . mainly because it must be remembered that there were only about 5 hours of flying time on our radical beast. But that it would be 'Duck Soup' for us to beat his flying time. That was one reason for the lengthy discussion we had at Wright Field. By then we knew what was what, and we also had the speed thing in the bag."

Another writer question: "I gather that General Arnold wasn't really mad at you for cracking up the new airplane. Is that correct?"

Kelsey was more than happy to respond to that. He often expressed some irritation with published information to the effect that the loss of the XP-38 had seriously delayed the entire program. "Right! Not a damn bit mad. I know he was not happy to lose the aircraft, but he was happy to see that I

ABOVE: Maj. Gen. H. H. Arnold (left), Brig. Gen. A. Warner Robins and 1st Lt. Benjamin Kelsey quietly consider a note or TWX as the XP-38 was being serviced. The fighter appeared to be remarkably clean after several hours of high-speed flight. Wright Field was a center of aeronautical excitement from that day forward. (WADC)

BELOW: Disaster! Wreckage of Lockheed's XP-38 reposed "in the rough" on the Cold Stream Golf Course on the approach to Mitchel Field, N.Y., after carburetors iced up during a lengthy (and unwarranted) approach behind some other slow-moving fighters. That experimental airplane was too beautiful to be reduced to a pile of junk. Photo was taken from a very low-flying aircraft. Kelsey sat bareheaded on left wing centersection.

was unhurt. I talked to him right afterward on February 11 by phone, and he told me to 'get down to Washington' the very next day. That was on Sunday. On Monday he took me around to see everybody. We went to see Secretary of War Henry (sic) Woodring and his key assistant, Louis B. Johnson, Gen. Delos Emmons and some very influential congressmen. Arnold would say, 'Kelsey, tell them what you told me.' For his purposes, justifying the go-ahead (with the P-38 program) was everything. If it was for a 400 mph fighter, he could not care less if it was good for 415 or 420. He had a 400 mph airplane; he had remarkable elapsed time on the clock; and he even had a newspaper article to wave around."

In spite of all critical commentary, Gen. Arnold was probably "Mr. Right" for his era.  He could cut his losses – as recommended in stock exchange dealings – without a whimper; better yet, he was decisive. Arnold and Kelsey made a good team. They may have been the only two Americans who really knew that the XP-38 crash would not set the entire program back.  In the long run, the program was actually promoted by the demonstrated prowess of the XP-38 and then by its early loss.  In a different era, it might seem doubtful that prototypes were lost with great regularity.  To pick a few at random – from that era, and without any real investigation –  it is possible to recall that the Douglas 7B, XP-47B of Republic, Boeing 299X (XB-17), North American NA-40B, and the Focke-Wulf Fw 187 V1 were destroyed in crashes.  One great loss, almost unrecognized, was the prototype Boeing B-307 Stratoliner.  It crashed with a large test crew aboard.  Untold others came perilously close to destruction in crash landings.  In the 1930s, losses were common.

Lockheed's XP-38 crashed on the Cold Stream Golf Course at Hempstead, Long Island, after slashing through a stand of trees.  The thing that seemed to cause the greatest damage was the golfer's nightmare, a big sand trap.    While the airplane appeared, at first glance, to be remarkably intact, virtually everything was twisted. It was truly more than a Class 26 airplane. As with most P-38s over a period of years, the main gondola came out of the crash in excellent condition. From a ground observer's standpoint, the crash was remarkable.  One person intimately involved was a well-known pilot and author, Col. Raymond Toliver, USAF (Ret.).  Here is his story as told to me in the mid 1970s.

"I was Officer-of-the-Day (OD) at Mitchel Field on that Saturday," the sharp-looking retired officer told me.  He was a young second lieutenant in 1939, an Alan Ladd look-a-like in appearance and stature.  "The tower or Operations called me to meet an incoming plane that was attempting to break some sort of a transcontinental speed record, as they put it.  We didn't know anything else about it except that it was something new and experimental.  Two – or maybe it was three – PB-2A fighters from Langley Field were coming in to land.  I remember that one was on base leg and one was on final.  The tower requested that Kelsey, by then identified as the pilot of that special aircraft, stretch out his base leg and take station behind the second of the PB-2As still in the air.  One pilot of those PB-2As, Joe Ambrose, was an old Air Corps classmate of mine.

"I stepped out in front of Operations to watch the plane land.  Both PB-2As were coming in from the southeast, and the closest was about one-half mile out.  The strange silver job was, by then, way out and pretty high.  I would estimate that he was about 6,000 feet as he banked for final.  When the tailend PB-2A cleared the fence, Kelsey was about 2 miles out and was, obviously, sinking rapidly.  He got down to what I guess was an alarmingly low altitude when one of the engines began to smoke, and I figured he was pouring the coal to it.  The nose went up but he continued to sink in spite of the power being turned on. Suddenly there was a whole lot of wood flying out of the trees.

"There was a tremendous cloud of smoke and dust going up, and I recall grabbing a soldier who was standing next to me and then heading for my car, which was an old Plymouth. The Army did not furnish cars for the OD in those days. Some other officer slammed out of the office, shouting 'He crashed . . . he crashed.' I drove my brakeless Plymouth like mad out of the North gate, drove about a quarter mile east, made that turn and headed a mile south to the Hempstead Highway.

"Saturday afternoon traffic was tremendous when we got to the intersection, where there was a traffic light. I ran the red light and headed the final half mile west to the crash site, then went off the road and onto the golf course. When I got to the plane, Ben Kelsey was sitting on the wing. It was unbelievable to me that he was not dead, or at least badly injured. He seemed to be rather disgruntled.

"Perhaps ten people at the crash site figured that if I went up to the aircraft it was okay for them to come close. Others began to show up with cameras within 10 minutes. What happened next seems funny as hell to me now. About 15 minutes after the plane hit, my squadron commanding officer in the 9th Bomb Wing arrived on the scene. Major 'Sudden Sam' Connell got there with about as much clamor as the XP-38 had created. He was a very bombastic type of person. He ran around shouting 'Take their cameras away. No pictures allowed. Take their film.' He tried to stop all of the photographers. 'It's a top secret airplane,' he yelled.

"Good Lord, but it was funny. It was totally hopeless because so many pictures had been taken."

Col. Toliver was a very good pilot, but one who was frustrated by events of the wartime years. Though he flew more than 200 different types of aircraft after being assigned to Wright Field following Pearl Harbor, he was unhappy that he never had the opportunity to become a combat fighter pilot . . . and perhaps an ace. It must be said that Ray Toliver did not particularly like the P-38, basically because he is rather small in stature, and, as he put it, "You had to be built like an ape to fly the P-38." Ben Kelsey, Cass Hough, Tony LeVier, Dick Bong, Jack Jenkins, Tommy McGuire and hundreds of others would probably take exception to that comment. But a man is entitled to his opinion.

Quite coincidentally, C. L. "Kelly" Johnson completed and signed Report No. 1483 out in California on the Monday following the loss of his dream airplane, turned into scrap by a sand trap. Although the document had been in preparation for a week, data transmitted by Kelsey by telephone from Dayton and from Hempstead were quickly worked into the report to provide some very enlightening and important performance figures. Speed information collected during some portions of the West-to-East flight, when everything was stabilized, was compared to data calculated by Johnson and his team earlier. The correlation was excellent, providing a solid base for substantiation of calculated data included in the report that was entitled "Preliminary Flight Tests – XP-38 Aircraft."

Johnson assumed that the aircraft took off in the overload condition and burned off 550 pounds of fuel (payload) during the climb to 18,000 feet. Starting with a weight of 15,000 pounds and a modest propeller efficiency of 78 percent, he expected to guarantee a top speed of 403 mph at critical altitude on 1150 brake horsepower per engine. When you realize that such performance guarantees were to be written into any contract involving the P-38, those people operating in the inner circles in Washington, Dayton and industry must have had a hard time absorbing and accepting the performance figures. Lockheed merely had to guarantee 360 mph.

Just for the sake of comparison, the absolute World's Landplane Speed Record recognized by the FAI in 1939 (at least in the early months of the year) was 352.2 mph. Howard Hughes had established that record near Santa Ana, California, a bit over 3 1/2 years earlier, flying his very special Richard Palmer-designed racing plane, the H-1. In the United Kingdom, a special Supermarine Spitfire was being developed to break that record, but a couple of test pilots from the Third Reich were destined to perform that feat as part of a propaganda campaign before the Speed Spitfire could be readied. The two German aircraft and the single RAF aircraft were as far removed from being combat types as Grand National Stock cars are from basic economy cars in a showroom. The top performing Messerschmitt bore little, if any, real relationship to a Bf 109 in squadron service. Neither of the two German record aircraft dared stray more than a few miles from the home airfield, and their top performance was at sea level. The XP-38 would not have provided a contest on the deck, but it was a fully capable military aircraft (for that particular period, prior to the Battle of Britain), designed to perform its primary mission at levels four or more miles above sea level.

Virtuosity and enterprise were two of Kelly Johnson's admirable traits. Although he was deeply involved in guiding several other military projects at the same time, he found it impossible to remain out of the P-38 picture. The following statement appearing in his new report serves as an illustration:

"As a result of research which has been done during the development of the airplane (the XP-38) and after its actual flight tests, it has become apparent that improvements can be made in the present airplane (configuration). Without going too greatly into detail, these changes may be summarized as leading to higher performance, lower weight and considerably better accessibility and ease of maintenance of the aircraft."

He provided a summary of those changes that were already scheduled for incorporation in the prototype following completion of early flight testing at March and Wright Fields. Redesign work had been completed on most items, and only the weight program would have been really difficult. Here are the summarized changes:

| ALTERATION RECOMMENDED | CALCULATED SPEED CHANGE |
| --- | --- |
| Redesign Prestone coolant radiators | plus 8 mph |
| Improved turbosupercharger installation | plus 4 mph |
| Revised oil cooler inlet (non-retracting) | plus 3 mph |
| Reduction in exhaust cooling duct size | plus 2 mph |
| Weight reduction of 800 to 1,000 pounds | plus 2 mph |
| Increase horizontal stabilizer area by 7 sq. ft. | minus 1.2 mph |
| Armament (muzzles protruding from nose) | minus 7.8 mph |
| Net change in High Speed | plus 10.0 mph |

Report 1483 detailed the conclusions that incorporation of all these specified changes would provide a guaranteed maximum speed of 413 mph at critical altitude. Remarkable! Upon reading his copy of the report . . . even after three years of intimate contact with the entire project . . . Hall Hibbard's suave, urbane facade melted before his new ebullience. He scribbled this note across the bottom of the last page of his copy before passing it on to Robert Gross:

"Note that without armament the top speed of the airplane is – 413 + 7.8 = 420.8 miles per hour – H.H."

He triple underlined the 420.8 figure.

Aviation magazine editors were sometimes rather gullible in prewar days, and some of their published misinformation was so bad that factual data became tainted by the backlash. As an example, the new Curtiss XP-40, essentially a P-36A with a pointed nose and an unsupercharged Allison C-series engine, was suddenly pictured and publicized as having a "2000 horsepower Allison and a speed in excess of 400 miles

per hour!" Rather incredibly, Europeans and Americans alike were more likely to believe reports of test pilot Lloyd Child's "575 mph dive" in an export Curtiss H.75A Hawk – a technical and actual impossibility – than they were to accept the reported 400 mph speed of the XP-38. Once again, truth was stranger than fiction.

On the day after his crash landing, Lt. Kelsey penned some comments that he believed would be useful in discussing the XP-38 with the VIP types he expected to meet the next day in Washington. The information in those notes is presented here as if it was an immediate post-flight mission debriefing:

SUBJECT: Speed flight of Lockheed XP-38 from March Field, Calif., to Mitchel Field, New York, on February 11, 1939.

The airplane was built as a Pursuit type, meeting standard strength requirements and having all normal operating equipment necessary for military use (except for replacement of the weapons with ballast).

The Allison vee-type Prestone-cooled engines are used with normal maximum power of 1000 hp each, but they are capable of delivering 1150 hp each for takeoff and for relatively short periods in the air. To maintain this power at high altitude, two General Electric exhaust-driven superchargers are installed.

The airplane develops its maximum performance at altitudes between 20,000 and 25,000 feet. On the leg from March Field, engineering data were recorded to show average operating conditions. For example, at 18,000 feet with each engine developing 755 hp, the true airspeed of the XP-38 was 350-mph. Converting by calculations to maximum conditions, the airplane is shown to be capable of 399 mph on 1250 hp per engine at 20,000 feet. Another run at 21,750 feet east of Pittsburgh, Pennsylvania, with each engine developing 865 hp, gave a true airspeed of 380 mph; converted to 1150 hp and 20,000 feet altitude, the aircraft would fly 394 mph.

Total elapsed time observed in the cockpit was 7 hours. and 43 minutes.; flying time for the flight, including takeoff and landing and climb to altitude was 7 hours flat. Total distance was approximately 2,460 miles. Average speed – deducting time for landing approaches and taxiing on the ground – was 365 miles per hour.

No effort was made to develop the maximum speed possible with the fuel supply available, there being more than 100 gallons left in the tanks at each stop. In losing altitude, the airplane was kept at speeds *below* the level flight high speed so that no benefit was derived from losing altitude.

Altitude was maintained between 18,000 and 22,000 feet. The total time flown above 18,000 feet was 5 1/2 to 6 hours.

Leaving Wright Field, the plane was over the Columbus, Ohio, Airport at 20,000 feet in fifteen minutes. The airport was 60 miles away, giving a speed in climb of 240 mph and a rate of climb of about 1,500 feet per minute.

The elapsed time for the 900 miles from March to Amarillo was 2 hrs. and 48 mins.; for the 1,020 miles from Amarillo to Wright Field, time was 2 hrs. and 45 mins.; for the 540 miles between Wright and Mitchel, 1 hr. and 25 mins.

With a helping tailwind, the ground speed from Enid, Oklahoma, to St. Louis, Missouri, was over 400 mph. Pittsburgh was reached from Wright Field in 33 minutes, giving a speed of 400 mph including the climb, while at altitude the airplane was actually making 420 mph.

Had the full capabilities of the new plane been used for the sole purpose of establishing a new record, it would have been possible to reduce the elapsed time by at least 45 minutes and the flying time by about 30 minutes. The aircraft would still be operating as a military – as opposed to racing – plane. The Hughes record would have been bettered by about one-half hour.

In spite of wing loading and performance superior to (all existing) racing planes, the airplane is perfectly usable as a military plane with normal flight characteristics. Due to the tricycle landing gear and other features, it is as easy to operate as more conventional types.

End of Lt. Benjamin Kelsey's personal comments. A tabulation of official U. S. Army Air Corps figures for the flight follows:

DISTANCE: 2400 miles*
ELAPSED TIME: 7 hours, 43 minutes
FLYING TIME: 7 hours, 2 minutes
AVERAGE SPEED: 350 miles per hour*

*When the starting and ending locations are taken into consideration for the Hughes flight (1937) and the Kelsey

LEFT: Carburetor icing in turbosupercharged aircraft was totally unexpected. But it had occurred previously in B-17Bs and Cs. Alas, the XP-38 was relegated to Class 26 or worse.
(LeRoy Weber from UPI)

RIGHT: Notice that the XP-38 gondola was hardly scathed. James Gerschler's structure was as tough as the Golden Gate Bridge. Trees and those sand trap gullies behind the tail constituted a wrecking crew.
(LeRoy Weber from UPI)

flight, the distances should be approximately the same. You might even suspect that the H-1 flew a shorter route since it was nonstop. Using the Air Corps "official" distance, the Hughes flight would have been over a greater distance. Also, using these time and distance figures, the average speed will not calculate out to an even 350 mph. In fact it seems to be somewhat in error.

| LANDING/TAKEOFF TIMES (ALL EASTERN STANDARD) | | |
|---|---|---|
| PLACE | DEPARTURE | ARRIVAL |
| March Field, California | 9:12 a.m. | |
| Amarillo, Texas | 12:45 p.m. | 12:22 p.m. |
| Wright Field, Ohio | 3:28 p.m. | 3:10 p.m. |
| Mitchel Field, New York | | 4:55 p.m. |

Ben Kelsey's own records indicated a total flight time of 6 hours and 58 minutes. NAA timing was revealed as 7 hours 0 minutes 36 seconds. NAA and Kelsey distance figures are 2,490 and 2,460, respectively. Howard Hughes was officially documented at 7 hours 28 minutes 25 seconds for a distance of 2,445 miles. That was nonstop. Even Ben Kelsey's own time figures from two different logs vary by two minutes. It all merely reflects the fact that the "speed flight" was not too well coordinated or documented.

One final coordination mystery remains. If the National Aeronautical Association can claim that it recorded the flight times until "touchdown" at Mitchel Field as 7 hours 0 minutes and 36 seconds, timing people had to be at all bases. If somebody at Dayton knew that all was being timed at least semi-officially, why wasn't Kelsey instructed to make a tower flyby before he left Wright Field? Why is it that nobody at the Mitchel tower or Operations Office was aware of the flight, especially if NAA timers were on the flight line or at Operations? And finally, why didn't the tower operator give Kelsey some sort of priority? For the want of a nail . . . .

Regulations required that Lt. Kelsey submit a comprehensive report about the accident soon after the crash. The pilot's information can constitute the only first-hand compilation of factual data and, unless an accident investigation committee's findings prove otherwise, it can provide valuable material for engineering analysis and action. Any commentary from other sources who had not studied the "Pilot's Statement" is essentially valueless. The XP-38 pilot's report on his memory and actions follow:

Departed from Wright Field at 3:25 p.m.; accident occurred while attempting landing at Mitchel Field at 4:50 p.m. Arriving over New York at 14,000 feet, the engines were throttled to low power, about 15 inches manifold pressure. The engines were running at this partial power for about 3 minutes and then throttled down and the plane slowed to get the gear down. After lowering the gear, partial power (at) about 20 inches manifold pressure and about 2,000 rpm was used in the turn for approach. The engines were (then) throttled completely and the plane slowed to about 120 mph to lower the flaps. After the flaps were down, the throttles were opened. The left engine started up partially, but the right (engine) continued to idle. The fuel capacity was checked, fuel pressure was steady at 4 pounds on both engines. Mixture controls were rich; the left engine was running at about 15 inches and 1,900 (rpm). The prop pitch was checked to be sure it was in low pitch. When it became obvious that with gear and flaps both down the plane would not glide into Mitchel Field, the flaps and gear handle were put in UP position in the hopes that with less drag it might coast in. When the speed got down under 120, further efforts to get one engine to go were abandoned since with the low speed and high drag the plane obviously could not be held if one engine came on full (power). The glide was slowed to about 100 (mph). It appeared that it might glide to a golf course across the road from Mitchel Field. As the trees were approached, the speed was kept at 90 to 95 and after passing through the tops of the trees, it (the XP-38) was pulled up sharply just before hitting. It landed in a normal altitude in the bottom of a gully (transverse) and slid up the bank. There was an impression that the main gear hit while partially extended. All items on the check list were checked on approach. The flaps were intentionally lowered so as to undershoot a little, (I was) figuring on pulling in with the engines so as to make the shortest possible landing due to the long ground run of the plane. The engines have to be completely throttled to get the flaps down without vibrating through the middle range (XP only).

Of the possible causes, the most likely seems to be the possibility of icing in the carburetors due to excessive intercooling at high speed and partial power. As far as could be ascertained in the time available, there was no apparent reason either in the operation of the controls or in the

41

*instrument indications of any mechanical failure or engine failure as such. The fact that both engines were partially out indicates that some general condition must have affected both. There is no control for carburetor heat since these engines have never given indication of icing, and with turbo installations there is normally sufficient heat of compression. However, in this case, the high speed, lower power condition may have cooled the air below normal conditions.*

(s) BENJAMIN S. KELSEY,
1st Lieutenant, Air Corps

It is pretty remarkable that Kelsey recognized that if the power came on full on one engine while the other idled, he would be unable to "hold" the aircraft from rolling violently. He was most likely the first pilot to encounter this possibility. With high torque and the wrong piloting technique, a flyer could get killed quickly on takeoff or landing if one engine failed at that time.

Carburetor de-icing techniques outlines in flight manuals published later on cannot work under the landing situation encountered by Ben Kelsey at Mitchel. If the ice has formed, you cannot possibly raise manifold pressure to 30 inches hg. Only the XP-38 had the flap problems that affected Kelsey's landing.

If nothing else, the Air Corps at least had a new record for its own service files. A transcontinental record had been set by Lt. H. L. Neely, flying a Seversky P-35 on July 28, 1938. No speed was listed, but the time recorded between San Francisco (Hamilton Field) and Mitchel Field, via Salt Lake City, Omaha and Cleveland was 9 hours 55 minutes.

Gen. "Hap" Arnold and Lt. Kelsey must have been pretty effective during their tour of VIP offices in Washington because a contract for 13 YP-38 service test airplanes was included in a vast award of aircraft contracts announced on April 27, 1939. Whatever went on behind the scenes, just a bit more than *60 days* elapsed between the conclusion of their tour to report on the XP-38 and the contract awards. Perhaps, and we can only speculate on that, officials in the War Department really began to worry about losing prototypes. They awarded a contract to Bell for thirteen YP-39s for service test. And just days after the order for a single Consolidated XB-24 prototype was placed, in the final week of March, seven service test YB-24s were ordered. It is not out of the realm of possibility to conclude that the XP-38 crash had such a profound impact on the Secretary of War, congressmen and Air Corps procurement specialists that they quickly revised their long-standing peacetime thinking.

Timing of the crash may just have been a remarkable coincidence at a time when President Roosevelt's military and naval expansion program was about to be initiated. But certain additional "coincidences" will be noted in the analysis of the YP-38, P-38, and P-38D story. Probably the true facts will never be known because of the complexities of so many crucial situations unfolding simultaneously.

With ominous war clouds gathering over Europe in mid-1939, there was precious little time left to get America's air arm out of the doldrums of long-standing indifference. Less than a month before the XP-38 made its cross-country dash, Maj. Gen. Frank M. Andrews – Chief of the General Headquarters Air Force of the Army – stated publicly that the U.S. had a fifth- or sixth-rate air force and that his own GHQ Air Force had just slightly more than 400 fighting planes. Rather interestingly, he was replaced by Brig. Gen. Delos C. Emmons in February, causing a considerable upheaval in Air Corps circles. It did, however, confirm that America's air arm was in deplorable condition. It also revealed what a great opportunist Gen. Arnold was, turning disaster into advantage.

Lockheed received an order amounting to $2,180,725 for that group of service test airplanes. At the same time, Bell received $1,073,445 for 13 YP-39s; Consolidated recorded a contract for $2,880,000 for procurement of seven YB-24s; and giant Curtiss – one of the "Big Four" of the aviation industry – walked off with the *grand prix* of $12,872,398 for the original production lot of P-40s . . . some 200 of them. Was it because they were going to be easy to produce since they were about 80 percent P-36/Hawk H.75 with vast tooling already in place? Or could it have been the fact that this giant organization was still fighting to recover from the tiny $2,886 net profit it had recorded for *all* of its corporate subsidiaries as reported in 1936? Well, it did have the required Allison engine; it was certainly very producible; it was faster than most *Armee de l'Air* fighters and as rapid as the Hurricane; and Curtiss-Wright Corporation certainly needed a financial boost to survive.

Concurrently, the Army announced the purchase of two "experimental" pursuits, one being the Bell XP-39 (!) and the other being the P-35 offspring, the Seversky XP-41. This was tantamount to being the first official public announcement of the Bell contract dating from 1937, while the XP-41 contract was an outgrowth of the fighter competition won by the XP-40 as 1939 dawned. In effect, it constituted what was the Army's first contract ever awarded for an aircooled monoplane pursuit equipped with a two-stage high-altitude mechanical supercharger.

Some 19 long months would elapse before the first Lockheed YP-38 was rolled of the former G.G.G. Distillery buildings purchased by Robert Gross, almost in desperation, in June 1939. A number of factors were responsible for that long delay, not the least of which was the increased complexity of the fighter because of lessons learned during the XP flight test program. A significant portion of Lockheed's problem was one that everybody would love to have; this company which was looked upon as a pipsqueak upstart by the likes of Douglas and Curtiss just two years earlier, was rapidly becoming the industry giant. Orders literally poured into Burbank for Hudsons, the upcoming Model 37, a new airliner and others. Buildings could not be constructed fast enough; entirely new methods of airframe construction had to be devised to compensate for a shortage of skilled personnel; massive new training programs had to be developed and implemented. Probably the most serious problem involved the extreme shortage of talented engineers and technicians. The Vega subsidiary of Lockheed was forced to abandon some of its minor programs to concentrate on design of Lockheed's Model 37 (soon named Ventura) developed from the Model 18 Lodestar airliner. Just 12 months after the XP-38 flight, the British ordered 25 of the Ventura bombers right off the drawing board. Design work on the Lockheed Model 122 (YP-38) was in direct competition for engineers with the Model 37 program.

Was Lockheed-Vega content with all of this sudden success?

Good Lord, no. In June, 1939 – just over 30 days after the YP-38 contract was acknowledged – they drove headlong into development of the Model 49 Constellation for TWA after having spent a great deal of time and effort on the Model 44 Excalibur for Pan American, without a reward it might be noted. Pan Am was "fishing" a lot in those days.

Jimmy Gerschler suffered under the intense pressures, and it was not long before a problem with alcoholism got the upper hand. He was replaced as P-38 project engineer by W. A. "Dick" Pulver, a man better equipped for management of a wildly burgeoning program. Even though Ben Kelsey was temporarily at arm's length from the project because his expertise was needed elsewhere, he soon recognized that Lockheed was not doing everything possible to solve the YP-38 and other P-38 situation anomalies.

# CHAPTER 5

# Second Thoughts - The YP

Activity at the intersection of San Fernando Road, Empire Avenue and Victory Place in the spring of 1939 was pretty intensive. AiRover, a new subsidiary of Lockheed, although it was not publicized as such at the time, had occupied the rather ugly red brick Empire China Co. factory right next door to Lockheed's main plant. Renovation began almost immediately in 1937 and by 1938 the plant was being expanded to produce a new feedliner. Reorganized as the Vega Airplane Co. in that same year, it continued to grow. When market analysis failed to reveal a market for the Vega Starliner, it was abandoned and Vega found itself with over 170,000 feet of floorspace that was being used in an unproductive manner. In the meantime, Lockheed was expanding along Empire Avenue almost as fast as steel could be delivered. It wasn't fast enough.

Production of Hudson bombers was the central theme at the main plant. That airplane was a real money maker and Lockheed management could hardly be faulted for concentrating on that model after the XP-38 had cost far more than it brought in. Viewing the 1939 Curtiss contract for the P-40, why should they expect to receive orders for more than 100 of the P-38s?

Looking around, Robert Gross found the aging G.G.G. Distillery on San Fernando Road, north of Union Air Terminal. He arranged to have lunch with the three owners, made an offer and it was accepted. Marked by a couple of grain towers, the odoriferous distillery was a real hodgepodge of random buildings. However, the shipping building was hangar-like, and the other areas were suitable for P-38 subassembly manufacturing. In June 1939, the G.G.G. organization was out; Lockheed took over and saved the day one more time. The lingering fragrance of bourbon mash hung on for a long time. Every Vega issue was more difficult to resolve, but a couple of the greatest manufacturing impacts in aviation history were about to strike the Gross brothers, Robert and Courtlandt, like a falling star.

Nobody could say that the P-38 series started life in elegant surroundings. The XP-38 had been constructed in a cluttered corner of one building; it was then partially dismantled and hauled down to March Field. Then it was decided to build the thirteen YP-38s and perhaps 60 or 70 production P-38s at the distillery about 3 miles away from the main factory. Was the airplane going to be treated like some unloved stepchild?

Technical requirements for a small number of service test and production P-38s came under discussion while the design of the XP-38 was being finalized and actual construction of the prototype was getting under way. Allison Engineering was showing considerable design improvement progress. Most early Allison V-1710s were in the C series, easily recognizable because of the lengthy nose gearcase carrying the epicyclic reduction gears. Fortunately for everybody concerned, General Motors had expanded the little Allison plant at Speedway, Indiana, and was at least working hard to convert the V-1710s into production entities. A great deal of effort went into development of a smaller, stronger set of spur reduction gears because the epicyclic gears were already in jeopardy. Testing revealed that the gears would be unable to handle projected

*Test pilot Marshall Headle taxied out to the L.A.T. runway in the first Lockheed YP-38 (c/n 2202) in the fall of 1940. That airplane and the Supermarine Spitfire were probably, without any doubt, the finest examples of aerodynamic cleanness in the world, at least among production aircraft. (Eric Miller - LAC)*

increases in power. Of course Lockheed engineers followed the engine manufacturer's progress closely, ultimately adopting the improved V-1710F series engine for use in the YP vehicles.

Several proposals for improving the pursuit airplanes were submitted via the Air Corps Project Office, including designs with and without turbosuperchargers. Consolidation of these proposals had led to the issuance of A.C. Type Specification No. C-615 on January 25, 1939, while the XP-38 was undergoing pre-flight testing. Nobody foresaw the loss of the prototype, so work on development of a thoroughly revised specification at Burbank progressed slowly. After all, everybody at the plant was completely engrossed in the bountiful Hudson effort, a program that was rapidly lifting Lockheed from relative obscurity to the top rank of aircraft manufacturers. Clarence Johnson and Hall Hibbard had, by the spectacular successes of their advanced designs, injected virility and vitality organisms into the entire Lockheed populations it seemed. Ideas, quality and spirit prevailed.

Close on the dispiriting heels of the crash at Hempstead, Long Island, came the hoped-for order for service test YP-38s. That gladdened the hearts of all, galvanizing the management team into action. The new Model 122-62-02 was born, and James Gerschler got Spec. No. 1611 completed by October 20. When Contract W535-ac-12523 was actually in hand, it called for design and construction of 13 aircraft and one airframe for structural testing.

YP-38s – Yippees to most company employees and to the California public – were equipped with the newest Allison V-1710-27 and -29 engines (F2R and F2L). The designers were enjoined from "messing with the external envelope" except for changes earlier mandated by Kelly Johnson in light of lessons learned during XP-38 flight testing and anything that had to be changed to be compatible with the revised engine installation. All P-38s had what was essentially the same wing that used the NACA 23016 section at the root (centerline of the fuselage gondola) and NACA 4412 section at the wing end (tip removed). In essence, the P-38s featured the NACA 0012-63 airfoil, giving the wing average chord/thickness ratio of 12 percent.

There was little commonality between the XP-38 and YP-38 power-plant installations. Bob Gross never believed, in 1937, that Lockheed would ever see orders for more than 60 of the "interceptors" because of Seversky and Curtiss experiences, not to mention the findings in the Baker Board report of 1934. And, as described in an earlier chapter, Army "brass" did not have much appreciation for fighters in the overall military picture. With such things in mind and with limited resources, Jimmy Gerschler did not commit the company to high-cost forgings in designing the XP-38 structure. That restriction was removed in designing the YP-38 airplane. Allison's F2-series engines were rated to 1150 bhp at 20,000 feet with new G.E. B-2 superchargers. Engine rotation was changed so that the propellers rotated outboard (at the top), thereby eliminating or at least reducing the downwash onto the wing centersection/fuselage juncture. There was, by then, no doubt that the disturbed airflow, trapped between the twin booms, was having an adverse effect on the horizontal stabilizer. No problem was encountered in reversing propeller rotation direction; they merely had to interchange the left and right engines.

Some of the key personnel involved in development of the YP-38 were W.A. "Dick" Pulver (who became P-38 Project Engineer for most of the wartime years), M. Carl Haddon (who headed up the XP-38A and XP-49 projects), Neil M. Harrison (a Vought engineer who was attracted by Lockheed products and California weather), J. Russell Daniel, John Margwarth and the proficient Ward Beman. Harrison eventually took over

the XP-58 project when both Lockheed and the military allowed it to drift aimlessly.

Meanwhile, armament thoughts were firmed up a bit and it was decided to concentrate on the M9 Browning 37-mm cannon with 15 rounds of explosive ammunition, two .50-caliber machine guns with 200 rounds per gun, and two .30-caliber machine guns, each with 500 rounds. There has been much speculation that the two long tube fairings seen on some YP-38s and P-38 models were false covers. Actually, the two top guns were .50-caliber Brownings mounted above the .30-calibers, and they projected so far that an attempt at streamlining resulted in the fairings being seen on only a few early Lightnings.

As restructured, the YP-38 had a design empty weight of 11,171 pounds and a design gross weight of 13,500 pounds. However, in order to carry that much needed extra 130 gallons of fuel – the so-called alternate load – in the reserve tanks, the maximum gross weight rose to 14,348 pounds. It is an absolute adage in aviation that you can't get something for nothing. Company engineers and management guaranteed a high speed of 405 mph at 20,000 feet, while time to climb to that level was set at a very satisfactory 6 minutes.

Robert Gross made the decision to plan for production of no less than 80 of the P-38 fighters, including the Yippees. Space in the G.G.G. Distillery was to be employed for manufacture of P-38 subassemblies and, if necessary, at least some of the YP-38s. In fact, the No. 1 airplane was built at that location. Expansion and reorganization of the main plant – a process that had just recently been completed for Hudson production – was started once more. Rapid hiring of engineers and draftsmen, and there were few with any real experience, brought on an entire family of problems. The situation was not aided one bit by Lockheed's proliferation of new projects. Draftsmen had to work from incomplete layouts, and production planners had to be "invented." Problems were so difficult to resolve that the release of initial drawings in July 1939 did not result in any fabrication work until February 1940. One humorous aspect of Lockheed's fantastic growth was the necessity for blueprint delivery clerks to resort to the use of roller skates to expedite the movement of paper.

Beginning in 1940, the world was to witness the most fabulous expansion of an entire aircraft and engine industry in the history of the world. But nowhere was the growth of any company comparable to that of the upstart outfit in Burbank. When Adolph Hitler launched World War II late in the summer of 1939, Lockheed and Vega counted almost 7,300 employees operating in a total plant area of 550,000 square feet. Most of that production and engineering area was still located in a tightly knit area around the old Lockheed buildings that were located at the corner of Empire and Victory Place. Many of the old buildings had more or less disappeared among and under

ABOVE: Milo Burcham had been hired to conduct high-altitude flights in the No.1 YP-38 after Headle was seriously injured in an altitude chamber accident. Lockheed had procured the first private altitude chamber in the country. Flight to more than 35,000 feet without benefit of a pressure cabin was challenging the aeronautical frontier in 1940. (Eric Miller - LAC)

OPPOSITE LEFT: As the first volume contracts for P-38 types were being generated and awarded approximately 60 days after the XP-38's engines failed to respond to throttle commands, the Lockheed plant began to look like a prosperous aircraft factory for the first time. The private airstrip looked about as good as it would ever get. That was on April 15, 1939. (LAC)

new buildings that sprang up virtually overnight. Buildings were spreading along both streets like algae in a stagnant pond.

Just an easy 2-mile walk out Empire Avenue to the west, the Union Air Terminal went quietly about its business, with airlines serving San Fernando Valley travelers and with one hangar (at least) housing Paul Mantz's Air Service. Burbank's pleasant Pioneer Park and the airport had hardly changed a bit since United Airport was dedicated in post-stock market crash days. Hold onto that pleasant picture.

Success of the Lockheed Model 18 Lodestar airliner, essentially a stretched Model 14, spawned a design for yet another new aircraft that was likely to please the RAF. Almost concurrently with the combined *Wehrmacht* and *Luftwaffe* attacks on Poland, Lockheed was submitting a proposal for a successor to the Hudson. After several variants of the original idea were put forth in responding to new wartime conditions, the British Purchasing Commission ordered 25 reconnaissance-bombers soon to be identified as the Model 32. That order was placed in February 1940. Ostensibly a hot-rodded Model 18 in early configurations, it was not long before it adopted its own personality as the Ventura.

Well, how was Lockheed going to handle this "kettle of fish"? With hardly a blink of the eye, the Gross brothers talked the city fathers of sleepy Burbank into selling them Pioneer Park. Robert Gross saw it as 30 acres of flat, virgin land. He also had a plan. Lockheed handed Mac Short, president of Vega Aircraft, a $4,500,000 subcontract to build those Venturas for the British. Short was a fine designer, but this new responsibility nearly caused him to have a stroke. Courtlandt

Gross came to the rescue and took over as president while Mac Short became Vice-President of Engineering, a job he much preferred. Almost immediately, work began on construction of a new 750,000-square-foot factory for Vega in the former park at the corner of Hollywood Way and Empire Avenue.

Back at the Lockheed administrative offices, more excitement was on the way. Hardly a day went by that some new plant construction revision was not on the table. The San Fernando Valley, spreading for miles west of the Union Air Terminal, was a vast desert-like area spotted with farms and suburban homes. Even in nearby North Hollywood, acres and acres of land usually only had two or three homes. On many avenues the only way to tell when you were in North Hollywood was to read the archway sign spanning the road. With great perception, Robert Gross visualized a tremendous change in that way of life, then decided to stockpile some of that valuable Burbank land by purchasing Union Air Terminal from United Air Lines. He was able to buy the airport with several hundred acres of land for $1.5 million just weeks later.

Anxiety at the Air Ministry drove them to seek greater performance out of the Model 32 bombers, and they opted for an upgraded Model 37-21-01 Ventura. Just three months later there was an add-on contract for 300 additional Venturas for the same customer. Lockheed suddenly increased its remarkable $4.5-million subcontract to Vega by about $54,500,000! It seemed absolutely astronomical, especially when it can be recalled that Curtiss had only recently received that $12.9 million "giant" order from the AAC for 200 of the new P-40s.

Members of the Allied Aircraft Purchasing Commission asked Lockheed to send a highly qualified delegation to New York to negotiate what they termed "most interesting contracts." Among those who flew to New York City via United Air Lines was James Gerschler, representing the P-38 team. It did not take long for the Air Ministry and the French equivalent representatives to convince Jimmy that they needed a great number of 400-mph fighters using exactly the same series of engines that powered their Curtiss H.81A/Tomahawk I fighters, then ordered in great numbers. Those Allisons ALL had right-handed rotation and epicyclic reduction gears; worse, they were flat-rated at 1040 bhp at SEA LEVEL! The Allies did not want turbosuperchargers. What they did want was the commonality of powerplants (complete) between the H.81As and the Lockheeds, defined as Model 322-B and 322-F. They were acutely aware of the problems that the War Department was having with delivery of turbosuperchargers, and they emphasized that they had enjoyed virtually zero experience with such devices.

More to the point, the so-called "Phoney War" had not given a clue to the need for high-altitude operations. The American fetish for turbosuperchargers was not shared by any other nation, they reasoned. (The commission's decision had absolutely – and that must be emphasized – nothing to do with any SECRET classification on General Electric superchargers. They weren't even classified RESTRICTED, but it was like pulling teeth to get one out of the manufacturer. Basically, the terms of that contract should have been rejected with a "Thanks, but no thanks for your offer." How in the world could they seriously consider guarantees of a speed of 400 mph at a critical altitude of 16,300 feet – in no way considered the P-38's bailiwick – on 200 horsepower less than the YP-38 was blessed with?

Even more improbable was the demand that ALL of the new airplanes be delivered in one short year. Comparison of the Model 322-61 with the Hudson when it came to simplicity of construction was an apples and oranges situation, and Jimmy Gerschler, of all people, must have known that. As for meeting that production delivery deadline, the closest thing Lockheed had to a P-38 production line in the spring of 1940 was the pungent 3Gs Distillery.

Why did the company negotiators accept the contract, and why did top-level management at Burbank confirm it? Probably because the offer was so astonishing that everybody was in a state of shock. The combined Franco-British offer was nearly $100,000,000 – yes, that is One Hundred Million dollars – for no less than 667 fighters! If anybody had thought it was some sort of flim-flam operation, they could hardly have been faulted. Remember, it was just over a year earlier that Maj. Gen. Andrews complained that the combat arm of the Army Air Corps, known as the GHQ Air Force, had just a little over 400 first-line aircraft for the defense of the United States of America. Not one of those airplanes was a P-38 or even a P-40.

It must be said that nobody in the corporation would ever provide details of those days in New York City, but Gerschler had been replaced as project engineer by Dick Pulver. Jimmy's career went into a decline from which he never recovered, although he remained on the project.

Almost buried by all of this excitement was the fact that back in 1939, just before war broke out in Europe, the Air Corps procurement people responded to presidential expansion plans by proceeding with an initial production contract for quantities of P-38s. Self-evident by then was the fact that long-leadtime items could prove to be a serious constraint on mass production. The predecessor of the civilian Office of Production Management (the OPM) was putting out storm warnings that could not logically be ignored. Among the worst dilemmas was Materiel Division's problems with General Electric and low production rates for turbosuperchargers.

Politics during the period of 1938 through the early part of 1940 had far more to do with the future of the American aircraft industry than any other factor. A book would be required just to cover the known surface elements; investigation of the underlying factors might require volumes. But it is necessary to touch lightly on the subject to have even a slight idea of what was transpiring behind the scenes. There is little doubt that President Roosevelt, in a historic meeting at the

White House, expressed the view that the Air Corps alone required a strength of 20,000 aircraft. At that time, the authorized strength of the Air Corps was between 2,320 and 4,120 total aircraft, including all training aircraft! Why the discrepancy in numbers? Most of it stemmed from the budget request sessions of January 1939, after the Chief Executive sent a special national defense message to Congress. The Chief of the Air Corps amazed everybody by only requesting money for 219 new aircraft because to ask for more would exceed the total authorized by the Air Corps Act of 1936.

In the meantime, the Army Chief of Staff, Gen. Malin Craig, had testified before Congress that the authorized strength was 4,120. Gen. Arnold was correct, but Craig's figure was based on his staff's interpretation, or misinterpretation, of the actual law. In the event, Congress did authorize procurement of 3,032 more airplanes in April 1939. That was to cost them $27 million for procurement. Events in Europe that summer resulted in authorizations rising to about $57,000,000. Passage of a supplemental appropriations bill in July added no less than $123,000,000 for procurement.

Materiel Division wasted no time. When the original fiscal year budget was approved, they had immediately ordered 200 Curtiss P-40s and those service test airplanes for about $19 million. Increases approved in July 1939 energized them to move by August 10 to order additional aircraft for $86,000,000. Contracts issued that day exceeded all orders actually received by the aircraft industry in any peacetime year until at least 1937! If America's aircraft and engine industry appeared to be under a deluge of money, it was the truth. The chief of Materiel's Production Engineering section, (then) Maj. K. B. Wolfe, stated that in 1940 alone his contracts section had made purchases of $1.6 billion.

Maj. Gen. Henry Arnold was not the highest ranking general officer in the Air Corps, but he was certainly the man for all seasons if ever there was one. He may not have been an engineer, but he was outstandingly fortunate in having a few men of Ben Kelsey's standing at his side. The previous comparison of the XP-38 and Halley's Comet was emphasized by the spectacular flight of the fighter and its rather ignoble demise on a golf course. However, just days later the matter was all but forgotten.

Lockheed's engineers, with the impetus of Clarence Johnson leading the way, had essentially redesigned the basic Model 22 for large-scale production in the final months of 1938. James Gerschler's prototype structure had been designed with economy definitely in mind because the official word from the Air Corps had been, "Do not expect total contracts for more than 60 aircraft." Johnson and Hibbard seemed to sense that production design should go hand in hand with technical changes acknowledged as necessary before the transcontinental flight. Even if the XP-38 had landed safely; even if Lt. Kelsey had been feted as aviation's current hero in New York, Dayton, and Burbank; and even if the XP-38 had flown hundreds of hours at Wright Field in 1939 and 1940, the die had been cast. All subsequent P-38s would have been very different. The XP-38 was, after all, a prototype just like the XB-24 and the XP-39. Those airplanes underwent even more radical changes before emerging as operational types.

D Scandal was the real word, not Secret. For many years after the actual event had long passed into history, the legend of the so-called deletion of the "Secret" turbosupercharger from British- and French-ordered Lockheed Model 322 airplanes was told and retold in magazines and books. With the passage of time, it appears to have been accepted as fact. Any guess about how that story was started has to remain a guess, but the truth is something entirely different. As for the device's secret status, it is only necessary to recall that Rateau, in France, was an early pioneer in developing turbosuperchargers. Brown-Boveri in Switzerland was a highly regarded developer of gas and water turbines. The truth was that America's big problem pertaining to G.E. turbosuperchargers at the time was critically insignificant production rates to provide units for B-17s, P-38s, P-43s, and B-24 aircraft. It should have rated as a national scandal.

Some 20 years after the U.S. Army Air Service had entered into a cooperative venture with General Electric (in 1919) for development of turbosuperchargers for aircraft engines, the Air Corps (successor the Air Service) became supremely disenchanted with the huge company's progress. Gen. Delos Emmons' Materiel Division warned G.E. that it had "performed in a manner completely unsatisfactory to the Air Corps," and that the company's lack of production facilities and its failures to correct delays jeopardizing production schedules were becoming more than "intolerable and embarrassing." Although the manufacturer was then under contract to deliver some 319 new superchargers for about $1 million – the contract having been awarded in April 1937 – only one single usable unit had been delivered in 1938!

General Electric executives didn't even bother to respond to the warning until the outbreak of war in Europe attracted their attention. Then they assured the Materiel Division that they would increase annual production rates to 1,200 units. (If the superchargers were only for B-17s and B-24s, total combined production of those aircraft on an annual basis could not have exceeded 200 with provision for spares.) The Industrial Planning Section, acting on instructions from an angry Maj. Gen. Oliver Echols, promptly informed G. E. management that oncoming wartime requirements would swell to eight or ten times that modest number. Considering the cavalier attitude exhibited by G.E. in the entire matter, it is incredible that some sort of punitive action was not initiated against the corporation or its managers.

In reassessing the reasons affecting the Allied Purchasing Commission's decision to procure Lockheed Model 322 airplanes sans turbosuperchargers, it is necessary to view their requirements objectively. Primary in those requirements was the maintenance of logistics simplicity. Since Allison V-1710C-15 engines were to be used in all Allied Curtiss Tomahawks, it seemed logical to use the same engines and propellers in the twin-engine fighters. In fact it was combined British and French purchases that were indirectly – if not directly – responsible for America's ability to produce Allison engines in quantity. As late as May 1939, Allison Engineering had managed to produce no more than a pitiful 20 engines of the V-1710 series. That was the total number.

In April, General Motors broke ground, in connection with Air Corps contracts, to build a new 390,000-square-foot factory and office near Indianapolis, Indiana, but a second plant was soon started under the auspices of the Anglo-French Purchasing Board. The Allies did not want to complicate matters by producing C series and F series engines, so great was their need. They must have been fully aware of the problems affecting G.E.'s delivery of superchargers, and that situation alone would have convinced them that it was one problem that was unwanted.

Negotiations in New York for procurement of the Model 322 airplanes must have been positively hectic. While neither the French nor British teams gave any consideration to the need for high-altitude performance – mainly because no such need had ever been established in the experience of either nation – when establishing their set of specifications, Lockheed had even less familiarity with low-level performance in a fighter. Simply stated, they had no experience with any V-1710C engine producing between 1040 and 1090 horsepower at critical altitudes of 14,000 to 16,000 feet.[1] Gerschler's team probably quoted data from Lockheed Report 1462 without noting that it referred to a more powerful engine, not the C-15 model.

Envisioned by the Air Ministry as a more viable aircraft than the Westland Whirlwind, the 322-61 was undoubtedly expected to replace that homegrown aircraft. Something that neither the Americans (nor Germans) were aware of early in May 1940 was that the Whirlwind had failed to make the grade even then. Consider these facts: (1) the first production P.9 Whirlwind had not yet been delivered to an RAF unit when the N.Y.C. meeting was convened; (2) the Ministry of Aircraft Production was already in the process of cancelling the second

---

1. One of Kelly Johnson's able assistants was young Ward Beman. His Lockheed Report 1462, completed in June 1939, provided a technical comparison table of six different powerplant combinations in a P-38-type airframe. He completed the report in response to an Air Corps Circular Proposal. All figures proved to be somewhat optimistic, especially for the one non-turbo version mentioned. Even then they referred to an F-series engine, 1150 bhp and a geared supercharger. Output figures for Allison V-1710C-15(-33) seemed to be variable, depending on whether Curtiss or Lockheed was the potential user. Ratings given for the P-40 or H.81A were generally centered on 1040 bhp at S.L./16,300 feet. Lockheed reported 1090 bhp at 14,000 feet. Beman was using a 15,000-foot critical altitude for the F-series engine used in his study.

Whirlwind contract and reducing the original contract, and (3) real combat experience (in the Battle of Britain) was yet to come, so the crucial altitude factor had not yet come to light.

As for the desperate French negotiators, they were privy to information that the Comite du Materiel and the *Armee de l'Air* had been looking upon an XP-38 derivative as a replacement for their Breguet 671 and 690C.1 deadly slow two-seat fighters for not quite a year. Just hearing the evening news report by H. B. Kaltenborn and others on the radio beginning on May 9 must have panicked members of the French team. Headlines in the papers literally screamed defeat after defeat on the Western Front. If Lockheed agreed to deliver hundreds of 322-Fs to stem the Nazi tide within a year, who were they to argue? Both parties were going to default on the contract in any event.

E Hollywood was in the midst of what, in later years, would be acknowledged as the greatest year in the production of great motion pictures. The studios produced something like 400 movies in that 12-month period. Most studies were not even in Hollywood; in fact, Warner Brothers and some others were far out Cahuenga Pass in the valley, on the fringes of Burbank. Lockheed, just a few miles out Hollywood Way, was even then beginning to outshine the film industry.

But it did not happen without strain and pain. Even as the aforementioned negotiators dealt with improbable production rates and what appeared to be an endless supply of pound note and francs, wildly expanding Lockheed was struggling to produce the first hand-built YP-38. And even as the Germans were bypassing the Maginot Line and streaming into northern France, that first YP was far from complete. Robert Gross and his staff had long since concluded that the 3Gs Distillery was not the place to mass produce aircraft. By then they were working toward establishment of four parallel production lines at the main factory. It took 19 long months to produce that initial Yippee before the other YP-38s began to move down the main production line.

Things were no less chaotic at burgeoning Wright and Patterson Fields in Dayton. Manpower, materials and components were sources of constant headaches everywhere. Factories were either rising or in the process of conversion

nationally. America, The Arsenal of Democracy, was then coming into the picture. Producers of the country's civilian products were being invited to convert partially or entirely to the manufacture of war materiel.

The spring of 1940 is best described as a period of major upheaval in the world at large. Everything seemed to be happening at once. Newspapers and newsreels – the latter a favored source of information on international events – could barely cope with the influx of important happenings on a day-to-day basis. Suddenly, Europe was reverberating to an anvil chorus of exploding bombs and shells, the rumble of track treads on tanks and the cries of anguished people. Reports of the use of "death rays" might be accepted or would bring guffaws, depending on the sophistication of the listeners. Spending an evening – and in some instances, the entire night – with an ear glued to the radio speaker in an attempt to reassure yourself that it was impossible for France and England to capitulate tended to raise one's metabolism to soaring levels. Great Britain and the Empire came under siege as it never had before. The *Luftwaffe*, after the initial collapse of the Allies, went after the RAF on the ground and in the air with a vengeance never witnessed anywhere.

When Reichsmarschall Hermann Göring unleashed his air assault against the Low Countries and France in support of the *Blitzkrieg* on May 10, Gen. H. H. Arnold decided that he must be fully apprised of what was going on and the appraisal had to be accurate and truthful. Therefore, early in the month he cancelled all of Col. Carl Spaatz's and Capt. Ben Kelsey's commitments and assigned them to TDY in England via Italy and France (Italy was still not involved) on what must have been America's first air intelligence mission of World War II. Kelsey lost contact with what the Allied Joint Purchasing Commission was doing.

France was attempting, through committee actions, to make up for years of indecision and errors of commission by spending hundreds of millions of dollars for weaponry in one week. It didn't buy much of anything for the French, but it surely alerted a great number of Americans to the need for a massive production effort. Unfortunately for the French people, their allotment of acceptable mistakes had been expended. In just six weeks after their purchase of Model 322-F fighters (airplanes not even really on the drawing boards, let alone in production) the Third Republic would cease to exist.

Col. "Tooey" Spaatz was chief of training and operations for the Air Corps in 1940. That seems like an inappreciable assignment, but the "operations" part meant all Air Corps operations. His assignment in England: Observe training methods and combat tactics employed by the Royal Air Force and – less openly – confer on British aircraft qualitative and quantitative requirements as they related to American production and training efforts. It certainly offered the colonel a wide latitude in the pursuit of information. The temporary duty assignment overseas lasted for no less than 18 weeks; incredibly, it coincided almost perfectly with the (then) oncoming Battle of Britain.

Spaatz and Kelsey arrived in London on Friday, May 31, 1940, when they flew over to Hendon Airport from beleaguered Orly Field in France. Based on what must have been fairly casual observation and interviews, Spaatz reported in the following week that the "P-36 (referring, of course, to the Hawk H.75As operated by the French) is still effective. Spitfire (is) superior to (the) Messerschmitt." (Aerial victories reported by the *Armee de l'Air* in the days before Germany launched the *Blitzkrieg* can be considered as suspect from either of two viewpoints. The flood of biased reports emanating from French sources in May and June contained little that would be viewed as credible material, and in the months comprising the "Sitzkrieg" period the Nazis were not revealing their true capabilities by using aggressive tactics.)

In one respect, Spaatz was probably correct in having a good opinion of the Hawk in service in France. That country's native first-line fighters – the Morane-Sauliner MS.406 and the Dewoitine D.520 – were lightly armed, lacked good armor protection, were nowhere near as rugged as the Curtiss machines and a first-class MS.406 was most likely hard pressed to attain 300 mph under the best of conditions.

The colonel was, in due time, to learn that the RAF Fighter Command – as a separate entity from the Advanced Air Striking Force based on the Continent – under the command of Air Commodore Hugh Dowding had only 446 aircraft that could be construed as being operationally serviceable. And of that force, only 331 were Hurricane and Spitfire models. Gen. Arnold's decision to send Spaatz and Kelsey to England to gather information had proven very timely and inspired. They observed the trauma of France's capitulation and the British Army's amazing withdrawal from Dunkirk. All signs of an organized defensive action had disappeared by June 17, and Marshal Petain surrendered on June 22.

Long-lasting false pride and an overabundance of inertia had been real enemies of France. If the Socialist government of that country had set out to sabotage their aircraft industry from the mid-1930s, it is doubtful if they could have done much more damage to it than they did.

As of mid-June, the Anglo-French Purchasing Board had placed orders for military supplies and equipment totalling an inconceivable (for that era) $1,600,000,000. Of that massive amount, more than half was expended by France in their drive to make up for the years of relative complacency. As if to emphasize the accuracy of that statement, more than $600,000,000 of the total in contract awards had been made in the last three weeks of May and the first two weeks of June 1940! No less than one billion dollars of that substantial total was for aircraft, some 8,500 of them having been ordered since 1938. The bad news was that only about $250,000,000 worth of munitions and aircraft had actually been delivered/shipped to the Allies by the time the powerful armies of the Nazis made their move. Perhaps some massive historical book will eventually make it clear as to why the Allies played the waiting game that the Germans were playing. If the declarations of war were politically motivated against the considerations of unpreparedness, they were virtually suicidal.

Within that framework, Col. Spaatz and Capt. Kelsey were most certainly in the right place and the timing was impeccable. As France showed the white flag, Britain embraced a new Prime Minister, Winston Churchill. Had Churchill been brought to power even a year earlier, the course of history would have been somewhat different. He had to start by preparing the British for the blow that he, at least, knew was yet to come as surely as the sun would rise.

Still, Hitler waited. Although the British Isles had been severely punished by early air attacks, the massive attempt to soften the defense for launching Operation Sea Lion did not come until August 12. It was on that date that the quintessential Battle of Britain began, a fight destined to continue almost unabated, even for a time, until at least November 3. The crucial delay of nearly two months – from June 22 to August 12 – had allowed Air Chief Marshal Dowding to increase his fighter strength to 704 operationally serviceable aircraft. That propitious increase included no less than 620 Hurricanes and Spitfires, with yet another 289 of those specific types in reserve . . . meaning that they were mostly down for repair but would soon be on line.

Hitler's delay was most likely a fatal mistake; the fact is that the delay was incurred, Dowding did build up his forces and Operation Sea Lion was nothing more than a threat in the annals of history. The threat of invasion was actually over by October, but in the interim the British had come frighteningly close to disaster.

History's first great conflict in the skies saw the RAF lose 915 prime aircraft, but the obsessive attackers lost no less than 1,733 bombers and fighters, not to mention a much larger number of trained aircrewmen. Unfortunately, the British had used up most of their first-line and reserve aircraft in the fray.

One side effect of the Battle of Britain was the damnation of any existing twin-engine, single-seat fighter as defined by the RAF and the Air Ministry. The first casualty was Westland's Whirlwind, which – in all truth – was on its way out before France capitulated in June. But the most important casualty was Lockheed's 322-61-04 Lightning I, as it had been named between the date of the contract and its first test flight in California. Of course that did not occur for nearly a year after the Battle of Britain. By that time the desperate need for any viable fighter capable of stemming the Nazi tide had passed into history.

As newer, higher-altitude-capable Hurricanes and Spitfires came into the picture, the need for low-altitude fighters or fighter-reconnaissance aircraft was capably handled by the North American Mustang I and certain models of the Spitfire. Curtiss began to deliver its H.81 Tomahawks to fulfill huge contract obligations, and all but a very few of those went to distant theaters of operation. No Tomahawk combat squadrons were assigned to the defense of England since the design was rapidly approaching obsolescence. Newer and more potent fighters were rising higher into the skies and higher on priority lists.

Capt. Kelsey returned to the U.S.A with the full and well-substantiated knowledge that his commitment to the high-altitude fighter was 100 percent correct from the outset. Much to his sorrow, the first YP-38 had made its initial flight during his absence. Reflecting Gen. Arnold's faith in Carl Spaatz, that officer received a promotion to the rank of Brigadier General as part of a now massive promotion scheme. Far greater things were in store for the new general officer.

Out in Los Angeles, in September 1940, a man by the name of Wendell Wilkie was aggressively campaigning for the presidency of the United States. The anti-war faction were probably his greatest supporters as the course of history was forcing President Roosevelt toward ever greater support for the Allied Nations.

Life was moving ahead in these United States in spite of the headlines and graphic newsreels. The new model 1941 cars – some of the best in years – were being previewed at major auto shows. Although there were signs of some mild inflationary spiral, almost everything was in plentiful supply. People making the move into defense industry jobs found that their purchasing power was escalating far faster than general inflation.

California was, then, the place to be, and that was especially true of Southern California. A local resident could purchase a neat three-bedroom home with a Mission-tile roof in the Los Angeles area for about $6,000-$6,500, while an upper-income citizen could buy a well-kept 12-room home – complete with two maids' rooms – in quiet, opulent Beverly Hills for about $16,000.

An ordinary buyer with little or no bargaining ability could get a used 1939 Lincoln Zephyr four-door sedan in great condition for under $800. If you did not demand the latest model, a 1937 Buick Phaeton (four-door convertible) with metallic blue paint – something new under the sun – for $599. Just two years later, people might fight just to buy that very desirable car, but in the post-Depression days of 1940 it was just another 4-year-old vehicle. In the industrialized northeast, you rarely saw older cars such as Model A Fords, but Californians held onto them with a passion, mainly because cars were licensed by weight, not value, in that state. Operating in such good weather, they did not rust out.

Housewives – and most wives were because few employment opportunities existed then – could purchase 2 pounds of grapes for 5 cents, an equal amount of Washington red apples for 9 cents and two solid heads of lettuce for 7 cents. A 12-ounce box of brand name shredded wheat went for 8 1/2 cents. Even top-grade prime rib cost no more than 31 cents per pound. Bachelors (and, of course, others) could eat out – if you didn't demand a Hollywood Restaurant – at the first-rate luncheon counters that were frequently a part of any large drug store. Memories of multi-course turkey dinners for no more than 75 cents still linger.

But the big, important news was out in Burbank. Lockheed's initial YP-38 left the ground for the first time at Lockheed Air Terminal – although most people still called it Union Air Terminal – on Tuesday, September 17, 1940.[2] Test pilot Marshall Headle, dressed most casually in a short-sleeve white shirt and a pair of dress slacks, slipped into his backpack chute and put on his earphones. No helmet protected his balding pate as he fired up the engines and taxied out for takeoff. The YP thundered past the tile-roofed terminal tower, circled over the beginnings of Valhalla Cemetery and continued on down toward Studio City. It was a very hot day, but the flight went like clockwork.

The final flight of the week took place on Friday. That was to be a "public demonstration flight" of the latest American fighter, with all of the press and radio people invited. However, any flight out of Lockheed Air Terminal had to be extremely public anyway. Airport security hardly existed in those days. Almost daily you could find people in their cars or up on the perimeter road embankment taking pictures as aircraft landed over the northern boundary fence. Large, clear pictures of the Yippee appeared on the front page and inside pages of the The Los Angeles Times and all other local and San Francisco newspapers. Accompanying an excellent takeoff picture of the gleaming duralumin airplane were statements to the effect that America could now proudly proclaim that it had a "500-mile-an-hour interceptor." Could that misguided statement have come from an overzealous corporation publicist? Other wild statements appearing in print that week included one that claimed the Army Air Corps had ordered $52,000,000 worth of P-38s. It just was not true at that time.

Although France could no longer be thought of as a viable ally with any plausibility, and with the British Royal Air Force totally engrossed in fighting for the salvation of the United Kingdom, one news article proclaimed that the "Allies have purchased 800 of the speedy fighters." It is bad enough that the quantity was incorrect, but the term "purchased" probably gave the impression to the masses that current delivery would be the order of the day. After all, when you "purchased" a car, you generally took immediate delivery. As with politics, the American people were quite naive about the manufacture of weapons of war.

During the 12 or 13 months between the time when the YP-38 contract was awarded and Benjamin Kelsey's air intelligence assignment in the United Kingdom, he was involved in any number of other projects. As Fighter Projects officer, he played a significant role in the January 1939 fighter competition at Wright Field . . . or at least in setting it in motion. Year end holidays went out the window with completion of the XP-38 because it was up to him to carry our the flight test program. Kelsey had made some flights in the prototype Curtiss XP-40, but it appears that the section chief at Wright – Lt. Col. Franklin O. Carroll – had responded to the increasing work loads by assigning Oscar Ritland as project officer on the XP-40 and Marcus Cooper to the P-39 project. A bit later on, Cooper moved over to the production P-40 program, but also was project officer on the P-39s. (One look at the Project Officer/Test Pilot Assignment Board revealed that most of the men wore several hats.)

As the months tumbled by, Kelsey became somewhat disenchanted with progress on the P-38 program as a result of his observations during visits to Burbank. Kelly Johnson was working diligently with Howard Hughes on the new Model 49 airliner after the Model 44 Excalibur had been put to rest. Robert Gross, at that time, was heavily involved with plant expansion, progress on Hudson assembly line growth and some "affiliation" program involving Menasco Motors. Lockheed Aircraft has not even mentioned the situation, but it seems that Robert Gross must have infused a considerable amount of money into Menasco to aid an expansion program right in Burbank. A close tie had been established between Vega Aircraft and Menasco when production of the Vega Unitwin-powered Starliner was seriously considered.

---

2. *Most, if not all, Lockheed records state that the YP-38 made its first flight on September 18. But how can you argue with a daily newspaper, the The Los Angeles Times, which reported flights on the 17th, 18th and Friday the 20th?*

Production of Menasco four- and six-cylinder engines was seriously curtailed when Vega dropped the Starliner and Model 35 programs, both of which were aligned with the use of Menasco powerplants. When the engine producer became heavily involved in the production of landing gear assemblies, either by choice or under pressure from the OPM or Lockheed-Vega, friction mounted between friendly business associates Al Menasco and Robert Gross. Whatever occurred, it must have been drastic. Menasco resigned and left the aircraft business to become owner of a Ford car dealership. (More than 40 years later, when Al Menasco was in his 90s, it was obvious that he was still bitter about the situation.)

G Beginning a year earlier in June 1939, some high-caliber Lockheed engineers became involved in the Model 49 project. It also appears that the real inception date for a true production P-38 came about with the release of Model Spec. No. 1459 for Lockheed's Model 222-62-02 on June 26. Less than a month later, a contract for no less than 66 of the "straight" P-38 airplanes was issued. August was the inception date for the Model 32, eventually to become the Model 37 before metal was cut. The summer of 1939 was really quite pleasant as the country recovered nicely from recession times. Hitler decided to spoil the fun, but a great number of Americans were determined not to let that happen. Later on, crowds lined up at theaters everywhere for hours to see *Gone With The Wind* in superb Technicolor. Perhaps the graphic war scenes made a long-lasting impression on large numbers of them.

Gross, Gerschler, Pulver and others were caught off guard by the contract award for 66 new production fighters. The 3G Distillery was obviously the wrong place in which to produce as many as 80 complex fighters. (Eventually, only c/n 2202 was completely built in that "new" facility.) Yet another expansion of the main plant was in store for them, almost immediately, if there was to be any hope of meeting the production schedules being bandied around in Washington and Dayton. If Gross had been without the foresight to buy Pioneer Park and launch construction of the Vega Aircraft plant (eventually Lockheed Plant A-1), the resulting chaos might have done them in. And just when Capt. Kelsey was about to fire a broadside at Lockheed for ignoring "his" project, Gen. Arnold sent him away to a summer in the British Isles.

Many years later, when all of this was discussed in detail with Brig. Gen. Kelsey, USAF (Ret.), the subject of the effect of the XP-38 crash on the overall program progress was brought up. Many statements have been published, to wit: the crash of the XP-38 set the interceptor program back more than a year. Most knowledgeable Lockheed employees were, for years, of the same opinion.

But according to the man who was in the best position to know all of the facts . . . that is, from the military customer's point of view . . . the loss of that prototype in this specific case actually expedited the program.

In 1973, Gen. Kelsey was pleased to have the opportunity to expound his views, to once and for all set the record straight. This is exactly what he had to say:

"Anyone even remotely connected with development and procurement as it was in Air Corps days, should be able to realize that the loss of the XP saved us about a year in getting the next series out. In fact, I think that the time between first flight and approval for service test go-ahead probably set an all time record.

"To elaborate just a bit, Hap (Arnold) didn't want to be cluttered up with all those damned technical details. He just wanted to be able to prove that he could get an airplane that had altitude and speed performance, and the delivery (record) flight – even ending in a ditch – did just that. The day after

the crackup (actually it was the second day after the crash), he took me all over Washington – starting with the Secretary of War – making me tell them (officials, politicians) what kind of machine it was. It was a lot easier to sell a qualitative evaluation on the basis of trust in the report than it would have been to sell it on hard data."

With a discordant note slipping into his tone, Kelsey seemed finally to have a chance to take issue with some of the media as he said, "Why most historians have never even been curious about how a washed-out airplane, with less than 12 hours total flight, could justify immediate go-ahead (for production) has always been a source of amazement to me. But then we had the same situation . . . in the loss of the demonstrator XB-17 (Model B-299). Its untimely loss saved us about two or three years in procurement.

"Getting back to the P-38, it must be recognized that there is no *single* P-38 story. There are thousands, and they are all valid. It was born of necessity to counter the dearth of funds for development of new engines. 'Kelly's' genius (referring to Johnson) added more evolutionary modifications in design and construction than were included in any plane until the next Lockheed quantum jump, the XF-12/SR-71."

While Capt. Kelsey still had a grandstand seat for the Battle of Britain in September 1940, the doors of Building 214 slid open on the eastern side of San Fernando Road, and the first of thirteen YP-38s was wheeled outside into bright sunlight. If the dural had been chrome plated it could not have gleamed more brilliantly in the sunlight. Two lengthy tubular gun covers were mounted on the highly polished nose section where the two .50-caliber machine guns would normally be located. Flush plates covered the other three gun ports. No "cuffs" had been installed on the Curtiss electric propeller, although it was very obvious that provisions had been made for them.

Emphasizing the importance placed on the P-38 program by the War Department, visitors on the scene that day included Maj. Gen. H. H. Arnold and Mr. William Knudsen, chief of the Office of Production Management (OPM). Of course, Robert Gross and other top-level Lockheed officials were on hand. Capt. Kelsey was still in England as aide to Col. Spaatz or he surely would have been present for the rollout. It is safe to presume that if Kelsey had not been the one to make the initial flight in YP-38 c/n 2202, he most certainly would have been at the controls for the second flight.

Even the most casual observer had to notice that the engine nacelles of the YP-38 were very different from those that had been used on the XP-38. In fact, the entire powerplant arrangement, except for the intercooler system in the wing leading edge, was different. At least two of the major reasons were abandonment of the Allison C-series engines and replacement of the tubular, built-up engine mounts with new forged mount bearers.

H In 1939, just two months after the YP service test airplanes were ordered, one of C. L. Johnson's bright young engineers, Ward Beman, completed Report No. 1462, prepared in response to Air Corps Circular Proposal 39-775. The true purpose of that particular CP had never been determined, but Lockheed's response provided performance data for a twin-engine fighter powered by any one pair of six tradeoff engines. In a rather archaic way, the report was titled "Comparison of Two Engine Interceptor Pursuit Proposals." There seemed to be some hesitancy in accepting the "fighter" terminology, even in 1940. Four of the proposed engines were V-1710F-series Allisons, ranging in Military Power ratings from 1150 to 1350 bhp for various critical altitudes. All of the high-altitude ratings were associated with turbosupercharged versions of the engine, while one 1150 bhp engine had only a basic single-stage mechanical supercharger. (A version of that last engine was never used in any combat version of the P-38, but ultimately powered numerous P-322-II trainer versions of the basic type.)

Adhering to some arbitrary limit on displacement, a turbo-boosted version of the R-1830 Twin Wasp was proposed for installation in the "XP-38 Type" aircraft involved. Some performance loss was involved, although reliability probably would have been improved in the European theater of operations. The data panel showed the best high speed for an uprated Allison version as 465 mph at a critical altitude of 25,000 feet. The figure seemed a bit optimistic, but nowhere near as optimistic as the figures for one of Curtiss-Wright Corporation's proposed engines, a radical 1800-cubic-inch unit.

Those figures relating to the V-1710 with geared supercharger were based on Allison data for an engine that was elected by North American to power its NA-73 fighter design that was initiated about a year hence. As with all F-series engines, it was equipped with spur reduction gears and the "supercharger" was essentially a diffusion blower. It was strictly a low-altitude engine as used in Curtiss P-40s.

The Pratt & Whitney R-1830 engine proposed for installation was comparable to the engines specified for Consolidated B-24Ds (and, of course, for later B-24s), although the Lockheed version may have been similar to the extended gearbox versions used in the Curtiss XP-42 and a new Vultee pursuit that came on the scene somewhat later as their Model 61 Vanguard prototype. The drag-reduction scheme devised by NACA was tested on various aircraft in perhaps a dozen different forms without any degree of success. Several Lockheed Excalibur and Constellation proposals featured a reverse flow, low-drag cowl design. Possibly that is what the Johnson-Beman plan was all about for the modified P-38. One sentence abstracted from the report is quoted herein to aid in clarification of tabular data: "To balance the airplane, the long nose (20-inch extension) engines were used, and the propeller plane is moved rearward approximately 10 inches."

Vultee displayed its new single-seater a few months later, variously as the Model 48X or 61, but there was no attempt to supercharge the Vanguard. Performance was hardly improved over that of the Hawk 75, but the aircraft was designed to be extremely producible. The R-1830 Twin Wasp was a marvelous unit, but it never showed any growth in power output during all of the wartime years.

Beman's *piece de resistance* in the proposal report – in retrospect it was more of a pie-in-the-sky, or even pie-in-the-face, item – was the Wright Aeronautical "cylindrical" engine that was later known as the Tornado. Unique in concept, the unit was essentially a liquid-cooled radial engine with six rows of seven cylinders each . . . at least in its initial form. With 42 cylinders, the rather small-diameter engine was intended to produce 2350 brake horsepower from the outset. Wright Aero claimed the engine could also be built with five rows of cylinders. In that particular form it would have had 35 cylinders with a total displacement of approximately 1,800 cubic inches. The designation for that version was XR-1800, and it had a power rating of 1850 bhp at a phenomenal 1200 revolutions per minute. Had it proven to be properly designed

and developed, it would have outpowered contemporary Allison engines by about 50 percent. Negative aspects included the need for considerably larger coolant radiators (more weight), a beefed-up structure (more weight) and a prolonged delay in delivery.

Why in the world Lt. Col. E. R. Page, chief of the Power Plant Branch and a long-time member of the Wright Field hierarchy, allowed himself and others to be so completely misled by Wright Aero is beyond comprehension. Surely the XR-2160 Tornado was more phantom than fact, and if it ever actually ran on a bench it was probably in single-cylinder form. Document CP39-775, under which Lockheed's powerplant proposal was submitted, apparently led directly to the production contract for Model 222-62-08 airplanes in July 1939. At a reputed price of about $10,000,000, that covered a total of 66 fighters under the designation P-38.

**ENGINE COMPARISON TABLE FOR CP39-775 (1939)**

| ENGINE TYPE SUPERCHARGER | ALLISON V-1710-F SERIES | | | | P&W R-1830 | WRIGHT TORNADO X-1800 |
|---|---|---|---|---|---|---|
| | Turbo | Turbo | Turbo | Geared | | |
| Military Rating (Brake Horsepower) | 1150 | 1150 | 1350 | 1150 | 1200 | 1850 |
| Propeller RPM | 3000 | 3000 | 3000 | 3000 | 2700 | 1200 |
| Critical Altitude (feet) | 20,000 | 25,000 | 25,000 | 15,000 | 25,000 | 25,000 |
| Airplane Gross Weight (pounds) | 13,500 | 13,500 | 14,500 | 13,500 | 3,500 | 16,500 |
| Airplane Empty Weight (pounds) | 11,094 | 1,094 | 11,741 | 10,776 | 1,114 | 13,881 |
| High Speed at Critical Altitude | 425 | 451 | 465 | 411 | 435 | 502 |
| High Speed at 20,000 feet | 425* | 425 | 439 | 400 | 419 | 490 |
| High Speed at 5,000 feet | 368* | 368 | 384 | 368 | 358 | 425 |
| Time to Climb to 20,000 feet | 5.94* | 5.94 | 5.60 | 5.97 | 5.70 | 4.95 |

Note appended to table: "*These values guaranteed, 6-21-39, for 39-775 – C.L.J. (C.L.J. being Clarence L. Johnson)

Construction of the three-quarter-million square foot Vega Aircraft plant was proceeding at a great rate adjacent to Lockheed Air Terminal in the final days of summer when the YP-38 made its first takeoff on September 17, 1940. All preflight tasks had been completed at the metal one-airplane hangar that was, then, located on the south side of the main east-west runway, almost directly across from the large United Air Lines maintenance hangar. Blade cuffs (soon to be deleted from all P-38 types) had been installed on the propellers and the two gun covers had been removed from the nose section so that a small yaw vane could be installed.

Curry Sanders, then assistant chief test pilot for the company, provided a first-hand account of Marshall Headle's early morning flight out of L.A.T. "He flew the job for the first time at 6 o'clock in the morning. Half of Lockheed's employees were at the air terminal to watch, and he was up for about an hour." Chief tester Headle was close to age 50 at the time, but he certainly had no trouble at all handling the YP. In his long and active career, he had never left an airplane in flight.

As for that little flight hangar, sometimes seemingly engulfed in a sea of Hudson bombers, it was transferred by a moving company to a location diagonally across the runway sometime late in 1940 or early in 1941. Portions of the seldom used short north-south runway became part of a huge tarmac

area (near the test hangar) for checkout of a great many Hudsons, Lightnings and subsequent aircraft. The longer north-south runway, heavily used, was lengthened.

Many hours of testing were accumulated on Yippee 2202 by test pilots Milo Burcham, Ralph Virden, Jimmy Mattern, and Swede Parker. Operations at Lockheed Burbank had a great deal to do with changing the image of a test pilot for millions of Americans. The swashbuckling Clark Gable image had been enforced by the popular motion picture *Test Pilot*. Some test pilots came close to fitting that image, but Headle, the boss, was a no-nonsense pilot. Terminal velocity dives and 9g pullouts, which attracted movie fans, became a thing of the past with aircraft like the YP-38.

Special test methods were developed by Headle, Burcham, and Dr. F. E. Poole (the medical director) to avoid newly recognized problems like anoxia, cold soak and vertigo plus aero embolism. In fact, flying over 25,000 feet up to the rarely encountered 40,000 feet was a new "ball game." Dr. Poole and Headle worked closely with the Mayo Clinic to develop methods by which they could cope with some extremely serious problems. Lockheed had a brand new altitude chamber constructed in order to test and certify new environmental devices. Aviation testing in the 1930s and 1940s was a terribly unsafe occupation. Man was rapidly pushing into a realm with which he was totally unfamiliar, pioneering in things that even scientists could not support with theoretical data. There were no ejection seats; oxygen systems were unreliable and even dangerous; data recording was just beginning to move from the "pad on knee and pencil" system. Solutions to flutter, for example, were often an outgrowth of in-flight failures, not a computer output.

As if to warn testers, a tragic accident occurred in the very test chamber designed to protect those intrepid aviation pioneers. As Marshall Headle was testing new flight equipment in the pressure chamber, something failed to work and there was a serious decompression accident. It ended the chief test pilot's career and brought suffering and a premature end to his life.

A gleaming jewel of a factory stood proudly at the corner of Hollywood Way and Empire Avenue by the end of 1940.

*ABOVE: A lesson had been learned. Headle patiently posed with the first YP-38 to compensate, in a way, for the failure to obtain a good series of photographs of the XP-38. (Washburn's ground views of the incomplete XP-38 were damaged in processing; no later full views were taken at March Field during weeks of testing, and nobody seemed to even think about flight photos.) (Eric Miller - LAC)*

*BELOW: With adoption of the F-series Allison engines, the powerplant structure was completely redesigned, largely for producibility reasons (see large forging). The thrust line moved up, changing the cowling lines. The P-38 airframe was several more times as complex as any contemporary fighter in the world. Hurricanes used a fairly "ancient" structure to expedite production. The Spitfire was a good compromise. (LAC)*

Actual fabrication of Vega Ventura bombers was under way inside, although 20 or 30 percent of the buildings were still under construction. That very large and modern factory was to become known as Plant A-1. The original Lockheed factory, located approximately two miles east, on Empire Avenue, became Plant B-1. No small amount of changes inside B-1 would ultimately provide for four parallel assembly lines for P-38-type airplanes. Twelve of the production lot of YP-38 airplanes were built on one of the production lines.

In many ways, the YPs were the most appealing of all P-38 models, the needle-pointed spinners combining with the natural metal finish and brilliant red tail stripes to add excitement. They surely were sleek airplanes. One big change between the XP-38 and the YP-38s was in the armament. As designed, the prototype was to have one 23-mm Madsen cannon with 50 rounds of ammunition and four .50-caliber machine guns with 200 rounds each. An alternate to the Madsen gun was an American .90-caliber T1 cannon, but it was never fully developed. Design of the YPs called for a 37-mm cannon with 15 rounds of ammunition and a pair of .50-caliber machine guns above the cannon, each with 200 rounds. Two .30-caliber machine guns with 500 rounds each flanked the cannon.

Reflecting the state of the art in this country's aviation industry in 1940, the YP series, like the prototype, carried all fuel in integral tanks. Self-sealing fuel cells were still to come. Main tank fuel capacity was (like the XP-38) 240 gallons – 120 on each side – and the so-called alternate load specified a reserve capacity of another 130 gallons (also stated as 140 gallons) carried in two tanks. There was, then, no provision for any external fuel to back up the 370-380-gallon capacity. Existing Air Corps policy and the contract specifications actually prohibited the use of external tanks. Those rules dated back to the early 1930s.

The small batch of YP-38s continued to trickle out of what was by then Plant B-1, with the last one scheduled to roll out in May 1941. America seemed to be literally throbbing with excitement, the desire to build and construct. Farm fields appeared to sprout new factories virtually overnight. There were mistakes beyond comprehension. But if Mr. President wanted 50,000 airplanes for the Army and Navy, he was going to get them. An arsenal, the likes of which had never been dreamed of, was being forged. Nobody could scan *Life* magazine; everybody read every word, burned the pictures into their brains. Shining Yippees could be seen in front of the little test hangar or in the pattern on almost any day after the first of the year. A terse message came from Wright Field, asking for details of P-38 performance. Project Officer Capt. Ben Kelsey responded with some enthusiasm on February 7:

> RADIO
> MAJOR K. B. WOLFE
> WRIGHT FIELD
> DAYTON, OHIO
>
> IF YOU ARE THE ONE WHO WANTS
> THE PERFORMANCE ON THE P-38
> NOBODY KNOWS EXACTLY BUT
> IT GOES LIKE HELL AND FLIES SWELL.
>
> KELSEY

Capt. Kelsey's boss was Lt. Col. F. O. Carroll, chief of Experimental Engineering. Lt. Col. (not Maj.) Kenneth B. Wolfe – soon thereafter to become a Brigadier General – was the chief of Production Engineering. It would soon be up to his organization to ride full herd on the production of Lockheed P-38s and everything else.[3] He reported to Gen. Oliver P. Echols, a remarkably competent officer.

No reports were ever made about Wolfe's reaction, but Kelsey was a full bird colonel a year later. (All who really knew Kelsey agree that he should have been a Lieutenant General when he retired.) K. B. Wolfe had a few YP-38s to test by that summer, but he did not have an adequate supply of testers. A few pilots from the First Pursuit Group at Selfridge Field, Michigan, got the assignment.

At long last, the P-38 Lightning was forming a cadre.

---

3. *In many circles of government and industry in 1940, it was "business as usual" and frustration was rampant. Nobody seemed to be in control. Just before Christmas, President Roosevelt established the Office of Production Management under William Knudsen as Director General. Among people recruited by Knudsen in 1941 was Al Bodie as a principal engineering consultant. He was assigned as special assistant to Gen. Oliver Echols, but seemed to get new assignments as "fires were put out." Bill Knudsen, up from the ranks in General Motors, had no trouble solving problems. His key response to a major problem at one time was, "How much capacity do you need? When do you need it?" When he was at the helm, things did get done. . . . in spite of bureaucratic interference.*

*As a realistic example of the problems that existed, by the thousands it seemed, nobody had foreseen the problems with facility (factory) financing in the face of emergency expansion. After Roosevelt had asked for 50,000 military aircraft in the spring of 1940, the Defense Plant Corp. (DPC) was set up to finance and build defense plants. As of August 1940, three months after the president's speech, the Air Corps had signed contracts for no more than 33 aircraft. Yes, that was thirty-three aircraft. Why? Contractors were reluctant to accept orders they could not possibly fill in existing plant area.*

*Can you even begin to imagine the impact of problems associated with something like the "expansion" of the Dodge Division (Chrysler), where the plant was expanded by . . . 6,750,000 square feet? That was even larger than the Willow Run Bomber Plant in Michigan. Can you visualize the problems involved in tooling that plant? Consultants like Al Bodie had the job of making certain it got finished. When the War Department reorganized in March 1942, Echols became commanding general of the new Materiel Command. Newly commissioned Maj. Al Bodie became Chief, Production Expediting Section. Late in 1943, Lt. Col. Bodie took an Air Service Group overseas to support the Lockheed P-38s. (Al Bodie was the author's father.)*

# CHAPTER 6

# At Long Last - Production and Trials

Burbank would never be the same. America was not at war, that's true, but the eastern end of the San Fernando Valley, hard against the Verdugo Mountains, was surely not at peace. How could it be peaceful in a town where the largest employer at the end of 1938 – having tucked the biggest aircraft contract in the U.S. into a vault – then had fewer than 3,000 employees but within two years would be boasting that no fewer than 16,900 wore Lockheed badges? Moreover, those numbers were due to pale by later comparison. Lockheed Aircraft was, at the dawn of 1941, finally rolling with production of YP-38s, P-38s and British 322-Bs in addition to the flow of twin-engine bombers.

When B. W. "Butch" Messer joined the company as an engineer back in those bleak days in 1933, he was a man in his mid twenties. Five years later, Messer was asked to recruit technical people as war clouds darkened over Europe. By 1941, "Butch" was in charge of all Lockheed recruiting. He was faced with a phenomenal recruitment and training task of unprecedented dimensions. At a later date he told an interviewer, "I was hiring as many as 500 people a day in 1941." How could any company find, process, train, and gainfully

*Tail buffeting, never flutter, was becoming a serious problem for Lockheed in mid-1941, and the first YP-38 encounter with compressibility tended to confuse the issue. Elevator flutter was named as the culprit by some Army pilots, so Lockheed had to add mass balances over the protests of Kelly Johnson. Taxiing YP-38 (AC39-689) showed them off for the first time. (LAC)*

employ that many people in a week, let alone one day? It was overwhelming, but somehow Lockheed did it.

Among the recruits in 1940 were famed aerobatic pilot Milo Burcham, airmail flyer Ralph Virden and distance flyer James Mattern. Burcham became chief in the test pilot group when Marshall Headle was totally disabled. The dapper and likeable new chief tester was soon flying the YPs up to at least 35,000 feet to demonstrate just what the twin-engine fighters were capable of achieving. If those pilots were not congregating at the stucco airport ranch house that served as the pilots' office. they were likely to be at the metal-clad test hangar waiting to wring out another airplane. Some 2,000 miles to the east, a few military pilots from the Production Engineering Branch of the Materiel Division or on TDY from Selfridge Field, Michigan, were subjecting the YPs to the rigors of an accelerated service test program.

B One of the service test pilots, Maj. Signa A. Gilkey, was an expert in his profession. A cross-country jaunt took him up to Selfridge, close by the shores of Lake St. Clair, in the early summer months. The major had been doing a lot of homework, having studied a report issued by Lockheed engineer Phil Colman at the behest of Kelly Johnson. A few Burbank engineers, alone in the aviation world, were battling the odds in attempting to convince everybody that fast aircraft flying at high altitudes were going to encounter an unrecognized and untamed factor called "compressibility." Nobody had encountered such an ogre before, so most people were disinclined to believe in it.

A Dr. Mach had developed a number theory that related speed of a moving object to the speed of sound. That speed number varied with temperature and the density of air. Unfortunately, nobody had developed an instrument to accurately measure that so-called Mach's Number outside of a laboratory. Now middle-aged Maj. Gilkey was no neophyte in aviation, having been rated as a Command Pilot since the mid 1930s; he also held Observer ratings and had been a military pilot since 1923. Gilkey had turned 40 just a couple of months earlier. Many things had to covered thoroughly in the Colman report (to be discussed in detail later), but there was nothing more important than his plan for conducting vertical dives from altitudes up to 35,000 feet. In 1940, that was the sort of thing you might expect from an H.G. Wells science fiction story.

Dive testing had hardly been approved when Maj. Gilkey decided to investigate the premises on his own. For unknown reasons, both engines on his test airplane were V-1710-F2Rs; therefore, both propellers were rotating in the same direction as they would have been on a British Model 322-B version. As in the XP-38, mass balances on the elevator on all YPs at that time were internal and there was no sign of any external balance weights. The wing-center fuselage juncture was quite abrupt in those days, showing only the barest evidence of a fillet at the leading edge.

With those conditions prevailing and with no hard evidence about what might occur, the Patterson Field pilot took the YP to an unspecified altitude. The major was a good test pilot, so he remembered that he must limit power and would have to remain below certain indicated airspeeds on the way down (if possible). Up to that moment, airplanes tended to act substantially the same when they entered a near vertical dive; acceleration was rather controlled by drag. Gilkey was to be the first man to find out that the Yippee did not act like other aircraft in that respect. It accelerated like a race car. Severe buffeting set in at 320 mph IAS (indicated airspeed), or somewhat above 400 mph TAS (true airspeed).

The major unexpectedly encountered two distinct (but interacting) phenomena at once, which tended to mask anything really identifiable. He swore, later on, that there was a lot of elevator flutter – most certainly because of things that were happening to the flight control column. Although Gilkey encountered "nose tuck" that gave the feeling of going over on his back and there was a terrific resistance to recovery from the dive, his subsequent report and diatribe concentrated on "tail flutter."

In retrospect, what really happened was that the wing center section ran into compressibility and the venturi effect created between the tail booms and the short center fuselage caused two things to happen simultaneously. (One of those "two" things was tail buffeting; it was resolved rather easily through a series of aerodynamic analyses and tests. The compressibility problem was extremely difficult to correct or modify. In the simplest of terms, nobody in science knew anything about it. That was true pioneering.) Here, essentially, is what was occurring: tail buffet was caused by badly

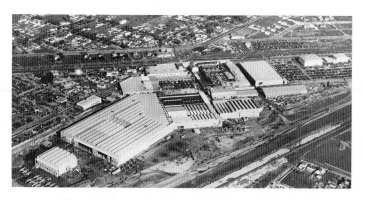

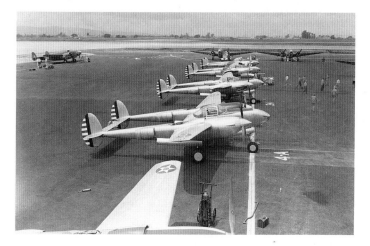

disturbed airflow passing through that "venturi" area at the lower midrange speeds and buffeting the empennage as if it was a sail that was "luffing." There was no clean airflow.

Compressibility effect was something entirely different. For the record, the speed of sound is attained at nearly 100 mph slower speed at altitudes above 32,000 feet than it is at sea level at standard temperatures. Since air density is lower at high altitudes, an aircraft is encountering less resistance to movement; therefore, it will move (accelerate) faster for a given amount of power or attitude. Suffice to say at this point that the relatively low-speed airfoil used on the P-38 design to afford a high climb rate and large internal fuel capacity was about 100 percent successful for those purposes.

But in 1936, only about one person knew what might happen to an inherently slow body attempting to move through a fluid (air) at high speed. Unanticipated was the problem wherein the wing began to enter the compressibility region and the center of pressure on the airfoil began to move aft. This stalled the wing, beginning with the airfoil between the tail booms, at high speed. (The air flow was considerably faster in the venturi realm.) Every pilot knows that a low-speed stall can provide a lot of anxious moments. At high speeds, a stall can induce all sorts of unpleasant effects. What occurred on the P-38? Normal downloads on the horizontal tailplane simply moved aft and left the elevator unloaded. Abracadabra! The tailplane wanted to come up and the nose wanted to go down. But the elevator wasn't going to do anything to overcome that situation.

Until a solution was found, pilots either reacted logically and survived to fly the plane another day, or they bailed out (with no guarantees of success), or they dove straight in. The amazing Maj. Gilkey did all the right things and survived. The old, bold pilot had certainly reached the P-38's limiting Mach No. of 0.68 without ever being aware of that fact. C. L. Johnson pegged it at M=0.68, and it makes no sense to argue the point. The biggest problem at that point in time: nobody knew what was happening.

The somewhat discomposed and irate major reported that he had encountered "tail flutter" at an indicated airspeed of 300 to 320 mph at 32,000 feet, but nothing was mentioned about G loading, which can be a critical factor. It was soon determined that the propeller rotation had no effect on the high-speed stall or the buffeting. Johnson and aerodynamicist Colman may have then guessed that Gilkey had encountered the fiendish compressibility situation, but they did not publicize it. (Just a few years later, everybody . . . well, almost everybody. . . was of the opinion that the "Sonic Barrier" was aerodynamically impenetrable. Any aircraft attempting to exceed the speed of sound [M=1.0] would be destroyed by the "wall." Actually, a few pilots did lose their lives and their aircraft in the Mach 1 realm because designers still had not resolved all aerodynamic problems.)

Responding to the demands from Col. Wolfe's office at Wright or Patterson, Lockheed equipped a new production P-38 (c/n 2218) with a set of external mass balances on the elevators. It was as if nobody even knew, outside of Burbank, that large mass balances were already fitted. They were beautifully concealed within the vertical stabilizers! One thing that was evidently overlooked in this matter was that the P-38s were the first production military aircraft anywhere to have all-metal control surfaces, something that would eventually become standard on all fast airplanes. Johnson and Colman knew that flutter was not one of their problems. But they set about to prove it to the customer.

Up went the P-38 with the test pilot (Burcham, Virden or Mattern) to 30,000 feet where he pushed over and accelerated to 350 mph (IAS) at 25,000. The test plane, of course, had normal propeller rotation, but Gilkey's problems were immediately duplicated. It was evident that the "compressibility tuck" and "tail flutter" conditions reported from Dayton were unrelated to the direction of propeller rotation. The test pilot reported that it was impos-

sible to maintain a grip on the control wheel as the control column oscillated violently back and forth. Recovery was effected in the same way that Maj. Gilkey recovered, i.e., the elevator trim tab was used to help overcome the air loads. Of course the pullout from the long dive, at low altitude, wasn't accomplished without the trauma of a 5g load on pilot and aircraft.

Once that test was out of the way, work proceeded on an entire series of external balance weight tests. With the Lockheed test pilot duplicating the test dive with every change in the teardrop weight arrangement, everybody tended to get a bit on edge. Finally, C. L. Johnson issued Report No. 2414; it was summarized as follows: "The results of tests on all of the balance weights were that absolutely no change in indicated airspeed at which the vibration developed could be noted. The violence of the vibration was unchanged and the diving tendency was naturally the same for all conditions."

Carrying the program a bit further (for insurance), Lockheed reskinned an elevator and stabilizer, using thicker aluminum sheet having a gauge thickness 63 percent greater than the standard covering. The resulting increase in rigidity had absolutely no effect on vibration. Elevator cable tension was checked at altitude with strain gauges, but nothing was amiss in that area. One unexpected finding was that the nose gear door would deflect enough to open about 4 inches at speeds in excess of 300 mph during the dive tests. Even with positive locks installed to prevent opening, there was no improvement in the buffet situation.

While new P-38s and RAF Model 322-Bs followed the last of the YP airplanes off the new assembly lines in a steadily increasing flow – only one YP was produced in 1940; production of 258 Lightnings was effected in 1941 – the testing program went on at a furious pace at L. A. T. Turbo exhaust hoods on YP-38 c/n 2202 were extensively modified to reduce intake area and attempt to change the airflow pattern. There was absolutely no change in the buffeting. Canopy fit, gondola skin roughness and canopy shape were tested on an accurate P-38 model in Lockheed's wind tunnel and on actual

*In what is probably the first P-38 production line photograph, dating to 1941, the last of the Model 122 service test airplanes (YP-38s) move down the assembly line as British contract Model 322-Bs take their place. Structurally, the RAF Lightnings were closer to the AAF's P-38E than to its P-38 and P-38D contemporaries on parallel lines. (LAC)*

aircraft. The wind tunnel model, built of mahogany, began to look like a terrible patchwork quilt as modifications were made with plaster of Paris.

By that time some major changes had taken place in Washington and at Wright-Patterson. Every facet of the Army Air Corps was revamped. With Gen. Arnold firmly at the controls, the United States Army Air Forces came into being on June 20, 1941. Arnold also retained the co-position of Army Deputy Chief of Staff. The two major organizations subordinate to the AAF were the Air Corps and the Air Force Combat Command. The former was under the Chief of the Air Corps, Maj. Gen. G. H. Brett, responsible for all service functions.

Oddly enough, old Air Corps thinking prevailed in some circles. The new Materiel Command got a bit tough with Lockheed as a result of prior experience, some inconclusive wind tunnel tests and, more to the point, frustration. Colonel Wolfe and company insisted that the manufacturer install the external balance weights on *all* P-38 type aircraft . . . or anticipate having the contracts cancelled. Kelly Johnson was unable to change their thinking, even though company tests, not yet completed, had provided unimpeachable proof that the external weights hadn't changed the buffeting by one iota. They reworked the aft fuselage (gondola) of AC40-747, extending the body about a foot beyond the trailing edge of the wing. That same type of modification was incorporated on the first Lightning I, a model 322-61-04 type, in September to help speed up the flight test program. Bearing RAF serial number AE978, the aircraft was heavily endowed with tufts for airflow analysis.

At one point the Lockheed team revised the fillet area aft of the cockpit side windows with large-radius fairings. None of these aerodynamic revisions had any perceptible effect on the so-called "tail flutter." Kelly Johnson was adamant then – and forever after – in stating that "no P-38 ever had tail flutter."

Aerodynamics engineer Phil Colman worked closely with test engineers Ward Beman and John Margwarth and a couple of wind tunnel specialists to find some solution to the buffeting. The over-worked wooden model was fitted (coated or slathered might be more appropriate) with a multitude of fillet shapes at the gondola/wing leading edge junction, all formed with plaster of Paris. Out in the experimental shop, they smoothed the entire nose section on the test P-38 as it had never been smoothed before. Then, fixed leading edge slots were mounted between the central nacelle (or gondola, if you prefer) and the engine nacelles. Those leading edge extensions provided the first tangible proof that disturbed airflow was the culprit, certainly not flutter.

While the results were promising, another problem was created: a center-of-gravity problem developed, and it could not be tolerated. Almost on the same day that flight testing revealed that the slotted wing was not the correct answer, the wind tunnel people ran tests with Tunnel Test No. 15 leading edge fillets. They liked the results. According to Johnson, pressure surveys provided some very interesting data. A very high airflow velocity was obtained at the wing-fuselage junction (where the chord/thickness ratio was the greatest on the P-38), with airflow accelerated as much as 40 percent above flight speed. In other words, if the aircraft was flying at 500 mph at 25,000 feet, the airflow speed at that point on the P-38 would be close to the speed of sound. It was certainly well over the limiting Mach number. Every test flight in the series had shown that the airplane always encountered the diving moment and onset of tail buffet at that specific flight speed, or a real indicated airspeed of 345-350 miles per hour.

The X-15 fillet was combined with the slotted leading edge on the test P-38, while the fillet alone (one on each side, of course) was installed on the No. 1 Model 322-B test plane. All of the dive testing for buffet and compressibility tuck

research was being conducted by Burcham, Mattern and Ralph Virden. But at a time when results were not producing acceptable results in the mind of a top executive, a decision was made to hire nationally famous test pilot Vance Breese to conduct dive tests and tender his solutions to the ongoing problem(s). Breese signed a lucrative contract. (Figures bandied about ranged all the way up to $40,000, even $60,000, a fortune in 1940-41, but no insider will even discuss it to this date.) His relationship with Lockheed was brief, unrewarding and the cause of much unhappiness among the company test pilots.

When the X-15 fillets were tested on the P-38 and 322-B, the buffet problem, at least, was annihilated. Every Lightning was fitted with the fillets as fast as they could be produced. The AAF cancelled the critical speed restriction that had been in force for a few months, but the external mass balances were required on every airplane . . . by order of the AAF. (In a much later, ultra-rare interview, Johnson said, "The only thing those external mass balances ever did was to kill a couple of good pilots who had been forced to bail out." He was inferring that the weights and pilots had collided during escape efforts.)

Over a lengthy period of time, Lockheed publicists and media writers everywhere gave the distinct impression that the various P-38 models only became successful in combat because the external "dive brake" was installed (before P-38s saw combat), correcting the compressibility problem. It was an erroneous impression at the very minimum. NACA wind tunnel testing and Lockheed creativity did not combine to provide that solution until 2 1/2 years later – at least in the combat theaters. The solution wasn't a "dive brake" at all, but a dive flap. The device – actually a folding "speed bump" – was tested successfully in 1943 (more about that later).

C Virtually concurrent development and production of the P-38/P-38D and 322-B airplanes yielded some interesting results that have never been expounded by Lockheed documents or any other sources. Although two parallel 322-B lines and two P-38 assembly lines within the Building 114-125-126 complex were operating by mid-1941, the situation at Plant B-1 was not without its troubles. YPs and P-38s, plus the first of the 322-Bs, were beginning to move along rather nicely. In the north bay, production of Hudsons, Super Electras and a mixed bag of Model 14 and Model 18 offshoots was proceeding with only minor interruptions as the "bull gangs" periodically rearranged equipment.

Things began to get so hectic at Plant B-1 West that much of the final production was being accomplished outdoors.  For the most part, California weather was cooperative.  However, outside production had to be fraught with any number of problems.  With hundreds of employees working in the open, an all-day rain storm could create chaotic conditions.

To provide some insight about conditions in Burbank, Lockheed Aircraft alone employed 17,626 people at the very beginning of 1941.  In some incredible manner, the number had grown to no less than 40,307 by November 30.  Vega, the subsidiary to Lockheed, started the year in its huge new plant at L. A. T. with 4,274 on board.  The Austin Co., engineers and builders, had poured the giant slab and erected nearly 750,000 square feet of so-called "Blackout" building (e.g., windowless) toward the end of 1940 in 90 to 120 days.  It was an astounding performance.

Employment at Vega nearly quadrupled by December 1941 to no less than 15,720.  Lockheed-Vega as a corporation employed no less than 53,427 workers – well, most were – as of November 30.  On that same date, the second largest aircraft employer in America was Douglas Aircraft with three plants (pretty well scattered) employing a mere 36,616 people.  It is well to recall Lockheed's status in the industry just a bit over three years earlier.

The OPM and Materiel Command could not manage to overcome all of the calamities nationwide because of politics, greed, throatcutting, and any number of other things.  Lockheed, in several months between autumn 1941 and later winter 1942, produced P-38s faster than Curtiss Propeller Division could deliver propellers.  (At one point, fighters were flown to assigned bases, props were removed and shipped back to Burbank to be installed on other aircraft.)  Not only that, but the Battle of Britain had strongly emphasized that it was foolhardy to go into battle with integral fuel tanks and minimal armor plate at crucial points, not to mention high-pressure oxygen systems, Plexiglas windshields and three different types of guns.

From an external aspect, the YP-38s, P-38s and P-38Ds were virtually indistinguishable . . . although no YPs were ever camouflaged unless the AAF painted one or two at a later date.  The major distinguishing marks of these airplanes were in the nose landing gear, supercharger shrouds and armament.  On the ground it could be seen that the nose gear door extended well forward of the main strut and the drag links were angled forward.  Model 322-B aircraft being produced on parallel lines were closer to newer P-38E models in many

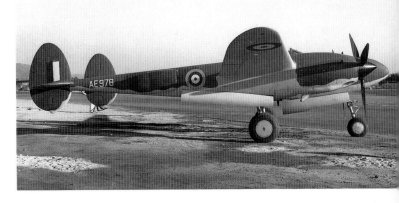

ways, especially in the nose landing gear arrangement.  Surprises could be found, however.  All YPs had sharply pointed spinners, but P-38s were supposed to have blunted spinners.  It wasn't always true.  At least a few  P-38/RP-38 types had pointed spinners.  Turbosupercharger hoods were used on all Yippees and on all P-38s and P-38Ds, after which they were supposedly deleted.  But for a few unexplained reasons, some P-38E aircraft were seen with the hoods in place.

The point had been made that one or two YPs had prominent gun enclosure tubes protecting the two .50-caliber machine guns while flush plates covered the other gun ports.  Actually, most YP-38s were flown without guns installed.  However, one of the types was flown up to Oscoda, Michigan, from Selfridge Field for gunnery testing.  All of the guns were installed, and the 37-mm Oldsmobile-manufactured Browning M9 cannon was fired many times.  It may have been a potent old weapon, but development had progressed at a snail's pace for years.  It was not really well suited for aircraft use.

A person could be reasonably certain that any Lightning having both upper machine guns protruding equally (or equipped with upper gun tubes) was a Yippee, P-38 or P-38D.

However, at least one P-38E was known to have flown with the P-38D machine gun arrangement. Logic seemed to have taken the day off.

Air Force planners decided to upgrade all aircraft then in production to incorporate items suddenly considered necessary if they were to be "combat capable." That decision was evidently made in the spring or early summer of 1941. As envisioned by the Combat Command and Air Materiel Command, all aircraft with this "combat capability" would have self-sealing fuel tanks, no magnesium flares, a low-pressure oxygen system, greatly improved armor protection and a plate of bulletproof glass. Unexpectedly, these changes on the Lockheed fighters seemed to have no negative effects on production.

The AAF specified that all aircraft with these capabilities would have a "D" suffix. As a result, there never was a P-38B or C. Beginning in August 1941, all production P-38s bore the new designation P-38D. A Change Order was issued to the existing P-38 contract, calling for 36 final airplanes in the lot to be built with self-sealing fuel cells, which reduced the total internal capacity from 390 gallons to 340 gallons. However, the increase in pilot safety was well worth the reduction in flying time. High-pressure oxygen systems had proven dangerous in combat and, even though it was a new item in the YP-38, low-pressure went into the D Model.

Lockheed's model designation 222-62-02 still applied to the newest version created by C.O. 3377. With the creation of the "combat capable" model, virtually all of the first 29 production aircraft in AAF inventory were redesignated as RP-38s. This new category meant that fighters were restricted in operation, essentially to training and familiarization. Unless the RP-38 was to be used for gunnery practice, they were almost always flown without guns being installed.

Although P-38s, RP-38s and some P-38Ds from Selfridge Field were active participants in Army-Navy joint summer maneuvers centered in Louisiana during the period September 11-26, few of them had any guns installed. Most of them had the tube fairings installed, but the guns went elsewhere. Because the P-38s were such complex machines, rumor had it that they were difficult to maintain. That, according to first-hand reports, was strictly in the "latrine rumor" category. Bell P-39Ds and Republic P-43s were fraught with problems, but the biggest headache awards went to the Douglas A-20s and early model North American B-25 Mitchells. Lockheed P-38Ds flown by the "experienced" 94PS (Pursuit Squadron) were virtually trouble free. No anti-buffet wing fillets had been installed by retrofit action, so it was not considered *de riguer* to perform high-altitude dives at more than 15 degrees or to exceed placarded speeds in a dive.

Second Lt. John W. "Bill" Weltman, assigned to the 27PS in the 1st Pursuit Group from Selfridge, logged some 38 hours in P-38s and P-38Ds in September. A large number of those hours were in connection with the maneuvers in the Southland. (It appears that Weltman spent most of November at the controls of some P-38 or other. He was in the air nearly every day at Beaumont, Texas, obviously on detached service or TDY.) In less than a year, he was Capt. Weltman, Operations Officer in the 1PG(F), and on his way to the United Kingdom - again at the controls of a Lightning.

Bell P-39D Airacobras involved in the war games seemed to be there in large numbers, but they were a source of much grief to pilots and ground crews. Although they carried six machine guns and a 37-mm shell gun, making them the most heavily armed fighters around, they were plagued with upper canopy panels departing in flight. Worse, side entry/exit doors often separated from the aircraft at embarrassing moments, as reported in a Memorandum Report from Lt. Col. F. O. Carroll's

Experimental Engineering Section at Wright Field. Although they were excellent ground support aircraft, even at that early date, it was extremely rare for a P-39D involved in a one-to-one dogfight above 12,000 feet not to get "waxed" in the process.

Rapid growth at Lockheed and modernized production and component manufacturing techniques resulted in a somewhat abrupt end to final assembly of that original batch of 80 pursuits authorized by Robert Gross. Summer 1941 had been nothing but hustle and bustle in Burbank. However, the changeover to P-38E production involved some rather significant changes to reflect the learning curve from results in European aerial warfare.

When the Air Corps people had decided to apply a letter D suffix on every fighter and bomber type that was supposed to embody all changes needed to make them suitable for combat, a great deal of foresight was missing. In the short number of months it took to complete 36 P-38Ds, the war and maneuvers taught them that they had erred. The plan went out the window. In mid-September it looked like the P-38E format was going to be the "combat ready" version of the Lightning. When the need finally arose, a few easily accomplished modifications converted those E versions into real fighters.

British official displeasure with the performance of the RAF Model 322-61-04 Lightning Is bubbled up. First it was the alleged "tail flutter" situation. Addition of the external balance weights on the elevator did nothing to solve the real problem: aerodynamic buffet. By that time, the Royal Air Force leadership had learned that many aircraft designed on the basis of prewar concepts were inadequate for the new job at hand. Following some negotiations in July, newly revised specifications were issued in connection with the British contract. Instead of procuring 667 Lightning Is, the RAF would only receive 143 of them; the remaining 524 aircraft would be updated versions of the USAAF P-38E, and that meant they would have turbosuperchargers and V-1710F series engines.

Suddenly, based on reports from an RAF evaluation pilot at Burbank, the Ministry of Supply stated that they would only accept three of the Lightning Is for evaluation in England, but would refuse to accept any more of that model. That could have brought at least two assembly lines to a halt. After consultations with his technical people, plus detailed reviews of the contract by contracts and legal executives, Robert Gross declared that Lockheed was going to deliver airplanes in accordance with the 1940 contract requirements. He ordered production to continue.

It became a standoff. As Lightning Is passed Lockheed flight trials, the airplanes were prepared for storage and wheeled into a nearby vacant lot. About $15,000,000 was involved, and Gross was not likely to let the British default on the contract. What happened next is not clear, but the bitterness that arose from discussions was not superficial. With no White House interference in spite of the obvious Roosevelt-Churchill friendliness, Lockheed was headed for litigation against the British. Whatever happened before December 7, it managed to garble Lockheed contractual records about the 322-61-04 airplanes. It might be assumed that the three Model 322-B airplanes that were sent to England would be the initial three registered as AE978 through AE980. In fact, it was frequently reported that AE978 was delivered to the RAF.

Three aircraft were ultimately shipped to the United Kingdom by the USAAF as follows: AF105 was sent to Cunliffe-Owen Aircraft Limited, at Swaythling, Southampton, for examination and experiments; AF106 was sent to the A&AEE at Boscombe Down for flight evaluation; AF107 was delivered to the Royal Aircraft Establishment at Farnborough for experi-

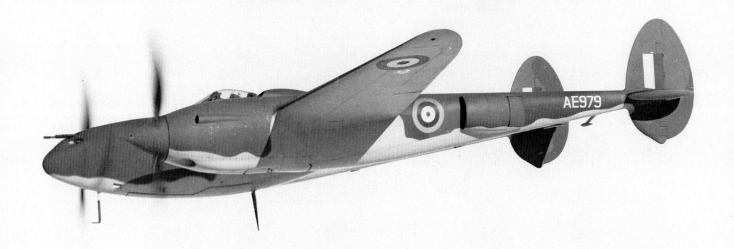

ments and evaluation. All three arrived by sea transport in March 1942.

It must be stressed that there never was any official acceptance of the type by the Royal Air Force or the Ministry of Supply. Most likely, the USAAF "temporarily loaned" the Lightning Is for test and evaluation. The three aircraft that were handed over were not from blocks comprising 22 airplanes in the AE serial block. Some rather strange things occurred in the post Pearl Harbor contract areas. All airplanes in the AF100-AF220 block were suddenly converted by Army Contract AC-31707 (121 airframes). Those planes and the AE series 322-Bs were delivered officially to the USAAF in January 1942. It is patently obvious that the RAF was never going to own those airplanes unless they were to be provided under Lend-Lease.

In actual fact, AF107 was returned to the AAF on December 2; AF105 was given back on July 1, 1943, and AF106 was turned over on the 10th of July. There was another strange happening that cannot be easily explained. One Lockheed Lightning II rolled out of the factory in August 1942 in full RAF colors and the RAF registry AF221, but it was a USAAF airplane. The constructor's number was 3144, and though the AAF number was 43-2035, that was never painted on the tail assembly. The British roundels passed into history by the next day, covered by the U.S. national insignia.

One more gremlin had remained undetected in this whole unpleasant episode, and it created an error in Lockheed records

Best view of Lightning gun arrangement through P-38D series shows up on this YP-38, No. 7. Upper machine guns protrude evenly, large-bore center gun is the 37-mm Browning. Size of large shells shows up well here as armament man holds clip. Site was reported as Oscoda, Michigan. (E. W. Howe)

mary – reveal that AF105 and AF106 were delivered in January 1942 (to the AAF), but AF107 stands out as a P-322-II (322-62-18) with a July 1942 delivery date. Records or not, that airplane went to England along with AF105 and AF106 in March 1942.

Without going into detail, disposition and rework of AE and AF prefix airplanes became a "hash" in that period, probably caused by the way they pulled aircraft out of storage and back from post-December 7, 1941, assignments for West Coast defense. (It may seem unimportant, but when consideration is given to the fact that it involved the largest single contract for one military type in the history of American aeronautics prior to 1942, loose ends are disturbing.) Additionally, the Lockheed P-38 Summary lists 174 Lightning IIs as P-38G-13-LOs, but AAF documents such as AFPI 41 indicate that there were no P-38G-13s at all, only P-38G-15-LO block aircraft. The company probably never bothered to update its records when some change order came through.

Whatever happened, it was certainly better than a prolonged legal battle between two allies. (It should be noted that P-322-II aircraft were not the same as Lightning IIs.)

As previously noted, production of P-38D versions of the Lightning ended in September. Although 38 of the twin-engine fighters were accepted by the Army Air Forces in August and September, production went absolutely flat in October. Only three P-38Es were sold off to the AAF Plant Representative in that month. The changeover to P-38E production obviously involved some major design changes and reorganization of subassembly and major component or assembly fabrication. By November the prime manufacturer of the day, probably blessed with superior weather, delivered no fewer than 74 much improved P-38E fighters to the AAF. Not one Lightning I was shown as being delivered (checked through final inspection as far as Contract A-242 was concerned) that month, but that situation only reveals that truth does not always exist in wartime documentation, official or otherwise.

*ABOVE: Taking off from the main plant strip in June 1941, the fourth P-38 (AC40-747) made its first routine shakedown flight. It then landed at the L.A.T. flight test activity for final checkout and delivery. That was to be one of the last flights from the old airstrip alongside the Southern Pacific railroad tracks. Interestingly enough, the last Bell YFM-1A was delivered in May. (P. M. Bowers)*

*BOTTOM: With a chrome-like finish, this YP-38 was on its way to Wright Field. It stopped briefly at Chanute Field and was photographed nicely at that training school. (Ed Wolak)*

that was never corrected. In fact, it may have never been detected. Uncharacteristically, the company "lost" a constructor's number (c/n) in the last batch of 374 Lightning IIs. No such happening has ever been noted among all other Lockheed contractual documents or records. In the final group of P-38G-15-LO airplanes, AAF serials run consecutively from AC43-2359 thru AC43-2558, accounting for 200 "Americanized" fighters. But, what happened to the constructor's numbers? In that same group they are tabulated as follows (for no apparent reason): c/n 3468 through 3500 and 3502 through 3668! What ever became of c/n 3501? No experimental P-38 of any kind answers to that number. Nobody can deny that it was uncharacteristic of Lockheed.

There were a couple of other oversights, but they might be explained away by the conditions that prevailed everywhere after the unexpected (except at the White House) attack on Pearl Harbor and the Philippines. Company records – at least on the fine-detail Lightning Model Sum-

Not only did Lockheed complete the very healthy group of AAF Lightnings in that hectic month, they completed all work on some 30 or 40 of the British-ordered version. In the contentious atmosphere that prevailed at that time in dealing with British officialdom, Robert Gross maintained his position and he intended to be paid in accordance with that contract.

The RAF was trading blows with the *Luftwaffe* in 1941, but that was merely a holding action. America was struggling mightily to forge itself into the Arsenal of Democracy, although a virtually full peacetime atmosphere prevailed. Completely restyled 1942-model cars came out on schedule; the new upscale General Motors cars were entirely revamped in design. While Churchill encountered a maze of serious problems in North Africa, Britain's financial situation was extremely precarious.

Americans were providing a great deal of wartime material under the Lend-Lease program, but the Lockheed 322-B contract was a totally different thing. That had been negotiated under the old Cash and Carry situation that prevailed before the fall of France and Britain's calamitous loss of weapons on the Continent. In retrospect, it seems incredible that the two governments looked lightly upon the problem that was festering. How could they stand by and watch Lockheed try to drag the British Ministry of Supply into court for default on a contract?

Unbelievably, as in some wild fiction story, new belligerents had intervened to settle the matter, or at least assume the unplanned role of *amicus curiae* in the potential litigation. They were the children of Emperor Hirohito; realistically, the Imperial Japanese Army and Navy.

E Almost immediately after the Japanese naval attack on Pearl Harbor, and coordinated attacks on Singapore, the Philippines and a host of Far East targets, Lockheed administrators reminded the Western Defense Command that at least 40 of the fast 322-B fighters were in temporary storage, many of them in a lot next to Buena Vista Street in Burbank. Armed and manned, they would certainly be superior to most combat aircraft that were likely to be available for West Coast defensive action. Only hours passed before War Emergency Powers came into effect, and the AAF – invoking the special powers granted to the Presidency – assumed direct title to the 40 aircraft available. Guns were installed, the fighters were serviced and checked out, and pilots from the Fourth Air Force were dispatched to Burbank to ferry the fighters, complete with full RAF markings, to bases such as Mines Field, North Island NAS and March Field.

The Alaska Defense Command (see Chapter 10) was unaffected by this action; the defense of West Coast cities and industrial sites became paramount in the eyes of the government. Quite truthfully, Alaska was at far greater risk than 99.9 percent of all Americans could have even guessed. Fuel was in terribly short supply; airfields (even those under construction) were not winterized; U.S. Navy presence was, factually, laughable; most AAF fighters (P-36s) were still in crates, awaiting assembly; and the bomber "force" consisted of a motley squadron or two of Douglas B-18s.

The crucial Panama Canal Zone was in similar straits, but there was little difficulty in ferrying Curtiss P-40 fighters from other bases. What was available to defend 1,200 miles of Pacific coastline and plants producing America's only truly modern fighters and the total supply of four-engine bombers? On December 8 all available P-38 fighters from the 1st Pursuit Group arrived at North Island Naval Air Station at San Diego, and the entire group had been transferred from Selfridge Field, Michigan, by the 22nd of December. Marine Air Wing 1 was also committed to the defense of the West Coast. (The most authoritative source on AAF history makes absolutely no mention of the 40 Lockheed 322-Bs and any part they played in defending California. Lockheed people say that it was a fact.)

Official sources have stated the defense of the key West Coast cities was vested in just 45 thoroughly modern fighters, ostensibly Lockheed P-38s, P-38Ds and some P-38Es. The 1st MAW fighters were, most likely, Grumman Wildcats, although they were probably still operating some Grumman F3F-3s, which could not in any way be considered as modern fighters. It is also possible that some of the 322-Bs were included in that batch of 45.[1]

Considering the deplorable condition of America's West Coast (and other) defenses after having viewed the devastation that could be wrought by any dedicated aggressor, it is hardly any wonder that no serious attempt was made to oversee the temporary destinies of 40 wanton Lightning Is.

Although it had been reported that four radar sets were located "strategically" on the West Coast, their performance capability was, at best, doubtful. On December 8, a complete blackout hit the San Francisco area and it lasted 3 hours. With no air raid sirens installed, police cars had to race around, sirens screaming, to alert the public. Radar supposedly tracked enemy aircraft coming in from 100 miles at sea. Even two days later, Lt. Gen. J. L. DeWitt was caustic in his criticism of those who disbelieved the reports of those hostile aircraft. He was, believe it or not, head of the Western Defense Command. An "invasion fleet" of 34 warships was reported off the California coast on December 9.

Were the Fourth Air Force's heavy bombers ready to attack them? Well, there were only ten heavy bombers deployed along the entire 1,200-mile coastline, and ammunition available was minimal. Fortunately, fourteen B-17 Flying For-

---

1. *What should constitute an infallible record of events, the Form 5 of a key 1st Fighter Group pilot, provides absolutely no insight to what really occurred. Lt. John Weltman's Form 5 shows that he flew a P-38 (his) back to Selfridge from Columbia, S.C., on November 29. His very next entry shows that he did 2 hours in a P-38 at North Island NAS! And that was on December 15, 1941. It is a 100 percent certainty that he did not leave his airplane in Michigan; it is equally certain that the aircraft was not dismantled and shipped by rail to San Diego. Therefore, some 15 days are not accounted for in his official records. (Weltman was with the 27PS, Fighter.) Reliance on official, but uncorrected, records after any number of years is not without inherent danger.*

*Most fortunately, however, Col. Ralph Garman's Form 5 (a copy) is in the hands of this author. It reveals some things evidently unknown to those in the Air Force history centers. Garman commanded the 1FG when it went to North Africa in 1942, after having been with that group from March 1938. He flew hundreds of hours in Seversky P-35 and Curtiss P-36 types, including XP-36D and E. Having logged some hours on a Republic YP-43 with the 27PS, he suddenly found himself involved in accelerated flight testing of a YP-38 from May 16, 1941, at FAD, identification for Fairfield Air Depot at Patterson Field, Ohio. It is very obvious from his log that he was piloting the YP-38 used in cannon tests at Alpena in June 1941.*

*This is where things get most interesting. Garman took off on a leisurely mission in his new P-38E (not alone, that seems certain) in the general direction of San Pedro, California, on the 5th of December, 1941, via Texas bases, and arrived at North Island NAS (San Diego) on the 8th! Was somebody psychic? If Garman was commanding the 94PS(F) on that date, he most certainly had the squadron with him, accounting for the shortleg cross-country flight. Weltman and the 27PS(F) surely were not far behind. It also points out that Weltman was probably flying a P-38D. He was just more casual about his Form 5.*

*(There was a period of time when Pursuit Squadron [Fighter] and Pursuit Group [Fighter] existed as an official designation form to achieve a smooth transition. Usually written as PS[F] and PG[F].)*

tresses were at March Field en route to the Southwest Pacific. Unfortunately their gun turrets were inoperative, there was absolutely no supply of oxygen to support high-altitude operation, there could be no fighter escort and they would have to attack warships with only a few 300-pound and 600-pound bombs that were available. America may have become the Arsenal of Democracy, but the guards were "out to lunch," a condition only too prevalent in a nation that had a 27-month warning period. Isolationism was as effective as sabotage.

Having disposed of the Lightning I delivery problems in short order, Lockheed and the Western Procurement District negotiated some new and useful contracts. In essence the contracts eliminated virtually all RAF association with the Lockheed Lightning, and that situation remained as a fact of life for the remaining years of the conflict. Various units of the RAF and some British Commonwealth squadrons flew most models of the Mustang and Thunderbolt during the war, but probably fewer than a half-dozen Lightnings ever operated with United Kingdom and Commonwealth units. One can only speculate that a tremendous amount of bitterness must have been generated by Ministry of Supply handling of the Lightning affair.

No clear picture of the Lockheed Lightning I story can be derived from Lockheed's Model Summary or from an updated AFPI Form 41 because there are definite conflicts. Worse, the Summary is unnumbered, undated and unsigned. Form 41 errs in listing all P-322-Is as having AE prefix numbers, P-322-IIs as having AF prefixes. That is absolutely incorrect. The best conclusion that can be drawn is that there were, at the end of 1942 or 1943, 22 Model 322-61-04 (P/RP-322-I) Lightning Is that remained unmodified. Concurrently, there were 121 Model 322-62-18 (P-322-II) trainers that had been reworked at Burbank as part and parcel of the AAF contract that covered conversion of Lightning IIs into regular service type P-38Fs and P-38Gs.

All P-322-II aircraft were provided with V-1710F-2 engines (unsupercharged). Most pilots and mechanics associated with the P-38F-13/F-15 or P-38G-15 airplanes probably never knew that they had been laid out as British fighters, and it appears that most of them were ultimately sent to combat zones. All of the P-322s operated with the Flying Training Command, primarily in the Fourth Air Force area. Several were still being used in 1945.

Around Burbank, and probably in Arizona (at the training bases), all P-322s were referred to as the "Castrated P-38s" because they were not equipped with turbosuperchargers. It would be unfair to presume that the P-322s were poor performers. In actual fact they proved to be faster at low altitudes (under 16,000 feet) than Curtiss Warhawks, North American Mustang Is and every Hawker Hurricane. Employed as transition/advanced trainers for pilots moving into the twin-engine type, P-322s never were known to acquire a bad reputation for handling, or for any other reason. They proved to be far easier and safer to fly than the much lower-powered Curtiss AT-9 trainers, a type that had to be withdrawn from service after a short operational career because they generated a fairly high fatality rate. (For the record, some of the fastest post-war racing P-38s had powerplant installations virtually duplicating those in the P-322-IIs.) The original Lightning Is, especially when painted in RAF colors, were rather handsome aircraft, even when at rest.

Knowledge that the original Model Spec. 2338 for the improved Lightning II was issued on August 5, 1941, totally invalidated any longstanding contention that the RAF "axed" the Lockheed fighters after completing initial flight tests in England. First tests at Boscombe Down could not possibly have been initiated before May 1942.

The three strongest factors in attempting to refuse delivery under contract provisions were (1) complete evaluation of the results of the Battle of Britain; (2) the condition of the British treasury, and (3) the uncertainty surrounding the so-called "tail flutter" condition. The first item revealed that original requirements established by the members of the Purchasing Commission were terribly flawed. Item 2 was probably the biggest factor of all; the "flutter" problem was solved more rapidly than most faults encountered with new airplanes.

The antagonism generated by the dispute certainly "poisoned the well" for more than a decade. To show how false pride can lead to lamentable waste, the RAF squandered a lot of money and technical effort in trying to develop the Westland Welkin. For a small fraction of the cost they could have re-engined a dozen Lightning Is for testing, using either the powerplants specified for the Welkin or the same engine model that was adopted for the P-51B. Demonstrating 5 minutes of combat between a Merlinized Lightning and the Welkin would have converted even the most hard-headed skeptic in the United Kingdom to the side of the Lightning.

*To perceive things in the germ is intelligence - Lao-Tsze.*

F In spite of the British camouflage and basic markings, the first Lightning II was officially a P-38F-13-LO under contract W535-ac-31707, and it was bailed to Lockheed for some crucial armament testing almost from the day of its acceptance. In its original AAF format, the contract called for production of P-38F-13-LO and -15-LO aircraft, but in the final analysis the procurements came out as follows:

P-38F-13-LO ......29 procured
Model 322-60-19  c/n 3144-3172

P-38F-15-LO.......121 procured
Model 322-60-19  c/n 3173-3293

*P-38G-13-LO.....174 procured
Model 322-68-19  c/n 3294-3467

P-38G-15-LO......33 procured
Model 322-68-19  c/n 3468-3500

P-38G-15-LO......167 procured
Model 322-68-19  c/n 3502-3668

*Note: *Air Force Report AFPI Form 41 had no reference to a P-38G-13-LO at all. There were 374 P-38G-15-LO airplanes delivered to the AAF.*

Probably the only thing that kept Lockheed from "losing" more of the airplanes in those feverish times was sheer bulk. With airplanes parked in vacant lots adjacent to main thoroughfares, spur-of-the-moment transfers to undesignated AAF units, absorption of entire groups of fighters without proper documentation, and as many as 500 new employees every day being assigned to jobs, it is some wonder that somebody didn't fly one out or truck it away.

In the midst of the melee the AAF splashed a multitude of priority programs for modification of large numbers of P-38s. Euphemisms for some of these programs included BOLERO, BRONZE, SUMAC, SNOWMAN and (unexpectedly) WILDFLOWER. The company never came out with any real explanation of what the programs were for (except for BOLERO), but random-selection airplanes were reworked on the line or on the ramps to include certain specialized equipment. The wonder is that most (hopefully) were sent to the correct destinations. It is only necessary to recall that Curtiss P-40s sent to the Philippines in December 1941 arrived without any Prestone coolant. Somebody decided that antifreeze would not be needed in that part of the world. Other P-40s that arrived later in Australia were missing gun chargers or some other key component, so the airplanes remained useless for weeks until the parts could be routed by air.

Initial deliveries on the P-38F Lightning IIs were made in August 1942 and production continued on those and the G version until the last of that type was delivered in March 1943. Under the impetus of combat requirements, many changes were introduced without being reflected in the block numbering system established by the WPB. (At Boeing, Douglas, Vega and Consolidated – primarily in connection with B-17 and B-24

heavy bomber production – block numbers were a way of life, changing almost by the week.) All P-38F-15-LOs were equipped with the "combat" or maneuvering flap system, allowing partial extension of the Lockheed-Fowler flaps at indicated airspeeds below 250 mph, something that worked out nicely at high altitudes or when combating slow-flying aircraft. (These should not be confused with the quick-acting dive flaps, an innovation introduced much later.) The major change introduced on all P-38G airplanes was installation of Allison V-1710F-10 engines in place of the F-5s. Although there was a complete change in the turbosupercharger (B-13) matched to the F-10 series engine, there was no increase in horsepower. It may have been an interim step to the more powerful F-17 engines that forced a redesign of the intercooler and Prestone coolant systems.

Most certainly there had to be a photo-reconnaissance version of the P-38G type, and the AAF procured 180 of them in groups of 20 or 60, interspersed with fighter deliveries. All of these were awarded the F-5A designation and, with few exceptions (if any), they had regular fighter-type camouflage paint instead of something in exotic blue. Anyone inclined to believe that Lockheed's photo versions did not provide extremely valuable services would have to be out of tune with various Army generals who considered them more valuable than the fighters. Many have voiced the opinion that more lives were saved by the F-4s and F-5s than by any fighter.

Somehow, it seems incredible that records of F-5F and F-5G airplanes in service (or acceptance) evidently do not exist in any comprehensive form. The production of F-5s ceased with the F-5B model, and all subsequent photo versions were

modification center products. At the end of the war, somebody made a tremendous mistake. Apparently records were discarded by plant managers with no regard at all for postwar requirements. Considering the detailed breakdown of AFPI Form 41, even to the point of including many "T" for Trainer prefixes such as TB-32 for the lamentable Dominator, there is nary a sign of the F-5F and F-5G. The latter absolutely had to be turned out in large numbers before the war came to an end. It wasn't pretty, but it was effective. (Civil mapping versions were still in use into the 1960s.)

No story about 322-B Lightning fighters would be complete without a few final comparisons and a couple of speculative thoughts. Lockheed, in the guise of Jimmy Gerschler, had guaranteed a top speed for the 322-B/F fighters at 400 mph at 16,900 feet, time to climb to 16,000 feet as 6.75 minutes and a normal gross weight of 14,467 pounds in 1940. Of course these figures appear in the type specification, but there are no reports that confirm actual performance.

Lockheed test pilots most certainly conducted performance tests on AE978 and AE979 if for no other reason than to

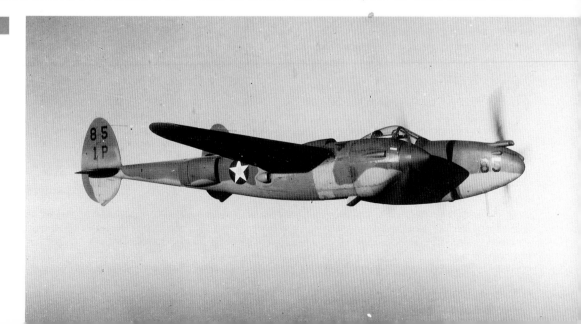

establish basic data to be used in buffet analysis testing that led to adoption of wing fillets. It has not been possible to gain access to any RAF flight test reports. Considering what happened to the Lightning I contracts, any results that revealed performance below guarantees would have to be verified by tests that were free from a bias.

Ron Harker, Rolls-Royce test pilot at Hucknall, England, had the opportunity to fly the first North American Mustang I belonging to the Air Fighting Development Unit at Duxford on April 30, 1942. In his opinion, the Mustang was far superior in performance to the Spitfire V in their normal operational altitude range (10,000 to 20,000 feet), even though Harker was no fan of the Allison V-1710. Although no true airspeed was recorded that day, it has been established that a nominal top speed for a Mustang I at about 13,000 feet was 386 mph. (A-36, P-51A and Mustang I performances varied widely at different altitudes, evidently dependent upon rated performance levels of the engine used.) And late model Curtiss P-40Ns could barely attain a TAS of 370 mph on military power a year later.

If the Lightning I was capable of attaining 400 mph – and Robert Gross evidently had some reliable data at hand to support his confidence level – in accordance with performance guarantees, the British reaction to the 322-B cannot be understood at all. The Lockheed type was obviously faster than a Mustang I, had greater load-carrying capacity (and probably greater range) and was ready for delivery in approximately the same time frame. What if the Hucknall people had tried Merlin 61s in a Lightning I as they did in the Mustang I? What if Col. Ben Kelsey had then flown the type and been so impressed that he enthusiastically "sold" the project to Brig. Gen. "Monk" Hunter and Gen. Arnold? Such things have changed the course of history more than once.

One highly respected contemporary RAF aircraft, the Bristol Beaufighter VIF, was similar to the Lightning I in size, had 50 percent more power, and had to carry a second crew member. If you believe the published performance figures for the popular Beaufighter, the best that could be seen was 333 mph at critical altitude. Beaufighters were tested with an entire covey of different engines, none of which evidently was able to drive the aircraft faster than 340 mph. Had the MoS done one-third as much experimentation with the 322-B, they might well have come up with a thoroughbred. Certainly the Lightning II would have outperformed any Beaufighter in most roles, by a wide margin and with a single crewman.

H A facet of the Purchasing Commission contract A-242 that is virtually unknown to the world at large is the fact that it had a direct impact on the creation of another Lockheed prototype fighter, the 6000+ horsepower XP-58 long-range escort fighter and, less directly, the XP-49. On April 12, 1940, the U.S. Government and Lockheed Aircraft signed a formal "foreign release" agreement. This was similar to the agreement involving the Purchasing Commission, North American Aviation and the USAAF that permitted the British to buy Mustang (originally Apache) fighters. In that situation, the AAC received two prototype XP-51s gratis.

Inasmuch as the P-38 type was already an Air Corps procurement item, the Lightning agreement called for devel-

opment of an "advanced version of the P-38 Lightning" to be delivered to Wright Field's Air Materiel Division for evaluation as an escort fighter. What was visualized was a bomber-escort fighter to be employed in a protective role approximately as described by Hap Arnold and Ira Eaker in their well-known doctrines. Engineers representing Brig. Gen. G. H. Brett's Air Materiel Division and Maj. Gen. Delos C. Emmons' Combat Command agreed that the new Lockheed, designated then as XP-58, could be either a one- or two-seat fighter. Powerplants were to be Continental IV-1440 (sic; actually IV-1430), one of a so-called group of "Hyper engines" being developed for the AAC. Like the XP-51s, the XP-58 was supposed to derive many parts from production P-38s. The end product appeared to be more closely related to the slightly later XP-61 Black Widow.[2]

In Lockheed parlance as related to their model identification system, it appears that the XP-38 design (Model 22) was preceded by the XP-58 because it was designated as Model 20. James Gerschler's personal problems prevented him from providing any responsible data years later, and that specific question was never put to Kelly Johnson. However, there are two things that would lead anyone to believe that is exactly what happened.

There had been some reason to presume that Lockheed's XFM-2 design was the Model 10D, but it may be more reasonable to believe it was the Model 17 or perhaps the preliminary Model 20 (since it was laid out as the bomber-escort fighter). Again, since the 37-mm cannon was the weapon of choice for the XFM-2 *and* the XP-58, the theory is even stronger. In a period when C. L. Johnson-Hall Hibbard designs were coming off the boards with unabated enthusiasm, only the Johnson-Hibbard-Gerschler triumvir could possibly know what form the original XP-58 design took. The second key point is that Jim Gerschler literally "pulled the XP-58 design out of a hat" when he produced those drawing for the Materiel and Combat Command engineers within hours of the establishment of a requirement.

Actually the second XP-58/Model 20 design was the only version ever discovered in the corporate files. That was the one that was obviously equipped with the prototype Pratt & Whitney X-1800 (military XH-2600) sleeve-valve engines, a development that was cancelled at the suggestion of United Aircraft Corporation's top official. (That large-displacement engine, just to add to general confusion – then hardly needed – had also been specified as the prime powerplant for

Lockheed's Model 522/XP-49 fighter in 1939. When the XH-2600 was dropped, the even less promising Wright XR-2160 was substituted.)

All logic seems to have gone out the window when the Wright Field engineers directed Gerschler to use Continental IV-1430 engines in the Model 20. Under those ridiculous ground rules, the very large XP-58 was to get two engines each having a displacement of 1430 cubic inches, while the P-38 derivative XP-49 was to have a pair of engines, each with a displacement of 2160 cubic inches (and considerably more horsepower). After a plethora of confrontational meetings and correspondence, the XP-49 eventually was the one equipped with Continentals and the XP-58 had a pair of 3000-horsepower Allison W-3420s swinging the propellers. Wright's XR-2160 never powered any airplane!

Kelly Johnson once tossed off this quip to unsettle the author: "The XP-58 was Lockheed's only 10-engine fighter!" He was alluding to the fact that no less than five different types of engines were specified for the XP-58 during its incubation or gestation period.

As if to emphasize the outstanding capabilities demonstrated by Benjamin Kelsey and Clarence Johnson, Air Materiel Division engineers followed their September 11, 1939, Request for Data (sent to engine manufacturers) with a detailed evaluation. Topping the list on their Figure of Merit for high-performance engines were (1) Pratt and Whitney's XH-2600 and (2) Wright's XR-2160 Tornado. Continental's GIV-1430 was eliminated for not meeting minimum horsepower requirements. Two versions of the Allison V-3420-A9R and -A10R were at the bottom of the list. Lt. Kelsey and Kelly Johnson were dismayed and scornful.

Of the six different engines, only the Continental and the Allisons could be considered even slightly successful. And only the Allisons were capable of producing 3000 brake horsepower or more. Both types of engines – the XH-2600 and XR-2160 – with a merit figure of 700 or more failed to power even a test aircraft according to official records. Unfortunately, that kind of unprofessional decision making and evaluation was prevalent on a wide scale during the war, causing America to fritter away hundreds of thousands of engineering and manufacturing hours. There can be absolutely no doubt that such decisions cost the country some outstanding aircraft.

Execution of North American Aviation's "Foreign Release" agreement eventually resulted in production of one of the world's finest fighters of all time, the P-51D Mustang. The efforts of Rolls-Royce's Ron Harker and the AAF's Lt. Col. Thomas Hitchcock in creating that weapon have not really been fully recognized. Lacking the foresight of these men, many persons of influence detrimentally affected the progress of such aircraft as the Lightning I and II, the XP-58 and a host of other designs, even as they pursued their chores without guilt. When financial gratuities are involved in such decision making, it jeopardizes the entire war effort. But even unrewarded bad decision making can court disaster.

*To mediocrity, genius is unforgivable* - E. Hibbard.

---

2. *The rather complex history of the XP-58 (Model 20) and of the Lightning-like XP-49 has been fully detailed in this writer's magazine articles published in 1980. The story involves bureaucratic bungling and indecision, political interference, thousands of wasted manhours and the decision to build dozens of Hughes XF-11 reconnaissance aircraft when a more suitable aircraft could have been available for production at least three years earlier. Logical direction of the project would have resulted in overcoming any and all difficulties. What any such project really needs is cooperative and efficient teamwork of the type exemplified by the Kelsey-Johnson relationship. Good engineering, a serving of pragmatism and firm, unrelenting leadership and cooperation can take on almost any challenge.*

# CHAPTER 7

# The Specters of War and Compressibility

Unidentified fighter pilots of an unidentified squadron in the 4th Interceptor Command are shown rushing toward their P-38Es as part of a practice interception in the autumn of 1941. This was obviously a media event, but it was within weeks of becoming the real thing. The "attack" on Los Angeles in February 1942 was a false alarm, but it did not stop the AA gunners from firing no less than 1,800 anti-aircraft shells at mysterious targets. (James Grose Coll.)

A October in Southern California is often punctuated by the sudden appearance of high winds blowing in from the deserts, winds that are pre-heated as they cross the desert landscape that has been scorched by the blazing sun. Summer in the southwest always seems to be off schedule from the rest of America, possibly extending from about mid-July to mid-October. Temperatures in Needles and Blythe can be over 100 $^0$ F at midnight, and car or house air-conditioning was as rare as television in 1941. But November in Los Angeles could be absolutely marvelous. Factories rarely, if ever, belched smoke; traffic jams were rarities; water pollution was not even a subject for discussion.

The aircraft industry was largely decentralized, with Lockheed-Vega located about 11 miles northwest of downtown Los Angeles, Douglas Long Beach's new "blackout" plant some 20 miles south of the city hall and the Santa Monica facility located almost on the western coastline. Douglas El Segundo was outside the Los Angeles city limits, but next to Mines Field where the nearly new North American plant had been built.

Southern California's aircraft industry started the year of 1941 with an explosive $1 billion backlog of orders and about 57,000 employees. Executives expected the total of employees to number about 100,000 by the end of the year. And yet . . . few people seemed to believe America would be at war in the foreseeable future. Typically, or so it seemed, this young person had a brand new 1941 Ford convertible, a well-paying job and there seemed to be no end of "dates" in spite of six-day work schedules. England was on every mind, every day. But it seemed to be 10,000 miles away. At least from Los Angeles County.

*A real wartime look was evident at the summer maneuvers in the south in 1941. Revetments there were certainly better protection than anything afforded for the defense of Hickam Field or Clark Air Base bombers or fighters five or six months later. Performance of AAF aircraft in 1942 in the Pacific areas (except Alaskan) was generally dismal for a dozen reasons. Training efforts for years had totally missed the actualities of war. (AAF)*

Probably nobody has the slightest idea of how many lives were totally changed by publication of *Fortune* magazine in March 1941, but that was a truly magnificent issue devoted to the American aviation industry. It opened with a color photograph of a London business street devastated by a bombing raid; then it went on to tell the story of air power and the aviation industry growth, especially in Southern California. But even the knowledgeable management of Time, Inc., failed to anticipate the reorganization of military forces that would create the United States Army Air Forces on June 22, under the command of Maj. Gen. H. H. Arnold. It was a master stroke at a crucial time.

November 4 was another one of those crisp, sparkling Southern California days that was looked upon as an indigenous part of the landscape by residents of the Los Angeles basin. There weren't any freeways, only the Arroyo Seco expressway and a new multi-lane highway under construction through Cahuenga Pass between Hollywood and the semi-arid San Fernando Valley. The populous east end of that valley, with its industry strung almost like parade flags along the route of San Fernando Road and the Southern Pacific Railroad main line, presented a remarkable contrast with the vast expanse of sparsely populated farmland and orchards of the middle and west valley areas.

San Fernando Road made a sharp turn across the northbound-southbound tracks of the SP at a junction with Empire Avenue and Victory Place, a venue called "Turkey Crossing." It was there, within yards of the entrance to Lockheed Aircraft's executive offices, that a fast freight and a truck bearing crates of turkeys met informally in the past.

In less than a decade, much of which involved the struggle of this nation to recover from the deepest depression in its entire history, Lockheed Aircraft Corporation had dug itself out of bankruptcy and expanded from its embarrassingly modest beginning in ramshackle buildings in a seemingly uncontrolled growth toward downtown Burbank to the southeast and North Hollywood to the west. Growth was so rapid that the private airstrip operated by the business had become partially swamped with half-completed P-38s, Hudsons and military Lodestars and could no longer be considered an airport. As a result, all aircraft had to be moved over city streets at night to Burbank's main airport, Lockheed Air Terminal. Historic corporate landmark buildings, like the Mission Glass Works and Empire China Company, disappeared behind new facades or under second-story additions. As the *Fortune* editors described California aircraft factories, they tended to

bear less resemblance to actual factories than to giant-sized sheds with sawtooth roofs.

The Vega subsidiary of Lockheed had relinquished its rather short occupancy of the old red brick Empire China building to the parent organization and was in the process of manufacturing Vega Ventura and B-34 bombers in its brand new 3/4-million-square-foot plant adjoining the air terminal's runways. Venturas were in full production, and the first of many hundreds of B-17s to be built under the so-called BVD Plan (actually B-D-V, for Boeing, Douglas, Vega) were moving down the assembly lines. Although there was at least one B-17E on display on November 4, it was a Boeing-built airplane. Vega did not deliver its first B-17, an F model, until June 1942.[1]

All across America, people were beginning to plan their Thanksgiving holiday, after which Christmas buying would begin in earnest. But American newspapers were crowded with headline stories of Nazi Germany's victories in Russia. The British had pretty well recovered from the *Luftwaffe* assault on the United Kingdom in that classical fight called the Battle of Britain, and bombing raids on Nazi-controlled Europe were increasing in intensity.

Short, balding Ralph Virden, at age 43 one of Lockheed's key test pilots, wasn't thinking of any of those things as he completed his briefing for a very special test flight. Engineers John Margwarth and Ward Beman had developed a specific flight profile based, to a large extent, on a report prepared by Phil Colman, a young aerodynamicist working for Kelly Johnson. That report, completed in July 1940, anticipated compressibility problems at a time when virtually every aerodynamics engineer in the world was oblivious to the problems. However, before the proposed test program could be initiated by Johnson, Maj. Signa Gilkey and his YP-38 had their historical encounter with both compressibility and tail buffet. By direction from Wright Field, the intensive buffet and compressibility identification and cure program was initiated on a priority basis. It became clear that there was a very real possibility that production of P-38s would be terminated if the "flutter"

---

1. *One post-war Lockheed document shows the Vega B-17 as a Model 17. That is a gross fiction, generated without contractual foundation. All actual B-17 bombers built at Plant A-1 were produced without any Lockheed-Vega corporate number being assigned. Only the single XB-38 and XB-40 airplanes had model numbers assigned, and they were Model 134 and 139 respectively. Any Model 17 assignment would have been back in 1937 or 1938 at the latest.*

and uncontrolled dive tendency (compressibility tuck) could not be solved . . . promptly.

As Margwarth and Beman talked, the terribly self-confident Virden was enjoying the sun while concentrating on this latest in a series of crucial tests in which he was a leading character. Together with his friends Milo Burcham and Jimmy Mattern, he was a key player in the trio of pilots considered to be "tops" on the Lockheed flight test team. The two test engineers, having been instrumental in developing the wing fillet that solved the buffet problem just weeks earlier, were extremely anxious to find out exactly what effect their newest device would have on dive recovery at higher altitudes.

The first YP-38 had not flown until September 1940, and was involved in such rigorous testing that it could not be committed to any dive program, especially the one developed by Phil Colman. In autumn of 1941 there were many Lightning types that could carry on with routine testing. Old 2202, that initial YP, had been remarkably successful in completing every test as a prototype. By September 1941, it had been totally committed to the compressibility program. Burcham, Mattern, and Virden took turns on the test program established by Colman, and according to Mattern the testing had gone well until November 3. In a revealing 1973 interview, the only surviving member of the testing trio (then) recalled that things got very "sticky."

According to Mattern, "We had been conducting dive tests in the 30-35,000-foot altitude range, reaching *indicated* airspeeds up to 295 mph. These speeds were coming very close to the absolute limit for the airframe." It is important to recall that Maj. Signa Gilkey had reported being in serious difficulty at 32,000 feet while noting an indicated airspeed of 300 to 320 mph. While it could be argued that such a speed would be in excess of a Mach's Number of 0.68 (Mach's number was the ONLY terminology in those days), there is very little chance that the indicator was calibrated for testing. Furthermore, Kelly Johnson has stated that the static source for instruments provided erroneous results in high-altitude dive conditions. (That latter point was a "key" to much of the contentious dialogue prevailing over the years.)

"The engineers wanted us to go on past 300 mph above 30,000 feet," Mattern continued, "but Burcham and I declined. But Virden was a very stubborn little guy and was determined to do it. We spent half the night trying to talk him out of it."

Although Mattern had lost the black, curly air he had in the early 1930s, he was so well known that it didn't matter that he looked more like a business executive than a test pilot. Milo Burcham would have been properly cast in motion pictures as a tester. But Virden didn't have notoriety as an asset and he looked like anything but a test pilot. However, his career story would probably rival fiction. No real detailed account can be provided because nobody could begin to recall all of the events in his flying lifetime.

After several years as a barnstorming flyer, he joined pioneering Pacific Air Transport in 1926 as a reserve pilot. Piloting fragile, underpowered mailplanes between San Francisco, Medford (Oregon) and Seattle (Washington), he built a fabulous reputation for safety. Virden rarely wore a parachute while at the controls of stuttering Ryan M-2, Boeing 40B-4 and Travel Air mail planes on routes over some of the worst territory along the West Coast. Weather was subject to unpredictable and radical changes; at times it was even necessary for the skimpy ground crews, assisted by the pilot, to literally dig the airplanes out of the snow. But Virden was renowned for his ability to fly on schedule and for never having lost an airplane. Later on he flew Boeing 80As and 247Ds, then moved on to Douglas DC-3s as the airline was folded into United Air Lines. His career as a mail and passenger pilot lasted for 13 years, and by 1941 he had logged approximately 15,500 hours in the air.

The Yippee that Virden was going to fly on November 4 had been fully instrumented, and a major change had been made in the elevator. It had been equipped with spring (servo) tabs, one at each extremity of the control surface. These large-area tabs were designed to come into operation only if the control yoke force exceeded 30 pounds. Whenever the higher forces were encountered, as they would be in high-speed dive recovery, the spring tabs would provide proportionally increased leverage to assist the pilot in overcoming the loads. Since high speeds and sharp maneuvers at low altitudes (where the air density was greater) would result in tremendous leverage (expressed as Q)², Virden was warned to restrict his low-altitude speed and maneuvering. A warning placard had even been taped to the instrument panel on Burcham's orders.

Why was it deemed necessary to experiment with spring tabs, wing-to-central nacelle fillets, elevator rigging changes and a host of other alterations to combat the obvious problems of compressibility? Frankly, there was virtually no information about the effects of compressibility on an airfoil. Few noted scientists were familiar with Dr. Mach's Number except that the speed of sound had a number of 1. Kelly Johnson's 1937 report reveals that he was warning aeronautical people that the compressibility phenomenon was going to be troublesome in the near future. He and his close associates were treading into an aviation minefield.

The P-38 design was a paradox. It was a remarkably clean

design, but one that had been mated with a high-lift, relatively thick wing as required by obsolete Air Corps requirements. If range on internal fuel and a very high rate of climb had not been mandated, Johnson would have employed an airfoil no thicker than the one used on Supermarine's Spitfire. But a fighter for America with a flight duration of less than two hours might as well have been constructed of lead.

Back in 1937, Clarence "Kelly" Johnson's report, endorsed by his immediate supervisor, Hall Hibbard, had been directed at Air Corps officials to warn that "as airplane speeds and operating altitudes increase . . . consideration must be given to the effects of compressibility." Army Air Corps engineering data of that era (and for years later) – data that rigidly controlled designers of aircraft – completely ignored compressibil-

---

2. *The seldom discussed Q factor is expressed as follows:*
$Q = \frac{1}{2} PV^2$, *where P equals air density and V equals velocity of airflow over an airfoil. Therefore, it can be seen that high speed at low level (dense air) increases airfoil deflection loads tremendously.*

ity effects, even after it was known that propellers were affected by compressibility. In an office memo to corporation president Robert Gross in December 1938, timed to coincide with completion of the XP-38 prototype, Hibbard had explained the problem in this manner: "In order to have the minimum possible drag, it is essential that air flow smoothly over any part of the aircraft structure. As the speed is increased, the air tends to be 'splashed' by the leading edge of the wing, more or less like the prow of a boat at high speed . . . As one approaches the compressibility range, the air is thrown so violently up and down that it does not have a chance to flow over the wing in a proper manner." Hibbard went on to state that the problem became "very serious at 500 mph (TAS) and over."

Rather logically, any person might ask – in late 1941 – why the problem had not affected other high-speed aircraft, e.g., the Mustang, P-47, Fw 190, Bf 109, Spitfire and Hurricane, among others. Two or three responsible answers pretty well cover the subject. The prototype NA-73X (Mustang) had flown for the first time less than a year earlier. It was considered a low-level aircraft, and was absolutely flat above 20,000 feet. Republic's XP-47B had not flown until May 6, 1941, at a time when the YP-38 was already deep into the trouble. As test pilot Ron Harker has said, the Spitfires (at least through the Mk. V type) were inferior to the Mustang I. They really were not combat capable above 25,000 feet until the Merlin 47 and 61 series engines (two-stage, two-speed supercharging) became available late in 1941. Favoring the Spitfire was a wing with a very low chord/thickness ratio. Also, the ailerons tended to float upward in a dive, acting as dive flaps.

The Hurricane had a very thick wing section, was never really a high-level combat aircraft and most certainly did not tend to accelerate rapidly into a dive from high altitudes. Little is known about Messerschmitt or Focke-Wulf encounters with compressibility, but in long dives they may well have lost many airplanes without really knowing the cause. It is well to remember that the Nazi aircraft were really not compelled to attacked Allied aircraft at high altitudes until the B-17 raids were well under way in 1943. Finally, it is important to remember that the P-38 type was really the first 400-mph (TAS) high-altitude fighter.

Everybody around Lockheed and Vega was in a pretty festive mood on November 4. Over at Plant B-1, the main Lockheed plant, some 25,000 employees had gathered together during the noontime lunch break for a rally. They were there to hear none other than Maj. Gen. H. H. "Hap" Arnold, the new chief of the Army Air Forces, praise the performance of the company team for its remarkable production accomplishments and for the quality of its products – with full knowledge that the "flutter" scare was a false alarm and that the buffet problem had been 90 percent eliminated. Arnold and other prominent officials were on hand, and a number of key Lockheed officials were also there. The general, who usually agreed with Ben Kelsey's technical opinions, had been greatly interested in the twin-boom Lightning almost from its inception date. One reason for his visit was to evaluate production progress and to inspire the workers to even greater efforts. P-38Es were being completed at an ever increasing

rate after the September-October changeover from the P-38D, which in spite of the D designation was not to be considered a "combat ready" aircraft. There were also numerous RAF 322-Bs to be seen in various stages of completion.

The definitive E model of the AAF Lightning did not, at that moment, have provision for carrying external drop tanks – in conformance with directives (and thinking) dating back to the early 1930s – but Kelsey and Kelly Johnson were already in the process of mixing an illegal brew called "range extension." Preliminary studies were conducted not long after Arnold's November visit to Burbank. As Kelsey said, "When the need for more range became imperative, we were ready because of initial unauthorized work accomplished by Lockheed at my request." That need was the need to prove that range extension was already a *fait accompli*, involving availability of engineering drawings, completion of tooling and at least a start on production. Such requirements were to become evident only too soon.

Three Hudson coastal-reconnaissance bombers with RAF markings, a brand new P-38E in full camouflage markings (and with the

newly adopted 20-mm cannon up front) and the first of many Vega Ventura bombers (with Jimmy Mattern at the controls) performed flyby demonstrations for the crowd. When the rally came to an end, employees and visitors alike returned to their routine activities.

John Margwarth had been outside most of the day, intent on obtaining valuable data from Virden's efforts. As usual there was a great deal of activity in and around the small metal flight test hangar, located a few hundred feet west of the old United Air Lines maintenance hangar. The rallies at Lockheed and at the new Vega plant had broken up, and the crowds had gone back to building airplanes.

"It was then," John related, "that we heard Virden's plane heading

*Five-cent daily newspapers appeared on Wednesday morning, November 5, 1941, carrying screaming headlines about a P-38 Lightning that had crashed in Glendale, California, on the previous afternoon. It involved a "500-mile-an-hour ride," said the picture caption. The facts: Test pilot Ralph Virden had crashed to his death in YP-38 c/n 2202. (Warren Bodie Archives)*

72

down toward Burbank. It was about 15 minutes after he had completed the last of the scheduled test dives. He was seen to pull up sharply, and something broke away from the aircraft. At the same time, the air was filled with a totally unfamiliar sound."

Immediately to the southeast of Burbank lay the moderately affluent city of Glendale, its famous Grand Central Air Terminal separated from huge and beautiful Griffith Park near the end of the Santa Monica Mountain chain by the infamous Los Angeles River. A local real estate dealer, I.C. Thomas, heard the familiar muffled Allison sound. He leaped from his desk as it seemed unusually near and ran outside just as a peculiar scream overwhelmed the typical engine roar. A piece of the P-38 empennage appeared to break off from the airplane as he caught sight of the Yippee.

"I could see the aluminum tailpiece glistening in the sun as it floated away from the rest of the airplane," Mr. Thomas reported. "The plane itself fell off on its side and started to zigzag to the earth. I just knew it was going to crash. 'There goes the tail . . . he can't possibly get out; he's going to crash!' I shouted to a friend who came running up." As an observer, Mr. Thomas was in the best of all positions to come to that astute conclusion. "The ship slammed into a house about 300 feet from my office," he said, "and people started to run in every direction. As soon as it hit the house at the front porch it burst into flames." The witness's eyes had been riveted to the YP as it fell to see if the pilot was going to be able to bail out, but it was in an inverted spin, "falling like a leaf," as he put it.

Glendale police and fire department vehicles converged

on Elm Street very quickly. Fires in the remains of the aircraft and two damaged houses were extinguished within minutes. The YP-38, minus the empennage, was on its back with one crumpled wing draped from the top of a stucco wall of the modest California bungalow like a silver shower curtain.

Within minutes the entire area was overrun with spectators and the curious trampling lawns and generally speculating on what had happened. Army Air Force student mechanics from the local civilian contract school that was based on the airport pressed close to the YP-38 remains. It was a rude introduction to what might be ahead for some of those same graduates of the Curtiss-Wright Institute when they arrived at their overseas stations. Elm Street on that spectacular Tuesday afternoon took on the appearance of Empire Avenue and San Fernando Road at a shift change instead of its normal look of a quiet, tree-lined residential lane.

Other witnesses were quoted as saying the YP-38 was booming westward at "blinding" speed in a shallow dive when the tail assembly "came off and simply floated away." One reliable witness was F. B. Berger, chief tower operator at nearby Grand Central Air Terminal. "I saw the plane in a dive at 1,500 feet," he said. "The tail was off and in the air." Many eye witnesses said there was no doubt that the entire tail assembly had broken away at about 3,000 feet. Conjecture was that the throttles had been pushed wide open by Virden, possibly in a last moment attempt to reach the open ground near the L.A. River or Griffith Park. Perhaps that accounted, at least in part, for the unusual sound made by the plane in those final moments before it crashed.

Kelly Johnson, on the other hand, had different thoughts. "I was back in my office when I heard Virden's plane screaming toward the plant. That most unusual sound probably resulted from the propellers striking the air at an angle abnormal to the line of flight," he speculated. "That is somewhat like the blade of a helicopter rotor changing sound when a cyclic-pitch change is made. It may also be that Virden's propeller tips went supersonic." Whatever caused it, the result was eerie.

Jack Jensen, owner of the house at 1147 Elm Street, played a most unusual role in the unfolding drama. By the time Police Captain W. E. Hegi managed to get to the crash scene, the Jensen house was burning and the roof and one side had been pretty badly damaged. Expecting the worst, the officer rushed inside to check on any victims. The kitchen had been demolished when one of the engines smashed through the flat roof. He was amazed to enter a bedroom and find the owner lying on the bed, but

*One wing of the Yippee (YP) lies mangled against a California bungalow at 1147 Elm Street in Glendale as many student mechanics from the Army contract school milled around. Weird sounds from the diving aircraft could be heard for miles before it crashed. The tailless fighter landed upside down and burned, but the slight fire went out quickly. (Warren Bodie Archives)*

73

with no evidence of injury. Actually, Jensen was still fast asleep! He had slept through the entire episode and was surprised when he finally saw what had happened.

Mr. Thomas was correct when he reported that the YP-38 was inverted when it was falling. It impacted upside down, burying the large canopy in soft earth. Although that did delay the removal of Virden from the cockpit, it had prevented the flames from reaching him. Among the early arrivals at the crash scene were engineer John Margwarth and P-38 Chief Project Engineer Dick Pulver. Although they were travelling in separate cars, both had scorched a path across Burbank on San Fernando Road, arriving in Glendale about the same time.

When interviewed, Margwarth remembered Virden as "being like a father to me. He would do anything within reason to please his army of friends and admirers." Also interviewed at the scene by newsmen, one Lockheed official – most likely Dick Pulver – was quoted as saying: "The airplane was valued at $75,000 to $100,000. It was the second P-38 built, having been completed in September 1940. It was no longer a production type." He was referring to the fact that, sequentially, the P-38, P-38D and the current P-38E type had replaced it in production.

(No other stories about the Virden crash appeared during the war, which engulfed America just a month later. When books and magazine articles began to appear in the years following the cessation of all hostilities, without exception it was reported that Virden was killed in a Lightning usually referred to as the "swoop-tail" P-38. That particular aircraft was actually a modified P-38E that did not even fly with the upswept tail until a year *after* Virden died.)

(Test pilot Tony LeVier's career was enhanced by the Virden crash. LeVier was working as a production test pilot and ferrying pilot from April 1941 until he was asked to join Experimental Flight Test in mid-1942 by Milo Burcham, ostensibly to replace Virden and to support Mattern, whose work load was rapidly increasing for a number of related reasons.)

It seems remarkable that even Dick Pulver did not know what the actual price of a YP-38 was at the time he was interviewed . . . unless that "official" was not Pulver. According to the respected *AAF Statistical Digest* (1945), the actual price of an "average" P-38 until the end of 1941 was $134,280. That first YP-38 and its 12 carbon copies actually cost $167,750 apiece, unless that initial handbuilt c/n 2202 was more expensive. (Observers of history should find it interesting that each Martin B-26 was priced almost exactly at twice the price of an "average" 1941 Lightning.)

The YP-38 in which Ralph Virden perished was a Model 122-62-02, Company c/n 2202, Air Corps serial AC39-689.

Calm, but visibly shaken, Lockheed president Robert Gross had consented to a press conference later that same day. "Ralph Virden," Gross said softly, "was a great pilot, but even greater, a man engaged in extremely dangerous work for his country."

Being a test pilot in those pioneering aviation days – and that is especially true in connection with testing of military aircraft – was extremely dangerous work. The general accident rate for aircraft in the 1930s was very high, while the tremendous push for higher performance that was in vogue in the 1940s made it highly unlikely that any prototype and development test aircraft would survive until retirement as a mechanics' trainer.

Designers were pushing the limits of aerodynamic knowledge and materials strength in their quest for performance, often exceeding the limits of their own ability to calculate solutions in advance. High-speed wind tunnel performance was falling behind actual aircraft performance. Working out most mathematical problems with a K&E slide rule or a Friden calculator was an agonizingly slow, tedious process.

There can be little argument about which YP-38s could be classed as the most famous – or perhaps that should be infamous. The one in which Virden lost his life (c/n 2202) was also the first to fly, by a margin of many months, and it certainly was the most photographed of all Yippees. Among the most famous airmen to fly it were Marshall Headle, Milo Burcham, James Mattern, Virden and "Swede" Parker. In its 14 months of existence, it had been subjected to an intensive flight regimen.

The service test fighter that Maj. Signa Gilkey had pulled out of that rather terrifying dive of more than 25,000 feet to recover at an altitude of only 7,000 feet was probably the first airplane in history to approach a Mach's Number of 0.70 (now, Mach No.). All evidence points to that airplane as being the second YP, c/n 2203, an airplane flown frequently during the service test phase by 1st Lt. Ralph Garman at Selfridge Field. Garman noted in his own records that the YP-38 was a maintenance headache when compared to the obsolescent Seversky P-35s and Curtiss P-36As, but that observation seems tainted by the old apples and oranges syndrome.

However, serious maintenance problems with the airplane could have explained why it had either two Allison F2R or F2L engines (both propellers rotating in one direction) when Gilkey had that first unsettling encounter with the new phenomenon of compressibility tuck. By December 1941,[3] that same aircraft was at Langley Field, Virginia, being prepared for mounting in the full-size wind tunnel. On December 11, it was securely positioned atop the tunnel supporting pylons for the first time in preparation for drag analysis tests and for studies of buffeting and diving tendencies associated with YP-38 airplanes.

Before delving into that troublesome issue, it is necessary to look at the probable cause of the Virden crash, take a comprehensive look at Phil Colman's 1940 test plan that led directly to the November 4 episode (and many others) and, finally, to learn about the outcome of Johnson's efforts to press

---

3. *Inexplicably, several Wartime Memo Reports by A. L. Erickson plainly refer to an NACA RMR dated March 1941 that states that a YP-38 was tested in the full-scale tunnel earlier in that same year. Photos of the second YP-38 taken immediately after it was mounted in the large tunnel on December 11, 1941, were clearly dated in that caption and on other pictures during the December test period. No YP-38 was available for tunnel testing in January- February 1941, and a second report by the same two authors was dated March 1942. It seems clear that a typographical date error was made on the one RMR and that the error was compounded in reference sections of several other reports. NASA has not been able to provide an answer.*

*OPPOSITE LEFT: Just a few miles up San Fernando Road from the Glendale crash site, Lockheed's factory looked like this as the California winter approached. The airstrip was no longer usable, especially for the P-38 types. Every airplane had to be towed over city streets to L.A.T. at night. The Buena Vista storage lot is at top right.*

*RIGHT: Full-scale (actual YP-38) Lightning sticks its nose into the Langley Field NACA wind tunnel on Christmas Eve, 1941. That fuselage extension had been grafted on, but there were no wing center section fillets because they had not yet been developed. (NACA)*

forward on the frontiers of aviation by getting NACA to do more of the pioneering work the committee was created to do originally.

Nobody will ever know what possessed Ralph Virden to make a final unauthorized dive toward Burbank that day. Some people concluded that he wanted to impress the rally crowds with a flashing flyby, but by the time he descended the crowds had dispersed. Since he had already completed the last test in his schedule with no reported difficulty, there would have been no connection with that dive. He was fully aware that a low-level pullout at high speed could not be accomplished successfully. That "Q factor" discussed earlier was unforgiving. Kelly Johnson concluded that the spring tab operating link broke before the tail came off, causing the elevator to go to full deflection. At an altitude of less than 2,000 feet, speed in excess of 300 mph would have loaded the tail booms far in excess of design criteria.

**B**Lockheed's Hibbard, Johnson and Colman wanted NACA to operate their Langley Memorial wind tunnel (full-size), their 8-foot high-speed unit and (eventually) the 16-foot Ames Aeronautical Laboratory wind tunnel at the highest possible speeds. NACA officials declined, contending that severe tunnel damage or destruction might occur. Therefore, the late 1941 testing for drag analysis and for buffet/diving tendency research was limited to 78 to 100 mph in the large LMAL tunnel. The engineers from Burbank considered such testing useless in pursuit of an answer to "compressibility tuck." By December 24, the fuselage gondola had been lengthened and the wing chord between the booms had been increased. Other tests eventually led to improved Prestone coolant scoops (as used on P-38J and L versions) and to rework of one P-38E into an airplane called "Swordfish." But several months were to pass before Johnson was able to enlist the support of General

Arnold for overruling NACA official objections to higher wind tunnel speeds.

Returning briefly to 1940, the month of July witnessed completion of the report by aerodynamicist Phil Colman that outlined the need for a pioneering dive test program to provide data – then unavailable – about the effects of compressibility and other critical problems "likely to be encountered by this new high-performance fighter." Colman's report, countersigned by Johnson, was issued nearly two months before the first YP-38 even left the ground. Although they knew that compressibility would tend to slow their aircraft in vertical dives, they knew nothing of the aerodynamic devilry lying in wait to teach them a lesson.

Colman laid out a program of vertical dives from 35,000 feet, using modest power application. It introduced a situation that had never been attempted before . . . anywhere. Few, if any, high-speed aircraft had ever ventured into that realm above the earth, and it is a certainty that no pilot of such an aircraft had ever even contemplated entering a vertical descent at the conclusion of a long climb. Lockheed's idea was to dive until reaching a constant indicated airspeed at 16,000 feet, continuing that dive at 13,000 feet and then executing a 3-4g constant-radius pullout. As Colman planned it:

(a) the pullout would be completed at about 7000 feet,
(b) in a vertical dive, the TAS would never exceed 570 mph,
(c) a true speed (TAS) of 568 mph would be equal to a TIAS of 450 mph, or approximately 438 mph indicated airspeed.*
*(Most certainly not at high altitude.)

He provided a specific example of what could be expected, although not even the scientists at Cal Tech could provide any specifics on what might be encountered. Little was known about Dr. Mach's Number; temperature effects were ignored for the most part; airspeed indicator calibration was known to be anything but accurate for scientific data, and variables were plentiful.

Colman's example is quoted: "If the constant TIAS is 400 mph, the TAS is 513 mph at 16,000 feet and 488 mph at 13,000 feet. Mach's Number is then 0.715 at 16,000 and 0.67 at 13,000. Predicted instrument IAS is 425 mph at 16,000 feet; 422 mph at 13,000 feet."

There wasn't a design team in the world that had a better grasp on what was likely to go on up there in the blue. Colman, for example, even specified the use of 750 bhp per engine at 2000 rpm. Three other dives were to be conducted in the series using various true indicated airspeeds down to a minimum of 300 mph for comparison purposes.

Months elapsed (in 1941) before Kelsey and Lockheed felt that enough P-38 aircraft were available to commit one to the dangerous dive program. One telephone call from Patterson Field had upset the applecart. Just a few weeks before Colman's program was to get under way, Maj. Gilkey came within a whisker of duplicating the company's test plan. The major even recovered from the terrifying dive at about 7,000 feet, just about where the aerodynamicist said recovery should occur. But what the AAF pilot and airplane encountered on that 28,000-foot descent had never been anticipated. Nature cooperated in every way as Lockheed threw its resources into the buffet and compressibility tuck program in the following weeks. Each test pilot learned that virtually every facet of the Gilkey flight was repeated like a carbon imprint.

Corporate politics briefly entered the picture that last peacetime summer, as was noted earlier, when famous test pilot Vance Breese was paid a gratuitous amount of money to aid in finding a solution to the problems quickly. Virtually no corroborative material is available to support a rash of rumors, but it appears that Breese would not take off unless every detail affecting the flight was perfect. Burcham and Mattern were not the least bit happy with the situation as Breese acted like a prima donna. There is no evidence that he contributed anything valid to the compressibility program. Nobody in any level at Lockheed wanted to talk about it nearly a half century later. Vance Breese was paid off and left the program under a cloud of discontent.

By way of contrast, it seems sad that the 40-year-old Gilkey was all but ignored. Yet, he was heroic in staying with his airplane and saving it although he was combating both the "flutter" (actually buffet) and almost totally unknown compressibility problems simultaneously. He was not alone in believing that the ol' demon flutter was in his YP-38 that day. Flutter had probably killed a battalion of pilots since World War I. (Col.

Gilkey was the first postwar commander of the test center at Muroc Army Air Field, later Edwards AFFTC.)

"Bird" Col. Ben Kelsey – he received rapid promotions in 1941-42 – was Kelly Johnson's close ally in gaining Gen. Arnold's support. It is likely that he got Arnold to apply the necessary pressure on NACA directorship that led to commitment of at least two wind tunnels to high-speed tests (up to Mach 0.75) early in 1942. Lockheed furnished a 1/6-scale mahogany P-38 model for testing in the 8-foot high-speed tunnel at Langley. A great many tests were conducted that winter, leading to an NACA report in May and a Lockheed report on the 4th of May.

Kelly Johnson's report, entitled "Study of Diving Characteristics of the P-38," was based on his analysis of the data flowing from Virginia early in 1942. It aimed at analyzing and explaining the problems of compressibility, especially as related to the effects of P-38s. Explaining the problems in those days was difficult; trying to correct the problems was far more difficult. As Johnson wrote, "Without elaborating on the technical causes . . . data will be presented to show:

"(1) The maximum speed that it is possible to attain . . . in a vertical (90 degree) dive from the service ceiling, using military power.

"(2) The airspeed at which buffeting will start at an acceleration of 1g.

"(3) The airspeed at which the dive tendency (tuck) is maximized.

"(4) The indicated airspeed at each altitude that it is possible to attain in level flight.

"(5) From the preceding, the margin of speed available for maneuvering without encountering either buffet or dive characteristics."

Johnson explained that at a critical value of airspeed, which varies with altitude, a condition exists at which airflow over the wing separates to produce a special form of stall. At higher airspeeds, the flow separation spreads over the upper surface and the airplane tends to become noseheavy because of a wing diving moment and a shift in the center of lift (aft). Downloads on the empennage virtually disappear rapidly and, of course, there is a loss of pitch control.

His figures revealed that at a Mach's No. of 0.65, airplane drag increased violently as a shock wave formed on the wing center section.

Actual testing proved that buffeting developed at a Mach's No. (M=) of 0.675 with an acceleration of 1g; at higher accelera-

*It doesn't look like much, but that formed piece of aluminum may have saved the military career of the P-38 from an early demise. It is the all-important wing-fuselage fillet that was added to prevent tail buffet, something that a few Wright Field chieftains insisted was tail flutter. Lockheed soon proved they were wrong, but that did not change their minds about installing the external weights on the elevator. Failure to ensure a tight fit of the fillet could lead to impaired flight characteristics. (LAC)*

tions, buffet was encountered at lower M= numbers. Shortly after buffet was encountered, the diving tendency (tuck) started. This tendency reached its zenith at M=0.74.

Wind tunnel tests indicated that a horizontal stabilizer angle revision, frequently described in publications as the "big solution" for the buffeting problem, was reset to its initial position. The report stated that it was necessary "to ensure the proper distribution of loads on the tail when the maximum tail load occurs." It seems to be obvious that any buffet improvement was more than offset by loads that could not be safely tolerated by the airframe. When intensive testing is conducted in a proper wind tunnel, many satisfactory solutions to a specific problem can be achieved in a matter of minutes or hours. But incorporating that same aerodynamic change in a production airframe might result in a major interruption of production or could even prove impossible to introduce into the design.

More practical solutions to the compressibility problem had to be found, but that did not happen until about a year later. While that specific performance problem plagued the P-38s in the ETO until the advent of P-38J-25-LOs and all subsequent aircraft, the problem really never manifested itself in the MTO, India, the Pacific arena, North Africa or the Aleutians. Enemy aircraft in those theaters of operation rarely were a cause for any combat above 25,000 feet. For a number of reasons, it was virtually impossible to encounter compressibility tuck in any P-38 types if the dive was entered at 25,000 feet or less. Numerous test flights confirmed that.

In the ETO, things were much different. U.S. Bomber Command tactics frequently involved very high-altitude operations. German fighters often had excellent performance at high levels, and operating in a zone, they could use high power in lengthy climbs, attack their targets until fuel and ammunition were exhausted, and then return to their local base for rearming. While the Lightnings were in their natural element high up, some pilots got into trouble with exuberant pursuit of a diving enemy target. Fortunes of war being what they are, P-38 pilots seldom were placed in a situation where they might encounter the phenomenon during combat. The vast majority of compressibility tuck encounters occurred when some pilots deliberately decided to find out what would occur if Tech Order limits were exceeded.

C Whenever the Lightning becomes the subject of conversation, one predominant question is usually asked: Why didn't they install Rolls-Royce Merlin engines in any P-38s? Considering the success of late series Mustangs powered by Merlins, it is a logical question.

Ward Beman was not empowered to include the Merlin in his 1939 alternate powerplant study for the P-38, but somewhat more than a year later Lockheed did complete a prophetic analytical study involving the relatively new (at that time) Rolls-Royce Merlin XX. Detroit's Packard Motors Co. had been selected by the British to produce several thousand of the liquid-cooled engines that featured a single-stage, two-speed mechanical supercharger. The Americanized version was designated Merlin 28. Compared to the Merlin 61 high-altitude engine that became available in 1943, the Series (Mark) XX was really a low-altitude engine. However, the Merlin XX was a first-rate engine in the time frame of the YP-38, 322-B, P-38 and P-38D. A summary comparison of the new Allison V-1710 F-series and the Merlin XX was completed and is included herein. Rather unexpectedly, the Allison-powered P-38 weighed in about 1,000 pounds less than the proposed Rolls-Royce version (at least on paper), and it had a superior rate of climb and service ceiling. Points in favor of the British engine were (a) higher speed in a broader altitude

| Analytical Study of P-38 Aircraft Using Allison F-Series and Rolls-Royce Merlin XX Supercharged Engines | | |
| --- | --- | --- |
| | Allison V-1710-F2 | Rolls-Royce Merlin XX |
| Supercharger Type | Turbo | Geardriven |
| Rating - Military | | |
| BHP | 1150 at 20,000 feet | 1170 at 21,000 feet |
| RPM | 3000 | 3000 |
| Critical Alt. | 20,000 ft. | 21,000 ft. |
| Rating - Continuous | | |
| BHP | 1000 at 20,000 ft. | 875 at 20,000 ft. |
| RPM | 2600 | 2650 |
| P-38 Gross Weight | 13,500 lbs. | 14,500 lbs. |
| High Speed at Critical Altitude | 425 mph | 431 mph |
| Time to climb | | |
| 15,000 ft. | — | 5 mins. |
| 20,000 ft. | 5.94 mins. | — |
| Takeoff over 50 ft. Obstacle | 2200 ft. | 2010 ft. |
| Takeoff Power | 1150 bhp | 1280 bhp |

envelope, (b) elimination of turbo intercoolers, (c) overall simpler installation and (d) increased reliability, at least over Europe. (In 1941, after the study was completed, nothing was known of that problem, so it was not even a factor in the report.)

Air Corps interest in the British Rolls-Royce engine at that time was absolutely minimal. Pure speculation would have to be involved in any analysis of the powerplant decisions at Wright Field in the late 1930s and early 1940s, but the blind dedication to such engines as the Wright Tornado, Pratt & Whitney XH-2600, Continental IV-1430 and one or two Lycomings must be laid at the feet of somebody. Lt. Col. Edwin R. Page, chief of the Power Plant Branch, had been an Army propulsion specialist since joining the old Aviation Section in 1918. He was a non-flying officer and was approaching age 60 when Pearl Harbor was attacked. It must be presumed that Page and his staff never went to England to personally investigate British engines because staff personnel obviously were even out of touch with Wright and P&W progress.

(Only a personal contact involving Gen. Arnold and Frederick Rentschler, Chairman of United Aircraft Corp., resulted in P&W dropping all of its work on liquid-cooled engines in 1940. It was a remarkable situation because Arnold and the Air Corps had become enamored with Prestone-cooled, small-frontal-area engines when the Allison began to come to the forefront in the mid years of the decade. Unfortunately, Arnold did not take a close look at Wright Aeronautical during the same facilities tour. If Rentschler had not been terribly candid when he broached the XH-2600 subject with Arnold, UAC might have eventually wasted thousands of manhours, a ton of money and a lot of machine time on their XH-2600 [X-1800] unit. It would have proved about as useful as the Hughes D-2 and the Wright Tornado.)

Most certainly there was a great deal of bias against British engine developments at Wright Field. You could almost taste it, just as you could sense the Army's bias against foreign weaponry. It was an era when foreign cars – sports or otherwise – were looked upon with the same disdain as anything that bore the label Made in Japan. Oh, there were perhaps a few Bugattis, Alfa-Romeos and Rolls-Royces in the big eastern cities, but they were about as rare as pet llamas. After the Great Depression, it was un-American to even think of buying foreign aircraft engines. Can't you visualize General Motors threatening to withdraw all support from Allison Engineering in 1939 if the Air Corps purchased some Merlin engines? By 1940, of course, the entire picture began to change because of Allied orders pouring into the U.S.A.

# CHAPTER 8

# Weapons of War and P-38 Spinoffs

As if by some infernal design – because of American's post-World War I traditional apathy for developing weaponry for fighting any future wars – the nation came very close to entering the Second World War without any explosive-shell-firing weapons under 3 inches in diameter. The highly touted "Arsenal of Democracy" at the end of the 1930s decade was close to having to fight any war with expletives and profanity. There was some inventory of automatic weaponry in the various armories that would be satisfactory for installation in aircraft or land vehicles and naval ships. Most consisted of aircooled .30- and .50-caliber machine guns of Browning design, and responsible Americans could thank Gen. "Black Jack" Pershing for the latter weapon because it was he who demanded its creation in World War I. Demands for armament improvements came rapidly after Pearl Harbor. Fortunately, a handful of men had made earlier decisions in peaceful times that would save thousands of lives.

What armored units the Army possessed were generally equipped with light tanks that mounted a "big" 37-mm cannon in a revolving turret. That particular weapon was really almost an accidental outgrowth of the World War I French Puteaux short-barrel cannon. Sometime after the Armistice, Baldwin-Poole Co. was awarded a contract to develop a 37-mm cannon for use in aircraft. As might be expected, it turned out to be virtually a copy of the Puteaux weapon. Specifications called for reduced weight, improved handling, and an increased rate of fire. One of the Baldwin guns was actually test fired from the nose gunner's position of a Martin MB-2 on the ground and in flight during the reign of Gen. William "Billy" Mitchell.

At a later date, when John Browning was hired by the Colt Patent Fire Arms Co. to serve as a consultant to critique the uninspiring Baldwin-Poole product, he could not help but suggest a number of much-needed improvements. It was obvious to him from the very start that little, if anything, had been done to re-engineer the Puteaux gun. Although John Browning was given a limited "go ahead" for design and development, he soon came up with a much-improved weapon that had an increased muzzle velocity, a higher rate of fire, greater reliability and a general arrangement that was far less cumbersome. When it was fired, it proved to be as reliable as any gun, regardless of caliber, that had been fully accepted for military service.

In spite of that, development crept on at a snail's pace in the early post-war years. Browning decided to shelve the project in 1925, reacting to the public's antagonism toward so-called "war mongers" and "dealers in death" as exemplified by the armaments firms. In America, the antiwar film released as *All Quiet on the Western Front* had an astonishing effect on most citizens. It was downright unpopular to be in the military or naval service.

Vickers-Armstrongs in England had acquired license rights to the 37-mm cannon by 1930, restoring the weapon to some semblance of usefulness. Virtually every Vickers gun manufactured in Great Britain eventually went to Spain – evidently in anticipation of the oncoming civil war – which became that

*ABOVE and OPPOSITE: Bazooka-type rocket launchers were pretty elementary as 1943 dawned, but a need existed for such a weapon for air-to-ground use. Lockheed developed a 12-tube arrangement for the Lightning, installing them in four clusters on a P-38G-15-LO (formerly, a Lightning II). Some kits were produced, and a few (at least) were used in combat zones. Results at the time were not encouraging. (LAC)*

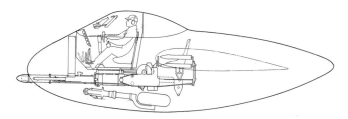
Proposed 75mm T-9 cannon installation on P-38 with automatic feed and 20 rounds of ammunition.

great testing ground for World War II weaponry. However, it appears to have been Lt. Ben Kelsey's strong desire to put some punch in American pursuit aircraft that actually saved the Colt-Browning blunderbuss from an ignominious disappearance. Kelsey's tenacious pursuit of plans to improve the firing rate, muzzle velocity and reduce weight led directly to adoption of a superior version for use in the Bell FM-1 series and P-39 Airacobra. The gun was initially specified for early versions of the Lockheed P-38 when neither the Army's .90-caliber T1 design nor any 25-mm cannon materialized. Some resistance to change in the Ordnance Department restricted development of rapid ammunition feed for the 37-mm cannon, inhibiting plans to use it widely in aircraft applications.

Meanwhile, the cannon – designated as the Browning (Colt) M4 – was improved, weighing in at 406 pounds with a 15-shot magazine. The cyclic firing rate improved to 135 shots per minute, while the muzzle velocity went up to 2,000 feet per second. Largely because of Kelsey's efforts, Ordnance came up with a better M9 version in 1939. However, back in 1936, when the young lieutenant became frustrated with Army indifference toward weapons development and a dearth of other automatic cannons specified in Circular Proposals X-608 and X-609 (plus subsequent revisions), he had settled on the M4 with reluctance. Absence of modern metallurgical techniques in manufacturing such weapons severely restricted appreciable increases in critical muzzle velocity, not to mention rate of fire.

Kelsey voiced displeasure with the 15-round magazine that was further handicapped with 5-round clips. As a result, he descended on ordnance officers at Aberdeen Proving Ground armed with a fistful of new theories and technical suggestions. In his opinion, the 5-shot clips might be fine for the armored cavalry (there was no real tank corps as such in the Army) with their pitiful M-5 light tanks and the few light anti-aircraft 37-mm weapons on hand, but the rate of fire would certainly have to be improved if the gun was to be effective as an aircraft weapon in the modern context. But Ben Kelsey, a man cut from the same cloth as Jimmy Doolittle – Kelsey had received his Engineering BA from MIT and both men had advanced degrees from the same university – soon learned that he had his work cut out for him.

"Why can't you Air Corps people be satisfied with this weapon as it is?" That was the plaintive protest of one lethargic artillery officer at Aberdeen. "You flyers never seem to be able to use what we already have." (He may have been referring to Spanish-American War Gatling guns or even flintlocks.)

Struggling against such retrogressive thinking, project officer Kelsey insisted on an automatic feed mechanism with a magazine holding no less than 50 shells, and the gun was required to have a muzzle velocity in the neighborhood of 3,000 feet per second. With no little difficulty, he got what he wanted, but not before the XP-38 had flown. That gun was the M9 version built by Colt. It weighed within one pound of the M4's weight, but the muzzle velocity rose from 2000 fps to as much as 3050 fps when an armor-piercing round was fired. (Starting in 1940, most of the M4/M9 production was vested in the Oldsmobile Division of General Motors Corporation.)

Although the Browning-Colt-Oldsmobile cannon was to pass from the scene at Lockheed with the P-38D series that was never to be considered as a real "combat-worthy" pursuit in the new Army Air Forces, one incident relating to the gun is worth relating. After serving as Assistant Military Attache for Air in London in 1940, Kelsey returned to project work at Wright Field. Just before being attached to VIIIth Fighter Command for work with the BOLERO Hq. "X" staff, he was spending a great deal of time at Lockheed in California on P-38 problem solving, range extension and development of the optimum weapons system. With the attack on Pearl Harbor, most existing priorities were scrapped and new ones were established, as they say, posthaste. Kelly Johnson and his staff had been able to resolve the dive buffet problem with a relatively simple fix. Some major production problems had been resolved, but there were still critical propeller and landing gear shortages.

Engineers plunged into the range extension episode with gusto and, of course, some of the top engineering talent was

assigned to the compressibility problem. Once the shock of Pearl Harbor was behind most Americans, resolute determination set in to replace overconfidence and fury. On the Plant B-1 production lines the 20-mm cannon had replaced the Colt M9 in all P-38E and F types after having been introduced on the British 322-B type. Testing of the M9 cannon did continue on a limited scale.

In later years, Kelsey enjoyed telling of one of those test flights. "Firing tests with the 37-mm cannon were carried out over the Pacific, somewhere between Ventura and Santa Barbara. While flying those missions, I was always looking for something – anything – to shoot at. The main idea was to use up the ammunition to test the feed mechanism. I got to the point where I was even shooting at things as small as seagulls. Late in the afternoon of one good day I returned to L.A.T. after the firing tests. We talked about rearming at 4:30 p.m., but finally decided to call it a day. The winter days are fairly short. It wasn't long before a Japanese sub surfaced and shelled some oil storage tanks near Santa Barbara. I have always wondered what might have happened if I had gone out just one more time that day and, just by accident, had stumbled onto that submarine."

One thing is certain. If Kelsey had been accurate with his fire and the submarine was sunk, it would have made spectacular headlines.

Bell Airacobras were, for the most part, equipped with the M4 or M9 cannons, and the P-63 Kingcobras either had the M4 or a later model, the M10. Entire batteries of the Browning (Colt) 37-mm cannon were scheduled to be used in such exotic designs as Lockheed's XP-58 Chain Lightning, McDonnell's XP-67 and the corpulent-bodied Brewster XA-32. However, as is so often the case, none of these projected installations actually materialized. Allied armies and navies all eventually used one shell-firing automatic cannon that had superior characteristics and could be used in a multitude of installations.

Few, if any, civilians – and we hate to add, an alarmingly small number of military men – in Great Britain and the United States were aware of the extremely narrow margin by which the Allies missed having to defend their ships or having to attack enemy targets without the punch of rapid-fire cannons. In fact it was only a few months after the RAF's Westland Whirlwind prototype first flew in October 1938 that the British – entering into a top-priority program – began to manufacture their own version of the French Hispano-Suiza (Birkigt design) Type 404 cannon (20-mm) at a new factory near Grantham.

It is important to recall that the Whirlwind was designed from the outset to carry four of the 20-mm guns in the nose. In keeping with the "shadow factory" scheme of the 1930s, the gun manufacturing plant was identified by the non-committal title of British Manufacture & Research Co. One of the key design features of the Whirlwind fighter was its battery of closely clustered cannons. They were called for in the specifications when the Royal Air Force didn't even have a modest grip on the 20-mm gun situation; in fact they had hardly a

*ABOVE: Company engineers had designed a yoke-type glider tow system that could accommodate more than one or two gliders at a time. Attach points were at the horizontal stabilizer tips (see photo). In all other respects the P-38G-3-LO (AC42-12791) was unchanged. Details of accident are sketchy, but breakage of both tail booms with nearly identical fractures indicated that a glider was still under tow when something stopped suddenly. (W-P AFB Photo)*

*OPPOSITE RIGHT: That initial Model 322-60-04 Lightning II (that was to be a rarity as the only turbosupercharged Lightning to carry full RAF markings) was classified as a P-38F-13-LO. On bailment to Lockheed from the USAAF, it was adapted for Lockheed's torpedo carrying and dropping demonstration. It easily carried two torpedoes or one 300-gallon drop tank and one torpedo. Formerly numbered AF221, it was more correctly identified as AC43-2035. (LAC)*

*BELOW: The one and only Lightning II ever to be seen in full RAF markings was AF221, shown taxiing away from Production Flight Test Building 304 on April 15, 1942. Almost immediately, it became P-38F-13-LO and was allocated AAF number AC43-2035. Only 29 of that model were delivered on Contract AC-31707. With only a change in the national markings, AF221 was bailed to Lockheed. (LAC)*

glimmer of expectation. The first BMRCo. cannon was produced in the same month that Lockheed completed fabrication of the XP-38 at Burbank. In order to understand what drove certain actions with regard to aircraft cannons in the 1930s, it is necessary to review the overall situation facing America and the United Kingdom.

Taking into consideration the attitude of the French toward the British and also the fact that France had a Socialist government in power, it seems amazing that a British commission had negotiated purchase of six 20-mm cannons from Societe Francaise Hispano-Suiza S.A. for an undisclosed sum in 1936. In contrast to some rather unproductive later negotiations with American buyers, Hispano offered to build a manufacturing plant in England . . . if an agreement to purchase at least 400 guns a year was consummated. Of course the British jumped at the offer, and that brought the BMRCo. into being. Had these negotiations ended in frustration, the RAF and the Royal Navy would have entered the war in 1939 with nothing better than Vickers and Browning machine guns, supported by a motley and outmoded collection of Lewis guns – all of .303 rifle caliber.

In the meantime, American Army and Navy ordnance attaches in Europe had detected the undercurrent of hectic development effort in automatic shell-firing weapons in the 1936-37 time frame. Navy staffers began to have many doubts about the ability of U.S. fleet commanders to defend warships against the latest design torpedo and dive-bombing aircraft then on the drawing boards. They would have been remiss in their responsibilities if they did not presume that the performance of projected aircraft being developed by unfriendly powers at least equalled capabilities of any design on American drawing boards. Under such circumstances, the prospects of defending vessels with .50-caliber machine guns and manually loaded 3-inch deck guns was disconcerting at best.

The fighter and bomber project offices at Wright Field were, at the same time, concentrating most of their efforts on the 37-mm cannon for lack of any more effective weapon becoming available within a decade. In their view, it would take forever to develop a new weapon, and getting it though the procurement chain was, historically, an endless process. Young Kelsey had, in the late thirties, gained respect among his superiors and, as a result, seemed to enjoy a relatively free hand in setting up specifications. He really was not enthusiastic about the multiseat fighter concept, but he realized that some respected people in the GHQ Air Force were strongly behind it.

Although Bell Aircraft's design had displayed several good features, the company had no track record at all where its own designs were involved. His personal view was that the less radical Lockheed XFM-2 competitive design was more likely to succeed. However, the rules of the game at that time favored Bell and Lockheed had lost out by a fractional percentage point. In both cases the 37-mm cannon was the weapon of choice. Kelsey's counterpart in Bomber Projects was Lt. Millard F. Harmon (later, Maj. Gen.), a young man who shared similar views about armament. Confirming that, the behemoth Dou-

glas XB-19 had a defensive forward-position turret that was to mount one of the 37-mm cannons.

Most likely because of pressures from key officers such as Gens. Oscar Westover and Frank A. Andrews, who paid heed to requests from the likes of Col. Henry Arnold and others, Army Ordnance finally decided to procure some foreign automatic cannons. Dealing through attaches in the overseas consulate offices, Ordnance managed to purchase approximately 20 weapons of (supposedly) the highest quality in the 20- to 25-mm range from various foreign manufacturers. The plan was, of course, to identify a suitable weapon and obtain manufacturing rights for that item. Those selected for active consideration included a 25-mm Hotchkiss gun from France, a Danish Madsen cannon, the German Rheinmettal-Borsig weapon, a Swiss Oerlikon and the Rheinmettal (Solothurn) cannon.

Were American gun designers incapable of designing good automatic cannons? U.S. inventors and designers constituted some of the finest ordnance engineers in the entire world, but Isolationism and the Depression had wreaked havoc on the weapons industry, even to a greater extent than they had on the aircraft industry. Therefore, we were compelled to look to Europe – even to a former, and perhaps current, enemy – for a cannon of modern technological concept. In a nation where purchase of foreign cars and aircraft was considered heretical (except by the ultra wealthy), any ideas about purchasing foreign weaponry could have stirred up a firestorm of protest if it had become public knowledge.

The elusive Hotchkiss 25-mm weapon, sometimes listed as a 25-mm Madsen – a cannon that never existed – was subsequently beyond reach since the French government had classified it as "Secret."

There is an almost unbelievable footnote to this French situation. Monsieur Hotchkiss was an American expatriate who had become so disenchanted and frustrated with the U.S. Army and Navy armament procurement policies in the years following the Civil War that he moved to France sometime around the turn of the century. French military authorities acclaimed his machine gun as the best in the world. They promptly adopted the Hotchkiss gun as their standard weapon throughout World War I and the post-war years.

Wright Field's Fighter Projects Office, essentially a one-man office in those lean post-Depression days, had specified a 25-mm automatic weapon in Circular Proposals X-608 and X-609 (for XP-38 and XP-39 respectively). The requirement probably assumed that the Hotchkiss gun could be procured. That requirement had to be revised in 1937 to substitute the 23-mm Madsen or the .90-cal. T1 Army Ordnance weapon (close to 23-mm) then under development. Fortunately for all concerned, the flaws in that latter weapon were of such magnitude that development was soon abandoned.

Four 23-mm Madsens were purchased from Dansk Industri Syndikat, Copenhagen, in 1936, and at least two of the guns were delivered to Wright Field. Installed in wing mounts on a Curtiss P-36, redesignated XP-36E, they soon proved to be considerably less reliable than their advance publicity indicated. Consideration of the Oerlikon cannon became a priority, but that program never proceeded for numerous political and technical reasons.

At times it seemed the Air Corps efforts to procure a satisfactory automatic cannon for fighters would never be productive. Finally, the Army convinced the Bendix Corporation that it was in the best interests of everyone for the manufacturer to negotiate procurement of a number of Hispano-Suiza Type 404 cannons and manufacturing rights for an American version. Neither the Army nor the Navy could ever determine exactly what their specific requirements would be, either for the job to be done or the quantities to be procured.

As the years passed and the OPM was able to convert more and more factories to the manufacture of war materials for the Allied Nations under our policy of becoming the Arsenal of Democracy, Bendix became increasingly frustrated with the Type 404 cannon. While the French became largely dependent on American production of aircraft, engines, and a thousand other items, Hispano-Suiza – through its Geneva (Switzerland) sales "front" identified as Suisse Brevets Aero Mecaniques – was quoting undulating and frequently outrageous prices for the 20-mm weapons.

And blindly true to America's "white hat cowboy" image, the U.S. government didn't even attempt to pirate or copy the weapons as it might have. The French firm had failed even to take out an American patent. (Marc Birkigt, designer of the H.S. Type 404, had not really invented anything new. In fact, all of the firing mechanism concepts employed in his weapon had been previously patented by Scotti – Alfredo Scotti of Brescia, Italy – and other people. Birkigt had merely taken the best design features and improved them in detail.)

Thoroughly disgusted with the situation, Bendix terminated the project to follow a less difficult course. They wanted nothing more to do with the flim-flammers from Geneva. The White House was forced to intervene in the matter, delegating the matter to the State Department. A contract for 33 cannons (20 for the Navy, 13 for the Army) was awarded to SBAM on December 14, 1939. That document called for payment of $3,490 per gun – a sum that would have bought any citizen a new LaSalle convertible coupe AND a new, much desired Ford Phaeton as a gift for that graduating senior at that time! Full rights for manufacturing the Type 404 were also specified in that contract. The initial delivery to the Aberdeen Proving Ground was made on February 20, 1940. A mere four months later, the worst of fates befell France and her continental Allies. The British fared only slightly better.

Less than 60 days later, the Navy Department strongly endorsed large-scale manufacturing of the weapon in the U.S.A. What remarkable foresight! With the entire world in a state of turmoil and knowledge that America was almost inevitably going to be drawn into the conflict, the admirals conceded that it was in the national interest to produce such a viable (and much needed) weapon. That from the Senior service.

Seizing the opportunity, Gen. Henry Arnold, Chief of the Air Corps, recommended that immediate steps be taken to initiate production in the U.S., and he managed to push through a purchase order for 400 of the French-design cannons – intended primarily for use in the P-38s and P-39s. For a new production contract, Bendix proved to be the low bidder.

Contracts for 1,202 guns were signed on September 23, 1940, just three months after French forces capitulated. It should not be too difficult to figure out who was advising Arnold.

In a nation of approximately 120,000,000 citizens, probably a half-dozen alert and alarmed men made the difference between survival or loss of literally thousands of soldiers and sailors during the years America was in the war. Because the handful of men did not value their career progress over the needs of the nation, the Ordnance Department M1 20-mm aircraft cannon was born. The rest is history.

Most Hispano-Suiza automatic weapons produced in the U.S.A. were of an improved type identified as the AN-M2 version. Nearly 10,000 Lockheed P-38s were ultimately to be constructed with the 20-mm cannon as the centerpiece weapon. While the Browning .50-cal. machine gun proved to be a roaring success throughout World War II, it had to be thoroughly satisfying to know that a totally reliable rapid-firing cannon was available. Versions of the gun were used in specialized applications on many carrier-based aircraft, but the most utterly visible demonstrations of the available firepower were to be seen in films/newsreels of American warships under attack by waves of Japanese Kamikaze aircraft. Banks of 20-mm cannons fired almost continuously at the attackers, knocking them out of the air in droves. Those were sights never to be forgotten. But the people should always remember how perilously close we came to not having the weapon.

No less than three alternate armament installations were proposed for the P-38 in March 1942. All involved substitution of four 20-mm cannons for the normal single-cannon/four-machine-gun armament. Each of the four-cannon installations had a different feeder system. Although the reworked noses were able to provide about a 50-percent munitions weight-per-second increase in firepower, total continuous firing time was reduced to as little as 5.13 seconds. A standard production installation in a P-38F provided a normal firing time of 40 seconds. One glance at the nose section of a Westland Whirlwind, featuring four of the 20-mm Hispano cannons, confirms suspicions that total firing time for that airplane could not possibly exceed 4 to 4-1/2 seconds. Advantage, Lightning.

One six-gun nose armament installation was tested on a P-38 in the same time frame. All four .50-caliber machine guns were retained in their normal positions, but two 20-mm cannons were located in the central area between the machine guns. The installation was proposed for the prototype XP-49, based on the Oldsmobile-built AN-M2 (Hispano-Suiza) cannons with 90 rounds of 20-mm ammunition for each gun. The shells were to be fed from two drums, while each of the machine guns were to have their normal supply of 500 rounds. Even the Lockheed engineers were astonished at the success of this arrangement for a modest increase in weight of 147.2 pounds, including the munitions. They gained a 35 percent increase in pounds of projectiles fired per second.

Any other advantages offered by the XP-49 were offset by program "drift" as the months ticked by, the decreasing need for the Continental engine (not to mention its lack of potential) and, of course, no real ability to produce the aircraft without interfering with much needed P-38 production. With Packard spewing out Merlin jewels, the Continental had no reason to exist. it still took it at least two years more to cancel it.

As the war progressed, it became increasingly evident that the 37-mm Browning (Colt) cannon was useful but had its limitations. Adaptation of a 75-mm cannon for aircraft use had meandered along at a snail's pace since one had been fired aboard a Douglas B-18 in pre-war days. It had been given very serious consideration as a main weapon for the oncoming Douglas A-26 program, but only a limited number of the Invaders actually had the gun installed. There can be little doubt that the Hispania-Suiza 20-mm cannon was a sparkling

success, but the even greater success of Gen. "Black Jack" Pershing's .50-caliber machine gun could hardly have been imagined. Those Brownings were everywhere. It did not take long for everyone to realize that .30-caliber machine guns were fine for infantry units, but for aerial warfare they were a relic of World War I. Modern aircraft had to be chewed up, not just peppered with pellets. The concentrated firepower in the nose of P-38 was nearly optimum. Once a pilot was able to get his sights on an enemy aircraft, a good burst from the 38's nose guns could generally be counted on to erase the competition.

B Referring back to the 75-mm cannon, it is a well-known fact that an autoloading version of that large-bore cannon (at least with respect to aircraft use) was definitely intended for installation in the Lockheed XP-58 and the Beech XA-38. Those airplanes came along relatively late in the war, created little interest and never came close to production status. However, development of the cannon autoloader proceeded with some little success. If nothing else, it was an impressive looking mechanism. Years later, when Kelly Johnson – by that time a board member and senior advisor after retiring from his more active role – was being interviewed in connection with this project, he was jolted by a chance remark about the 75-mm weapon. An innocent question was asked: What did he think of the proposal to install a 75-mm cannon in one version of the P-38?

For a moment, he looked nonplussed or annoyed with the question. Then with gentlemanly patience he replied, "There was no 75-mm cannon installation proposed for the P-38." He may have presumed that I was confusing that with the XP-58 installation. "There is no way that a large gun like that could be installed in a P-38. In fact, if they installed that huge gun with its feeder in the nose, it would plow a furrow just trying to get off the ground."

A look of utter disbelief came across his face when a set of professional drawings from the National Archives, evidently prepared by aeronautical engineers at Wright Field, was placed on his desk. One drawing showed an elaborate inboard profile of a radically revised (but somewhat familiar) gondola fuselage containing details of a 75-mm cannon identified as the T-9 and a once-secret automatic feeder with provisions for 20 rounds of

explosive shells. A single .50-caliber machine gun was mounted on each side of the cannon barrel for target alignment and for a touch of defense. Each machine gun had 300 rounds of ammunition. Its basic airframe design appeared to be the P-38F; in fact, it appeared that much of the contouring aft of the wing leading edge may have come almost directly from Lockheed's P-38E Swordfish and from NACA wind tunnel testing.

The cannon muzzle barely protruded from the modified nose section, and the entire barrel ran beneath the pilot's floor. The large feeder occupied the exact area where the pilot normally sat. Little doubt existed in Johnson's mind that the pilot enjoyed a much improved view, his space provisions were exactly the same and that no c.g. problem was involved.

Even Kelly Johnson could not stifle a "Well, I'll be damned!" Nobody seems to have any idea about what became of the proposal, but Lockheed never became involved with it.

C Lightnings, even as early as mid-1942, were demonstrating their great versatility, a direct outgrowth of the compromise wing section adopted by Kelly Johnson. Early in 1942, a glider-towing system was designed for application to the Lightning. Slightly revamped horizontal stabilizer tip assemblies contained attachment points for a yoke-like cable. Another cable with a pulley was connected to the yoke in such a manner as to allow the pulley to travel freely across the yoke. That second cable was then attached to a glider release system. It allowed the glider to move laterally over a range of about 60 degrees while vertical movement could be as much as 45 degrees above or below the P-38's line of flight. At least one full period of tests was conducted at a test base in Orlando, Florida, with a fairly large number of observers witnessing the event. A single Waco CG-4A was towed aloft and released, but a Lockheed proposal document had depicted no less than three gliders being towed by one P-38E type.

During a subsequent test of the system as installed on one of twelve P-38G-3-LOs built, there was a serious accident. It is not clear exactly what occurred, but all evidence points to one of two situations:

(1) They were attempting to tow a glider (or gliders) from the lush turf in front of the main hangars at Wright Field and the glider(s) upended and dug in. Both P-38 tail booms snapped at the same boom stations, the nose gear strut broke off and the nose dug into the sod. Both propellers tore the gear cases loose and the props flew wildly.

(2) After takeoff in a routine manner, the glider release failed to work. The P-38G pilot was forced to land in the turf area with the CG-4A still in tow. Either the glider dug in or the nose wheel on the P-38 broke off or buried itself. The results were the same. The P-38 was, of course, written off.

So successful was the company-designed (in late 1941) wing pylon/drop tank installation that it was not long before Lockheed was hanging virtually everything on the shackles. Various bailment P-38s began, in 1942, to haul assorted loads into the air from Burbank.

With the disappearance of observation-class airplanes for Army ground forces support, a need arose after Pearl Harbor for aircraft to lay smoke screens in support of future land assaults. Some standard smoke generators – evidently the same model used a few years earlier on Northrop A-17s – were hung from the pylons of the former Lightning II (AF211) after it was redesignated P-38F-13-LO. Tests were conducted at altitude and on the deck in the desert country near Muroc, and a few Lightnings may have dispensed smoke screens in combat areas, but most activity of that nature in the Pacific was carried out by naval aircraft.

Lockheed's experimental department had to be operating on a 24-hour day, seven-day-per-week schedule to keep up with the multitude of wildly innovative design changes that were being produced. Anthony "Tony" LeVier moved from production test to experimental flight testing in that busy era, becoming irrevocably wedded to the P-38 Lightning program. Among the most interesting test programs was a 12-tube rocket-launcher installation, the P-38E with elongated, two-seat gondola, pressure-cockpit XP-38A, 300/310-gallon drop tank tests, and the P-38 with two aerial torpedoes.

As 1942 came to an end, a new P-38G-15-LO, c/n 3404, was equipped with no less than twelve 5-inch (possibly 4.5-inch) HVAR launcher tubes and two 165-gallon drop tanks. Whatever the results were, no attempt was made to put the installation kit into mass production. Two groups of three tubes were mounted close inboard to the fuselage (gondola) and two additional three-tube clusters were mounted on the left and right wings outboard of the propeller arcs. With the regular nose armament, the firepower must have been quite impressive.

(Weapons systems always seemed to fascinate young men, so there was an endless flow of suggestions on ways to improve what was already available. Why anybody pursued the .60-caliber machine gun concept, at least through 1945, is beyond comprehension, but considerable time and effort went into the project. Three of those long-barrel weapons were mounted in the nose section of P-38L-1-LO, AC44-23601, and some tests were conducted at Wright Field, Ohio, and evidently at Orlando and Eglin Field in Florida. All three barrels protruded several feet in front of the nose cap.

The Lightning with possibly the greatest volume of firepower was P-38L-1-LO, AC44-24649. In a direct takeoff from the eight-gun nose B-25J in 1944-45, the Lightning was fitted with no less than eight .50-cal. machine guns in the gondola nose. Then, out at the attach points used for the zero-length rocket trees, twin .50-cal. machine guns were installed, one under each wing. It appeared to be a standardized pod used on Douglas A-26s of that same period. As with the B-25 and A-26 arrangements, the firepower had to be withering.)

Excitement at Burbank never seemed to cease. Whether it was watching Kelly Johnson shoehorn himself into a piggy-back P-38 for some hair-raising flight or observing some new prototype roll out of a hangar for the first time, life was never dull. Even being part of a work shift change in the afternoon was akin to being caught in a cattle stampede. It was awesome. Just about one year after the U.S. and Japanese forces started to fling themselves at one another, Lockheed received a contract to test the Lightning in a torpedo-launching role. Some marvelously interesting sights and results came out of the subsequent experimental program.

The basic idea was to determine if the P-38F was a suitable platform for launching aerial torpedoes. Although the Battle of Midway was history by the time the contract was secured, nobody was certain that another serious naval attack of that magnitude could not take place. Although the AAF had used four Martin B-26 bombers to attempt torpedo attacks at Midway, they had not been any more successful than the squadrons of Douglas TBDs and a few Grumman TBFs in scoring hits on the enemy warships. There had to be some more successful launching platform. The company responded to the need with the initial Lightning II, a Model 322-60-19 aircraft taken over by the AAF from a British contract. As P-38F-13-LO, AC43-2035, the airplane was still in its British camouflage paint, and the serial number AF221 remained conspicuous.

Both external fuel tank pylons were modified to handle two 1-ton dummy torpedoes, one under each wing center section, by including a saddlelike cradle on each drop tank/bomb pylon. Each 1,927-pound torpedo was locked into the saddle by two cables. Both cables were supported at the inboard ends by a spring-loaded hook arrangement and at the outer ends by a standard bomb shackle. Both mechanical and electrical release mechanisms were employed to guarantee positive release of the weapon. When shackle actuation occurred, the outer ends of the support cables fell away and, as the cables relaxed, the springs at the inboard hooks allowed the cables to fall away with the torpedo.

Carrying a full load of ammunition and 300 gallons of internal fuel, the P-38F had a then-astonishing gross takeoff weight of 19,970 pounds. For comparison, the contemporary Westland Whirlwind had a maximum gross weight of 11,388 pounds combined with a maximum top speed at critical altitude of only 270 mph when two small 500-pound bombs were being carried underwing. In contrast, the Lightning without greatly increased horsepower and relatively little more wing area, was soon to demonstrate the ability to fly simulated combat missions with two torpedoes at a takeoff weight of nearly 10 tons.

Test pilots selected for the torpedo hauling/dropping experiments included James White, Tony LeVier and Joe Towle, with the latter being the only one in the group to make an actual torpedo drop. That particular event took place in December 1942, at a time when the much improved P-38G series fighters were coming off the production lines in large numbers. Largely unknown or ignored in that same time frame were two situations that reveal just how important the

P-38 Lightning was to this nation. The two facts that are incontrovertible are:

(a) All North American P-51/NA-73 Mustang deliveries ended in September 1942 and were not resumed until March 1943! (It is most likely that without the intervention of Lt. Col. Thomas Hitchcock, production of the Mustangs would have been permanently canceled. It is an absolute certainty that, at the very least, no P-51 airframes would have been produced for at least a year.)

(b) P-38s were the only turbosupercharged Allison-powered fighters produced during the war. Thus, they were the *only* high-altitude Allison-engined fighters ever placed into production. If Col. Kelsey had ever allowed the P-38 to follow the path dictated by others for the Bell P-39 and P-63, it would have fallen from grace at some stage of the war.

Equipped with two 1150-bhp Allison V-1710F-5 engines, the P-38F airplane made its initial test flight with the two saddle-type torpedo supports and sway braces in place for calibration purposes. All speed runs were conducted at 10,000 feet, an altitude well below the Lightning's optimum. A speed loss of 6.7 percent was measured. Both 1,927-pound dummy torpedoes were installed for the second flight, and the fighter took off from Lockheed Air Terminal (before the runways were extended) to head for Muroc.

Handling characteristics and stability were evaluated at indicated airspeeds up to 300 miles per hour! (Although true airspeeds reported in Lockheed LR3000 were only recorded during maximum – range tests that limited the TAS to 215 mph, shorter range mathematical conversions revealed that the probable true airspeed for short ranges was 364 mph – with two ponderous torpedoes in place. Speed loss attributable to the double installation was approximately 16.7 percent.)

Flight testing revealed that the maximum combat range, based on the launching of both torpedoes at the turnaround point, was 1,000 miles. True indicated airspeed on the way out was only 175 mph. The return leg was flown at a TIAS of 185 mph, giving a TRUE airspeed of 215 mph. Total flight time on that mission was 4 hours 28 minutes for a range of 960 miles. Test mission No. 5 was a far more practical demonstration. One 310-gallon fuel tank, only recently developed by Lockheed at that time, was installed in place of one torpedo. Their idea was to fly to a target rendezvous on the fuel in that large external tank, drop the torpedo and tank and return to base by cruising at about 1600 rpm.

Those successfully conducted mission profiles proved to be impressive beyond the wildest dreams of many. Results showed a zero-wind range of 2,160 miles, demonstrating a radius of action of 1,080 miles! No special attempt was made to improve on the fuel consumption figures on the return leg of the flight by climbing to critical altitude for optimum cruise. Average fuel consumption was approximately 63 gallons per

ABOVE: Approaching the Muroc Dry Lake bombing range with one dummy (weighted) aerial torpedo in place on the left pylon, the P-38F prepared to launch from 3,000 feet altitude. Number on tail is last two digits of constructor's number. Definitely unauthorized in government circles. (LAC)

BELOW: Reality. Those might have been dummy units, but they weighed as much as the real thing. Air Ministry decision to refuse Lightning delivery smacks of politics and finance more than performance. It could not have been worth the bad feelings generated. (LAC)

hour during the mission flight time of 10.33 hours! Landing weight was 14,100 pounds with a full load of ammunition aboard. Even Ben Kelsey had to be impressed at the thought of a 63-pound-per-square-foot wing loading at takeoff. With the drag of one torpedo and the oversize drop tank accentuated by about 4,000 pounds of additional weight, speed loss only amounted to 12.6 percent.

Post-flight calculations revealed that the single drop tank would be jettisoned after all fuel was used after about 4 1/2 hours. That alone would have increased the radius of action to about 1,150 miles. It is also well to remember that the P-38E lugged that torpedo and the empty drop tank all the way back to Burbank on Mission 5, and they were still attached when the fighter taxied back to the flight test area apron. The P-38 was at a very high gross weight for landing.

Test pilot Joe Towle performed the final flight test of the torpedo demonstration program on December 8, 1942. The purpose of the flight was to show that a naval torpedo could be successfully launched from a P-38. Towle made the following comments about that historic flight:

"I had one full-weighted torpedo on the left side and nothing on the right (pylon). There was just a slight change in trim of the ship at takeoff, but not enough to bother. In the air the ship would trim hands off

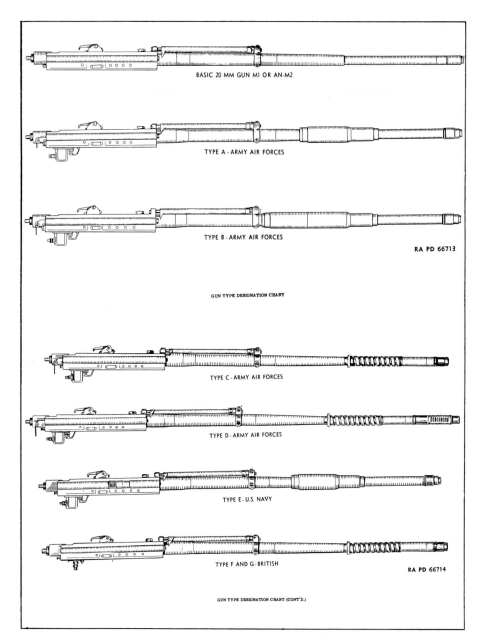

BASIC 20 MM GUN M1 OR AN-M2

TYPE A - ARMY AIR FORCES

TYPE B - ARMY AIR FORCES

RA PD 66713

GUN TYPE DESIGNATION CHART

TYPE C - ARMY AIR FORCES

TYPE D - ARMY AIR FORCES

TYPE E - U.S. NAVY

TYPE F AND G - BRITISH

RA PD 66714

GUN TYPE DESIGNATION CHART (CONT'D.)

*Several versions of the Hispano-Suiza 404 cannon were eventually adopted by U.S. and Great Britain. Conversion of the gun to U.S. standards created many production problems, but with a 3/4-in. diameter shell, it carried a hefty punch, making it worth the effort. Most of the main versions are depicted in this illustration. As fate would have it, the French - reluctant at first to share the 20-mm gun - had little opportunity to use their Model 404 in the shooting war.*

malfunction on that one flight. But when the electrical release failed to work, Towle simply pulled the jettison handle for manual release. It worked perfectly.

The motion picture footage showed that the weapon separated cleanly, dropped in a near-level attitude for about 75 feet and then slowly nosed down slightly. At the moment of impact with the desert sands, the "tin fish" was in a 45-degree nose down attitude. There could be little doubt that, if needed, the P-38 airplanes would be a first-rate torpedo launch aircraft and possibly the best land-based aircraft for that mission.

Available intelligence by year end resulted in many strategy changes. There was no doubt that the Imperial Japanese Navy had suffered major manpower, aircraft and vessel losses in the Battle of Midway. U.S. Navy warship availability was on the ascendancy and the character of battle was tending away from torpedo-launching aircraft.

Further testing showed that any P-38 could even be equipped retrospectively in the field to carry no less than six 500-pound bombs, and that sort of load began to appear on Lightnings fairly frequently in the MTO.

More to the point, stateside follow-on tests were initiated early in 1943 when the Burbank plant received a request for demonstration of an ability to successfully carry (and drop) a 2,000-pound (standard) bomb. Of course the workhorse P-38F-1-LO, c/n 5540, was selected for the job because it had been involved with other bomb and external tank tests. Armament experts in Experimental Flight Test devised special mounting lugs to match the existing 14-inch spacing of the shackle used with the 300-gallon drop tanks. They soon recognized that sway braces would be required to prevent rocking of the bomb. Company pilots did not actually conduct drop tests of the 1,100- and 2,000-pound bombs (actual weight 2,043 pounds), but the bomb kit was sent to Eglin Field, Florida, for evaluation. Testing conducted at the Eglin range proved to be quite successful. Results and drawings eventually found their way to VIIIth Fighter Command Headquarters and to the Technical Operations Unit. Later model P-38s were used by that organization to drop the 2,000-pound variety on the nearly impregnable Nazi submarine pens in Holland and at St. Nazaire in France.

Press and magazine reports pertaining to the Lockheed P-38 and the Republic P-47s in 1941 and 1942 – especially those originating in the United Kingdom – were often critical

with about 5 to 7 degrees of aileron tab . . . it was very stable," he said. "The ship jumped a little when the torpedo was dropped. Immediately afterwards, I made several high-speed turns without retrimming the airplane. It was slightly wing-heavy, but not enough so that I had to retrim the airplane immediately."

(It is significant that the P-38F was certainly not the strongest or best model of the P-38 by any stretch of the imagination. Original-concept wing leading edge intercoolers, never designed [in 1936-37] to handle 1300-1600 horsepower per engine, proved to be a power-limiting factor in high-altitude combat. Allison was not yet getting high power or reliability out of the F-5 engines, while dive flaps and boosted controls had not yet been developed. Weight increases were not then being overcome by horsepower increases.)

Towle had flown out to the Muroc bombing range while accompanied by a Lockheed Hudson carrying company photo ace Eric MilLer and several test observers. His Lockheed approached the bombing range at 3,000 feet because there was little interest in what the torpedo could do after it was entirely clear of the aircraft. Operation of the release mechanism was of paramount importance. Of course they had a of the "enormous" or "gigantic" sizes of the two aircraft. However, when the shooting ended in 1945, the tally of fighters that could consistently fly deep into Europe to fight included only those two types and, eventually, the Merlin-powered North American P-51s. In the other direction, no *Luftwaffe* first-rate fighters were fighting over the United Kingdom once the Nazis were pushed out of France and the Low Countries. They most certainly were not long-range types.

A very high percentage of the experiments implemented at Burbank bore lucrative fruit. It appears that the P-38F models came along at just the right time. Certainly the campaign in North Africa would have had some other outcome if the Lightnings had not arrived. The Northwest African Allied Air Forces (NAAF) were in poor shape early in 1943, primarily because of maintenance, tactics and logistics problems. Of 600 combat aircraft of all types in North Africa, Gen. James Doolittle could not muster more than 200 of them at any given time for battle. When 1st Fighter Group P-38s had to fly escort formation with the Boeing B-17Es and Fs, they invariably had high attrition in the early seconds of an attack. Members of the 14FG did not fare better, and the 82FG had to overcome some morale and discipline problems before it became one of the finest AAF groups. The total number of P-38F and G models available for use (including those "down" for maintenance) at any given time in North Africa probably never reached one hundred. Despite that shortcoming, they carried the war to the enemy with vigor.

*RIGHT: In the best naval tradition, the Lockheed test pilot launches his torpedo from 3,000 feet to provide a safety margin for the aircraft in the event that the torpedo hit the Lightning during separation. Test date was December 8, 1942. (LAC)*

*BELOW: One of the most unusual gun installations tested on a P-38 was this two cannon, four machine gun arrangement. Tested in connection with the XP-49 program, the guns (including two short-barrel 20-mm cannons) were mounted in P-38G-5-LO number AC42-12866. One later model P-38 was equipped with eight .50-cal. guns in the nose, while still another had a trio of long-barrel .60-cal. machine guns. That odd caliber gun was not seen on any other type. Basic gun arrangement on all P-38s was nearly optimum. (LAC)*

# CHAPTER 9

# War! And a North Atlantic BOLERO

America, the sleeping giant of the 1930s, was rudely awakened one Sunday morning to find an assailant giving it a merciless beating. The victim grabbed its well-publicized weaponry and tried to fight back. But peacetime Curtiss P-36s and a facelifted version of the same airframe redesignated P-40 may have impressed the American public far more than it did a misunderstood Asiatic enemy. The U.S. Army and Navy fighters didn't get much respect from the long denigrated Japanese. If the United States was going to defeat this upstart antagonist, it was not going to be done with those Curtiss and Brewster "flying baggage compartments." What was needed at the moment was a number of squadrons of fighters with heavy armament, armor plate, self-sealing fuel tanks, a top speed in excess of 350 mph and a decent combat radius of action. The newly formed Army Air Forces, as of December 7, 1941, could not claim to possess more than a couple of Mustangs (P-51s) and one prototype P-47 Thunderbolt. Brave pilots might go into battle in a P-43A Lancer or a Brewster F2A Buffalo with confidence, but if they were fortunate enough to survive that combat they were not anxious to try it a second time. Such aircraft were not going to provide a license to longevity.

There were really only two fighters in production for the Army Air Forces on that day that were going to give a pilot a reasonable chance of outclassing a determined enemy. One type was Lockheed's P-38E and the other might be the Curtiss P-40D/E or Bell's P-39D and companion P-400 export type. While the Bell was newer and more potent in the armament

ABOVE: This heavy cloud cover was "good weather" on the way to Europe! At least the pilots could see the other airplanes in their flight. Lt. Gen. John Gerhart, a member of the "Fuddy-Duddy Four" element, reported that he "was scared stiff" when the other airplanes disappeared in the fog between Bluie West 1 and INDIGO (Reykjavik, Iceland). (LAC)

RIGHT: Mass production of P-38s, at last. Many wartime P-38 pilots, like Lt. James Kunkle who saw combat with the 370FG, which was activated in July, 1943, were introduced to the Lightning while working on these assembly lines in 1941-42. The airplanes shown are P-38F-13-LOs, originally ordered by the RAF, in 1940, as Lightning IIs. (LAC)

department, twice as many P-40s were being produced at the time. (As time went on, the various P-40 versions always seemed to have a better combat record for a variety of reasons, hardly any one of which would explain the situation.) The Navy was not going to win the war with Grumman F4Fs, and it was counterproductive to even use the Brewsters as fighter-trainers.

When all of the facts were taken into consideration, the only fighter in the American arsenal that could successfully tackle the role of air-to-air battler against the best Nazi fighters and Japanese Navy and Army types on a daily basis was the Lockheed Lightning. That was a truism for the first 18 months of the war after Pearl Harbor. But 18 months in any war is an eternity. No P-40 of any model could be pitted against German fighters over the European Continent; they did reasonably well in the Aleutians; Kittyhawks and Warhawks proved to be very useful in North Africa, but they were never going to gain air superiority in Italy or the Southwest Pacific theater. Gen. George Kenney recognized the fact at a very early date. He carried out a tenacious battle with USAAF headquarters for months to get every available P-38 that could be sent his way. Lightnings suited his war requirements in almost every way, even after P-47Ds became available much later. Range and firepower were predominant requirements in the far reaches of the southwestern Pacific Ocean region. If – and that would be a hard *if* to validate – the P-47C or D proved to be more maneuverable, it was still incapable of coming close to matching the range of any P-38 for any period of the war. Curtiss P-40s and Bell P-39s lacked range or maneuverability or altitude capability or all three. What about the Grumman F6F Hellcat? When it eventually picked up the cudgel for the Navy it did a superb job. But it never had to do battle with Messerschmitts or Focke-Wulfs over France, Germany, Italy or Rumania – or any other place for that matter.

None of those arguments are meant too cast aspersions on any of those valuable American fighters. The majority of them performed their jobs in a soldierly manner wherever they were committed to battle (except for the Brewster fiasco), but only in certain time frames for the most part. But up to mid-1943, those that were available were only capable of carrying out a "holding action." Until the P-47Ds and P-51Cs and Ds were available in group strength in the major theaters of operation, the P-38 types were the only fighters that were going to carry the battle to the enemy in an effective manner.

One major event, more than any oth... supports this thesis because it reve... facet of the P-38's capabilities in an... manner. The event was every bit as spec... the Doolittle Raid on Japan, although it wa... given one-one-hundredth of the publicity. This... tacular operation was the aircraft delivery phase of BOLE... , the program for buildup of American armed forces in the ETO. The aerial delivery phase involved, in 1942, transfer of a large number of Boeing B-17Es, Douglas C-47s, and Lockheed P-38Fs (and evidently a few modified P-38Es) over North Atlantic air routes to the United Kingdom. Such delivery of fighter aircraft en masse had never been considered before, let alone reaching a successful conclusion.

When Col. Ben Kelsey took it upon his own shoulders to authorize a serious program for P-38 range extension sometime late in 1941, he was taking a long chance that his military career would not be seriously curtailed. His decision was not based on support from General Arnold in any way. In fact, what he was about to do was a clear violation of AAF longstanding policy and War Department direction. What actually triggered Kelsey's action is not entirely clear, but it is logical to assume that it began with Col. George W. Goddard's staff suggestion at Wright Field. They pointed out that U.S. forces were essentially without any photo-reconnaissance aircraft that could be sent into a combat zone.

What they did have was a handful of Beech C-45A/AT-7 light transports/navigational trainers modestly reworked for photo work. These airplanes, designated F-2, were distinguished by a door-within-a-door on the left side. By opening that panel, large aerial cameras could be aimed at likely objectives. To send such an airplane on a combat mission anywhere would have been a homicidal action. What they wanted was the new "combat-ready" P-38E with some cameras installed in lieu of regular armament and some extra fuel tanks in place of normal ammunition loads. By means of Change Order 11 to Contract AC-15646, they were to obtain P-38E types without guns and redesignated F-4-1-LO.

Lockheed immediately began experiments with some new Bell P-39 belly tanks that had proven to be indispensable during the summer maneuvers in the south. Without drop tanks, the Airacobras could not be operated effectively. Therefore, Kelsey had some precedent to work from. Kelly Johnson determined that the 75-gallon tanks were virtually useless, if

top speed at critical altitude of 390 mph. Whatever problems plagued the aircraft proved insurmountable. Only three aircraft were ever converted to the F-3 configuration before the war engulfed this nation.

Long ignored, Col. Goddard was suddenly being heard. The long-range, high-speed photographic airplane was critical in waging global warfare. In fact it was indispensable. But the AAF and the USN did not have even one under construction. As if by magic, Johnson's team produced drawings of a P-38E type with four K-17 cameras conveniently installed in the nose section in lieu of guns. Perhaps it was not perfect, but it worked. Goddard liked what he saw.

Top priority was given to setting up a modification center, but a rather long time elapsed before any photo versions of the P-38 flowed from the mod center established in Dallas, Texas. Neither Lockheed nor Goddard let this deter them. Contract revisions soon caused diversion of no less than 100 of the badly needed P-38Es into the new Lockheed Plant B-6 area for conversion to an F-4-1-LO configuration (222-62-13). One airplane in that group served as the prototype, at least from the equipment standpoint, for the F-5A type. In fact, it was given the odd designation of F-5A-2-LO before the block numbering system went into effect in 1942.

Twenty additional F-4 types came along later in the year, bearing the designation F-4A-1-LO. Modification of P-38Es for range extension, whether it was for the Aleutian or African campaigns that were soon to be come significant parts of the overall picture or for reconnaissance purposes, was not simple. It involved major changes in the fuel transfer system, addition of mounting shackles and installation of mechanical and electrical controls.

Once the initial shock of Pearl Harbor wore off, range extension was given an A1A priority at Burbank. From a technical standpoint, some 330 Lockheed P-38E types were built before Contract AC-15646 was revamped again. But, as noted, there were 100 of the F-4s and twenty F-4As created from P-38E airframes. All of those Es came off the B-1 assembly lines looking just alike. Rather than try to make the changes in production and slow up the line, camera installation and fuel system rework was accomplished in B-6 at Lockheed Air Terminal (the term "Burbank Airport" never existed) or at the Van Nuys Modification Center located about 7 miles to the west. After 330 airplanes on AC-15646 had been built, numerous changes were made in production – including a change to Allison V-1710F-5 engines – to create the improved P-38F model (basically 222-60-09).

Even then it was necessary to divert them through modification to fit them out for the BOLERO mission when it became a priority project. Although information relating to Projects SUMAC, BRONZE and BOLERO reveals exactly what modifications were involved, no documentation exists to clarify the meanings of projects such as BRONZE, SUMAC and SNOWMAN. One thing that seems clear, however, is the fact that nobody can positively state that the Lockheed drop tanks contained 150 or 165 gallons of fuel.[1] Tanks from different

**ABOVE:** *Virtually unnoticed in the hectic days of 1941 was the birth of the war's best photo-recon aircraft. The 116th Lockheed P-38E was converted to an F-4 camera plane about the time of the Pearl Harbor attack. Armament was deleted and four cameras were installed. One of the original F-4s, c/n 222-5316, was cloaked in a special blue paint disguise. Conversion of Douglas A-20s to an F-3 format had not been very successful. Officially, this airplane was an F-4-1-LO, converted at Burbank. (LAC)*

**BELOW:** *One camera installation involved use of large mapping cameras, including the trimetrigon type. The forward unit in this installation appears to be a K-22 with a 12-inch or 24-inch telephoto lens. (LAC)*

not a real handicap. He instructed his engineers to double the capacity to at least 150 gallons and to adopt the new laminar-flow concept that was gaining great popularity. They finalized a design within days and, of course, it was tested in the wind tunnel. Bingo! It proved to be an optimum design, even to the point that separation from the aircraft when empty or partly full was rarely a problem.

As 1942 dawned, there was anger, dismay and frustration everywhere. Colonel Goddard and his team had, a year or so earlier, tried to adapt the early series Douglas A-20 to the reconnaissance role. Several of the earliest A-20s had turbo-supercharged R-2600 engines, supposedly giving that type a

---

*1. The terms 150- or 165-gallon and 300- or 310-gallon tanks are used interchangeably because of common usage and the absence of a specific gallonage. The numbers really define a capacity range.*

subcontractors had varying capacities because of manufacturing differences. Lightnings soon proved to be the best weight-lifting fighters of the war, so an extra 30-gallons of gasoline was hardly noticed. Mountings located the jettisonable tanks very close to the c.g.

The haste with which Lockheed designed, developed and produced a successful range-extension system for the Lightning was remarkable. Republic encountered a plethora of problems in attempting to design low-drag shackles and tanks for the Thunderbolt. Eventually the only really successful operational tanks ever used on the P-47 were the "paper" tanks of various capacities developed by Col. Cass Hough's Technical Operations Unit and the Lockheed P-38-type tanks used on certain SWPA P-47s and large numbers of P-47Ns late in the war. (The Lockheed tank design was so good that in late war years and in post-war years it was not at all unusual to see such tanks on Consolidated PBY-5As, Bell P-63 racers, Boeing B-17Gs and North American's record breaking P-82B "Betty Jo" and numerous later P-82E fighters. And, of course, large numbers of Lockheed P-80As and T-33s used the same design.)

Consider the situation in 1942 when a typical P-40 or P-39 standard fighter in the USAAF could only carry external fuel in a 52- or 75-gallon drop tank. Total internal fuel in virtually any P-40/Kittyhawk/Warhawk was almost exactly the same as a P-38 Lightning carried in a single standard drop tank. Most P-38s carried two of the tanks as a standard operational component, and it was not long before it became rather common to see a mix of one 165-gallon tank and one 300-gallon tank or even two of the latter.

Trials with non-jettisonable drop tanks for ferrying Hawker Hurricanes were initiated early in 1940, but it was not until later in the year that the program really became a priority item. Fixed 44-gallon ferry tanks were fitted under each wing of the Hurricane II type when the aircraft were sorely needed in Africa. In due time, jettisonable 44-gallon tanks were used for combat operations, while two fixed 88-gallon external tanks were eventually used for the ferrying effort. When the fixed 44-gallon or 88-gallon tanks were fitted for those long flights, no ammunition was carried for the guns. Needless to say, the Germans were developing external tanks for the Bf 109 and Fw 190 types about the same time. Large tanks were also developed for the Messerschmitt Bf 110 in the same time frame, but troubles encountered were momentous.

While the range capabilities of Lightnings became legendary in the years 1943 through 1945, two major episodes occurred in 1942 that were absolutely phenomenal in any context. Almost unheralded, either triumph certainly would have placed the P-38 on a roll of honor in an aviation hall of fame.

Once upon a time – it was in March 1942 to be exact – there was a typical high-level dinner gathering in the shadow of the White House, or at least the Washington Monument. One of the attendees seated alongside Maj. Gen. Henry Arnold aimed a topical question at the tactful Chief of the Army Air Forces. "With shipping as it is (in the face of the Nazi U-boat menace), how can we get more fighters to England?" Arnold, flashing one of his dazzling grins, reportedly purred, "I guess we will just have to fly them over."

We don't know who the diner was, but less than 48 hours later the "off-the-cuff" remark came back to haunt him. "Hap," President Roosevelt asked, "can you really fly them over?"

Arnold was under so much pressure from so many directions in those disheartening days that nobody really knows if his flippant rejoinder was based on solid knowledge of aircraft capabilities or if he was merely hoping to blunt another attack on his decimated air arm. We choose to believe that the general remembered that Ben Kelsey had told him that currently produced P-38F fighters had demonstrated outstanding range performance. Arnold was well aware of Kelsey's enthusiasm for the big fighters. Now he would ask for realistic evidence that would allow him to respond affirmatively to the Chief Executive. Hap Arnold was not unaware that his aide had been carrying out unauthorized experimentation with range extension. It is highly likely that Col. Goddard, another with a maverick personality, had discussed it with one or two senior officers.

Once he was unmasked, Col. Kelsey was forced to blurt out his story of the conspiracy with Lockheed's Kelly Johnson regarding the somewhat illicit fuel system revisions required to install external fuel tanks on Lightnings, at least for test purposes. The engineers had tested some 31 different designs by that time, limited only to the 150-gallon units, before settling on the optimum design. Not only that, calculations revealed that the P-38F (and, of course, later versions) had a realistic capability of flying with two 300/310-gallon drop tanks in operational service.

A set of 300-gallon tanks was fabricated and test flown with mixed results. Although there was no trouble in lifting the weight, the initial design concept was poor in comparison to the smaller tanks. The engineers then proceeded to scale up the 165-gallon tank to carry 300-310 gallons. It, too, proved to be a success from the first test. Ben Kelsey stated that the P-38s would have a viable ferrying range of at least 2,500 miles. A skeptical Gen. Arnold had not yet learned to reckon with the likes of Kelsey and Johnson. He recalled that the initial P-38 design specified a range of 1,000 miles in 1936, and installation of self-sealing tanks obviously had to reduce that figure. What was the P-38's then current range?

Having only unverified second-hand information in mind when he made the offhand remark to his inquisitive dinner associate in March, Arnold was possibly only half serious in answering. Whatever the situation may have been, it was only a matter of hours after he had conversed with President Roosevelt and, subsequently, Col. Kelsey that Brig. Gen. Oliver P. Echols – the top man at Materiel Command – requested that Lockheed expedite conversion of all P-38s to include extended-range equipment. As soon as General Arnold was confident that his earlier statement was, indeed, factual, he called the President to assure him that fighters could be flown to the United Kingdom. At that moment, the most serious problems would be landing field construction and major navigational problems. After disposing of a problem he, himself, had created while dining, Arnold then proceeded to "pin the tail" on an unsuspecting Brig. Gen. Carl "Tooey" Spaatz, chief of the then vast Eighth Air Force that was sprinkled throughout the Carolinas and Georgia. His friend of many years, Brig. Gen. Frank O'Driscoll Hunter – easily recognized because of his Jerry Colona mustache – was based at Charleston, S.C., as head of VIIIth Fighter Command. Although "Monk" Hunter, a native of nearby Savannah, Georgia, was the fifth or sixth highest-scoring surviving American ace from World War I with eight victories to his credit, he was not one of the better-known aviators outside of AAF circles. A veteran of the 103rd Aero Squadron, skilled racing pilot and test pilot, Hunter was evidently a retiring personality of "Old South" gentility. He had survived many years of harrowing flight operations in a vast selection of devilish airplanes, including the treacherous Thomas-Morse R-4 racer. A man in his forties, he still liked to fly fighters. Galvanized into action by commands from Arnold, General Spaatz gave this open-ended instruction to Hunter: "Plan, expedite and execute the mass delivery of five AAF fighter groups, comprising about 85 aircraft each, by aerial route to Great Britain so that we can start the damn war."

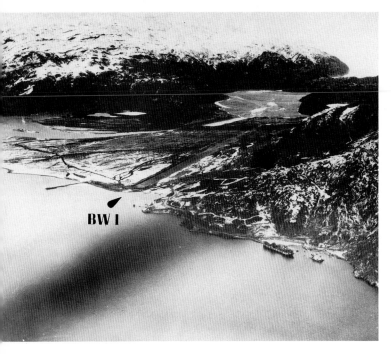

BW 1

ABOVE: Located 779 miles from Goose Bay and 919 miles from Gander, Bluie West One (BW1) presents an uninviting aspect to approaching pilots, especially with the prospects of summer fogs, terrible radio reception, and 5,000-foot mountains in the immediate vicinity of the "strip." The only practical approach was up a jagged - edged fjord to the 4,000-foot runway on a northeast heading. Radio call was "Tiptop." View here is looking almost due north. Camouflaged ship is tied up at pier. (Col. Cass Hough)

BELOW: Goose Bay, Labrador – May, 1942. Newly carved out of the wilderness, Goose was hardly ready to handle nearly 200 aircraft – arriving in relays – for the pioneering trek across an unfriendly Atlantic Ocean. Only one runway had been completed, and there was proper parking for no more than four aircraft at a time. Basic buildings are at 3 o'clock position in photo. Crude as the base appeared, it was only necessary to recall that Allied tankers and freighters were being sunk by Nazi U-boats at the rate of nearly a half-million tons per month, and every aircraft lost with those unlucky ships was a crisis initiator. (Col. Cass Hough)

Then he added, "Now!" We suspect that "Monk" reached for a bottle. Like Churchill, he was known to like a drink, now and then.

Only one time in the entire history of the Air Corps/Air Forces had the service made an attempt to fly a fighter (pursuit) aircraft to any part of the United Kingdom. Notice: that was "a" fighter. Not 425 of them. The one attempt was made some years after Charles Lindbergh had made his solo non-stop trip to Paris. Air Corps Captain Bert Hassell made the multi-stop attempt, only to crash on that inhospitable Greenland icecap. Quite coincidentally, Col. Kelsey had proposed and planned a nonstop U.S. transcontinental flight of P-38s for the summer or autumn of 1941, a flight which would have contributed immensely in planning and executing a transocean flight.

Ironically, Germany had developed airfields in Iceland and had even surveyed numerous "commercial" landing sites in Greenland in the 1930s, supposedly for Lufthansa. Almost nine-tenths of the giant island's raw surface was covered by a massive sheet of ice, but coastal areas could easily be converted into airfields. When war broke out in 1939, the Nazis had the most comprehensive data anywhere about conditions in Greenland.

Great Britain was not long in setting up a ferrying service to expedite transfer of much needed aircraft to the United Kingdom by air. The Atlantic ferrying organization (later, ATFERO) had established a major route across the North Atlantic from Gander Lake to Prestwick in Scotland. Most aircraft using that route were Lockheed Hudsons, Consolidated Catalinas and a few Consolidated LB-30s. On May 29, 1941, the Air Corps Ferrying Command (ACFC) was established by the AAC to take on the major function of delivering aircraft across the North and South Atlantic routes. Gander Lake, Newfoundland, was far from an ideal departure point because of location and weather, and that became even more critical once the idea of ferrying fighters across the Atlantic developed out of the embryonic stage.

There were already two British-developed airports in Iceland, but it was up to the USAAF to develop fields in Greenland and a better departure point in Canada. Sites ultimately selected for development were Presque Isle, Me., Goose Bay, Labrador, and Bluie West 1 and 8 in Greenland. Needless to say, once the newest needs were established, construction work moved ahead at a feverish pace bordering on panic. Crews attacked the Labrador site in much the same manner that Marines and Army infantry would eventually launch invasions all over the globe. In the summer months they waded ashore, cut trees to fabricate rafts, floated equipment to the beach that was approachable; then they proceeded to hack out a roadway extending 100 miles inland. They leveled an area in a rough triangle for their airfield site. But with only one runway completed and rudimentary facilities constructed, the Canadian winter arrived with a vengeance. Although a packed snow runway was used sporadically during the winter, construction crews had to retreat and await the coming of spring.

Even as the crews struggled to build the road to Goose Bay, a ship dropped anchor at a place soon to be known as Bluie West 1 (BW-1) to put work crews and equipment ashore. Work began almost immediately to lay down one runway at the head of Tunugdliarfik Fjord to serve as the main stopoff on the route to Scotland. About 450 miles to the north, other crews started work on an alternate strip identified as Bluie West 8 (BW-8). Construction of BW-8 was not to be completed – certainly not by choice – until the autumn of 1942.

As if to emphasize the critical importance of such bases, German U-boats were sinking Allied shipping at the rate of 6 million tons a year, and a large percentage of the cargo

consisted of fighter aircraft. It was not until March 1942 that the first aircraft headed for Europe (not a fighter) even managed to land at Goose Bay. However, it was destined to be the first of many hundreds, even thousands of aircraft to be delivered over North Atlantic routes.

Meanwhile, initial work was completed on an airfield in Charleston, S.C., which was to serve as headquarters for VIIIth Fighter Command. Spaatz had located his command center at Bolling Field and Hunter was ordered to join him at that headquarters. Three of his key subordinates charged into the massive task at HQ "X" (Charleston). They were Col. Lawrence P. Hickey, Lt. Col. John N. Stone and a middle-aged reservist, 2nd Lt. Cass Hough (pronounced Huff). He was a highly regarded, prominent manufacturing executive from Michigan. (Although Hough was only a 2nd Lt. in 1941, he was placed in command of the HQ and HQ Squadron in the 3rd Air Base Group at Selfridge Field. His total nonmilitary flying time was an overwhelming 4,971.5 hours, much of it in multi-engine aircraft. Hough was also a skilled astronomer, engineer and navigator.) This trio was soon joined by Lt. Col. Robert Landry in planning the BOLERO mission.

Every new day seemed to generate a new conspiracy to force constant change in the overall plan. Gen. Arnold's edict had called for no less than five fighter groups to make the initial crossing. Three groups – the 1st, 14th, and 78th Pursuit Groups – were to be completely equipped with the latest modified P-38F series, newly capable of ferrying flight of more than 1,700 miles (plus reserves) with their new 150-gallon drop tanks. If the even larger tanks of 310-gallons capacity could be provided in time, ferry range could be increased to approximately 2,500 statute miles, plus a reserve allowance.

Two additional groups (the 31PG and 52PG) were to receive the newest Bell P-39F Airacobras, hopefully embodying many new improvements over the then standard P-39D. At least one P-39 test airplane was being flown with a large "slipper"-type belly tank, but the drag counts proved to be extremely high. The three P-38 groups and two P-39 groups were intended to comprise the basic VIIIth Fighter Command in the U.K. in connection with the long-term plan referred to as RAINBOW NO. 5. In essence, BOLERO was a defined operational aspect of the plan.

Up to April 1942, America's only real production of fighters was centered on Curtiss P-40s and Bell P-39s (see Table 9-1). Bell, located in Buffalo, had turned out about 1,200 Airacobras in Model 14 (export) and P-39D and F formats. Approximately one-third of the fighters had been shipped to the Pacific Ocean arena; the remainder constituted the main body of interceptor commands for air defense of the Western Hemisphere, although some were reposing disconsolately in England, unloved and unwanted by the Royal Air Force now that the Battle of Britain was a part of history.

Units of the 97th Bomb Group were already set to fly their new B-17E Fortresses to Europe, and revised plans called for a single B-17 to lead each section of four P-38Fs or P-39Fs, thereby furnishing the necessary navigational services. That action would relieve the fighter pilots of a chore for which some were ill prepared or untalented. The 60th Air Transport Group, then newly equipped with Douglas C-47 Skytrains, was committed to carrying all necessary equipment for the groups to England, or to shuttle needed items to bases along the North Atlantic Ferry Route.

| TABLE 9-1 PRODUCTION OF AIRCRAFT [1] | | | | | | | | | | | | | |
|---|---|---|---|---|---|---|---|---|---|---|---|---|---|
| **1941** | | | | | | | | | | | | | |
| | J | F | M | A | M | J | J | A | S | O | N | D | TOTAL |
| P-38/322-B | 1 | – | 2 | 4 | 4 | 4 | 23 | 26 | 12 | 3 | 74 | 52 | 205 |
| F-4 [2] | – | – | – | – | – | – | – | – | – | – | 2 | 2 | 2 |
| P-39/Model 14 | 3 | 6 | 11 | 1 | 15 | 37 | 50 | 158 | 128 | 198 | 128 | 191 | 926 |
| XP-47B | – | – | – | – | – | – | – | – | – | – | – | 1 | 1 |
| NA-73/P-51 | – | – | – | – | – | – | 1 | 6 | 25 | 37 | 67 | 136 | |
| **1942** | | | | | | | | | | | | | |
| | J | F | M | A | M | J | J | A | S | O | N | D | TOTAL |
| P-38/322-B | 32 | 113 | 80 | 100 | 100 | 85 | 170 | 60 | 132 | 145 | 124 | 123 | 1264 |
| F-4/F-5 [3] | 84 | 14 | 20 | – | – | 20 | – | 20 | – | – | 20 | 36 | 214 |
| P-39/P-400 | 179 | 113 | 141 | 52 | 86 | 227 | 185 | 188 | 93 | 129 | 277 | 302 | 1972 |
| P-47 | – | – | 5 | – | 10 | 26 | 38 | 61 | 66 | 64 | 114 | 140 | 524 |
| NA-73/P-51 | 84 | 84 | 52 | 86 | 84 | 84 | 76 | 22 | 60 | – | – | – | 632 |

1. Acceptances
2. The ONLY two photographic-reconnaissance airplanes received by the USAAF or the USN
3. Three Douglas F-3s comprised the remaining total of photo-recon airplanes delivered, although there were a few field conversions of B-17 aircraft.

*NOTE: Rarely noticed is the fact that all production of North American P-51 Mustangs had ceased in September/October 1942 in spite of a dire need for fighter aircraft. Improved performance of the Packard-built Rolls-Royce Merlin version warranted the restart of production in 1943.*

Something that would have been an acceptable script for an Orson Welles radio program just a year earlier suddenly attracted serious consideration in the hectic days of 1942. Word arrived at Headquarters "X" and Bolling Field that the proposed installation of 150-gallon "pregnant belly" tanks proposed for the P-39Fs would not be available for use before June or July. (Even if the tank installations had worked well, it is extremely doubtful that the kits would have been available before the northern route was shut down for the winter.) Suddenly the five-group effort was in serious trouble.

The desperate Orson Wellesian proposal that was submitted by someone with enough clout to be heard involved transporting the 31PG Airacobras by aircraft carrier to a point about 900 miles off the British coast . . . two squadrons at a time. At that point they would be launched á la Doolittle style for the hop to an English base. After some serious analysis, an official "Go" came down from topside. Subsequent events killed that plan, but it had been based on an earlier plan to launch the P-39s to support the original TORCH invasion of North Africa that was scheduled for July 4, 1942. Lt. Hough had worked on that project, but had never been at all happy with the launching prospects. (A co-equal operation when TORCH finally became a high-priority project was the carrier launch of Curtiss P-40Fs from the U.S.S. *Ranger*. The fact that P-39s were not used for the launch in January 1943 speaks rather loudly in support of Lt. Hough's findings.)

By April 9, 1942, movement of the Eighth Air Force ground echelons to England had become a fact. VIIIth Fighter Command HQ was stripped of Hickey, Stone, Hough and Landry, all of whom reported to Gen. Hunter in the "game room" at Bolling Field. It was in that room that all came face to face with the overwhelming odds against which they were pitted. If anyone believed that negotiating the 500- to 800-mile stages across the North Atlantic was no more difficult than completing an overland cross-country flight from Wright Field in Ohio to Bolling Field in the District of Columbia, they were in for a rude awakening.

A simplified review of conditions would bring these facts to light:

(a) Nobody had established a basic functional system for gathering crucial weather data.

(b) Radio transmission and reception were subject to unpredictable fadeouts at the latitudes over which the crossing would be made. However, since no Allied radio facilities were, at that time, located in either Greenland or Labrador, the problem was really a nonentity.

(c) Airstrips – they could hardly qualify as airfields – at key locations were only about 30 percent completed in mid-April.

(d) Flight path proximity to the north magnetic pole tended to make a fighter's compass spin like a top.

(e) So-called foehn winds, the fierce 150-mph winds that swept the Greenland icecap nearly every week, would appear so unpredictably that no more than 4 hours of warning could be expected . . . even if radio contact could be established.

(f) and the *Luftwaffe*, predictably, could be expected to transmit totally erroneous commands and weather reports. There was always the possibility that one of the far-ranging Focke-Wulf Fw 200C Condor raiders would come slashing out of a massive cloudbank to break up the ferrying formations, sending the fighter pilots into disarray.

(g) North Atlantic weather was notorious for shifting from CAVU to zero-zero conditions almost in the blink of an eye. As pioneering aviator Jimmy Mattern learned in 1933, a heavy coating of ice might be thrown in for good measure.

As if all of that was not sufficient to give everybody second thoughts about the viability of aerial delivery of fighters, somebody asked what would happen to a young pilot with little formation and navigation experience when visibility rapidly deteriorated. If he was forced down in water that averaged about 37 $^0$ F with little more than an inflatable raft under him, his survival chances would be seriously limited.

In the Operations Building at Bolling Field, lights generally burned into the late hours as much of the planning, coordination, logistics and technical load fell on the shoulders of Jack Stone and Cass Hough. And it was even later every night when "Monk" Hunter and Hickey reviewed the day's output of data. "BOLERO" began to appear on crates and packing cases in great profusion. Rumors made the rounds like an inter-urban train.

Out on the West Coast, 100 new P-38Fs were abruptly shunted off to Building 304 at Lockheed Air Terminal beginning on April 15 for modification, a feverish activity that went on for 24 hours a day. The big range-extension program begun by Col. Kelsey was suddenly one of the most important programs in the country. Furthermore, it paid other handsome dividends about 45 days later when 25 slightly older P-38Es from the 54PS out of Paine Field, Washington, suddenly descended on Lockheed for similar modifications. Those Lightnings were to play a decisive role in countering a Japanese invasion of the Aleutian Islands and Alaska.

Pessimism engulfed the team at Bolling when Lt. Col. Milton W. Arnold from Air Transport Ferrying Command came in with some officers from BW-1 in Greenland. He had been making survey flights of the proposed fighter delivery routes in a Consolidated B-24A. The reports they made to Gen. Hunter's people were far from encouraging. "The weather over Greenland," they stated, "was totally unsuited for operations with any type of fighter aircraft – even with skilled pilots at the controls." With this knowledge in hand, how could Hunter bring himself to risk the lives of hundreds of critically needed young fighter pilots, not to mention the hundreds of fighters of unparalleled quality in the AAF inventory? (Col. Arnold eventually went on to command the 389th Bomb Group, known as the "Sky Scorpions," at Hethel in 1944.)

Brig. Gen. Muir S. Fairchild's office – he was the Director of Military Requirements – in the old Munitions Building was the scene of an important conference. Present were Gens. Arnold, Stratameyer, Spaatz, Miller, Hunter and Duncan, supported by numerous notable colonels. But nobody at that key meeting was more important than the very amiable 36-year-old 2nd Lt. Cass Hough. His work was crucial to the lives of many young pilots. Subject of the meeting: BOLERO delivery.

Later that afternoon, Gen. Arnold, looking more grim than usual in those frequently disastrous days, drifted into the Operations Building overlooking the confluence of the Potomac and Anacostia rivers. He slumped down into a chair opposite Hunter's desk.

"Monk," he growled, "it looks pretty bad. It's damn near impossible; we may have to pull in our horns."

"I'll admit it looks bad," Hunter drawled in that pleasant Savannah dialect, "but I don't think it could possibly be as bad as that."

Turning to Lt. Hough, Arnold calmly asked, "What do you think about it, Cass?"

Any challenge to Cass Hough was something to be solved with precision, probably a demeanor tied in with his astronomy training. He spoke crisply: "I think it is entirely feasible." Jack Stone added his 2-cents worth. "Let Cass and me take a couple of P-38s up there to prove that it can be done."

Gen. Arnold left without really responding to that suggestion. He mulled it over in his mind for a few hours. Hap decided that his men knew what they were doing. Calling Hunter, he supported their thesis by telling him to keep on the course already established.

On May 17, Col. (later Lt. Gen.) James E. Briggs, a senior officer who was then teaching freshman algebra at West Point,

left the U.S. Military Academy under orders to report to HQ "X" at Charleston, S.C. Virtually nothing remained of VIII FC at that location; only one person was there. Briggs was designated A-3 (Assistant Chief of Air Staff, Training), replacing Jack Stone, reassigned to the 1st Pursuit Group (F), then under command of Maj. John Zahn. (Actually, Briggs was placed in charge of operations and requirements, not training as such. To place things in proper context for the period, Hoyt Vandenberg was also a colonel at the time, as was Harold L. George.)

Just as Lockheed was putting the finishing touches on the first hundred P-38Fs for BOLERO, which might give the technicians a breather from the long hours and weeks without a day off, word was flashed to 1st Lt. Clarence "Shoopie" Shoop in the AAF Plant Representative's Office to prepare the next 100 production airplanes for another group, the 14PG. Lt. Shoop was a former California National Guard sergeant who was at Burbank in the capacity of AAF acceptance pilot. (In later years, as a General officer, he went on to command the California Air National Guard at Van Nuys.)

According to Maj. Ralph Garman's records, the 1st Pursuit Group – none of the groups converted to the "Fighter Group" designation until July, it seems – began to receive their BOLERO P-38Fs in mid-April. By that time, the 1PG was operating out of Grand Central Air Terminal in Glendale and out of Mines Field next to Inglewood and El Segundo.

Lockheed had the seemingly impossible task of manufacturing no fewer than 1,200 brand new 165-gallon drop tanks by May 15. At least 400 of the tanks would be required for installation on the 200 BOLERO aircraft that were to cross the Atlantic. And no less than 800 tanks would be needed to provide (initially) two sets of spares when they started on combat operations in the ETO. As for the Bell Airacobras, one group was carrying out fuel consumption tests near New Orleans, La., using the regular 75-gallon belly tanks. It seems that Bell could not possibly deliver the first 150-gallon tanks until July 1, but the P-39D pilots were able to cruise on 38 gallons per hour at 10,000 feet. "Scuttlebutt" had it that seven hours of flying time far exceeded that of the P-38F fighters. Subsequent events revealed exactly how inaccurate such rumors can be.

Pilots of the 31PG(F), then flying P-39Ds, were scheduled to acquire a full complement of new P-39Fs at Niagara Falls, N.Y., within a few days. Just to add to the confusion of the HQ "X" team, the Battle of Midway and several reports on shabby P-39 performance in Southwest Pacific combat convinced Gen. Arnold that it was illogical to put the Bell Airacobra into combat over Northern Europe against Nazi airpower.[2]

---

2. In later years, Lt. Gen. Briggs responded to my question in the following manner: "It had been decided that the Airacobra, or P-39, was no match for German aircraft in the European Theater of Operations (ETO). All of the aircraft were taken from the 31st and the 52nd to be sent 'somewhere.'" He obviously was not an admirer of the Bell fighter.

**ABOVE LEFT:** Operation BOLERO proved to be far more successful than anyone dared hope. Loss ratio was extremely low for a mission of that nature. An impenetrable weather front caused six P-38Fs and two B-17Es to run completely out of fuel over the Greenland ice cap. Lt. Brad McManus's airplane was the only one critically damaged. Landing with wheels down, fuel ran out and the nosewheel hit a crevasse. The airplane flipped, but they dug McManus out. (Russ Rajani, Pursuits Unlimited)

**ABOVE RIGHT:** This 94FS Lightning, flown by Lt. Dallas "Spider" Webb, landed with the props still churning. Result: two propellers and two gear cases back there behind the tail. As usual, the central gondola was hardly scratched. Webb's airplane was fitted with the long-barrel 20-mm cannon. (Russ Rajani, Pursuits Unlimited)

**BELOW ;** Aerial view of one P-38F-1-LO on the ice cap, taken from a recon Consolidated LB-30, shows the approximate final condition of at least five of the "Tomcat Yellow" Section which McManus was leading. Missions designed to "rescue" the downed aircraft found them in the mid 1980s . . . . under more than 200 feet of snow and ice. (Russ Rajani, Pursuits Unlimited)

Before that order came down, the 52PG(F)[3] under command of Lt. Col. Dixon M. "Dick" Allison, had moved its complement of P-39Fs (and a few Ds) to Grenier Field close by the Merrimack River at Manchester, N.H., in a staging prelude to the BOLERO mission. Of course Allison had no inkling that all of the familiarization effort with the Airacobras would go for naught. Sans the P-39s, his men would be on their way to the British Isles aboard ship by July. Most of the pilots would be winging over England in Spitfires before the year ended.

As for the P-38Fs, things were going along pretty well . . . except for critical shortages of some much needed components. Lockheed was forced to deliver some BOLERO-modification aircraft without key items that were on the planning tickets. Staff people at HQ "X" were taxed to the limit in attempting to locate misdirected shipments or trying to correct personnel errors. Just one example is cited, giving but a clue to a multitude of similar problems:

Lockheed P-38Fs modified for BOLERO had RAF-style VHF radios substituted for the HF radios used by the AAF organizations in the States. One clue was the "pylon" antenna that replaced the pitot-static tube staff just forward of the nosegear doors. Unfortunately, throat-type microphones worn by AAF pilots were not compatible with the British radios. The bulky microphones that worked with the VHF transmitters were, again unfortunately, part of a British pilot's helmet. Somebody had decided that the RAF-type helmets would never be used stateside, so they were all being shipped overseas. The BOLERO team located a major shipment in Montreal, Canada, already in the shipping channels (on time, for once, of course). They diverted enough of them to outfit all of the P-38 pilots.

After Milton Arnold had reported on his surveys of conditions over the North Atlantic routes, Capt. Michael "Flash" Gordon was dispatched to check out conditions at the airfields involved in the BOLERO aerial delivery operation. That involved checking facilities, supplies and overall conditions. He was appalled to find that Goose Bay still had parking places for no more than four aircraft; the contractor was warned that parking spaces must be provided for no less than 80 aircraft, and that included four-engine bombers and C-47s. Up at Bluie West 1, he learned that the Signal Corps section was overwhelmed with the volume of coded messages to be sent by

radio instead of by key or teletype. Gordon discovered that whenever the operators failed to contact Goose Bay radio, they simply proceeded to transmit the messages anyway, then promptly put it our of their minds! No guilt! It should have resulted in courts martial actions.

During his visit to Presque Isle, Maine, which was HQ, North Atlantic Wing of ATC, "Flash" Gordon discovered 300,000 pounds of priority equipment – mostly radio equipment and aircraft spare parts – piled up and waiting shipment. Intended for Goose Bay and Greenland destination points, it had merely accumulated since the ice had closed in on Goose in November 1941. Every bit of the 150 tons of material had to be at the prescribed destinations before any of the fighters could be flown out of the staging areas. It was not recorded that "Flash" used his disintegrator ray gun on anybody.

Having been appointed Assistant Chief of Staff-Operations, Col. Briggs promptly moved out of Charleston as May came to a close. He planned to take up his duties at Grenier Field, N.H., but had become seriously ill from the effects of Yellow Fever shots that he said were "badly attenuated." That brought Col. John K. Gerhart into the picture. Like Briggs, he had little or no experiences with P-38s; he was essentially a "bomber" man. But Gen. Hunter needed his expertise as Operations Officer/Eighth Air Force to bolster Briggs' suddenly threatened planning activities. Designated "control officers" were especially needed to regulate the flow of aircraft. They had become key elements in this operation, and the ultimate success of the movement of fighter aircraft stands as a tribute to their abilities.

Immediately after the 52PG(F) moved its Bell P-39s to Grenier Field in New Hampshire, the 1PG(F) was ordered to move to Dow Field (Bangor AAB) in Maine for initial staging. Their plans and timetables were upset when Gen. George Marshall, Army Chief of Staff, became alarmed at what he found during an inspection tour on the West Coast. He felt that the Western Defense Command was in deplorable condition. Therefore, on June 1 he ordered all eastward movement of the Eighth Air Force suspended; in fact, the 97BG(H) was ordered to fly its B-17Es back to the West Coast. Information gathered by Naval Intelligence and other agencies convinced everyone that the Imperial Japanese Navy (IJN) would not let the Doolittle B-25 raid go unavenged, while fleet movements and decoded messages pointed in that direction.

Officials became so alarmed about an IJN invasion of the West Coast that they ordered all equipment of the 1PG(F) loaded aboard American Airlines DC-3s at Bangor. It all went off in the direction of March Field. At 9:15 a.m. on June 3, no

---

3. Officially, pursuit and interceptor groups and squadrons were redesignated as fighter groups/squadrons on May 15; many did not change from PG(F) and PS(F) until July.

*The personal mount of Col. Ben Kelsey for the long overwater hop to England was this P-38F-1-LO, serial No. AC41-7631, assigned to the 71FS. Like the B-17E leadship, it still had the U.S. Army legend painted on the lower surfaces of the wing. Cass Hough's aircraft, AC41-7635, is parked in the background at Goxhill on the afternoon of July 28 as they prepared to depart for Hendon. (Bodie Archives, via Roger Freeman)*

less than 95 Lightnings of the group were set to leave for the opposite coast via Morris Field, North Carolina. Every member of the group not flying an aircraft climbed aboard twenty-one C-47 Skytrains of the 60TG. Col. Hickey received a last-minute telephone call from General Hunter at Bolling Field.

"Larry," Hunter said with solemnity, "I want Jack Stone to take over command of the group. They are to depart immediately, RON (remain over night) at Charlotte and be ready to move on to March Field." Within the hour the P-38Fs were headed south with a new commander in charge. He was promoted to bird colonel within days. (When Hickey turned to Lt. Col. Stone and told him to take command of the 1PG, Maj. John O. Zahn, up to that moment the group commander, demanded "What happens to me?" Hickey, caught off guard, blurted out, "I'll be goddamned if I know!")

Weather at Charlotte turned sour, so the group movement was held up temporarily. By June 5 the Battle of Midway, known only to Gen. Hunter in that command, had been decided in favor of the U.S. Navy. Then Gen. Arnold flashed a message to send the P-38s and all personnel and equipment back to Dow Field – an exercise that was not completed until June 11. Yes, things were tumultuous in 1942.

In less than two weeks the 1st Pursuit Group (F) would be taking off on the initial phase of the BOLERO fighter delivery mission, so Hunter quickly moved his "transient" headquarters north to Presque Isle Army Air Field in Maine. Facilities at PIAAF were very good.

A hint of what might be in store for the Lightning pilots came when a weather reconnaissance B-17E, returning to Greenland from Iceland, ran into "potato soup" weather. They decided to opt for Bluie West 8 (BW-8) and headed north. As the weather worsened, the plane commander reversed course for BW-1, but feeding a B-17's voracious appetite was turning into a problem. By some miracle they found a stretch of sandy beach and the pilot managed an excellent landing. The crew existed on apples and some onions for five days until a Coast Guard cutter could bring in 800 gallons of fuel. They took off and finally made it to BW-1. But Mother Nature decided to give them a hint that could not be ignored or handled with such ease.

Ten B-17E bombers from the 97BG flew out of Goose Bay at 8:30 p.m. on June 26 and headed northeast for Bluie West 1, some 779 miles distant. Unfortunately, the Air Controllers had not yet been assigned to perform their new duties. Acceptable weather was forecast entirely on the basis of poorly translated coded messages. Actually the weather was deteriorating rapidly. When the Fortresses were about 400 miles from Goose, they were swallowed by cold, gray fog. Just as all crews lost visual contact with any other aircraft, Greenland radio WYXE advised all pilots to return to Goose Bay. To make matters worse, radio reception was poor to dismal. Some crews heard a portion of the message, but others heard none of it.

Four of the ten B-17s were low on fuel and could not make it back to Goose. They headed for Bluie West 8. One bomber crash landed on the ice cap; nobody was hurt and they were all rescued. Another B-17 found its way to BW-8 and made a safe landing, but a third crash landed on a rocky beach near Edgesmunde, 240 miles north of BW-1. The 10 men were rescued by the Coast Guard. The fourth airplane ditched between a small island and the mainland shore. As the Boeing sank, crewmen climbed into a dinghy and paddled to clear the aircraft. Suddenly they were pulled toward the B-17 and the dinghy began to go down with the airplane. It was still tied to the fuselage. Somebody reacted well and cut the rope. They made it to the island and were picked up by a Coast Guard cutter.

Real depression swept over Hap Arnold. If 10 of our best bombers with the finest of navigation equipment could not

ABOVE: On July 6, 1942, Bill Weltman's contingent arrived at Reykjavik, Iceland, with high hopes of landing in England within hours. In the event, the 27FS was retained in Iceland for a time to provide air defense for the base in support of P-40s flown by the 33FS. Lockheed P-38F "17598" (AC41-7598) in the foreground is tentatively identified as Weltman's airplane. (Air Force Museum)

BELOW: Aircraft arriving in the British Isles by ship in 1942 were assembled at Lockheed-staffed bases such as the British Reassembly Division (BRD), Speke, or the BRD at Renfrew, Scotland. A larger facility, Langford Lodge at Belfast, Northern Ireland, was operated by Lockheed Overseas Corporation. A P-38F-15-LO and an F-5A-3-LO photo-recce aircraft are shown at Speke Aerodrome, just outside Liverpool.

the Air Corps number 41-9085, and it constituted the vanguard of the initial group of forty-nine B-17Es, eighty P-38Fs, and fifty-two Douglas C-47s to fly the North Atlantic route to Great Britain as the initial phase of BOLERO.

The mass movement was on. About a week earlier, on June 23, seven P-38s departed Presque Isle and headed for Goose, flying the 571-mile leg in formation with two of the Boeings. Weather was excellent and they landed at their destination without incident. Weather to the east was unfavorable, causing Goose Bay airport to become clogged with fighters and bombers. A good report came in for the night of July 1-2, so no less than 24 of the P-38s assigned to the 27FS (finally, the official designation) and 1FG Hq. squadron took off in company with the six B-17Es. They were on their way to Bluie West 1, at least 779 miles away.

Operations personnel at BW-1 were suddenly jolted by "May Fly, May Fly, this is B-17 leader with 24, I say twenty-four P-38 fighters and five, I say five B-17 bombers requesting landing instructions," crackling out of the radio loudspeakers. Finally, the big day had arrived as the first eight Lightnings smacked down on the steel Marston mats of the one and only active runway. As the last flight came up Tunugdliarfik Fjord, one plane was missing. Minutes later it was spotted trailing the others by several miles. One engine was dead, the prop feathered. Just like a C-47, it limped in on one engine to fly another day.

Young Lt. Peyton Mathis, Jr., had covered more than 70 percent of the course to Greenland when the Allison coughed its last. After completing his shutdown procedure, Mathis boosted power on the other side in an attempt to keep the others in sight. There was really only one suitable approach up the fjord to line up with the 4,500-foot steel plank runway because it was bordered on the south by 3,000-foot-high cliffs.

With drop tanks still in place, he managed to climb to 5,000 feet, circled for position, dropped gear and flaps for a down-wind approach at 150 mph. He had to do it right the first time because it wouldn't be good policy to go around on one engine under prevailing conditions. Chunks of rubber flew from the screeching tires, and his brakes belched smoke as Mathis sought to get that big fighter stopped in less than 4,000 feet. Just 20 feet from the end of the Marston mat, the Lightning slid to a halt. The pilot's biggest complaint: those swarms of local mosquitoes attacked him with a vengeance when he opened the canopy. But that was in keeping with the crude conditions at BW-1. The mess hall was a shack and the crew quarters were cramped and few in number.

When the 27FS had departed, the next squadron to arrive was the famed 94FS, the old "Hat-in-the-Ring" outfit. It was not the kind of XC flight that any of the pilots would ever want to repeat. July 6, 1942, was the kind of day that will age any pilot. All difficulties stemmed directly from one of those defective weather forecasts. Divided into four sections – Tomcat Black, White, Yellow and Green – to fly with four B-17E lead ships, the 94th squadron left Goose Bay in acceptable weather conditions. Tomcat Black section was composed of pilots Harmon, Widen, Ilfrey and Pringle; Tomcat White section had Williams, McWherter, Sutcliffe, and Hille in its P-38s.[4]

Halfway across Davis Strait was an

even make it to BW-1, how could a bunch of young fighter pilots hope to get close? He picked up the phone and called Hunter to find out if he favored abandoning the project. (It must be remembered that Arnold was far more affected by politics than any fighter command general would be.)

"Hell!," Hunter exploded, "we haven't even started yet. If we could get rid of those damn B-17s, we'd go right on across." It was pretty obvious that Hunter was a career pursuit officer.

"Monk" had already been prodded by Gen. Carl Spaatz after the latter had flown the route on an inspection tour days earlier. "Tooey" had been irked by what he found, compounding "Flash" Gordon's findings. He sent a radiogram of significant length to Hunter. What it said, in effect, was that: (1) None of the airfields have been finished . . . (2) None of the special communications systems required are in . . . (3) Weather reports are skimpy and inaccurate . . . (4) Gas and oil stocks are very low. But, GET MOVING!

Arnold's confidence in Hunter might have been flagging, but he had overlooked the capabilities of Briggs, Hough, Gerhart, Hickey and a few hundred young pilots who were more than ready to fight. On July 1 the first American-crewed combat aircraft to reach the United Kingdom by air in World War II landed at Prestwick, Scotland. It was a B-17E bearing

unexpected overcast. They climbed to 25,000 feet, but the P-38s were staggering under loads of ice. Then Lt. Harmon lost sight of the lead B-17E and was forced to made a quick decision. He continued on to BW-1 himself, a "gutsy decision." When the Fortress turned back for Goose Bay, the other three pilots went right along with it, having no idea of what became of Harmon.

Tomcat White section left Goose within 10 minutes of Black section's departure. Flying at an indicated airspeed of about 180 mph in formation with the bomber (about 23-in. Hg. manifold pressure and 1700 rpm), they encountered the same cloud bank after 2 hours in the air. All five aircraft climbed to 28,000 feet without finding a top. In the meantime, the dynamotor supplying power to the B-17's radio caught fire and was ruined. Then supercharger trouble developed in one engine.

At the same time, all four P-38 pilots asked for navigation instructions; of course there was no reply. The big Boeing made a slow turn back toward the mainland, but Lt. Sutcliffe was the only one who managed to stay with it in poor visibility. Hille turned 180 degrees and hoped for the best. He got it. By a stroke of good fortune he was passing over a hole in the overcast as the struggling Fortress went past. He quickly formed up with Sutcliffe. Williams and McWherter managed to pick up the D/F range on Simiutak Island for the flight into BW-1.

Tomcat Yellow section with pilots Webb, Starbuck, Harry Smith and R. H. Wilson departed Goose Bay, followed closely by Tomcat Green section with Lts. McManus, Rudder, R. B. Wilson and Lentz.[5] When the two B-17s and eight P-38s hit the white wall with only about 150 miles to go to BW-1, the Yellow leader could not contact AACS because of typical radio blackout so common to the route. After they climbed to 20,000 feet and found a top, they also saw another cloud bank up ahead, but it seemed to break off to the north. Meanwhile, Yellow section dropped down to 10,000 feet and located a break in the clouds. However, Tomcat Green followed them and went on past to the deck without finding a break in the weather. As they climbed back to 4,000 feet, they picked up some ice, but they did settle between cloud layers. Yellow leader radioed Green leader to report they were going into BW-1, but the latter suspected it might be a phoney Nazi message (a not uncommon situation).

Forgetting how far they had come from Goose, Green section leader radioed his counterpart that he was returning to the mainland. Several hours later, that navigator made his Labrador landfall . . . but this time he was all of 350 miles north of the isolated base at Goose. Quickly he contacted the 38s to find out if they had enough fuel to make it, but he even botched that one by asking, "Do you have 30 minutes of fuel remaining?" It was hardly likely that the P-38s could do 350 miles in 30 minutes. Of course everyone increased power, expecting to see the base heave into sight very soon. (The B-17 navigator should have had his pilot head for Gander or Presque Isle.)

Suddenly, Lt. Rudder's Lightning rolled and headed for whatever lay below. His arms felt like lead. He fumbled for the oxygen controls, somehow managing to get the right ones. As

his head cleared, he looked around and found his wingmates clustered nearby. His was the only plane in the section that did not have full tanks when he took off, so they were all concerned that he had gone dry.

"Where is Goose?" they demanded of the B-17 navigator. He replied that they should be there in about an hour. Back came the power setting on eight Allisons and they all slowed to about 150 mph. If that navigator miscalculated again, five aircraft were going to be lost and a few hot-tempered pilots would be out for blood.

Some really tired fighter pilots landed at the RCAF-operated base after battling miserable weather and worse navigation for just about eight hours! They had flown off the gravel runway at 11 a.m., only to return to that same runway after a long day. Some had to be lifted out of their cockpit seats. It was estimated that they had covered about 1,500 miles.

Tomcat Yellow section had hardly been cheered by the intercepted radio message from Green leader, and prevailing weather conditions did not look encouraging. However, flying at 20,000 to 25,000 feet for another hour, they broke out of the overcast about 15 miles from the coast of Greenland. They landed after some seven long hours. Commanding officer Col. Bernt Balchen, himself a famed pioneer aviator, and his staff did not have a clue that the 94FS fighters were on their way. Bad communications were, once more, the culprit.

On July 10, Lockheed P-38Fs from Tomcat Green, accompanied by the stray "cats" from Black and White sections, flew to BW-1 in good weather.

Even as the first of two entire groups of P-38 fighters proceeded to fly the treacherous North Atlantic air route in sections, the Air Controller assigned to Greenland, Lt. Col. Robert Landry, received a message about a *Luftwaffe* attack against Reykjavik, Iceland. He immediately committed 13 of the *in transitu* Lightnings to air defense and put them on alert status. Tons of 500- and 1,000-pound bombs were spotted around the base for rapid loading into B-17Es of the 97BG as a precautionary move against a possible attack by sea. Other enemy aircraft "sightings" and rotten radio communications tended to make everybody edgy. Landry soon learned that the "air attack" had been a false alarm. However, he decided to keep one P-38 airborne over the base at all times and kept another four fighters on a ready alert status. The rest were permitted to continue on their way.

Tomcat Green and Tomcat Yellow section pilots had rejoined forces by July 14, 1942, up at Bluie West 8. They were alerted to prepare for the 845-mile overwater/glacier flight to Reykjavik, Iceland. One B-17E weather ship took off at 3 a.m. on July 15, with the main body of seven P-38s and one lead bomber following about 30 minutes later. Lt. Starbuck's P-38 had suffered a damaged rudder when the ground crew of another aircraft caused a minor collision as the aircraft were spotted for takeoff. A low battery charge forced Lt. Lentz to return to BW-8 on one engine after he had a propeller run away (overspeed).

Weather reports from the BW-8 reconnaissance plane and from another Fortress westbound from Iceland were favorable, but nobody reported that a thick weather front was moving down from the north. One flight scheduled to leave BW-8 that morning had been told about the front, but somebody "just happened to forget" to relay the message to anybody departing with the latest mission involving an expanded Tomcat Yellow section. By that time, six P-38s – flown by Lts. Rudder, Smith, Webb, McManus and the two Wilsons – together with a single B-17 piloted by Lt. Staples were headed for Iceland. The simple communications "oversight" was eventually to prove very expensive, not to mention the fact that men's lives were at stake.

Somewhat ironically, while tremendous reliance was placed

---

4. *Pilots in Tomcat Black were Lts. James Harmon, Norman I. Widen, Jack M. Ilfrey and Wesley M. Pringle, Jr; Tomcat White section had Lts. Robert E. Williams, Richard W. McWherter, George W. Sutcliffe and Earl W. Hille, Jr.*

5. *94FS pilots in Tomcat Yellow were Lts. Dallas "Spider" Webb, Donald O. Starbuck, Harry L. Smith, Jr., Robert H. Wilson; Tomcat Green pilots were Lts. Joseph B. McManus, Carl F. Rudder, Robert B. Wilson and J. C. H. Lentz.*

on the crews of the 97th Bomb Group for leadership, one of the BOLERO mission planners had pointed out that the B-17 he was following was piloted by a young officer just 3 months out of flight school. Worse, the man in the copilot's seat had graduated from flight school only 1 month before he was on his way to the United Kingdom. As a saving grace, it had become standard procedure to have a seasoned Northeast Airlines pilot flying along with the "green" airmen as an "advisor" to provide some element of confidence.

While Tomcat Yellow flew over a terrifying and seemingly endless icecap, the weather was not threatening. Crossing the eastern coast, they headed out over the cold, gray Atlantic. A little over an hour later, the weather suddenly turned sour. In heavy murk, they climbed to 22,000 feet without finding a top. A report, supposedly from Iceland, said that Reykjavik was closing down rapidly. (Later on there was sufficient evidence to support a contention that at least this particular transmission had, indeed, come from a Nazi source . . . most likely a U-boat.)

After nearly five hours of flight they would normally have expected to be ready for a landing in Iceland, but a decision was made to return to BW-8. More bad luck. When they were still two hours away from the Greenland base another towering weather front rose in front of them. Worse, BW-8 radio WYTK reported that "zero-zero" conditions prevailed at the base. That was absolutely unexpected. Normally there was only one foggy day per year, with perhaps 3 inches of rain and 8 inches of snow in the same

period. The air was usually very dry. Pilots in the reconstituted Tomcat Yellow section were still about 350 miles away from BW-8, but BW-1 was even farther away. Once again a B-17 leader had erred; they were not going to make it to either base because the P-38s – after 8 1/2 hours of flight – only had about 30 minutes of fuel left in their tanks. Weather at BW-1 was reported in code as "clear."

The Boeing pilot turned south toward BW-1, which probably should have been their destination as soon as they turned back from the Iceland area. Most of the P-38 pilots had already suffered through one maximum-duration flight within the last 10 days, but each of them now suspected that they had pushed their luck too far. Not only had they flown somewhere between 1,500 and 1,600 miles, they had been forced to climb to more than 22,000 feet a couple of times. Never had they seen their fuel level readings so low. Up to that moment, a few wondered if they were doomed to a lifetime of flying in circles over the North Atlantic route.

Section leader McManus, his tanks nearly dry, descended to look for any suitable emergency landing site. He dropped the landing gear to reduce speed as he swept down over the trackless, gray-white wasteland. It can only be described as "brutal." Like the others, McManus had jettisoned his external tanks to reduce drag to a minimum. At close range, the ice was seen to be full of ruts and crevices. As McManus opened his throttles to climb away, both engines quit after coughing and sputtering briefly. He was not about to look for a better landing spot or attempt to turn with both engines powerless and windmilling. He was faced with much the same situation that faced Lt. Ben Kelsey 3 1/2 years earlier in the cockpit of the XP-38.

Penetrating the crust, the main wheels slowed the P-38 rapidly, but the nosewheel dug in. The draglink or uplock broke and the wheel snapped backward. Gears, shaft and the lefthand propeller tore loose and went spinning through the snow. Up and over went the nearly new fighter. As it landed inverted, the left tailboom broke and the entire canopy disappeared in the snow. Somewhat remarkably, McManus survived with hardly more than a sprained shoulder, but the P-38F suffered major damage.

With little fuel remaining, the other five P-38 pilots fanned out for belly landings, wisely leaving the landing gears up. They all "pancaked" down on the snow and slid to a quick halt without further incident. One of the two Boeings continued to circle until the fuel was nearly exhausted, sending out an SOS signal all the while. Finally, the pilot proceeded to make a smooth belly landing. Radio operators at BW-1 and BW-8 managed to get a point fix on the downed B-17, but the weather was not cooperating. Some of those dreaded foehn winds were forecast for the area. As a consequence, all of the PBYs, C-47s and a B-17 were tied down to weather out of the blasts of the storm. There was no improvement the next day; in fact it was worse.

By July 17 things had scarcely improved, but a small rescue party headed for the coast in the vicinity of the forced landing site. They were traveling in a mostly open power boat, but they managed to rendezvous with the USCG cutter *Northland*. The cutter acted as an icebreaker for the rescue boat – it was too small to be called a vessel – so that it could approach within a reasonable distance of the downed aircraft and land a rescue team.

A Douglas C-47 headed west out of Reykjavik was the first aircraft to locate the downed aircraft. After they circled the cold, tired and hungry airmen and sent off a message to the cutter and to BW-1, the C-47 crew dropped a food package by parachute. Howling winds blew it across the icecap and totally out of reach in a minute. Their second package drop proved to be more successful, providing the stranded crewmen with a fair food supply. Sleeping bags, blankets and medical supplies – including a supply of whiskey, for medicinal purposes of course – followed with considerable success.

Guided by the Consolidated PBY-5A amphibian that orbited the area, the rescue team proceeded 15 miles inland with a dogsled, reaching the survivors on July 19. Lt. McManus and the two Norden bombsights rode out on the sled. The lieutenant's injury made it too difficult for him to trudge through the snow. While most of the survivors attempted to carry their own personal gear out, it was not long before they abandoned almost everything, including some expensive tailormade uniforms. The 15-mile trek seemed like 100 miles in the hard going. McManus's injury was the only one suffered by anybody, although several men had a severe case of snow blindness by the time they were rescued. With nice weather prevailing at the coast, it was a rather pleasant ride in the small rescue boat out to the *Northland*, anchored and with its Grumman J2F-2 Duck biplane secured on the fantail. Everyone transferred to the PBY amphibian as soon as they got to ice-free waters.

As things turned out, that was the only serious loss sustained in the entire BOLERO fighter aerial delivery program. A few Fortresses were lost, but no C-47s were even seriously damaged. Operation BOLERO was the code name for a major campaign, namely the Eighth Air Force's combined assault against *Festung Europa*, and the delivery program was the result of a serious shortage of ships and a high attrition resulting from the terribly successful U-boat campaign then in full swing.

If anybody still had any doubts at all about the superior qualities of the Lockheed P-38 as a long-range weapon with great potential, it had to be dispelled by that pioneering operation. Actual losses were entirely due to operational errors, poor navigation and the weather. The young fighter pilots never flinched. The Allisons were extremely reliable – flying on American fuels – and the Lockheed external tanks could hardly have performed better. Another case of the right thing being at the right place at the right time.

There were, of course, many harrowing and even humorous incidents involved in the transfer of the 1st and 14th Fighter Groups to Europe that summer. Lt. Col. Landry was even goaded into placing a few of the "wilder" P-38 pilots under restriction to quarters as a result of some of their uninhibited adventures at BW-1. Nearly 200 pilots were involved in flying the P-38Fs to the United Kingdom in that unparalleled effort. Although the vast majority of pilots participating in the transfer of Lockheed P-38s, B-17s and C-47s to the ETO were probably under the age of 23, men like Lt. Col. John Stone (commander of the 1FG), Maj. Ralph Garman (flying pursuits since early 1938) and Capt. John "Bill" Weltman were over 25 years of age. They may have been referred to universally as the "old men" in each case when the lieutenants spoke of them (but not at them). But some of the real old timers were yet to be heard of.

It is difficult to fully appreciate the true magnitude of the achievement of the Army Air Forces in delivering hundreds of aircraft to the fledgling Eighth Air Force in England. And the climactic delivery of nearly 200 single-seat fighters over the North Atlantic routes in the summer of 1942 was totally unprecedented. Everybody said that it couldn't be done . . . so they did it.

Just for comparison purposes, it was exactly five years earlier that Pan American Airways and the British Imperial

Airways each managed to have one North American transocean survey flight succeed over that approximate route. Neither of the big four-engine flying boats used carried any significant payload on the flights. Is it any wonder that many people viewed the P-38 fighter as a quantum leap forward?

D It was time for the "Fuddy Duddies" to make their move. By that time, some other old timers had left their marks in aviation history. Col. James Doolittle was right up front earlier in the year when several B-25 Mitchell bombers hit Tokyo. He was 45 years old at the time. Col. Signa Gilkey was doing terminal velocity dives in the P-38s at age 40.

Up at Presque Isle, a relatively ancient Col. James Briggs was just recovering from the effects of some "bad" Yellow Fever shots he had received. Depression had set in because he expected to miss the BOLERO overseas movement entirely. (When Lt. Gen. Briggs was interviewed some years later, he expressed his views on how important the mission was to him. "My greatest fear was that I would wind up in some Training Command billet in the U.S.A. and miss the entire war.")

He pled his case to "Monk" Hunter. "Buster," Hunter said, "you can go along with the Headquarters Flight when I go, but only if: (1) the Flight Surgeon will clear you, (2) you can rack up 5 hours in a P-38 (Briggs had zero), (3) you can make five nighttime landings in a P-38 and (4) that at least 2 of the 5 hours must be logged at night." Now, it is important to know that Col. Briggs was at least as old as Doolittle. Therefore, he was either one terrific pilot or the Lockheed Lightning was a beauty to fly (or both). Briggs managed to meet all of the Hunter requirements at Presque Isle.

Brig. Gen. Hunter, also older than Doolittle, was set to lead the "ancient aviators" to England in one of the B-17Es (AC41-9119). Those staff aviators included Col. Benjamin S. Kelsey – who had already completed one impromptu round trip to Bluie West 1 in a P-38 – from Wright Field, Col. John Gerhart, Col. James Briggs and Capt. Cass Hough (at the time, recently promoted from 2nd Lt., but already a major because another promotion had come through two days before their liftoff for GB). Hough was the one Service Pilot in this select group, meaning that he had been commissioned before the war on the basis of his extensive civilian flight experience and management capabilities. When he went on active duty at Selfridge Field in 1940, he was one of a select group in the Air Corps with any significant multi-engine time logged.

Each with a huge grin on his face, the self-deprecatory "Fuddy Duddies" charged off the runway at ZQ (Presque Isle) at 1410 hours GMT on July 18, taking a bearing for Goose Bay. The relatively short flight of 2 hours 50 minutes was accomplished without incident. Following a siege of bad weather that finally broke on July 23, Lightheart Red flight (their formal call identification) eased off the runway for the 779-mile overwater flight to BW-1. They touched down on the single runway a bit over 4 hours later. Hough had become separated from the others in a thick cloudbank, climbed to 28,000 feet and soon linked up with two of the other Lightnings. The weather at BW-1 was beautiful that day, prompting a bit of horseplay on the part of the "old, bold aviators."

Cass Hough's personal account of the adventure from Goose Bay to INDIGO (code for Reykjavik) to Stornoway, Scotland, is certainly the most accurate record (Cass was a meticulous record keeper). His narrative is presented verbatim (with a bit of clarification, as required):

The general's ship took off from YR (Goose Bay) first, and it was supposed to circle the airfield at 8,000 feet until we could form up. My canopy decided to let go at that time, so I had to go back and fix it, which took about 15 minutes. I guess the B-17 crew miscounted, so they left for Greenland without me. By pulling all the power that was permitted (until I learned better during flight testing), I caught them just as they left the coast of Labrador.

About 250 miles out of YR, with everybody in loose formation (200 yards or more apart), I suddenly saw the B-17 disappear into the mists with Johnny Gerhart in tow. They were swallowed up by what had been an absolutely invisible overcast because of the tricky mists and a glare from the sea. So there I was at 10,000 feet over the middle of the ocean and buried in overcast. I turned northwest and went to full power to climb. Besides being on instruments – in a fighter – I soon found that the airplane was completely coated with rime ice. I broke out on top at 27,000 feet, losing the ice almost immediately . . . to my everlasting relief. About 20 minutes later, another P-38 popped out of the overcast no more than 200 yards in front of me and, of course, I had found my good friend, Ben Kelsey. It was most comforting to have his professional company.

Not more than 10 minutes later, another P-38 appeared directly ahead, and we soon identified it as Buster Briggs' airplane. We closed up and had a neat three-plane element headed for Greenland, but I was damned cold. I could hardly move. It was 30 below out there and my cockpit heater wasn't working! (One major wartime problem with the P-38, never satisfactorily corrected, was the extremely poor heat distribution to the cockpit.) After another half-hour we spotted a B-17 and formed up with it, wondering where Johnny Gerhart was. Naturally it didn't turn out to be 'our' B-17 at all, but another one bound for BW-1. Gerhart – who recollected being pretty well scared – stuck to Gen. Hunter's B-17 like a leech.[6]

The next day – July 24 – we joined the B-17 at 10,000 feet over that gray-white icecap, but we were somewhat disturbed to find the bomber had started some 30 degrees

off course. By the time we reached the east coast of Greenland, we were 55 miles off course . . . in a 90-mile trip! You must admit that it was pretty damn poor navigation. Ben and I consulted with each other, asked the B-17 operator if they knew where they were. The pilot said that we were crazy and that our navigation was wrong. At least Ben and I agreed that our headings were identical and that the B-17's heading was 25 to 30 degrees off at 109.

We continued off course for an hour and 30 minutes, and we were nearly 95 miles off course by that time. I must admit that Ben and I were getting a bit desperate by that time, especially since we were then picking up the southwest leg of the Iceland (INDIGO) radio beam, which we never should have reached. When the Lightheart Red leader B-17 continued across it to the 'N' zone, I radioed (in the clear) that I was leaving the flight in 30 minutes to go it alone into Reykjavik. Ben supported my stand and agreed to leave with me (Kelsey was Lightheart Red 4, Hough was Red 5). That fool pilot in the B-17 wasn't even trying to find where he really was.

By then General Hunter was becoming more than a bit concerned because of our announced intentions to leave (the formation) and because the weather was positively stinking. We weren't any too happy about things ourselves, having been on instruments for nearly an hour in tight formation. We were icing up; we were irritated by this totally ridiculous situation; and then Schmoldt (B-17 pilot), probably at the prodding of Hunter, wanted to know, 'if you are really sure of your position,' just to make things worse.

I managed to control my temper, telling him that if we all turned 40 degrees north we'd soon hit Iceland. Otherwise, it was on to Norway and internment for the duration. Red leader radioed Reyjkavik, then turned 38 degrees north. Within 42 minutes we broke out of the clouds over the coast of Iceland. I wasn't a bit sorry to see the end of that tough bit of flying.

After a good night's sleep, they flew to Stornoway (radio call: Pigsty II) and then on to Ayr, Scotland (radio call: Greenherd), where the four plus one P-38Fs – Lt. Don Starbuck of the 94FS had joined them on the last leg – in a vitriolic retaliatory gesture led the B-17E over the base, but then forced it to land first in the presence of a large welcoming committee of AAF and RAF dignitaries on hand to greet the VIIIFC commander. The B-17 pilot, Schmoldt, was furious, but Cass Hough says that Hunter roared with laughter about their avenging shenanigans. The "Fuddy Duddy Four" had made it, as if there had really ever been any doubt that they (of all P-38 pilots) would, ending a milestone phase in American – and indeed, the world – aviation.

Lightheart Red 2 and 3 – Briggs and Gerhart – went on to become Lieutenant Generals. In the ETO, Gerhart soon commanded the 95BG(H), the only Eighth Air Force group to receive three Distinguished Unit Citations. It was the first group to bomb Berlin, March 4, 1944. Gerhart later commanded a Combat Bomb Wing. Kelsey, for various reasons, moved back and forth between the U.S. and U.K. on assignments. Most everybody agrees that Ben should have become a three-star general; yet he remained a colonel throughout the war, retiring years later as a Brigadier General. Cass Hough shared command of the Technical Operations Section (eventu-

---

6. *About 30 minutes after joining up with the lone B-17, they spotted the Hunter airplane in the thinning mists. Gerhart's P-38 was tucked closely under the wing. All elements of Lightheart Red joined forces to fly into BW-1.*

ally known as Operational Engineering) with Kelsey and also became a full colonel by the end of 1943.

Considering Kelsey's talent and magnificent contributions to aviation progress, it is doubtful that anybody – even Arnold and Doolittle had no explanation – could ever explain why he did not progress to at least Lieutenant General level. Kelsey himself said, "I did not want a desk job. I preferred to fly and to be involved in day-to-day detail." It may have been as simple as that.

E August 1942 was the beginning of an important era for the Lockheed P-38 Lightning. Far out toward the end of the seemingly endless chain of barren islands known as the Aleutians, a pair of P-38Es shot down two – almost certainly three – large four-engine Kawanishi Mavis flying boat patrol bombers near Atka on August 4. It was the first aerial victory for P-38s in the war. That victory, gained in the winterly summer skies near Siberia, was achieved near the 55th parallel.

Ten short days later at a spot nearly half-way around the world at the 20th longitude and above the 60th parallel, another P-38 gained the first victory for the AAF in the ETO after an assist from another P-38F and a P-40. A very aggressive Focke-Wulf Fw 200 Condor four-engine recon-bomber was the Nazi culprit that fell victim to a P-38's guns. Icelandic skies were the scene of that aerial combat action, with the Lightnings coming up from Keflavik. Members of the BOLERO movement were involved, so there was a direct tie-in with that venture. Fortunately for this narrative, an eye witness account of the event was provided by a participant. Details of that very accurate, participant account follow.

After a 4 hour and 45 minute flight from BW-1 to Reykjavik, Capt. John Weltman learned that the 27FS was going to be held in Iceland to add support to the aging P-40Cs of the 33FS. That force had been on duty there since 1941, primarily at Keflavik, a crude, one-runway airfield on a site that was rocky and boring. Most of the active field was surfaced with oiled gravel; there were a couple of Nissan huts and a characterless Operations building. Young "Bill" Weltman was squadron commander when the unit was moved to Keflavik.

He was idling away the uneventful hours in the Ops Office when the jangling telephone broke the silence. Reykjavik control center was reporting a Focke-Wulf Condor over Icelandic territory. This was not a practice or a false alarm. Weltman, a West Virginian who had received his Air Corps wings in 1939 and had been posted to pursuits/fighters since that time, picked up another phone to call a friend, Woody Korges, at Reykjavik.

"What's up Woody?," Weltman wanted to know.

"We spotted a big Fw 200 in the area, so I scrambled a couple of your P-38s. I've also scrambled a couple of the 33rd's P-40s," Korges replied.

"Well, Hell," Weltman burst out excitedly, "I'll get my wingman and just go up and see if I can nail him!"

According to Weltman, the Condor reconnaissance-bombers had been overflying the airfields with impunity for months. Bell P-39s and the 33rd's Curtiss P-40Cs had proved to be totally ineffective against the fast raiders.

Weltman's following narrative is the only first-hand account of the AAF/8AF's initial ETO victory in combat in World War II:

"There was a broken overcast – between 8/10 and 9/10 coverage – at 1,500 feet over the field. I grabbed my wingman, 2nd. Lt. Elza Shahan, by the arm and we sprinted for our airplanes. Well, when we got fired up and went off into the wild blue through the low cover, there

was our boy (the Condor) right in front of us . . . just like it had been planned. So I took out right after him.

"Had he turned south, as I expected he would, he would have gone into the clouds, but to my surprise he turned north over the bay. The weather up that way was clear as a bell. Anyway, the one P-40 that had been chasing him (and has evidently been given half credit in the records) had given up the chase by that time, so Shahan and I set up a regular gunnery pattern. The ol' boy was just a lumbering clunk (to us) because we were really much faster." (It is quite possible that, on August 14, the Germans did not know that P-38s had been assigned to an interception role.) "Both of us were banging away at him with everything we had, shooting as if it (the Condor) was a big sleeve target.

"As I bored in to point-blank range, I saw those tracers coming at me from the top turrets and someplace in the tail area. But just like the RAF boys said they would, the tracers seemed to curve away. About that time, my guns jammed and one engine got a bit rough on me." (Upon landing, Weltman discovered that two large-caliber bullets had smashed the forward ammunition cans. Other bullets had shortened the tip of one propeller blade by 4 inches.)

"I told Shahan to stick with the Condor until I could go down and get another P-38. Elza stuck with him for another 5 minutes, but then decided he might get away. By that time the German was smoking a bit and there wasn't much return fire (indicating that the raider had been hit, possibly seriously). As Elza closed in on him, the Condor just blew up and he had to fly through a lot of debris.

"One of the crew was washed up on the shore later on, and he was found to be full of bullets. So we knew we had been scoring an awful lot of hits on that big clunk. Shahan and the P-40C pilot, 2nd. Lt. Joseph Shaffer, each got half credit for the kill."

Bill Weltman became Executive Officer of the 1FG in North Africa early in 1943; by May he had been assigned – personally by Gen. Doolittle and Gen. Vandenberg – to command the 82FG at Berteaux. He led the development of P-38 dive bombing, and completed his 50th combat mission on June 12, 1943, with the 95FS. Gen. Doolittle sent a personal commendation to Weltman in July. In August, Lt. Gen. Carl Spaatz informed Gen. Arnold that the young colonel would be working under his (Spaatz's) command. Bill's last flight in a P-38 was in an L model on October 17, 1945. He had flown virtually every model since his first YP-38 flight on June 23, 1941.

By the end of August 1942, no fewer than 164 Lockheed P-38s had flown across the treacherous North Atlantic to England in the first group of 386 fighters, bombers and transports that had made it safely. All told, a magnificent group of no less than 920 aircraft (including one small flight of Republic P-47Cs equipped with P-38 drop tanks) had attempted the crossing by the end of 1942. Losses were quite small, with 892 airplanes arriving safely at their stations in the UK. Of that total, approximately 700 belonged to the Eighth Air Force.

Other than the six P-38Fs forced down in Greenland by bad weather and an accompanying poor navigational decision, only one other P-38 was lost on BOLERO. Exactly 100 percent of the P-38s were flown by their own combat crews, or remarkably, by planning staff officers. Not one ferry pilot was involved. Although the AAF had expected to lose up to 10 percent of the 920 airplanes committed, the loss percentage was only 5.2 percent. In December, the North Atlantic route was closed to all air traffic until Springtime 1943.

# CHAPTER 10

## From the Aleutians to Eagle Farm – the Fight for Time

If America had been fortunate enough to have General Simon Bolivar Buckner, Jr., as the Hawaiian Defense Commander at Pearl Harbor, TH, on the morning of December 7, 1941, the outcome of the Japanese attack probably would have been significantly different. Unlike Gen. Short and Fleet Admiral Kimmel, Buckner was firmly of the opinion that the Japanese would ultimately attack the United States territories. As a result, he was doing everything in his limited power in the nearly forgotten Alaskan Territory to be prepared to counter such an attack. Buckner was in command of the minuscule Alaskan Defense Command (Army). He was almost an unheard voice in the wilderness; perhaps he had even been sent there as a punishment for being too vociferous. In the event, he had absolutely nothing to do with defending Hawaii.

Simon Buckner was not the sort of soldier who would allow himself to be put down by the opposition. And what was unusual for a U.S. Army Infantry senior command officer in the 1940-41 era, he seemed to sense that air power was crucial to the defense mechanism of his entire remote command. Aside from less significant detractors in the Army, the general had three major antagonists to contend with in those days: the U.S. Navy, the weather and the Imperial Japanese Navy – probably in that relative order. Interservice rivalry was so deeply ingrained in officers intent on furthering their own careers that any real adversary was often forgotten. Gen. William "Billy" Mitchell could have attested to that.

Somewhat fortunately, Alaska's top Army officer had two or three major allies to combat the "enemies." Those allies were shrewdness, the remote location and civilian construction teams. Navy opponents were constantly lobbying Congress and the War Department to outlaw Buckner's determined battle to fly long-range reconnaissance missions over Alaska's outer waters. They opposed or blocked every effort on his part to build a string of airfields beyond his mainland command far out in the virtually unchartered and unpopulated Aleutian Island chain. After all, the Navy contended, their base at Dutch Harbor was the center of their defensive hub, while their Sitka-based patrol bombers were capable of patrolling the ocean expanse and bombing the enemy.

Those patrol "bombers" they alluded to were a truly pitiful handful of Consolidated PBY-2 flying boats, not based in Alaska at all but on detached service from Seattle, Washington. With a calm weather top speed of 156 mph (as opposed to roughly 250 to 290 mph for the general's early-series B-17s and LB-30/B-24Ds) coupled to an insignificant bomb load, the plodding flying boats were hardly ideal for Alaskan defense. They definitely were not optimum for any assault on a determined enemy invasion force.

Of course there was the "might" of the U.S. Navy's North-

ern Pacific Fleet to be taken into consideration too. But as late as the spring of 1941, the "fleet" consisted of one new gunboat – the U.S.S. *Charleston*, flagship of the Navy officer-in-charge – and three commercial fishing boats painted gray! Rather coincidentally, they were called "Yippee" boats, but that had absolutely no connection with a tag that was widely applied to the popular YP-38s. The boats had taken on the mantle of patrol boats (YPs) upon application of the traditional paint of the day. That was the Alaska sector naval force in 1940-41 under command of Capt. Ralph C. Parker. Evidently he was a pragmatic man for he happened to be a supporter of Gen. Buckner and his unconventional ideas.

The Army commander's prime ally, shrewdness (it might be read as deceitfulness), was to manifest itself – happily for Americans – in the willful diversion of funds from Alaskan mainland projects to the building of Army airfields out in the Aleutians. Going so far as to set up sham fish canning companies (shades of Col. North and the infamous Irangate scandal), Buckner had bogus civilian construction crews start to build the military installation at Cold Bay at the western extremity of the Alaskan Peninsula. That was in August 1941, proving that at least Buckner was paying attention to communications from Washington and newspaper articles. His actions were those of a desperate man. A bit later he began work with another illegitimate spinoff company to start construction of an airstrip on the distant Umnak Island, a desolate spot with a total population of 50.

Just 10 days before the Pearl Harbor debacle, official authorization suddenly came through from Washington; Buckner could now officially proceed with building air bases at Cold Bay and at Umnak Island! The Cold Bay facility became the military Fort Randall, while the Umnak base became Fort Glenn. Somewhat amazingly, Gen. H. H. Arnold's new Army Air Forces combat command was totally unprepared to supply defensive fighters and bombers to man those stations, so the authorization to build was an empty gesture and a hollow victory for Buckner.

Tundra – hardly a roadbuilder's ideal turf. The only viable location for an airstrip on Umnak that would be worthwhile for the defense of Dutch Harbor in the Aleutian Islands was a place called Otter Point. Exposed to the elements, it was composed of spongy tundra which was incapable of supporting an aircraft let alone a squadron. Col. Ben Talley and his 807th Engineer Corps solved the problem with one of Gen. Hap Arnold's pet devices that had proven to be so useful in the "Battle of the Carolinas" training maneuvers just a couple of

*ABOVE: Only BOLEROized P-38Fs (and a few P-38Es and P-38Gs) flew in the United Kingdom in 1942, and hardly anyone realized that P-38Es were already engaged in battle in the frigid Aleutians chain that stretched 1,000 miles or so out toward Russia and Japan. These 11th Air Force Lightnings were photographed during a mission out of Adak to Amchitka. The 54th FS fighting leopard insignia was painted on Prestone coolant scoops. (USAAF)*

*BELOW: Modern mount in primitive conditions. As the Battle of Midway and the Aleutian Campaign formed ominously like a typhoon on a distant horizon, the 54th Fighter Squadron's P-38Es were taking up defensive positions near Anchorage, Alaska, because Washington officialdom expected Adm. Yamamoto to attack Alaska and the U.S. West Coast cities. En route from California, the Lightnings refueled at Watson Lake's primitive airstrip, each pilot servicing his own aircraft, pumping over 600 gallons per P-38 by hand from 55-gallon drums. (Col. Stanley A. Long)*

months earlier – the Marston mats. These perforated steel planks with interlocking edges could support a fleet of new B-24s. Buckner had ordered 70 acres of Marston mat planks for the 300,000-square-foot strip and hardstands at Otter Point (and for other contemplated base construction).

On March 31, 1942, the Douglas C-53 transport of Brig. Gen. William D. Butler, the new commanding general of the Eleventh Air Force, became the first airplane to touch down at Fort Glenn's airstrip, Umnak Island. With uncanny anticipation, Gen. Buckner had put the Alaska Defense Command on War Alert as of December 1, 1941! It was certainly not his fault that nobody in America was farsighted enough to have at least a handful of new Lockheed
P-38s dispatched to man the new base, the one at Fort Randall or at Elmendorf AAB until impending war became a reality or faded away.

Being preoccupied with isolationism, most Americans had learned little of importance about militaristic nations in Europe or Asia. The only combat-worthy fighters in the U.S.A. that could do battle in the far north were Curtiss P-40s and probably less than two dozen Lightnings. That was it.

The powerful U.S. Navy, which had literally fought Buckner because they considered the defense perimeter to be their bailiwick, had manned Dutch Harbor – their key installation – with an awesome force of 67 men! They had perhaps another 300 at nearby Kodiak and 180 way off at Sitka. Total naval airpower for the tremendous Alaskan expanse was vested in a "fleet" of six Consolidated PBY Catalina flying boats. By that time the surface fleet had been bolstered with no less than six World War I four-stack destroyers – probably some rejected by the Royal Navy when offered under Lend-Lease.

In the days immediately following the murderous attack on Oahu and other Western Pacific targets, Gen. Arnold sent some P-38s directly from Lockheed's Burbank factory to Fairbanks and Anchorage. Presumedly they consisted mainly of P-38Ds, which could not be considered to be fully combat worthy, and probably some P-38Es. It is important to recall that the D model was set up for the 37-mm cannon while the E model had the Oldsmobile (Hispano) 20-mm cannon.

Fortunately for Butler's defense forces, the Japanese had seriously underestimated American weakness because of faulty espionage. They failed to foresee the benefits to be derived from launching a coordinated invasion of Alaska in December 1941. It is a good bet that their intelligence people were fooled by Gen. Buckner's truculent approach and possibly believed that he had the full support of Washington in his assertive actions. There is little doubt that a force of 10,000 IJA troops or Marines, supported by two light carriers and their defensive warships, could have overwhelmed Dutch Harbor, Kodiak and Juneau while laying waste to Cold Harbor and Elmendorf Air Base within the first week of the war. Even one battleship in such a force might have been unstoppable. Alaska would have been lost and Western Canada would have been seriously threatened.

The psychological effect on America's West Coast popula-

A 54FS Lightning sits in the quagmire that was called "Longview." This Adak, Aleutian airfield was only 250 miles from the Japanese-held Kiska, providing an ideal base from which to launch multiple strikes. Second Lieutenant Stanley A. Long arrived at Adak's new strip on September 13, 1942. Living conditions were best described as miserable. Snow was not a major problem in conducting operations, but ice and fog made life very unpleasant. You didn't try to climb above the clouds in the Aleutians because the higher you went, the worse the ice became. Ice changed the airfoil shape and added hundreds of pounds of weight to the aircraft. (Col. Stanley A. Long)

tion would have been far more serious than anyone can imagine. Possibly thousands of aircraft and shipyard workers would have deserted their California and Washington homes and headed east. The Japanese soon would have had bombers within 3 hours' flight time of the Boeing plants at Seattle and Renton, and Bremerton Naval Shipyard would have been a prime target as well. (Many vessels damaged at Pearl Harbor were eventually repaired or refitted at Bremerton.) The enemy intelligence and command errors related to Alaska may have been a fatal blow to the entire Japanese war effort.

Thousands of miles from Anchorage, some cryptographers in the office of Naval Intelligence at Pearl Harbor had intercepted many Japanese coded messages referring to Operation MI. By May 15, 1942, the information was in the hands of Pacific Fleet Admiral Nimitz and his staff. They concluded that the IJN, commanded by Admiral Isoruko Yamamoto, would attempt to overwhelm Midway Island in the Central Pacific while launching a (belated) major diversionary thrust at the Aleutians and possibly mainland Alaska.

In the United States, Chief-of-Staff Gen. George Marshall issued an order that emphasized just how seriously the Japanese plans were taken (by then) at the highest levels. He ordered Gen. Arnold to have two entire P-38 fighter groups – the 1st and the 14th – abort their in-progress Operation BOLERO mass movement to England. They were to fly immediately to the West Coast for combat against any imminent attempt by the enemy to invade the mainland.[1] That order was cancelled before the Lightnings were deployed for effec-

---

1. USAAF pilots who were in classes that graduated between the latter half of 1941 and 1944 either loved, feared or disliked P-38 airplanes, but the tendency toward criticism was 99 percent based on comparison with the fighters they were then (in 1943-45) currently flying. One very important fact always seems to have escaped them, however: total production of P-38Es in 1941 was about 100 units; exactly one experimental P-47 was built; precisely two XP-51 token tributes were exacted from the British Mustang I quantities. Only the proven (but seriously limited-capability) P-40s were available in quantity, and the Lightnings were really the only American fighters capable of taking on the best of German and Japanese combat aircraft everywhere on earth. They fought effectively in the Southwest Pacific in the jungle environment; they were the only types with the range and capabilities to defend the Aleutians; with no P-38s remaining in the U.K. once Operation TORCH took priority, the AAF had no effective fighter aircraft to carry the fight to continental Europe; and finally, they were the only fighter type the Allies had that could effectively escort the heavy bombers or carry out strike missions at 300 miles or more combat radius of action as late as December 1943.

Even in the face of the awesome handicap of totally inexperienced pilots facing off against some of the Luftwaffe's most experienced and skilled warriors in war-proven aircraft, early P-38s more than held their own. Think about supply lines thousands of miles in length when some minor part is needed and clouds of sand are encountered daily. When it came to firepower, range, survivability and maneuverability for air-to-air combat throughout 1942 and 1943, only the P-38 had it all!

tive defense following the determination that Midway Island was the main target.

Five long months after war was declared on Japan, on May 23 to be precise, the 54th Fighter Squadron was separated from the 55th Fighter Group at Paine Field, Washington, and all of its P-38Es headed south toward Burbank, California, for modification. Many of the Lightnings, including one piloted by Lt. Stanley Long, arrived over the San Fernando Valley after dark. Somebody had not done their job. With no advance notification of their arrival, Los Angeles went to a full blackout condition.

Lt. Long, totally unfamiliar with the Burbank airport (but well aware of the dangerous surrounding Verdugo Mountains) contemplated heading west toward the Pacific and bailing out. He was nearly out of fuel. Suddenly a light appeared below. Long recognized it as the landing lights of a commercial DC-3 airliner. Pitching into a turn, he swung around, dove in behind the Douglas and followed that aircraft in for a hasty landing at Lockheed Air Terminal. Several of his squadron mates followed him when his landing light extended. Viewing the surrounding mountains the next morning, Long realized that he was lucky to be alive.

By May 29, factory teams had done a remarkable job. All of the P-38E fighters had been modified with external fuel tank-bomb pylons (of the type made standard on P-38Fs at that time), winterization equipment, and more than a dozen other small-scale modifications. Lt. Long retrieved his updated aircraft, thundered down the field past the bustling Lockheed buildings and the new Vega aircraft plant, made a sweeping turn over downtown Burbank and headed north for Hamilton Field past San Francisco Bay. With a few squadron mates in formation, they made the trip in approximately 80 minutes.

At Hamilton their orders were confirmed to head for Elmendorf AAB at Anchorage, Alaska, by way of Felts Field in Edmonton and Watson Lake, both in Canada. The weather at Watson was beautiful. After landing on the good-weather gravel strip, Long and the others had to service their own aircraft. It was necessary to pump fuel by means of hand pumps from 55-gallon drums. By June 2 he and his P-38 were members of the 11th Air Force at Elmendorf, assigned to a mixture of training and patrol flights. Rather strangely, Long and his squadron mates were totally unaware of any impending Japanese attack. But far to the west, enemy naval and army units were within hours of launching a belated invasion.

Maj. William M. Jackson's 54th Fighter Squadron was assigned to the 343rd Fighter Group, and on June 15 the squadron was deployed to Cold Bay (Ft. Randall), soon followed by another important move to the noisy Marston mats at Fort Glenn in the Fox Island group. Umnak Island was about 600 miles from Kiska, which the diversionary Japanese force

*ABOVE: Missions out of "Longview" were usually limited in scope in 1942, but unlike missions over Continental Europe, any small force of bombers had some escorting fighters. This Consolidated B-24D and Lockheed P-38F duo typify the equipment available in the Far North for 11th Air Force operations. (Col. Harry Dayhuff)*

*BELOW: Two Lockheed F-5A-1-LO photo-recon airplanes (of three assigned to Alaska) remain parked in dirt revetments on a base of Marston steel mats as five P-38G fighters taxi out to escort a single B-24D on Arctic strike mission. The F-5As were considerably improved versions of the pioneering F-4s, having additional horsepower and better camera arrangements. First F-5A deliveries were made in August 1942, along with the initial batch of P-38Gs (from which they were derived). This photograph was probably taken in September when the G versions were rushed to the Aleutians. On August 4, Lts. Ambrose and Long, flying wing on a mission leader B-17E near Atka, caught three Kawanishi H6K4 Type 97 Mavis four-engine flying boats as they attempted to attack U.S. Navy installations at Dutch Harbor in the Aleutian chain. In the ensuing attack, one Mavis went down in flames and one fell out of control in a death dive. The third flying boat was set on fire. These were the first aerial victories of the war for P-38s. Lt. Stan Long survived the war and eventually flew P-51Ds in the Korean War. His early-type P-38E mounts performed superbly during the many months he flew them under the most adverse conditions. P-38Es were formally Lockheed Model 222-62-09 versions. Only 210 were built before production was switched to the improved P-38F type. (Col. Stanley A. Long)*

had invaded and captured during the first week of June. Weather permitting – which meant infrequently – the obvious target of the 54FS was the Japanese task force at Kiska. Even when excellent weather prevailed, a combat radius of 600 miles was hardly a safe situation in any early series P-38s; it was downright impossible for contemporary fighters.

Within days "weather permitting" was interpreted to mean that if you could locate the runway for takeoff in the persistent fog you went. Without any doubt, the Aleutian weather had to qualify as about the worst in the world. Winds could howl up to 80 mph while, at the same time, fog was thick enough to limit visibility to six feet! A cloud front could coat a B-24 bomber with a ton of ice in minutes. Temperatures in the B-17, B-24, and P-38E cockpits at 20,000 feet were recorded at 60 degrees below zero. Rubber parts frequently shattered like glass. Hydraulic fluids were close to solidifying in the lines.

Navigation was a nightmare. All existing American navigational charts were either based on a Russian survey of 1864 or some Rand McNally road maps. Large volcanic islands that poked up high into the clouds were often mislocated by more than 50 miles. Jetstream winds were such that a mission to Kiska sometimes meant 2 hours outbound for a B-24D followed by a return trip of 9 hours during which the eyes were constantly snapping back to the instrument panel.

Lt. Long recalled that his first landing at Fort Glenn on the semi-rigid Marston mats was a real eye opener. The mats rattled like a thousand tin cans as he rolled along, and a pilot could get seasick from the undulations of the Martson strip runway as the tundra progressively gave way under the weight of each aircraft.

Supporting the IJN task force of Vice-Admiral Boshiro

Hosogaya in its two-pronged assault on the Aleutians in early June was a small fleet of Kawanishi Mavis flying boats. Six of the large Kawanishi H6K4 Type 97 four-engine patrol bombers – a mid-1930s type that appeared to be a contemporary combination of the 1935 French Loire-et-Olivier H.246.1 and an American Sikorsky S-42 – had flown out from Paramushiro in the Northern Kuriles. Under command of IJN Capt. Sukemitsu Ito, they comprised the primary bombing force available to Hosogaya, particularly after the admiral had offloaded numerous Nakajima A6M2-4 Rufe seaplane fighters at Kiska before taking his carriers to other waters.

The totally unexpected defeat of major portions of the Japanese fleet at Midway Island mandated his prompt return to the Western Pacific frontier. Adding to the problems plaguing the remaining units at Kiska was the loss of three of Capt. Ito's six Kawanishi bombers to the elements during the invasion of Kiska, Adak, and Attu.

Ito led the flight of the three remaining Mavis boats as they flew 600 miles to the Fox Islands on August 3. He was determined to sink the U.S.S. *Gillis*, a seaplane tender (the AVD12) that had been converted from an old World War I flush-deck destroyer. The *Gillis* had been dispatched to the area to service USN Catalina flying boats operating from that base. A destroyer and the tender, caught within Harold's Bay, managed to avoid bombs dropped by the big Mavises. It all added to Ito's frustration. He then decided to repeat the raid the very next day, hoping to catch the Americans off guard as he had done the first day.

Equally determined to put an end to the Japanese bombing attacks, the AAF bomber commander, Col. William Eareckson, was busy setting up a proper defense. He would use a few of his bombers as combat command centers and

P-38Es of the 54th Squadron as interceptors. Those Lightnings had flown into the new airstrip at Ft. Glenn (on Umnak) in July after making a 2-hour hop from Ft. Randall. Eareckson adopted the BOLERO technique in which a bomber crew uses their navigational and scouting expertise to advantage by leading fighters to an intercept point. A strike force of one four-engine bomber and two P-38 fighters comprised each interceptor flight. Squadron commander Jackson was ordered to furnish three of the flights for the morning of August 4. Lts. Kenneth Ambrose and Stanley Long were the intercept team of the third flight.

Col. Eareckson personally briefed Lts. M. H. McWilliams (B-17 pilot), Ambrose and Long. He told them that Maj. Miller had taken off earlier in a B-24 with a brace of P-38s in trail. "We'll run the patrols all day," said the colonel. "He's (Miller) going to stay there until you relieve him. Takeoff is at eight, and I don't mean 5 minutes later. Ambrose will answer to the call sign 'Skylark' and Long, you're 'Robin.' Got that? Good luck and stay away from their tail guns," he admonished them. (Kawanishi Mavis flying boats had armament consisting of a 20-mm tail gun in addition to rifle-caliber machine guns at nose and midsection locations.)

McWilliams took off and headed out toward Harold's Bay in a long climb, while Ambrose and Long darted around between cloud layers at 3,500 and 9,000 feet. They spotted Miller's B-24 just as his escorting P-38s turned back for home. Near Great Mountain, the B-17 bomber crew spotted a couple of specks at a distance of about 10 miles. They were heading toward the bay. After the initial alerts, there was a call from the B-17. "Skylark! Skylark! Do you see them now?" The Fortress crewmen had lost contact.

"Nope, no sign of them yet." was the reply from Ambrose. Yet the P-38s were headed right at their target.

As the B-17 crew went to battle stations at about 15,000 feet, the P-38 pilots switched on their guns and sights, ripping off a few bursts to warm the guns. Suddenly the targets, two big flying boats, reappeared against the sea of white clouds at about 7,000 feet.

Lockheed's P-38s were about to get their first taste of air-to-air combat, nearly eight months after the attack on Pearl. (It was several days later that, half-way around the world, Capt. John Weltman and Lt. Elza Shahan would attack a Nazi Focke-Wulf Fw 200 Condor raider over Icelandic waters, scoring America's first victory against the *Luftwaffe*.)

Ambrose took the Mavis to the left while Long assaulted the enemy on the right. Ambrose missed with his first burst, but Stan Long saw his slugs hitting both flying boats as they came closer together instead of splitting away. His .50-caliber slugs and 20-mm shells tore into the cockpit enclosure of the right aircraft. Both P-38s sizzled past the Mavis boats, drawing defensive fire. Ambrose's fighter sustained some hits. Long was fascinated by those large red meatballs painted on the Jap aircraft, but Ambrose spotted smoke trailing from the wing of his target, the result of Stan Long's hits. Both Kawanishis droned toward a fogbank at 3,500 feet as the two Lightnings clawed around for another pass. It was to be a low approach in an effort to avoid return fire.

Long's gunnery was top notch. Once again his slugs ripped into the hull of his target, working in close to the flight deck. The Mavis jerked violently as the crew was decimated by gunfire; then it wobbled drunkenly out of control, rolled over and plunged toward the waters of Nazan Bay. Stan Long had hardly wasted a bullet or shell.

On his second pass, Ambrose put full bursts into the wings of his target, causing one of the radial engines to explode in flames. A long tongue of flame ate away at the fabric on the tail. Bombs were seen to jettison from the flying

for lack of targets – the aerial bombardment threat to Dutch Harbor and the American fleet units evaporated into the ever-present mists. Capt. Ito flew his patched up Mavis back to Paramushiro, having lost five aircraft and scoring only cosmetic damage to the American installations and ships.

The most important event to take place in subsequent weeks was the invasion of Adak Island. If the U.S. forces were to drive the Japanese from Kiska and Attu, they couldn't possibly do it from far away Ft. Glenn. On the same day that Ambrose and Long chalked up their historic victories, Eareckson's bomber fleet – a motley collection of bailing-wire B-17s and B-24s – having declined to a force of less than a dozen in number, was in a battle to sustain operations. Most losses were the result of accidents. Those 1,200-mile grinds through "ice looking for a place to form," impenetrable fog and lava-rock-filled clouds had taken a fearful toll. The enemy had large concentrations of antiaircraft guns at Kiska and Attu, and there were the Rufes – floatplane versions of the fabled Zero.

But for the terrible storm that raged during the invasion of Adak and for four days afterward, the victory would have been a "walk-in." Not one Japanese soldier or sailor contested the retaking of Adak, and when the weather finally cleared, P-38s flew constant air cover missions over the barren island. After a quick survey of the site, Army Engineers under command of Col. Carlin Whitesell built a complete new airfield in a handy lagoon – the only possible site – by draining the entire area which was part of Sweeper Cove. Marston mats could not be used as a base because the entire supply of perforated metal planks – part of that initial order placed by Gen. Buckner in 1941 – went to the bottom in icy waters when storm winds capsized the cargo barge. Improvising quickly, the Engineer Corps used hard-packed sand for the runway and hardstands as an interim measure.

boat as it headed straight into the fogbank, flaming like a funeral pyre. There could be no doubt about its ultimate fate.

As the victorious P-38s circled, McWilliams reported spotting what he thought was another brace (unlikely) of Kawanishi Type 97s going into a cloud bank. He cranked the B-17 around and followed the target into the mists. About 25 minutes later, the B-17 was spotted unbelievably chasing one Mavis out of the cloud, straight at the two P-38s. In the heat of the battle, Ambrose and Long positively reported that this third Jap was mortally wounded, but neither could claim a positive victory. They had no way of knowing that the damaged patrol bomber was piloted by none other than Capt. Ito. Had they known, they would have taken desperate steps to attain certain victory. Ito managed to nurse the badly damaged Kawanishi back to Kiska some 5 hours later. The Mavis force was done.

By the middle of August – after Col. Eareckson had discontinued his defensive patrols over Umnak and Unalaska islands

On the 2nd and 3rd of September, Lt. Long and others in the 54FS flew back-to-back missions of 5 hours, 30 minutes and 6 hours, 30 minutes to attack Kiska installations. They had to operate from Ft. Glenn. Just a few days earlier, a single P-38E had shot up about a half-dozen Rufe floatplane fighters as they lay at anchor in the bay. In a scornful, provocative act, the P-38 then loitered over the base for a few hours in hopes of catching some incoming enemy aircraft. That bordered on foolishness. The pilot was fortunate in that he encountered no headwinds on the way back to the base, but his landing was made with just 5 minutes of fuel left after a mission of close to 9 hours. This was not a mission over unfriendly lands; it was over freezing arctic waters in possibly the worst weather region of the world. The Lockheed Lightning had made a point.

Col. Eareckson was the first pilot to land at the new Adak base, code named "Longview," on September 10, 1942, in the van of the dozen remaining bombers of the 36th Bombardment Squadron. They were escorted by 18 fighters, including some P-38Es from the 54FS. Lt. Long arrived with a few more on the 13th. At about the same time, a ship arrived with a load of Marston planks, which the Engineers laid and linked in an overnight frenzy of work.

Putting his entire force of bombers up, Eareckson headed for Kiska on the morning of the 14th. Fourteen P-38Es, led by Maj. William Jackson, were joined by an equal number of Bell P-39F Airacobras that had just joined the mixed-breed 343rd Fighter Group under Col. Jack Chennault. All of the aircraft involved went to Kiska at deck level, hoping to surprise the defenders. It didn't work.

Spotters picked up the incoming waves of aircraft and the bombers were met with a hail of flak. Nevertheless, within minutes the bombers plastered the base and sank two ships. While some of the P-38s and P-39s went up to fly top cover, four of the Lightnings used another half-dozen Nakajima Navy Type 2 (Rufe) floatplane fighters for target practice. They destroyed all six at anchor along with an unidentified flying boat (not a Mavis). The top cover P-38Es and P-39Fs tore into five of the Rufe fighters attempting to break up the attacking formations. Firepower of the AAF fighters was devastating, causing the Jap fighters to break up in the air or explode in flames.

In one of those unaccountable accidents that can be compared to the later loss of Maj. Thomas McGuire in the Philippines and Col. Harold Rau's victory over a silver Bf 109 which, in its death gyrations, wiped out a passing P-38, two American pilots were killed at Kiska. Maj. Jackson's P-38 and another Lightning flown by Lt. Dewey Crowe collided while pursuing a diving Rufe floatplane. Both AAF pilots perished.

After that initial pioneering raid from Longview, daily assaults on Kiska became routine, but the Japs were tough and were not about to give up without a real fight. Adding to the tribulation, the lagoon-based airfield tended to return to its former status at times. Fighters and bombers alike tended to emulate Catalina flying boats during landing and takeoff in foot-deep water. If the water got deeper, operations were forced to cease.

The Eleventh Air Force, in the autumn of 1942, summarized combat losses of only nine fighters and bombers. However, no less than 60 airplanes of all types (B-17, B-24, LB-30, B-26, C-47, P-38 and P-39, P-40 and OA-10) became victims of the horrific weather or mechanical failures during that same time period. Several of the aircraft simply flew into unchartered mountains in the blinding fog. As has been pointed out, one of the worst enemies was the unpredictable weather. In the same time frame, that polar weather was insidiously assaulting P-38 and B-17 pilots participating in Operation BOLERO on the opposite side of the globe.

Attacks on Japanese installations continued until the enemy finally was forced to withdraw completely in the face of overwhelming odds by the end of July 1943. The enemy simply faded into the ice fog that surrounded Kiska.

In accordance with Army Regulation 95-5, issued and promulgated on June 20, 1941, the United States moved haltingly into the modern age of aerial warfare potential by creating the United States Army Air Forces. As it turned out, it was not a minute too soon.

In the succeeding months, there was some considerable confusion about things like the remaining Air Corps, the GHQ Air Force, the Combat Command, etc. If it was not accompanied by infighting and rancor, it would be unique in history.

The new commanding general, Henry H. Arnold, was a good executive, a fervent airman and he was truly committed to formation of an independent air force, whenever that could be managed. But he was not Merlin the Magician, and he – individually – could not identify all of the deadwood in his command. After years of tight rations and the demise of Brig.

Gen. William Mitchell, there were men who would never risk their careers in the interests of crusading against poor performance, wherever it was evident.

That all come home to roost on December 7, 1941.

The debacle at Pearl Harbor and in the Philippines could have been reduced substantially if several commanders at high levels had paid even minimal attention to history, let alone the available intelligence and espionage data that had to be available to them. To what degree they were derelict in their duties will never really be known to the general populace.

In the face of broken treaties and, ultimately, war in Europe, the known propensity for the Japanese to seek expansion in the Orient, or any psychological understanding of mankind and the effects of isolationism in America, American leadership should have at least been on full alert. The cost would have been minuscule.

Were these men so engrossed in their own career movement that they were afraid to be accused of mild saber rattling? Evidently.

During summer war maneuvers in the Carolinas, airplanes were generally dispersed and often placed in revetments, as it was expected they would be in any emergency. Supposedly, that is what maneuvers are all about. At Pearl Harbor, the Navy lined its ships up like ducks in a gallery, and orders were

*Although the shining black P-38M two-seaters of 1945 have always been considered the sole night-fighter version of the Lightning series, two radar-equipped P-38Fs fought the Japanese in the Pacific at Guadalcanal and in New Guinea as early as February 1943. Incomplete records indicate that these aircraft were limited to a total of two, both being converted at Port Moresby or in Australia in January. Assigned to the 6th Night Fighter Squadron with other P-38Fs and some Douglas P-70s, they operated with the Seventh Air Force in the 15th Fighter Group. However, at least some records indicate that they may have operated as Detachment A with the 8th Fighter Squadron of the famed 49FG. Another P-38 detachment of the 6NFS operated with the Thirteenth Air Force at Guadalcanal at about the same time. The squadron insignia, official from 1924, was a skull on a spinning propeller background. Yagi-type antennas were fitted to the nose section, and an SCR540 radar set was installed. Two of the .50-caliber machine guns were relocated forward (a very difficult task). (Phil Narzisi)*

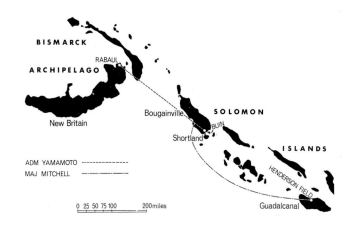

*"Most Remarkable Long-range Mission of the War."* Typical of the accolades applied to the Yamamoto Mission in April 1943, this probably applies even when compared to the outstanding Doolittle Tokyo Raid because of its superb timing, total surprise, and absolute achievement of its original goal. Maj. John W. Mitchell (339FS C.O.) who planned and led the mission, was the real hero of the day. Working with a limited number of operational aircraft and having to assume that the enemy would be punctual, his attack plan called for flying nearly 600 miles on the outbound leg over an arcing route at sea level to avoid detection. Expecting heavy fighter escort for Yamamoto, he set up a four-plane "killer" flight of pilots from the 70FS to be protected by a much larger high-level team. The timing was perfect beyond belief, results went according to plan, and American losses were virtually nil. It was so elegantly executed that the Japanese never suspected that their codes had been broken. The only real flaw was in the bickering over who shot down the admiral. Three Betty bombers were claimed, but records prove that only two were actually involved. The Japanese escort was relatively small, and their losses were almost 100 percent. Needless to say, only the Lockheed P-38 was capable of flying the Yamamoto Mission.

actually issued not to disperse airplanes in order to deter anticipated sabotage. It seems that the American militarist of the day was contemptuous of the Japanese, based almost entirely on a total lack of understanding of the Asiatic mind.

At Army Air Force fields such as Hickam, it seemed like business as usual. For those who lived near military bases or airfields in the 1930s and 1940s, it was accepted fact that the draft act had not made Americans love those in uniform. And military pay scales were abysmally low, giving many enlisted men little to do but go out and get drunk and get into trouble. Close order drill may look great to an officer who is several years out of West Point or The Citadel, but it was useless to a fault in a "kill or be killed" situation, soon to be commonplace as 1941 rolled on.

Like it or not, Brig. Gen. Billy Mitchell, in his own way, was right. Coupled with his departure from the service, political roadblocks to "real" interservice war games – something that never *really* did happen – American AAF men flying bombers were virtually uneducated in the techniques needed to bomb ships on the move. Did they believe that dive bombing was invented just for the thrill, or that torpedo bombing was developed because it was easier than dropping a 2,000-pounder from high in the sky? One look at Navy indifference about level bombing should at least have provided a clue. Dedicated commanders were driven crazy when engaged in evaluating the true effectiveness of AAF medium and heavy bomber attacks against moving warships. Gen. Arnold had every right to be in a bad temper.

Ultimately in 1942, the greatest effectiveness of the American heavy bomber in Pacific Ocean areas was in the previously ignored science of long-range reconnaissance. Oh, yes, the Army had concentrated on observation. With a big Oh? What good was a Douglas O-46A or a North American O-47A over the Coral Sea? But the B-17 crews quickly learned how important "photo-recon" was.

Quite frankly, some great administrative generals and colonels were total misfits when given command of an understrength, poorly equipped force that had to fight committed, trained and properly equipped enemy troops, ships and planes. Heroism is not enough in such situations. And false claims of success – such as the completely erroneous Colin Kelly episode – only served to deflate those who were doing a real job. Kelly gave his life in attempting to do the best he could, but the system had handicapped him from the start. The lessons of trench warfare in Europe in World War I and our own war between the states seemed to have been forgotten or totally ignored in an Isolationist atmosphere.

How well did our Army Air Forces perform in the days and months following December 7, at least in the Western Pacific areas?

Not well at all. In the first place, there were really no air forces in being at the time. Not, at least, as the conception of the AAF had suggested they would be. Wrangling over the form to be assumed by the AAF occurred by higher levels. On the surface, training looked acceptable, but it was chaotic.

As for aircraft production, suddenly attempting to reach a level of more than 50,000 airplanes a year, the question might be asked: Why did Lockheed Aircraft come from a position of virtually laughable obscurity to become the largest aircraft manufacturer by the end of 1941, all in the course of three short years? It was mainly because the management respected talent and utilized it with zeal, and because they committed their own limited funds to factory expansion when others insisted on governmental funding first.

However, all that aside, how did America do in conducting the war far west of Pearl Harbor?

Well, on December 7, the Japanese hit Hickam, Wheeler and Bellows Fields at 0755 hours, destroying 64 of 231 airplanes of the Hawaiian Air Force. Of the 167 remaining, nearly half were severely damaged – out of commission. (The U.S. Navy lost 50 percent of their 169 assorted aircraft.)

One miracle stands out. Not one *new* U.S. Navy battleship or even the most ancient of aircraft carriers was even near Pearl Harbor on December 7. Miracle or coincidence, it certainly makes food for thought about the home base lack of preparedness. It all lacks credibility.

There was, at that time, a Far East Air Force (to be reborn, of necessity, in 1944). Whatever transpired and the whys, whats and wherefores aside, preparedness and execution of defense actions read like a Greek Tragedy. Interception flights could not even locate slow-moving Japanese bombers approaching Philippine bases after American radar had supposedly located them. When U.S. fighters came back for fuel, well coordinated attacks caught them in helpless confusion.

By all accounts, Clark, Iba and Nichols Fields had been defused, all but annihilated by December 9. The scoreboard: 18 of 35 Boeing B-17s destroyed; 55 Curtiss P-40s pulverized; 30 Martin B-10 and Douglas B-18 bombers (?), plus some observation planes, turned into junk. Even three Republic (not Severskys) P-35As were wiped out.

Meanwhile, up in Alaskan Defense Command headquarters, questions arose on how a half dozen Douglas B-18s and a dozen 5-year-old Curtiss P-36s were going to confront an invasion of Alaska and, of course, western Canada. Finally, after repeated demands were transmitted to the highest authority, the 77th Bomb Squadron and the 11th Pursuit Squadron arrived at year end. It was frightening to contemplate.

Down, once more, to the South Pacific arena, initial fighter planes for the fledgling Far East Air Force, consisting of eighteen P-40s, were flown in to Australia. They belonged to the 17th Pursuit Squadron.

Previously, there were some comments on the structures of the Air Forces. On February 5, 1942, several existing air forces were dissolved, and the Fifth, Sixth, Seventh and Eleventh Air Forces were created. Now for the truth; at any given time within the following year, an entire air force might be a thousand miles away from its designated area of responsibility and that same "air force" might consist of as few as six aircraft!

On February 12, the Tenth Air Force was established. Where? At Patterson Field, Ohio.

The Fifth AF sent out ten P-40s on February 19 from Darwin to defend Allied troops against aggressive attack by Japanese bombers. Virtually all of the P-40 force was wiped out in combat with the IJN fighters.

Two days later, Gen. George Brett, CG of Allied Air Forces (SWPA), was forced to pull the Fifth Air Force out of Java HQ and he reported that 11 of the 20 AAF bombing strikes were complete failures. In two more days, Gen. L. H. Brereton was forced to pull his Fifth Air Force HQ back to India.

On February 27, the Battle of the Java Sea had turned into a rout and a disaster. AAF personnel had to quickly destroy 27 crated P-40s that had just arrived in Java by ship. They also learned that on February 23, the U.S.S. *Langley*, carrying 32 new Curtiss P-40s and their pilots, was sunk. Most of the pilots were rescued, only to be lost when the rescue ships were also sunk. Only two pilots of the group survived.

Out in the Southwest Pacific and mid-Pacific, the Japanese Navy and Army steamrollered forward in (roughly) a 220-degree arc. AAF attacks on warships achieved less than 10 percent effectiveness. Our own heavy bombers sometimes attacked American or Allied shipping.

By March 5, the new Tenth Air Force, having moved to India, was composed of eight tactical aircraft. All were B-17s, and it would have been remarkable if all were on flying status. Brereton assumed command.

Just a few days later, the USAAF reached a reasonably viable organizational status, eliminating the Air Corps and the Combat Command.

On April 9, Bataan fell. The Battle of the Coral Sea, calling up a new kind of warfare, raged from May 4th to the 8th. Despite limited resources, the U.S. Navy turned the tide. AAF bombing effect: pitiful.

Skipping over other disasters, we came to the Battle of Midway. It was essentially a naval victory, with AAF participation not likely to put a smile on Hap Arnold's face.

Up to that time, little was heard about Lockheed P-38s, except in the ETO and in the Aleutians. But, on September 3, 1942, Lightnings participated in a long overwater assault on the enemy, the longest such mission over water up to that time in World War II. Lightnings escorted Boeing B-17s on a 1,260-mile operation. Those P-38Es and Fs encountered weather that was so bad, five of the six B-17s were forced to turn back. The mission: from Umnak, in the Aleutians, to Kiska and back. In the SWPA, Maj. Gen. George Kenney took command of the Fifth Air Force.

The first reported P-38 operation with the Fifth Air Force, against Buna and Gona, came on December 8, 1942! About six weeks later, the initial Thirteenth Air Force Lockheed P-38 mission was reported.

At long last, the Lightnings were in action in the SWPA.

With fewer than 100 Lockheed P-38s operating in different air forces having to contend with their own responsibilities, the impact of their presence was severely muted. However, Gen. George Kenney merely increased his pressure to obtain more P-38 aircraft, and he was gradually rewarded for his efforts. Optimism began to increase with the new year of 1943. Within a short time, a mere dozen or so Lightnings were to have a tremendous impact on the overall course of the war. Not that the operations in the Aleutians were unimportant, or that Operation BOLERO wasn't a great event in history. Additionally, the key to success in Operation TORCH and the subsequent battle of northwest Africa was the P-38. But a mission right out of fiction was about to become one of the most successful operations of World War II. From that point on, it was as if the Allisons in all P-38s had shifted into high blower.

D There is little doubt that it was one of the most beautifully planned and brilliantly executed combat missions of the entire war. Although there was a dearth of parametric or demonstrated data upon which to draw in planning the escapade, this did not deter the primary planner one iota. Fortunately for those involved, a small contingent of then current production P-38s had been delivered to the Thirteenth Air Force just a matter of weeks earlier. Otherwise, there was not an AAF or Navy aircraft that could perform the feat at all, let alone have some remote chance of success. The exploit to which we refer was the intriguing "Yamamoto Mission."

*Having returned to the U.S. from Guadalcanal for some R&R (rest and relaxation) and to promote the sale of war bonds, Maj. John H. Mitchell (r) and Capt. Thomas G. Lanphier, Jr., made a stop at Randolph Field, Texas. Mitchell demonstrates the techniques he employed in shooting down several Japanese aircraft to become an ace (11 aircraft by war's end). Lanphier, credited with the destruction of Adm. Yamamoto's transport aircraft and the admiral's death, had a final total of five aircraft. Both men received the Navy Cross for their participation in that spectacular mission. Mitchell flew with the 347th FG, Lanphier with the 18th FG.*

114

U.S. Navy cryptographers (whose work should have saved Pearl Harbor and was the hinge-pin for success at Midway) had broken yet another Japanese secret code by early 1943. Interception of messages sent in that code disclosed plans for Fleet Admiral Isoroku Yamamoto and his staff to pay a flying visit from Rabaul to the Bougainville base at Buin on April 18, 1943. The key message was intercepted only a few days earlier, on April 13. Now ordinarily it would have been only of academic interest with no chance to capitalize on it. However, some quick-witted personnel realized that here existed a diminutive but real opportunity to – in the appropriate context – assassinate the supreme command officer in the Imperial Japanese Navy, the man who planned the attack on Pearl Harbor.

Initially a Navy-Marine operational effort, the format was altered to include the AAF when it was quickly calculated that no naval aircraft types available could fly the necessary mission profile with any hope of returning to a friendly base. Only the P-38 Lightning had a remote chance, based on its range, to intercept and destroy the flag officer's airplanes with their valuable cargo.

What made such a mission so difficult to carry out?

First, any direct route to Empress Augusta Bay and Buin meant that the aircraft would be flying over enemy territory and enemy surface vessels for most of the distance, with total probability that the intended prey would be warned off and the attackers would fly into an ambush. Second, the admiral's transporting aircraft would surely be escorted by fighter aircraft and would undoubtedly be met by as many as 100 friendly fighters from Kahili upon arrival. Third, the distance on any route that might avoid early warning would be about 450 to 500 miles, one way – a distance that no other fighter aircraft in the world could negotiate in early 1943 with any chance of success, especially with a requirement to fly at sea level and with allowance for at least 15 minutes of combat required at the target area.

To Maj. John Mitchell, C.O. of the 339FS, fell the task of devising and leading the Yamamoto mission. Mitchell planned to have a "hit" team of modest size (four P-38s) attack the incoming transports carrying Yamamoto and his staff officers (including the valuable Adm. Ugaki), while a larger group would fly high cover to ward off the expected swarm of Navy Mitsubishi Zeke fighters rising from Kahili airfield. The P-38s would have to fly "on the deck" all the way to avoid radar or visual contact, thereby increasing fuel consumption far above normal levels that could be expected when operating at high level. The P-38 drag characteristic was not at its best at low altitudes, and the turbosuperchargers almost became a liability.

(Most accounts attribute the mission to the 339th Fighter Squadron, but it is only fair to point out that the original four "killer" pilots were from the 70th FS and eight of the escorts were from the 12th FS. The 18th and the 347th Fighter Groups were involved.)

Two aborts very early in the mission struck the "hit" team. Lt. James McLanahan's P-38G blew a tire on takeoff, while Lt. Joseph Moore was unable to get his external fuel tanks to feed. That left two original members of the team, Capt. Thomas G. Lanphier, Jr., and Lt. Rex T. Barber, to carry on. By previous arrangements, Lts. Besby F. Holmes and Ray Hine of the 339th FS peeled off from the escort formation to join them. Thus, the covering team was reduced to 10 aircraft.

Rather amazingly, the two Mitsubishi G4M2 Betty bomber-transports, converted from a bomber type that was the mainstay of the Japanese Navy's bomber force, arrived over the destination almost precisely at the minute specified in the intercepted messages. Even more amazingly, Mitchell's P-38G Lightnings arrived within 30 seconds of the admiral's contingent, which included six protective fighters. No swarm of escort fighters had risen from the Kahili Airfield at that moment, although many were warming up to participate in a formal escort.

Lanphier swung in instantly to attack the leading Betty with Rex Barber flying as his wingman. With enemy fighters outnumbering them, and with the two bombers (that had to be shot down at all costs) splitting off in different directions in evasive maneuvers, there was a considerable amount of post-mission controversy being generated about victory claims. But it was certain that the two bomber-transports went down to crash heavily, and that most of the fighter escort for Yamamoto suffered the same fate.

The controversy over who actually shot Admiral Yamamoto's aircraft out of the sky and how many aircraft were

consider that the very new 310-gallon drop tanks had never been used in the Pacific before and that about a dozen pilots would be taking off for the first time with the equivalent of two 2,000-pound bombs or asymmetrical loads on the bomb pylons in Army Hot Day conditions, the odds looked even worse.

Sixteen P-38Fs and Gs from the 70th Fighter Squadron of the 18th Fighter Group, 12th FS of the same group, and the 339th FS from the 347th Fighter Group took off on that April 18, precisely at 7:10 a.m. and 14 of the pilots arrived on time over Bougainville.

If the Lockheed P-38 had done nothing more in the war, its contribution over Empress Augusta Bay was at least equal to the value of the Tokyo Raid a year earlier, conducted by B-25 Mitchells (no relationship). Unfortunately, secrecy was far more important at the time than any amount of publicity, so the news was suppressed, just as Operation BOLERO had proceeded without publicity.

actually destroyed may never be settled to the satisfaction of all participants or historians. It was argued for years that no less than three bombers went down, but that contention was eventually disproven.

What is undeniable in the light of post-war analysis is that:

(1) Yamamoto was killed in the aircraft that crashed in the jungle (his body was recovered).

(2) Two Betty aircraft were involved, not three, and both were shot down.

(3) At least five Zero fighters were destroyed in the attack.

(4) Only one P-38 was lost as a result of the combat mission (Lt. Ray Hine).

(5) Maj. John Mitchell did plan and execute a near perfect mission that achieved 100 percent of its objectives, no matter whose slugs killed the admiral.

In the face of much rancor, Capt. Lanphier is – on the basis of eyewitness accounts and post-mission claims and publicity – credited with shooting down the Yamamoto airplane. The official records, though far from being conclusive, also stand to support the claim. Lt. Rex Barber (now Col., USAF, Ret.), who was in the thick of the fight, generally supported the claims of Lanphier (at the time), but disagrees in much detail. (Some 45 years – long years – after that remarkable mission was concluded, a concerted effort was launched to arrive at a definitive settlement of the controversy.)

Odds against success of the action were enormous. On the basis of probable "foul ups" alone (information leaks, weather, incorrect information, bad planning, aircraft malfunctions), the mission had little chance to succeed. When you

The AAF Tactical Center at Orlando, Florida, tested the capability of a Lockheed P-38H to carry two 1000-pound bombs during March, 1944, Shortly after D-Day, the Kelsey-Hough team was carrying two 2000-pound bombs on combat missions. Hans Groenhoff-NASM

# CHAPTER 11

# Experiments Galore

There is an old adage to the effect that necessity is the mother of invention. Never was that ancient maxim more appropriate than in the early months of World War II in the far reaches of the Pacific Ocean. Japan had smashed most British and Dutch forces on the Asian mainland, and American forces on land and at sea had generally been overwhelmed by superior forces. Until the marvelous success of U.S. naval forces in the Battle of Midway, nothing was going right for Allied forces west of Hawaii. In the most remote reaches of that huge ocean, Lt. Gen. George H. Brett (later, Lt. Gen. George C. Kenney), commanding the Allied Air Forces in the Southwest Pacific region, desperately needed fighter aircraft that could cope with Imperial Japanese Navy and Army airpower. The pitifully inadequate collection of outclassed fighters then available lacked the performance needed to attack higher-flying Japanese bombers, let alone the capabilities to stave off the ubiquitous Mitsubishi Zekes (when all Japanese monoplane fighters were referred to as Zeros).

There simply were not any production Republic P-47s of any denomination built as yet, the Bell P-39s and P-400s did not act like cobras – even against twin-engine bombers – and Curtiss P-40s could barely hold their own. They were unlikely to even wrest air superiority from the Japanese. What was sorely needed was at least a group of Lockheed P-38 Lightnings. But the question was, "How do we get them to Australia to whip them into a true fighting force?" Shipping capacity was, perforce, strained to the ultimate limit, and the shipping lanes were anything but safe. Even the long-legged P-38Fs and Gs were not miracle workers; distances between bases were just too great.

Informal discussions involving Col. Kelsey, Kelly Johnson and Hall Hibbard somehow led to a seemingly improbable concept for ferrying Lightnings almost anywhere in the Pacific. (The problem of overwater navigational difficulties was evidently put aside until the immediate technical problems could be addressed.) Their solution, kept under a thorough veil of outstanding secrecy, was never fathomed by any outsider and few insiders until many

*ABOVE: The P-38E pictured (c/n 5204) on the Friday after Pearl Harbor was attacked stayed at Lockheed on bailment for experimental flight test. Building 304 structure rising in background was just a portion of new Production Flight Test. (LAC)*

*RIGHT: Company-generated artwork depicts floatplane version of P-38E as proposed for transpacific air delivery. One of several drawings, it shows upswept tail boom appearance. Projected nonstop range was 5000 miles, probably more than most pilots could endure. (LAC)*

years later.[1] Calculations showed that, with an adequate takeoff run, the P-38F could lift enough fuel to fly approximately 5,000 miles without refueling. Airports and, of course, pilot pain thresholds being the limiting factor at the time, they had to find an alternate launching capability. Waterways were soon determined to be the only option open to them. If the P-38 could be mounted on temporary floats with any success, that part of the problem could be solved. It would not even be necessary to hang external tanks under the wings because all of the extra fuel could be carried in the twin floats.

Johnson foresaw the possibilities of attaching the floats, one under each boom, while retaining all components of the normal landing gear in the retracted position. It would be relatively simple to jettison the floats in flight by using explosive bolts or some other mechanical device for cutting the attaching hardware. If en route refueling was required, the airplane could land in a protected waterway, even at a remote island. Tank car size neoprene bladder cells had been developed for carrying liquids on flat cars, and it was found that they could be towed by a ship when filled with liquids that were lighter than water. The team was convinced that P-38s could be refueled in a cove or river from such fuel containers.

After operating characteristics were evaluated, the only problem that bothered Johnson was the probability that the large horizontal tailplane would be immersed in nearly solid spray or would be in the water. Could they raise the empennage without creating insurmountable problems? They concluded that it was out of the question, but somebody suggested "bending" the tail booms.

Young G. H. "Bert" Estabrook was called in and asked if he could move the entire empennage upward and aft. Bert found a remote corner of a new factory building and set up shop, with

---

1. *Some thirty years later, this writer pressed Gen. Kelsey about a major technical aspect of the solution. He seemed genuinely surprised to find that at least one person not associated with the project had figured out the true reason for major modifications to the tail booms on one Lightning aircraft. He soon revealed the real story about that modification. But for the revealing interview, details and facts of the venture would never have been divulged publicly*

walls made from heavy brown paper supported by a wooden framework. He designed the first version – there were two separate and distinct configurations ultimately – on yellow sketchpad paper so that work could be rushed to the Experimental Shop. Estabrook remembered that "we added a stovepipe section, raising the tail 16 inches (actually it was 18 inches) and moving it aft 24 inches." Within hours they were constructing a wooden mockup in full scale. Another crew went to work modifying the 1/6-scale wind tunnel model. As soon as results showed that there would be no real adverse effects on flight characteristics, aircraft conversion work began.

P-38E c/n 5204 (AC41-1986) was the designated test aircraft. Without delay, the entire tail assembly was detached from the booms at the aft attach point. A strong, angled stovepipe affair was inserted and the empennage was reattached. Smooth, compound-curved skins were then fitted to complete a longer, upswept structure. Photographs were taken at Lockheed Air Terminal on March 3, 1942, and the airplane was flown for the first time that week. Numerous flights were made over a period of months, frequently with Tony LeVier or Milo Burcham at the controls. This early "Skunk Works" type of operation was indicative of the way in which Kelly Johnson's team actually got results.

In the spirit of that family-like operation, Bert Estabrook was given the opportunity to fly in No. 5204, which Johnson had earlier converted to the piggy-back configuration for first-hand test observation. Johnson, himself, was a not-infrequent flight test observer. Bert related his story. "I went on a piggy-back ride in one of the raised tail versions with Tony LeVier. What a ride! I remember that Dick Pulver told me to be sure and tell Tony not to roll the ship with one engine out. Can you imagine me telling Tony what not to do with his flying?" Bert received

*Empennage on the P-38E was moved aft 24 inches, raised either 16 or 18 inches (arguable). Bert Estabrook designed the structure and headed up modification team. Notice unchanged pre-war insignia. (G. H. Estabrook)*

a P-38 "Piggy Backer" diploma, a highly regarded document.

With the victory at Midway, the crisis evaporated and seaborne shipment of P-38s to Australia moved ahead. But when the buffeting problem was resolved without any solution in sight for the compressibility flaw, Johnson and Colman decided that raising the horizontal tailplane even higher might at least change the characteristics. However, they certainly did not want the temporary extended tailbooms.

Estabrook was asked to raise the horizontal tail by 33 inches, but there could be no increase in the aircraft length. When the P-38E went back into the shop, the tail booms were amputated right at the trailing edge of the Prestone cooling scoop outlets and completely new boom extensions were created. One unanticipated reward was the addition of some ventral fin area, but the effect went largely unnoticed in the

search for resolution to the big "compressibility tuck" problems. Venerable 5204 received a complete and updated paint job before it was rolled out in December.

Earlier test data indicated that tail buffeting might also be reduced by raising the tail, but it did not take much time to prove that there was no aerodynamic gain. There was a loss of 3 mph in top end speed because of the modification and, of course, the airframe basic weight increased. Visually it was no thing of beauty. The tests with Kelly Johnson along as test engineer were conclusive: there was no improvement in the realm of compressibility.

Because few people had observed the original "bent boom" version and virtually nobody at Lockheed had ever been told the reason for the modification, the project was quickly forgotten. When the tailplane was raised 33 inches, most employees had become aware of the intensive program established to defeat the buffet problem. Every causal observer immediately concluded that the raised tail was concocted exclusively for aerodynamic purposes. After all, who would have ever even thought of a P-38 floatplane?

Throughout the year, c/n 5204 had been flown more than one hundred times in connection with aerodynamic tests, and that was long after the original purpose for the "sweeping" change had become history. One very interesting sidelight was that one year to the day after U.S. forces and installations were attacked in Hawaii, Kelly Johnson flew in the P-38E in the tight space behind Milo Burcham. With the tail raised 33 inches, Test Flight No. 55 was being conducted for V-g demonstration. Showing real confidence in his products, designer Johnson was

*LEFT: After the floatplane requirement evaporated (Battle of Midway Is.), Kelly Johnson chose to conduct some dive tests. It was decided to restore normal boom length, but raise the tail 33 inches. Picture shows the booms were amputated at Prestone coolers and restructured. It should be noted that 5204 was also the first Piggy-Back Lightning. (G. H. Estabrook)*

*OPPOSITE RIGHT: Piggy-Back P-38E with swooptail version No. 2 was painted and rolled out on December 2, 1942, about 13 months after Virden's crash in the YP-38. Johnson flew as flight test engineer in aft position many times. Test pilots included Milo Burcham, Col. Ben Kelsey, Capt. Frank Jenks and Tony LeVier. Estabrook flew with LeVier to witness effects of additional sideplate area and tail position. X-15 fillets had been standardized. (LAC)*

participating in a high-speed dive from altitude to 10,000 feet at a time when compressibility tuck was unsolved and a fearful situation. Old 5204 had no dive flaps (not yet invented), and it would have been impossible for Johnson to bail out in the event of some crisis. Following the dive, Burcham feathered one engine to fly comparison profiles against unmodified aircraft.

Kelly Johnson submitted his written report on the flight, including the following commentary: "A number of wing-engine maneuvers, including rolls, were made and the airplane seemed to handle normally. A landing was made at approximately 11:05, keeping the left engine feathered." Keeping in mind that the main reason for initially raising the tailplane was not for compressibility investigation at all, Johnson stated that "it seems that no benefit is obtained from these modifications and the airplane is in several regards worse than a standard P-38." Flight Test Report No. 55 for that series of tests was signed by C. L. Johnson. Just one day after the Burcham-Johnson dive and single-engine landing was made in the "bent boom" P-38E, pilot Joe Towle made the test flight on December 8, 1942, during which he dropped a one-ton torpedo from a normal P-38F onto the Muroc bombing range. The versatility of the Lightning seemed to have no limits.

B A reference was made earlier to the fact that Gen. Hap Arnold was in a bad temper during the early days of 1942 because his highly touted AAF was tasting defeat on virtually every front. He could derive little solace from the Battle of Midway because Martin B-26s were ineffective as torpedo airplanes. Flying Fortresses had proved that high-level bombers were almost useless against fast-moving warships. That had become evident in the Coral Sea battle. And while patriotism motivated most Americans, a few flim-flam operators surfaced almost every day with "war winning aircraft concepts." Fortunately, most of them never got past the artist's sketch stage. Although he had great faith in Ben Kelsey, Arnold remained a sincere skeptic. Even as Lockheed's 165-gallon drop tanks were proving to be a roaring success, ultimately leading to the success of BOLERO, he wavered in his faith. Kelsey's talk of a 2,500-mile ferry range for a top-line fighter was, to be blunt, hard to swallow.

It was not long before the general proved his skepticism. A message arrived at the Burbank executive offices ordering Lockheed to proceed with a carefully documented demonstration of the maximum range capability of the P-38F. Engineers had approached the problem of carrying fuel in 300-gallon tanks of various shapes during the early months of 1942, but none were very efficient.

The laminar-flow shape of the 165-gallon tank was proving to be unbeatable. Various subcontractors were invited to produce their versions of that tank in a 300-310 gallon size. Certainly the most efficient version was a beautifully formed and flush-riveted unit which evidently was produced in some numbers later on. One tank, tested later on a P-38G-10-LO (c/n 7370), was created by splitting a 165-gallon tank longitudinally and inserting an airfoil-like "plug" between the halves. It was cheap to manufacture and it carried more than 325 gallons of gasoline. However, its drag counts were high.

As BOLERO's aerial delivery program was approaching a climax, the second P-38F-5-LO, bearing serial number 7002, was being prepared for the rigorous range demonstration program. Strangely, it was drawn from a group of 100 that comprised the last of the Model 222 series powered with V-1710F-5 Allisons. Remaining aircraft of that model (in the 222-68 block) had the improved F-10 engines, and they were then designated as P-38G or F-5A, depending on the combat role assigned. Apparently there was an inadequate number of F-10 engines delivered by August 27, 1942, the target flight demonstration date, although P-38G-1-LOs were being accepted by the AAF Plant Representative.

Kelly Johnson selected Milo Burcham to conduct the demonstration. Milo was more experienced than Tony LeVier, and Mattern was deeply involved in his special training mission. The smoothest new 300-gallon dural drop tanks were hung on the pylon mounts, but the fuel load gives a clearcut clue as to why they were usually referred to as 310-gallon tanks. Burcham's combat-equipped mount, c/n 7002, was fueled with 300 gallons of internal gas and no less than 638 gallons were used to top off the two externally mounted tanks. A full load of 26 gallons of oil was on board. Armor plate was not removed, and it has been verified that the regular armament was in place. Instrumentation required use of the regular underwing pitot tube plus the pre-BOLERO type immediately forward of the nosewheel. Takeoff weight was verified at 19,128 pounds, a rather prodigious load for those rather early F-series Allisons.

Avoiding a takeoff over populated areas for obvious reasons, Burcham lifted the P-38F from Palmdale's runway, out in the Mohave Desert, at 4:30 a.m., using no more than 35 inches of manifold pressure. He climbed to 10,000 feet over tiny Daggett, near Barstow, before settling to cruise power near Kingman, Arizona.

Power was reduced a bit more over Oklahoma City at 9:36 a.m. (PST). If Burcham had chosen to continue on that flight path, he would have arrived over Norfolk, Virginia, at about 3 p.m. (PST). However, logistics plans had not been established for a transcontinental flight, so he turned 180 degrees and headed back toward Palmdale, arriving there about 3:18 p.m. (PST).

Fuel in both drop tanks had run out near the Colorado River, so Milo switched over to the 180-gallons remaining in the aft internal tanks. He then cruised on to Burbank, still maintaining a 10,000-foot altitude, and cut south toward San Diego. Turning near North Island, he cruised back to L.A.T. at 4:33 p.m. before heading up U.S. 99 toward Bakersfield. The aircraft was still performing flawlessly and transfer to the forward internal tanks occurred at about 4:53 p.m.

Shimmering in the scorching August sun, the San Joaquin Valley city of Bakersfield came into view at 5:08 p.m. Those Allisons had not even sniffled as the plane turned and Milo set his course for Burbank one more time. Fuel consumption levels were still excellent (even at a time when long-range cruise control was still anything but a science) as he passed over the San Gabriel Mountains and the camouflaged Lockheed plant came into sight. Although our intrepid pilot was "saddle sore" beyond description, he again veered away from home base and headed toward Oxnard on the coast at 5:55 p.m. He circled past Pt. Mugu and headed back down the San Fernando Valley to L.A.T. as evening shadows lengthened. With 38 gallons of gasoline remaining in the tanks, he cut the throttles in front of Building 304, having touched down at 6:09 p.m. after a long day in the "office." Incredibly, those Allisons had consumed no more than one and a half gallons of oil.

The amazing Milo Burcham crawled out onto the wing after having been aloft for a flesh-and-bone-numbing 13.67 hours while covering a distance of 2,907 miles. Yet he still had reserve fuel that could have provided an additional 119 miles for a total range of 3,026 miles. His speed over the ground had worked out at 213 mph instead of the planned speed of 204 mph. Turbulence had forced Burcham to fly at a higher speed. They calculated that the lower speed would have extended the range capability to 3,167 miles. No additional allowances were made to compensate for the four sweeping 180-degree and one 90-degree turns. Had the pilot been permitted to jettison the two huge fuel tanks at the Colorado River, speed would have increased significantly with no increase in fuel consumption. They might have gained an additional 100 miles during the final 3.5 hours. In its report, Lockheed stated that the following ranges could be expected in early-series P-38s:

| | |
|---|---|
| Normal range................................. | 1,300 miles |
| With 2x150 gal. drop tanks.... | 2,200 miles |
| With 2x300 gal. drop tanks.... | 3,200 miles |

A round trip from London to Berlin is 1,296 miles, while a similar flight from Paris to Moscow and return is 2,082 miles. Johnson and Col. Kelsey had proven their point in spades. Lockheed medical director Dr. F. E. Poole, who was responsible for checking Burcham before and after the lengthy flight, certified that the pilot was in excellent condition and that all vital signs were back to normal within a few hours after landing.

Nobody can say with any certainty that Gen. Arnold's opinions about Kelsey and Johnson skyrocketed or that he was even secretly satisfied with the Lockheed performance. It certainly gave him a great deal of "firepower" whenever the subject of P-38s or range requirements came to the fore. The airplane may have been up to the job, but not every pilot could have endured the pain of 13½ hours in that bucket seat. Burcham deserved a medal, but he didn't even get a mention in the newspapers. In retrospect it would seem that the AAF should have publicized the event to give the Nazis something to think about. It was a remarkable test of man and airplane.

C Whether or not it was the support of Carl Green and his staff at Wright Field that helped motivate work on pressurized cockpits, a certain amount of high-priority effort went into pressurized cabin work after Pearl Harbor, once the G. E. turbosupercharger production problems began to clear up. Types such as the North American XB-28, Consolidated's XB-32, Republic's XP-47E and XP-69 all attempted to gain more advantage from that fire-breathing supercharger by incorporating cabin pressurization. Sealing up the airframe was difficult, but cabin supercharging

*ABOVE: Anticipating a Gen. Hap Arnold question, Lockheed manufactured 300/310-gallon drop tanks and installed them on P-38F-5-LO c/n 7002, not long after the Battle of Midway. On August 27, Milo Burcham taxied out without any fanfare, took off with ease and proceeded to demonstrate a 3,000-plus mile ferry range. Even with power-limited V-1710F-5 engines, short runways at Burbank might have been okay, but it was decided that a 19,128-pound takeoff should be made from isolated Palmdale. With wartime security, there was no publicity. (LAC)*

*RIGHT: Lockheed was a pioneer in pressure cabin work with the XC-35, C-69 Constellation and with the XP-38A. That single P-38 type was really just a testbed for the XP-49. Carrying LAC model designation of 622-62-10, the XP-38A was a straightforward conversion of the 19th P-38 on Contract AC-13205. It was obvious that X-15 version fillets were added after the fighter was converted and painted. (LAC)*

was even more difficult. Long Island did not even get to see one XP-69 takeoff and the XP-47E project encountered a multitude of seemingly insoluble problems. North American got nowhere with the XB-28, and Consolidated must have encountered far more problems than were ever revealed. As the war progressed, the initial version of the XB-32 was evidently 95 percent redesigned. The pressure cabin was among the first casualties.

Lockheed entered the quest with at least two airplanes, both of which were essentially P-38s. Under Contract AC-13205, Change Order 8, one of the first batch of production P-38s (no suffix) was taken from the assembly line (such as it was at the time) and reworked to incorporate a pressure cabin. A completely redesigned windshield and canopy assembly was installed, using a simple movable clamshell portion for entering and leaving the cockpit. Heavily structured, the clamshell section closed down on rubber seals to provide an airtight assembly. Designer Nathan Price's "home-grown" cabin supercharger worked fairly well, but its high-pitched sound tended to become a bit annoying on longer flights.

This project moved forward in 1941-42 under the direction of M. Carl Haddon, who also was the project engineer on the XP-49. In reality, the XP-38A (AC40-762) was merely a flight test bed for the XP-49 pressure cabin. Once again the corporation model resignations tended to cloud the issue. Originally, the XP-38A was Model 222-62-08 aircraft, becoming the one and only 622-62-10 as reworked. However, the XP-49 was Model 522-66-07 under a different contract, of course . . . AC-13476.

All test flights were conducted out of L.A.T. between May and December 1942. Joe Towle did all of the test work, completing approximately 30 test flights during that period. For unexplained reasons, the highest altitude attained by Towle was 36,500 feet, an altitude exceeded by numerous pilots with conventional oxygen systems while flying standard P-38 models.

One other P-38 modification project that is worth mentioning was "Swordfish." It appeared in the same general time frame in which the XF-5D, the first Droop Snoot and the asymmetrical-cockpit P-38 came into being. Kelly Johnson's aerodynamicists, drawing upon the wind tunnel testing that was completed by NACA as Lockheed searched for a solution to both the annoying buffet and compressibility tuck problems, jointly and separately, were convinced that certain fuselage modifications would greatly improve the Lightning's flight characteristics. In spite of the heavy work load in early 1943, approval and funding for the work was received.

A well-used RP-38E (c/n 5226) was bailed to Lockheed early in 1943, and work progressed fairly rapidly in the experimental shop that might be looked upon as ancestral to the famed "Skunk Works." The forward gondola section was carefully amputated, moved forward approximately 30 inches, and reconnected with a "plug" section. It immediately became the Lightning with the longest wheelbase on record. All pilot controls were moved forward 36 inches into a new cockpit area. The original cockpit became the co-pilot/observer/test engineer station. There was no intention of anyone flying the Swordfish from that position except in an emergency. A new flat-panel windshield was installed for a greatly narrowed canopy arrangement. That windshield was the predecessor of the type eventually appearing on late-model P-38Js and all L models, but it apparently was more sharply raked. Instead of the central gondola ending at the wing trailing edge, it was extended about 48 inches aft by a beautifully shaped conical section. The standard radio antenna remained on the bottom of the fuselage, but was moved slightly aft of the wing trailing edge. An early series P-38D pitot tube was installed at its former location just forward of the nose gear door.

Swordfish flew for the first time on June 2, 1943, at Lockheed Air Terminal, and it was almost immediately involved in the high-speed dive and maneuverability program. Carl Schmidt was most often the flight test engineer, and the special panel of test pilots for the airplane included Milo Burcham, Tony LeVier, Joe Towle and James White. Dives were conducted up to Mach 0.68, with pullouts generally limited to less than 2g. All of the recorded data was compared to that obtained with the P-38G that had been fitted with the first set of dive flaps, the ultimate "fix" for compressibility tuck.

Lockheed eventually bought the RP-38E from the War Assets Administration, in March 1946, paying $1,200; the tail still bore the incorrect 412048 AAF number that had been applied by company painters sometime in 1944. All camouflage paint had been stripped and a P-38L style marking arrangement was applied. The correct tail number for AC41-2048 should have been 12048. Reregistered as NX91300, Swordfish was involved in dropping models of the supersonic XP-90 before eventual sale to Hycon Aerial Surveys for "$10 and other valuable considerations" on August 27, 1954.

**E**meanwhile, Phil Colman's 1940 dive report contributed significantly to the conduct of buffet and compressibility tuck aerodynamic tests throughout 1941. By midsummer 1942, Lockheed had plunged through P-38E and F production alongside British-ordered Model 322-B versions, moved on to the G series and was headed into P-38H production. Those types were salted liberally with 180 photo-recon airplanes in the F-5A series. (With this rapidly expanding and changing picture, it is appropriate to refer to the comprehensive, detailed P-38 Model Designation, Serial Number and Delivery tabular data tables provided in the Appendix section for definitive information.)

A constant stream of refinements, combat theater revisions and state-of-the-art improvements were being incorporated in airframes as rapidly as solutions to problems could be devised, tested and fabricated. During that first full year of war for America, Lightnings were performing some remarkable feats overseas, especially in the North Atlantic delivery operation, in air-to-air combat in the North African invasion and in early missions against the Japanese in the Southwestern and Northern Pacific. Of course the operations in the Mediterranean and Pacific theaters were in their infancy in late 1942, but they were establishing a base of successful performances in 1943.

**F**ust before C. L. Johnson's "Study of Diving Characteristics of the P-38" report was completed in May 1942, Col. Kelsey and Wg Cdr Mike Crossley participated in an interesting competition of sorts at Wright Field. The colonel was flying a P-38F – possibly the one that he flew to the U.K. in July – while Crossley was at the controls of one of the two XP-51s. (Brig. Gen. Kelsey was unable to located his Form 5 at a later date to confirm some of the technical details and exact date.) Since combat was to be limited to a maximum altitude of 22,000 feet at the critical altitude of the XP-51, the P-38 was not given a true test of its capabilities.

At no time did Kelsey encounter any diving tendency, and the buffet was "quite normal for a pursuit aircraft," according to his report. His comments had to be considered valid because there were few fighters of any importance that Kelsey had not flown (including captured enemy aircraft). During the mock attack, indicated airspeeds were as high as 400 mph with positive accelerations up to 5g. The entire idea of that mock combat episode was to test the practicality of the new P-38F as a viable combat aircraft. Sadly, the Lightning was not flown against the then new Supermarine Spitfire IX. Kelsey was not at all displeased with the P-38F performance, but it was obvious that he wished for a more competitive aircraft for an opponent.

Not long thereafter, Col. Kelsey went to Great Britain with the pioneering BOLERO movement. By July 29 he was visiting the Air Fighting Development Unit at Duxford in company with Gens. Carl Spaatz and F. O'D. "Monk" Hunter. The latter, a member of Spaatz's staff, was a World War I fighter ace. Like Brig. Gen. William Kepner, who succeeded Hunter as commander of VIIIth Fighter Command, he was one of the oldest active officers in the Eighth Air Force. At Duxford, more mock combat took place with the assistance of Wg Cdr Campbell-

NACA wind tunnel tests suggested that a lengthened fuselage would reduce buffeting and, perhaps, delay compressibility tuck. A modification of one RP-38E was authorized. The result was a very slick two-seater with the pilot moved forward of the wing leading edge in a narrower canopy. Riveting of gondola structure was not yet complete on "Swordfish" when this rare photograph was taken in 1942. (LAC)

Orde, who was chief of the AFDU. By July 30, they had all moved on to Farnborough, where Kelsey hoped to fly in and against the Focke-Wulf Fw 190A that had been captured. Much to his chagrin, the Nazi fighter was out of commission for parts replacement. While the colonel was gaining first-hand knowledge of competing aircraft, he was obviously enjoying his work.

**G**s P-38Ds, P-38Es and RAF 322-Bs moved down the production lines side by side in Burbank and were delivered to the new Army Air Force, the AAF fighters went to long-established units. Most of the peacetime pilots were either considered very good when they were trainees or they had flown the best of America's pursuit planes. Between the relatively few "hot" airplanes that were delivered in 1941 and the first half of 1942 and the experienced pilots that were available, there was no real fear of the P-38 airplane type.

But all of that was due for a rude change of status. With the outbreak of war in the Pacific, a real need for lightning-like expansion of the armed forces, and the tremendous crush of new recruits, there was a sudden realization that the AAF training establishment was going to be a bottleneck. As the Army Air Forces was formatted in 1941, there was a Combat Command and an Air Corps under Gen. Arnold's command. The A.C. had Materiel and Training & Operations, all under the command of Maj. Gen. George Brett.

The training organization was, in 1941, preparing to expand pilot training from the prevailing 12,000 each year to 30,000 each year, starting in September. Imagine the pandemonium that existed the day after December 7, 1941. Every plan was "out the window." If the U.S. government was unprepared for war, the new pilots who would have to fly P-38s in combat, perhaps no more than 10 months later, were even less prepared. Here was a 7 1/2-ton, 2300-horsepower charger that was crown prince of the world's fastest fighters, probably more rightly the king. Nobody could hope to get even a minute of dual-control flight time on something with a speed potential of 400 mph. There was little likelihood that every cadet was going to be up to the challenge.

The airpower inventory of high-performance twin-engine aircraft was almost non-existent in those days, particularly when it came to training aircraft. New Douglas A-20 attack bombers might have been used, but they were sorely needed by first-line squadrons and could hardly have been adapted for transitional training; they were also having their own teething troubles, as revealed during the summer maneuvers of 1941. If an aspiring fighter pilot could get any time in the cockpit of a Lockheed C-40 military version of the Lockheed 12A light transport or with AT-7, he had a leg up in the competition, but there were few of these types. Meanwhile, transition from the best of the single-engined trainers, ...ance twin-engine P-38 was akin to ...s Ford to an Indianapolis race car. ...Air Corps let Curtiss-Wright talk ...AT-9 Jeep trainers that were ... make the move into P-38s ...dvanced Martin B-26 me- ...twin-engine aircraft, but ...selage to lessen asym- ...failed. They did not have ...the wing was merely a bee... ...ne CW-21 export fighter ... ...m AT-9 crashes reached s... ...of the fact that the three-t... ...n level flight. Even the Be... ...that, so it wasn't long ... ...oo dangerous for cadets to fly ... ...disappeared from most advanced tr... ...the time OVERLORD was launched aga...

Still desperate for ...ced twin-engine trainer, ... ...SAAF realized that a relatively simple rework of their small fleet of semi-idle Lockheed 322-Bs, originally built for the RAF as the Lightning Mk I without turbosupercharging for its engines, might do the trick. By substituting Allison F-2 series engines for the less reliable and less powerful C-15 engines, the 322-Bs would provide new pilots with the opportunity to become well acquainted with the P-38's characteristics before they had to cope with the complexities of high altitude, high-performance flight and unfamiliar turbosuperchargers. The change was a workable alternative and few novice fighter pilots ever had serious problems flying the resulting P-322-II. A handful of the older P-322-I types remained in use for a year or two; they retained the earlier C-15 engines. Pilots always flew P-322s after a period of intense

*ABOVE: "Swordfish" (or "Nosey") was a long-lived Lightning, undergoing many dive tests, aiding the XR60-1 Constitution program and the XP-90 jet fighter program. Lockheed bought the airplane as surplus after the war, and it was used for years by Hycon Aerial Surveys. When paint was stripped, number was painted incorrectly on tail. It should have been 12048, representing AC41-2048.*

*BELOW: An improved "Swordfish" gondola on a P-38L airframe would have been an optimum nightfighter or pathfinder conversion. Tony LeVier said it was the best diving P-38 of all. Envision it with a bubble canopy. (LAC)*

125

cockpit checkout on the ground, the instructor giving directions from a position on the wing centersection.

Although many pilots seemed to have difficulty in coping with the psyche-domineering P-38, old line fighter group pilots did not. If a pilot had much time on a Republic P-43 or the Bell P-39D, or even a P-40, he seemed to encounter little trouble jumping to the P-38. However, prior to 1941, there were relatively few multi-engine pilots in the U.S.A. The most skillful of them probably had piloted Lockheed Model 14 and Electra airliners, airplanes with relatively high performance, but not in the P-38's class.

Certainly the Douglas B-18 bombers were unlikely to prepare a pilot for P-38 fighter operation. In those days, it was pretty easy to convince a youthful pilot that Lightnings were demonic airplanes. Hadn't one or two experimental test versions crashed with skilled pilots at the controls? It was also logical to concede that you had better stay out of a P-38 if you had a Stearman PT-17 philosophy. Not everybody could be adept at driving a race car; likewise, not all pilots were really well adapted mentally to flying P-38s. And so a consensus began to emerge. If you were happy in a Lightning and did not get in frequent trouble, your confidence level was probably very high, your reaction times were great, and you loved to take a chance on life.

Each month that went by in 1942 dramatically increased the exposure of new pilots to P-38s and Martin B-26s. Both airplanes had extremely high wing loadings for the period, even in America where large, paved airfields were commonplace. Vast numbers of airfields in the rest of the world had sod runways, and to believe that all of them were absolutely flat was folly, particularly in the United Kingdom. A first-rate airport in Algeria might be looked upon as a poor emergency field in the United States and in all of metropolitan France in 1939 there was only one concrete runway.

In 1942, the typical P-38 could call upon 2300 horsepower; there wasn't an experimental or operational fighter in the world with that much power. Even the brand new XP-47B was lucky to see 1850 horsepower. Martin's B-26A bomber was propelled by nothing short of 3700 horsepower, and the loss of half that power on one side was more than a bit frightening if you didn't

have some altitude under you. With every new crash of a P-38 or B-26 – inevitable in a wartime scenario – the rumor mills churned out terrorizing stories about both aircraft.

Taking into consideration the effects of a frenetic wartime expansion and the emotional feeling of an American public thoroughly indoctrinated with the belief that they could whip the Japanese in a matter of weeks without half trying – only to find themselves on the canvas about three times in the first round – it was no wonder that accident rates in every phase of the training and war production buildup burgeoned. With an unskilled labor force, it was quite common for members of riveting teams – working on either side of an aircraft's skin – to suddenly have the drill punch through the aluminum and into the body of their partner. All this was the result of carelessness, fatigue, a too rapid buildup and the high-pressure training that often neglected to cover even the rudiments of a craft.

By the end of 1942, Flying Training Command was experiencing similar woes as the accident rate with P-38s threatened to outpace production. Most were not fatal, but the number of deaths that resulted was alarming. At least a new pilot in a B-26 was not in the air by himself. He had his instructor. In the P-38 he was on his own as soon as the canopy closed, following the ground checkout. And it was not lost on Air Force instructors that prior to taking control of a 2300-horsepower Lightning, the most powerful machine a new pilot might have previously handled a few months earlier was probably a 90-horsepower Ford V-8.

Balding air adventurer and Lockheed test pilot Jimmy Mattern was quick to visualize a potential in the P-38E for

RIGHT: All spruced up, "Piggie-Back I" was ready for another lengthy demonstration tour as Tony LeVier was concluding his 6-month tour in the United Kingdom. Operation OVERLORD was merely days away. It must be concluded that Mattern was very easy on his aircraft. (LAC)

BELOW: Jimmy Mattern posed with his P-38F-1-LO, wearing one of his special jump suits, at Lockheed Air Terminal. It is difficult to believe that a very intensive war was going on. Many pilots, including Col. Jack S. Jenkins (C.O., 55FG) affirm that they owe their lives to the lessons learned from Mattern. Jenkins says that the complete emergency procedures saved his life in a P-38 and in a B-25. (Eric Miller)

improving student pilot confidence. In his own inimitable style, he bypassed Lockheed management to go directly to Gen. Barney M. Giles, a real power in the training command, with a proposal to use P-38s that were modified to duplicate the special two-man "Piggy Back" version that was an outgrowth of the company's flight test program.

Giles was quickly convinced that Mattern's proposal was the shortest route to a solution to the training problem. He acted immediately to launch Mattern on a whirlwind tour of bases wherein the old master could demonstrate the P-38's vast array of capabilities in solo flight. That was to be followed by a series of dramatic demonstration maneuvers preceding a number of awe-inspiring but short rides with student pilots peering over his shoulder. An order was soon issued to all training commanders to provide every assistance to the popular Lockheed pilot, who promptly adapted a P-38F-1-LO (AC41-7485) to his particular needs, decorating it with a distinctive flash on its nose and a neat bucking bronco insignia on each tail boom.

The adventurous record setter also had some special flight suits tailored for his training tour. Although his flight demonstrations seemed remarkably daring and aggressive, they were really well thought out and executed. For example, he would roll the P-38 into a "dead" engine immediately after take-off at low altitude, but only when he keyed on a safe speed. While these maneuvers were almost frightening to observe, Mattern knew he was safe even in the face of real emergencies (within logical limits, of course). Everything he did was plotted out in advance and performed many times at a safe altitude.

Lockheed top management was somewhat unhappy with Jimmy Mattern's methodology in arranging for the demonstrations via the back door while he was on their payroll, but the ultimate success of his exhibitions could hardly be ignored. Within 4 or 5 months of the first training session, the accident rate at training bases involved with the P-38s was cut from an index figure of 6.5 down to 1.5 or less. When other AAF P-38s were locally converted to the piggy-back configuration, Mattern's tired P-38F eventually went back to Burbank for overhaul. It was stripped, polished to a chrome-like finish and decorated with new trim paint. The name "Piggie-Back I" [sic] was added; pre-war type Air Corps tail stripes were painted on the twin rudders to give the aircraft a YP-38 appearance, but the bucking bronco emblems disappeared. Internally, new engines were installed in anticipation of many more hours of rapid power setting changes.

Mattern's demonstrations had all but eliminated the feeling that the dreaded loss of an engine during takeoff had to be fatal. In fact, one pilot admitted to losing three successive P-38s over a period of months at Muroc Army Air Field, California, when engines failed at crucial moments. Having benefitted from the Mattern demonstrations, he survived every time. In general terms, this was the recommended procedure to follow during takeoff when a P-38's engine fails just as the landing gear is retracted, or is in the retraction cycle:

a. Raise landing gear at 90 mph IAS, using takeoff power.

b. If engine fails during climbout, don't maintain full power; don't try to feather dead engine propeller (you may get the wrong one).

c. Typically, if right engine fails, correct yaw action by closing throttle on the "live" (left) engine (or close both throttles if unsure). Increase power on left (good) engine and simultaneously apply as much left rudder as necessary to maintain straight ahead flight. Continue climb out at 125 mph IAS.

d. Obtain radio clearance for emergency landing. Proceed with single-engine approach procedure, but with only 50 percent flaps. Do not extend full flaps until certain that a/c will reach runway.

Of course every situation will vary to some extent. Army hot day conditions could inhibit a climbout, forcing a straight-ahead approach and gear-up landing. Mattern acknowledged that a normal reaction would be to immediately apply maximum power to the "live" engine as the other fails, but with the P-38 at full power, it was impossible to control the yaw or counteract torque immediately. As Mattern continually stressed, the first thing to do was "get the airplane under control, and then apply power as needed." The old balding eagle remarked that this was an easy procedure to practice at moderate altitude. And it was not lost on P-38 pilots that (generally) the Curtiss Electric props required an eternity to feather.

Because of his unstinting, confidence-building activities, Gen. Giles recommended that a Civil Medal of Merit be awarded to Mattern for his demonstrations, which undoubtedly saved many lives and airplanes.

Lockheed had its wartime successes and failures, and two of the most depressing failures were remotely tied to the P-38 program. It is only fair to say that neither of those failed aircraft types – the Model 20 (or XP-58) and the Model 522-66-07 (or XP-49) – had even a remote connection with Col. Kelsey (except that he inherited them in disarray in a remote way in mid-1943). The Model 20 was Lockheed's contribution to the frantic orders placed by the Allies in 1940 when Nazi forces attacked France and the Low Countries. When orders were placed by the British for production of the Apache/Mustang, a "foreign release agreement" was placed in effect. As a result, the USAAF received two of the airplanes as "exacted tribute."

A similar agreement was involved when the British and French procurement teams placed the enormous order for close to 700 Model 322-B and 322-F airplanes as the German *Wehrmacht* stormed through the Allied armies almost with impunity. In that negotiation, the AAF was to obtain a prototype airplane that would fill a niche in that family of fighter aircraft called for by Gen. Arnold back in 1939. That particular design was to be a multi-seat fighter for bomber escort work. There appeared to be no real connection with the Model 322 except in the most superficial way.

Air Corps procurement of new, advanced aircraft in that era began with a requirement, either from the tactical organizations or from a board of staff officers. Then the Experimental Engineering Section of Materiel Command at Wright Field issued detailed specifications for the new type. What evidently occurred with regard to the Model 20 was that it was either designed in response to an obscure specification or that Lockheed had submitted the design in hopes of generating a requirement. Originally, it was to be powered by two of the so-called "Hyper" engines under development contracts issued by Materiel. The engine specified was Continental Motors' inverted IV-1430, having a target horsepower of 1600 bhp in production trim. (No Lockheed drawings of that version have even been uncovered or seen in company archives since wartime.) The "new" Model 20 thrown into the hopper by Jimmy Gerschler in East Coast negotiations with the Allied Purchasing Commission was powered by a P&W "paper" engine, the X-1800 sleeve-valved design that was given the military designations XH-2600. Obviously it was going to have nearly twice the displacement of the Continental unit. Subsequent events tend to lead to the belief that Materiel Division engineers were still tied to the IV-1430-powered version of the Model 20 . . . mainly because of the morass that engulfed that program and (unfortunately) an intersecting program (the XP-49 project). It was soon to become obvious that Lt. Col. Edwin Page (at Wright Field) was not about to relax his inflexible attitudes about the Hyper engines.

Virtual confirmation of those assumptions can be seen in any detailed analysis of the interwoven XP-58 and XP-49 projects, a story related in periodicals. Even the details of the XP-49 history are far too complex to relate in this narrative, but the airframe was quite closely related to Lockheed's Model 222 and 622 airplanes (P-38E and XP-38A respectively).

Following the call by Maj. Gen. H. H. Arnold in June 1939 for a complete family of fighter designs, Lockheed proposed a very-high-altitude fighter embodying a pressure cabin. Notice must be taken of the facts that it was to incorporate most features of

*Early flights with LeVier at the controls of the XP-49 revealed a serious loss of directional control attributable to lengthened nacelles. Haddon's crew increased fin and rudder area with "plugs" to restore stability. Wright Field's addiction to the XIV-1430 cannot be understood. True, the Allison V-1710 problems in Europe were not yet known, but information interchange would have revealed the success Rolls-Royce was having with the Merlin. (LAC)*

the P-38, but it would be powered by a pair of Pratt & Whitney X-1800 engines! There we have the seeds of utter chaos. A larger Model 20 in its initial form was to have Allison V-1710s; as proposed by Lockheed (via Gerschler), it was to be powered by P&W X-1800s; as specifications were drawn up at a May 6, 1940, conference at Wright Field, the aircraft was to be powered by those Continental IV-1440s [sic]. It appeared to be a situation out of control. Two small IV-1430s in the large aircraft and two large (but totally undeveloped) and complex engines – almost 900 cubic inches larger than an Allison in a standard P-38 – were to be hung on an airframe that was 90 percent P-38.

Eventually, and unhappily, specification changes dictated by Wright Field called for no fewer than five totally different engines as powerplants for the XP-58. It is no wonder that Kelly Johnson once referred to Lockheed's "only ten-engine fighter." Of course it was an "inside" joke.

Lockheed's Model 522 was, in actual fact, a response to Materiel Division's Circular Proposal 39-775 issued on March 11, 1939, at the request of Combat Command, GHQ Air Force. Evidence pointed to the desire for a new interceptor, albeit one with most components of an existing aircraft. However, it was to have uprated engines or completely different engines and higher altitude ratings. In response to the request for a proposal sent to competitors, it should be noted that the two winning designs had at least a two-thirds commonality with existing airframes. That was, basically, a farce, for one of the airframes was in mass production and the other was an unproven, eventually unsuccessful USN fighter that was plagued with problems. Highest on points was the Lockheed 522, provided with the military designation XP-49.

As of that date it is important to recall that the Seversky-cum-Republic XP-47 and XP-47A designs were lightweight fighter proposals based on Allison V-1710 power. The Curtiss XP-46 was a comparable design in that same class. Second place on points in the CP39-775 contest was Grumman's Model 41, a revamped, upgraded and land-based version of the struggling XF5F-1 Skyrocket that had been built for the Navy. That design was still powered by Wright Cyclones, but it did have an extended nose carrying the components for a tricycle landing gear, and the engines were boosted by turbosuperchargers.

Burbank engineers were not to be faulted for incorporating an engine that ran off with top honors in Air Materiel Command's evaluation of powerplants on September 11. However, it is most likely that the Lockheed men did it *cum grano salis*, although they probably phrased it "with a grain of salt." Incredibly, the military panel that selected the Model 522 anticipated that the Wright Tornado – that multi-row, cylindrical, liquid-cooled radial that

ABOVE: *Aerial view of Lockheed Building 304 (Production Test) at L.A.T. in early 1943 reveals more than 30 Lightnings and other Lockheed types being processed. This was merely one area of intensive activity at Lockheed. Boeing-Vega B-17s, Hudsons, Venturas, etc., were all being produced in the same two-mile circle. Burbank was always a beehive of activity. (LAC)*

BELOW: *Requirements for the XP-49 and Grumman's XP-50 were sadly flawed. If pressurization was a key, it missed the Grumman plane. The same applies if the Continental IV-1430 was a main factor. C. L. Johnson's contemporary proposal for a Merlin-powered P-38 made far more sense. Yet it was "sluffed off." Production versions of the Merlin (60 and 70 series) were attaining 1,600-plus bhp early in 1942. Packard could have been producing them in a matter of months or even weeks. (LAC)*

never really existed – would be powering the production P-49A.

The military board then agreed that the prototype could be powered by the new Pratt & Whitney X-1800, soon to gain the military designation XH-2600. To the credit of United Aircraft Corporation, at least a few hand-built XH-2600s were constructed. One senior executive in P&W engineering had pushed

the X-1800 project very hard because he had been overly impressed by the British Napier firm's prototype Sabre engine during a visit to England. Not only was the X-1800 project started late, Pratt & Whitney tackled the sleeve-valve engine concept, which was almost an unknown technology in America. As proposed to the Air Corps in 1939, 2000 to 2200 horsepower could be expected at a prop speed of 1200 rpm for takeoff. With a rating of 1850 bhp at 20,000 feet, the XP-49 was expected to attain a speed of 473 mph at that altitude.

Fortunately for all concerned, Frederick B. Rentschler was a man of vision and pragmatism. As chairman of the board at UAC, he had the power to make all-powerful decisions. In the fall of 1940, during one of Maj. Gen. H. H. Arnold's visits, Rentschler spoke out with splendid candor against continuation of the X-1800 project. Being totally objective, he pointed out every shortcoming of the engine and what its continuation would mean to the available manpower at P&W. Arnold was extremely impressed with such candor. He agreed to order immediate cancellation of all work on that project. (Just weeks before that decision was made, it must be recalled that general arrangement drawings of the XP-58 "foreign release agreement" airplane proposed by James Gerschler in New York were based on the P&W XH-2600/X-1800 engine. It must be presumed that the May 6 decision made at Wright Field to switch to Continentals for the XP-58 had no effect on the XP-49 program. The magnetic attraction of Wright's XR-2160 Tornado was its comparatively small diameter.) If it seems inconceivable that Lockheed propulsion engineers would not raise all sorts of red warning flags about those fighter engine convulsions, high-level executive preoccupation with overwhelming production programs and diversion of Capt. Kelsey to the United Kingdom with Col. Spaatz were factors that had a profound effect on decision making.

Grumman Aircraft received their contract for a single prototype XP-50 on January 17, 1940, and that was close to 90 days before the Navy's XF5F-1 made its initial takeoff. In spite of great publicity about the carrier-based interceptor, performance was actually disappointing. The Bethpage factory had the Air Corps' Model 41 – designated XP-50 in its Army format – ready to fly in May 1941, something over two years after the first Lockheed XP-38 flight. However, it turned out to be a long time after the XP-50 flew that the XP-49 would take to the air. After years of outstanding success with its naval aircraft, Grumman was in a deep slump. Their venture with the XP-50 did nothing to relieve the pressure. On that first test flight, the supercharger for the right engine exploded, forcing the test pilot, Bob Hall, to bail out. Little, if anything, was learned about the Model 41's characteristics before it plunged, burning, into Long Island Sound.

After a series of meetings in July 1940, powerplant problems plaguing both the "no cost" XP-58 and the single XP-49 attracted much attention. The obvious became evident. Bigger engines were needed for the XP-58, an aircraft that was more nearly medium bomber size than something viewed as a fighter. There can be no doubt that Lockheed people had recognized that fact in their haste to replace the V-1710s with P&W X-1800 units.

Just as obviously, the Power Plant Branch (official designation) under Lt. Col. E. R. Page was trying to find homes for the numerous, but mostly phantom, "Hyper" (for high performance) engines that were being developed under that organization's contracts and direction. But Robert Gross and Hall Hibbard prevailed; by September 10, 1940, XP-58 Spec. 1870 had been revised to reflect their choice of the XH-2600 (X-1800-SA2-G). How could the Lockheed or Materiel Division have known what revolutionary ideas had been formed in the mind of Fred Rentschler 3,200 miles away? Even P&W types who may have been in the meetings could not have guessed.

But at last there was some real logic – or so it seemed – entering the overall picture. All parties agreed that the Model 522/XP-49 would be powered by Continental GIV-1430-9 and 11 opposite-rotation engines. At the same time, P&W engineers would concentrate on a new, very large displacement aircooled radial, the R-4360 corncob engine. Lockheed was caught in the concussion. Forces of evil conspired to creep into the minds of the planners. The brilliant decision was made to design the XP-58 around that "pie-in-the-sky" Wright Tornado . . . immediately! The question of the day should have been "Has anyone even seen a mockup of the Wright Tornado?"

Why didn't anyone suggest the use of a turbosupercharged version of the oncoming P&W R-2800? Lockheed had more experience than anybody when it came to supercharged engines. Their XC-35 was a major prize winner. It certainly had to be easier to put an extended driveshaft on the R-2800 than to develop the Wright XR-2160 Tornado, if such extension shafts were likely to contribute to XP-58 performance. Most of those huge cooling scoops could have been removed from the big fighter and the aircraft could have been developed rapidly.

Of course some pseudo-logical arguments would have contended that there would be no airframe for the Tornado, but that had no validity at all. And where could they have built production versions of the XP-58? Eventually the XP-58 flew with Allison V-3420 engines, taking to the air at Burbank for the first time on an appropriate day . . . June 6, 1944. By that time it had become an airplane looking for a real mission, about 4 years and a month after it became something more or less real. If engines had not killed the P-58, a stake would have been driven into its heart by committees trying to figure out if there was, indeed, a mission available. There was, but politics and access to the President's ear via one of his sons allowed Howard Hughes to win a contract that never should ever have received consideration.

The XP-58 slowly rotted in a remote corner of Patterson Field in 1946. Perhaps only the Lord has any ideas of the cost absorbed by Lockheed, but AAF Change Orders cost the government $451,566. A second XP-58 was less than two-thirds complete when it was abandoned, but it had cost the AAF $1,893,551, a not insignificant amount of money during the war. That amount would have procured no less than fifteen P-38Ls! In fact the total cost would have supplied a squadron with P-38s and all necessary spares.

As for the XP-49, it did not leave the ground on its maiden flight until November 14, 1942. Even then it was in the air for just over 30 minutes. Wrangling over the Continental engines, the pressurization system and maintainability weighed heavily on the program. Had anyone been smart enough to put R-2800s or R-3350s in the XP-49 (or the XP-58), it might well have proven to be a winner. Such an airplane would have been a close contemporary of Northrop's P-61, an aircraft featuring the same engines, sans turbosuperchargers until much later when the C model went into production.

An R-2800-powered P-49A would have been a contemporary of the similarly powered P-47 Thunderbolt, albeit with considerably longer range capabilities. Equipped with reliable R-2800s, deck-mounted turbosuperchargers, no Prestone cooling system and at least 4000 horsepower in early 1943, that clean-lined Lockheed would have been churning out 450 mph speeds (at least) and could be flown with 310-gallon external tanks without difficulty. How does a 1,200-mile combat radius sound? With great available, reliable engines and a producible airframe having 60 percent or more power than production P-38s of the same time frame, it would have been a sure-fire winner.

What did the Continental Motors engine or its derivatives contribute to the war effort? Virtually nothing. As an old saying went, "It was not worth a continental," making reference to a piece of paper money issued by the Continental Congress in the

1770s. As for the airframe, it wound up on the end of a drop-test rig cable in 1945. Faulty specifications and Col. Page's enchantment with the pre-war Hyper engine concept most certainly handcuffed the Model 522 from the very beginning. Improvement of the breed is what won the war, not chasing the elusive phantom of far-out concepts. What did the Curtiss XP-55, Fisher XP-75, Northrop XP-56, McDonnell XP-67 (with Continentals) or Vultee XP-54 do in any way that might contribute to the war – unless that war might have lasted another five years? Nothing! America kept a tight rein on the wasting of materials. Yet it frittered away valuable manpower as if there was a never-ending supply.

By mid-1943, there were some good things happening in the aircraft industry. Production costs of fighters, bombers, and transports were coming down significantly. Typical "flyaway" costs, at the factory (including armament), for major AAF fighter aircraft looked like this:

| | |
|---|---|
| Bell P-39 | $60,000 |
| Curtiss P-40 | $49,449 |
| Lockheed P-38 | $105,567* |
| Republic P-47 | $104,258 |

*   *The P-38H model was in production at that time.*

Lt. Col. Franklin O. Carroll headed up the Experimental Engineering Section – including its flight test branch under Maj. Stanley Umstead – in 1941 at the time the Air Corps was reorganized into the Army Air Forces. He made a statement that could easily be overlooked in the "big" picture, but it strikes at the heart of all that was good and all that was bad in America's Army aircraft. Lt. Col. Carroll wrote, "Air Corps specifications leave very little to the designer's imagination regarding the plane's general type and purpose, but urge him to employ his utmost ingenuity on design details."

Furthermore, he wrote, "The 'idea men' (originators of the specifications) must take care not to demand more than is possible of the designer. The aircraft engine is one of the design's limiting factors." Carroll certainly spoke the truth. When young Lt. Ben Kelsey laid down the specifications for the XP-38 and XP-39, he was *the* man moving America's "pursuit" aircraft forward in a quantum leap in spite of two decades of political constraints. Kelly Johnson surely recognized this.

The people at Bell Aircraft made a decent start with the XP-39, but no man can carry two major programs at the same time. Kelsey stayed with the Lightning and George Price took over on the P-39. Removal of the turbosupercharger can be attributed to Price. Later on, Cols. Price and Howard Bogert were frequently at loggerheads over the XP-58 Chain Lightning project, and their opposing views did nothing to get that Lightning unchained. It all goes to prove that even when the original specification is valid, faulty revisions will undermine everything. Personal ambition surely played a part in some of the bad decisions of the war. As things turned out, the Lockheed XP-58 would have been more logically named "Chained Lightning."

*ABOVE: Grumman's XP-50 competition against the XP-49 was this revamped Navy XF5F-1 concept. The latter had been "Kelseyized" with tricycle landing gear and turbos. The test pilot had to bail out on the initial flight when a turbosupercharger failed. Instead of having any winner, the competition got terminal indifference. (Grumman)*

*BELOW: A terrible case of political infighting seemed to poison the large XP-58 design from the start. It is doubtful that the British ever adhered to their "foreign release" agreement to pay for two XP-58s. Serious attempts to force no fewer than five (that's 5) different engines upon the design led to Kelly Johnson referring to it as "our only 10-engine fighter." It finally wound up with Allison V-3420s for a total of 6,000 (plus or minus) horsepower.*

*Constantly changing mission requirements plagued the XP-58 Chain Lightning for its entire life. Flown for the first time on D-Day in 1944, it eventually went to Wright Field where it was allowed to deteriorate rapidly. There can hardly be any excuse for the four unproductive years between the June 1940 agreement and the June 1944 first flight date. (LAC)*

# CHAPTER 12

# Oh, To Be In England

When a P-38 lands with everything out, it is reminiscent of a gigantic eagle or shrike at the moment of striking its prey while in full flight. Here a P-38F-13-LO prepares to touch down at Goxhill or Ibsley in England, August 1942, becoming the first U.S. fighter in strength capable of combat with modern Axis fighters.

A With a minimum of fanfare, Eighth Air Force Head-quarters was formally established in Great Britain at Bushy Park, southwest of London, on June 18, 1942. Code name for that HQ was WIDEWING. Not un-expectedly, Maj. Gen. Carl Spaatz became the first commander, but the rapidly changing war situation often forced him to move on to other critical command functions. Within days after Brig. Gen. Frank O'D. Hunter arrived in England aboard his B-17E, he moved into his own headquarters at Bushey Hall as commander of the VIIIth Fighter Command. Other than small numbers of ex-RAF Supermarine Spitfires and Bell P-39s/P-400s, his key fighter strength was vested in Lockheed P-38Fs.

Squadrons of the famed 1st Fighter Group, after having been long-time residents of Selfridge Field, Michigan, had moved to England in the van of others involved in the BOLERO movement, starting in June 1942. Their British stations were to include Goxhill, Atcham, High Ercall, Colerne and Ibsley . . . at least until the latter part of October, but nobody in the squadrons had any knowledge of that. The 27FS had diverted from their scheduled course to Reykjavik for rein-forcement of the fairly weak Icelandic defensive force. There, the 27th's P-38Fs were a huge improvement on the early series Curtiss P-40s and Bell P-39s then on station at the North Atlantic island. Those airplanes from the 1FG were ultimately to remain there for approximately three months.

Fourteenth Fighter Group (all pursuit groups and squad-rons were in the process of making the technical transition to "fighter" groups and squadrons) airplanes joined the BOLERO movement in August. The squadrons settled in at Atcham, but the 50FS was soon sent on detached service to Iceland to

relieve the 27FS. Squadrons of the 82FG made their way to the United Kingdom by sea routes for assignment to bases in Northern Ireland. Pilots and aircraft never reached operational status in the U.K. after their arrival in October. When their P-38s arrived by ship, their primary basing was at Langford Lodge.

Part of that massive private estate had been converted into a large airfield system, originally as an assembly and overhaul facility operated by Lockheed Overseas Corporation. (Lockheed had been operating the British Reassembly Division [BRD] for their British employers since 1941.) Longtime Lockheed executive Carl Squier was placed in charge of the Langford Lodge base, located about 20 miles west of Belfast. Eventually the base spread out over several hundred acres of the estate of the late Gen. Sir Edward Packenham, an officer who had been defeated in the Battle of New Orleans by Andrew Jackson decades earlier.

Last of those early P-38 groups to arrive for duty in Great Britain was the 78FG, composed of the 82nd, 83rd and 84th Fighter Squadrons. They were based at Goxhill from December 1. Squadrons of the 78FG were equipped with P-38Gs, the newest model that had been received at March Field, California. Generally speaking, G Model airplanes, including 374 aircraft taken over from British Contract A-242, were different from other P-38s in having Allison V-1710F-10 (-51 and -55) engines. As for basic P-38Gs on Contract AC-21217, they were essentially duplicates of the "takeover" aircraft, but 180 were accepted at Burbank equipped as F-5A reconnaissance aircraft based on a single prototype, the F-5A-2-LO (originally F-5-1-LO). They differed from F-4 types in having five cameras instead of four and, of course, numerous technical changes. One identifying feature of G airplanes was a canopy revision, the top panel opening longitudinally instead of laterally. However, it is not a positive clue since there were notable exceptions.

After a few days of visiting major British installations with Gen. Spaatz, Col. Kelsey went on a tour of fighter bases populated by the youthful P-38 jockeys. He would nearly always demonstrate the capabilities of the P-38F. There was no doubt about it; Kelsey just loved to fly airplanes. While many of the young pilots had misgivings about some of the airplane's characteristics – largely predicated on rumors, inaccurate accident reports and accidents eventually traced to absolutely illegal flying actions – they were all encouraged by his demonstrations and enthusiasm. After all, this old "Fuddy Duddy" obviously performed with such aplomb and smoothness that it just had to be easy.

B Mention must be made of two brand new prototype single-seater, twin-engine fighters that made their first flights in Great Britain just a couple of months after the VIIIth Fighter Command established itself in headquarters known as AJAX near London. Westland's P.14 Welkin was a giant-size high-altitude, single-seater featuring a pressure cabin à la Lockheed's XP-38A. The quagmire environment surrounding the XP-49

notwithstanding, the fighter had managed to fly in exactly the same time frame as the two British pressure-cabin types.

That second RAF type was the Vickers Type 432, an airplane seemingly designed only with ellipse guides and no straight edges; the Vickers also appeared to be of relatively modest size, but with two outsized powerplant nacelles. It had at least 40 percent more power than P-38Fs stationed in England, conventional – even C-47 Dakota-like – landing gear, and 20-mm cannons located in a belly pannier positioned about midway between the nose cap and tail cone. The Vickers featured an odd cockpit canopy that looked exactly like a B-24 navigator's sighting dome. Supposedly capable of 440 mph at 28,000 feet, the Type 432 went nowhere.

Designer W.E.W. Petter led the Welkin design team, with hardly a french curve in sight, in designing an airplane that was as conventional as the Vickers in general concept, but it must have been about 25 percent larger. In fact, the 70-foot span put its wing exactly on a par with that of Lockheed's XP-58, an airplane with more than twice the gross weight. Although the Welkin outpowered the early production P-38s by 50 percent, its top speed was comparable to the slowest P-38s built. In spite of huge ailerons, the rate-of-roll was deadly slow and it was unable to switch rolling direction.

And, suddenly, there it was. That ogre called compressibility. Even in a shallow dive of 15 degrees the Welkin encountered the problem so compellingly that a D.H. Mosquito could dive away from it with ease. Although 67 were ordered into production, it appears that the contract was either not fulfilled or was cancelled. If the Welkin could not exceed 387 mph at critical altitude, one wonders how the Vickers could hope to attain 440 mph on less horsepower.

*Trained AAF ground crews were on hand to greet pilots of the 14FG arriving at Atcham in August 1942. The group was commanded by Col. Thayer S. Olds. This P-38F-1-LO was typical of all equipment provided to the 1FG, 14FG and 82FG of the Eighth Air Force. (IWM)*

Remember, even with those marvelous Merlin 61 and 70 series engines powering the Westland and Vickers fighters (in prototype form), they were either slower or no faster than the XP-38 that had flown almost exactly 4 years earlier. A fighter also has to be maneuverable, it has to be producible and . . . more to the point . . . it has to be there when its target problem exists. Specifications that led directly to the P.14 and Type 432 fighters were totally predicated upon a very-high-altitude fighter requirement, dating back at least to 1940.

It does not take much detective work to figure out that the Rolls-Royce Merlin 60/70 series engines were going to be desperately needed for airframes meeting the specifications. Why, then wasn't somebody imaginative (we phrase it gently) enough to see that the RAF already had an airframe that was "aching" for those 1600 bhp high-altitude engines. A couple of 322-B airframes could have been tested with the Merlins, and production activity could have been modified at Lockheed to wed the Merlin 61 to that airframe. (Cass Hough and others were flying up to 41,000+ feet in 1942 with ordinary low-pressure oxygen systems. That was about the target altitude for the RAF fighters.) Yes, hindsight is subject to criticism, but so is lack of foresight when it is emblazoned in front of someone. It was a golden opportunity lost.

C Major Hough did most of his flying in the first half of August in an Airspeed Oxford (dead slow), a Miles Master and a Spitfire at Northolt. It was then back to his P-38F at Atcham and High Ercall. By that time, General Hunter had – with the approval of Spaatz – asked Kelsey and Hough to form a special development organization for the specific purpose of matching his fighter aircraft to any combat environment that was likely to be encountered. Hough was assigned to the VIIIth FC, but it appears that Kelsey (for the moment) was assigned to the Ninth Air Force.

The initial organization established at Bovingdon was originally named Technical Services Section, but the select outfit was destined to have a variety of official names over a period of time. Hunter obviously believed that his P-38 groups would soon be locked in combat with the *Luftwaffe* over the European countryside. After spending some time flying his

P-38F at Atcham and High Ercall, Hough evidently participated in two fighter sweeps in September for insight purposes. He was 37 at the time. But there would be many more combat missions for him before he finally returned home.

Unknown to Hunter or Hough, some major political decisions were to affect VIIIth FC, upsetting some well-laid plans. SUPER GYMNAST, soon to be replaced by an operation identified as TORCH, increased in importance, while the bomber offensive on *Festung Europa* showed definite signs of losing support. In all truth, TORCH had already been put into motion if for no other reason than its massive logistical complexity. Up to that time, there had never been any seaborne invasion to challenge it for sheer size. TORCH was the invasion of North Africa.

Boeing B-17E Flying Fortresses of the 97BG launched their first Eighth Air Force raid on the Continent on August 17, 1942, sans any fighter support beyond the French coastline. The recently arrived P-38 airplanes and their pilots were hardly settled into their new bases, let alone having attained proficiency that would allow them to claim operational readiness. As of mid-August, no 1FG pilots were even ready to think of fighter sweeps. Their P-38s were going to be the only fighters in the U.K. that were capable of escorting bombers deep into France and maybe venturing into Germany. Not one Republic P-47 Thunderbolt was going to appear on the scene in Great Britain until January 1943, and even then few C models would be capable of operating against the Nazis until at least April. They lacked useful command radios, did not feature water injection (limiting power) and range capability was hardly better than that of the contemporary Spitfires.

Cass Hough's special unit – by that time renamed Air Technical Section – was an operating branch of AJAX with facilities at Bovingdon. Another promotion had come with that responsibility; his promotion to Lieutenant Colonel was hardly unwarranted. Although Col. Kelsey was attached to the Ninth Air Force for operations, he was still Chief of the Fighter Branch at Wright Field, responsible for development and procurement of all fighters. Sometime in January or February 1943, he returned to the U.S.A., where he nearly lost his life in California. In the meantime, Hough had his first and second encounters with the infamous "compressibility tuck" problem, once in a P-38 and once in a P-47. Capt. Robert Shafer, a pre-war enlisted man at Selfridge Field, and Hough were tackling their greatest problem after the initial P-47s arrived at the docks of Liverpool: How to provide the Thunderbolts with enough range to escort the hard-pressed B-17 formations over Europe. By that time, most of the P-38 Lightning problems had gone away, far away . . . literally.

A fairly steady stream of P-38s was directed toward the United Kingdom ports of Liverpool and Belfast in the final months of 1942. Work shifts operated around the clock at Speke Aerodrome (BRD) outside of Liverpool, up north at Langford Lodge (LOC) and at a second BRD at Renfrew, Scotland. At least one battered P-38G, mounted on an assault craft to save space aboard ship, had been towed into Dufferin Docks at Belfast. The assault landing craft – at least part of it – had been found by a British Navy corvette about 300 miles from Northern Ireland on November 25. Part of the craft had been torn off when it went overboard with the P-38 tethered to it. The gondola nose section had taken a terrible battering, but crews at Langford Lodge managed to repair the Lightning and return it to service.

Generally representative of established routines for USAAF groups, ground crews and support personnel were on hand when the leading P-38F fighters of 14FG arrived by air at Atcham in August. Command of the group was in the hands of Col. Thayer S. Olds. After sorting out a multitude of technical and operational problems associated with arriving at an overseas base with differences in standards, intensive training regimens were established to ready the squadrons for tackling the Nazi fighters. Within a week the 1st and 14th

Fighter Groups were at least initially geared to carry out fighter sweeps over France and the Low Countries and to escort bomber formations at the earliest possible date.

In fact, after relying heavily upon the Royal Air Force for training support, the men of the 1FG took their Lightnings on the first real mission on September 2. Mission operations continued with no encounters until October 25, and the *Luftwaffe* assiduously avoided confrontations with the Lockheeds during that entire period. Whatever the reasons for avoiding combat, the Germans failed to put up any challenge to the American penetrations of the European airspace. The 71FS and 94FS had been flying out of Ibsley and the 27FS out of Colerne since August with no great difficulties. One fighter was lost on operations – missing in action, probably the result of a navigational problem or bad weather.

By mid-September IT had become a fact of life: the first two P-38 groups to arrive in the U.K. were quietly assigned to the Twelfth Air Force. In fact, Brig. Gen. James Doolittle assumed command on September 23; Col. Hoyt Vandenberg was his chief of staff. As late as mid-October, only the highest ranking officers knew for certain that the 1FG and 14FG were no longer part of the Eighth Air Force. Rumors were rampant, especially when aircraft of the 1FG flew to Chivenor for staging activities that were a usual part of activities prior to shipping out. As October came to an end, TORCH was still virtually an unknown name.

On November 8, 1942, everybody knew where they were going as radio reports were overwhelming listeners with the news of a massive North African invasion. If there was any lingering doubt in the minds of the "top brass" about P-38F capabilities, it was nowhere to be seen or heard. Col. Stone informed his pilots that they were going to fly nonstop from England's South Coast area via an indirect route to Oran, Algeria. They were to fly past Gibraltar, using it only as an emergency stop en route. In other words, their route was not going to be the shortest distance between two points.

Firm orders were given that they were not to fly over Portugal or Spain for any reason. To land in either place meant loss of the airplane and internment. For the record, Gibraltar's

*During part of the summer of 1942, the 71st Fighter Squadron of the 1FG (the latter under command of Lt. Col. John N. Stone) was based at Ibsley. They were actually assigned to XII Fighter Command, but remained under VIIIth FC. All began with some strafing operations in September, and the group flew a few bomber escort missions. Capt. Francis "Bucky" Harris is pilot fifth from the right, standing. The exigencies of war soon forced their departure for North Africa. (Kenneth Sumney)*

airfield was 1,200 miles away and Oran was 1,500 miles from their jumping-off point at Portreath. There was going to be little flexibility for doing things incorrectly.

Basics of the flight plan dictated that all P-38s would carry maximum fuel in all tanks, including two 165-gallon drop tanks. Eight aircraft would make up each fighter element, and they were to fly formation with a Martin B-26, although there is proof that North American B-25s led some of the flights. Official records state that Col. Olds' 14FG airplanes flew out of Portreath first, followed by 1FG fighters commanded by Col. Stone. Again, there is strong evidence that at least some 1FG airplanes flew out on the first day.

French (Vichy) forces decided to resist, so the first fighters to go into battle for TORCH were Spitfires of the 31FG flying out of Gibraltar. On November 9, Spitfires of the 52FG escorted Brig. Gen. Doolittle's B-17 on the flight from Gibraltar to Algeria. French forces at Oran finally surrendered before the Allied onslaught on November 10, and that was the official signal to launch the P-38s from England. No other single-seat fighter type in the world that was a first-line combat aircraft

*ABOVE  Lockheed P-38Gs of the 78FG, such as "Mackie" (possibly flown by Maj. Harry Dayhuff), were available too late to fly the North Atlantic route before conditions became unsafe.  Assigned to the 82FS at Goxhill after arriving via sea routes, it was soon flown to North Africa as a replacement aircraft. (Col. Jack Oberhansly)*

*BELOW LEFT: On early model P-38s, a three-point landing (especially on undulating runways or sod fields) sometimes broke the nose gear yoke.  Damage to the fuselage and ground-down strut indicated this pilot actually hit on the nose wheel first.  Aircraft is a P-38G-1-LO.  (LeRoy Weber)*

*BELOW RIGHT:  Rather typical of fighters being flown by the Americans in the Eagle Squadrons and by other AAF groups which had arrived in the U.K. sans aircraft was this Supermarine Spitfire Mk. 5b. Very few U.S. pilots did not like the Spitfire.  (Vickers-Armstrongs Ltd.)*

was capable of making that flight nonstop. Lockheed's 165-gallon teardrop external tanks performed their function beautifully, making Gen. Arnold's earlier gamble all worthwhile. Official records indicate that the air movement of the Twelfth AF from England actually began on November 7, but that must have applied primarily to bombers headed for Casablanca in French Morocco.

(Approximately 125 Bell P-39s/P-400s were equipped with large centerline tanks, allowing them to be ferried to North Africa a bit later. However, Eighth AF organizations were poorly equipped in any way to erect and service Bell P-39D-1s and the P-400s that were originally destined to go to Russia. Squadrons of the 68th Observation Group plus the 350th and 81st Fighter Groups had trained on those types, primarily for ground support. Unfortunately for Twelfth AF operations, several of the Airacobras were out of commission. About a score went down in Portugal because of "winds and mechanical failures." Of course, they were promptly interned. First mention of P-39 action with the Twelfth AF was on January 22, 1943, as a result of those losses and training problems. In the Battle of Kasserine Pass, the valuable airfield at Thelepte, Tunisia, had to be abandoned with the loss of 18 aircraft that could not be moved. Most, if not all, were Airacobras. None of that was very encouraging because it had been learned months earlier that P-39s and P-400s were no match for any of the Japanese types in the Solomon Islands. The Royal Air Force appraisal of P-400 performance in European operations at an earlier date should have been heeded. Deletion of the turbo-supercharger early on had dealt a troubled aircraft a death blow.)

A young Texan, Lt. Jack Ilfrey, was – on the surface, at least – more or less typical of the 1941-type AAF fighter pilot. In some other respects he was not entirely typical. He did tend to get into trouble with his superior officers on occasion. Another pilot, Lt. Richard Bong, had some of the same character "flaws." In the summer months of 1942, Ilfrey had flown his 94th "Hat-in-the-Ring" Squadron P-38F across the extremely dangerous North Atlantic ferry route as part of the BOLERO operation.

Such a flight could, in the early 1940s, be a trial for the most experienced pilots. Yet 2nd Lt. Ilfrey (and many of his contemporaries) had still been a cadet in training on December 7, 1941. He was 21 years of age when he flew the first leg of BOLERO on July 4, Independence Day. Between the day he received his wings and headed for the (then) 94PS(F) and that national holiday, Jack contends that he – and his squadron mates – became veteran P-38 pilots. Nobody can deny that they logged many hours in cross-country flights and in exercises down south.

Ilfrey's personal tale of his flight from England's Portreath base to Oran reveals that everything does not go according to the best formulated plans. It also reveals something of Ilfrey's character and why he became (arguably) the first ace in the Twelfth Air Force, the first P-38 ace anywhere, and certainly the first ace in the 1FG in World War II. And all of that happened before January 1, 1943. (Lt. Virgil Smith may have beaten Ilfrey out as the first Twelfth Air Force ace by a matter of hours, but there never has been any conclusive proof.)

Fortunately for the historical record, Jack Ilfrey narrated his thoughts and memories before they began to fade from his memory bank.[1] He related the story as he lived it in November 1942:

It was November 9, 1942, and I was about to embark on an unknown future. The invasion of North Africa had just begun the day before and I knew we were going to be something besides guinea pigs. Sometimes a few guinea pigs survive.

Our instructions sounded simple enough when we had heard them in the briefing room the night before. We were to fly in groups of eight, with a B-26 bomber leading us. The route kept hammering in my brain: fly across the Bay of Biscay, hit the Spanish coast, fly down the Spanish and Portuguese coast, turn left, and go through the Straits of Gibraltar. Hit the Spanish Moroccan coast and fly around this coast into French Morocco and then into Oran.

Colonel Stone had told us at briefing that it was uncertain as to where the enemy might be on our route, and we were cautioned to be exceptionally alert and warned again and again that Gibraltar should be our first emergency stop.

I learned much later that some of the American Spitfire groups and P-40 groups had flown off carriers at Casablanca, but the P-38s were the first to fly down to Africa. It looked pretty simple, but it turned out otherwise.

As I turned away from the base at Land's End, I had a true feeling of "This is it." We knew things were rugged in North Africa, and we knew the chance of survival was going to be hard. But you didn't think about death – you only thought of living. And you thought of a lot of other things too. I wondered what my mother was doing in Houston and by now it was difficult to picture in my mind's eye what my mother looked like. When you're off at war, everything becomes abstract. You don't have vivid mental pictures of things back home.

It was now 7 o'clock in the morning and I was beginning to feel a little tired. We had left England around 6:30, just at daylight was breaking, and I had been up since 2 a.m. Morning in England had been cool and damp and misty.

Strict radio silence was being maintained across the Bay of Biscay, and we were flying low, just above the wave tops so we could not be detected by the enemy. We saw no German planes, but several days later some long-range Luftwaffe fighters came out and shot down a few of our planes going to North Africa.[2]

This was a bigger adventure than flying over the Atlantic. We felt this time we were going to get into real combat and later events proved to be more than correct in this respect. Of course, the old American custom of joking and laughing it off prevailed. Everything was so new to us – England had seemed quite different from the United States, and yet we were to find that the British Isles were very much like our own country when compared with other countries we saw.

Suddenly I felt a slight jolt and by the time I realized what had happened, my right engine went out. One of my long-range belly tanks containing 150 gallons of gasoline had fallen off. Automatically, I switched to another tank and the right engine caught on again. But it was clear that I had lost 150 gallons of gasoline. I was still flying low. And then I saw Tony Syroi coming close to me and in his hand he was waving a map for me to see. In large letters, he had printed ONE BELLY TANK. I nodded that I understood and then my mind got really busy. I didn't want to go back to England. I wanted to stay with my

---

1. *Capt. Jack Ilfrey scored six victories (officially), but could not prove he had other "kills" because early P-38s had the gun camera mounted in the nose section, adjacent to the vibrating guns. Jack's early notes were published in* Happy Jack's Go Buggy, *published in 1979. He happily granted permission for us to quote excerpts from his manuscript.*

2. *That was a conundrum for any intercepted pilot. With external tanks on, he was a sitting duck. If he dropped his tanks, there might not be enough fuel left after a fight to get to land. Either way, he was probably out of luck.*

*Oh, to be in England! Emerging from the dense, clammy, bone-chilling fog, a line of P-38Fs dominates the streets of Liverpool early in the morning after being offloaded at the big port on the northwest coast of England in 1942. Truncated Leyland trucks were adapted to tow the P-38s from Garston Docks on the Mersey River – and sometimes clear across Liverpool from Bootle Docks if Garston couldn't handle the load – out to Speke Airport at the southern end of the Cheshire town.*

come true. One minute I decided to bail out; the next minute I figured I would crash land on the coastline. Suddenly I came to the mouth of the Tagus River, which, according to my map, ran 20 or 30 miles direct to Lisbon. Our briefing about what to do if we were forced down in Spain or Portugal had been poor. I vaguely recalled someone saying the Portuguese were friendlier than the Spaniards. A bribe might get you out of the country. I also knew it was the duty of every pilot to destroy his plane and equipment. Still uncertain about what to do, I turned inland and headed for Lisbon.

Soon I saw a beautiful airdrome just outside the city of Lisbon, with long, paved runways and modern buildings. I put my wheels down, circled and landed. As I completed my landing roll, six men on horseback galloped out to meet me. Those horsemen looked like something out of a picture book; big, plumed hats, sabers, pistols and brightly colored trousers. Gesturing wildly, the men motioned for me to taxi my plane toward the administration building. I was busy tearing up my maps, charts and papers . . . tossing them into the wind. Other frantic gestures got me to stop. People came from every direction as the horsemen surrounded the P-38.

When I asked if anyone spoke English, a young fellow (who looked sort of ex officio) came over and said he did. "You are American, yes?" I confirmed that I was. He smiled and said, "Yes, I thought so. I see the star on your airplane. It is the first American warship that I have seen? In trouble?"

I confirmed that there was trouble and that I needed gas.

outfit. I got out my maps and charts and decided I had enough gasoline to get me as far as Gibraltar. I was not going to miss out on the operations in Africa or be separated from the gang.

We kept on flying and when the B-26, which was leading, dodged a thunderhead, I had the feeling we were getting off course. I flew for another hour and began to get a little worried. After another hour passed I began to get alarmed. My gas was running low as we had used a great deal of fuel dodging thunderheads. But still no coastline in sight. We were pretty far out to sea. Worse, we were flying in a southwesterly direction. I decided to leave the group as my gas would not last much longer. Turning southeastward, I hope to hell I would run across the Spanish or Portuguese coast. The clouds were dispersing and as the sun came out, I saw it from about 8,000 to 10,000 altitude. I got my maps out and saw that I was close to a point on the coast at the Spanish-Portuguese border. Flying parallel to the coast, my fuel gauges indicated I would never make it to Gibraltar.

There are no words to describe the feeling you have when you are going to be out of fuel at any moment. You have a kind of paralysis with part of your mind still functioning, making you hope for something that cannot

Lt. Ilfrey was taken into the restaurant and served cake and coffee. He recalled that the cake was awful and the coffee was even worse. There were German pilots from airliners seen outside; Douglas DC-3s in full German swastika markings, something that made Ilfrey mad. In a short time, he was being questioned by Portuguese officials. He remained mute in response to all questions. More excited officials arrived and it was obvious that they did not appreciate his rather stony silence. With a lot of Germans gathered around and the determined questioning and grim faces, Ilfrey knew he was certainly in anything but a neutral nation. He could feel the hatred of the officials.

One of the Portuguese questioners suddenly stepped over to Ilfrey and, in perfect English, advised him that their country's neutral policy was to intern all foreign pilots and their planes. Ilfrey continues with the story in his own words:

That was a shock, suddenly realizing my serious problems. If I ever felt alone, it was at that moment. My friends had gone on. I surely would not see them for a long time. I was out of the war and the adventure had come to an end. And my airplane would be taken away. That hurt. A plane is as close to a pilot's heart as a ship is to a sailor. I never had a desire to fight a war, but my country needed help and that was all I knew. Now, here I was in Portugal and about to be interned . . . cut off completely. I'd never get any mail, and I'd never know what was really going on.

A Portuguese pilot came in and asked me if I would show him something about the P-38. He said he had never seen one before and that he was amazed at its looks. He told me that their air force was made up mainly of German, British and French planes. He was going to take my plane and fly it to a military airfield. He asked me what type of fuel the P-38 used, and when I told him it was 100 octane he looked uncomfortable. "Would 85 octane do?," he wanted to know. After thinking it over, I finally told him it was OK. When the pilot asked me to show him the various mechanisms, I really saw nothing wrong with that.

Mechanics finished gassing up the plane as I climbed into the cockpit. My Mae West was gone and my parachute was gone. I had stuffed by billfold with my AGO (identification card) and overnight bag behind the seat, but they had also been removed. There were a few maps, however, still in the cockpit.

The "student" pilot sat on the wing while I explained the various switches that go into the operation of a P-38. As I talked, my conscience kept bothering me. I kept thinking (that) I should have destroyed my plane. I had a feeling of disloyalty because we had been told to destroy the airplane if we were forced to land. Suddenly I heard a familiar, but faint, sound. I looked up and saw a lone P-38, in trouble and making preparations to land. All six guards on horseback dashed off. The '38 had his wheels down and was landing on one engine.

A sudden thought hit me. "Ilfrey, what the hell are you waiting for?" I threw on all of the switches. While I was doing that, the Portuguese pilot guessed what I had in mind; he tried to reach inside the cockpit to turn off some of the switches. My left propeller was already turning and the engine started, blowing the pilot's hat off. When he struggled to get a getter grip on the plane, I managed to start the right engine. I revved up the left engine while holding the brakes. My idea was to blow the pilot off the wing center section; luckily, it worked. I slammed the canopy shut, gave the plane full power and, without looking back, went straight across the

field, disregarding runways and everything in my path.

As I was leaving the field, I saw the identification mark on the Lightning that had just landed. That plane belonged to Jim Harman, a flyer in my squadron. Once I got into the air, full realization of that harrowing takeoff fairly shook me. I had no parachute, no helmet, and most of my personal belongings were gone. My heading was on an estimated course for Gibraltar, a course which would take me across Portugal and Spain, a forbidden course. I just hoped they had put in enough fuel for the 400-mile flight.

Ilfrey must have had homing pigeon instincts. The "Rock" loomed ahead and he had no trouble at all finding the airdrome. Several other 1FG pilots were there, having been forced to stop at Gibraltar for various reasons. Most everyone, including the Operations Officer, had looks of disbelief on their faces. It wasn't long before Ilfrey stood before Colonel Willis, a pilot in the Lafayette Escadrille in World War I. The story put him in a blind, furious rage; according to Ilfrey, Willis was incoherent and the lieutenant was speechless. After the 45-minute tongue-lashing, the colonel broke into a laughing spasm. Unofficially he was pretty well impressed with Ilfrey's actions. The AAF played their little communications games, and young Texas Jack was sent off in the direction of Oran, Algeria.

Wartime press reports flowed like wine to fill an insatiable home front appetite for information. For a multitude of reasons, many of the stories were reported inaccurately; some of them were downright fabrications. For example, Lt. Ray Crawford was cavalierly credited with shooting down five enemy fighters "before breakfast" one day. The 82FG ace says he never even saw five enemy fighters before any breakfast, and he absolutely never knocked down five of the enemy in a single encounter.

Once in a while a story would be sent over the wires by overly zealous military public relations types who had failed to verify the story with the pilot or crewman involved. If it was a particularly "hot" story, exaggeration seemed to be the controlling factor. Much to the consternation of one serious engineer pilot in 1943, an action that had occurred in September 1942 fell into that category. The pilot was Lt. Col. Cass Hough, the man deeply involved in the daily operation of the new Eighth Air Force's Technical Services Section. His problem with press stories stemmed from his own great desire to get at the root of an ongoing problem that threatened the success of Lockheed P-38s in ETO operations, if not the lives of numerous pilots. Hough was not entirely faultless in the matter because he was – like Maj. Signa Gilkey of Wright Field a year earlier – pioneering in the field of aerodynamics.

He had instrumentation that was a few years in arrears of the needed technology; he had incomplete information on a subject not even understood by aircraft builders or the respected NACA; and he had no way at all of knowing that a flawed performance test report would ever get into the hands of publicists who knew absolutely nothing about the subject. Hough was probably more guiltless than test pilot Lloyd Child was about three years earlier when it was reported that he dove a Curtiss Hawk 75 at 575 mph, "a new world's record,"

*Typically P-38 in concept, this cockpit belongs to one of the F-4-1-LO photo-recon airplanes that was used extensively in connection with Operation TORCH. (LAC)*

the paper said. Absolutely ridiculous! No Curtiss Hawk ever came close to attaining such a speed, straight down or otherwise. But it made headlines.

Colonel Hough's problem started innocently with a non-routine test and a report submitted through channels to headquarters at AJAX. It then languished for months before somebody decided that the Eighth AF needed some good publicity for a change in 1943. Bomber Command was taking a beating, and VIIIth Fighter Command hardly existed in force. A morale booster was sorely needed. AAF airplanes had done little in Europe to impress either the British or the Germans in late 1942 or early 1943. The only mistake made by the colonel was in reporting his indicated airspeeds in a dive as he saw them. He did not add any "disclaimer" because few would have understood it anyway. The most highly qualified pilots in the world reported high-altitude indicated airspeeds as they saw them, mainly because they believed what they saw. In fact, their instruments were technically crude. If they had not been calibrated frequently, and if post-flight correction factors were not included, the data – at least the raw data – were subject to misinterpretation.

Scores of World War II pilots reported, in all sincerity, seeing indicated airspeeds of 500, 600 and even 750 mph at altitudes above 25,000 feet. All such reports were without foundation. Recalling that, Hough's new mission was to improve the operational capability of fighter aircraft in the command by direction of General Hunter. One of the most vexing problems was something entirely new to pilots of VIIIth FC; indeed, it was new to the AAF and to the aviation world at large. Newly arrived P-38 pilots undergoing intensive training in the U.K. in the fall and winter of 1942 were, with increasing frequency, encountering "control freezing" in dives from high altitude. Evidently nobody in the GAF had encountered the problem with Bf 109s or Fw 190s, and the first experimental RAF type to have such a problem was the almost unheard of Westland Welkin. It seemed to be a problem unique to the P-38s, although not many months would pass before the "virus" infected Republic P-47s as well.

Flying over England, more than one pilot found that he was incapable of wresting his hurtling fighter out of a dive from very high altitude. If he did not panic and attempt to bail out, he was lucky. He would find that the higher-density air at low altitude would retard the aircraft speed and the control surfaces would again be able to "bite" for control of the aircraft. It was a phenomenon not even really understood by scientists and the finest engineering talent in the aircraft industry. At least the people in Burbank knew it existed; they just did not know how to fight it. The rest of the world hardly knew about it. Some years would pass before anybody would even mention a new term, "The Sonic Barrier." It had not been encountered by any pilot.

During his mid-1942 tour of British establishments, Col. Ben Kelsey reported that "the most astute British scientists and engineers with whom I came in contact at Farnborough seemed to be totally unaware of the (compressibility) problems. Even worse, they seemed loath to discuss it or even acknowledge that it existed."

Just when the first "compressibility" chart appeared in AAF training manuals and flight operation manuals is unknown, but it is almost a certainty that few combat area pilots ever even had access to a Pilot's Flight Operating Instructions manual or a Pilot Training Manual that included a speed limitation chart before 1944 – at least one that even mentioned compressibility. (As an example, Pacific Area fighter pilot Tom Lanphier, made it clear that he and all of his squadron mates had made the transition from Bell P-39s to the P-38G without ever having seen a P-38 handbook of any kind.)

The immediate problem facing Lt. Col. Hough was an almost total lack of any relevant information, compounded by reports of unexplained fatal accidents or of "control freezing"

*ABOVE: Lockheed had established the British Reassembly Division (BRD) at Speke Airport toward the end of 1938 to complete work on Hudson Coastal Command airplanes shipped by sea from America. BRD, overlooking the Mersey at its widest point (about 4 miles), was the headquarters for several Americans who had joined the Lockheed team at this British facility to put finishing touches on Hudsons, Venturas and P-38s. (LAC)*

*RIGHT: In the shadow of an ancient, brooding Garston Docks warehouse, a transient P-38F grinds to a halt – crippled. Magnesium wheels, exposed to the briny seas on the decks of nearly submerged tankers crossing the stormy North Atlantic in winter, frequently disintegrated. The right wheel of this airplane shows severe signs of distress. Lightnings such as this one were among the first to see action in North Africa after being flown down. (LAC)*

in a dive. It wasn't his nature to sit back and wait for data to trickle in from the U.S.A. through channels or via the rumor mill. Young pilots were, in increasing numbers, reflecting a loss of faith in their chances for survival in a P-38. They had all encountered unfamiliar problems because the Lightning was like no other aircraft in any arsenal. It was a "quantum leap" forward in the technology at that time. Training accident rates in America, not yet challenged by Jimmy Mattern's unique flying exhibitions, were climbing at an alarming rate. Most of that was really attributable to rising demands for combat pilots, uncoordinated training programs and a host of other causes. After all, Americans were still trying to recover from the shock of the early defeats . . . something that had been totally foreign to their thinking. Replacement pilots arriving in the United Kingdom and North Africa were, in many cases, virulent rumor-plague carriers.

Aware that he had to put an end to such rumors immediately, determine what happens in the diving realm and find a way to combat it, Hough decided the only way it could be done was by a direct encounter with the problem. His own P-38F-1-LO, nicknamed "Skunky" for unexplained reasons, was set up with full combat ammunition loading, fuel and oil. The only minor change was substitution of a whip antenna for the VHF mast antenna under the nose.

Hough's credentials for such a test were impeccable. He had logged just under 5,000 hours in non-military aircraft and close to 500 hours in military types, with far above average time in multi-engine aircraft. He had a Master's degree in astronomy and had been top executive in his own reputable manufacturing company in America. He related the story of

*Westland Aircraft's design team tried to produce a viable high-altitude replacement for the failed Whirlwind. Powered by two Rolls-Royce Merlins of 1650 bhp each, with 50 percent more power it was about 30 mph slower than a contemporary P-38H; rate-of-roll was dead slow, and it ran into compressibility at lower speeds than any P-38. Flying for the first time in November 1942 (about 8 months after the 322-Bs arrived from America), its ceiling was just about where Col. Cass Hough had been flying in his P-38F without a pressure cabin. Hardly mentioned in the British press was the fact that it weighed about the same as a P-38J and the wing span was no less than 18 feet greater than any P-38. Remember the chiding about the huge size of P-38s and P-47s? What goes around comes around. (USAF)*

the P-38 dive test as it happened on September 27, 1942, in the Bushey Hall area.

"The Met (meterological) boys told me that ground temperatures were 10 $^0$ C and I could expect -58 $^0$ C (about -78 $^0$ F) at 40,000 feet. Five layers of broken clouds would be encountered between 5,000 and 22,000 feet during my climb to 41,500 feet. At that altitude, indications were 25-inches manifold pressure at 2800 rpm, producing the desired 180 IAS on the nose. I half-rolled "Skunky" into a nearly vertical dive."

"Skunky" had normal P-38F instrumentation, not calibrated to research standards. The pitot tube was in the normal BOLERO (standard from then on) position under the

Unique design marked the Supermarine-style Vickers Type 432; there wasn't one straight line to be seen in wing, tail or fuselage. Designed to the same specification as the Welkin, it was much smaller and far faster on less horsepower. But those 1,565 bhp Merlin 61s would have pushed the modified (wishful thinking) 322-B along just about as fast. And the 322s were already built. Only one Type 432 was built. (Vickers-Armstrongs)

left wing and no error calibration chart had been prepared (facilities were not yet available at Bovingdon). Hough, who was not tall, found that the location of the airspeed indicator made it difficult to read in the higher ranges. He had difficulty in estimating the indicated speed as the needle got toward the end of the scale. And indicator "windup" (probably because of the static pressure source) could be fierce.

"At 35,000 feet, the speed built up to 350 or 360 mph (IAS) when some buffeting set in," Hough continued. "As I pulled back gently on the wheel, the buffet increased (natural, as g force increased), but there was no indication of any tendency to recover from the dive. At 30,000 feet, the IAS was over 500 mph."[3]

In retrospect, it is easy to evaluate the data and recognize that the colonel's P-38F was very close to its critical Mach's Number. However, this is the situation as Cass Hough saw it in 1942. "Up to this point there was no tendency for the nose to drop further, but the elevator felt sloppy and the other controls were heavy. I retarded the throttles and the nose started under, but it came back to vertical as power was increased."

At that point, he was somewhat concerned by an increase in propeller speed to 3500 rpm and manifold pressure was at 40 inches. However, he did not reduce prop speed because he had no idea what the results would be.

"By the time I was at 28,000 feet, I was really being jolted around. The control column was vibrating through an arc of

about 4 inches. Trying to pull back on the wheel only made things worse because of increased acceleration forces. Between 27,000 and 28,000 feet, I rotated the elevator trim control two full turns for nose-up trim, but it had absolutely no effect. I was beginning to get pretty scared that the airplace would not recover at all. By the time I had descended to 20,000 feet, the airspeed was still reading over 500 mph and I felt some small amount of acceleration, something that was most welcome."

(NOTE: Hough was reporting just what he saw. However, that was the core of the reporting problem. When the Compressibility Chart was published in the Pilot Training Manual, and other manuals, it would be easy to see that an IAS of only 360 mph at 20,000 feet was the absolute red-line, and just a bit more was at a Mach's No. of 0.68. That was the P-38 fighter's limiting Mach's Number according to Kelly Johnson. Because there have been reports of attaining higher M=numbers, especially in other aircraft... it might have been possible with a P-47 or a P-51... it is only fair to make one or two important facts known: There were no Mach meters in any aircraft in World War II; the best instruments in the war, referring only to airspeed indicators, worked from the pitot tube and a source of static pressure. There were no compensating devices to offset differences in air density at S.L. vs. 40,000 feet.)

---

3. An indicated airspeed of 180 mph at 41,200 feet works out at a true airspeed (TAS) of 360 mph and a Mach's No. of 0.55. That is just about what should be expected. However, the 500 mph indicated that the colonel reported (from direct observation) is where the press report problem began in the 1943 newspaper stories. Instrument error played a significant part in the erroneous stories that were printed in that year.

As an experimental pilot, he eased off about three-quarters of a turn on the elevator trim tab control because he feared that too much trim had been cranked in and what its effects might be in the dense air of lower altitude.

"Below 15,000 feet, the airplane began to recover by itself, and at 13,000 feet it was practically in level flight again with airspeed of about 400 mph. 'Skunky' had actually attained a slight climbing attitude."

Nobody had forced Lt. Col. Hough to risk his life in a highly experimental situation. With the information available in England at that time and in view of fatal and near fatal dive accidents, he certainly was at risk. To presume that Hough was seeking publicity fringes on lunacy. Here was a retiring personality involved in a test that was unknown to more than a half-dozen men. His "P-38 Dive Report" was classified CONFIDENTIAL and it was not even declassified until 1957. It was treated in the manner of all wartime classified documents. The only person he ever really discussed it with in detail was Hall Hibbard at Lockheed during a trip to the U.S.A. in March 1943.

What seems to have been ignored in the entire matter is that the man proved without any doubt that:

No compressibility dive problem had to result in either a damaged aircraft or a fatality. As long as you were not over a mountainous area, recovery between 15,000 feet and 7,000 feet could be accomplished with relative ease. Obviously, the worst enemy was panic.

Until a solution to the problem was forthcoming, a combat pilot should have, at all costs, avoided any attempt to pursue a diving enemy aircraft at high speed from altitudes above (at least) 25,000 feet.

Patience and familiarity with updated, current information were the best assets a P-38 pilot could have at that time.

Diligent study and analysis over a decade or more has revealed that all negative aspects of the dive story originated with, of all people, Hall Hibbard. Lt. Col. Hough after completing the P-38 dive test and a subsequent P-47C comparison test, returned to the United States for direct contact with engineering personnel at Burbank and Farmingdale. He met with Hibbard between March 21 and 25, at which time he presented his test report and personal commentary. It is of special interest to know that Hough managed to log just under eight and a half hours of flight time on a Lockheed P-38H during that visit to Burbank. Every hour that Hough had logged to that time was on the P-38F model, so he was probably delighted to fly a new, more powerful model that had many innovations.

Hibbard's interest in what happened to Hough and "Skunky" in 1942 must have been overwhelming. In his excitement, he evidently forgot everything he knew about indicated airspeeds and the compressibility factor. Whatever occurred, it did not turn out to be the best thing for aeronautical science. Evidently he met almost immediately after his interview with Hough – probably while Cass was flying the P-38H – with the head of Lockheed's public relations department. It is important to be aware that Hibbard was a vice-president and chief engineer at Lockheed on that day. His story was almost immediately published in the *Lockheed Star*, an employee publication. Communication with AJAX in a London suburb apparently led VIIIth FC to issue a communication to all media that the Distinguished Flying Cross for "flights which took him knowingly into unexplored fields in 1942" had been awarded to Col. Hough. Then the big story broke.

Hough's picture appeared on the front page of hundreds of newspapers along with this headline: World Record P-38 Dive Told For First Time. There it was again, the old "world record" theme. Everybody quoted Hall Hibbard. "He told me he went straight down – vertical – in a full power dive. Everything wide open, and that he hollered like a banshee all the way down from 43,000 to 18,000." Good Lord! Did he really say 43,000 feet? With everything wide open? No wonder Tony LeVier and his test pilot associates got their feathers ruffled. If Kelly Johnson did not chide his boss for the statements (afterward, of course), it would be most unlike him.

By the time the news hit the front pages, LeVier and Burcham had probably made dozens of such dives in the modified P-38G. It was a part of insider information that Maj. Signa Gilkey and Jimmy Mattern had most certainly survived comparable dive tests; in fact, Mattern once made the statement, "And I really bent the airplane." Far worse from a technical standpoint, Hibbard also said, "it was the longest dive in history – nearly five miles – made at 780 miles an hour." The press then went on to say that "The previous power dive speed record was 725 miles an hour, set in a Thunderbolt single-engine fighter," quoting Hibbard. (Just for the record, 780 miles per hour TAS, extrapolated of course from indicated speeds as if they were factual, works out at about Mach 1.04! Altitude is a big factor. Even using Hough's written report as the source, 500+ mph [IAS] at 27,000 feet, assuming -38.5 $^0$ C at that altitude that day, 505 mph would have produced a TAS of 710 mph, or M=1.04.)

The newspapers then added their own little white lies. The major article stated that Hough and other officers "accompanied by scores of other P-38 aircraft and convoying bombers *flying in mass formation*" had crossed the Atlantic a year earlier.

Just about two weeks later, Col. Ben Kelsey was at Burbank to fly the P-38G that was fitted with the first set of dive flaps for inhibiting compressibility problems in the P-38. It was his job as Chief for Development and Procurement, Fighter Branch, to approve that major change in P-38 design. That episode, to be narrated in detail later, nearly cost Kelsey his life. After he recovered from his injury, he was appointed to the post of Chief of the Flight Research Branch, Flight Test Division, at Wright Field. Hough had returned to Farmingdale for some P-47 flights in early April before returning to intensive activity at Bovingdon, England. For the record, it was Hough who did the compressibility dive testing on the P-47C in England.

F Lightning pilots of the 1FG, 14FG and 82FG (plus transferees from the 78FG back in England) operating in the Twelfth and Fifteenth Air Forces in North Africa and throughout the MTO from late 1942 until at least mid-1944 were rarely plagued by the compressibility problem because of their mission profiles. Whether flying cover for B-17s or for B-25s, B-26s or A-20/DB-7 types, their altitude maximums were rarely over 15,000 feet. Lightnings even flew cover for Bell P-39 ground strafers on occasion. Missions taking them above 27,000 feet over Austria and southern Germany were not very frequent, while missions over Yugoslavia and Rumania were more than likely low-level or dive-bomber missions. Almost none of the best Italian fighters could be considered as high-altitude combat planes. Above 16,000 feet, both the P-47 and P-38, even the early models, would just climb away from the highly rated Macchi C.202.

While a P-38 wasn't *nonpareil* in speed contests below its critical altitude (because of that thick, fuel-carrying wing, which also gave it the high rate of climb), the compressibility problem just evaporated. Those "interim" P-38G and H models in the MTO were not at their best, but were less inhibited by restrictions imposed by the leading edge supercharger intercoolers. Their counterparts operating in the ETO in 1943 and 1944 were at a disadvantage until J and L models featuring core-type intercoolers came on line. At that time, Fifteenth Air Force units were happy to get the castoffs of the Eighth Air Force, so the early model P-38s found a good home.

Anyone who has been deluded into believing that Republic P-47s and North American P-51s through the K model were unaffected by compressibility or allied aerodynamic problems will be shocked to learn that some very serious problems existed. A limited study conducted by an AAF safety officer in 1944 showed that losses of P-47s and P-51s as a result of encounters with compressibility were on a par with P-38 incidents. Mustangs also suffered from a wing weakness that was compounded by a landing gear uplock failure problem. To be realistic and fair, these difficulties all needed attention leading to correction, but accidents and loss of life attributable to compressibility in P-38s, P-47s and P-51s were not really significant.

The real significance was in an ongoing problem afflicting P-38s in the ETO prior to installation (at a production change point or by retrofit) of dive flaps because an enemy aircraft could escape by split-essing into a dive. A smart P-38 pilot would not try to follow, preferring to await a new opportunity. But, once again, it was primarily at ETO problem.

G Col. Ben Kelsey was once quoted as saying, "this comfortable old clunk will fly like hell, fight like a wasp upstairs and land like a butterfly. As a fighting ship, it's just like a big girl you have to take on your lap and manhandle. It's an extremely honest airplane; it doesn't bite and doesn't do dishonest things." John Wayne could not have phrased it better.

Of course Kelsey spoke from a position of an MIT graduate engineer, and from considerable association with the best of test and combat pilots. He was most certainly no "desk jockey" commander, having flown at least 22 combat missions in the ETO.

The P-38 won immediate and nearly unanimous acceptance in the South Pacific zones and in the Aleutian Islands. It overcame incredibly bad operational conditions in the 1942-43 North African desert war against some of the *Luftwaffe's* best pilots (including members of the impressively effective Hermann Göring Staffel) to gain a reputation as a fine, viable fighting aircraft.

That was no simple achievement in the face of a semiglobal logistics problem, total unpreparedness (lack of training and equipment) for desert warfare and, of course, command and management problems that invariably afflict armies engaged in unfamiliar combat for the first time. Lightning fighters and the new F-4 and F-5 photo-reconnaissance versions soon earned a "workhorse" *nom de guerre* for feats in the Sicilian and Italian campaigns, even though it is a well-known fact that the U.S. Army's effort in attacking the "soft underbelly" of Europe through Italy was badly undercapitalized.

Only in northern Europe did the Lightning come off – in the fighter role, at least – as just somewhat better than the enemy fighting in his "own ballpark." Everyone agrees that it is easier to blame failure on inanimate objects than on favored humans. If a tiny number of Lockheed P-38s was not very successful in defending a large fleet of B-17s and B-24s (without any help from other "protectors"), it sprang from a true lack of commitment to the Lightnings on the part of Gen. Eaker's staff because, from the outset, there had been great hopes for the Republic P-47 Thunderbolt. (It is terribly paradoxical that the two American fighter types – Lightnings and Mustangs – that received the least favorable initial reception in the ETO ultimately became the *only* ones of the trio that could provide fighter cover for the "heavies" on deep penetration raids against German industrial targets.)

By the time *Luftwaffe* actions presaged a failure of POINTBLANK and caused a rising clamor for return of the Lightnings to the Eighth Air Force, Maj. Gen. George C. Kenney was winning a long-standing battle with the War Department to gain increased deliveries of his favorite fighter to the Southwest Pacific war zone. He knew that P-40s and P-47s were, in 1943-44, unlikely to perform the required job of flying long-range missions dictated by the island-hopping campaign being waged in the far western crescent of the Pacific Ocean. After all, the reason that the B-29 project had been force fed so intensively was the fact that the planners knew that neither the B-17 nor B-24 was up to the job, and they knew that even before December 1941 was a memory. The "short legs" inherent in the mass-produced P-40s and P-47s really limited them to an interim role at best.

Kenney seemed to instinctively know that the P-38 type was going to be a winner for him. (He had also been instrumental in commending the Martin B-26 more than once in 1942 when production of the type was halted three different times as contract termination was considered. Kenney's words were not ignored by Gen. Arnold, and the B-26 soon proved – by way of its performance in North Africa – that he had been correct one more time.)

The Eighth Air Force never fielded more than four groups of P-38s, and the eventual deluge of P-47s and P-51s nudged the P-38s into the shadows. Policy makers in Washington must certainly be faulted for providing dual-source manufacturing for P-47s, P-51s and B-26s while all but ignoring the more complex P-38 for such consideration until the war in Europe just about became history. No knowledgeable person will ever reveal exactly why the War Production Board failed dismally to establish a second production source for P-38s as early as 1942 or 1943. The failure to produce Packard Merlin versions of the Lightning while wasting time, manpower and money on Continental and Lycoming "hyper" engines in the 1600-horsepower range for most of the war years defies understanding.

"Mickey" was the name on a P-38F that landed on Gibraltar en route to North Africa in connection with TORCH. One of the 14FG's airplanes, it landed on November 10. Maj. Ralph Garman flew direct from England to La Senia (south of Oran) in 8 hours, 10 minutes, nonstop. Garman was soon in command of the 1FG. (Army Signal Corps)

*Lockheed Orion 9C Special N12222, Ex-Shellightning. Warren Bodie Photo, 1950 (Long Beach, CA)*

*Lockheed Vega 1, N965Y. Painted to represent Continental Airlines Vega 5.*

*First Lockheed YP-38 c/n 2202, September 1940. LAC*

ABOVE: Lockheed
YP-38. Maj. Signa
Gilkey - Pilot,
1941. Rudy Arnold
- NASM Photo

LEFT: Lockheed
YP-38 Lineup,
August 1941.
Eric Miller - LAC

Lockheed YP-38 c/n 2202.
Ralph Virden - Pilot, November
1941. Eric Miller - LAC

Republic YP-43.
USAAF contemporary
of the YP-38, P-38
and P-38D. Used by
1PG, 55PG, etc.
in 1941. NASM

Test Pilot Jimmy
Mattern and Lockheed
P-38D, September 1941.
Eric Miller - LAC

Lockheed 322-B,
RAF AE979,
Model 322-61-04
Lightning I. LAC

Lockheed P-38F-5-LO and
Supermarine Spitfire F.Va
at Burbank, 1942.
Photo LN5004, LAC

Lockheed P-38E, Model 222-62-09.
1942. Hans Groenhoff Photo

*Lockheed P-38H-5-LO, AC42-66979, w/165-gallon drop tanks, September 1943.*

*Lockheed F-5A-1-LO AC42-12668, NAAF, Telergma, North Africa, 1943.*

*Lockheed P-38H-5-LO, AC42-67079, 1943. Eric Miller - LAC*

Lockheed P-38H-5-LO, c/n 1550.
Lt. M. C. "Chris" Pennell, 20th FG,
55th FS, Wittering, England.
October 1943. AFM

Lockheed P-38H Pilot Lt. Royal Frey,
20th FG, 55th FS, Wittering, England.
October 1943. AFM

Lockheed P-38 Pilot Capt. William Haning, Jr.,
Hq Squadron 475FG, Fifth Air Force, SWPA,
Port Moresby, N.G.,

*ABOVE: Lockheed P-38J-5-LO and F-5B-1-LO near Burbank, CA, Autumn 1943. Eric Miller - LAC*

*RIGHT: Lockheed F-5B-1-LO and P-38J-5-LO near Burbank, CA, Autumn 1943. Eric Miller - LAC*

*Lockheed P-38F-1-LO
"Piggie Back I" [sic],
AC41-7485, Jimmy
Mattern - Pilot. LAC*

*Lockheed P-38F-1-LO
"Piggie Back I" [sic],
Jimmy Mattern - Pilot,
Burbank, CA. LAC*

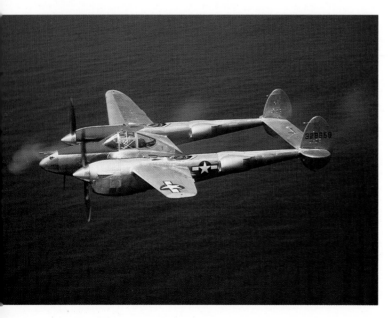

*Lockheed P-38J-15-LO,
Lt. Col. Clarence Shoop,
firing guns, December
1943. LAC*

ABOVE: *Lockheed F-5B-1-LO AC42-67332, Autumn 1943. Eric Miller - LAC*          BELOW: *Lockheed P-38Hs, 20FG, 55th FS, Wittering, England. 1943. AFM*

ABOVE: *Lockheed P-38H-5-LO w/two 1,000-pound bombs, Orlando, FL, 1944. NASM* BELOW: *Lockheed P-38J-15-LO , AC42-103979. First J-15 airplane. E. Miller - LA*

Lockheed P-38J-15-LO
AC43-28859, early 1944.
Eric Miller - LAC

P-38J Pilot Capt. Thomas
McGuire, Jr., Multi-ace
with "Pudgy III" at
Dobodura, N. G., 1944.
Dennis G. Cooper

Lockheed P-38J-20-LO
"YIPPEE," May 17, 1944,
5,000th P-38 built.
Milo Burcham - Pilot,
Photo LN5006.
Eric Miller - LAC

ABOVE: Lockheed
XP-58 Chain Lightning.
Eric Miller - LAC

RIGHT: Lockheed
P-38J-20-LO "YIPPEE."
At L.A.T., May 17, 1944.
E. Miller - LAC

*Lockheed P-38L-5-LO,
September 1977 Symposium.
Dave Tallichet - Pilot/Owner
(Photo LN5736)
Courtesy Split-S Society,
W. M. Bodie*

*BELOW: Lockheed
P-38L-5-LO,
September 1977 Symposium.
Dave Tallichet - Pilot/Owner.
(Photo LN5739)
Courtesy Split-S Society,
W. M. Bodie*

158

ABOVE:  Lockheed P-38J Restoration "Joltin Josie."  Eric Schulzinger Photo - LAC          BELOW:  Lockheed P-38J Restoration "Joltin Josie."  Eric Schulzinger Photo

Lockheed P-38J-20-LO.
Burbank, May 17, 1944,

Lockheed P-38Js escorting
Boeing B-17Gs in bombing
assault on Festung Europa
in 1944. Charles Hodgson
Painting - Lockheed
Photo LN7158.

160

# CHAPTER 13

## TORCH Lights the Way to AVALANCHE

*Lt. Col. Ralph Garman, newly promoted to group commander in the 1st Fighter Group, is shown in flight over their newest base at Chateaudun-du-Rhumel in his recently acquired P-38G carrying the markings HV *G on the booms. His wingman here is the 94FS commander. It seemed strange to have the Fifteenth Air Force headquarters rating the P-38 as having a combat radius of 350 miles in the 1943-44 period when the C.O. of the 1FG was logging missions of up to 6 hours and more in his P-38G. That translates to somewhere between 1,200 and 1,600 miles! Four-hour missions were common.*
*(Col. Ralph Garman)*

DISCLOSURE – From the outset, it has been the purpose of this narrative to reveal all of the underlying, salient, technical and operational facts about Lockheed's unique P-38 Lightning family of aircraft. Heavy emphasis has been placed on the aircraft characteristics, but it is of equal importance to proclaim the parts played by many men in bringing the fighter type to the fore and to emphasize the roles played by numerous military pilots in bringing the war to a satisfactory conclusion. That is especially true of those who overwhelmed a combat-wise and experienced enemy while they, themselves, were trying to learn the rules of the game.

Naturally there is a pervasive and overwhelming desire to relate all details of every important mission flown by those airmen. But that would be the modern-day equivalent to jousting with windmills. If that sort of coverage had been attempted, this narrative would never have seen the light of day. It seemed wiser in every way to concentrate on a few episodes from each theater of operation to provide the flavor of the ongoing warfare in that particular part of the world. Many other books have been written and will be written which concentrate on the aerial battles in a particular theater of operation, or they may just concentrate on the exploits of one squadron or one individual.

Therefore, only some representative tales – reasonably accurate stories, if you will – are included in this monograph. Much of what appears in subsequent paragraphs is based on firsthand accounts as related to the author. And, while they are especially significant, they are often tales that have not even been touched upon in other narratives. We trust that these well-flavored episodes will satiate your tastes.

A There is really nothing simple or clearcut regarding the manner in which an aircraft, especially a fighter aircraft, gains a reputation, be it good, bad or indifferent. In the final analysis, it is the demonstrated capability for destroying numerous enemy opponents in air-to-air combat, on the ground or while still being manufactured in a factory. At the same time, that aircraft must sustain relatively light losses to avoid a "jinx" reputation. Even so, the performance of an aircraft as flown by one pilot may bear little resemblance to its record in the hands of another. Gaining even nominal respectability, however, can be inhibited by poor organizational leadership, logistics problems, low morale among pilots and ground crews, to say nothing of the numbers, types and qualities of aircraft being flown by the opposing force. When the capabilities of opposing pilots are factored in – and that may be the most important element – there is a far clearer picture of the real qualities of a fighter. Anybody who believes that a point defense interceptor aircraft can be compared to a long-range bomber escort fighter on equal terms would be content comparing an ear of corn to a pomegranate or a mouse to a giraffe. It is one thing for a pilot, be he an RAF type or a *Luftwaffe* youngster, to be flying over his familiar home territory on a one-hour interception mission, while it is

ABOVE: *Anybody who was closely associated with the P-38 knew it was a very tough airplane, but some of the pilots were even tougher. For example, young Lt. Benton Miller of the 94FS, who was given the award that made him Knight of the White Knuckle. Miller, off on his first mission against Rommel's Panzer units, was flying this Lockheed P-38F-15-LO (AC43-2092) on low-level strafing runs. What the Nazis could not do, a common telephone pole tried to do. Upon impact, the left propeller tore loose and smashed into the gun bay, bending the access panel into a forward speed brake. The pole tore into the wing and glanced off the spar before breaking. The entire outer wing panel was bent backwards several degrees besides having the dihedral reversed into anhedral. With his disbelieving wingman doing all he could do to help, Miller flew many miles back to Biskra, Algeria, and (with drop tanks still in place) made a perfect landing. Lt. Col. Garman, looking into the cockpit, still contends that "there is no way that airplane could fly." (Kenneth Sumney)*

BELOW: *Lt. Jack Ilfrey, wearing a British battle jacket, was surveying damage to "The Texas Terror," his P-38F that was punctuated with about 150 random holes. "Happy Jack" quickly became an ace while flying with the 94FS. He has to be regarded as the first P-38 ace in World War II, although some contend that Lt. Virgil Smith beat him out of that honor by a few hours. Smith was KIA shortly thereafter. (Kenneth Sumney)*

something far different to be a young pilot tied to a bomber formation for the better part of 3 1/2 to 4 hours out of a 7- or 8-hour mission. The latter, far from home, over territory peopled by decidedly unfriendly antagonists, tired by frequent short battles with enemy aircraft, still has to fly home to a base that may be engulfed in bad weather. If he loses his way and disappears forever, what happens? His airplane becomes a statistic in which the real cause for its loss goes out of focus. It just becomes another digit in the overall "Loss" column.

What really weeds out the bad, fair or poor aircraft from those that go on to moderate or total success are inherently poor systems designs or aerodynamic flaws that absolutely cannot be corrected by retrofit action or by production changes that will not bring the production lines to a halt for weeks or months. The North American Mustang, Republic Thunderbolt and Lockheed Lightning were three types that had "sprung leaks" in their development cycles, but the problems were not insurmountable and the upgraded aircraft were far superior to the competition. Aircraft like the Curtiss Caravan, Brewster Buffalo and Westland Welkin were either all wrong from the start or nothing short of major redesign could save them.

A majority – but certainly not all – of the shortcomings attributed to the P-38 were based on myth or personal annoyance, not fact. What would seem to be a plague to most pilots in a given theater of operations – loss of the single generator, bailout procedures, lack of adequate cockpit heat, or loss of an engine – might not have even been a point of discussion at the local pub or bar in another part of the globe. Some pilots complained about the cramped cockpit in an airplane that could easily carry another person merely by deleting a bit of equipment that was at least a foot away from the pilot's head. It would have been nigh on to impossible to squeeze two uniformed men into the cockpit of a Spitfire or Hurricane, but Lightnings sometimes were flown long distances with two men sharing the control actions. And the men were delighted that at least one of them did not have to set up residence in some *Stalagluft* or spend weeks attempting to escape to England.

It is almost incomprehensible that some pilots even condemned the supposed lack of firepower. All but the most blasé combat pilots were impressed with the powerful concentra-

tion of firepower spewed by the closely grouped weapons. Unfortunately for most AAF pilots, deficiencies in gunnery training in 1942-43 resulted in sending them into combat with little, if any, air-to-air gunnery training with high-performance aircraft. Once a P-38 pilot mastered the situation, results were impressive. An early fighter ace in the 82nd Fighter Group, Lt. Ray Crawford, remembers that he was literally sickened by the destruction wrought by his P-38G's guns one day when his squadron caught a fleet of Junkers Ju 52/3m slow-moving transports out over the Mediterranean. It turned out to be a "turkey shoot." Crawford blasted one of the trimotor monoplanes, causing it to explode almost immediately. His next salvo caused a second transport to break up in the air, scattering *Wehrmacht* troops over the surface like confetti, the forward half of the Junkers cartwheeling as it hit the water. Crawford has never forgotten that awesome sight. His official score at the end of 50 combat missions in three months was six confirmed victories.

An adequately trained and properly supported P-38 pilot, given some competent leadership, had a very good chance of surviving one or more of the 50-mission tours in combat. Those missions ranged from dive bombing or skip bombing to escorting bomber formations to strafing attacks on tactical targets. The Lightning was a tough aircraft, and the two-engine format was frequently a substantial asset. One pilot took a flak hit from Rommel's ground defenses directly in the gun bay doors during a low-level strafing run. The explosion blew both gun bay doors open where the airstream forced them back over the windshield. With his forward vision completely obstructed, the pilot wisely went into a climb on instruments. A couple of squadron mates flew formation with him to guide the pilot back to his base, nearly 100 miles distant across the rugged

North African desert. Guided by his flight leader, he made a blind landing that was textbook perfect.

Another persisting rumor, which had some validity if a pilot did everything against the book, was that nobody could survive a bailout attempt without hitting the tailplane. Capt. Ted Runyon, who had flown from the U.S.A. as a member of Col. Jack Stone's 1FG and had eventually arrived in North Africa during the second week of November, soon learned that bailout was not really all that difficult. While attacking a large concentration of *Wehrmacht* ground targets at rooftop level, Runyon's P-38 absorbed crippling flak strikes, one of which severely injured his leg. One engine seized immediately as power began to fail on the second engine. Former naval aviator Runyon zoomed to about 500 feet and dropped out of the inverted cockpit as the mortally wounded aircraft faltered. The seriously wounded captain was, of course, captured and spent the rest of the war as a prisoner. However, it did verify that a pilot could leave a P-38 in flight, even at minimum altitude. Dropping out of an inverted Lightning was a favored escape procedure. It rarely, if ever, failed.

During the early months of the Northwest African campaign, the war without Capt. William J. Hoelle (pronounced Holly) would have been like Bob Hope's friend Jerry Colonna without a mustache. He was a cut above the average fighter pilot in proficiency and nerve, enjoyed a tremendous amount of good luck, and was adept at getting fantastic mileage out of his publicity opportunities. Hoelle did not qualify as a talent equal to Richard Bong or Tommy McGuire in a P-38 – at least in his theater of war – but he did have his very good moments.

Bill Hoelle was a member of the 14FG when he had the first of two encounters that left some permanent impressions locked into his memory. As the final days of 1942 tolled away, a dozen P-38 fighters – including Hoelle's P-38F "Maxie" – were "suckered" into attacking a fleet of Junkers trimotors. There were promptly ambushed by no less than 50 German fighters that came right out of the sun. Hoelle (a lieutenant at that time) reacted by attacking a quartet of Messerschmitts. He fired pointblank into one of the Nazi fighters, causing it to spin out of control and crash. Unfortunately, nobody broke with Hoelle to protect his flank in those first hectic seconds,

giving the other three enemy pilots the opportunity to gain position advantage. They all bored in at him, scoring dozens of hits. The ex-Stanford University student from San Mateo, California, departed from "Maxie" at about 400 feet altitude, while it was still under fire. Luck was with him; the parachute opened without delay, and he landed at some great distance from his base at Youks-les-Bains. Anticipating reward, some local Arabs helped him make his way back to the airfield.

That other memorable encounter was with a hapless telephone pole. There seemed to be something about the desert landscape that caused more than a few Lightnings to collide with telephone poles at attack velocity. Lt. Hoelle made contact with one such pole but published reports tended to be in direct conflict with most of the facts. Some published reports said he was upside down, flying at a speed of 400 mph after colliding with that pole. The news correspondent said, "He was close enough, literally, to reach down and touch the earth flashing past." No way, not even figuratively! Well, it made a good story.

According to Hoelle, a member of the 49th Fighter Squadron, he was in a flight that was strafing tanks and trucks when the C.O. of the squadron became the victim of ground fire. The lieutenant said that he glanced back to confirm that identity, and his flight path carried him into a line of telephone poles. In one wartime interview, he stated that the tail of his P-38 had hit the pole, but closeup pictures absolutely revealed that it was the wing centersection that took the blow. That, of course, could not have happened without first separating the propeller from the engine, which Hoelle never mentioned. A detailed photograph shows the pole slashed through the leading edge of the wing as far as the front spar.

At that point, the pole lost the battle and broke, but not before the P-38 went completely over on its back, very close to the ground. Reacting instantly, Hoelle kicked full rudder and full left aileron to force that airplane back into some semblance of level flight, but his speed dropped to under 200 miles per hour. Forced to hold full left aileron, the pilot worked up a good set of blisters during the 2-hour flight back home to base, which was 360 miles away at the time of his collision. In spite of reports, it is unlikely that Hoelle's Lightning could have been repaired because such concentrated damage in that area of the airframe would have required return to a facility like Burtonwood Air Depot or Langford Lodge, something that was not available in the MTO.

In a comparable accident, A P-38F-15-LO – which, oddly enough, had incorrect radio call numbers on the tail – also

smashed into one of the seemingly overabundant telephone poles with even more devastating results. Young Lt. Benton Miller had joined the 1st Fighter Group at Biskra early in 1943 as a new replacement pilot. Off on a typical strafing mission (on an unrecorded date) with a first mission pilot, Lt. Louis Murdock, as his wingman, Miller went to deck level to shoot up some enemy vehicles. It is probable that he never even saw the pole. The left propeller made contact first, sending at least one blade broadside at the fuselage gondola. Hitting the aft

section of the gun bay, it smashed in so hard that the forward two-thirds was bent outward. It created a very badly located airbrake.

The pole then slashed into the wing leading edge intercooler area. Penetrating back to at least the 30 percent chord line, it smashed into the spar, bending the outer wing backward and downward. Miller's aircraft, identified as UN*C (a 94FS marking), must have been thrown into a wild skid, at the very least, less than two dozen feet from the desert floor. Severely jarred, Miller managed to recover and joined up with the unbelieving Murdock to return to base, a considerable distance away.

With aerodynamic drag nearly equal to an additional tricycle landing gear caused by the protruding left gunbay door, the left prop and spinner completely missing, and the left wing twisted, swept back and bent downward several degrees (anhedral) – not to mention a large airscoop hole ending at a bent spar web – it must have required full right rudder to maintain a straight heading. In spite of all that, Lt. Miller made a near perfect landing. He could have been excused if he had blown even one tire. Neither of the two 165-gallon external drop tanks and been knocked loose, and Miller was too preoccupied with saving himself to remember to jettison the tanks.

When the new group commander, Lt. Col. Ralph Garman, made a detailed inspection of the bent Lightning, he could hardly believe that Miller had managed to keep it in the air. After having flown every main P-38 model since the accelerated flight test trials with the YP-38, Garman was one of the more experienced Lightning pilots. According to him, "there was no way that Miller's bent up P-38 could possibly fly." Of course, he was being rhetorical in his statement, but it would probably have been a totally correct opinion in 95 percent of the cases.

Benton Miller's personal thoughts and comments on the return flight after the accident were never, unfortunately, recorded. Even the excellent photograph was never circulated to the media. It all goes to help in proving that many of the greatest exploits of the war were probably never even known to the public.

When Lt. Hoelle hit one telephone pole, he had been attempting to see what happened to his squadron commander, Capt. Thomas Morris. Evidently other reports confirmed that Morris could not have survived the December 31 crash. Immediately after that New Year's activities, Hoelle was promoted to captain and assumed command of the 49FS. Morris had been his good friend, so there was no elation at taking over the squadron. By the end of the month, Capt. Hoelle had three

confirmed victories over enemy aircraft plus several classed as "probables." He had also completed his 50-mission requirement, and was returned to the United States in February 1943.

Although Ray Crawford tended to "walk on the wild side" to some degree, he was well qualified to be a fighter pilot. He seemed to have developed a fondness for the P-38, and was soon confirmed as an ace. At the end of his 50-mission tour, he volunteered for a second tour of duty in the MTO. However, Crawford withdrew that request because of the blatant pomposity and overbearing attitude of some non-combat administrative officer. He was returned to duty in America. During the period when he was still flying missions in North Africa, Crawford began to accumulate data that allowed him to analyze the reasons for P-38 losses in combat. Two highlights of Ray Crawford's observations were:

1. If a pilot survived his first 10 missions, he could count on about a 90 to 100 percent chance of finishing 50 or more missions without becoming a statistic.

2. About 85 percent of the losses occurring in the first 10 missions could be traced to pilots who, for various reasons, tended to straggle behind the formation. Reasons for straggling ranged from inability to hold formation because of aircraft damage, wounds or loss of an engine, to getting lost or trying to become a "hot shot" by going after a single "lame duck" enemy aircraft. Such "ducks" were usually bait on the end of a line leading to a few German fighters.

Many pilots were found to curse their own lack of gunnery ability and the fact that their training in air-to-air gunnery (if they had been given any at all) had little or no connection with a P-38. Crawford, like his entire group of replacement pilots assigned to General Spaatz's Northwest African Air Force, had somewhat less than 40 hours in a P-38 and absolutely no simulated combat training. Unfortunately for all, the USAAF had – because of pervasive bullheaded political attitudes and downright stupidity about world affairs – failed in its real mission during the Army Air Corps days. As pointed out earlier, the Air Corps was a tenth-rate power in pre-war years. Playing "catch-up" to the Nazi war machine head start of five years or more in 1942 was almost a panic situation. It has to be obvious that members of the U.S. armed forces had to overcome some very serious disadvantages in those first months of combat in the Mediterranean Sea area.

Fortunately, Air Chief Marshal Tedder, Maj. Gen. Carl Spaatz and Brig. Gen James Doolittle were in charge of West-

*Navigation was crucial to success in the winter weather conditions prevailing in North Africa. Engineers laid out a satisfactory compass rose for accurate swinging of the compasses on fighters like this P-38G from the 82nd Fighter Group. Repositioning was accomplished by taxiing the aircraft into the blocks, after which it was towed out for respotting by the ubiquitous Cletrac. (USAAF)*

ern Desert affairs, and after Kasserine Pass was history, things began to improve tremendously. The RAF's Air Marshal Coningham was probably correct when he contended that the Allies suffered from mutual petulance at many levels when forces were committed to TORCH. In planning for that expedition, all earlier lessons of the Western Desert warfare had been ignored, resulting in widespread misuse of airpower in the first months of Tunisian operations.

**B**Intercoolers and World War II were really some things that were unlikely to be problems as the year 1937 rolled along. Clarence Johnson and his tiny team of powerplant specialists had been pretty clever in 1936 when they chose to make the P-38 wing leading edge do double duty by serving as turbosupercharger intercoolers. That was pioneering at its best. Normally those hollow wing leading edges were so much wasted space, serving primarily to make the airflow do the right things to provide lift. They even upstaged aviation magazine artist and story teller Frank Tinsley, because his mythical Bill Barnes character had science fiction fighters (named Snorter and Stormer) featuring a less advanced form of cooling.

The basic purpose of an intercooler is to lower the temperature of the turbosupercharger's hot compressed air at the carburetor, thereby increasing the air density for improved aspiration. However, the zero-drag penalty system had its shortcomings in that it could not cope with totally unforeseen and unprojected increases in horsepower that would show up within five years. By the time Lockheed was preparing to produce P-38G and H models in the early 1940s, leading-edge intercoolers could no longer handle the required heat rejection.

For a given displacement, Allison engines had seen power rise from about 960 in 1939 to more than 1700 by 1943. As a result, manifold pressures had to be restricted because inlet temperatures at the carburetors were becoming excessive. Power was restricted as temperatures rose and Grade 100-115 gasoline – about the best at that time – was prone to detonate under high manifold pressures. Lower grade fuels could be a disaster at high power settings.

New pilots were being instructed to obey engine limitations in combat or to expect dire circumstances, at least with F-10 and F-17 engines. It was not long before the P-38G and H pilots found themselves at a great disadvantage at high altitudes. While the so-called "maneuvering flap" revision of the Fowler flap system came along originally in the Lightning II (British contract, P-38F-13-LO) series, it could not be used to advantage at high altitudes on P-38Hs because of the power limitation.

Lockheed's Model 422 airplanes came into the picture as P-38H-1-LO (and subsequent) fighters, and they featured the V-1710F-17 engines. Horsepower had jumped to 1425 rated bhp, and they could produce 1600 bhp at War Emergency Power. However, the intercoolers could not adequately handle more than the 1150 horsepower attributed to P-38Fs. Several model changes in turbosuperchargers were made in 1943, and it is sometimes difficult to know which supercharger type was in which airplane model. (It was the appearance of P-38H models in the ETO that really made the Lightning subject to a lot of pilot criticism. In spite of the "book rules" that were to be observed, more and more pilots encountered that old bugaboo, compressibility tuck. In the heat of battle, they just slipped into those high-speed dive attitudes. Because of mission profiles, cockpit heat . . . the lack of it . . . and power limitations were a real headache.)

As early as springtime in 1942, Lockheed engineers were faced with introduction of Allisons with a WEP rating of up to 1725 bhp. Even the military power rating of 1425 bhp constituted about a 30 percent increase in power. Key personnel readily determined that it would be possible to use that power only through complete redesign of the intercooler system and the Prestone (ethylene-glycol) coolant system. Very serious consideration was given to substituting the Rolls-Royce Merlin 61 engine, a version of which was being manufactured in Detroit. Numerous factors forced Lockheed to abandon any such plans. Paramount among them was the fact that the USAAF had invested vast assets in developing and manufacturing the Allison.

(Politics seem to overrule logic, even when war events are turning against a nation. Production of various Bell P-39s and

P-63s continued well into 1945 despite early British negative evaluations that were substantiated in the Pacific and Mediterranean areas. It was not until very late in the war that a handful of Lockheed P-38s were manufactured in a second-source factory. AAF usage of the P-39, and especially the P-63, in combat was extremely limited from mid-1943; yet, large-scale production continued. Probably the biggest factor in that was the influence of Harry Hopkins in "gifting" P-39s and P-63s to the Russians.)

The ultimate approach taken by Lockheed engineers working under the direction of W.A. "Dick" Pulver, by then established as Chief Project Engineer, was anything but novel. And it did little for the esthetics of the Lightning, just as Vokes desert filters did not improve the looks of the Spitfire. However, the approach was effective. Wind tunnel tests showed that the Curtiss P-40F cowl/inlet arrangement was not unduly high in drag counts. NACA wind tunnel tests conducted at LMAL Langley Field, Virginia, had revealed that poor airflow characteristics through the Prestone cooling scoops on the YP-38 created unwanted drag. Work in that area produced the more bulbous, larger scoops employed on later P-38J and L models. Looks are deceiving. The fatter scoops produced much lower drag and actually were more effective in cooling the Prestone.

One interesting aspect of the Prestone cooler scoops on late P-38 models is that the inlet design was nearly duplicated in the jet engine inlet design of the P-80A. However, for some unknown reason, the boundary layer bleed duct was not used on XP-80A and YP-80A airplanes until tests showed that it was absolutely required. In the case of the Lightning, every P-38J-type coolant scoop was fitted with the bleed duct. It must be assumed that the forward position of the XP-80A inlets led the "Skunk Works" design team, working under extreme pressure, to calculate that boundary layer bleed air would not be a problem. It did not take them long to find out that the bleed air duct was required.

Engineers Willis Hawkins and Ward Beman made every

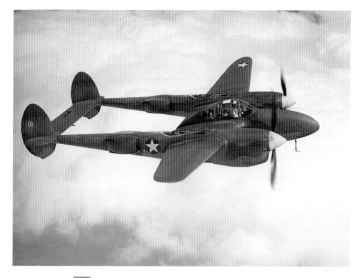

*Number 01 must have been a recognition expert's nightmare. The odd aircraft, having most features of a P-38J, was really a P-38E that was better know as "The Mule." It most certainly was the only J-type with the early-style Prestone cooler scoops, 1942 version of the national insignia and a pitot tube under the nose. Identifiable as AC41-1983, the P-38E was used to test the new nose-mounted intercooler radiators for the more powerful Allison F-17 series engines.*

possible effort to see that the Allisons were replaced by Merlin 61-type engines. They felt that Allison engineers were not making diligent efforts to overcome detonation problems and other faults associated with turbosupercharged versions of the V-1710 engines that were unique to the P-38. By switching to the Merlin high-altitude engine, Lightnings could eliminate all of the intercooling problems, gain reliability and eliminate the General Electric superchargers and associated regulator prob-

*RIGHT: Changes in technology made it unlikely that scenes like this shift change at Lockheed-Vega Plant A-1 (and all aircraft plants) will ever the repeated. It was February 3, 1943, and the North African campaign was in full fury. The view is looking north on Hollywood Way in Burbank from a long-gone overpass. (LAC)*

*OPPOSITE LEFT: Never previously published, this photo shows the remains of Col. Ben Kelsey's P-38G-10-LO (AC42-12937) less than an hour after it crashed on April 9, 1943. The site is a Calabasas, California, hillside very close to the location of Lockheed's new corporate offices. It was only a few hundred feet from old U.S. 101. Kelsey was making one final test run with the first dive flap installation before granting approval for production. One wing and the entire tail came off in an inverted spin. Kelsey suffered a broken ankle. (Lockheed via NASM)*

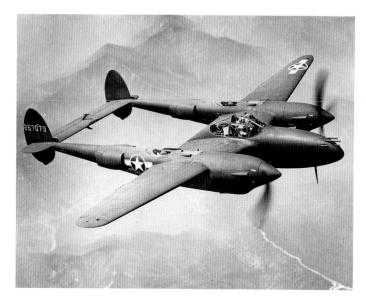

lems. Critical altitude for the Merlin 61 was a notch higher than the Allisons, but preliminary calculations revealed that the Merlin-powered fighter was almost 1,000 pounds heavier. It would be illogical to presume that could not be reversed in final design.

Unfortunately, Kelly Johnson was forced to point out that the War Production Board was not going to allow production of P-38s to decay while a major retooling effort was put in place. Lockheed's automated production line (automated in the vernacular of that era) was geared to turn out one fighter per hour, and they actually managed to attain that rate on occasion. Decisions of the WPB were frequently at odds with combat commanders' requirements and the wishes of the Engineering Division at Wright Field.

No real proof exists, but it must be a fact of life that Lt. Gen. Knudsen was not going to do anything that would hurt General Motors. After all, he had been a top executive with that corporation for years until he had accepted his appointment to the Office of Production Management at the beginning of the new decade. It would be ludicrous to believe that he would throw more plums to competitor Packard (builder of the Merlins) at the expense of G.M., and it is also likely that

Knudsen held a large block of stock in the corporation. (In those days, it was not necessary to give up your stock holdings where a "conflict of interest" might occur.)

There was one interesting aspect of all this that has generally been overlooked. Allison Division of G.M. produced 69,305 of the V-1710s during the war years; Packard Motors, starting later, produced 54,714 Americanized Merlins. While Continental Motors in Muskegon, Michigan, did produce some 28,800 engines, all of them were rated at less than 225 horsepower! But that corporation did manufacture 23 of their inverted vee IV-1430 engines and (surprise) 797 of the Americanized Merlins. (Continental only needed 4 years to do this!)

In Burbank, the cries of anguish about performance problems and the need for greater production rates emanating from the War Department, from the war zone commanders and – closer to home, but perhaps somewhat toned down – from Col. Kelsey must have sounded like the Anvil Chorus. Dick Pulver's engineers and the test pilots huddled and regrouped every week.

Lockheed took delivery of a batch of development engines in the 1400 bhp class early in 1942. One of the P-38E development airplanes was committed for modification; it turned out to be the first one of the series, AC41-1983. That Lightning had been redesignated RP-38E, signifying that it was in a restricted category. Basics of the airplane remained as it had been constructed, but the standard intercooler system was blocked off and core-type intercoolers were installed below and in front of the engines. The cowling lines appeared to be a cross between those used on the Curtiss P-40E and F models, and all panels had been formed by using thin steel sheets. Everybody referred to the airplane as "The Mule." Nobody cared about the fact that it was a pretty crude-looking airplane; they were only interested in learning about the performance of the core-type intercoolers. It was absolutely the only Lightning built that combined the new P-38J cowling lines with Prestone cooling scoops used on all previous Lightnings from the YP-38 through the last P-38H-5-LO series.

All-round performance of "The Mule" was greatly im-

proved. While the top speed below 20,000 feet did not increase appreciably under the impetus of several hundred additional horsepower, high-altitude performance soared, closely paralleling performance characteristics of the projected design that was to be powered by Rolls-Royce Merlin 61s. Before long, the RP-38E was reworked with the initial sets of modernized Prestone cooler scoops. There was, by that time, no doubt that the major intercooling problem was solved. A multilateral decision was made to convert all new production P-38s over to the Allison V-1710F-17 engine with a basic power rating of 1425 horsepower.

Maj. Gen. O.P. Echols' staff at Materiel Division authorized a change order to Contract AC-21217 to create a Model 422-81 series of airplanes. One dozen airplanes were designated as prototypes, and a new serial number group (c/n 1001 through 1012, initially) was assigned. The main feature was the use of Allison's V-1710F-17 engines. Unfortunately, Lockheed's reach exceeded its grasp. It soon become evident that there would be an intolerable delay in production if the parallel production lines were brought to a halt until all new components of the modernized intercooler system could be stocked in sufficient quantities to support a production rate of at least 15 airplanes a day at Burbank.

Although company records fail to reveal what occurred, the evidence supports the following conclusion. Logistically, half of the assembly lines could be supported by the core intercooler and powerplant component subcontractors for a period that would not exceed, perhaps, six months. The decision was made to produce an unplanned P-38H series of fighters powered by the available F-17 engines, but with existing wing intercoolers and the old-style Prestone coolant ducts. Therefore, of the one dozen new prototype aircraft, one was physically unchanged from its predecessors (G models) although it was equipped with the newest engines. That airplane, c/n 1005, became the first P-38H-1-LO (recognized in the company as a Model 422-81-20). Flight testing of that fighter was primarily to establish performance criteria that would then be included in the Pilot's Flight Operating Manual.

The government soon authorized production of 600 of that model, with all deliveries to be completed by the end of the year (1943).

C Engineers at Lockheed also proposed another model in lieu of any Rolls-Royce/Packard Merlin-powered version. The resulting product was an airplane that resembled the P-38J like a twin brother but was a better performer in most categories. That airplane was the Lockheed P-38K-1-LO, bearing Air Corps serial number 42-13558. This supposedly "one-off" airplane was probably the least known of all Lightnings that saw the light of day. Again, it was an airframe taken from the proximate-dozen Model 422-81 airplanes that were to be essentially

service test types for a production P-38J that was to utilize Allison V-1710F-17 engines.

However, the single P-38K-1-LO (c/n 1004) was actually set up for V-1710F-15 engines and was the only P-38 designed to have -15 units installed. Reduction gear ratio changes were made in that type engine to accommodate the Hamilton-Standard Hydromatic propellers with high-activity blades for better altitude performance. Curtiss Electric propellers used on the P-38J had a normal gear ratio of 2.00 to 1; the gear ratio used to swing the Hamilton-Standard units was 2.36 to 1. Based on reliable test data, the production P-38K was expected to have a ceiling well above 46,000 feet. That's correct; above 46,000 feet!

Rather amazingly, high speed at critical altitude (29,600 feet) was 432 mph, or about 14 mph faster than a P-38J-1-LO tested in the same time frame. At 40,000 feet, the P-38K proved to be faster by 40 mph! That turned out to be a true airspeed of 384 mph at that altitude, using military power. Another 9 or 10 mph could be expected with War Emergency Power (WEP). We are not speaking of an airplane with a pressure cabin; that was not projected performance, but actual

ABOVE: Capt. James J. Hagenback (possibly still a lieutenant at the time) proudly posed with the P-38F, "Bat Out of Hell" (UN*G) on a Sardinian airfield in 1943. Other P-38s seem to have borne different versions of that name and devilish face. (Kenneth Sumney)

BELOW LEFT: That diligent worker, "The Mule," appeared with wooden weapons, a new paint job, authentic late-model Prestone scoops . . . and most unusual propellers. Kelly Johnson verified that this was the old P-38E (c/n 5201) converted to XP-38K format and fitted with high-activity Hamilton-Standard propellers. There was also one P-38K-1-LO bearing the AAF number AC42-13558, built by Lockheed as c/n 1004. The K model had excellent performance high up and in climb. The War Production Board could not authorize production, supposedly because it would require a revision in the engine cowlings. No pictures of the P-38K-1 version exist. (LAC)

BELOW RIGHT: It was the old "hat in the ring trick," leading to a bunch of important medals for Lts. Richard Lee, Ralph Thiesen and Robert Vrilakas in 1943. Yes, that is a Silver Star worn by Lt. Thiesen. Obviously, these men were members of the famed 94th Fighter Squadron. (Col. Robert Vrilakas)

170

performance using an airplane with weighty and rough camouflage paint.

All attempts to get the P-38K-1-LO into production failed for one apparently insignificant reason. To accommodate the H-S Hydromatic propellers, it was necessary to increase propeller spinner diameters slightly, thereby affecting the top cowling lines and the interface at the oil cooler/intercooler inlet. Evidently the WPB was not about to accept any production delays beyond the autumn of 1943, already having been forced to accept the stopgap P-38H. So, the high-performance P-38K and Merlinized P-38 were never even close to attaining production status. (A second operating production facility was sorely needed.)

There are several interesting aspects of the P-38K program that have rarely, if ever, been touched upon by historians or even engineers. All initial K-configuration flight testing was conducted using the tired old "mule" airplane, that extensively reworked RP-38E (c/n 5201). With its battered and stretched handmade cowlings, it had demonstrated the viability of a core-type intercooler to create the P-38J series. With additional hammering and forming, the cowlings were revised again to accept Hamilton-Standard propellers. At the same time, those initial low-drag Prestone cooler scoops were installed.

By that time it was necessary to repaint the "Mule", complete with correct tail numbers. Therein lies the tale of why so many Lockheed employees who were aware of the project became terribly confused. The RP-38E, complete with white paint on the spinners and wooden machine guns protruding from the nose for correct aerodynamic simulation, was often referred to as the XP-38K. It never carried any such identity. To make matters worse, nobody ever thought to photograph the real P-38K-l-LO. Tony LeVier, who conducted some the test flights on the "K-Mule" airplane (for want of any better designation) has stated that several aircraft configurations were never photographed under wartime pressures. Other test pilots who conducted flight tests on the RP-38E/K were Joe Towle and Jim White.

Kelly Johnson's Engineering Flight Test Group conducted all the P-38K-format tests between February 24 and April 30, 1943. Remembering that the RP-38E had been converted to a "Piggy Back" configuration in 1942 when buffeting testing was initiated, all of the tests were observed by engineers John Margwarth and Norm Pultz with a single exception. One test was planned for a climb to maximum altitude, and a Lt. Col. Lovelace from the AF Plant Representative's office went along as observer. Because there was a severe temperature inversion over Los Angeles County that day, it become necessary to extend the maneuvering flaps to offset Army Hot Day conditions, thus limiting maximum altitude to a mere(!) 45,000 feet. It was concluded that on a standard day (with a clean airplane condition . . . flaps retracted) the airplane would climb several thousand feet higher.

The real P-38K-1-LO (c/n 1004) was sent to Eglin Field, Florida, for performance evaluation. It was then demonstrated that in high-speed and climb performance, it was superior –

outstandingly superior – to the best fighter models in contention. Every manufacturer of AAF fighters had submitted their best and latest models for the evaluation. Among its capabilities, the P-38K-1-LO could take off and climb to 20,000 feet in 5 minutes flat, with an initial rate of climb of 4800 fpm.

Lightnings may have been getting older, but they were also getting better. In retrospect, it would have probably been logical to dedicate one or two assembly lines to production of the P-38K, even though some production delay – possibly a few weeks for final delivery – would have been incurred because of the 1-inch higher cowl line of the F-15 engines used on the K model.

D With adoption of the P-38J as the standard production Lightning in late 1942, a new era had dawned. Literally hundreds of changes in systems and equipment were incorporated at various intervals in production, every one intended to eliminate some problem or improve that fighting capability of the aircraft. As an example, the flat-panel windshield was not introduced on the first blocks of P-38Js, nor did the wing leading edge fuel tanks occupy the spaces available when those AiResearch core intercoolers replaced the leading edge surface intercoolers. Lockheed had to wait until adequate stockpiles of materials and vendor components accumulated.

Dive flaps and aileron boosters came along at a later date. Hardly anyone would suspect that with the firm commitment of the P-38J-5-LO to production – with first AAF acceptances in August 1943 – that 70 percent of all P-38 Lightnings still remained to be constructed. Between December 1938 and December 1943, only 2,943 Lightnings (XP-38 through P-38H-5-LO) had been delivered to the USAAF, but between August 1943 and the end of hostilities in August 1945, Lockheed alone produced 6,981 improved Lightnings (P-38J-5-LO and subsequent) plus the family XP-49.

America had been at war a little over one year when Tedder, Spaatz and Doolittle used their precise talents to properly organize their available manpower in the MTO. Heavy fighting in North Africa was to persist for a while, but AVALANCHE, the plan for an amphibious assault on Salerno, Italy, was entering the final preparation phase. In the meantime, two of the most important projects ready for implementation were FLAX (a concerted attack on Axis airborne support of the Tunisian campaign) and HUSKY, (the Allied invasion of Sicily). It would be but a matter of weeks before the Germans and Italians were defeated, especially in the critical Tunisian campaign.

Spaatz and Doolittle concluded that it would be necessary to give the battered 14th Fighter Group a respite from battle for reorganization and rebuilding. In the meantime, the load would fall on the 1FG and the 82FG with P-38s, the only MTO groups equipped with those aircraft. Events in the ETO and the Southwest Pacific area were soon to put great demands on Lockheed for delivery of their long-range fighter, leaving precious few available for the MTO. Curtiss P-40s, Bell P-39s and Supermarine Spitfires were available in much larger numbers, but after the successful invasion of Sicily their usefulness for the air war in Italy would go into rapid decline as greater numbers of Republic P-47s flowed from production lines in Farmingdale and Evansville. Only P-38s could carry out the major long-range fighter missions in the MTO.

Although the long-range and load-carrying characteristics of the Lightning, together with its demonstrated ability to take on the best *Luftwaffe* fighters in the MTO on better than even terms, made it an optimum aircraft for use in Italy, there would never be enough of them available for the job in hand.

# CHAPTER 14

# About Face: The Nazis Head North

Allied forces gained the momentum in 1943 to expel the Axis from North Africa after more than 3 years of seesaw warfare. Perhaps the operation known as FLAX played a larger part in defeating the Germans than we will ever know. Originally planned for March 1943, to interdict the aerial supply line that was obviously critical to Axis survival in Tunisia, FLAX had been delayed by events at Kasserine Pass. Everything was right on April 5, and it all got under way when 26 patrolling NAAF P-38s pounced on a mixed bag of trimotor transports, six Stukas, 24 single engine fighters and – if it is to be believed – a single Focke-Wulf Fw 187A. It was promptly shot down by the Lightning pilots, along with eleven Ju 52/3m transports, two Bf 109s and two Ju 87 Stukas, and there is confirmation that many of the surviving aircraft suffered serious damage.

This kind of action became somewhat typical throughout April, with everything from P-40s to B-25s carrying out spectacular assaults on the *Luftwaffe* aircraft. There is no doubt about it, the Nazis were desperate. The aerial supply line was essentially halted with the destruction of an entire convoy of Messerschmitt Me 323 giant transport aircraft by a mixed force of Spitfires and South African Curtiss Kittyhawks. In the meantime, bombers of the Northwest African Strategic Air Force (NASAF) were bombing German airfields in Italy, Sicily and Sardinia. Destruction of enemy aircraft on the ground exceeded even the fabulously successful air-to-air interceptions. The Allies had achieved air superiority over Tunisia by April 22, although some *Luftwaffe* aircraft still defended the bridgehead into the first days of May.

One large force of the *Afrika Korps* in the Tunis bridgehead was shelled into surrender of May 11, and Col. Gen. Jurgen von Arnim showed the white flag at Ste. Marie du Zit the very next day. The last stubborn defender of Mareth, Gen. Giovanni Messe, was subjected to a very intensive bombing attack that day, and finally gave up on the 13th. so it was, nearly six months to the day, that Operation TORCH finally ground to a halt.

All eyes now turned toward Sicily and Italy. British-American domination of the air over the entire Mediterranean resulted in cancellation of plans for invading Sardinia and Corsica, and the assault on Sicily, Operation HUSKY, was carried out with great success. Then almost without a pause to regroup, the British Eighth Army launched Operation BAYTOWN near Reggio di Calabria at the toe of the Italian "boot."

A few days later, the American Fifth Army landed in force at Salerno to begin AVALANCHE on September 9. One thing often overlooked in evaluating the Salerno invasion is that Axis air defense fighters were based on numerous airfields at Naples and Foggia. Allied air support over the target area was at severe handicap because of distances from the nearest

*Lt. Edward S. Newbury of the 27FS had a long-lived relationship with this P-38F displaying the name "Dear John." The association began on April 15, 1942 as preparations were being made for Operation BOLERO. After two ETO missions, the team flew to North Africa to participate in TORCH. "Newby" scored his first aerial victory over a Bf 109F and he then proceeded to clobber a Siebel Ferry in the Straits of Sicily in April 1943. By August he had logged more than 300 combat hours at the controls of that same Lightning. By that time he was Capt. Newbury. (USAF)*

bases. Based on realistic NAAF evaluations, the following fighter radius-of-action figures applied to the situation, providing for 10 minutes of aerial combat and assuming that at least one drop tank was to be carried by each fighter:

| | |
|---|---|
| Lockheed P-38 . . . . . . . . | 350 miles |
| North American A-36 . . . . . | 200 miles |
| Supermarine Spitfire . . . . | 180 miles |
| Bell P-39 . . . . . . . . . | 150 miles |
| Curtiss P-40 . . . . . . . . | 150 miles |
| Bristol Beaufighter . . . . . | 300 miles |

(Beaufighters for night ops only)

*NOTE: All figures are relatively conservative.*

It is important to notice that there were no Thunderbolts available for operations in the MTO. Not only that, Eisenhower and Spaatz encountered fierce opposition from every quarter when they tried to obtain B-17s or B-24s on short loan. They also needed A-20s or RAF Wellingtons, but that could not even be arranged.

Far worse, as far as Spaatz was concerned, was the word received just before AVALANCHE was to be initiated that he could not expect any more P-38s before at least October. In spite of heavy Lightning losses (60 in August and 24 in the second week of September), the general had found them to be invaluable in escorting bombers and ship convoys, providing cover at assault areas, cutting lines of communication, supporting ground troops and destroying enemy transport. He regarded the P-38 as being "in a class by itself." His big problem was that there were fewer than 250 Lightnings in the NAAF at that time. (The situation really never got to be much better.)

One look at the radius-of-action figures reveals something that rarely, if ever, became a point of discussion. While 50 missions were the normal cutoff point for pilots on operations, it immediately becomes evident that virtually every P-38 pilot was in the air for two or two and one-half times as long as a Curtiss P-40, Bell P-39 or Spitfire pilot during the 50-mission period. More time in the air equals greater chance of an encounter and certainly greater fatigue.

After the beachheads were secured and the U.S. Fifth and British Eighth Armies had attained most of their objectives, things literally bogged down in the following miserable Italian winter. In spite of the bad weather 12th and 15th Air Force missions continued to grow in power and stature. The major responsibility for carrying out the fighter air war during 1943 fell entirely on three basic types of aircraft: P-38s, P-40s and Spitfires. If the radius of action went beyond 150 miles the Spitfire and P-40 fighters were pretty much out of the picture.

Reorganization and consolidation seemed to be the order of the day in the MTO as autumn turned to winter. Early in October, Maj. Gen. Gordon Saville – Col. Kelsey's long-time friendly associate from Wright Field – assumed command of the XIIth Fighter Command in Italy. Creation of the new Fifteenth Air Force on November 1, 1943, resulted in transfer of XIIBC to the new air force. Gen. Arnold also created the Allied Expeditionary Air Force (AEAF) in the ETO, and the Ninth Air Force came under operational control of the AEAF. With the creation of the 15th Air Force, Maj. Gen. Doolittle was appointed commanding general. It would be many weeks before the three P-38 groups in the MTO would get any assistance in escorting heavy and medium bombers, not to mention having to carry out all missions where the radius of action was over 180 miles. The first appearances of Republic Thunderbolts in the MTO with the 12th and 15th Air Forces came in mid-December. In the final days of December, the Mediterranean Allied Air Force (MAAF) was created under

Tedder. Spaatz moved back to England to take command of U.S. Strategic Air Forces in Europe; Eaker was to take command of Allied Air Forces in the MTO, and Doolittle was ordered to become the new commanding general of the Eighth Air Force.

As 1944 dawned, Republic P-47s began to fill out the ranks of the longer-ranging aircraft in the MTO in company with newer Lockheed P-38J models, all welcome additions. Thunderbolts also joined the 12th Air Force, replacing the venerable Curtiss P-40Fs and Ls (and whatever other model might be serviceable), Supermarine Spitfires and North American A-36s. Bell P-39s had, more or less, disappeared from the scene after Salerno except for observation functions.

That presents a gross view of activities that took place after the AAF received its initiation with the launching of TORCH. The successful conclusion of the operation was really merely a beginning. With few exceptions, the Italians were virtually out of the picture with the full capitulation of Axis forces in Tunisia. But the Germans were another story. Literally thousands of events involving Lockheed P-38s occurred in the months leading up to AVALANCHE. Some of these events must be covered in detail if for no other reason than to add color to the gross picture.

One event that occurred in the early months of 1943 had as its setting the San Fernando Valley of Southern California. Its significance lies in the fact that it involved something that proved to be the ultimate solution to that fascinating ogre, "compressibility tuck." But that ogre was to have one final, almost fatal swipe at the Lightning before giving in to progress and invention.

As Chief, Fighter Branch, at Wright Field in April 1943, Col. Ben Kelsey was on TDY at Burbank to settle some technical matters related to increased production rates, resolution of aircraft change orders and to discuss the new P-38J and K airplanes. On a Friday afternoon, he was set to return to Dayton, Ohio, for some Monday meetings. However, he was not entirely satisfied with one item for which he was about to provide full production authority.

Although Tony LeVier had carried out a very comprehensive flight test program to evaluate Lockheed's new compressibility dive flap, one possible – even probable – situation had not been included in the tests. As designed, the flap control was to be actuated immediately before the P-38 was committed to diving from high altitude. LeVier's tests, using a modified P-38G-10-LO (AC42-12937), were conducted from various altitudes up to about 35,000 feet. In that final test, he recorded test data that he contends took him to a Mach's Number of 0.72, a number that would be on the high side for a P-38. According to Kelly Johnson, the limit was between 0.68 and 0.70. LeVier had done some things in that dive that resulted in a 7.5g load on the aircraft during the pullout. His boss, Milo Burcham, was not very happy about that, but the dive flap was known to be effective and the aircraft appeared to be undamaged.

What Kelsey was uneasy about was the fact that the dive flap had never been deployed *after* the aircraft had accelerated to critical speed in a dive. Learning that the P-38G was ready for flight, Kelsey delayed his return to Ohio and decided to fly the test Lightning. That first test P-38 was different from planned production models in that flap actuation was by means of hydraulic drive. The Bendix four-way hydraulic valve had an extension welded to the normally short handle. (Youthful engineer Ken Pittman had designed the production system around an electrically driven actuator arrangement. A 1⅓ horsepower electric motor, turning at 15,000 rpm, would drive each flap down to a 35-degree angle in just 1½ seconds. Each of the two dive flaps was located on the main spar, outboard of each engine nacelle. Flap length was 58 inches.)

The weather was beautiful as Kelsey took off southbound over Valhalla Cemetery after passing over the Southern Pacific Railroad tracks. Turning westward, he began a sawtooth climb to 35,000 feet. At that altitude he was between the San Fernando and Conejo Valleys, over largely unpopulated terrain. The only town out that way was Calabasas, not much more than a sleepy gas station on Highway 101. The colonel cinched his seat belt, checked the instruments, and rolled into a steep dive. Once the nose started to go under, indicating that the normal lift point of the wing had moved aft under the effects of compressibility shock waves, he would deploy the dive flaps. (the dive flaps did not decrease aircraft speed in a dive. They merely altered the airflow over the wing surface so that the wing would not lose its lift.)

Ben Kelsey, like Jimmy Doolittle, was an old, bold pilot on that afternoon of April 9, but he was also the curious engineer. If this dive flap did everything it was supposed to do, the compressibility bugaboo would not plague combat pilots any more. The device had been tested by other Lockheed pilots, namely Stan Beltz, Herman Salmon and Milo Burcham sharing duties with LeVier. As of that date, Kelsey had never been involved in a compressibility dive situation, but he had discussed it at length with LeVier, Cass Hough, and others. The P-38G accelerated rapidly and soon the controls became ineffective for controlling the dive attitude. It was time to deploy the flaps. He pulled on the handle extension. Nothing happened!

Surprised, Kelsey really bent to the task at hand. Literally. With no warning, the handle extension broke. The Command Pilot was suddenly sorry that he had not gone out over the ocean. He was going to need every foot of altitude to recover, and the foothills of the Santa Monica Mountains were starting up at him. He could not move the elevator, of course, and the trim tab was ineffective. At that moment, he was ready to try anything, so he ap-

plied full rudder and aileron at the same time. He really was not expecting anything to happen because of his discussions with Cass Hough.

Kelsey was totally unaware of LeVier's 7.5g pullout in the recent days, but it probably would not have affected his thinking about any approach to recovery efforts. C-R-A-A-A-ck! Suddenly some parts left the aircraft and the pilot reached quickly for the canopy release. The canopy opened a bit, them slammed shut. He was in an inverted spin.

It was really time to leave. Kelsey unsnapped the seat belt, got his feet into the seat and forced his shoulders against

LEFT: Camouflage paint, as on this P-38J-10-LO in 1943, was to be deleted toward the end of that year, reducing weight and surface friction. Insignia on the nose indicates that it was a memorial aircraft to an employee on military leave who was KIA or MIA, or to a close relative of a current employee at the time. Flatplate armor glass windshield was introduced on the J-10 model. (LAC)

*BELOW: Now there was a pilot with a hot hand. Lt. Herbert B. Hatch from Birmingham, Michigan, shot down no fewer than five Focke-Wulf Fw 190As in about 1 1/4 minutes over Ploesti. it was on June 27, 1944. Hatch was a member of the 71st Fighter Squadron. (USAAF)*

the canopy. At that moment, a wing came off and the colonel was suddenly catapulted out as the canopy blew out. His parachute opened almost immediately. He looked down to the springtime green of the hills coming up at him. Then he looked up. What he saw left a deep impression, and he related the incident three decades later with total recall.

"The human mind works in strange ways. It does not see or recall events in a continuous sequence as you would normally think. Things come back, more or less, in a stop-action sequence. I recall looking up and seeing this small panel fluttering toward me from above, like a falling piece of paper. Only the vision came in still-picture flashes.

"Suddenly that panel was level with me, and as it went past I realized that it was the entire outer wing panel. Luckily it didn't hit me (or the parachute). A few other pieces went by and the ground was coming up fast."

Col. Kelsey landed on a hillside near the remains of the P-38G, which had landed flat on its back (sans the tail). There was some mid-section fire, but it either burned itself out or the flames were put down by a California Highway Patrol officer. Kelsey landed on the hill in such a way that the impact broke his ankle, but he believed his leg was broken. A motorist answered his request for a splint by bringing an entire fencepost.

Although there was absolutely no connection with the flawed test flight, Kelsey was named Chief of Flight Research Branch at the Flight Test Division in July. It was a new organization that had not previously existed. With all the reorganization within the MTO and ETO commands occurring as the year wore on, Kelsey was assigned as Deputy Chief of Staff to Gen. Brereton's IXth Fighter Command (Brig. Gen. E. R. Quesada did not assume command of IXth Fighter Command until mid-December, so there may have been a temporary "dead spot" in the chain of command.)

In the peacetime environment of 1937 in the United States, neither 1st Lt. Ben Kelsey nor Clarence Johnson ever envisioned the new XP-38 interceptor design performing functions normally accorded some Navy specialized types such as the Curtiss SBC-3 or Northrop BT-1 dive bombers. Kelsey had gone out of his way to eliminate the "sometime" requirement for 25-pound bombs. A requirement for such bombs had even been included in specifications for the original XP-47A (never past the drawing board).

In 1940, when Col. Goddard foresaw the possibilities of using the P-38 for photographic missions, his bit of prognostication eventually led to the installation of several large cameras in the ideal nose section of the Lightning. But even more importantly, Goddard's requirements eventually led to the installation of external mounts for range-extension fuel tanks on the wing centersection. Those pylon mounts were ultimately adapted to carrying bombs weighing up to 2,000 pounds each.

Adaptation of the P-38 for operation as a premier-grade dive and skip bomber had its beginning in North Africa in connection with TORCH operations. In 1943, that unanticipated mission requirement was devised to cope with a very special problem that was causing loss of sleep for Gens. Doolittle and J.H. Atkinson, not to mention plaguing Air Chief Marshal Sir Arthur Tedder. The problem manifested itself in

*Unusual formation in the MTO included a B-24J, P-38J, B-17G and P-51C. The Lightning belonged to the 95FS of the 82nd Fighter Group. All of these aircraft were in the Fifteenth Air Force. (AFM)*

the form of a fleet of small, rather ungainly self-propelled barges that had originally been constructed for Hitler's Operation SEA LION, the invasion of the British Isles, in 1940-41. Those Siebel Ferries – floating flak stations – were the Nemesis of fighters and bombers bent on interdicting the flow of troops and materials to North Africa. Tedder's Mediterranean Air Command (MAC) requested that Lt. Col. Ralph Garman attempt to develop a solution to the problem presented by the Siebel Ferries.

Garman, commanding the 1st Fighter Group, was already faced with the extremely serious problems that were stretching his group almost to the breaking point. There was the Kasserine Pass crisis, watching the 14FG pull out of the offensive and defensive missions for reorganization and rebuilding, and a stated commitment to a big forthcoming operation that had the code name FLAX. Garman promptly delegated the Siebel Ferry matter to his Executive Officer, Maj. John "Bill" Weltman.

This was close to the same time that the 14FG, commanded by Col. Thayer Olds, had been reduced to no more than 12 operational P-38s . . . for the entire group. Out of the original 54 fighter pilots who had flown to Africa in connection with the opening of TORCH, only 39 were left in the group. A command decision was made to rotate Olds and all of the pilots back to the U.S.A. from their base at Berteaux, Algeria. Only the newer replacement pilots would remain in North Africa, and they were assigned (with the remaining aircraft) to the recent arrival, the 82FG. Maj. Weltman was not sorry to see Olds leave because they could hardly be thought of as friendly. However, he was certainly not happy to see the 14th pulled out of action.

Of course, there was, in effect, a replacement group for the 14FG; it was the 82FG which had arrived in the United Kingdom by sea transport when the oncoming winter of 1942-43 closed down the BOLERO route. Hard weather had scattered B-25s and B-26s like tenpins along the entire route, so it would have been suicide to send the one-man P-38s over the route. Lt. Col. William E. Covington, commander of the 82nd since it formed up in California, was still in charge when they arrived by air in North Africa.

It was an unusual group in that in the original formation of the organization, many of the pilots were enlisted men (flying sergeants). Most of them eventually became flight officers or lieutenants. Before the group could be deployed to North Africa, all of their assigned P-38s had to be replaced because the majority of them had been lost at sea. (Perhaps the damaged P-38 towed into the U.K. by a corvette was one of those intended for delivery to the 82nd. Secured to a landing craft that split in half and broke loose from a cargo ship, the P-38 suffered from salt water immersion and collision damage to the central nose section.)

Sometime in the early spring of 1943, the Germans began to run the air and sea blockade to Tunis and Bizerte for resupply of Rommel's troops, using a great number of the Siebel Ferries. Those "little devils" (in the parlance of young Weltman) were motorized floating flak stations, each equipped with up to four of the famous high-velocity 88s and a veritable hedgehog array of lighter-caliber weapons. When the Twelfth Air force B-17s and B-25s tried to knock them out from nearly any altitude, the plodding Siebels proved to be a bit too nimble to be a good target for level bombing. Some low-level attacks by B-25s were more successful, but the risk increased tremendously. The flak barges could make the skies unbearable. Finally, the risk became too great to warrant continuation of the bomber raids, but the high command could not afford to allow the resupply operations to continue unabated. That was when Garman was given the assignment to put an end to the Siebel Ferry rampage.

It was during the initial development phase of a program to find a way to neutralize the Siebels that Maj. Weltman, the man Garman had committed to that specific task, was ordered to report to Gen. Doolittle. The general remembered that it turned out to be somewhat of an amusing incident.

"Bill," said Gen. Doolittle, with an unusually affable tone for somebody in the position of commanding the entire NASAF,* "we want you to take over the 82nd from Bill Covington." Weltman, a fervent West Virginian, was a bit quick on the trigger when responding to the even stronger-minded Doolittle.

"The 82nd! Hell no, I don't want to take that outfit!" His next thought was to wonder what terrible thing he had done to warrant such cruel punishment. Then another figure stepped out of an unlighted corner of the conference room. The handsome officer spoke with determination.

"Bill, we aren't asking you to take over. We're telling you to take over." The speaker was Brig. Gen. Hoyt Vandeberg, then commander of the XIIth Fighter Command in North Africa, according to Doolittle's account.

*(The 12th AF had become an administrative organization. Spaatz commanded NAAF and Doolittle headed NASAF.)

Weltman's story tallied very well with Doolittle's. "My answer to Vandenberg's statement was, 'Yes, sir.' It was probably the smartest think I ever did."

All that the reassignment really did was to provide Weltman with an entirely new group of fresh pilots to work out the problems of developing new tactics to be used against the Siebels and Rommel's supply vessels. He had only managed to fly one or two anti-shipping missions with the 27FS before transferring to Headquarters Squadron of the 82FG. For flying operations, he was attached to the 95FS at Berteaux. "Now I'm no engineer," said Weltman, who was by then certainly one of the youngest lieutenant colonels in the AAF as a result of that meeting with Doolittle and Vandenberg, "and we ran into some real technical problems. But those there 82nd boys couldn't be stopped. We got along just great, and worked out all the problems together," the West Virginian commented.

They flew several 3- to 4-hour escort missions for the first half of the month in their P-38G-10-LO airplanes before doing some skip-bombing on May 21. the welcoming committee was not at all friendly.

"We tried skip-bombing on those Siebel Ferries, but I'll tell you that that was no damn fun. Even with 38s coming in from at least three directions at once, the Germans threw up enough flak at us on the run-in to make life downright uncomfortable," Weltman recalled with a touch of the old excitement. "Crossing over the Siebels was murder, absolute murder. And sometimes the bomb skipped right over those devils. We also had trouble with the tail fuses breaking off, and if the bomb went off at impact, it would have blown us up too."

The results forced the 82nd to regroup and concentrate all efforts on dive-bombing tactics. Somebody worried about the bombs running into the props after release during the dive. Technical people would have been able to tell them that the bombs would not accelerate after release, but Weltman's commentary was more to the point. "Hell, the way the P-38 dove, those bombs couldn't even keep up with us once they were loose. The problem never materialized."

He had learned very early in his 1st Fighter Group days that the clean design and acceleration of the P-38 (downright extraordinary for those years) had been responsible for more dead pilots than compressibility ever would be. From force of habit, all of the former P-35, P-36 and P-43 pilots routinely started half-rolling maneuvers at 7,000 to 8,000 feet, diving down and split-essing out with no trouble at all and with altitude to spare. "When the YP-38s and P-38s (first production models) arrived at Selfridge Field," Weltman told me, "one of the pilots attempted a split-ess at about 7,000 feet and went straight into the ground. He probably lost 6,000 feet before he even began his recovery.

*ABOVE: Honors for what must have been the most totally-damaged-in-flight yet intact Lightning would have to be awarded to this F-5B-1-LO (AC42-67318) after it had a mid-air collision with a British RAF Handley Page Halifax four-engine bomber. The first inclination is to suspect that it was a ground collision, but there is no sign of debris or parts on the ground, and the F-5B's landing skid marks are very clearly visible. The big Halifax left one complete vertical tail embedded in the Lightning's left outer wing as its fuselage attempted to amputate the smaller aircraft's right wing. It introduced what appears to be about a 30-degree sweepback into that wing, the hard way. The pilot of the '38 never got No. 2 engine feathered as it probably froze in position when the engine seized. Somehow the recon pilot managed to get the airplane on the ground without collapsing the gear, and walked away from the forlorn Class 26 airplane. What became of the amputated Halifax remains unrecorded.*

*BELOW: With a jump in production, re-equipment of the Fifteenth Air Force began in earnest, probably as a concession to Gen. Eaker and ties to the Doolittle decision to go exclusively with the Mustang as bomber escort aircraft for the Eighth Air Force. Either that or it was a remarkable coincidence. This P-38J-15-LO shows a major battle markings change at the same time, although this 94FS aircraft had not had the spinners painted or plane-in-group number added. (Kenneth Sumney)*

"I remember on Easter Sunday in 1942, I had a nice kid by the name of Ben Bridges in the squadron. He was out flying on a beautiful day, did a split-ess maneuver at about 8,000 feet, and also wound up going right into the ground. He lit near Sepulveda Boulevard and about one mile north of Mines Field (which became Los Angeles International airport after the war). We had a piloting problem in that we didn't know that the P-38 was so damn clean that if we half-rolled into a dive below 12,000 feet we could not pull out of it in time. We needed at least 12,000 feet under us." (Training was such that the same kinds of errors were still being made in 1944.)

Under the circumstances, the dive-bombing problem was one of having to develop the best techniques and altitudes for entering a dive, perfecting simple but effective aiming devices and adhering to the rules for observing a minimum pullout altitude. Rarely would a dive begin below 12,000 feet, but even more rarely above 20,000 feet. They could, in that manner, avoid getting into compressibility. According to Weltman's Form 5, the first dive-bomber attack was launched on May 31, 1943.

Within a very short time, the P-38G became one of the finest dive-bombing platforms of the entire war. After rolling into a dive attitude, pilots discovered that the airplane could be lined up rapidly as if it was a pole jutting from the target. Corrections were simple to crank in by minute movement of the controls. The fighter moved so quickly that the final approach time – where the airplane was committed to a single path, thereby becoming a relatively predictable target for enemy gunners – proved to be of very short duration. Bombs were released on the direct run-in so that upon recovery from the dive the pilot could take effective evasive action immediately.

One of the first pilots to destroy a Siebel Ferry was 1st Lt. Edward S. Newbury, piloting a 1FG Lightning named "Dear John." It was a P-38F-1-LO (AC41-7544) that he had picked up in California on April 15, 1942. It had carried him through a multitude of adventures since that time. Newbury and "Dear John" had crossed the North Atlantic as part of BOLERO, flown on the earliest missions in England, and ventured to North Africa at the very beginning of TORCH.

In fact, the team of Newbury and the hardy P-38F were still together after no less than 75 missions, including some 300+ hours of combat operations as of August 1943. That was an admirable achievement for man and airplane. Newbury and the other pilots in his group caught some of the Siebel flak ships in the Sicilian Strait, with "Dear John" delivering the message. The armored ferry was not actually hit, but the near miss virtually capsized the vessel, causing it to break up and sink very quickly.

Meanwhile, morale in the 82FG climbed rapidly to a new high under Weltman's leadership. The Siebels began to have a very discouraging time of it. Pilots soon learned that the

most effective method for sinking the barges was, as Newbury had discovered, to score a near miss and let the concussion cave in the hull by external pressure. A direct hit might create havoc on the superstructure (which was very heavily armor plated) or even put a clean hole through the hull, but in either case the vessel might still get away. A powerful near miss would either capsize the shallow-draft Siebel or tear up enough hull plates to sink it in minutes.

Group commander John Weltman – always Bill or Willy to his friends – was not the sort of C.O. to remain at his desk. He preferred to fly combat missions and, since he loved the P-38, he instilled great confidence in his pilots. They were never going to hear a disparaging word about the Lightning from that man. Every man in the group knew that he had been flying the "hot" fighter for two solid years and had posted nearly 1,000 hours on fighters since he was commissioned. He knew the P-38 better than most military aviators.

Weltman was unequivocally not a man of large physical stature, and at least a couple of the smaller Lightning jockeys had relayed their complaints about the cockpit layout. Ray Toliver, for instance, complained that "You have to be built like an ape to fly the P-38 the way the cockpit is laid out." Young Weltman, on the other hand, happily completed his 50th combat mission in Lightnings on June 12, 1943. Fittingly, it was his seventh dive-bombing mission, and virtually all of those flights exceeded 3 hours in duration. In 1943 it was notable when any pilot of a traditional fighter logged more than 3 hours on any flight, much less on a mission involving the use of military or war-emergency power for 10 to 15 minutes.

And if those single-engine fighters carried large bombs in place of drop tanks, the 3-hour mission just never happened. But here was a 25-year-old group commander who had flown in every major Lightning type from the YP-38 to the P-38G-10-LO, the final model of the Lightning that he flew in combat. Considering the fact that his first active squadron duty had been at the controls of Boeing P-26s in Panama, the young man had made the transition to very high-performance fighters with a minimum of trauma.

Bill Weltman commanded the 27th Pursuit Squadron (F) at Mines Field in California early in 1942, and he is extremely proud of the fact that he led his squadron of 28 pilots and their P-38Fs over the BOLERO route to England – with a brief pause at an Icelandic base – without the loss or severe damage to even one aircraft or pilot. It is no wonder that Jimmy Doolittle held him in such high regard. He displayed all character traits that the general regarded as necessary in a fighter pilot.

Weltman received a special commendation from Doolittle in early July, and for unexplained reasons he spent most of his flying hours in that month at the controls of a North American B-25C and B-25D. He did manage to get in five P-38G combat missions before Doolittle sent him back to "Uncle Sugar" (the U.S.A.).

However, before his combat career was ended, he led a very active life at the controls of P-38s. One incident serves to reveal how effective the Lightning could be as a maritime raider. At the same time, it proved out some of Weltman's theories and techniques, gave Fighter Command a big boost at a time when it was sorely needed, and gained the man a Silver Star. On April 13, he led a flight of four other P-38Gs of the 1FG – his transfer to the 82FG had not been completed – on one of those experimental dive-bombing development missions. Although the techniques were being developed under fire, they went after the Italian naval cruiser *Gorizia*, a unit from Admiral Arturo Riccardi's ostensibly inactive navy, although there was every expectation that it would challenge Allied forces in the forthcoming invasion operations that were identified as CORKSCREW (Pantelleria), FIREBRAND (Corsica), HUSKY (Sicily) and AVALANCHE (Italy). At that particular time, the German hold on Tunisia was precarious at best in the face of a two-pronged assault by the British Eighth Army and the American forces led by Gen. Patton.

Each of the P-38Gs carried a 1,000-pound bomb as they arrived at La Maddalena precisely at 1000 hours. Their plan of attack called for Weltman to come in "on the deck" and attempt to skip-bomb the *Gorizia*, while the other four fighter-bombers, including one piloted by Capt. David Stentz, made dive-bombing assaults from four different positions of advantage. Three bombs headed downward as the four Lightnings pulled up; one bomb failed to respond to the release signal. Stentz's bomb landed squarely on the stern of the cruiser, while the other two bombs exploded nearby in the water. Weltman had miscalculated his approach and failed to line up properly for his drop. Unflustered, he remained low and headed for Porto Torres, having spotted two freighters there. They proved to be a misleading target.

"When I went in for the freighters, the Italians seemed to have a couple of hundred machine guns and 20-mm cannons around the dock areas," Weltman reported upon his return to base as he attempted to explain the numerous gaping holes in his airplane. "I didn't want to waste that half-ton bomb after carrying it all the way to Sardinia. I decided to look for a more suitable target when I noticed the two motor vessels at a small pier in Porto Torres. Hell, I couldn't have been a couple of hundred feet up when I went over the dock area, and I saw my bomb go clean through the side of one ship and explode inside the second. Then the whole works burst into flames. I guess the second boat was loaded with ammunition or gasoline."

Captain Stentz confirmed that the vessel burned furiously.

According to Weltman's Form 5, that was a 4-hour 35-minute combat mission, far more dangerous than any missions where the prime targets turned out to be Junkers Ju 52/3ms, no matter how many victories could be confirmed for a pilot. Interdiction missions against armed vessels are dangerous enough – as the single surviving crewmember of Torpedo 8 might attest – for the attacker, but compound that by having the ship in a well-defended port and the attacker is at even greater risk. Weltman's crew had to replace one entire wing panel and apply several other patches to his P-38G. Confirmed enemy losses included serious damage to a naval cruiser, one freighter and adjoining dockage areas. No Lightnings were lost, no pilots were injured, and one 1,000-pound bomb was returned to the armorers at Chateaudun du Rhumel. but the Lockheeds were not done for the day. That afternoon, in CAVU weather, a veteran Lockheed F-4 recon aircraft of the 3rd Photo Group – Col. Elliot Roosevelt's outfit – was escorted to La Maddalena to record the results of the strike. They orbited the area between 1310 and 1600 hours, located the sunken ship and nine other boats, and obtained some photo evidence. It was confirmed that the *Gorizia* had been towed from the scene.

Several active months were to pass before the Northwest-

*Perhaps 60 Lockheed F-4 and F-5 photo-recon airplanes were used by the Twelfth and Fifteenth Air Forces in peak-level operations with the MAAF. Literally millions of photographs were printed for evaluation during 1943-45 from pictures taken by Lightnings of the 3rd and 5th Photo Groups. One squadron, the 12PS, completed 3,000 missions by April 1945, mostly in support of the Fifth Army. All F-4s and F-5s from the 3rd Photo Group, like this F-5E-2-LO flew every sortie without guns for protection.*

ern African Air Forces (NAAF) organization was disbanded, accompanied by the movement of fighter groups to Italian bases. When Lt. Col. Weltman took command of the 82nd Fighter Group in North Africa for about three months, he was still averaging in the neighborhood of 30 hours of combat flying each month, but it tapered off in June and was severely reduced in July. He flew P-38 combat missions on July 8, 9 and 10, and managed a long escort mission on July 14. The 15 administrative flights made in that same month were all in a Mitchell medium bomber because the end of his combat career was at hand.

Rare was the day when more than two P-38 groups were involved in MTO combat operations. The influx of pilots and airplanes was far from adequate to maintain three active groups of Lightnings in the role assigned in the Strategic Air Force (specifically the Northwest African Strategic Air Force or NASAF). Most pilots were attaining the 50-mission replacement level in less than four months of action. It had not mattered much that the 78FG in the U.K. had lost all of its P-38s, together with most of its pilots, to Operation TORCH as replacements for 1FG and 14FG losses in the first two months of action.

So great was the need to mount the invasion that it appears nobody in the USAAF had anticipated the deteriorative effects of blowing sand and bottomless mud on aircraft operating from third-class airports or "improved" landing grounds. Nothing akin to the British Vokes filters was ever fitted to any P-38, P-40 or B-17 aircraft (or any other AAF types). When it appeared that Rommel's forces were on the verge of routing the British after many lengthy seesaw battles, TORCH was mounted in haste. Army supply lines – thousands of miles in length – failed, and the only solution had been to strip the Eighth Air Force in the United Kingdom of virtually all of its fighters and most of its bombers to fill the gaps in the battle of North Africa.

The exigencies of war were probably responsible for Lt. Col. Weltman flying P-38s in combat after he chalked up that 50th mission. There was certainly no letup in the war around the Mediterranean after the Axis forces capitulated in May. Typically, on July 21, the entire 82FG escorted North American Mitchell medium bombers to Salerno and to Battaglia on the Italian mainland. That mission constituted the initial opera-

*Gen. Nathan Twining, in command of the XVth Air Force, used his fighters and bombers with intensity and some effective razzle-dazzle. Although Ploesti's oil refineries were hit dozens of times, it seemed that results were less than satisfactory. With Russian occupation of the Ploesti fields in September 1944, as the Nazi Wehrmacht retreated from the Balkans, it was found that 90 percent of oil production had been knocked out in Rumania. P-38Js, like Maj. Tom Rafael's from the 27FS, shared long-range escort duties with Eighth Air Force P-51s and performed outstandingly as the AAF's best dive bomber, the P-47 being better at low-level strafing attacks. (USAAF)*

tion by any P-38 unit over Italy's mainland. Some key railroad installations were destroyed that day. Just three days earlier the 82nd had escorted B-25s over Golfo Aranci, Sardinia, with somewhat different results. Approximately 40 or 50 enemy fighters attacked the formations with a vengeance, but the 82nd pilots were in winning form. They scored 16 solid victories, with all of the aircraft downed being confirmed as single-seat fighters. At least two "probables" were claimed and eight other enemy fighters were known to have been damaged by gunfire.

Nobody denied that 82FG pilots had experienced more productive days – such as the destruction of 32 enemy aircraft on a day in April. However, virtually all of those victories had been over multiengined transports intercepted at low altitude; victories over enemy fighters were much sweeter, much more satisfying to the ego. It was evident that the 82nd under Weltman was right up there with the best of them. As many as three separate major missions in a single day were being flown by members of 82FG as the Allied forces pounded through Sicily.

Under pressure from above, Weltman had flown his last P-38 combat mission – a bomber escort assignment – with the 95FS on July 14. Within days he was to become one of the youngest full colonels in the AAF. Gen. Spaatz ordered him to report to Gen. Arnold in the United States, hoping to get him back within a reasonable time. It wasn't to be. Bill Weltman spent the rest of the war commanding a combat crew training

*ABOVE: A "little friend" P-38J from the 82nd Fighter Group, 95FS, moves in close to a Consolidated B-24J during a typical escort mission. (AFM)*

*BELOW RIGHT: Lt. Richard E. Willsie sits on the lap of Flt. Off. Richard T. Andrews in the latter's P-38J at a base in Russia in August 1944, after pulling off a hair-raising "Great Escape" at Focsani, Rumania. When Lt. Willsie was shot down, he bellied into a farm pasture and was rescued by his squadron buddy, Andrews. Flying for more than 2 hours in the cramped cockpit, the two pilots came through a torrential rainstorm to a safe haven. In attempting to demonstrate "how they did it," according to Stumpy Hollinger, they found it took more than 10 minutes of effort to close the canopy under ideal conditions. (Lockheed Aircraft Corp.)*

school in California. As the war ground down to a weary end, he was commended for running an operation wherein his trainees flew no less than 24,029 hours in P-38s without a single fatal aircraft accident. That proved to be a record for the Fourth Air Force, and it certainly proved that the Lockheed Lightning, when flown by properly trained and inspired pilots, was a remarkably safe airplane to fly.

D Split-second decisions were an absolute necessity for survival in combat. Prudence and survival hardly went hand-in-hand where fighter aircraft were involved. Captain Newell O. Roberts, one of the pioneers in the NAAF, was not the sort of person to mince words or include prudence in his decisions. He generally tended to lay things right on the line. One thing that stood out in pronounced fashion in his traditionally straightforward commentary about flying P-38s in combat was his candor and style that assured you that his information was totally reliable. Roberts maintained the traditions of the famed Rickenbacker "Hat-in-the-Ring" squadron from the time he joined it back in the U.S.A. to fly his P-38F to England in the wake of Col. John Stone, then the commander of 1st Fighter Group.

"I learned one thing from the first Jerry I shot down," Capt. Roberts grunted. "In a fight with a Messerschmitt, 3 seconds is all you have to either live or die. People seem to think that fighter pilots of the World War II variety zoom, dive and twist like a swarm of bees, spitting bullets right and left. It isn't like that at all," the captain said emphatically.

Roberts then pointedly told his version of what air combat is really like. "You take off in your Lightning for a 3- to 5-hour flight for patrolling, strafing, bombing or escorting a larger flock of heavies (four-engine bombers). Altogether you have

just about 3 minutes' worth of shooting in the ammo cans up front feeding the most heavily concentrated firepower of any service fighter. When attacking, you hold your fire until you are no more than 100 yards from your enemy. Then you let go with 3-second bursts. In that time, you can squirt out about 300 bullets and shells. Either you get him or he gets you.

"My first Jerry (victim) was one of a pair of Messerschmitt Me 110s* that were cruising over the town of Gabes at the southern end of Tunisia. I was flight leader as we patrolled that part of the Mediterranean to keep the German U-boats under water. We had also been ordered to strafe German field concentrations around Gabes. I saw the Jerries above us, going in our direction. We had the speed to overhaul them, but there was no time to maneuver. I gave my engines the 'blossom,' pulled my nose up to get one of the Me 110s in my sights and gave him a quick squirt. He immediately burst into flames. My wingman was equally successful in getting the other one. The whole job took about as long as it took to tell about it," he stated, almost with disinterest.

(*Correct designation is Bf 110. Another is Bf 109. But in WW II, most spoke only of Me 110 or Me 109 Nazi fighters.)

Roberts had a fiercely determined belief that air warfare was a percentage game when you fought as a team; otherwise, you were dead wrong and very dead. Of course there are many pilots who will disagree with his contention that "they'll shoot you down any time you go into aerobatic maneuvers. There isn't any room for grudge fighting. Almost all of the pilots we lost were fellows who let themselves be suckered out of formation. The Jerries love to send one of their planes out in front and down low as a decoy. If one of our men went after the decoy, a whole team of Me 109s would go after him in a flash. But if our whole team went after the bait, those Jerries usually chose to stay out of it. We could outfly and outshoot them," Roberts contended, not showing any sign of bravado. His words were, perhaps, entirely true for 1943 and that theater of operations at a time when the P-38F and G models dominated the scene. Even Axis pilots – especially those in the *Luftwaffe* – would concede that operational tactics and conditions in the Mediterranean area would be distinctly different from those prevailing in northern Europe.

Many stories related by Capt. Roberts were distinctly worthy of publication, but so were the exciting tales emanating from literally dozens of other pilots who were masters of their craft. But Roberts did have some succinct and pointed words that epitomized his personal feelings:

"The only limit to what you can do with the Lightning is the endurance of the pilot himself. The armchair strategists think that if you fly for 3 hours escorting bombers, fight for 3 minutes, then fly back home for 3 hours that it is an easy day's

*Over some forbidding, frozen terrain of Italy or, perhaps, Austria, an 82FG P-38L-1-LO was photographed probably from the aft gunner's station of a B-25J from the 5th PRS. These Model 422-87-23 fighters had 3450 WEP horsepower on tap in an emergency. Top speed on normal rated power was 421 mph, so they could probably attain around 440 mph on WEP for about 5 minutes (an eternity in combat). Absolute ceiling in a P-38L was 44,000 feet, a not inconsiderable height. Deliveries began in October 1944. (USAAF)*

work. I can't even begin to describe to you just how wrong they are. When we hit North Africa, the Jerries had control of the air; no doubt about it. We took it away from them because we were better trained and had a better plane. Considering what we were able to do with only a handful of them, you'll have to agree." Lending more support to Roberts' contentions were a few equally important items that he neglected to mention. A high percentage of the Nazi pilots, if not the Italians, had up to 3 years of combat experience by the time the TORCH aircraft arrived, their logistics problems were considerably smaller (at least in the first few months), and they, like their British counterparts, had equipped their aircraft with desert air filters.

Ill-informed critics of the Lightning evidently got more mileage out of misinformation and pure fabrication than they could out of the facts in those early months of the European war and the battle of North Africa. After all, the range capabilities of the P-38 type far outstripped anything else that could be put into the air *en mass*. That fact did not seem to be important to such critics.

Everybody involved felt that it sure was one hell of a long way to go – or so it seemed at the time – just to strafe a target. It then appeared to be all the more illogical when it became patently evident that 150 rapidly tiring P-38Fs, Gs and Hs were going to have to do the job. Up to a few months before the orders came down from HQ, the P-38 was still considered to be the Allied world's most controversial fighter. (Its single-engine contemporary, the Bell P-39 Airacobra, had already been "written off" as a first-line combat type.) But now the rookies and veterans alike had developed a healthy faith in their

Lockheed mounts that would tend to make a 530-mile (each way) flight to the target seem like an easy cross-country training flight, even if the operation would take them over hostile territory during a major portion of the mission.

No doubt about it, the mission would be a big one. Over a period of months, beginning with the spring offensive that had been launched to finally drive the *Wehrmacht* and the dangerous Rommel from Tunisia, Lt. Gen. Carl Spaatz's NAAF had assaulted the *Luftwaffe* and Axis forces 24 hours a day. The Allies had gained mastery of the air, thanks to the performance of the P-38s, P-40s and Spitfires. The "Desert Fox's" aerial supply routes had not infrequently lost between 25 and 30 aircraft in a single encounter. Meanwhile the information about skip-bombing and dive-bombing techniques developed by the 82FG was passed to the 1FG and the 14FG, the latter having been (finally) rebuilt to full strength with three squadrons early in May 1943.

Several times it appeared that the Italian Air Force was scattering to the winds, only to launch large formations of Macchi C.202s and Reggiani Re.2001s for attack on Allied medium and light bombers with evident bravura. Some of the Italian pilots displayed real fighting talent. However, for the most part, the IAF lacked the skill, spirit and equipment

*Luftwaffe* fighters and bombers were based on Sardinia, Corsica, in southern France and on the Italian mainland. A-2 believed that a large percentage of those airplanes were in Italy proper, mostly below the 42nd parallel in the vicinity of Foggia's 10 airfields. Then everyone concluded that one final all-out assault on the Foggia Complex would break the back of Axis aerial resistance.

After three days of intensive training in the art of low-level attack, the 1st and 82nd groups took off from their Tunisian bases and headed out past Pantelleria, then over Sicily and the Tyrrehenian Sea toward the Italian boot. At about the same time, Consolidated B-24s swept northward out of Bengazi, crossing the Ionian and Adriatic seas in the direction of the same target area.

Flying close to the tops of the waves to reduce the chances of detection as they approached the Italian coastline, the vast fleet of P-38s offered an unprecedented and awesome sight in the MTO. Colonel MacNichol, generally credited with planning and leading the raid, quickly become aware that they had achieved almost complete surprise as his two groups split into attack formations. Of course it was virtually impossible for the six squadrons of Lightnings to effectively hit all of the satellite bases, but the planners had allowed for that. The P-38s smashed dispersed aircraft in multiple passes, catching the defenders with more than 230 aircraft on the ground. So complete was the surprise that pilots observed men on the ground actually throwing rocks at the twin-engine fighters out of pure frustration.

What were the actual achievements of Maj. Gen. James Doolittle's Northwest African Strategic Air Force (NASAF)? They had launched 140 Lightnings, 65 coming from the 1FG and a full 75 launched by the 82FG. By the time the "Famous First" departed the Foggia area, no less than 88 enemy aircraft were known to have been totally destroyed or seriously damaged. What ammunition had not been expended at the main target was used to strafe other targets of opportunity as they streaked back to Tunisia. Only two fighters had been lost by the entire group. Although the score racked up by the 82nd did not match the impressive numbers garnered by the 1FG, they did mount a highly successful attack.

necessary to establish an effective defense. They still had to be dealt with as a major factor in any large-scale raid.

Plans for that first long-range mass operation, a low-level strafing mission, involved an attack with a mission profile of approximately 1,100 miles, allowing for at least 20 minutes of combat at the target area at maximum rated power settings. Two of the three Lightning groups active in the MTO at the time – the 1FG, still under command of Col. Ralph Garman and the 82FG commanded by Lt. Col. George M. MacNichol after Doolittle and Spaatz sent Weltman back to the U.S.A – were assigned to the strafing attack.

At the same time. Lt. Col. Troy Keith's resurgent 14th Fighter Group was given the task of escorting a major attack force of approximately 150 Boeing B-17Fs on a followup raid on the same target later in the day. (It should be noted that Col. Garman did not lead his group on the August 25 raid. After logging more than 600 hours of flight time on P-38s and a total of 1,505 hours on pursuit/fighter aircraft, he had flown his final combat mission on July 20 to the Palermo-Naples area. As soon as a replacement commander arrived, he was to be rotated home.)

Once Operation HUSKY, that invasion of Sicily, was launched, all air units in the Mediterranean area had been flying missions virtually around the clock in support of British and American ground forces and their naval support units. Few of those missions could be classed as "milk runs."

Allied Intelligence people were reasonably certain that the number of Axis combat aircraft facing the Twelfth Air force and NASAF amounted to approximately 1,600 first-line operational aircraft to oppose the AVALANCHE and BAYTOWN forces. It was concluded that 950 Italian Air Force and 650

Not long after the two strafing groups set off on a course for their home base, the B-24 Liberators arrived on the scene to pound the railroad marshaling yards. Later on that day, Boeing B-17s from Tunis and Bizerte came over at 25,000 feet to hit airfield structures and facilities, using 500-pound bombs and clusters of 20-pound fragmentation bombs. The Fortresses were attacked by nearly 100 Axis fighters as they turned away from the target area to head for home, but P-38s of the 14th Fighter Group waded in to provide an effective defense. Air-to-air combat accounted for no less than 26 enemy aircraft. Post attack assessments of GAF and IAF losses amounted to about 150 aircraft destroyed or severely damaged on the ground. Even when A-2 included all losses from NAAF operations that day (including missions flown against Taranto by RAF and Canadian bombers), only 15 aircraft were lost.

Once again the Lightning had demonstrated its great ability for operating over lengthy routes in a combat environment, assaulting very heavily defended targets as if they were only about 30 minutes away from home base and combating a wide assortment of short-range defensive fighters at parity after having flown nearly 600 miles while frequently having to "thatch" (weaving back and forth) while escorting the slower B-17s. In the following two years, P-38s would not only continue to demonstrate the virtues of the design configuration on a daily basis and in many areas of the global conflict, but the newer models of the type embodied virtually all of the improvements desired by combat pilots, plus many that they hadn't even thought of.

Even as the Lockheed fighters carried out the stringent demands of the Foggia mission, Republic P-47s in the ETO were just barely beginning to overcome the limited range problems that prevented them from providing necessary defensive cover for the growing number of heavy bombers being committed to the Combined Bomber Offensive, better known as POINTBLANK. Following the Regensburg and Schweinfurt debacle – losses in the order of 20 percent per mission could no longer be tolerated – on August 17, VIIIth Fighter Command realized that without P-38s to perform escort duties until the Thunderbolt range problems could be overcome, daylight bombing might well succumb to congressional pressures. Whatever history has told us, the P-38 buildup in the ETO began once again in earnest after a year of neglect.

In recognition of their participation in the audacious low-level strafing attacks on the Axis airdromes at Foggia on August 25, 1943, both the 1st and 82nd Fighter Groups were awarded Distinguished Unit Citations. Just five days later, the 1FG performed so bravely and brilliantly in protecting bomber aircraft that they were awarded a second DUC.

Thousands of miles away in Burbank, the weather was wonderful and production of the new P-38J-5-LO was beginning to move into high gear. Introduction of the new core-type intercoolers permitted lifting of power restrictions on the F-17 series Allison engines. Although that did not cure all problems afflicting the Allisons, it did give the P-38s renewed life. First deliveries of the new J model occurred in the same month (August) that top MTO and ETO commanders discovered just how valuable the P-38 Lightnings, even in the early model form, were. Not only could they function brilliantly as long-range fighter-bombers or bomber escorts, they could more than hold their own against Axis short-range interceptors operating very close to their own home bases.

Major errors in modernizing training techniques, failure to accept the twin-engine fighter at face value because of obsolete thinking, high command vacillation about commitment of the P-38 in the ETO – partly because of their total misjudgments on the Bell P-39 – and overconfidence that the P-47C/D Thunderbolt would fulfill established requirements by mid-1943 all affected decisions about the Lightning. One of the worst decisions was ultra-late commitment of a second-source production facility for an aircraft known to be difficult to manufacture. (There was no validity to any argument about availability of engines, or even turbosuperchargers. Numerous available Packard Merlins would have quickly overcome any such argument. The P-38 was almost infinitely adaptable.)

TABLE 14-1

**AIRPLANE ACCEPTANCES 1943-44**

| Type | J | F | M | A | M | J | J | A | S | O | N | D | Totals |
|------|---|---|---|---|---|---|---|---|---|---|---|---|--------|
| **1943** | | | | | | | | | | | | | |
| LOCKHEED P-38 | 151 | 168 | 133 | 122 | 84 | 180 | 264 | 102 | 66 | 350 | 387 | 206 | 2213 |
| LOCKHEED F-5 | 24 | – | 60 | – | – | – | – | 89 | 1 | – | 110 | | 284 |
| BELL P-39 | 330 | 385 | 472 | 511 | 312 | 437 | 503 | 501 | 280 | 420 | 403 | 391 | 4945 |
| CURTISS P-40 | 315 | 314 | 324 | 325 | 380 | 400 | 337 | 463 | 400 | 378 | 422 | 200 | 4258 |
| *REPUBLIC P-47 | 160 | 151 | 232 | 244 | 307 | 307 | 381 | 434 | 496 | 496 | 548 | 660 | 4426 |
| *NAA P-51 | – | – | 70 | 121 | 121 | 20 | 91 | 175 | 201 | 284 | 295 | 332 | 1710 |
| BELL P-63 | – | – | – | – | – | – | – | – | 7 | 10 | 11 | | 28 |
| NORTHROP P-61 | – | – | – | – | – | – | – | 7 | 6 | 3 | 6 | 10 | 32 |

\* DUAL MANUFACTURING PLANTS

| Type | J | F | M | A | M | J | J | A | S | O | N | D | Totals |
|------|---|---|---|---|---|---|---|---|---|---|---|---|--------|
| **1944** | | | | | | | | | | | | | |
| LOCKHEED P-38 | 317 | 313 | 352 | 342 | 352 | 355 | 367 | 402 | 397 | 364 | 325 | 300 | 4186 |
| BELL P-39 | 351 | 350 | 300 | 252 | 201 | 150 | 112 | 13 | – | – | – | – | 1729 |
| BELL P-63 | 28 | 50 | 50 | 72 | 110 | 160 | 210 | 260 | 101 | 252 | 255 | 240 | 1786 |
| CURTISS P-40 | 275 | 241 | 283 | 202 | 200 | 73 | 97 | 155 | 202 | 193 | 80 | – | 2001 |
| *REPUBLIC P-47 | 650 | 633 | 648 | 623** | 601 | 600 | 600 | 600 | 593 | 494 | 377 | 644 | 7063 |
| *NAA P-51 | 370 | 380 | 482 | 407 | 580 | 579 | 569 | 700 | 663 | 763 | 709 | 702 | 6904 |
| NORTHROP P-61 | 12 | 20 | 23 | 31 | 15 | 48 | 21 | 50 | 50 | 59 | 65 | 55 | 449 |
| LOCKHEED P-80 | – | – | – | – | – | – | – | – | – | 1 | 4 | 5 | 5 |

*Dual manufacturing plants
**Production of P-47Gs at Curtiss Buffalo Cancelled

**WASTED PRODUCTION CAPACITY/EFFORT**

| | J | F | M | A | M | J | J | A | S | O | N | D | Totals |
|------|---|---|---|---|---|---|---|---|---|---|---|---|--------|
| **1943** | | | | | | | | | | | | | |
| DOUGLAS RA-24B | – | – | 1 | 8 | 19 | 35 | 65 | 75 | 103 | 81 | 114 | 114 | 615 |
| VULTEE A-31/V-72/A-35 | 39 | 56 | 93 | 86 | 56 | 75 | 80 | 80 | 80 | 80 | 80 | 70 | 875 |
| CURTISS SO3C-4 | 50 | 43 | 53 | 45 | 42 | 39 | 26 | 20 | 32 | 26 | 47 | 27 | 450 |
| CURTISS C-76 | – | 1 | – | – | – | – | – | – | 9 | 3 | 2 | – | 15 |
| BREWSTER SB2A | 45 | 38 | 9 | 41 | 76 | 78 | 89 | 54 | 73 | 25 | 7 | 29 | 567 |

**WASTED PRODUCTION CAPACITY/EFFORT**

| | J | F | M | A | M | J | J | A | S | O | N | D | Totals |
|------|---|---|---|---|---|---|---|---|---|---|---|---|--------|
| **1944** | | | | | | | | | | | | | |
| CURTISS P-60 | – | – | – | – | – | – | – | – | 1 | – | – | | 1 |
| FISHER P-75 | (buildup to production) | | | | | | | | | 2 | – | | 2 |
| CURTISS SO3C | 43 | (production terminated) | | | | | | | | | | | 43 |
| CURTISS C-76 | 5 | 4 | 1 | (plant fully tooled) | | | | | | | | | 10 |
| VULTEE A-35 | 70 | 68 | 60 | 39 | 29 | 4 | (plant conversion) | | | | | | 270 |
| BREWSTER SB2A | 32 | 2 | – | 1 | – | – | – | – | – | – | – | | 35 |
| CONSOLIDATED TBY-2 | (plant conversion) | | | | | | | | | | 1 | 1 | 2 |
| BUDD RB-1 | – | – | 1 | – | 3 | 1 | 2 | 4 | 3 | 3 | – | – | 17 |

**NOTES:**
Douglas RA-24Bs, equivalent of the Navy SBD Dauntless dive bomber, were rejected out-of-hand by Gen. Kenney in the face of excessive combat losses. His arguments: P-38s could fly farther, carry a larger bomb load, could fight their way out of any defense and only needed one crew member.
The unloved Vultee A-31/A-35 dive bombers were generally used as advanced trainers throughout the war.
Ranger V-770 engines downed far more aircraft in which they were mounted than all Axis air forces combined. The Curtiss SO3C Seamew was a bad aircraft powered by a dismal engine. Ranger had the poorest engine production record of any engine company.
Brewster's SB2A-2, in production even before Pearl Harbor for export, also served as the -4 version. Production continued at a leisurely pace clear into 1944. There is no record of any in combat.
Wooden Curtiss C-76 Caravans literally fell apart in the air. A major debacle.

185

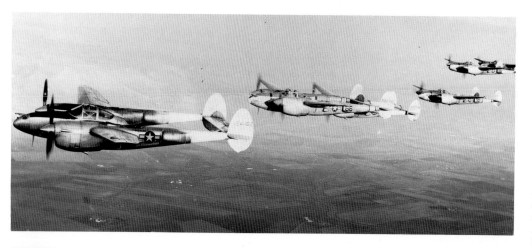

G In the meantime, activities in the Mediterranean Theater of Operations accelerated steadily with the launching of Operations BAYTOWN and AVA-LANCHE in September 1943. Little consideration has been given to the fact that throughout the 12 months of 1943 and, generally, the first few months of 1944, commanders in the MTO were equipped with something less than optimum weapons. For the most part, fighters were Curtiss P-40 Warhawks, Bell P-39 and P-400 Airacobras, Supermarine Spitfires from the RAF on reverse Lend-Lease, North American A-36A Invaders and Lockheed P-38s.

The Lightnings included everything from P-38F models to P-38Hs, some F-4 and F-5 recon aircraft, but not one of the improved P-38Js. (in fact, Lockheed Aircraft was still manufacturing the H-5 models [50 percent of production] until early December 1943.) New P-38J-5-LOs were being accepted by the AAF beginning in August, and the first of them began to arrive in the United Kingdom in December. Some of those new Lightnings may have been reaching the NAAF as early as November, but the numbers were few. Even the newest North American Mustangs, powered by the Merlin, did not arrive on the scene in Italy until springtime 1944 when new P-51B models began to replace Spitfires and P-40s. Razorback Republic P-47Ds flew operationally in Italy for the first time in December in the hands of 57FG and 325FG pilots.

Any thoughts that fighter and fighter-bomber attrition during that period in the MTO was insignificant could not be further removed from the truth. Losses to ground fire and flak from Siebel Ferries were, at times, intolerable. Once again it must be emphasized that virtually every time a Lightning was doing battle over the Italian mainland, the brave pilots had already flown several hundred miles just to be there. Whatever transpired, they still had a long way to go just to get some much needed rest. When the 1FG and the 82FG shot up the Foggia airfields, there was strong evidence that no less than 88 Axis aircraft had been destroyed or had suffered major damage that would be difficult, if not impossible under the circumstances, to repair. Unfortunately, few of those aircraft were fighters. That became all too evident on August 30. On that day, the 1st Fighter Group put up 48 Lightnings to escort a force of Martin B-26s attacking Aversa. The defenders put up something on the order of 60 to 75 fighters. The USAAF fighters claimed eight destroyed plus three probables, but no fewer than 13 of the P-38s were lost in the fierce running battle.

On September 3, the 82FG sent out a major escort force of 72 Lockheeds in support of a North American B-25 Mitchell force, equaling the P-38 effort in scale. Their target was the railroad marshaling yards at Cancello. Approximately 60 German and Italian fighters went after the B-25s, even firing rockets into the bomber formation. Given better odds, the

P-38s tangled with the enemy aircraft with great vigor. Pilots of the 82nd claimed no fewer than 23 "kills" and added five probables. True, some ten P-38s failed to return to base, but a rate of two and a half to one was pretty favorable, especially with prevailing circumstances.

Those Axis fighter losses must have proven unacceptable because opposition to subsequent raids in September greatly diminished. In another attempt to reduce opposing fighter forces even more, the 14FG and the 82FG launched still another strafing attack on the Foggia satellite bases on September 14, but most of the aircraft knocked out on the ground were Junkers Ju 88 types. Almost everybody has ignored the fact that the 350FG (comprising three squadrons) had joined in on the TORCH invasion and, a few months later, partially assumed the mantel of a P-38 group. Losses of Bell P-39 and P-400 types, plus the need to fly some missions that had profiles well beyond the capabilities of any other types in the theater, resulted in transfer of a small number of P-38s to the 350FG. Though tiny in numbers, the P-38s acquitted themselves well and scored several victories that included some Messerschmitt Bf 109Fs. (As P-47s became more plentiful, the 350th converted to that type in 1944.)

The point is that the Italian campaign was anything but a "milk run" for a very long time. There never seemed to be enough aircraft to do a proper job, and it became quite common for the NAAF, and the main successor organization – the Fifteenth Air Force – to get older, used aircraft as replacements, at least with respect to Lockheed P-38s.

When Lt. William H. Caughlin reported to 27th Fighter Squadron at Foggia on April 2, 1944, the self-effacing youngster was, in many ways, typical of a largely unheralded force of fighter jockeys who constituted the basic mass of combat fliers in every theater of operations. At age 22, most of his flight time in operational-type aircraft had been in Bell P-39Qs, logging about 76 hours total. When he arrived at Salsola (Foggia No. 3) as a replacement pilot assigned to the 1FG, his log showed just over 30 hours on P-38s, which turns out to be just about average for pilots moving into combat units in 1943-44.

It can be said that most of Caughlin's 50 plus combat missions in the MTO's Fifteenth Air Force were lengthy, truculent and exhausting . . . the mixture of missions where a flier could accumulate 300 hours or more of combat time in 3 or 4 months. He just barely missed being a member of that select group who became official aces, having been credited with four confirmed victories over enemy fighter aircraft. Two of the *Jagd* (GAF fighter or pursuit) he shot down within seconds of each other were Focke-Wulf Fw 190s, and he scored hits on at least six others (without confirmed positive results) in the same battle. Caughlin was fortunate in having a virtually new P-38J-15-LO as his mount, it being among the first really new-model P-38s to be allocated to the Fifteenth Air Force.

One mission that stands out in Caughlin's mind was launched about a month and a half after he joined the 27FS at

Salsola. On May 18, 1944, the entire group – then under the command of Col. Robert B. Richard – was dispatched to provide protective cover for the withdrawal phase of B-17s from an HB formation of 146 aircraft that had been launched to attack Ploesti's Romana-Americana (isn't that an incongruity?) oil refinery. Several previous attacks on that same target had confirmed that the entire refinery was very heavily defended. Defenses consisted of a multitude of fighter aircraft, a most effective flak network, and a smoke screen laid down by hundreds of smoke generators.

As the May 18 mission progressed, weather en route degraded until it was terrible; so bad, in fact, that strong consideration was being given to aborting the mission. However, the group leader, thinking of the heavies coming out, decided to forge onward to provide a defense for any bombers that might have pressed on to the target area. Although navigational equipment in a P-38J was inadequate for dead reckoning navigation in such conditions, the 64 twin-engine fighters managed to maintain formation discipline, arriving at the rendezvous point some 450 miles distant from Salsola.

Incredibly, their timing was nearly perfect. In spite of the foul weather, one of the four bomber groups had made its way to the drop zone, bombed the target with determination, and that single group was under vicious coordinated attack by no fewer than 80 assorted *Jagd*. Six of the Boeing Fortresses had already fallen to the fighters. Lt. Caughlin and the other P-38 pilots immediately forgot about their own difficulties with flying conditions during the past 2 hours and charged into the larger force of *Luftwaffe* and Rumanian aircraft.

Once the fight at odds was joined, everything seemed to be working for the Lightnings, and that was combined with the aggressive spirit of the P-38 pilots that day. The B-17s managed to slip away without further losses, and the target defenders suddenly found themselves fighting for survival. While Caughlin, for some reason, did not score any confirmed victories in the melee, his squadron companions and the rest of the 1FG pilots managed to knock out 10 of the Axis warplanes. Three more were claimed as probable, and six other *Jagd* were hit hard enough to be considered as seriously damaged.

The Salsola team came out without one P-38 being shot down, although one of the Lockheeds was so severely damaged that the pilot was forced to bail out after stretching his flight beyond enemy territory. Many, having been at War Emergency Power settings for well over 10 minutes, ran low on fuel and had to land on the Isle of Vis off the coast of Yugoslavia. There they were refueled by Partisan soldiers and sent on their way back to the Foggia complex. Considering what had transpired in about 4 1/2 to 5 hours, the attrition rate was far below average.

Two months later, on July 18, Caughlin was leading a flight of the P-38Js over the Alps, heading for the Dornier aircraft production center at Friedrichshafen, Germany, when he spotted a large swarm of *Luftwaffe* fighters assaulting the heavy bomber groups that were participating in Operation ARGUMENT (the joint 8th and 15th Air Force air offensive against the German aircraft industry). No less than 75 German fighter aircraft were involved. The small force of 14 Lightnings

*A favor returned. This 27FS (1FG) Lockheed P-38J-15-LO was returning from an escort mission to Ploesti on May 5, 1944. Having suffered hits, and low on fuel, he flew with 15AF Liberators for protection. With the Adriatic in sight, he headed for Foggia.*
*(1st Fighter Group Association)*

of the 27FS was quickly committed, wading into the fray at full power.

Describing the encounter, Bill Caughlin said, "I shot at least eight of them – hits registered – and two of the Fw 190s went down. All of the Jerries that I didn't get, my own flight got. Every man in my flight got at least one enemy fighter." The men of the 27th scored 14 confirmed victories that day, deep into enemy territory, and outnumbered nearly four to one. Here is what the official AAF record for that day says:

"200 B-24s and B-17s attack the Memmingen airfield (and facilities), Dornier aircraft works at Manzell, and Casarsa della Delizia railroad bridge. Between 250 and 300 fighters oppose the formations attacking the targets in Germany, beginning interception at the North Adriatic coast, continuing to the targets and back as far as the Brenner Pass. Twenty U.S. aircraft are lost. HBs (heavies) and escorting fighters claim 66 *Jagd* shot down."

On the following day, the Eighth Air Force launched a massive raid of 1,100 bombers and 731 escorting fighters. From bases in Italy, the 15AF launched more than 400 B-17s and B-24s, with P-51s and P-38s able to provide 300 sorties in support. Air Defense over the target areas was reported as "weak." Evidently the fighters of the Mediterranean Allied Air Forces (MAAF) had helped put a severe dent in the *Luftwaffe's* capability to defend even its most important targets.

One fact relating to that small-scale escort force put up by the 27FS on July 18 that could easily be overlooked was that the B-17 gunners were down to their last few rounds of ammunition as a result of the sustained attacks throughout the entire mission. Without the timely intervention of Caughlin and his squadron mates, most of the Fortresses might well have fallen in one of the greatest disasters of the entire daylight bombing campaign.

187

One of Caughlin's friends was a B-17 pilot on that fateful day, and he told Bill that it was that small group of Lightnings that had saved them from certain destruction. Within a few more seconds they would have been defenseless. Strangely enough, it was one of the remarkable happenstances of the war when the 27th intervened. As Caughlin remembers the event, the bombers that they were sent to escort had not been at the rendezvous point; the bombers his flight had saved were from an entirely different group.

Such was Caughlin's 48th combat mission, certainly one of the most gratifying events in his life.

All of the foregoing brings up one of the most perplexing situations of the war. One P-38 pilot, James S. Alford, served in the 1st Fighter Group, 27th Fighter Squadron, from August 23, 1943, until the latter part of September 1944. He then moved to the 305th Wing Headquarters until December, basing at Foggia, where the wing controlled activities of all P-38s in the XVth Fighter Command. Alford had flown 53 combat missions, logging 250 combat hours in the process. He was credited with three confirmed victories and two damaged enemy aircraft. As an especially astute observer of combat activities (and serious historian in later years), Alford made the following commentary:

"In the Mediterranean, in early 1944, we began to hear some rumors about this (referring to problems with P-38s in the Eighth Air Force), but nothing very specific until some of our pilots went to Nuthampstead to bring back some P-38H models. They (the Eighth Air Force pilots) reported dissatisfaction with the airplane, blowing up engines . . . slow rate of roll and so forth.

"We were very glad to get the H models as our old G models were becoming worn out. We still had a few older F models, which, being lighter, still flew excellently. The reason we were so slow in obtaining newer models in the Mediterranean area was a matter of priorities. After the Salerno Invasion in September 1943, priorities shifted to the U.K. for the buildup for invasion (Operation OVERLORD) so that we received none of the newer models until the spring and summer of 1944.[1]

"I am still amazed to hear about the troubles they (VIIIth Fighter Command) had with the Allison engine. We had nothing of that kind. I think we flew, on the whole, somewhat longer missions and just as high as they did. I think we were more accustomed to leaning back and saving fuel, thus saving our engines by not keeping on high power settings over the distances we traveled."

Alford then referred to one incident, which was probably connected with the May 18 Ploesti raid. He gave all facts except the date. "One of our 27th Squadron pilots, Lt. Frank Williams, lost his right engine on a Ploesti mission (in the combat action), and later he lost his oil pressure on the left. He flew for 30 minutes on that left engine with no oil pressure showing at all, which was enough to get him over the Adriatic, where be bailed out. He was picked up . . . in 10 minutes by a Walrus ASR airplane of the RAF."

There was certainly one very good reason, or combination of reasons, why MTO pilots suffered few of the problems encountered in the ETO with Lightnings. Most of the incoming replacement pilots were indoctrinated by 1FG, 14FG and 82FG pilots who had been with P-38s for a long time. From observation, it appears that most of those men liked the P-38 and it had served men like Garman, Weltman, Newbury,

Hoelle, Crawford, Caughlin and Alford very well. Therefore, there was no rumor mill to scare the hell out of new pilots.

In the ETO, it is a fact that the rumor mills flourished and some commanders did nothing to stem the rumors. Therefore, the command problem cannot be discounted. Gasoline available in the MTO obviously came from a different source, probably direct from the U.S.A., and it is a well-known fact that fuel in the United Kingdom was of poor quality. If you but remember that the Allisons were not turbosupercharged in any fighters except the P-38s and that no Merlin had such supercharging, it becomes rather evident that fuel quality could easily have been one of the most important culprits.

Turbo regulation was a serious problem in the Eighth Air Force, but it is rarely even mentioned as a problem in the Fifteenth Air Force. Was weather the difference? Not at 30,000 feet and up. In that realm, the temperatures are just about the same wherever you are. Were the winters more difficult in England than in northern Italy? Hardly.

Were U.K. problems afflicting the P-38 encountered in the Aleutians? In the South Pacific? In India or China? Rarely. If there seems to be any uncommon denominator, it was in the widespread rumor mill and abject fear of the P-38 that prevailed in the Eighth Air Force. Those conditions were so obvious to at least one respected Lockheed employee in England that his telegraphed request to have Tony LeVier dispatched to the ETO for a demonstration and training program was accepted by top management and Gen. H. H. Arnold's office almost instantly. As LeVier soon found out, the fear was pervasive and some commanders were not only ignoring the situation, they were actually adding to the problems. (Circumstances relating to LeVier's trip to the ETO will be discussed in Chapter 15.)

H Certainly one of the most exciting "cliffhanger" rescue operations of the war involved two P-38 pilots flying with the 82nd Fighter Group on a shuttle mission between Foggia, Italy, and Poltava, Russia. A plea from the Soviets for a strike mission, which became part of an operation that was code named FRANTIC, was partially answered by a mission launched on August 4, 1944. More than seventy P-38 and P-51 fighters participated in that particular mission.

According to plan, the fighter force hit a Nazi airfield at Focsani, Rumania, severely damaging communications facilities nearby. During his run-in at the target, Lt. Richard E. Willsie, a combat veteran of about eight months in the MTO despite his tender age of 23, was hit by concentrated ground fire. His left engine quit and the right engine was clearly streaming coolant fluid and oil by the time a squadron mate, Flt. Off. Richard T. Andrews, spotted him.

"Head for the pasture," Andrews shouted into his microphone, "and I'll pick you up." Willsie quickly dropped his landing gear and flaps, and rather easily slipped the mortally wounded P-38J onto the soggy cow pasture and slid to a halt. As Andrews lined up for a straight-in approach, an entire staffel of Messerschmitt Bf 109s (that's nine airplanes) seemed bent on decommissioning the two Lightnings on the spot. All of the enemy pilots evidently forgot about the other American fighters in their vengeful desire to destroy two "sitting ducks." Andrews touched down just as several P-38s opened fire on the Messerschmitts. Lt. Nat A. Pate bagged one of the 109s, and within seconds had damaged another. Suddenly aware that their intended prey had a lot of friends with sharp teeth, the German or Rumanian pilots broke off their attack.

Willsie started to run for the idling Lockheed, remembered that he still had his parachute on and ran back to throw it on the damaged aircraft. He was unsuccessful in attempting to

---

1. In the big picture (officially), summer and fall 8AF bomber losses in 1943 caused redirection of all P-38 and scheduled P-51B deliveries from the MAAF to the ETO. When General Hunter was replaced by General Kepner, short-range P-47s went to the MTO in place of the planned-for Lightnings and Mustangs.

set fire to the airplane. Meantime, Andrews unfastened his chute and threw it overboard, dropped the stirrup and strongly urged the 190-pound lieutenant to get aboard. Andrews, who weighed in at about 160 pounds, climbed back into the cockpit as his friend retracted the stirrup.

"He sat on my lap," Andrews recalled with a chuckle, "wiped some blood out of his eyes and managed to slam the canopy shut as I ducked. The cockpit was a bit crowded, but Dick managed to get his feet on the pedals and opened the throttles."

No less than three truckloads of Axis troops were speeding toward the pasture by that time from the direction of Focsani airfield. They were quickly spotted by the men in the circling umbrella of P-38s, and one pilot dropped down to make a firing run. In an uncontested attack, it is hard to imagine a P-38 pilot not being perfectly zeroed in, but in this case the gunnery was "way off target." The oncoming troops evidently were not trying to judge accuracy, however; they bolted from the careening trucks just as Andrews' P-38J was lifting off.

That, however, was hardly the end of their ordeal. Heading off on a course for the landing ground at Poltava, still some 250 miles away, Willsie had to contend with a blinding rainstorm pummelling the Lightning with torrents of water. The team flew on instruments for most of the following hour. Excitement at the Russian base was running extremely high after they made a pretty fair landing and the two men managed (with some difficulty) to wriggle their way out of the cockpit. Back slapping, hand shaking and a bit of "whooping it up" went on for about 10 minutes.

In later days it all came to an anti-climax when Maj. Gen. Nathan Twining, who had flown to the eastern terminus of the shuttle operation, presented Flt. Off. Andrews with the coveted Silver Star for "gallantry in action." Lockheed Service Representative "Stumpy" Hollinger, one of the company's more proficient reps in the field, reported that in the course of taking pictures of the two fliers in the P-38J cockpit, they made several attempts to close the canopy to show how cramped it was in the cockpit. Without the urgency of avoiding capture or even death, Willsie and Andrews spent almost 15 minutes trying to get the canopy latched!

Such "hard day at the office" events were not new to Andrews. On June 10, he had participated in a joint P-51 and P-38 combination escort, strafing and dive-bombing attack on Ploesti's often-attacked Romano-Americana oil refinery. As he began his bombing run, he ran into a wall of flak. His aircraft garnered an arsenal of enemy shrapnel, and one engine was knocked out of action. Without wavering, he pressed on to complete his dive and drop the bombs. It was necessary for him to fight his way out through a blanket of enemy fighters before setting course back to Vincenzo airfield, figuratively a million miles away. The surviving Allison V-1710 kept on churning and he made it safely back to Foggia. For his part in that Ploesti mission, he was awarded the Distinguished Flying Cross.

In the face of a radically changed command, the appearance of the P-51D in the ETO, the success of Col. Cass Hough's drop tanks in extending the range of Republic P-47s and Doolittle's desire to reduce the selection of fighter types in the ETO's Eighth Air Force to one – if possible – the fact that the P-38 had proved to be the proverbial workhorse in the MTO had little effect on its destiny. The Mustang-mit-Merlin was the "new boy on the block." And it was truly becoming one of the greatest fighters of all time. Twining was happy to get whatever he could for his tough role in the Mediterranean area, and everybody in the Pacific Theater was beginning to be rewarded with a flow of long-ranging Lightnings with virtually every improvement any pilot desired.

# CHAPTER 15

# From Piccadilly Circus to OVERLORD via POINTBLANK

Following months of interminable training in the Northwest, these senior officers were urgently ordered to take the outfit overseas in September 1943. Lt. Col. Frank James (C.O.) is at center of the group. Maj. Jack S. Jenkins is to his left; Jenkins would succeed James within 6 months. Capt. Dallas "Spider" Webb, far right, had departed for the U.K. more than a year earlier with the 1st Fighter Group in Operation BOLERO. However, his P-38F and five others (plus two B-17Es) had been forced down on the Greenland icecap. "Wabbit" (shown here) was a P-38G-13-LO, a former RAF-ordered Lightning II. (AAF)

A Command Decisions; they must seem like the weight of the world. When a man is faced with making the most critical of such decisions, those who will be affected have to pray that he has the guts and knowledge to make the correct ones. For a multitude of reasons and fate, America's top military and political leaders seemed to encounter the need for making some of the most compelling decisions as the winter holiday season – Christmas and New Year – approached in four consecutive years. In 1941, the Pearl Harbor attack turned America upside down. As the holiday season loomed in 1942, Operation TORCH and all that went with it topped the agenda. The need to launch that invasion literally sabotaged critical long-term plans for operations in Northern Europe. From the viewpoint of the general public in Allied nations, the events of 1943's season were far more subtle. After a year of intense fighting in Northwest Africa, the Allies had finally prevailed over a dedicated enemy and were moving into the struggle for Italy and control of southern Europe. However, what lay ahead meant that some earthshaking decisions had to be made.

The invasion of Italy was destined to be a major undertaking, but with the Operation OVERLORD timetable clocks ticking away, the dramatically important daylight bomber offensive in Europe was not going well or according to plan. Massive changes in command were triggered, starting officially in December 1943, but already in motion a bit earlier. One affected a general who, along with Gen. Arnold, had been a leader in the creation of the daylight bombing concept, Ira Eaker.

Just about everything changed in the Mediterranean Theater with formation of the Mediterranean Allied Air Forces. Gen. Arnold created the United States Strategic Air Forces in Europe (USAFE, soon to be reidentified as USSTAF), putting Gen. Carl Spaatz in charge of that. His precise aim was to maintain effective control over something called Operation POINTBLANK, or more technically the Combined Bomber Offensive (CBO).

Nobody could overlook the jobs done by Gen. Doolittle in the Pacific and in the North Africa/MTO arena, and he promptly replaced Gen. Eaker as commanding general of the Eighth Air Force. Eaker, after a short command coordination period, moved to Italy to command the relatively new MAAF that had

been under the RAF's ACM Tedder for a month. Maj. Gen. Nathan Twining became the new CG of the recently created Fifteenth Air Force.

Although the reasons for all of these changes are multitudinous and complex, the Eighth Air Force was attempting to prove out a doctrine of daylight bombing that was dear to the heart of Arnold. The Royal Air Force had attempted daylight bombing much earlier, but the results convinced them that the cost was too great. Germany's *Luftwaffe* had enjoyed even less success, albeit in the face of better odds.

Something that nobody ever seems to readily acknowledge is the fact that the AAF did have suitable long-range fighters available to escort the heavy bombers in the autumn of 1942, and they were based in the United Kingdom. If the Lockheed P-38 Lightnings had enjoyed the same break-in period accorded the Republic P-47 Thunderbolts (in 1943), it is easy to speculate that the disasters of Regensburg and Schweinfurt (and others) might have been averted. Those same airplanes and pilots went to the rescue in the North African crisis in a totally unexpected move that did not really have long-term planning behind it. As previously noted, just the air filter and logistics problems alone were to have a great impact on P-38 (and other aircraft) performance in the MTO. Even with such handicaps, the Lightnings prevailed.

With no deviation from the facts, it must be acknowledged that when the P-38s arrived in the United Kingdom in July-August 1942, the aircraft easily demonstrated that, regardless of pilot proficiency, the combat radius of action was at least 350 miles. Radius of action, it must be remembered, provides for 10 to 15 minutes of high-power combat over the mission route. That was more than double the radius attributed to Curtiss P-40s, also with external fuel. Republic P-47Cs and Ds did not exist. Something less than 200 of the B models had been delivered to the AAF, and it was certainly anything but combat worthy.

Twelve long months later – eternity in a war – when the 4th, 56th and 78th Fighter Groups had been supplied with the best Thunderbolts available, they could hardly fly a mission beyond the shoreline of continental Europe. When, in early August 1943, the Ben Kelsey/Cass Hough-directed Air Technical Section developed the metal 75-gallon and impregnated-paper 108-gallon pressurized drop tanks for use on the Thunderbolt, it was as if the P-47 had finally been unleashed. Even then, they usually could not penetrate more than 85-100 miles over the Continent. But it made a great difference . . . a remarkable difference. . . in B-24 and B-17 losses on big raids. Lightnings were capable of going in another 150 miles and more . . . a year earlier! Another 6 to 7 months would elapse before the first P-51Bs would even begin to match the P-38H range capability, as 1943 ended.

Soon after the disastrous raids of August 1943, the call went out to bring in something that could escort the bombers, mediums and heavies, over Occupied France and the German fatherland, wherever they were needed. As in 1942, there was but a single choice. Maj. Gen. William Kepner had just replaced Maj. Gen. Hunter as CG of the VIIIth Fighter Command on August 3.

Half a world away, the 55FG, way out at McChord Field in the state of Washington, had cooled its collective heels for a year. One squadron had been pulled out and sent to the Pacific Theater in 1942 and a second of three squadrons had been shipped to North Africa to aid in rebuilding the battered 14FG. New squadrons had been assigned, of course, to replace the reassigned 37th and 54th Fighter Squadrons. Just three short weeks after Kepner assumed command of VIIIth Fighter Command, the 55FG shipped out and headed for Europe via Camp Kilmer, NJ. Can anybody argue that the 55th was not ready to go to Europe back in 1942? The squadrons that went

to the Southwest Pacific and Northwest Africa had just been part of a well-oiled machine commanded by Lt. Col. Frank James. Suddenly jerked upright, the 55FG was being thrown into a very tough war against a mighty and determined and growing *Luftwaffe*.

If Gen. Frank Hunter had not had the good sense to let Col. Ben Kelsey and Lt. Col. Cass Hough set up the Air Technical Section at Bovingdon soon after their arrival in the U.K. in 1942, things might have been much different over Europe in the fall and winter of 1943. Neither Republic nor Air Materiel Command had developed anything that even resembled a combat-useful external fuel tank. Col. Hough and Capt. Bob Shafer conceived and developed a 108-gallon tank that was to become a standard for the P-47s and P-51s until Germany surrendered (and later). Mustangs usually carried two of the 108-gallon paper tanks and Thunderbolts carried anything from one 75-gallon "Curtiss or Bell"-type central tank to three of the big paper tanks. (It must be noted that in the Pacific Theater, the later P-47N model fighters were mostly equipped with two 165-gallon Lockheed P-38-type tanks, although the pylon mounts used on the Thunderbolts were not nearly as clean as the pylons employed since 1942 on the Lightnings.)

And how was it that World War I ace Frank O'D. Hunter decided to charge forward with development of the paper external tank for the P-47? The man who knows the story from its day of inception, Cass Hough, flatly stated that he told Gen. Hunter that the P-47 was never going to do the job (as a useful escort fighter) unless it had more range. The mustachioed veteran quipped, "Figure out a way to do it." In somewhat less than 60 days from that initial order, the first 75-gallon metal tanks (pressurized) and the pressurized 108-gallon paper tanks were being flown in operations over France and the Low Countries.

Indicative of much that was wrong with some command decisions was a teletype received by Gen. Doolittle almost exactly one year after those first tanks were used operationally. It said, among other things, "these tanks (tested by Air Materiel Command) are unfit for operational use." Thunderbolt pilots had already dropped tens of thousands of them over the European countryside! A thousand kudos for the likes of Hunter, Hough and Shafer.

Although the Combined Bomber Offensive (POINTBLANK) truly had its beginnings as of June 1943, it really could not become a real CBO until the Fifteenth Air Force was established in the MTO. That air force could not be considered as "big" in any sense; as of the first of January it consisted of no more than six heavy bomber (HB) groups and four fighter groups. Four of the bomber groups flew B-17s and two were structured around B-24s. The three veteran groups flew P-38Gs and Hs, while the 325th Fighter Group flew razorback "Jugs." That was it! Any day that the 15th could field 250 fighters was most likely considered an exceptional day. And in the eyes of many, it was a toss-up as to whether more fighters or more HBs were actually bombing the Ploesti oil refineries.

Concurrently, the Eighth Air Force had 26 HB groups operational on the same New Year's Day. When the 20FG had been declared operational just a couple of days earlier, Kepner's VIIIth FC was able to provide a maximum force of 11 fighter groups. However, only two of those 11 groups were flying Lightnings, and they had far more H models than new J models. Even though power-boosted ailerons and dive flaps were yet to come, the P-38Js could count on having greater horsepower and fewer limitations than the earlier type because the new intercooler setup kept the carburetor heat rise down to acceptable levels.

Pressures on the commanders had been extreme since August 1943, but that was about to get worse. On January 5, 1944, an Eighth Air Force report – probably generated by the

Operational Research Section that was formed in the previous October – declared that "the bombing program against Germany will be threatened unless steps are taken to reduce the enemy's fighter force, which has been increasing in strength . . ." It presented a most dismal view.

On the very next day, Gen. James Doolittle assumed command of that air force, replacing (officially) Gen. Eaker. He soon found that the figurative and actual flow of blood had hardly been stemmed; it was obvious that he and Gen. Kepner were going to have to improve the bomber escort situation by some massive factor. Doolittle had barely unpacked when he was fully briefed on the critical issues at hand. Tremendous losses of heavy bombers as in October 1943 would doom the bomber offensive unless fighter escorts could be provided.

The Eighth Air Force raid on Schweinfurt on October 14th proved to be the climactic episode. Unescorted and penetrating deep into Germany, a force of 230 Boeing B-17Fs and Gs attacked the important ball bearing manufacturing center. Having stubbornly refused to acknowledge reports that the *Luftwaffe* was becoming more formidable, VIIIth Bomber Command still believed the formation defense concept was valid. Nearly 300 of the HBs had been launched, but some had to abort for various reasons and some were lost on the way to the target. No fewer than 60 of the bombers were shot down by enemy fighters and flak.

The biggest daylight bombing raid was launched on December 30 when no fewer than 658 Fortresses and Liberators attacked their target at Ludwigshafen. This time things went a bit differently. Fighter escort was provided by VIIIth FC and IXth FC, using P-47s, P-51Bs and P-38Hs, with only the P-51s and P-38s able to provide target area escort. The new 20FG provided its escort protection for the first time, but only in the penetration and withdrawal phases. Thunderbolts, still short on range, provided escort duties no further than Compiegne, France. While some 28 heavy bombers and 13 fighters were lost, the loss ratio showed a substantial reduction.

After a short overnight rest, the Lightnings and Mustangs were off to Bordeaux, France, in one of the longest Eighth Air Force missions to that date. (That mission will be described in detail later.) Total losses to fighters and flak were reported at about 5 percent, a big improvement over those missions flown in the autumn months. Following moderately sized attacks launched on the 4th and 7th of January, in which the heavies sustained losses of 3 percent or less, a maximum effort was called for on the 11th. More than 650 bombers took off, but with the weather deteriorating rapidly, only about 570 of them ever found the three targets. Fighter cover was to be provided by the two P-38 groups and the initial Ninth

Air Force P-51B outfit (354FG) assigned to that role.

Almost 50 Lightnings of the new 20FG left Kings Cliffe, located rather a long distance from the coastline, and ran into thick weather just minutes after takeoff. At 34,000 feet they were still in thick cloud cover, and the leader ordered that the mission be scrubbed. They all returned to base. Only one squadron of the 55FG P-38s managed to find any of the bomb groups. As a result, something less than 50 Mustangs were available to protect the force of bombers that was headed for Oschersleben. Of the 174 HBs sent to that target, 34 were downed by a furious onslaught of German fighters. In fact, the *Luftwaffe* had evidently gathered about 500 interceptors of all kinds in the reasonably good weather prevailing in the east. That number of fighters was almost equal to the entire mass of operational P-47s, P-38s and P-51s available in Gen. Kepner's VIIIth FC.

Nearly concurrent estimates provided by intelligence sources estimated that the Germans could field no fewer than 1,500 interceptors against the Eighth Air Force. It would be folly to overlook the fact that many of the available *Jagdgeschwader* and *Zerstörergeschwader* aircraft could engage, land and (after replenishing fuel and ammunition) attack the retreating bombers. That was particularly true on the 11th, since most of the returning aircraft encountered 90-mph headwinds. American bombers lost that day amounted to 60 aircraft, including the first Consolidated B-24 Pathfinder types used in that capacity. It was bad enough that about 10 percent of the initial force was lost to enemy weapons, but many other aircraft were so badly damaged that they never flew again after return to base. A recall order had been transmitted, but only a portion of the bombers and fighters heeded the call. Just one squadron (out of two groups) of P-38s managed to join up with bombers to defend over a target area; it was very fortunate for the Oschersleben bombers that the Eighth Air

*BELOW LEFT: Lockheed pioneered in new manufacturing methods in 1941-42. Here workers were installing a complete Allison power "egg" on a P-38H in the Burbank factory. (LAC)*

*BELOW RIGHT: After settling in at Nuthhampstead, England, the 55FG was equipped with new P-38Hs in September/October 1943. Lt. Col. Jenkins was, by then, Deputy C. O., leading operational missions starting in October. He named his airplane "Texas Ranger" within days of its arrival. His maintenance crew joined Jenkins and his airplane for this publicity photo. (Col. Jack Jenkins)*

*This inflight plan view of a P-38J-10-LO reveals a non-standard feature, one round item near each wingtip. Stains aft of each one indicate that they were fuel tank caps for the leading edge fuel cells. This aircraft, then, was probably the test airplane used for fit and operation of the new tanks. Production-type tanks each carried 55 gallons of fuel. (AAF)*

Force had the support of IXth FC and their new P-51Bs, or losses might have been significantly higher. There was one great compensating situation: large numbers of the bombers that did get to their assigned targets pressed their attacks to the extreme and bombing accuracy was outstanding.

Weather conditions over the Continent were dismal for many days after that painful day; in combination with the arrival of a new CG, and because of USAAF losses, no more missions were launched at German targets in the Fatherland until January 24. Forecasts of weather conditions proved to be faulty, and only 56 of the 857 heavy bombers dispatched that morning managed to strike an alternate target.

As pointed out previously, command decisions were momentous in that January period. With Doolittle in place, Gen. Carl Spaatz moved into command of USSAFE at WIDEWING, a cryptogram for Bushy Park, and on January 16, Gen. Dwight Eisenhower became commander, actually Supreme Commander, of the AEF. Evidently based on fast-growing production rates of the AAF's newest operational fighter and on the logic of equipping the 15 planned/existing fighter groups with a single type, the decision came down to re-equip *all* VIIIth FC groups with North American P-51s. The plan provided for transfer of all Lockheed P-38s and Republic P-47s to the rapidly expanding Ninth Air Force. Lockheed's real winner, the P-38L model, was not even coming off the production line at that time; the few P-38J-25-LO fighters – actually production proofing models of the P-38L – that were turned out did not even equal one month's production of P-51s at Inglewood, and the first of the J-25s and L-1s were not ready for delivery until June 1944.

But by that fateful January 24 date, P-51D production was under way at Inglewood and at Dallas, Texas, with deliveries totalling about 375 airplanes a month and accelerating. Total production of P-38J-25-LOs amounted to no more than 210 airframes. Here was the most complex fighter in America's inventory being produced in one single factory. Even the ultra-simple Grumman F4F-4 was being produced at two locations; yet some of the top management people in the War Production Board were making decisions to produce aircraft that no rational combat commander wanted. At that same time, it took nearly 13 months – in the heat of all the war drama that surrounded these men – to incorporate the newly proven dive flap into production P-38s along with leading edge wing tanks and the powered ailerons. The AAF was still accepting deliveries of Curtiss RA-25A Helldivers (R stood for Restricted) and Vultee A-35B Vengeance dive bombers right up to the day that the first P-38L was accepted by that same air force.

Who wanted RA-25As? Who could possibly have wanted the Vultee A-35s, even as trainers? Just as the Battle of the Bulge burst on American troops, the first Consolidated TBY-2 Seawolfs were being delivered (received with great reluctance). Vought had been struggling from pre-war days to develop and produce that torpedo-bomber without success. After some 18 months had slipped away, Consolidated-Vultee contracted to build hundreds in a brand new factory, but another 14 months went by the board before the first one was delivered. By that time it was obsolete. Finally, after high-level vacuity had prevailed for years, a second-source for P-38s rolled out its first Lightning in January 1945! Six long, frustration-filled years after the XP-38 was being readied for that all-important first flight, the WPB finally cancelled the C-V Vengeance production at Nashville in mid-1944 so that P-38Ls could be produced there. It was a sad commentary on the efficiency of the WPB in time of crisis.

Obviously there were many command decisions that not only prolonged the war, they might have even lost the war for the Allies.

The month of October 1943 had been an especially significant one in the chronological history of the Lockheed Lightning. A small selection of fighter groups equipped with the P-38 were being rushed into operation with Maj. Gen. William Kepner's VIIIth Fighter Command. Why two of the four P-38 groups finally integrated into the ETO command had languished in the U.S.A. while the need for long-range escorts was so overwhelming for months on end may never be known. It was a tragic oversight. At the very extreme, there were no more than 150 operational P-38s in England in the final three months of 1943. Even at that, half of those only became operational after Christmas Day. When viewed in the clear light of day, the great efforts put forth by the likes of Tommy Hitchcock (Merlin P-51s), the Rolls-Royce engineers at Hucknall, and drop tank entrepreneurs Hough and Shafer at Bovingdon were the equal of last-minute place kicks in some championship football games. They made the difference between victory and a failure to gain air superiority, perhaps even defeat.

Gen. Kepner's "hand's on" leadership gave him what was probably the best analytical viewpoint of the entire Eighth Air Force support problems. In his opinion, P-38s did a superior job, one that no other fighter available to the Allies was

capable of performing in a period of feverish pre-invasion assaults on German's industrial might. There can be no doubt that the crucial period for success or failure of strategic bombing in Europe – at least for daylight precision bombing – was in the year preceding June 6, 1944.

However, there was only an initial 3-month period late in 1943 when target area fighter cover could be provided, and the only aircraft that could provide that coverage in the ranks of the Eighth Air Force was the P-38H. That meant that the entire load fell on a single fighter group, the 55th, with an absolute maximum strength (never available) of 75 aircraft. Seventy-five fighters in the entire United Kingdom that could protect the heavy bombers on deep penetration raids over Germany! Even when the Mustangs of the 354FG of the new Ninth Air Force joined them in the first week of December, it hardly doubled their numbers. The 354th was not up to full strength at that time. During the same weeks, the P-38s of the untested 20FG came on line to help carry the load. In a worst-case situation, the defensive fighters might find themselves facing odds of up to 10 to 1. The wonder is that far more bombers and protective cover fighters were not lost.

In the meantime, the Thunderbolt was managing to stretch its range so that intermediate and withdrawal coverage could be provided with great effect.[1] Not to detract at all from the role played by the P-51D Mustangs, it must be pointed out that Operation POINTBLANK was fast becoming history on the day that OVERLORD was launched. From that day on, much of the responsibility for destruction of the *Luftwaffe's* supply of fighters shifted to the Ninth Air Force. As a result, the attacks became more tactical than strategic.

Hardly less important to the AAF in October 1943 was the introduction into service of the significantly revised P-38J model. Far more horsepower was available upon introduction of the core-type intercoolers, and literally dozens of smaller, but nevertheless important, changes were incorporated in production. All of that was combined with multiple assembly lines that were essentially "automated." On average, beginning in October the production rate was intrinsically doubled. The WPB stated that the "Lockheed System" became a model for sub-contracted manufacture of a complex assembly.

According to all the best plans "of mice and men," the

Lightnings that should have gone to Europe with the 55FG and the 20FG would have been P-38J versions that were equipped with Allison V-1710F-17 engines rated at 1425 bhp and a War Emergency Power rating of 1600 bhp. However, it was necessary to manufacture 600 airplanes in a bastardized version that was never intended for production. That was the P-38H model, essentially featuring the G airframe fitted with the new F-17 engines. Because the wing leading edge intercoolers were even hard pressed to handle the power of the Allison F-10 engines used in the G model, there was a maximum power restriction of 1150 bhp arbitrarily applied to the H airplanes.

It is easy to see that a total of 550 bhp could not be used with any degree of safety, and to use the WEP rating exposed the pilot to destructive detonation in the engines, the product of uncontrolled heat rise at the carburetors. (More than one pilot, including Col. Hough, learned through experience that the power restrictions were artificially low. If the aircraft and engines were properly maintained – a function of ground crew capabilities – far more power could be "pulled" without suffering engine failures.) Externally, these Model 422-81-20 (P-38H) airplanes were identical to P-38Gs (Model 322-68 and 222-68 series). Lockheed was compelled to produce the P-38Hs between May and December 1943 because of delivery delays involving core-type intercooler radiators.

With the introduction of the P-38J-10-LO version in October, following delivery of 210 of the J-5-LO airplanes, the external configuration of the Lightning remained essentially unchanged (except for reconnaissance and night fighter versions of the basic airframe) until production was terminated at the end of the war. The main identifying feature was the flat-plate windshield composed of armor-glass. Considering the widespread deployment of the Lightning up to introduction of P-38J-10-LOs in October, coupled with the fact that production deliveries had begun more than three long years earlier, it is almost impossible to believe that only 2,719 Lightnings in the fighter configuration had been manufactured. By the time production came to an end about 21 months later, Lockheed would have produced about 8,500 of the fighters out of a grand total of 9,925 airframes stemming from the original Model 22. (That fighter total does not include photo-recon versions or the P-322 trainer models converted from the British-French 322 airframes.)

The October event that allowed Lockheed to step up production so dramatically was a massive conversion of all Lockheed-Vega production facilities, especially those at the original Lockheed facility that was to be known, henceforth, as

---

1. *Considering the fact that General Kepner had great hopes for the P-47s that he favored, it seems incongruous that the Thunderbolt reached its zenith just as he and Doolittle decided to concentrate on the Mustang for virtually exclusive use.*

Plant B. Everything not related to the P-38 program was moved out, with final production of B-17s, Lodestar versions, B-37s and the PV series (for the most part) being accomplished at the large, modern, more integrated Vega factory that became logically identified as Plant A-1. Since there were several Plant B fabrication, test and delivery buildings located at Lockheed Air Terminal north of the east-west runway, the sprawling main facility laying about two miles to the east of the airport was identified as Plant B-1. All of the allied buildings at L.A.T. were then identified as Plant B-6. (Lockheed had some other facilities scattered about the state, and many other subcontractors were involved in Lockheed production programs.)

One of Lockheed's major subcontractors on the P-38J program was Consolidated-Vultee's Nashville (Tenn.) plant. Even as A-35B Vengeance attack-bomber production continued there, Lightning fuselage-wing centersection production became a major effort. That makes it even more difficult to understand the ultra-late transition to full P-38L production at Nashville. If the people in Washington and Dayton failed to recognize that P-38 production requirements far outstripped any need for A-35s, it was either because of inattention or plain bad judgment. (Investigation of other possible reasons was never initiated.) C-V built only 113 Lightnings!

Production of all types based on the Model 14 design ended in May, and the records reveal that the AAF continued to receive some RB-37 bombers into mid-1943, despite the fact that the aircraft was never successful as an operational type in combat. Although Ventura and B-34 production had ceased, the Navy's PV-1 (and, eventually, a revised PV-2 version) patrol bomber continued in outside production at Plant B-1. Some versions of the basic Model 18 Lodestar continued in production for a limited time.

C Over in the ETO, tremendous pressure mounted to get the Lightnings on combat operations in support of the strategic bomber force. By October 14, only the 55FG was in place with enough aircraft to be considered fully operational. The group, under command of Col. Frank James and his deputy, Lt. Col. Jack Jenkins, was committed to support a huge effort of maximum intensity against a far distant objective – Schweinfurt. As fate would have it, rain fell heavily at Nuthampstead that morning and orders came down to scrub the mission. James and Jenkins were terribly depressed when they learned how badly the mission had gone that day.

It is not difficult to understand why headquarters would frequently scrub a mission for one or more groups scheduled to participate. Forming up – as the formation assembly operation was known – was difficult enough even in clear weather if conditions created long-lasting contrails. Rain and/or a heavy cloud cover could create chaos. Mid-air collisions became numerous, and problems multiplied when squadrons, groups or wings became intermixed during the "forming up" process.

Poor to terrible weather over Great Britain and over the Continent, especially in winter months, had a tremendous impact on accurate bombing. And it did little to assist fighter pilots in rendezvousing with the bombers. While weather ranked well up the scale of problems facing VIIIth FC, combat range was probably an even greater problem. Just consider the problems of cruise control, low-drag shackles, fuel feed at high altitudes, positive drop tank separation and an adequate supply of drop tanks. Lockheed alone among all manufacturers had taken the problem seriously as early as 1941. The tank shapes proved to be so good that they were still being used on jet fighters up to the time of the Korean War. Evidently the system developed for fuel delivery at very high altitudes was near perfect. The volume of Unsatisfactory Reports (URs) submitted on the system was minimal.

Just what was *combat range* in World War II? *Combat radius* of action? Range capability? Did range figures in the Pacific Theater dovetail with those encountered in the ETO? Given comparable pilot capabilities, any matchup of the P47C/D, P-51B/D and P-38H/J airplanes, the Thunderbolts were unmatched champions for the "short-range" crown, and that remained a truism even after they were adapted to carry one or more 108-gallon drop tanks.

For the record, Materiel Command and AAF Procurement Office officials under the command of Gen. Oliver P. Echols drew up plans to absolutely terminate Thunderbolt production in the final quarter of 1944 in the backwash of Operation OVERLORD. They considered P-47D/M range capabilities wholly inadequate for the Pacific Theater of Operations. (As of their determination date, they were dealing almost exclusively with P-47D-25-RE/RA model aircraft equipped with greater internal fuel capacity and up to three external fuel tanks. For comparison at that time, they used the P-51D-25 and P-38L-1/P-38J-25 aircraft as logical comparative aircraft. Early P-38J/P-51Bs had already shown an 1150+ mile ETO capability, and combat range in the Pacific was generally less demanding. Under ETO conditions, a P-47D with one 108-gallon glue-impregnated-paper tank demonstrated a simulated combat range (under U.S. conditions in the Deep South) of 860 miles.

The gross recommendation was to limit that target in the ETO to 800 miles, interjecting some allowances for weather, pilot capabilities, and combat factors. (They did not treat other types differently.) Total internal fuel in that model was 370 gallons as opposed to 305 gallons in P-47s through the D-23-RE/RA production run (all "razor-backs").

In general terms, combat range was virtually double the combat radius figure, of course. Takeoff was on internal fuel; climb to 25,000 feet and cruise to target area was at medium to high cruise power; tanks were dropped when empty (hopefully); they allowed for two combats for a total of 20 minutes at high power; return to base was at low to medium power settings; and, finally, there was a 30-minute reserve in the tanks. Flight to and from the target was considered to be under full formation conditions.

When the 4FG made their first mission as far as Aachen, which is roughly 280 miles from Debden airfield, their P-47s carried about 100 gallons of fuel in bulky, unpressurized belly tanks. Using that external fuel, they could not fly above 23,000 feet. On the July 28 effort, the group did not drop the belly tanks at the coastline of Europe (an adopted procedure), thereby eking out an extraordinary 150-round-trip miles over the best they could expect without external tankage. It had been a real gamble to go that far, but they succeeded. VIIIth Fighter Command generally recommended that combat radius for P-47s be limited to about 240 miles when using a pressurized 108-gallon centerline tank. That was far more practical when dealing with pilots displaying varied talents. Nobody relished the idea of losing numerous $105,000 Thunderbolts on the basis of fuel exhaustion. Another year would pass before improved P-47Ds with greater internal fuel capability and two

*With Col. Cass Hough at the aircraft controls and Col. Don Ostrander doing the sighting, this P-38J-10-LO Droop Snoot bomber performed the original test drop, using small practice bombs. Two accompanying P-38J fighters (with Col. Kelsey believed to be at the controls of one) made their drops by visual formation light signals from the leader. In the early days, those signal lights were not considered satisfactory. Since Air Materiel Command was an "outsider" in the Droop Snoot program, there was no coordinated plan for recording exactly how many aircraft received the modification kit installations. (Col. Cass Hough)*

or three drop tanks would be venturing (or at least have the need to venture) as far as Kiel and Stuttgart. Mustangs would be travelling that far with some regularity, and P-38Ls would be capable of lugging a 1,000-pound bomb at least that far. Those late model Lightnings were more likely to be limited by a pilot's durability on missions lasting more than nine or ten long hours.

Battle conditions in the ETO and MTO were, in general, not dissimilar. And yet, the methods used to solve range problems in the VIIIth and VXth FCs were somewhat different. However, in those two theaters of operation, every commander worked on the assumption that there would be at least 20 minutes of combat at maximum power at the higher altitudes. A P-38H might burn approximately 320 gallons of fuel per hour at the highest power settings, translating to about 107 gallons in 20 minutes of air-to-air combat. A razorback Thunderbolt would likely use 80 gallons during that same combat time.

But even those suppositions could easily be rendered

invalid. If there was a running battle along the withdrawal route, or even sporadic battles, range capabilities might not be endangered, but any lengthy battle that tended to carry the aircraft eastward could create a serious problem for the fighter pilots. Few seem to have taken notice that it was a P-38 fighter group – the 20th – that was located farthest of all from the coastline, something on the order of 80 miles. That meant that some P-47 and P-51 groups enjoyed up to a 140-mile combat range advantage over those pilots flying out of Kings Cliffe. At the end of a lengthy mission, it was quite likely that 20FG airplanes were well represented at a vast assortment of fighter and bomber airfields several miles from home.

D At just about the time Gen. Doolittle moved into his headquarters digs in the U.K., Lt. Col. Jack S. Jenkins (as deputy commander of the 55th Fighter Group at Nuthampstead) was rather emphatically elaborating on the subject of combat range to the commander of the 67th Fighter Wing. In fact he touched on the very subject of simulated combat range testing in the continental United States, employing specialized test pilots to conduct the tests. He emphasized that such tests were not at all relevant. The reasons: VIIIth Fighter Command was dealing with a mixture of experienced and new or inadequately trained pilots flying together under the pressure of knowing that they might well be under attack not just once during a mission but perhaps several times. They were also flying in weather conditions that they rarely encountered in America. Weather, deteriorating late in the day, along with rapidly dwindling fuel supplies, battle damage, wounds and failing equipment, conspired to degrade the decision-making abilities of those pilots.

Jenkins summed up his commentary in a rather pithy document:

". . . it is the opinion of the experienced pilots in the Lightning groups that with favorable – or at least not unfavorable – winds, we can successfully execute a target cover mission to (distant) coastal targets, such as Kiel (Germany) or Bordeaux (France), each some 400 miles from the English coast (actually close to 475 miles from the base, Auth.). However, we take a dim view of doing target support at a greater distance than our maximum range (sic: actually, radius of action) if the target is well inland and enemy air superiority is certain."

A typical P-38H mission format and the operational characteristics of the aircraft must be thoroughly understood before any comparison of fighter capabilities has any validity. With two of the 150-gallon drop tanks installed (but with actual standard capacity of 165-gallons which helps to explain apparent errors in the data), external and internal fuel capacity for P-38H airplanes was 600 gallons (630). The commanders allowed for expenditure of 40 gallons for takeoff and landing (using external fuel only). They also planned on burning 107 gallons during a 20-minute period of combat at military power after reaching the target rendezvous, using fuel from the drop tanks during the penetration phase. All combat, of course, would be on internal fuel after the drop tanks were jettisoned. Tanks were usually dropped from P-38s at a predetermined location or as soon as the fuel was depleted, unless they clashed with the enemy. Then the tanks had to go, no matter how much fuel remained in them.

All fighters were extremely sluggish at or above 30,000 feet with external drop tanks in place. It was considered *de rigueur* to jettison tanks at any altitude with the appearance of hostile fighters. In fact, it was foolhardy not to drop them in the face of combat. After the allowances made for takeoff/landing, climb to altitude and formation flight to the target, only 260 gallons remained available for combat (20 minutes)

ABOVE: When Cols. Cass Hough and Don Ostrander conceived the idea of using the P-38 as a "medium/heavy bomber" in 1943, they went to Lockheed Overseas Corporation's (LOC) base at Langford Lodge to get their ideas translated into hardware. George McCutcheon did most of the design work. A wooden mockup was fabricated to aid in layout of accommodation and equipment. LOC constructed a wood and metal aerodynamic mockup of the Droop Snoot nose, mounting it on a P-38H-5-LO for flight testing because there was no wind tunnel available. Airplane AC42-67086 proved that the aerodynamic shape was nearly perfect. Work began immediately on fabrication of an airframe modification kit for a prototype. (LOC)

BELOW: Prior to testing, the prototype P-38J Droop Snoot airplane was displayed for interested officials at Langford Lodge. As planned, the Droop-Snoot lead airplane and certain of the following fighters would carry up to 4,000 pounds of bombs to continental targets. All bomb aiming could be handled by one or two leader aircraft with Norden bomb sights and qualified bombardiers. The concept involved true carpet bombing techniques. Carrying one 2,000-pound bomb and a 310-gallon drop tank, a P-38L could handle most long-range missions normally assigned to B-17s and B-24s. Instead of 10 men in each aircraft, there was only one. Even doubling the number of aircraft involved provided a tremendous reduction in possible casualties. Because of the speed, interception was more difficult, and when the bombs and tanks were dropped, they could provide their own defensive force. (LOC)

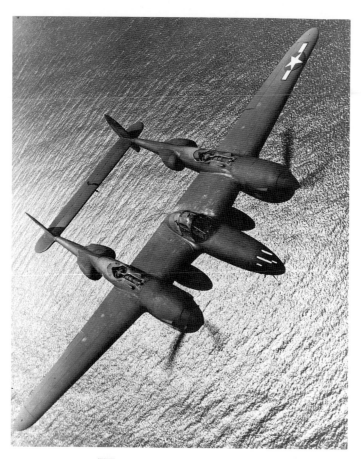

By November 1943, final deliveries of painted P-38Js were coming to an end. Unpainted P-38s were about 60 pounds lighter, on average, and many man-hours were saved. All Lightnings after the P-38J-5-LO production was history had optically flat external windshields. (LAC)

remain in the target rendezvous area for anything in excess of 20 minutes.

Everything was different, however, on a 300-mile mission to Bremen. Most of the flight was over land . . . territory that was defensible with relative ease. The Lightning pilots and heavy bomber crews had to fight every mile of the way through the target area during the penetration time and during withdrawal, warding off enemy attacks on the way home with some frequency. That was especially true if engine failures or combat damage increased the numbers of "lame ducks." Perfectly good aircraft sometimes had to be ditched in the English Channel because of absolutely dry fuel tanks.

Among World War II targets, the seaport town of Bordeaux – mostly associated with production of wines – far south of the industrialized areas such as the Ruhr and Saarland was rarely even thought of as a prime target. Distance and location were the keys to that thinking. A mission against Bordeaux necessitated a flight of close to 475 miles from the famous Dover cliffs, and that was after climbing away from Nuthampstead and completing their assembly operation. The base itself, not far from Cambridge, was about 80 air miles from the Dover coast. In a fair estimate, the combat radius of action on a Bordeaux mission was 550 miles.[2]

According to their calculations, they reckoned that was something more than 50 miles beyond the P-38H one-way flight capability. Enemy opposition on the first Bordeaux mission was only about 5 percent of what might be expected on a Bremen run, and Lt. Col. Jenkins was thankful for that small favor. "It would be impossible to complete one of those Bordeaux missions if we meet one-fourth the opposition that we meet at Bremen," he noted.

"We stayed in the Bordeaux area for 15 minutes on December 31," he commented, "and then (the 55FG) withdrew along the bomber route." Some of the pilots dropped their tanks soon after the arrival at the coastal target, and they were forced to cut down their power to minimum cruise in order to return to England. (Long-range cruise control data were sadly lacking, and training in the science of cruise control was minimal. Back in the summer of 1942, some of the pilots on the BOLERO mission – especially the men in Tomcat Yellow flight – found that they had burned fuel at a far greater rate than expected. Worse, they may not have found out why. Even the specialized ATC Flight Test Unit was not yet set up to concentrate on cruise control until nearly two years later.) Jenkins mentioned that on the final mission of 1943, the 55th crossed 325 miles of occupied France during the withdrawal phase. If five or six aggressive *Luftwaffe* pilots had attacked, he is certain that half of his force would have been lost because of fuel exhaustion.

At least one thing could have been done to alleviate the problem of fuel shortage on the Bordeaux cover missions and probably on the Kiel missions, but it would have possibly generated two or three other problems. Their P-38Hs could have been fitted with one Lockheed-type 300-gallon drop tank in place of one of the normal external tanks. However, the Fifteenth Air Force P-38 pilots had not, as of year end, flown any missions from Foggia, assignments on which they were to become the European pioneers in the use of those capacious 300(+)-gallon drop tanks.

P-38Hs were powered by the high-horsepower F-17 Allisons

and the return flight to the British Isles. Hardly anyone could feel comfortable with only 153 gallons of fuel remaining to cope with the known and the unknown. Every pilot had to anticipate the possibility of some Nazi fighters "bouncing" his formation, or that it might become necessary to protect some straggler or a limping bomber from certain destruction. Under the circumstances, it was necessary to plan for a return trip at cruise power where 120 gallons of gasoline would be burned. That converted to 1 hour and 16 minutes (maximum) at 210 mph (indicated) at about 20,000 feet, or roughly 350 miles.

In actual tests conducted by the 55th Fighter Group, pilots demonstrated that they could climb to 25,000 feet and go out 450 miles from the English coastline on external fuel (after takeoff and climb on internal supplies) before the drop tanks ran dry. With no simulated combat, the return flight was accomplished on about 153 gallons at cruise settings (no climb), or about 50 percent of the external supply used on the outbound leg. That was mostly attributable to reduced drag (no tanks) and lower weight.

As Jenkins had indicated, there was a significant difference in missions that were mostly flown over the seas – such as a mission to Kiel – and one that was predominantly over Nazi-occupied territory, where numerous airfields could be located and there would, logically, be many flak sites. As of January 1944, he believed there would be little chance of interception by fighters, even though the target might be more than 400 miles from the British shoreline. Even under that circumstance, he believed that no group should be expected to

---

2. *There are definite differences in reported and measured distances that can't be readily explained. Straightline map distances, not allowing for deviations from that course, exceed reported distances by 75 miles or more, each way. Also, distance from the coast is nearly irrelevant, especially if a group was operating from Kings Cliffe, far inland, to a target in eastern Germany.*

targeted for the newer J models, and the limitations attributed to the leading edge intercoolers should not have proven to be any handicap to pulling more power during takeoff and early climb mode. (The wing intercoolers did contribute to an excessive heat rise at the carburetors when rated power was pulled at high altitude. Cass Hough found from experience that redline restrictions were often arbitrary. It was his contention that, for the most part, they could be exceeded for short periods without undue concern.) Even with trepidation about the P-38 beginning to fester in the ETO, the 55FG men did not seem to be victims of that plague in 1943. They might well have proven to be the ideal outfit to try out the 300-gallon tanks in that asymmetrical configuration.

It is likely that nobody suggested the use of those larger tanks at the time, and perhaps there was no real supply of them available. Fortunately, Bordeaux was not the sort of target that had to be bombed repeatedly, i.e., on a weekly basis. An even greater asset was the limited number of *Luftwaffe* defensive fighters in that area.

E Combat range problems really began to evaporate rapidly as the new year dawned. Newer bubble canopy Thunderbolts had an abundant supply of the Hough/Shafer paper drop tanks by then, and the installation of bulky, but useful, Republic bomb/tank pylons on the wings permitted late-model P-47Ds to carry up to three drop tanks. As early as March 1944, Lightnings and the new Mustangs were venturing afar to Berlin on escort duty.

But brand new aircraft are rarely assimilated into combat without some kind of serious difficulty arising. Bubble canopy Mustangs and Thunderbolts needed extra sideplate area for stability. Both types soon had dorsal finds added. Model J Lightnings were a great departure from all previous P-38s, hundreds of changes having been incorporated. With the ability to extract 1600 bhp War Emergency Power (WEP) from the Allisons, poor maintenance could not be tolerated. Coupled with the fuel problem that apparently existed in the U.K., faulty spark plugs and problems that had not appeared in stateside testing, V-1710F-17 failures suddenly skyrocketed. That just happened to coincide with the arrival of many new and inexperienced pilots from the U.S.A. It took several months to correct such problems, and the Eighth Air Force couldn't wait. Gen. Doolittle had made his decision to replace Thunderbolts and Lightnings with the ever increasing numbers of Merlin-powered Mustangs.

However, in wartime it is possible for conditions to change direction virtually overnight. In something considerably less than a year after the Schweinfurt-Regensburg

crisis of unescorted bombers had threatened the very survival of POINTBLANK, Allied dominance of the air over the Continent became a reality. Everything began to change, and escort missions were no longer the great imperative. Thousand-plane day and night raids were certain to have a major impact on the enemy's ability to fight back. Those bombers were not just breaking windows and potholing fields, they were seriously damaging German industrial capacity and forcing major changes in arrangement of the Nazi production scheme. When Maj. Gen. William Kepner's "boys" shifted to the "Down to earth" policy in 1944, the entire complexion of the war in the ETO changed radically.

Doolittle's decision to concentrate on one primary fighter type may not have been a unilateral decision. The resurgence of the Ninth Air Force coincided – as a result of one of those important command decisions – with the updated plans and, as a result, none of the Thunderbolts or Lightnings were wanting for a new home. In fact, both types were found to be well suited to their new career: interdiction of the *Wehrmacht's* armor and troop movements. That unleashed a flood of aircraft at low level to shoot up trains, bomb bridges and airfields, and generally make life miserable for anyone and anything that moved on the surface of Europe.

And for the first time, airmen in the MTO and SWPA theaters of action did not have to anticipate a diet of second-hand fighters . . . or worse, none at all. Brand new P-38Ls and P-47Ds were soon arriving for immediate assignment to operational groups.

It may be that P-38/Allison problems never vanished entirely, but pilot confidence in the Lightning changed almost overnight in the ETO. Possible crisis became annoyance. Nothing more. Republic P-47s, flying from bases much nearer prime targets, were suddenly operating with just one drop tank and a couple of 500-pound bombs under the wings. Mustangs found fame in flying sweeps over just about any location that was selected for them, and they did it with a certain amount of impunity.

For the record, Lockheed Lightning production never fal-

*Production Flight Test Building 304 was usually a short-term home for up to two days' output of P-38s. AAF Constellations (C-69s) were assembled at the east end of the large clear-span building.*

tered or was endangered by command decisions concerning production. In fact, the orders increased and production in 1944 and 1945 swelled. The P-47 became an endangered species; a major decision was made to terminate all Thunderbolt production because the type was lacking necessary range for use against Japan. Republic was not content to let that happen, and their engineers produced the long-ranging P-47N version. Carrying greater internal fuel, two 165-gallon Lockheed-type drop tanks and even a belly drop tank, the N-model Thunderbolts benefitted from a more powerful engine to become an important factor in the Pacific.

North American P-51Ds and P-51Ks already had excellent range characteristics. It was fortunate because there was virtually no way that they were going to be adapted to carry any more internal or external fuel. Lockheed's P-38L was in great shape. Engine reliability in the far reaches of the Southwestern and Western Pacific areas never became an issue. Range was actually being increased greatly because of extra fuel capacity in the wing leading edge tanks, and few pilots were unable to cope with the extra weight (at takeoff) of one or two 310-gallon centersection drop tanks. It became fairly commonplace to see an entire group operating with one 165-gallon drop tank and one 310-gallon tank on each P-38. With the benefits of cruise control information, P-38Ls were unmatched for range capability.

F It's early in the day when a squadron-sized group of Lightnings approaches the coastline of continental Europe, their polished noses gleaming in the weak sunlight. They turn as one, taking a new heading directly toward some cavernous submarine pens along two edges of a well-defined harbor. The German flak crews only give the fighters perfunctory consideration. After all, the P-38s are probably the most identifiable aircraft in the ETO. Surely, no fighter pilot could have more than a tourist's interest in the giant monolithic structures housing submarines undergoing resupply, repair or construction. There is no need to throw up a vast curtain of flak in a serious attempt to drive those Lightnings off.

Suddenly, the lead aircraft leaps upward several feet as two ugly black missiles fall from its underside. Almost immediately a pair of identical shapes leave one or two of the trailing P-38s, while a single object falls from every twin-boom fighter in the formation. The planes pitch to the right as one, increasing speed and climbing away. Those big black objects fall toward the concrete pens and several of them score direct hits. There is some delay; then there are explosions, massive explosions as several tons of RDX are detonated. Some of those missiles were 2000-pound armor-piercing bombs. The majority were 1000-pounders. It didn't seem possible. Incredibly, a couple of those P-38s had each dropped a pair of one-ton bombs. Nobody would ever expect such accuracy

from fighters in level flight. The Droop Snoot had struck.

Many months earlier – sometime in mid-1943 – Col. Cass Hough got together with Col. Don Ostrander (a brilliant armament and ordnance specialist) to hatch an idea at Bovingdon that was soon to catch the imagination of the current Eighth Air Force commanding general, Ira C. Eaker. Lockheed had already demonstrated that the P-38 could lug almost any standard American ordnance to a target and drop it with some reasonable accuracy. Acting as a dive bomber or a skip bomber, the P-38s were big leaguers, demonstrated consistently in the MTO. The Hough-Ostrander duo saw yet another way to employ the Lightning at a time when B-17s and B-24s were suffering devastating losses.

"Why not build a batch of pathfinding P-38s that could guide other Lightning fighters to a target at speeds up to 100 mph faster than could be attained by B-17s and B-24s on comparable missions?" they more or less inquired of each other. In practice over enemy territory, the medium bombers were not appreciably faster than the HBs, and the mediums were not well adapted to carrying one-ton bombs. An even greater negative aspect was that bombers carried crews ranging from 8 to 13 men just to carry 1 or 2 tons of bombs to many targets. Usually flying at no more than 180 mph, it took many hours of flying over defended territory to deliver the loads, and every airborne hour subjected the crews to potential attack. Not only that, VIIIth Fighter Command was then struggling desperately to find a way to provide an umbrella of protective fighters to escort the bombers when they were most likely to be attacked. The long-standing and deeply embedded Air Corps theory that heavily armed bombers in formation could provide their own defensive network was, in mid-1943, found to be seriously flawed and obsolete.

*OPPOSITE RIGHT: Close to the time when Col. Ben Kelsey's Technical Operations organization was preparing to prove out the effectiveness of the Droop Snoot led group as a carpet bombing weapon, the AAF Tactical Center at Orlando, Florida, was beginning experiments with a P-38H-5-LO carrying two 1,000-pound bombs. Kelsey and Hough already had proven the feasibility of each P-38 carrying twice that weight in bombs. (Hans Groenhoff)*

*BELOW LEFT & RIGHT: Half a world away from Italy and the sands of North Africa, the AAF was testing the practicality of flying P-38s from frozen lakes and snow-covered landing grounds. Following some successful wind tunnel tests, a P-38G-5-LO was equipped with retractable Federal skis at Ladd Field, Alaska. A Republic P-47G fitted with fixed skis and a North American P-51 fitted with retractable skis were tested in the winter of 1943-44 at Wright Field. Although this P-38G suffered some damage when the ski gear collapsed during a landing in January 1944, it was flying again within a few days. Tests were sufficiently encouraging to warrant the conversion of a P-38J for trials. (ATSC)*

Hough and Ostrander had not been raised on such philosophy, so their "engineering" minds reasoned that the P-38s could match practical bomb loads of a B-17 on short missions, and probably exceed B-26 bomb loading on medium-range missions. By doubling the number of fighters, they could provide a very effective escort, and the pseudo bombers could also fight their way out after dispensing the bomb loads. Fighter Command would not even have to supply other fighters during the withdrawal, and only minimal P-47 coverage during the penetration haste. Most importantly, great numbers of "defensive" crewmen would not be put at risk. The two colonels reasoned that navigation would also be the responsibility of the lead bombardier-navigators – a select group – for the most part, relieving the fighter pilots of that often worrisome task.

Colonels Ben Kelsey and Hough were convinced that the optimum load for a medium-to-long-range bombing mission flown by Lightnings would be one 2000-pound bomb and one 310-gallon external tank. This would provide a pretty well balanced load during the critical takeoff and climb stage, and the one external tank would provide approximately the same range characteristic as two 165-gallon tanks. While all three men conceded that pilot proficiency on such missions would have to be of the highest order, they knew that most pilots would rise to the challenge. It would not have required the proficiency displayed by B-25 pilots on the Tokyo raid.

Pooling their individual ideas, Hough and Ostrander drew up a rough set of specifications relating to the concept and to the modifications required on a P-38. The plan was readily approved by officials at WIDEWING, and they provided authorization to proceed with a prototype. Also – if it was successful – authority was granted to supply kits to rework additional Lightnings for operational use. Col. Hough left immediately for Langford Lodge in Northern Ireland to discuss their needs with Lockheed Overseas Corp. engineering personnel. James E. Boyce was Engineering Manager, while his chief design engineer was J. D. "Jack" Hawkins. George McCutcheon was given responsibility for preliminary and production design. In the practice of the day, they assigned the project name Droop Snoot to LOC Project P-3819. (Even

McCutcheon could not recall where that name came from.)

McCutcheon prepared the drawings within days, and work on a mockup for equipment location and bombardier-navigator space provisions began as soon as the drawings were released. They were faced with the necessity for accommodating one crewman in relative comfort for up to 8 hours of flight, a Norden bombsight, a bomb-aiming position enjoying good visibility, plus navigation equipment and instrument and control panel items. Oxygen was required for at least 6 hours at 30,000 feet, and some alternate bomb releasing mechanisms were provided.

Lockheed's design included $1/2$-inch thick armor plates on both sides of the nose section, overhead, on the seat back and seat pan, and on the floor. That was needed as much for maintaining a proper center of gravity as it was to protect the bombardier. Even with all that, they had to add a lead plate in the floor aft of the bomb-aiming glass panel plus 80 pounds of lead ballast immediately beneath the bomb sight.

They constructed a skeletal wooden mockup containing every item that was to be in a converted P-38. Jack Hawkins personally spent several hours inside the mockup to make sure that everything was satisfactory. Except for the flat bomb-aiming panel, they hardly altered the aerodynamic shape. Since there was no wind tunnel available to check on any drag changes, they merely removed the gun nose from a P-38H-5-LO and built a wooden nose shape over a metal frame in its place. It was constructed of white pine strips attached to the framework, just as Glenn Curtiss built many of his flying boat hulls more than a quarter of a century earlier. Sanded smooth and varnished, it was bolted onto the P-38H structure. LOC test pilot George "Pappy" Clark flew the ballasted airplane to check on speed and handling characteristics. If there was any reduction in speed, it was not discernible.

Using a simple jig, a nose section was fabricated for installation on one of the early model P-38Js. That "proofing" aircraft was weighed in February 1944, giving an empty weight of 14,206 pounds. Official Lockheed figures for the P-38J-5-LO quoted an empty weight of 12,780 pounds, complete with camouflage paint, and stated that the "alternate" (with full external tanks) gross weight was 18,635 pounds. Lockheed Overseas Corp. scales showed an alternate gross weight for the first Droop Snoop at 19,291 pounds in their report dated February 26.[3] One interesting sidelight: the new Droop Snoot P-38J gross weight was almost exactly equal to that of a fully loaded Douglas DB-7 Havoc I light bomber. Even with external tanks installed, the P-38 was some 30 to 40 mph faster than a "clean" DB-7, and its *combat range* exceeded the normal *cruise range* of the DB-7 by least 75 miles.

Shortly thereafter, Gen. Doolittle authorized the "go ahead" construction of three Droop Snoots, later increasing the order to include 15 aircraft modification kits. According to Jack Hawkins, no less than 22 Lightnings were modified into the lead bomber format at Langford Lodge. George McCutcheon's records indicated that he had been instructed to design the package for Fourth Echelon (Depot) modification, based on fabrication of no less than 100 kits. It is a known fact that other Droop Snoot mod kits were built in India.

That first Droop Snoot left the ground at Langford Lodge on its maiden flight in the final days of February, again with "Pappy" Clark at the controls. Jack Hawkins made sure that

he was going to be in the bomb aimer's seat on that first flight. He recalled that the view afforded the second crew member in a P-38 Droop Snoot was magnificent.

Tests conducted with a later model P-38J Droop Snoot at Bovingdon included formation bombing operations. With two P-38J fighters flying in vee formation, Cols. Hough and Ostrander tried out a system of wing trailing edge lights to signal the following pilots when to release their bombs. The setup included "Ready; Aim; Drop" lights. Results left something to be desired, at least in the minds of Technical Operations people. They then attempted to work out a radio release signal, automatically releasing bombs from the trailing fighters. That system proved to be far less successful, so they concentrated on improving the light system.

G Droop Snoots first went into action as early as April 19, 1944, in the ETO, providing good to moderate results. That pioneering operation was flown by the 20FG as their Mission 45. Maj. Herbert Johnson, Jr., piloted that P-38J Droop Snoot and Lt. Herschel "Easy" Ezell, Jr., was at the Norden bomb sight in the nose. Although there were several paint additions, it is possible that their aircraft, named "EZE Does It" was the first P-38J Droop Snoot turned out up there in Northern Ireland. No fewer than 43 of the Lightnings took off from Kings Cliffe on that morning of April 10, at 0730 with Maj. Johnson in the lead. The operational plan called for a high-level precision bombing attack on Florennes Airfield in Belgium. Twenty-eight of the Lightnings were each carrying a 1000-pound bomb and a single 165-gallon drop tank; the other 15 fighters carried two drop tanks each. Former B-17 bombardier Ezell found 10/10th solid overcast at the target area. The 20th finally salvoed over the Channel on a radio signal from Ezell, at least giving the opportunity to check on the pattern. It was frustrating, but nothing that hadn't happened to Fortress and Liberator groups after a lengthy flight over Europe. All of the Lightnings returned safely to Kings Cliffe and prepared for a second mission of the day.

With the aircraft rearmed and refueled, Lt. Col. Harold Rau led 38 Lockheeds on a mission to Gutersloh, Germany, at 1415 hours. Razorback Thunderbolts of the 359th FG out of East Wretham were dispatched to provide fighter cover over the target area. The 20th bombed from 20,000 feet while flying a tight formation of 28 aircraft (eight aircraft had returned to base for various reasons). It may have been a small force, but they dropped 26,000 pounds of bombs in a concentrated area among the many hangars, good results being observed. Only one aircraft failed to return, that being flown by Maj. Donald Willis from the 67th Fighter Wing; he was also a former Eagle Squadron and 4FG pilot. Willis is believed to have bailed out over Holland.

Not incidentally that day, 20FG aircraft accounted for eight enemy aircraft in the air and no less than 46 on the ground. Maj. Willis was the only USAAF casualty of the day.

Droop Snoot P-38s were used successfully by the Eighth, Ninth and Fifteenth Air Forces on bombing missions with relative success. At least a few appeared on the CBI, although they may not have been used as bombers.

Possibly the most important mission/operational test of the Droop Snoot was conducted when the three key members of the Technical Operations Section – then under command of Col. Ben Kelsey – actually led P-38s of the 20FG group over Antwerp for a precision bombing attack. Deputy C.O. Cass Hough was at the controls of the Droop Snoot P-38J and Col. Ostrander was the bombardier. Flying wing was Kelsey, with the fighter cover being provided by the aircraft of the 20th. It was a remarkable mission in that the Kelsey and Hough

---

3. *Any lengthy association with the aircraft industry and knowledge of data in design specifications leads one to the assumption that actual weights of single examples (or any dozen) are likely to vary widely from the design data. The discrepancies cannot all be based on paint thickness. Differences in performance are easier to understand. Many significant factors are involved in performance.*

Lockheeds were each carrying two 2000-pound bombs on the wing shackles. Two P-38s with four tons of bombs!

But that was not the entire picture. Each of the Kings Cliffe fighters was carrying two of the 1000-pound bombs. Bombing was carried out from 16,000 feet and enemy defensive action was extremely light, but the bombing attack provided only moderate success against the large drydocks which were attacked. Whatever the reasons were for not having a spectacular success that day, none could be attributed to some failure on the part of the P-38s. They did their job.

The Hough/Ostrander theory about using P-38s to supplant the B-17s and B-24s was never taken seriously by Doolittle or his staff. The idea would have flown in the face of the commitment to a bomber offensive on the part of Gens. Spaatz, Arnold and Eaker. With OVERLORD less than 60 days in the offing, P-38s already in short supply, and with massive production programs committed to the B-17 and B-24, who could be expected to make any commitment to the idea? (Nobody should forget that just a year earlier, virtually no one in the Eighth Air Force really knew how to use the Martin B-26 Marauders in the ETO.)

*ABOVE: One of the lesser-known experimental versions of the P-38/F-5 series was the one and only XF-5D. Nicknamed "Bobbie," the airplane was derived from the G-series fighter, a recon type that was designated F-5A-10-LO in its original form. First flown in the spring of 1943, the XF-5D was actually the inadvertent progenitor of the famous Droop Snoot and Pathfinder P-38s. Engineered by the Air Technical Service Command, it carried a photo-navigator up front, a vertical camera, and retained two .50-caliber machine guns that would have deafened the navigator if fired. Nose was clear Plexiglas. (USAAF)*

There is one interesting sidelight to the Droop Snoot concept. A few thousand miles away at Dayton, Ohio, there was a telephone conversation between Maj. C. H. Terhune, Jr., working for Brig. Gen. F. O. Carroll's Engineering Division, and Capt. C. E. Reichert, working for Col. Paul H. Kemmer in the Aircraft Laboratory. That was on July 20, 1943, very close to the time that Col. Cass Hough was starting on the Droop Snoot project. Terhune and Reichert initiated work on conversion of a P-38G fighter into a very specialized photographic airplane designed to operate at low altitude (under 12,000 feet). The turbosuper-chargers were to be deleted, along with all oxygen equipment, and an observer/photographer was to be located in the nose section. A K-17 camera and vertical viewfinder were to be located in that nose section, and there was to be a K-24 or K-25 camera mounted in one tailboom. Two .50-caliber machine guns would be repositioned in the nose section, but all other guns and ammunition would be removed.

A subsequent conversation with Lt. Col. H. L. Nadeau (AAF Reconnaissance Branch, Washington) resulted in plans to use a P-38J and retain the turbosuperchargers (and oxygen). Upper and lower escape hatches had to be incorporated for the observer. Armor plate and two additional machine guns were considered on August 4, and work on a conversion began on a F-5A because a priority would be needed to obtain a P-38J. The prototype, designated XF-5D, did not differ

radically from the first Droop Snoot in appearance. No P-38J was ever modified in the same manner, and it had to be presumed that once the Wright Field people learned of progress on the Droop Snoot, their own project fell out of favor.

There seemed to be plenty of projects for all at Wright Field as the war progressed. When North American Aviation proposed a long-ranging escort fighter for Pacific operations, their intention was to mate two P-51s of the D or H series by means of a new intermediate wing section, using more than 75 percent of Mustang components for the remainder of the fighter. Kelly Johnson had discarded the idea back in 1936 or 1937 when his Model 22 (XP-38) was on the drawing board.

As proposed and originally built, North American's XP-82 offered some benefits over the forthcoming P-38L, but with the end of hostilities that soon evaporated. The latest Rolls-Royce Merlins were not utilized, even in the development airplanes, and most production versions were powered by an even more

*Moderate success with the Federal ski landing gear on a P-38G led to installing a similar set on one of the ten P-38J-1-LOs that were built for accelerated service testing of the new intercoolers and unrestricted V-1710F-17 engines. Lockheed's Model Designation 422-81-14 applied to the small group of aircraft. By the time that tests were completed (after the March 8, 1944, starting date), any need for operation from frozen lakes had long since vanished. (LAC)*

complex version of the Allison V-1710. Once again, Lockheed had two versions of the P-38 projected that could have been produced in 1944, and both had high-altitude performance that at least equalled that of the much later F-82E and F. One of the Lockheeds was the P-38K and the other was a Merlin powered version that was never even built.

As for the XP-82 design, the AAF Aero-medical people were greatly concerned about dynamic effects on a pilot located well away from the true centerline of an aircraft with very high performance. They were not optimistic about the situation at all. There was bound to be some sort of centrifuge effect. Consequently, they obtained an old model P-38 (no suffix) for modification, one that has been consistently misunderstood. All turbosupercharger components were removed from the engines, which were then fitted with conventional exhaust stacks. Rather crude carburetor scoops were stuck up into the airstream and a special pseudo-bubble cockpit was created where the left supercharger had been situated. Although no flight controls were fitted, the person riding in that left boom position could certainly feel all of the dynamic loads that were imposed as the aircraft was maneuvered by the pilot in the basic central position. Evidently the problem was not one that created insurmountable difficulties because North American P-82s were eventually manufactured and delivered to the AAF. Evidently, though, not one was ever constructed as a single-seat fighter.

I As progenitor of the P-82, the P-51B through P-51D models of the sleek Mustang were not too different from the P-38 in some ways. Just for the record, Merlin-powered P-51s went through a period of wing failure problems during pullouts from combat dives. And, amazingly, the number of pilots lost in P-51s and P-47s as a result of compressibility dives during an intense investigative period was found to exceed P-38 losses from the same cause.

The wing failure problems were evidently a factor in effecting the transfer of Col. Ben Kelsey from his then current Wright Field assignment back to England for duty as Deputy Chief of Staff in the IXth Fighter Command. He reported for duty in November 1943, after the Ninth Air Force had been reactivated a month earlier under command of Maj. Gen. Lewis Brereton. Kelsey's appointment did not turn out to be one of long duration.

Less than three months later, when Lt. Gen. James Doolittle had settled in as CG of the Eighth Air Force, he insistently requested transfer of Kelsey to his command. Months earlier when Gen. Kepner replaced "Monk" Hunter as chief of VIIIth Fighter Command while Gen. Eaker struggled to overcome massive problems within his command, he retained Col. Hough's organization at Bovingdon without change. Doolittle had other ideas. He quickly dissolved the VIIIth FC Technical Services Section in the initial weeks of 1944 and instructed Kelsey to reconstitute it directly under the Eighth Air Force as Maintenance and Technical Services. It was intentionally a name to disguise its true purpose.

*The business asketh silent secrecy:* Shakespeare.

Cass Hough, who had just received his eagles (as full colonel) was designated as Deputy Director under Kelsey, and Doolittle immediately expanded the scope of their activities to "investigate and take corrective action" to overcome all major aircraft problems afflicting the Eighth Air Force. One problem that only the general could resolve: for unknown reasons, all P-51Bs and Cs were slated for the Ninth Air Force. In order to get the newest, inexperienced Mustang group, Doolittle offered to trade a P-47 group that could boast of extensive combat experience. It was, in the eyes of many, a gamble. Gamble or not, it was the beginning of the end for Lightnings and Thunderbolts as probable *ne plus ultra* fighters of the VIIIth Fighter Command. While that prestigious organization was destined to see little, if anything, of the best Lightnings (P-38L), pilots of the Ninth and Fifteenth Air Forces (to name but a few) became the beneficiaries of the situation. Perhaps the greatest benefits went to the men of the Far East Air Force, where pilots like Richard West were eager to take on any enemy, including the vaunted Nakajima Ki-84 (Frank), and others, who flew missions involving a combat RADIUS of action of 950 miles or more. The only pilots who feared the Lightning out there were those flying aircraft bearing red Hinomuras (meatballs).

# CHAPTER 16

# Tidal Wave Over FESTUNG EUROPA

Young, impressionable pilots freshly arrived in England and assigned to the transitional training group at Goxhill or directly to an operational squadron were usually made aware of the flood of adverse rumors about troubles with the P-38. The rumors may have become self-fulfilling; there was a rather sudden and dramatic increase in the accident rate at Goxhill early in 1944. Had all the good work performed earlier by Jim Mattern gone for naught? Rumor mills could be found in every theater of operations, but the subjects were varied. Only in the ETO was there a real fear of the P-38 by someone other than the enemy.

Commanders of a few P-38 units, either having a mental block about the P-38 type or having a strong emotional attachment for some fighter type they flew previously, permitted their personal attitudes to infiltrate into the ranks of those rookie pilots. The enemy could hardly have been more effective in sabotaging morale. Fortunately, there were several clever tacticians like Harold Rau, John Weltman, Ralph Garman, Jack S. Jenkins, Oliver "Obie" Taylor, John Stone, Cy Wilson, Kyle Riddle and – in a war zone thousands of miles removed from the ETO – Charles MacDonald who set marvelous examples for their young charges. They were all adroit in their ability to impart confidence and to master their mounts. It did not go unnoticed that all of those leaders were anything but "wallflowers" when it came to participation in combat. Weltman, for example, was perhaps even smaller in stature than Ray Toliver, but he embraced the P-38 from the beginning and frequently demonstrated his "tigerish" attitude. More often than not, all of those commanders were right up there in the thick of the action, encouraging their men to win.

Maj. Gen. William Kepner was sort of a "circuit rider" CG, and was, therefore, keenly aware of two major problems affecting Lightning performance early in 1944. There was no doubt that the influx of P-38H and J airplanes with their new V-1710F-17 series engines had been accompanied by a significant percentage increase in engine failure, at least in the ETO. He was also acutely aware that morale in the ranks of young replacement pilots was possibly headed for bankruptcy. But

*Superimposed against a patchwork of small villages and tilled fields, a Lockheed F-5E-2-LO from the 34th Photo Recon Squadron of the First Tactical Air Force (out of Chateaudun, France) presents a melange of markings in post-Invasion days. Black stripes on the wings have faded and the white stripes have disappeared, but tail boom markings are still bright. Radio call numbers on the tailplane are incorrect; the number should be 328624 because the aircraft was converted from a P-38J-15-LO, AC43-28624. Capt. Bosworth was flying the F-5E somewhere between Orleans and Chateaudun in August 1944. (T/Sgt. Jack Quinn)*

he had a couple of things going in his favor. He would not hesitate to approach Doolittle to gain his support for something a bit "offbeat." And, keeping an open mind, he had listened intently when word got to him about Lockheed engineer Ward Beman's constructive suggestion.

Kepner asked the new CG of the Eighth Air Force – Lt. Gen. James Doolittle – to request that Washington officials have test pilot Tony LeVier fly to England for accelerated engine test work and to conduct special training and demonstration flights. There is strong evidence that this had all been pushed through the chain of command by civilian Lockheed engineer Ward Beman, assigned to duty in the U.K. with Tech Rep Phil Nelsen to support the 55FG and other new groups scheduled for duty. One of the company's best crew chiefs, Glenn Fulkerson, was also there. All were working to improve P-38H performance and also support the new P-38Js that began to arrive in England in December.

Ex-racing pilot Anthony LeVier had been hired by Lockheed as a ferry pilot in May 1941, and "Tony" worked as a production test pilot until he was inducted into the newly formed Engineering Flight Test Group in July 1942. He got along very well with the chief test pilot, Milo Burcham, sharing some of the most important P-38 test work with him. By the time LeVier

was told to pack up and head for Europe, he and Burcham were probably the most experienced men in the world in the matter of compressibility effect on aircraft. Certainly there wasn't one military pilot anywhere who knew one-tenth as much about compressibility and the P-38. Over a period of months, Tony had shared the entire compressibility dive flap test program with Burcham, with some assistance from other Lockheed test pilots.

Virtually every P-38 or P-47 pilot who had encountered the dreaded phenomena had either been locked into it by mistake, by uninformed curiosity, or had intentionally flown into it one time in order to find out how it could be countered. Some were lucky and did the right things (by mistake or circumstance, allowing the aircraft to gradually recover in the denser air at lower altitude) and survived. Some were forced to bail out when the control column oscillated wildly or everything went wrong. More than a few died. Cass Hough had recovered successfully in a P-38F and in a P-47C, mainly through outstanding piloting ability and a cool engineering perspective.

Still smarting from some trouble he had gotten into by "attacking" a flight of naval Vought F4U Corsairs near San Diego, Tony LeVier was accosted by Col. Clarence Shoop at Burbank. The AAF Plant Representative said that Hall Hibbard and Kelly Johnson wanted to see him, post haste. Tony guessed that he was scheduled for termination. Actually, they were very friendly and wanted to know if he would like to go to the United Kingdom and boost morale by demonstrating how well the P-38 could fly, if operated properly.

In addition to compressibility problems, Johnson was obviously concerned about rapidly disintegrating confidence in the P-38's engines. Allison V-1710F-17 engines were, "suddenly blowing up all over the U.K.," and General Doolittle was under pressure to pull the P-38s out of VIIIth Fighter Command. While Allison knew it had a serious problem, they weren't really doing everything possible to correct it. Ward Beman and Phil Nelson were trying any number of potential fixes at Nuthampstead, but needed a test pilot to prove them out, so the ways were greased for LeVier's rapid departure to the war zone.

The recipient of 2-weeks' worth of inoculations in only 2 days, on January 26, 1944, Tony went to Washington to arrange for transportation and was soon over the Atlantic in a C-54. By the time he landed in Newfoundland, influenza

ABOVE LEFT: *Lockheed test pilot Tony LeVier posed with his modified (w/retrofit kit) P-38J-10-LO (AC42-68006) named "Snafuperman" during his six-month tour in the United Kingdom. The civilian with him was Glenn Fulkerson, a top-rung technical representative.*

ABOVE RIGHT: *"Major" Tony LeVier, flying tech rep, relaxed in his basic office during the January-June 1944 demonstration and evaluation tour of the United Kingdom. (Anthony LeVier)*

symptoms from the accelerated series of shots were making him very ill. He was almost too sick to continue when he got to Greenland, but after reaching Scotland, he felt better and caught a train for London.

There were some interesting sidelights to LeVier's demonstration tour, a few of which are related here . . . just to show what was occurring as viewed from a different viewpoint.

Lt. Col. Jack Jenkins, soon to be designated to command the 55FG as Lt. Col. Frank James moved over to AJAX to a staff level function, wrote some of the following items in his personal diary: His January 27 entry stated that they received another flight of P-38Js from (Langford Lodge) Northern Ireland. "I'll take one of these and hope that I keep it until I finish the war. It is Number 825 and will be 'Texas Ranger IV'."

February 2. "I came home (to Nuthampstead) to find that AJAX had sent Ben Kelsey, Cass Hough and some Lockheed servicemen up here to stay about a week." (Among the "servicemen" from Lockheed was Tony LeVier.)

Four days later, Jenkins took command of the group and the base. It seems amazing that on January 31, both James and Jenkins were involved in a wild dogfight over Holland. The P-38s were to cover P-47s dive bombing an airfield. They tangled with thirteen Bf 109s, and seven of them were shot down. Jenkins learned later that six P-38s were MIA.

The first day of his group command, Jenkins and the 55FG went to Dijon, near the Swiss border. He reported one pilot lost because he flew too tight in formation. Consequently, he was not looking around, and the *Luftwaffe* pilots picked him off. One P-38 went all the way home from Dijon on one engine. Another pilot collided with a Jenkins wingman. The errant pilot lost a fin and rudder; later on, over the Channel, he suddenly spun out and was lost. The other P-38 had two damaged engines, but made it home on one of them.

February 7. "We have had seven long missions in eight days and we are tired. We've lost about 35 percent of our group since we arrived. Not good at all."

By March 2. Jenkins calculated that they had lost 40 percent of the original group members. He commented that the engines were throwing (connecting) rods and failing left and right. Although nothing like it was reported from any other theater of operation, including the MTO, the February to May period was almost disastrous as far as the engines were concerned. Morale in the 55th was getting well down because of the stress involved with lots of long-distance missions, the constant threat of an engine failure, and the fact that poor cockpit heating and the associated windshield fogging was making it a certainty that the P-38 was not the right airplane

for high-altitude work. (At least in the ETO.) Col. Jenkins reported that turbosupercharger regulators were a major culprit.

It is only fair to listen to another viewpoint. Col. Hough went along on P-47 missions and P-38 missions as often as he felt it was necessary. He stated, without equivocation, that the majority of the problems stemmed from morale and stubborn determination to ignore certain instructions. Cass Hough said that many P-38 pilots refused to fly at high manifold pressure and low rpm because "it gave them a rough ride." He proved that it was the best way to go for range, engine saving and for not being a sitting duck if attacked. That was exactly what Charles Lindbergh proved half-way around the world . . . later that year!

Hough attributes much of the P-38 morale problem to his former boss, Brig. Gen. Hunter. "I couldn't get Gen. Hunter into a P-38," he says. Hunter was absolutely delighted when the Lightnings went to North Africa for Operation TORCH. No wonder they didn't bring the 55GF and 20FG over from stateside as replacements for groups lost to TORCH. So what did Hunter have for his VIIIth Fighter Command? Short-legged Spitfire Mk Vs and a handful of useless P-39Fs that dared not tangle with Messerschmitts or Focke-Wulfs. How about his Thunderbolts? There were no P-47s available at all in the ETO for group deployment until at least early January and February 1943. And those were P-47Cs (earliest blocks) with no belly or wing tank provisions (attach points). From coastal bases in England, a P-47C might have been adjudged to have a combat radius of action of 275 miles, compared to about 180 miles for a Spitfire. However, many pilots could not squeeze out a 225-mile radius in a P-47C in formation. Hough proved that he could get to Aachen or the Rhine River on a "combat radius" mission while carrying an experimental 108-gallon drop tank *but not using the fuel*. "But you had to use the right manifold pressure and rpm, and many young pilots just wouldn't do it right." (With a 75-gallon drop tank, an early P-47D had a combat radius of 410 miles. In the same time frame, P-38s were going out 600 miles and more.)

Col. Hough said it did not do much good to carry three drop tanks (on late model P-47Ds) because their combined drag defeated the purpose. In January 1943, long-legged P-51Bs were not much more than a dream. The first ones came on the scene nearly a year later. Lockheed P-38s were the only fighters that could do the long-range escort job, but it is easy to see that the opportunity was wasted. It isn't fanciful opinion either. A detailed review of the record shows it to be factual. As pointed out earlier, command decisions were of paramount importance in the overall scheme of things.

A jeep whisked Tony LeVier out of London to VIIIth Fighter Command headquarters at Bushey Hall, where he drew his flight gear and was soon on his way to Nuthampstead, north of London. After Tony talked with Colonels Mark Bradley (P-47 project) and Ben Kelsey, Ward Beman arranged to have him fly Maj. Dallas "Spider" Webb's new P-38J on a simulated long-range, full-bore combat mission. Of course he was to remain over England while he did so, but he was to operate as if he were flying escort for heavy bombers to Germany.

Webb's aircraft had been modified with a revamped induction system, which Beman and Nelson hoped would solve the prevailing detonation problem. With minimal briefing and very little sleep, Tony took off on February 3 with a full load, drawing all fuel from the 165-gallon drop tanks. He was in cruise climb to 30,000 feet, and would be required to perform several minutes of combat maneuvers at full rated power (Military and WEP).

When climbing through 29,000 feet at cruise, the right engine chose to emulate a fragmentation grenade. As the saying goes: "There I was at 30,000 feet and . . . " Still flying at a fairly high gross weight for one engine, LeVier switched to the main tanks but chose not to jettison the drop tanks. Because the airfields in East Anglia were closely spaced, radio communication on the emergency channels could be confusing. When Tony saw what appeared to be his field below, he got interrupted instructions for landing.

Almost forced into stalling by the extra weight of the tanks, he had to choose another runway when he saw there was a strong crosswind. As luck would have it, the field turned out to be that of a B-26 group. Tony left the P-38 on a taxi strip, where it had rolled, and the chagrined pilot finally got back to the 55FG's base in an ambulance. That was most appropriate because the medics checked him out and put him in the infirmary for a week. On the same day that LeVier's test ended so abruptly, Lt. Col. Frank James moved out as group commander and transferred to a staff function at HQ. While LeVier caught up on his rest, Lt. Col. Jack S. Jenkins moved into the slot as commander of the 55th. (Col. Jenkins's diary gives absolutely no clue that he even knew LeVier was at Nuthampstead.)

Evidently having little else to go on, the top brass pointed to the cold temperatures in northern Europe, including the British Isles, as the real culprit for the P-38's engine problems. Everybody seemed to have ignored the fact that Eleventh Air Force pilots operation in the Far North encountered some of the worst weather on earth, including surface temperatures that could rival those encountered elsewhere at 30,000 feet. There is no evidence that Eighth Air Force meteorologists claimed that temperatures above 32,000 feet were lower over Europe than anywhere else around the globe. Certainly the temperatures encountered by Fifteenth Air Force pilots over the Alps were hardly warmer than those over Denmark.

It seems more likely that the Lockheed engineers were on the right track, but they appeared to lack the "clout" needed to be heard. Everybody seemed to know that just

as the Merlin engine was not at all compatible with turbosupercharging, evidence points to the fact that the Allison V-1710 had its problems in the related induction system. In a letter from an APO in early 1944, Lt. Col. Al Bodie told that Champion spark plugs being delivered to AAF units overseas were faulty in more than 50 percent of the cases. That could have been one serious problem. It is the author's opinion that British fuels furnished to the Eighth Air Force were improperly blended at the time, and the tetraethyl lead compound was separating out of the gasoline in the Allison manifolds. Nobody seemed to give that possibility much consideration in 1944. Yet, who ever heard any great hue and cry from the Russians about Allison failures in Bell P-39 and P-63 aircraft? All their operations were in cold weather, but those aircraft had no turbosupercharging!

Following his discharge from the infirmary, LeVier went to the base of the new 364FG, just forming at Honington (AAF Sta. 375). The pilots, for the most part, were just out of OTUs (Operational Training Units). LeVier gave a number of lectures, including some on his 31st birthday, February 14. Asked to give a flight demonstration in a P-38J that next day, he was more than happy to oblige. It was at this time that the supposedly "key" test operations all but evaporated, and the emphasis went on lectures and the flight demonstrations. As if by magic, a P-47 wandered by at about 2,000 feet, both pilots indicated interest, and they promptly engaged in mock combat. LeVier says that "I swarmed all over the guy." That certainly made the Honington P-38 pilots very happy.

On one checkout flight, LeVier lost his radio just about the time that it began to snow. With low visibility, he spotted an airfield and promptly decided to land. The field had no real runways, being one of those sod airfields common to England in the 1930s. Grass and snow were not good surfaces to brake on, and the P-38 pirouetted through 180 or more degrees before stopping. Tony spotted numerous De Havilland Tiger Moth trainers parked near the buildings. It turned out to be a unique site. He had landed at Hucknall, the Rolls-Royce experimental base, which also served as a primary training facility.

LeVier's next stop was a return to Bovingdon, the den of Col. Cass Hough. General Doolittle had just recently asked Ben Kelsey to expand the former VIIIth Fighter Command operation functions under the aegis of his Eighth Air Force. Deputy C.O. Cass Hough was their operational leader because Ben Kelsey had duties in the U.S. at the same time. While in England, Tony was in the position of reporting and being responsible to Hough (and, of course, Kelsey). Billeted at Bushey Hall, LeVier flew several aircraft for the Technical Operations Section (it had probably become Maintenance and Technical Services by that time) at Bovingdon, including a new Mustang. He went to lunch one day with Kelsey, who asked what he thought about the new dive flaps. Tony rendered his opinion that it was the best thing to happen to the P-38. LeVier expresses the opinion, now, that he feels that his comments had convinced Kelsey to push the dive flap program forward. However, the discussion was in late February 1944, and Lockheed was already producing dive flap assemblies at a high rate.

Unfortunately, during the LeVier tour, a Douglas C-54 that was carrying more than 200 sets of dive flap retrofit kits to be installed on virtually all P-38J-10-LO through -20-LO fighters in the U.K. was shot down by an overzealous RAF pilot who mistook the Skymaster for a Focke-Wulf Condor. (In all fairness, it must be pointed out that in the same general time frame some P-47 and P-38 pilots shot down three Spitfires and severely damaged two P-51s over Europe, having mistaken them for German Messerschmitts. Some very serious problems existed in the field of aircraft identification.) Somebody who had never heard of "Murphy's Law" or gremlins had every available kit loaded into that one C-54 flying the North Atlantic run. It was a catastrophic mistake. Inability to modify those 200+ fighters possibly cost untold loss of pilots and aircraft in combat.

LeVier was incorrect in believing that he had played a major role in convincing Col. Kelsey that he should authorize adoption of the dive flaps for the Lightning program. Way back in April 1943, as Kelsey recuperated from the broken ankle received when he bailed out of the P-38G test plane over Calabasas, he had authorized full production and retrofit installation of the anti-compressibility flaps. (According to Kelsey, he had planned from the outset to sign the authorization anyway, based on the flight test data compiled by Burcham, LeVier and the few other test pilots involved. It was only a last-minute decision to investigate what might happen if the dive flaps were deployed well after a Lightning was already into a compressibility dive. On that particular occasion, the experimental hydraulic drive failed to work – it couldn't handle the loads – as designed. The P-38G – already a very tired, overstressed aircraft – broke up in the air. LeVier's comments only served to confirm to Kelsey that he had made the correct decision early on.)

Very few days passed during LeVier's 4-month tour in the United Kingdom without some interesting or exciting happening. To illustrate, one young pilot accosted Tony, excitedly shouting, "Tony, you saved my life." He explained that after hearing LeVier describe the phenomena of compressibility and prescribed survival actions, he was in a group of four P-38s venturing for their very first time up to 30,000 feet. Tony had been informed that very few new P-38 pilots coming from the ZI had ever flown above 20,000 feet. It was not entirely clear as to whether the flight leader suffered from an oxygen problem or had deliberately entered a steep dive, but the other three pilots dutifully followed. This one pilot remembered LeVier's instructions about putting the props into full low pitch, pulling back on the power, and using a moderate pulling pressure on the control yoke. He managed to recover safely at about 2,000 feet. Evidently one pilot bailed out, but the other two dove straight in. Tony's admirer was the sole survivor, according to his story. None of the P-38s involved was equipped with dive flaps.

Right after the incident, LeVier was ordered to head for the huge Lockheed Overseas Corporation

*ABOVE: Making an exceptionally low pass over the 466th Bomb Group base at Attlebridge, a Lockheed F-5B, which probably had flown over from Mount Farm or Wormingford, was captured by an alert photographer as he "buzzed" the field. Winter snows coated the bomber base. (Kenneth Pittman)*

*BELOW: A 364FG Lockheed P-38J-15-LO, assigned to the 383FS, carried the name "Betty A III" when it closed up to a Boeing B-17 that it had been assigned to escort. The fighter was operating out of Honington. Tail markings shown came into general use in March 1944. (IWM)*

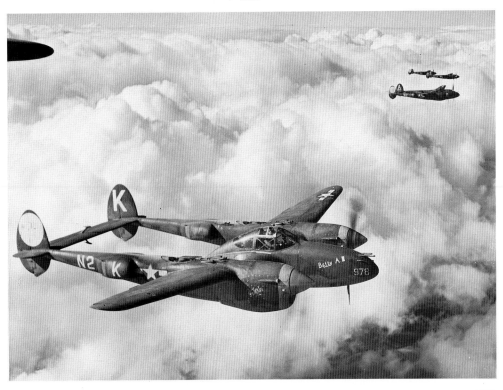

modification facility at Langford Lodge near Belfast, Northern Ireland. A new P-38J-10-LO named "Snafuperman" (complete with nose art) was assigned to him. It was newly modified with all of the latest P-38J-25-LO/P-38L retrofit changes, bringing it up to definitive P-38L standards. It was at that time that LeVier was requested to give a special flight demonstration for military pilots at the base (and for the large civilian crew).

Some AAF pilot had put on a show shortly before, got in over his head and crashed. The display that LeVier put on in March had to be seen to be believed. Fortunately, much of it was filmed as he maneuvered at treetop level. There was a very low ceiling that day, and if he ventured much above 300 feet, he disappeared into the cloud cover. Most of the flying was done within the airfield perimeter, frequently on one engine. More often than not, he would bank into the "dead" engine, something that would never be done if it could be avoided. Most of the short-radius vertical turns at about 100 feet altitude were completed to the cheers and applause of the crowd. At the low speeds involved at times, there was no chance of faking. It was a classic demonstration.

Sometime in the next few day, LeVier went back to England with "Snafuperman" to visit new bases and to return for lectures or demonstrations at Bovingdon, Nuthampstead, Kings Cliffe, Wittering, Honington and Goxhill. He also visited Harwell, where Col. Roosevelt's recon group was located. Only happenings during three or four of those visits can be related here, but there was always something new occurring at the bases.

He went back to Nuthampstead in April to demonstrate the dive flap improvement against a P-47D and a new P-51. They had to abandon the comparison against the Mustang because the Merlin would not shift into high blower at 22,000 feet. The Thunderbolt pilot was "Jake" Oberhansly, possibly at the controls of his well-known "Iron Ass." Jake, a long time member of the 78FG, was officially an ace. He and LeVier took off together and climbed to high altitude. They were to evaluate the ability of the P-38 to dive with the P-47, something that was as difficult as performing a clean split-ess in the average P-38. Republic's design had the advantage of being three and a half years newer in design and it met a requirement that was at least four years newer than the P-38 requirement.

The two airplanes completed at least two dives from altitudes above 25,000 feet. Tony reported that, "The P-47 was a bit faster in the dives because I had put out the dive flaps before pushing over." Oberhansly was more than a bit surprised to see LeVier pull alongside after each dive. That was a major improvement. And prior to the design change, it was very difficult for anyone to perform a split-ess maneuver at high altitude. Tony had proven to himself that it was "no sweat" at all in the modified Lightnings. On the other side of the coin, P-47s suffered from severe aileron oscillation in dives, causing the control stick to brutally beat a pilot's inside thighs. Colonel Oberhansly reported that he had encountered that problem in his final dive of the day. LeVier felt confident in stating that the "improved model J" was absolutely superior in maneuverability at low altitudes, except for a well-piloted Spitfire Mk IX.

Lectures by LeVier did not seem to stir up much interest among the pilots at Kings Cliffe on April 9. Frustration and the sky-lit evenings prompted him to leave the Officers' Club and crank up the P-38J. He took off and climbed to a goodly altitude over the airfield, popped the dive flaps and headed down. Everybody heard what they presumed was the death dive of another unfortunate P-38 pilot, not knowing that Tony was happily "throwing down the gauntlet." Every building emptied as people rushed out to witness the inevitable crash. "Snafuperman" pulled out smoothly and skimmed the length of the field. Having gained their attention, he proceeded to treat everybody to a late-evening version of the Langford Lodge demonstration. Needless to say, it provided everybody with more excitement than they expected in a week.

About 10 days later, he was sent over to Goxhill, home of the 496th Fighter Training Group under the command of Col. Harry W. Magee. It seemed that the 554FS, a P-38 outfit based there, was in real trouble. As LeVier reported it, they were losing nearly one P-38 every day, and there were some associated fatalities. Many of the crashes were attributed to engine failures on takeoff, and it was evident that the pilots had not been exposed to the Jimmy Mattern plan.

It was at Goxhill that LeVier personally encountered a situation for which he was totally unprepared. Having a drink with the group/base commander in the "O" club that evening, Tony was terribly disturbed when the man stated that he was a "P-40 man and did not like the P-38." Now it must be made clear that Tony failed to record the man's name . . . or even his rank, but he made a point of the fact that it was a bad situation to have somebody commanding any P-38 outfit – especially an operational training squadron – who made no bones about disliking the airplanes. (It can be confirmed that the only commanding officer ever assigned to the 496FTG at Goxhill, and later at Halesworth, was Col. Magee. His group had two squadrons . . . one with P-38s and one with P-51s.)

As the avalanche of Mustangs descended on the U.K. from the first days of summer 1944, the Lightnings and Thunderbolts generally moved over to the fast-growing IXth and XIXth Air Commands

*Landing out in the rough with any aircraft having a long nosewheel strut had to be accomplished with care. However, in emergencies that just did not happen. This P-38J (5Y\*F-) had obviously participated in many escort missions prior to this incident. The 364th Fighter Group pilot was given a bit of aid at Honington on March 30, 1944. (AFM)*

of the Ninth Air Force. Even the complexion of the war in Europe was changing, with tactical air support soon outstripping strategic bombing in importance. Gen. Kepner's "down to earth" policy for the VIIIth Fighter Command allowed that command's fighters to devote a far greater amount of their attention to shooting up anything on the ground that even looked a bit suspicious. Tanks, trains, troops and transportation soon joined the airfields as favored targets as the *Luftwaffe* struggled to put up even small defensive forces against the giant heavy bomber raids. The onslaught of RAF bombers at night, followed by massive daylight raids by the Eighth and Fifteenth Air Force heavies was rapidly destroying the German ability to fight, if not the will. Virtually every P-38 and P-47 that had been assigned to the VIIIth Fighter Command had been transferred to the Tactical Air Commands under General Brereton by October 1944.

Kepner's A-2 decided that with OVERLORD at hand, LeVier's presence would not be an asset. Most objectives had been attained, and morale was certain to have been improved. Perhaps Allison had been moved to take more action; at least everybody had learned that the airplane itself was capable of taking on the best fighters. More than one commander had shown that the P-38 was, indeed, a weapon of substance. Arrangements were made for Tony's departure.

Allison's problems faded; at least they did not really seem to be a point of discussion or serious consideration as the autumn of 1944 made its appearance. Lightnings of the Ninth Air Force operated all winter out of hastily patched up captured airfields with minimal maintenance facilities. Droop Snoot P-38s were mixed in with the fighters, and it is presumed they were utilized. Even a few of the newer Pathfinder P-38s appeared on the scene, helping to overcome that bad winter weather of 1944-45.

As LeVier warmed to the job at hand in Europe, something special was taking place thousands of miles away in Burbank. In spectacular contrast to the thousands of camouflaged airplanes, tanks, armored cars and just commonplace staff cars, a vermilion-colored P-38J-10-LO streaked out of the sunny California sky, swooshing low over the upturned faces of about 15,000 Lockheed employees. There were excited cheers of approval when the giant sized word "YIPPEE" was seen, spread from wingtip to wingtip. It was the 5,000th P-38 manufactured by Lockheed, participating in the award of an Army-Navy "E" citation. . . E standing for excellence. It was also symbolizing the 13,000th warplane turned out by Lockheed.

Chief Test Pilot Milo Burcham ended the pass with a

The exclamation "Yippee" had its origins back in September 1940 when Marshall Headle took off on the first flight in the YP-38 after Lockheed had struggled for close to 18 months to redesign the Model 22 and manufacture it as a new prototype. The Model 122-62-02 (LAC identification for the design of the YP-38) was the most complex fighter – possibly the most complex military aircraft – ever built anywhere at the time of that first flight. No military aircraft had ever boasted of an absolutely flush-riveted, butt-joint skinning and metal control surfaces. So, it was not unexpected for a chorus of "Yippees" to be shouted by the morning crowd that witnessed the takeoff. This vermilion P-38J-20-LO was the 5,000th Lightning to be manufactured in Southern California. It made its colorful flight on May 17, 1944, a little more than five years after the contract award for thirteen YP-38s. (Eric Miller - LAC)

climbing spiral until he disappeared from view. He made a similar pass at Lockheed's Plant B-1, just a couple of miles down the road toward Burbank (where the P-38s were actually built), and then went on to buzz other Lockheed branch facilities. It was most fortunate that Lockheed sent a photographer up to record the beauty of that brilliant red airplane. In wartime, it was really one of a kind. In less than a year and a half, Lockheed would build almost another 5,000 Lightnings (production stopping just a couple of days short).

There will forever be considerable potential for argument about the actual performance capabilities of every World War II aircraft, and quoting unverified, undocumented official figures is akin to pouring water on powdered magnesium. In general, it is counterproductive to argue with test data obtained through flight testing programs conducted at Wright Field, Eglin Field or Orlando AAF under strictly controlled conditions. but even that sort of data can sometimes be subjected to derision by combat pilots who fought for their lives in virtually identical fighters. Most certainly some combat theater maintenance was lacking in quality. Just as pilots and navigators varied in competence, crew chiefs and mechanics in general had varying degrees of skill and commitment.

Experienced combat pilots were disinclined to worry about technical manual limitations during the heat of battle. For example, multi-ace Richard L. West, a Fifth Air Force pilot of considerable talent, admits (with some relish) that he often resorted to actions totally opposed to any recommendations/instructions when engaged in a fight. While on a lengthy mission from the Halmahera base in the Moluccas to northern Mindoro (south of Bataan), West spotted a Nakajima Oscar

above and behind him, closing slowly. Fuel was getting tight, but West and his wingman went for him. West did the unthinkable; he slowed way down in the climb, dropped full landing flaps and turned into the Oscar while climbing steeply. Having ultimate confidence in his P-38L, at something less than 100 mph, he went to full power to hang the Lightning on its props as the surprised Oscar pilot broke to the right and upward.

As West phrased it, "I left the flaps down, and stuck the nose at a spot I though he might be at pretty soon . . .Sure enough, he rolled it out at the top of an Immelmann. Neither of us is doing 65 mph, and that old L hung on the props and didn't even shudder." West blazed away with all guns, and the frail Oscar began to shed skin like a molting snake. The 35th Fighter Squadron pilot expressed his opinion about flight manuals and rules this way: "If you and I were in combat against each other and I could get you interested in manifold pressure and rpm readings . . . your ass (would be) mine!" Ah, yes. A point well taken. As a Pacific ace with at least a dozen confirmed victories, West is not bragging when he says "A '38L was a special kind of cat and one hell of a weapon in the hands of an experienced pilot. I would try one-on-one (against)

any airplane made in that era with any pilot, and bet whatever money I had I'd kill him." In the heat of battle, you do what you have to do.

Erroneous figures on performance have frequently been published since World War II, and it becomes exceedingly difficult for anyone to determine what might be even semi-reliable data. Interestingly, a similar problem plagued official observers in the midst of that war. It seems that manufacturer and user flight tests were often conducted with airplanes not entirely typical of random production examples. Not only that, it seemed apparent to combat pilots that they were often unable to match performance with what they expected, basing their expectations on formalized technical data furnished to them (e.g., Flight Characteristics Handbook or Flight Operating Manuals).

Late in 1943, the Experimental Engineering Division, Fighter Branch, under command of Maj. Charles Terhune, wanted to obtain directly comparable performance figures for the contemporary P-38J-10, P-47D-10, P-39Q-5 and P-51B fighters, all flown at combat gross weight (not maximum gross). All aircraft were to be selected at random from factory production delivery batches. No special preparations were to be allowed.

Lockheed P-38J-10-LO, AC42-67869, was allotted to the Fighter Flight Test Branch on December 2, committed to a 30-hour accelerated flight test program. Three different captains flew the airplane, using war emergency power (WEP) ratings, in an effort to avoid personal opinions. Their findings were that it had a high rate of climb and performed very well at high altitudes. They flew as high as 40,500 feet in the test series. Takeoff gross weight was 16,597 pounds, including full ammunition ballast. Extra ballast was carried to maintain what was them believed to be the maximum allowable rearward cg. Later tests revealed that they could move the cg further aft by as much as an additional 3 1/2 percent. Power settings were at 60 inches Hg manifold pressure and 3000 rpm. Everything being considered, it was remarkable that not one of the pilots made any reference at all to compressibility tuck. Some nose heaviness was noted in high-speed dives if they did not ad here to the limiting airspeeds published in the operating handbook. Testers mentioned a tendency toward tail buffet at high airspeeds – even in level flight above 30,000 feet. (It is a fair bet that the leading edge wing-fuselage fairings were improperly secured.)

They did feel that the turn radius was "fairly large for a fighter." Rate of roll was considered fair at medium speed, but slow at high speed. (With introduction of aileron power boost and dive flaps on P-38J-25-LO and subsequent airplanes, or retrofit of earlier Js, there was a remarkable improvement in

the roll rate and turn.) It is suspected that turning ability was more a matter of feeling than actual measurement. The following is a summary of figures presented in the formal test report, approved and signed by Brig. Gen. Franklin O. Carroll, Commanding:

Maximum horsepower at 60.8 inches Hg manifold pressure, 3000 rpm, was listed at 1612 bhp per engine at critical altitude, which was controlled by a limiting turbine speed of 26,4000 rpm and 60 inches Hg pressure.

Maximum SL speed . . . . . . 345 mph
Maximum crit. alt. speed . . 421.5 mph (WEP) (25,800 ft.)
Rate of climb (SL) . . . . . . . 4000 fpm
Rate of climb (crit. alt.) . . . 2900 fpm (23,400 ft.)
Time to crit. alt. . . . . . . . . . 6.19 mins. (23,400 ft.)
Service ceiling . . . . . . . . . 40,000 ft.

*NOTE: Two of the Allison F-17 engines failed (at different times) during the test program. After both engines had been changed, it was found to be 5 mph slower, probably attributable to cowl fit and ducting losses. (WEP rating for the P-38L series was 1725 bhp.)*

*OPPOSITE LEFT: Lt. Col. Rau's 20th Fighter Group (all three squadrons, they say) was led to a target by the colonel piloting "EZE Does It," a P-38J Droop Snoot on a "toggleer" mission. Capt. Herschel F. Ezell was a well-qualified bombardier, and the bomb-laden fighters in very good formation released their loads at his "bombs away" signal. In the ETO and MTO, regular bomb loads carried by the fighter contingent ranged from a single 500-pounder and 165-gallon tank to six 500-pounders and even to two 2,000-pounders (rarely) for sub pen bashing. The Rau-Ezell mission depicted was in June 1944. (AAF)*

Unfortunately, that specific report did not provide comparison figures for the other types tested in that program. However, earlier comparison tests of the P-38F and P-38G against earlier versions of the same manufacturers' products produced very good marks for the Lightnings.

As might be expected, the P-38J, as tested, was not nearly as fast on the deck as it was at critical altitude, but even the clean-lined P-51A and Spitfire Mk 5 low-altitude fighters were only marginally faster at the same level or at their low critical altitudes. Test pilots' opinions notwithstanding, good, capable pilots in the P-38J and L series airplanes could consistently cope with the best German fighters, maneuver for maneuver, below 25,000 feet. Even the very late model Focke-Wulf Fw 190D was officially rated at 357 mph at sea level, while the plentiful Fw 190A series fighters were rate as 2 mph slower, or just 10 mph faster than a P-38J-10-LO low down. Far more important is the fact that the highly regarded Fw 190A's critical altitude was below 21,000 feet when using their equivalent of WEP. Even at that level, it was 13 mph slower than the J-10 was 5,000 feet higher. Two balance factors existed: the German was over his own territory, and the F-17 Allison was no Merlin.

Of more than passing interest was the performance of a P-38G in earlier tests at Eglin Field in the spring of 1943. Lockheed had restricted the peak manifold pressure on that model to 44.5 in. Hg at 2800 rpm (because of intercooler limitations). Top speed attained in that test series was 385.5 mph at 25,000 feet. Above 30,000 feet, those leading edge intercoolers were considered critical. That particular test data helps explain some of the problems experienced by the 55FG and the 20FG in the period between mid-October 1943 and February 1944. (Perhaps it should be pointed out that although P-38Fs had Allison F-5 series engines and P-38Gs had F-10 engines, rated power on both types was 1150 bhp. Even the Fs could pull as much as 1325 bhp for a few minutes for combat. It must be obvious that if the P-38G performance was constrained by intercooling capacity, the H model was in even worse shape.)

Lest anyone should ever reach the conclusion that *only* P-38s had any problems, a survey of Unsatisfactory Reports (URs) or discussions with engineering officers and field service representatives would be most enlightening. Operational capability is what counts. (History is loaded with examples.) Notice the relatively short period of time that airlines could afford to operate Boeing 377 Stratocruisers with their R-4360 engines. The USAF could afford to maintain them, but not the airlines. Also note the great rapidity with which most of the post-war British airliners disappeared from the scene, at least in the first post-war decade. Of all the R-R Merlin-powered airliners built, only the Canadair DC-4M was reasonably successful.

Test pilot evaluations often made it extremely difficult to understand the reasons for some commentary in their reports. When P-38Fs were tested at Eglin Field in 1942, they attained (on average) 392 mph at 25,000 feet, using only 40.5 in. Hg manifold pressure and 2800 rpm. Later on, the test pilot who flew the P-38G looked upon the airplane as an "also ran" against what was basically the same competition. But here is the commentary from Eglin pilots in 1942:

"Against the P-39D, P-51, P-40F and P-47D-1, the P-38F had an equal or shorter radius of turn . . . from 15,000 feet on up.

"(It) would outclimb all other types in the test. For a general combination of rate of climb, range, endurance, speed, altitude and fire power, the P-38F is the best production line fighter tested to date at this station." Hardly faint praise.

Objectivity in evaluation was often a missing component. Consider the ultimate results: How many Allied fighter types could venture 600+ miles from the White Cliffs of Dover to Berlin, take on fresh pilots in short-range interceptors and maintain a better-than-1:1 kill ratio . . . and do it day after day? History says there were only two such fighter types. Lightnings constituted half of that team. How many heavy bomber types were able to venture over almost any target area in Europe (especially Germany) in broad daylight with even a modicum of success. True, there weren't many types that could try it; even fewer dared to try it for more than a few days.

That was the true test. As every fighting pilot know, testing and combat action are two entirely different things. Each has his important niche in the picture, and one is no good without the other. It's that simple.

One final set of relevant test information, circa 1942 (autumn), is provided for comparison with P-38F, P-38G and P-38J-10 data. Tested by RAF pilots of the Air Fighting Development Unit (AFDU), a captured Focke-Wulf Fw 190A3 demonstrated the following capabilities:

Max. speed at 4500 ft. altitude . . . . . . . . . .326 mph
Max. speed at 20,000 ft. altitude . . . . . . . . 389 mph*
Max. rate of climb at 4500 ft. altitude . . . . . 3050 fpm
Max. rate of climb at 17,500 ft. altitude . . . .3280 fpm

*Indicates override boost on supercharger for maximum performance.*

Notice that the low-level rate of climb on supercharger was about 75 percent of P-38 capability (virtually any model). At 23,000 feet, an Fw 190A and a P-38J (early series) had roughly comparable rates of climb. Maximum range of later Fw 190As (not combat range) with two underwing drop tanks was only 650 miles.

All of this gives credence to some of the most often overlooked factors in writing about the performance of various aircraft. In the final analysis, the key factors involved in attaining superiority in the air were pilot competence (training, experience, confidence, technique, aggressiveness), time and distance flown from base to target area (and the intensity of enemy resistance), maintenance conditions, overall performance of the aircraft flown, command quality, and combat tactics. Obviously it involves a complex equation, not just the performance of the aircraft as it is stated in specifications. If an aircraft is misused, it will not attain its full potential and may be viewed as "just another airplane." The Messerschmitt Me 262A was an excellent example of misuse of a remarkable airplane.

Even with all the initial handicaps afflicting it, the P-38 recorded some 2,500 "kills" in aerial combat in the ETO for the loss of 1,750 Lightnings from all aerial combat causes. That included all types of flak, aerial collisions, air-to-air combat, engine malfunctions and even pilot error. When an aircraft failed to return from a mission, it was tabulated as a combat loss. Therefore, the P-38 can probably boast of a 2 to 1 combat advantage over the best fighting types of the opposition over his own playing field, and mostly before the USAAF had air superiority over the Continent.

At the same time, ETO Lightnings flew 130,000 sorties at a loss factor of 1.3 percent. More clearly stated, that is 1.3 of the P-38s lost to ALL causes for every 100 aircraft dispatched on combat missions. All of that against a very determined enemy who destroyed 25 percent or more of the tough Boeing B-17s deployed on numerous missions. All factors considered, that is a pretty impressive performance in the face of unbalanced odds.

Some exploration of pro and con viewpoints of combat pilots about the Lockheed P-38 seems worth pursuing in view of the fact that the Lightning was such a departure in fighter airplane design and was controversial. Lt. Col. Mark Hubbard, commander of the 20th Fighter Group for about 15 days from March 3 to March 18, 1944, had come aboard as replacement for Lt. Col. Barton M. Russell. Although squadrons and elements/flights of the 20th's squadrons had flown combat missions while attached to the 55th Fighter Group in the final months of 1943, the group did not become operational until December 28. Hubbard was not an admirer of the P-38, and – at least in the ETO – he was not alone in that opinion.

On the ground and in the air at the 55FG, Capt. Chet Patterson studied the airplane's potential in depth and was more successful in utilizing that potential. Patterson thought that the Lightning was a very good combat machine in spite of several shortcomings. Perhaps he realized that the Bf 109, Bf 110, Fw 190A and Fw 190D all had an abundance of their own deficiencies. The Bf 109 was inclined to snap roll out of control if banked very sharply in the wrong direction; it was heavy on the controls in a high-speed dive; and it was a "bear" to land and take off. Neither it nor the Fw 190 could outrun a P-38. Patterson scored at least four confirmed victories over Europe in those days prior to OVERLORD. He knows he downed at least six enemy aircraft, but that old bugaboo, the camera in the nose section, precluded any chance of proving those tallies. (At a later date, Patterson served on Doolittle's staff at Eighth Air Force HQ.)

Lt. Col. Hubbard, on the other hand, was snakebit by the Lightning. He was not a bit reticent in post-war days in referring to his deep-seated ill will against the P-38, similar to attitudes of some pilots in 4th Fighter Group when they had to forgo flying Spitfire Mk 5s in favor of Republic P-47Cs in April 1943. Hubbard was convinced that the Lightning was all wrong in being a twin-engine fighter and that it was not a first-rate combat airplane.

Just for comparison, Lt. Arthur W. Heiden of the 79FS in the 20th Fighter Group worships the P-38 as a type, and with good reason. His personal mount, named "Lucky Lady," racked up more than 324 combat hours without suffering a single mission abort. There was not one single engine change performed in that entire period of operation! Heiden, forever the self-effacing battler of the 79th, attributes his own success entirely to the expertise of his crew chief, T/Sgt. Max Pyles. Art Heiden was being too generous. Those Allison engines were babied or maltreated by the pilots, depending on how well they understood the limitations of a mechanical device. (For the record, "Ace" Heiden was still flying expensive corporate aircraft into the 1990s.)

But, returning to the dissonant opinions of Mark Hubbard, it is only fair to present his commentary as he expressed it. While the full breadth of his remarks cannot be presented in this story, nothing is taken out of context. (If his comments were disproved by some person or action, some responsible comments may be interjected at that point. The source will be noted.)

Hubbard went on record to say, "It was a mistake to build a twin-engine aircraft, regardless of the role it was called on to perform."

RIGHT: *Air Force Plant Rep. Maj. Clarence Shoop, who would eventually rise to the rank of a general officer as commander of the California Air National Guard (from the ranks), is shown on a gun-firing mission on a P-38J-15-LO. Flying over the Pacific, shell casings fell harmlessly. Notice that they cannot be seen exiting as often shown in artist renderings. (LAC)*

ABOVE: *Having returned from his tour de force with the Eighth Air Force, Tony LeVier posed with his boss, Kelly Johnson, and the prized dive flaps then being installed at the factory on all P-38J-25-LO and P-38L fighters. Retrofit kits were being sent out for earlier series P-38Js. Engineer Kenneth Pittman was primarily responsible for the electrically actuated drive system. Dive flaps did not act as speed brakes; they, above all, affected the center of pressure distribution on the wing as compressibility came into play. (LAC)*

BELOW: *Compressibility chart relating specifically to the P-38 Lightning was taken from the AAF Pilot Training Manual. It is based on actual test data compiled by Milo Burcham and his team. To ignore this chart was pure lunacy; it did not lie and the airplane was quick to prove it to a pilot. One interesting point that has never been taken into account is that a P-38L-5-LO, enjoying up to 1,725 bhp per engine at War Emergency Power settings, must have been coming very close to its critical Mach Number of 0.68 in level flight at its critical altitude. WEP speed at 20,000-23,500 feet was probably as high as 443 mph (TAS).*

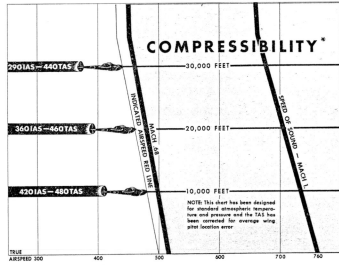

COMPRESSIBILITY*

290 IAS – 440 TAS
30,000 FEET

360 IAS – 460 TAS
20,000 FEET

420 IAS – 480 TAS
10,000 FEET

INDICATED AIRSPEED RED LINE

MACH .68

SPEED OF SOUND – MACH 1.

NOTE: This chart has been designed for standard atmospheric temperature and pressure and the TAS has been corrected for average wing pitot location error.

TRUE AIRSPEED 300    400    500    600    700    760

* FROM USAAF P-38 PILOT TRAINING MANUAL

Well, it is obvious that Gen. Kenney in the Far East did not share such thoughts, and Gen. Doolittle was glad to have those fighters in Northwest Africa in 1942 and 1943. The fully contemporary single-engine Bell P-39s were not going to defeat the *Luftwaffe* or *Wehrmacht* there, nor were the Curtiss P-40s, Supermarine Spitfires, Hawker Hurricanes going to overwhelm the enemy in the MTO. If Gen. Eaker did not have enough long-range P-38s to serve as escorts for the B-17s and B-24s, that cannot be blamed on the constructors or the designers. Command decisions in those upper echelons had far more to do with it. The War Department, Congress, U.S. Army generals, and Navy admirals of the 1920s and 1930s were the culprits in the American abdication from competitiveness in the arena of world air power. (By the time America had a single engine that equalled the two V-1710s in a P-38 for power, it was about 1946. And it was not a bit more reliable than the V-1710. Maintaining it in a combat environment would have been . . . shall we say, difficult.)

Some of Hubbard's condemnation, after the war, included his faulting of the fighter for not having two generators, "compressibility, incorrect intercoolers, and props rotating in the wrong direction." Instead of a group commander, Hubbard sounds more like a replacement second lieutenant after his first few missions. His knowledge of compressibility was obviously very limited, and the intercooler problems stemmed almost entirely from failure of the War Production Board to set up a second production source early in the program. Had that been done (instead of building a magnificent plant for fabrication of Fisher P-75As, which started off with a completely erroneous conception, and became an end-of-the war fighter with performance that could not match that of a P-38L) in the summer of 1941 or early in 1942, the USAAF could have had the P-38K and/or a Merlin-powered version that certainly would have been a world beater.

Criticism of poor cockpit heat, windshield fogging, a camera gun placement in the nose, and turbo regulation was certainly valid. But, if the Materiel Command would not authorize a change, or if the vendor could not improve his product (and there were no others), or if the using commands failed to submit a flood of URs, why blame the designers?

As for being critical of Lockheed for not solving the compressibility problem, neither Dr. Albert Einstein nor Dr. Theodore von Karman could even suggest a solution, let alone develop one. NACA blocked progress for months for fear they just might damage their wind tunnels, a fear that eventually proved groundless. Nobody in the AAF ever presented a valid solution. (Such criticism is akin to blaming the medical profession for polio or a failure to find an earlier cure. Necessity is the mother of invention, but sometimes mom is not fertile.) Highly regarded Caltech could not offer even basic advice.

When Lockheed's Kelly Johnson designed the Model 22, the powerplants available were unlikely to produce more than 1060 bhp in the foreseeable future. Not only that, the Army Air Corps never presented any hope of ordering more than 60 airplanes. The intercooler design was a zero-drag item and considered to be adequate for the job. By D-Day, 1944, P-38Ls were flying with engines capable of producing at least 60 percent more power than was ever envisioned by anybody in 1937 or 1939 or 1941. No, the thermodynamicists had not planned for such heat transfer problems. If Alex Kartveli had ever been told that his P-47 design was going to require a combat radius of action of more than 700 miles, his famed Thunderbolt would have been even bigger. And that would have been criticized. Initiated by a British contract, why wasn't the Mustang based on a Merlin (Packard-built) engine from the beginning?

In criticizing the failure of somebody to authorize and fund a second production source for P-38s, there is substantial evidence in fact to support the criticism. Boeing managed to produce up to fifteen B-17s a day in their Washington factory. Boeing-Douglas-Vega, at their peak levels, could produce more than 500 Fortresses a month. Lockheed P-38 production only managed to get above 400 a month (for a one-place fighter) in one month of 1944. Assuming that one modern four-line facility only half the size of Willow Run could easily produce a minimum of 200 fighters a month, at least 15,000 Lightnings could have been produced before August 1945. And that with the new plant only operating from mid-1943. With that huge Ford Willow Run plant built from scratch, B-24Es were being delivered by the autumn of 1942.

Orders that Lockheed had received for the L version alone reveals that the War Production Board, itself, believed that Allison could produce an adequate supply of engines for all P-38s that could be built. And there were, by that time, at least three manufacturers producing turbosuperchargers.

Packard seemed to have monumental flexibility for production of the Merlin. Example: In April 1943, the company produced and shipped no less that 606 engines. The following month saw 1,222 Merlins shipped! If two lines in a modern P-38 plant produced P-38Ks and two lines produced Merlin-powered P-38s – with all of the latter types going only to the ETO – there would have been one remarkable impact on the course of history. (Whatever Lt. Col. Thomas Hitchcock did for the success of the P-51 Mustang, it appears that Brig. Gen. Frank Hunter was extremely effective in handicapping the Lightning to an equal extent. Power corrupts. Like it or not, the AAF shot itself in the foot.)

Curtiss Airplane Division, certainly not the most progressive manufacturer from the engineering aspect, showed that transition back and forth between Allisons and Merlins was a minuscule problem. They proved that with the P-40 series. If Lockheed, in 1941, could produce non-turbo Lightnings (322-Bs with a different engine configuration) on parallel assembly lines with AAF P-38s and have virtually no problems stemming from that, the same thing could have transpired with Merlin-versus-Allison assembly lines.

Untrumpeted excuses for not Merlinizing P-38s do not ring true, just as the reasons expounded for not producing the P-38K (a mere one-inch difference in the height of the top cowl) sound pitifully unconvincing. If there is no real advocacy from a powerful personage for movement in a certain direction, there is no movement. The British Ministry of Supply (or whatever agency was responsible) proved that with the 322-B, an aircraft for which they had placed absolutely massive orders. Even when the Battle of Britain and the Westland Whirlwind showed that the unsupercharged powerplant specified for the 322-B was a glaring error, there wasn't even the slightest movement toward an obvious solution. Rolls-Royce (Hucknall) could have easily equipped an initial group of 322-Bs with various Merlin engines, even with their limited resources. Lockheed (Robert Gross) would have been most cooperative, and the WPB did not even have to be involved. (Of course that effort might have been aborted by the December 7 attack on Hawaii.)

Be that as it may, criticism of the WPB/AAF actions relating to the P-38 have tremendous validity. By contrast, many of Lt. Col. Hubbard's criticisms of P-38 flaws are not based on sound engineering principles, let alone knowledge of WPB, Materiel Command, or War Department decisions totally unknown to officers operating at his level. Even more to the point, these errors constituted only a tiny, insignificant fraction of all the errors made by men at many levels throughout the war.

Lt. Col. Hubbard, after spending about 15 months in a German prison camp, did not hesitate to express the following views, although he never flew a P-38L in combat. (There is no indication that he ever flew any P-47 or P-51 in combat theaters, certainly not in the ETO.):

ABOVE: A single-aircraft hangar, virtually destroyed in Allied attacks, could provide little protection at this former Luftwaffe base. Droop Snoot P-38s were in more widespread use than most people ever realized. "Colorado Belle" was another P-38J conversion, already armed with two 500-pound bombs for a tactical support mission. (James Kunkle)

BELOW: Crew Chief T/Sgt. Max D. Pyles received a Bronze Star for his expert maintenance of 1st Lt. Art Heiden's P-38J "Lucky Lady." That Lightning logged 300 combat hours without a single aborted mission. Cowl panel shows that the airplane had seen a great deal of action. (Arthur Heiden)

"Regardless of how well the P-38 performed in a variety of roles, it was the third best fighter in Europe – fifth best if you include the 109 and 190, and fifth best in the Pacific behind the F6F, F4U, P-47 and P-51."

Now isn't it marvelous that a man who never had a conversation with Bong, McGuire, MacDonald, West, Westbrook, ad infinitum and ad nauseam, about the P-38 – not to mention a plethora of Navy and Marine Corps pilots – can be so certain about his viewpoint. The P-51D was not even a factor in the Far East Air Force until the final months of 1944 (almost 9 months after Hubbard went down in Nazi territory). Some F-6Cs had been operating in the CBI Theater, and F-6Ds were evidently the initial Mustang (Merlin-engined) types assigned to far western Pacific units. (All F-series Mustangs were for photo-recon work.)

Regarding SWPA Thunderbolts, most of those received in that area in 1943 had the most limited provisions for carrying even one drop tank. As late as February 1944, air depots in the SWPA were "jury rigging" P-47Ds to carry two 165-gallon drop tanks under the wings. When P-47D-23 razorback versions were among the latest arrivals in the CBI, they were invariably seen flying with the P-38 drop tanks. Stating the facts about P-47 usage, there were some squadrons of P-47Ds operating with Eastern Air Command in 1944-45, and it seems that about three RAF squadrons had Thunderbolts (D models) for operations in Burma, etc.

As for the long-ranging P-47Ns, a maximum of three groups employed them in the Japan Air Offensive. It appears

that the 413FG and the 507FG together only had five squadrons. The 318FG was an older unit with five acknowledged squadrons, but perhaps not all at the same time. Worse, they flew a mix of P-38s, P-47s and P-51s, with no certainty that they ever had the P-47N model. The Twentieth Air Force planned to use P-47Ns for B-29 escort duty, but that plan was never implemented. The Seventh Air Force P-47Ns operating out of Ie Shima rarely flew any escort missions. Lifting off at a gross weight of about 10 tons, including two 165-gallon P-38-style wing tanks and a 75-gallon belly tank, they operated mostly in an interdiction role. Virtually all P-47N missions and P-51D missions were flown in 1945.

Fact upon fact, it is certainly obvious that Lt. Col. Hubbard had a difficult time with objectivity.

"Incidentally, I enjoyed flying the P-38 below 20,000 feet when not in combat," Hubbard commented. "It was the most comfortable of all prop types I flew because of the cockpit layout, two fans (props), and long legs (range)." Faint praise.

As March 17, 1944, dawned Hubbard had logged just under 55 hours of combat time in the ETO. His eleventh mission was to be Mission 37 for the 20FG. Lt. Col. Russell had logged just 11 missions. This was also to be Mark Hubbard's last mission of the war.

"We introduced a new tactic that day, something we called the 'bouncing squadron.' That squadron was to follow the enemy down as far as it could, hoping to keep them in sight since they always split-essed away and outdove the hell out of us without any compressibility factor. The other two squadrons were to provide top cover. We ran into 30 or 40, and sure enough, about half of them split-essed. We managed to keep some in sight until we got down to tree-top level," said Hubbard in his downhome manner.

"I wound up chasing a flight of four, then three, then two. There were more targets than we could shoot at. After about 10 minutes, the five tracers came out,[1] so I called my wingman and said, 'We're going home.' We had gotten three (enemy aircraft) without apparent harm to us," he recalled.

"There were several chasing us, quite well back, so (we) stayed on the ground to build up speed. Saw 350 mph on the

clock and pulled up to zoom into broken/solid clouds at about 2,500 feet. Hadn't paid much attention to what was ahead of us . . . you know fighter pilots fly backwards. Looked down dead ahead and saw a large city – which was Augsburg – in flames and smoke. Pushed down again to fly around it since I had no desire to test their flak," the colonel remembered without joy.

"Thud! I heard a distant, heavy thud in what I took to be the nose. Believed I had taken a non-explosive round there. Within 15 seconds there was an explosion in the left engine, with the cowl pushing up and a nice long stream of flame trailing." When Hubbard's proximity to the city is taken into consideration, he probably took hits from secondary flak batteries or was struck by shrapnel from some low-burst shell. The fact that the engine explosion followed a primary "thud" within seconds would certainly indicate something different than an engine self-destruction tendency, but an emergency of that nature at very low level does not provide much time for analysis of the situation.

Hubbard continued with his memories. "Pulled back on both throttles and the left mixture control. Then pushed both throttles forward, but had no power from either engine. Was down to about 50 feet altitude at something over 300 mph. Thought of setting it down on the belly because there was lots of snow. Then it occurred to me that there might be some stone fences in those fields, and that gunsight was right in front of my face. I pulled up, released the canopy, rolled (the P-38) on its back and she began to shudder. Pushed out with my legs tucked well in and I saw the tail go by, so I pulled the cord. My chute popped open fast . . . thank God, and I had only

---

1. Indicating ammunition exhaustion was close at hand.

one-half swing before hitting. That sprained my ankle badly."

Thinking back, the former group commander reflected on what had actually happened in those fleeting seconds. "I have thought about this many times, believe me. I could have taken a hit in the left engine. Did not remember to open the intercooler shutters when we got down on the deck, so I think maybe the carburetor heat got too high. Or it could have been the good old Allison 'Time Bomb' again. I believe it was the latter, becoming my third engine failure in twelve (?) missions." (As a P-38 pilot, Mark Hubbard had recorded 59 hours 20 minutes of combat time.) "As to the failure of the right-hand engine, I believe I pulled back the mixture control on the wrong engine."

Well, it is patently obvious that Lt. Col. Hubbard was unlikely ever to be happy with P-38s, and his bit him. (More than one copilot in a multi-engine aircraft has received a severe tongue lashing for having feathered the wrong propeller or pulling back the wrong throttle or mixture control.)

What happened to the 20th Fighter Group in the following days and months was not on the negative side at all. Lt. Col. Harold Rau was sent up to Kings Cliffe as replacement for the MIA Mark Hubbard. Eventually word got back that Hubbard was a POW in Germany.

During the period when Lt. Col. Hubbard was decrying Lightning performance, he had Capt. James M. "Slick" Morris on board as a flight commander in the 77FS, and the captain's performance should have convinced Hubbard that the P-38 had something going for it that he did not understand. On Mission No. 18, some 50 Lightnings of the 20FG were escorting 3rd Division B-17s to conduct a raid on Frankfurt, but no fewer than 14 of the P-38s aborted and returned to base, revealing a serious problem at the maintenance level. The remaining fighters escorted the bombers over the target and during withdrawal.

Looking for targets of opportunity on the way home, they did some effective low-level work. 1st Lt. Morris (promoted after the mission) became the first Eighth Air Force pilot to be credited with shooting down four enemy aircraft on one mission. Two were Bf 109F/G fighters and two were Fw 190A fighters. "Slick" Morris also managed to blow up a locomotive on that same mission. Before he became a POW on July 7, he was credited with seven aerial victories plus a 1/3rd credit for a Heinkel He 111 bomber.

E Whereas Lt. Col. Barton Russell had a countenance that appeared to have been chiseled from granite, Lt. Col. Rau was more like a friendly sheepdog. He was unique in several ways, one being that he was one of the taller pilots. He also went home after the war, having flown P-47s, P-38s and P-51s in combat

in the ETO, all without much difficulty. Although his P-38J "Gentle Annie" had markings showing five air-to-air victories, he did not gain formal "ace" status. Evidently he only received a partial official recognition for one of the victories. It is only fair to say that "Hal" Rau was a rather popular commander, and overall performance of the historical 20th Fighter Group improved tremendously under his command. He was aided immensely by having men like Maj. Cy Wilson as commander of the 55FS and Maj. Russell Gustke to command the 77FS.

In those early months after Gen. Doolittle took command of the Eighth, luck and leadership prevailed for the general. Even as he implemented the actions that would eventually lead to a single tier (P-51s only) fighter force, a strange thing happened. Performance of the P-38 groups improved rapidly for a number of reasons, even though it would be the Ninth Air Force which would benefit from having the "definitized P-38 Lightning," namely the P-38J-25-LO and P-38L series. (In essence, the 210 production P-38J-25s were proofing aircraft for planned retrofit of a couple of thousand early J versions that were already in service. The "Murphy's Law" destruction of that AAF Douglas C-54 by an RAF fighter deprived all VIIIth Fighter Command groups of an opportunity to out-dive and split-ess with the Luftwaffe's top fighters to that enemy's sorrow.) Not only that, the Republic P-47D-25 "bubble canopy" series, with much improved range and capability performance, came on the scene at about the same time as the P-51Ds were becoming very plentiful. Just as the new Thunderbolts were enabled to fly with nearly 300 gallons of external fuel, many of them could suddenly operate from airfields on the continent. As has been stated, everything was happening in rapid-fire sequence in 1944.

Col. Roy W. Osborn, operating out of Honington, brought the 364FG onto line operationally on March 3. And the 479th Group, known as "Riddle's Raiders," flew its first operational mission on March 26. That outfit was commanded by Lt. Col. Kyle L. Riddle.

There were a couple of unusual incidents involving the last two groups mentioned. During the operational training phase, the commanding officer of the 364FG, Lt. Col. Fred Grambo, was killed in action just 3 days before the group reached operational status, and Col. Osborn was thrown into the breach. As for the intrepid Lt. Col. Riddle, he was shot

*With Field Marshal Von Rundstedt's forces less than 15 miles away, P-38Js loaded with 500-pounders taxi out from tight quarters on ice and snow to the runway. The P-38J with checkerboard nose markings was assigned to the 485FS. Named "California Cutie," it was loaded and ready to go. It could not have been an especially enjoyable holiday time, but the Lightnings helped turn the tide. (Al Meryman)*

down on August 10 in his Lightning. Two days later, Col. Hubert "Hub" Zemke, twice commander of the famed 56th Fighter Group, assumed command of the 479FG and began flying P-38s. "Riddle's Raiders" continued to fly P-38s until conversion to P-51Ds was completed on Sept. 28. In the meantime, Kyle Riddle had evaded capture and was returned to England, but Col. Zemke and his new P-51 went down over Europe on October 30. He became a POW. Riddle, having made the conversion to P-51s, again took over as commander of the group to which he had given his name.

F In the remarkable February-through-April period preceding Operation OVERLORD, three P-38 groups joined the Ninth Air Force's IXth Fighter Command under the guidance of Maj. Gen. Elwood "Pete" Quesada, a man with AAF roots clear back to the U.S. Army Air Service days. Unlike his VIIIth Fighter Command contemporary (circa 1943), Frank O'D, Hunter, who never flew a P-38 at all, Quesada never shied sway from flying Lightnings. His 367th, 370th and 474th Fighter Groups started out with P-38Js and soon made the easy transition to the spectacular L version. Updated with dive flaps, boosted aileron controls (the first fighters in history to have them) and engines that could belt out 1725 bhp in the War Emergency mode, the Lightning had progressed from its Recession year beginnings (1937) in a drawing office with a leaking roof to become one of the three great AAF fighters of the war.

Once the Ninth Air Force began to fly from captured airfields in Belgium (and even more advanced bases on the Continent), it became more commonplace for the Lightnings to tote bombs (usually in the 500- to 1,000-pound category) than external fuel tanks. In the ETO, the need for extended range became of secondary importance to inflicting damage.

As the perimeter around the German ground forces shrank, emphasis on the Pacific war against Japan increased dramatically. Even P-51 pilots in the ETO commands began to log time on P-47s anticipating the need to fly the extended range P-47N fighter in that forthcoming assault against the Land of the Rising Sun. As take-off gross weights for the P-38L Lightning

and the P-47N Thunderbolt climbed relentlessly toward 12 tons, there was little doubt that both types would combine forces with the newer P-51H (and slightly older D) Mustangs in an expected massive invasion. Lengthy overwater flight would be the norm. In general, most fighter missions in the 1945 Pacific arena were flown below 25,000 feet. Certainly the Allison failure rate had little bearing on the so-called island-hopping campaign. Fuel consumption management was a more important subject.

Unheralded, Lockheed was flying test aircraft on a virtual, "round-the-clock" basis in the most intensive accelerated testing program ever initiated up to that time. It must be assumed that Allison was working closely with the Burbank people and the Air Materiel Command (AMC) to incorporate every conceivable improvement that would make the V-1710 engines more reliable everywhere, but especially so in northern European skies. Missions in excess of 9 hours became relatively routine in the Far East, but there was no hue and cry about engine failure rates from that quarter. Whether it was operating technique, climatic conditions, fuel supplies or powerplant improvements that made the difference will probably never by known. (Best possible guess: operating techniques combined with fuel quality and constant cold soak, on the ground and at altitude, had combined to plague P-38 operations in Northern Europe.)

Col. Jack Jenkins observed and noted the effect that operating technique had on aerial losses. His memories were in sharp contrast to the contemporary techniques stressed by Col. Curtiss LeMay, commander of the 305BG about a year earlier. LeMay demanded maintenance of the formation defensive boxes. In sharp contrast, Jenkins noted that his group was assigned to escort Consolidated B-24s – three combat wings (three 60-plane formations) that were to be in boxes with about two miles between wings – on a Friedrichshafen raid and during withdrawal.

"They were strung out over 40 miles, and we couldn't cover them. They had bombed the target and were going home; we were about at the limit of our endurance when about thirty Me 109s and Fw 190s came in." The colonel said he saw several B-24s and B-17s (?) shot up and many parachutes opened. He said that it was "a hell of a long trip home with some flak (encountered). A 5 hours [sic] and 15 minutes trip." That was on March 19, 1944. The point: If formation discipline was not maintained, or if the required technique was beyond the operational capabilities of the pilots, losses were bound to escalate. There was literal proof that many pilots – be it fighter or bomber – could not develop the required technique for survival, even when their lives were in jeopardy. (According to official records, the mission was on March 18. Auth.)

G April 8, 1944, began in a less than auspicious manner. No fewer than 644 heavy bombers were sent out to attack aircraft assembly plants (Brunswick), *Luftwaffe* bases and control centers at four other cities deep in Germany. Lt. Col. Hal Rau's group was assigned to provide target cover for the 1st Bombardment Division, but foul weather descended on Kings Cliffe and the group was forced to stand down. The colonel was not happy with this turn of events, and when the weather cleared later in the morning he called VIIIth Fighter Command HQ at Bushey Hall. They gave him permission to lead a strafing mission against airfields and other targets in an area about 80 miles west of Berlin. The target area was known to be very heavily defended. The Eighth Air Force had not attempted any similar venture where no other covering squadrons would be involved.

As the 20FG broke ground at Kings Cliffe for Mission No. 43 on that fateful April 8 at 1402 hours, Col Rau had only one thing in mind: He was determined to clobber the hell out of anything that moved west of the German frontier. Arriving over Salzwedel at 1554 hours at an altitude of 7,000 feet with Rau leading White Section of their 79FS, the group split up. While the 79th went after an airfield north of Salzwedel, the 77FS attacked an airfield south of the town. Maj. McAuley led the 55FS in an attack on locomotives and industrial targets.

Led by Maj. Franklin, four pilots from Yellow and Blue

sections of the 79th enjoyed catching a big Heinkel He 177 bomber in the landing pattern. Hit by devastating firepower, the long-range bomber smashed into the ground in a spectacular cartwheel that ended in a fiery explosion.

Ignoring increasingly intense ground fire on each pass, Rau – in the lead – took White and Yellow sections through four separate assaults on the bomber base. These two sections alone destroyed or seriously damaged seven Ju 88s, two He 177s, one He 111, one Ju 52/3m and two unidentified twin-engine aircraft. Red section swept in on several hundred soldiers marching in close order drill on a large parade ground. Caught by surprise – the Lightning could quietly sneak up on you – with no available cover in sight – the soldiers suffered as many as 300 casualties on the first pass. It was too good to be true, so Lt. Col. Rau's section was called in on the R/T to hit the same target. Every barracks building was shot up thoroughly in the sustained onslaught, adding substantially to the casualty list.

Maj. Donald McAuley's 55th Fighter Squadron had knocked out no less than eight locomotives in its initial sweep before going on to shoot up flak towers and ammo or gasoline storage facilities. Rau and Franklin (79FS) intercepted two trains headed in opposite directions, and each proceeded to demolish the locomotives and strafe the strings of railcars. For their part, the 77FS claimed three locos destroyed and three more damaged.

Seven silver-colored Bf 109s charged into the busy P-38 flights as they rampaged over the countryside. They knocked Lt. Esau out in their first pass. Fortunately for Esau, in Rau's section, he was able to bail out. Rau, reacting quickly, zoomed to 4,000 feet, snapped over and caught one of the Messerschmitts as it was intent on attacking Lt. M. P. Snow's aircraft. Evidently the German pilot was killed instantly by the hail of lead from the colonel's Lightning because the 109 went straight into Snow's P-38. Both aircraft exploded on impact, and neither pilot was seen to escape. Rau tallied another Bf 109 just as Maj. Franklin and Lt. LeFevre blasted two more silver bandits into terminal dives.

Meanwhile, on the south side of Salzwedel, the 77FS caught a Heinkel He 177 in the pattern on final approach. Maj. Johnson closed to within 200 feet before opening fire. The helpless heavy bomber never made it to the runway, crashing heavily and burning furiously. The calling card left by the 77th was eight enemy aircraft claimed as destroyed and 21 more damaged. Lt. Claude Horne followed a flaming P-38, a victim of concentrated ground fire, and saw it crash. As he turned

*Developed as a natural extension of the Droop Snoot concept, P-38L Pathfinders relied on BTO radar for inclement weather bomb direction. This P-38L-1-LO, seen at L.A.T. in Burbank, was evidently the second Pathfinder produced by Lockheed. It was, unexpectedly, displayed on November 2, 1944. The company's first conversion was completed on a P-38J. There evidently is absolutely no record of the number of Lightnings that were modified to use AN/APS-15 radar in this manner. Considering the extent of modification in equipment and mission, the lack of some different designation was unexplainable. (LAC)*

away, he found himself headed straight at an onrushing Fw 190. It broke to the left and Horne reacted instantly, triggering a long burst that turned the Focke-Wulf into a flamer. It went down in a rather sloppy split-ess. Capt. James Morris enjoyed shooting up another locomotive. Perhaps that was even more important than shooting down a fighter or two because about 20 gasoline- or oil-filled tank cars went up with it. Loco busting could become habit forming.

The Republic P-47 Thunderbolt emerged from the war with a reputation as being the reigning champion of strafing aircraft. While its firepower was a major reason for that reputation, it was also an extremely rugged and dependable aircraft. That powerful P&W R-2800 up front brought more than one P-47 home even when one or two cylinders were missing completely.

However well deserved that reputation was, it is important to know that one P-38 group in the ETO and one in the MTO became relatively famous as the "Loco Boys" (20FG) and the "Loco Busters" (82FG) because of their outstanding success in locomotive destruction and overall strafing efficiency. Since the Thunderbolt groups outnumbered the P-38 groups in the Eighth, Ninth and Fifteenth Air Forces by a margin of five or six to one, their publicity exposure was much greater. Lightnings continued to rack up impressive "shoot 'em up" scores until the supply of available P-38s dwindled to a trickle in the ETO. With the guns well harmonized, firepower out to maximum gun range was concentrated in a neat pattern.

In the months following April 8 and Mission No. 43, performances of most P-38 pilots in 20FG improved considerably. Hal Rau was a definite asset, and even when he was returned (for a time) to the Zone of the Interior (ZI) for a well-deserved rest, the very able Cy Wilson made certain that the group did not miss a beat. On that one day in April, the 20th had lashed out at the *Luftwaffe* and *Wehrmacht* in what began as an impromptu mission with 42 Lightnings. Before they headed home, they had fired 21,475 rounds of .50-caliber ammunition and 3,850 rounds of 20-mm cannon shells in approximately 30 minutes of low-level combat action. If, indeed, there was a need to turn a tide of effectiveness, it was done in just a little over 4 hours . . . once and for all. Never again would the Germans feel safe from sustained, multiple attacks on even the most unlikely targets in the deepest recesses of their homeland. Seven *Luftwaffe* aircraft had been destroyed in aerial combat; 21 other aircraft – assorted bombers for the most part – had been destroyed on the ground; and another 23 aircraft on the ground were damaged, some very extensively. At least 13 locomotives and more than 50 railroad cars had been wiped out. For all the intensity and fury of their attack, only four P-38s failed to return to Kings Cliffe, a loss rate of less than 10 percent. One of those had been knocked out by secondary flak batteries, and one was rammed by a Messerschmitt with a dead pilot at the controls.

H While Kings Cliffe and Mount Farm may have up-scale names, there was one serious annoyance factor about operating from those bases that is rarely, if ever, mentioned. Lockheed Lightnings were provided with a "built-in headwind" in having to operate from those locations. No other AAF (and probably RAF) fighter-class aircraft operating against the Continent had to fly so far just to cross the English coastline, going and coming back. Depending on the location of the target area, something like 82 to 100 miles was added to a mission just to fly from those two bases. Kings Cliffe, home to the 20th Fighter Group, was located even farther west of London than AJAX (VIIIth Fighter Group HQ), and Mount Farm – 7th Photo Group base – was literally 15 miles west of AJAX. Therefore,

---

**TABLE 16-1**

**GROUPS AND SQUADRONS OF THE
ETO AND MTO**

**USAAF**
  Major P-38/F-4/F-5 Combat assignments - ETO/MTO 1942-1945. Standard Group strength (Fighters) was 75 airplanes

**EIGHTH AIR FORCE/TWELFTH AIR FORCE/FIFTEENTH AIR FORCE**
1st Fighter Group
  *AF
    27th Fighter Sqdn.
    71st Fighter Sqdn.
    94th Fighter Sqdn.

**EIGHTH AIR FORCE/TWELFTH AIR FORCE/FIFTEENTH AIR FORCE**
14 Fighter Group
  *AF
    37th Fighter Sqdn.
    48th Fighter Sqdn.
    49th Fighter Sqdn.
    50th Fighter Sqdn.

**EIGHTH AIR FORCE**
20th Fighter Group
    55th Fighter Sqdn.
    77th Fighter Sqdn.
    79th Fighter Sqdn.

**EIGHTH AIR FORCE**
55th Fighter Group
    38th Fighter Sqdn.
    338th Fighter Sqdn.
    343rd Fighter Sqdn.

**EIGHTH AIR FORCE/TWELFTH AIR FORCE/FIFTEENTH AIR FORCE**
82nd Fighter Group
  *AF
    95th Fighter Sqdn.
    96th Fighter Sqdn.
    97th Fighter Sqdn.

**EIGHTH AIR FORCE**
78th Fighter Group
    82nd Fighter Sqdn.}
    83rd Fighter Sqdn.} *
    84th Fighter Sqdn.}

**EIGHTH AIR FORCE/TWELFTH AIR FORCE**
**350th Fighter Group
    345th Fighter Sqdn.}
    346th Fighter Sqdn.} ***
    347th Fighter Sqdn.}

**EIGHTH AIR FORCE**
364th Fighter Group
    383rd Fighter Sqdn.
    384th Fighter Sqdn.
    385th Fighter Sqdn.

**NINTH AIR FORCE**
367th Fighter Group
    392nd Fighter Sqdn.
    393rd Fighter Sqdn.
    394th Fighter Sqdn.

**NINTH AIR FORCE**
370 Fighter Group
    401st Fighter Sqdn.
    402nd Fighter Sqdn.
    485th Fighter Sqdn.

**NINTH AIR FORCE**
494th Fighter Group
    434th Fighter Sqdn.
    435th Fighter Sqdn.
    436th Fighter Sqdn.

**EIGHTH AIR FORCE**
7th Photographic Reconnaissance Group
    13th Photo-Recon Sqdn.
    14th Photo-Recon Sqdn.
    22nd Photo-Recon Sqdn.
    27th Photo-Recon Sqdn.

**NINTH AIR FORCE**
10th Photographic Group
    30th Photo-Recon Sqdn.
(assigned 67 TRG)
    31st Photo-Recon Sqdn.
    33rd Photo-Recon Sqdn.
    34th Photo-Recon Sqdn.

**NINTH AIR FORCE**
67th Tactical Reconnaissance Group
    33rd Photo-Recon Sqdn.

**NINTH AIR FORCE**
9th Tactical Reconnaissance Group
    39th Photo-Recon Sqdn.

**NAAF/FIFTEENTH AIR FORCE**
154th Tactical Recon Sqdn.
    (Weather Reconnaissance)

**TWELFTH AIR FORCE/FIFTEENTH AIR FORCE**
3rd Photographic Group (Recon)
    5th Photo-Recon Sqdn.
    12th Photo-Recon Sqdn.
    23rd Photo-Recon Sqdn.

**TWELFTH AIR FORCE/FIFTEENTH AIR FORCE**
5th Photo-Reconnaissance Group
    15th Photo-Recon Sqdn.
    32nd Photo-Recon Sqdn.
    37th Photo-Recon Sqdn.

* All P-38s sent to NWAAF as replacements. 78FG converted to P-47s in U.K.

** This was a mixed aircraft fighter group, with a few P-38s employed for specialized assignments. Exact allocations of P-38s not known.

*** Squadrons composed of P-38, P-39, and P-400 aircraft in 1943.

Col. Rau's group had to travel about 575 miles just to reach the Salzwedel target area, and nobody seemed the least bit concerned about flying at maximum rated power (or perhaps at WEP) for at least a half-hour. Still air conditions must have prevailed because flying time was only about two hours in each direction. (On several of the missions the big fighters encountered 120 mph westerly winds, requiring a bit of extra care in planning for the return flight.) It was not uncommon for the entire group of fighters from the inland bases to land at Attlebridge, Horsham St. Faith, Hethel or Metfield on the way home with as little as 5 minutes of fuel remaining.

There can be little doubt that P-38Js equipped with the two 55-gallon wing leading edge tanks (standard from J-25 onward) and two 310-gallon drop tanks (rarely available in the U.K. it seems) might have been able to hit Prague or even Warsaw. After March 3, 1944, Berliners were to become very familiar with the shape of P-38s and P-51s.

The aggressiveness and kindly demeanor of Harold Rau had, without a doubt, provided that spark so badly needed by the 20FG. He was, for the Lightnings, what Zemke, Blakeslee, Schilling and Chesley Peterson (among others) were for Thunderbolts, Mustangs and Spitfires.

A few other P-38/ETO items are of particular interest. Capt. Arthur Jeffrey, a 479FG pilot flying a P-38J on July 29, chased a Messerschmitt Me 163B Komet rocket-powered, tailless interceptor while returning home from a mission to Merseburg. That was the first recorded encounter between an AAF fighter and a jet- or rocket-propelled *Luftwaffe* aircraft. Making a deflection shot, Jeffrey scored hits on the Komet, which went into a near vertical descent below 500 feet and plunged into cloud cover. Since the P-38 pilot suffered blackout from a high-g pullout in order to avoid crashing, it would be difficult to believe that the German rocket aircraft was able to pull out of that dive. Jeffrey was awarded credit for destroying the enemy aircraft, but a review of captured German records failed to provide confirmation.

The 479th, late getting into combat, was most notable for being recognized through award of two Distinguished Unit Citations while flying P-38 Lightnings, although the second DUC was received for operations during the transition to Mustangs. The only question: How many P-38s participated in the September 26, 1944, mission? The last 479FG mission for Lightnings occurred the next day. Lightnings were most certainly involved, though, in tallying no fewer than 19 *Luftwaffe* aircraft on that memorable 26th day of September action for which the highly regarded award was made.

In Europe, only the 474FG retained its Lockheed P-38s until cessation of hostilities became a fact.

Gen. H. H. Arnold had stated in the early months of 1944 that the advent of the long-range fighter was at "just the saving moment. He was not being very candid or accurate. The saving moment for many bomber crews in a period of potential disaster – it may be recalled – was more likely placed in the last quarter of 1943. Arnold's delayed statement has been taken to mean assimilation of Mustangs into VIIIth Fighter Command. The Combined Bomber Offensive was in dire straits when Gen. Doolittle became Eighth Air Force CG in January 1944, and it had been in that condition for months. And the *Luftwaffe*, according to intelligence reports, was stronger than ever in the first quarter or so of 1944. If the CBO was not successful in attaining its aims, OVERLORD would have been all but impossible. POINTBLANK most certainly could not wait until the first week of June to prove that it was a success. Until February 11, the only long-range fighters operational in the ETO were P-38Hs in the 20FG and the 55FG. The first Eighth Air Force Mustangs to become fully operational belonged to the transferred 357FG. Two more P-38 groups became operational in the ETO

before D-Day and they were joined by three more P-51 groups.

If Arnold had been specific and totally honest in his statement, he would have made it clear that Lightnings and Mustangs shared in that accolade, fifty-fifty. As interpreted in the press, it sometimes appeared that the P-47s were sharing with the Mustangs. But it was only Lightnings and Mustangs that were seen over Berlin until much later in 1945.

So speaking, proper credit for the first penetration of fighters to Berlin (the bombers failed to show) goes to the 55th Fighter Group, an event that made outstanding headline news on Saturday, March 4, 1944. "FIRST U.S. FIGHTERS REACH BERLIN," was the banner-like headline on the *New York Times*. Newspaper stories are always somewhat suspect as to accuracy. Who might have had a ringside seat? Our vote goes to Lt. Col. Jack S. Jenkins, the man who led the 55FG mission on March 3. Excerpts taken directly from the Jenkins wartime diary provide the best possible idea of what occurred that day.

"S-2 called early – a big mission is on. It was the long awaited show to Berlin. Six months ago, General Kepner told me that we would go there, and today we did it!

"I led the group in and flew with the 38th (Fighter) Squadron. We went straight in and got pretty well shot up by flak over Magdeburg, Hannover, etc. We kept calling the bombers but couldn't contact them. I had a rough right engine and wondered if I would make it in. The (other) boys had engine trouble and dropped out like flies. We got into Berlin with only about half our group. We saw a few unidentified airplanes on the way in but they didn't bother us. We stooged around Berlin city limits for 15 minutes waiting for our big friends (B-17s), but couldn't see them. We started out and came by Leipzig, dropped our tanks and about that time I had to drop down with my flight (to warmer outside temperatures) due to right engine trouble. I lost one boy when I did a 360-degree turn. Lt. Kreft and I came out alone. We had to outrun about 15 Huns. Doing this with one bad engine wasn't fun.

"The bombers turned back at Hamburg (we learned later), so we were the only Allied planes to reach Berlin! I got so cold that my crew chief had to help lift me out of the cockpit. God, let's get this war over!

"P.S. It took only 1 hour and 45 minutes to make the trip to Berlin."

Between March 4 and March 22, the 55FG made five more missions to the Berlin area. Jack Jenkins led three of them. That is, at a minimum, a 1200-mile round trip, amounting to a 650-675 mile radius of action.

On April 10, just before the group was scheduled to move to Wormingford, Col. Jenkins made one too many strafing passes at a *Luftwaffe* airfield. His P-38 took hits. Losing his engines, he made a belly landing. A while later, after some time in a hospital not far from Paris, Jenkins eventually was sent to a *Stalagluft*.

Just short of 13 months after he was the victim of vicious flak, the war in Europe ground to a halt. That isn't exactly the way Jenkins planned it when he made his diary entry on March 3, 1944.

The last gasp Battle of the Bulge episode left the Nazi forces in the west a thoroughly whipped giant, but the serpent died slowly. Heavy bomber losses did not just fade away, but those terrible days between the summer of 1943 and the launching of OVERLORD in 1944 – a time when most missions had to remain unescorted over the targets – were just recurring nightmares.

Perhaps one little boy did prevent the flooding of Holland by stopping a leak in the dike; and there is a strong possibility that one group of P-38 fighters – the 55th – prevented a mere crisis from turning into an unconstrained disaster. Nobody will ever know for certain. But who really wants to argue with success?

# CHAPTER 17

# With Honor, With Distinction

A Combat flights ended quietly for the 475th Fighter Group, known widely as "Satan's Angels," on July 21, 1945, with their scoreboard indicating the air-to-air destruction of 551 enemy aircraft in 87 engagements for the total combat expenditure of only 56 P-38s and the unfortunate loss of 27 pilots. (There were a few more pilots who lost their lives, but not as a result of enemy action.) That was the record of the Fifth Air Force's only fighter group that was, from the outset, composed entirely of Lockheed Lightnings. A unique status had been maintained since the spring of 1943 when the group was created in the far reaches of the Southwest Pacific theater of operations at one of the most crucial periods of the War. General George C. Kenney knew when his day of reckoning was upon him in the grim months of 1942, and he uncompromisingly and steadfastly tied his wagon to the Lockheed star.

Literally flying in the face of overwhelming pressure generated by the marginally desperate 1943 requirements of Doolittle's Twelfth Air Force in the Mediterranean Theater and of Eaker's crisis-plagued Eighth Air Force daylight bombing program in the European Theater, Kenney knew that his and Gen. MacArthur's chances of success in combating the Japanese forces depended on the fighting capabilities of the P-38. Nearly 2 years after he took this stance, the fighter pilots of the Fifth Air Force were constantly proving how sagacious the general had been.

Probably the purest example of the general's wisdom was the record attained by the 475th Group in a 2-month period during November-December 1944, in the tenuous and often desperate Philippines Campaign. The three combat squadrons, plus elements of Headquarters squadron, assigned to the 475th totally destroyed 169 enemy aircraft in the air for the loss of only nine P-38s and no more than four pilots. The enemy aircraft kill ratio rose to a fantastic 11 to 1 at that time, a classic figure comparable to the 14 to 1 ratio later attained by the famous North American F-86Es and Fs during the Korean War. All of this was in the face of primitive maintenance and living conditions and a Kamikaze-minded enemy who was not the victim of some "turkey shoot" syndrome. In a period when the Japanese pilots were imbued with a fatalistic fanaticism for ramming American aircraft, the AAF pilots surely could not be accused of attacking a reticent or incompetent enemy.

In fact quite the opposite was often true. While the abilities of the average pilot had decreased somewhat (just as many of our pilots had been poorly trained in 1942), their attitudes were intense and their airplanes had far better performance than those of their predecessors. In keeping with this improvement in enemy capabilities, several late-model P-38J and L aircraft had literally been stressed beyond repair as a result of extremely vigorous maneuvering in pursuit of individual enemy fighters.

Although a few pilots in the 475th Fighter Group (and the companion 49FG) had fabulous scores at the end of hostilities, the dominance of the P-38 was not limited to just a few pilots with exceptional talents. Quite the contrary. Forty-two pilots in the 475th Group attained "ace" status, while more than 40 pilots in the 49th Group shot down five or more Japanese aircraft. Unlike their Navy counterparts in the same general

*Newly painted blue spinner shows up well on this P-38H-5-LO of the 433rd Fighter Squadron (475FG), the "Blue Devils" of the famed "Satan's Angels" group. Non-standard drop tanks may have been fabricated at one of the depots in Australia. They appear to be somewhat less finished than the tanks made by Lockheed subcontractors. (H. N. Madison)*

theater of operations in 1944-45, Lightning pilots rarely participated in base defensive intercept missions. In that respect, their sorties/missions tended to be more closely akin to those flown by P-38, P-51 and P-47 pilots in the MTO in 1944-45.

Perhaps it had something to do with the nearly absolute dearth of civilized (?) distractions that were always close at hand in the United Kingdom. Many other factors are to be considered, but camaraderie and associated leadership were major factors in the aerial warfare in that area of the world that was almost totally unknown to Americans before Pearl Harbor. The popularity and success of Robert Westbrook is but one example. Col. Charles MacDonald was almost fanatic in stressing the importance of aerial gunnery, and especially deflection shooting. Moreover he was right in there with his men, proving time and again the validity of his preaching. Leading ace Richard Bong was rotated back to the ZI on the pretext of giving him some special training in the art of aerial gunnery, something he had missed out on almost completely when he was a second lieutenant. (He probably never would have asked for R&R on his own.) Not intending to brag at all, Bong flatly stated (after scoring 40 victories) that if he had been trained in aerial gunnery prior to his first tour he probably would have scored twice as many victories. (When British experience was transmitted first-hand to AAF pilots, it really was as if a new climax had been placed in the "book of knowledge.)

ABOVE: Popular Capt. Danny Roberts commanded the 433FS of the Fifth Air Force's 475FG in New Guinea. He is shown in his P-38H (No. 197), but that aircraft was down for maintenance on November 9, 1943, so the captain was flying No. 198. After a major encounter with IJN aircraft, Roberts pursued a lone Mitsubishi A6M2 Zeke. It banked sharply; Roberts turned with it, and his wingman collided with Roberts's airplane, shearing a tail boom. Both pilots perished in the low-level collision.
(Dennis G. Cooper)

BELOW; An engineering officer and crew of mechanics contemplate the situation before making their next move to get a bellied-in P-38H-1-LO from the 433FS back on its landing gear. The airplane skidded off the coral runway, losing a prop when it bounced over the drainage ditch.
(H.N. Madison)

1944, when pilots like Robert DeHaven scored heavily in P-40Ks and P-40Ns. Those later P-40s had good firepower to offset their limited maneuverability and critically short range. Best of all, AAF pilots had learned what tactics would work against the Mitsubishis and Nakajimas. On the negative side it was a certainty that Bell Airacobras were not going to gain mastery of the air over the products of Nippon.

B Maps cannot provide any real sense of the tremendous distances that had to be spanned in the Southwest Pacific arena to attack enemy targets. General MacArthur's island-hopping campaign was only viable in 1942 and 1943 because there was a handful of Lockheed P-38s in that faraway theater of operations. Just to impart a feeling of some of the logistics problems that existed, the distance from Brisbane to Darwin, Australia, was about the same as the distance from Darwin to the Philippine Islands, or 2,500 miles. No railroad connected Brisbane and Darwin, and a crude, rough motor road cut through the desert ended 300 miles short of Darwin. Much of Australia in 1941 was as remote as Borneo.

To make matters worse, Lt. Gen. George Brett, the man in charge of AAF operations in the SWPA, was an excellent administrative officer but lacked knowhow in carrying out an air war even with topnotch equipment, but he did not have that sort of material. Gen. Hap Arnold replaced him with Maj. Gen. George C. Kenney in the summer of 1942. While it took some time to get things turned around, Kenney was the man to get the AAF back on the right track.

Eventually, the 8th, 35th, 49th and 475th Fighter Groups carried the battle to the enemy across the deadly expanse of New Guinea, an island of mind-boggling size. In fact, it is the world's second largest island mass. One of the niceties of flying in that area was that you were either flying over shark-infested waters or jungles populated by headhunters or other less-than-civilized cannibals.

Clawing their way through determined Nipponese pilots in a variety of fighters designed to dogfight in the classic style, pilots of the 475th, as but one example, performed well beyond all expectations. Much later, by the time the Philippines had been secured, it was only a matter of bombing Japan's survivors into submission. The fight that had been initiated in the face of overwhelming odds had become history. If nothing else, it revealed that, once again, Gen. Arnold had made the right choice when he selected George Kenney to save the day.

Port Moresby, Dobodura, Nadzab, Hollandia, Biak, Dulag, Lingayen, Luzon were names that could hardly be described as American household words. But they had become indelibly

Colonel MacDonald, among other leaders, insisted that combat pilots did tend to totally misjudge their range when closing on enemy aircraft in the heat of an attack. He, McGuire and Bong all emphasized the need to close on the enemy "until you can read his instruments." They needed to fire sparingly, making certain that they did not waste that precious supply of ammo. Even when the American pilots cranked in a lot of "lead" on an enemy aircraft at sharp angles of deflection, if they fired at 2,000 or even 1,000 feet they could watch their bullets trail off with no effect at all. For those who scored profusely, it was not unusual to come home with parts from the enemy aircraft (and even Japanese maps) embedded in some portion of their P-38s.

Who could ever count on that kind of leadership attention from certain ETO commanders who admittedly disliked the P-38? Many pilots in the Far East owed their lives to that extra engine on the Lightning, and they did not hesitate to express affection for it. Perhaps they had serious thoughts about those shark-infested waters, to be avoided at all costs.

The scores chalked up by Fifth and Thirteenth Air Force fighter pilots in the last 18 months of the war had not been at all that commonplace in the perilous reaches of the SWPA early in the war. In that stressful first year or so after the fall of Bataan, most pilots had to face the Asiatic enemy in various model Curtiss P-40s and Bell P-39/P-400 types. While some of the pilots managed to do quite well against the Japanese Navy fighters and bombers while flying P-40s, the Airacobras were just plain outclassed. Actually, the best Warhawk performances and accomplishments seem to have come about in impressed into the minds of those pilots and supporting crews who had suffered through what seemed like a neverending battle for survival.

Nearly forgotten in the mists of time and location, that relatively small but critical campaign in the Aleutians had ultimately faded away when Imperial Japanese forces departed in silence. The air war in the Aleutian chain of islands had often brought American bomber and fighter pilots closer to the Japanese homeland than they were to the U.S. territorial mainland. The part played by P-38E and F fighters in defeating enemy attempts to attack Alaska proper and the Canadian and U.S. western coast areas has been described in detail. It was most fortunate that the Japanese had underestimated America's ability to stave off the attacks, which, from the outset, lacked the strength and equipment to overwhelm the AAF forces that were thrown into the breach, thanks to the foresight of Gen. Simon Bolivar Buckner, Jr. Without the initial preparations set into motion by Buckner, who has any idea of what successes the Japanese might have enjoyed? Had Lockheed Aircraft failed to complete the task of adapting early P-38Es to the far north environment in a matter of a few dozen hours, and had the P-38 failed to perform spectacularly in a role for which it was never designed, the outcome of the World War II in the Western Hemisphere certainly would not read as it has been described in this book.

The late Col. Stanley A. Long, first AAF pilot of a P-38 to shoot down an enemy aircraft, recalled that the Lightning was ideally suited to warfare in that arena. (If that seems a bit optimistic, a consideration of the options would be enlightening.) When Long was asked to enumerate the P-38's attributes and faults, he replied that "the P-38 didn't have any faults!" His perspective was not faulty. He recalled the many times, in a later war, when he was leading P-51D Mustang missions over Korea about a decade after his encounters in the Aleutians, that he frequently found himself wishing he was back in a P-38. It is hard to believe that Long was flying a modified P-38E in absolutely primitive conditions, not an improved J or L version. American facilities at key points in the Aleutian chain eventually began to look more and more like stateside bases than waterfilled sink holes as they had in 1942. At the

*America's second-highest scoring ace, Maj. Thomas McGuire, Jr., compares notes with occasional combat sweep associate Charles Lindbergh at an advance "Satan's Angels" base in the summer of 1944. "Slim" abhorred publicity photographers, but Maj. Dennis Glen Cooper was permitted to take numerous candid pictures while Lindbergh flew with the 475FG. Contrary to the widespread published reports, Lindbergh was not on tour to teach long-range cruise control procedures for P-38s. His primary objective was to evaluate the performance of single-engine vs. twin-engine fighters in battle for United Aircraft Corporation. Being a first-rate pilot with some special savoir-faire, he quickly discovered that few pilots managed their power controls properly. He was soon granted permission to teach the young pilots the correct methodology of cruise control. "Slim" shot up numerous barges and small ships, and had a least one confirmed (but unrecorded) aerial victory over a Japanese fighter. Five- to seven-hour missions were the norm, rather than the exception, for the 42-year-old airman in that young man's environment. Although he had no previous association with the P-38 or Allison engines prior to his arrival at Nadzab, New Guinea, his inherent ability to manage fuel consumption allowed him to return to base from missions with as much as 210 gallons of unused fuel while his wingman was coming in on the fumes. (475th Fighter Group Association)*

*Pre-war type tailstripes on this SWPA Lightning that had ditched on the final approach to its home base has led some writers to identify it has a "converted YP-38," an absolutely ridiculous association. Actually, Lt. James A. Posten, a member of the famed 9FS of the 49FG was returning from a combat mission after suffering battle damage. Both engines quit before he reached the airstrip, but he managed to walk (or swim) away from the wreck. Correct nose and coolant scoop ID numbers do not match the tail number, possibly indicating prior damage repair. Posten's mount was really a P-38J-15-LO. (USAF)*

end of the war, adequate numbers of wide-ranging P-38Js and Ls were available for nearly any emergency. One tiny detail that has never been mentioned before was the fact that P-38Ls, the fighter variety, were equipped with radio direction-finding (D/F) loop antennas. While some F-5Gs in the Far East Air Force had ADF loop antennas, the Lightning fighters featuring D/F loops were a rare breed.

Few Lightnings ever became available for operation in the Tenth Air Force assigned to the India-Burma Theater of Operations prior to 1945 for a variety of reasons – primarily because the threats were greater elsewhere, and possibly because mission profiles could be flown by other types of aircraft. However, the "Green Dragons" (459FS) of the 80th Fighter Group managed to chalk up numerous aerial victories over enemy aircraft. This was accomplished in spite of the fact that from the early days of 1943, photo-reconnaissance F-4 and F-5 versions of the Lightning were in great demand and appeared to be more commonplace. They evidently operated with outstanding results in the CBI.

Somewhat like poor relatives, Burma-India commanders had to conduct operations with a mixed bag of aircraft throughout the war. It included Mustang Is, P-47Ds (razorback and bubble versions), P-51Ds, Spitfires, Beaufighters, Mosquitos, Warhawks, Kittyhawks and the unloved Vultee Vengeance series.

Following creation of the Far East Air Force in June 1944, Lightning photo-recon and fighter versions of the Fourteenth Air Force carried out important operational activities from rudimentary bases in various areas of China. Operational techniques and requirements in the CBI were, for the most part, considerably different from those employed in the Southwest Pacific, the MTO and the ETO. No massive escorted bombing formations

*ABOVE RIGHT: In front of Col. Charles MacDonald's P-38J named "Putt Putt Maru," neophyte Lightning pilot Charles Lindbergh is shown at the Hollandia base in 1944 (June). "Slim's" wingman on one of his early combat missions was none other than Thomas McGuire. It was evident that the ex-colonel had made the transition to twin-engine fighters with minimal difficulty. (Dennis Glen Cooper)*

*ABOVE LEFT: This team of pilots, gathered on Biak Island in October 1944, could intimidate any group with their prowess. At least six of the eight men were aces, some of them several times over (the second man from the right was a visitor from the 475th Fighter Group - Maj. Thomas McGuire, Jr.). The hot fighter pilots were (l to r) Col. George Walker, Col. Robert Morrissey, Lt. Col. Gerald R. Johnson (22), Capt. Milden Mathre (5), Maj. Wallace Jordan (6), Maj. Richard I. Bong (40), Maj. McGuire (38), and Capt. Robert De Haven (14). The P-38J is from the 9th Fighter Squadron, and was reportedly Bong's personal mount. (Don C. Bong)*

were involved; air-to-air combat was relatively low key and on a small scale; large cities were seldom in the picture and mechanized warfare was not a dominant theme.

It is difficult to categorize one other aspect of P-38 participation on World War II. Where do we address the many P-38/F-5 operations conducted in the Caribbean? Hundreds of photo-recon missions were flown from Central and South American bases, mostly in connection with anti-submarine warfare operations. The activities were about evenly divided between fighter and reconnaissance flights, with the fighters

*Handsome Lt. Col. Robert B. Westbrook, from Hollywood, California, became the top fighter ace in the Thirteenth Air Force. Initially flying Curtiss P-40s, he switched to P-38s and eventually ran up a score of 20 enemy aircraft. Westbrook flew with the 44th FS of the 18th Fighter Group. Many sources fail to indicate that the "Vampires" of the 44th flew P-38s for nearly two years. Westbrook was extremely popular with his fellow airmen and the ground troops as well. The odds eventually caught up with him after many tours of duty, and he failed to return from a strafing mission. (USAF)*

*Four victories over e.a. are displayed on the pilot's nacelle of this Tenth Air Force P-38L-1-LO. Although the manufacturer stopped camouflaging the swift fighters during the P-38J production run, many later models were painted in the CBI Theater of Operations. "Geronimo II" was a fine example of that program. The unknown pilot was a member of the 459th FS, 80th Fighter Group.*

often being involved in protective surveillance flights over Allied convoys.

All in all, the P-38 type had to be rated as among the most effective of AAF fighter aircraft in use in 1942 through 1944. Let's look at the picture in the clear light of day. Take 1942 as an example. At Eglin Field, Florida, AAF test reports indicated a clear superiority of P-38 and P-47 fighters over all other American types. Yet, only the P-38 (of the two) was involved in actual combat, demonstrating its prowess over the enemy in North Africa, the ETO – in Iceland, for example – in the Aleutians, and in the Southwest Pacific. Not even the top AAF fighter in the ETO at that time – the Spitfire Mk V, a borrowed type in somewhat restricted usage – could handle the jobs allocated to the P-38 in North Africa, the Aleutian Theater, and especially in the crucial effort of stopping the Japanese incursions in New Guinea and the Solomon Islands.

Yet, Spitfire production in one month at that time outstripped Lockheed P-38 production for a year. Moreover, the Spitfire was poorly suited to the geographic conditions in which that conflict was being waged. As a consequence, all of the slack had to be absorbed by P-40Es and Ks and the demoralizing Bell P-39s and P-400s assigned to island defensive forces. Notice that the Mustang remains unmentioned. Only a few P-51s and the dive-bombing A-36s participated in any degree in the North African campaign, while the British restricted their use to low-level interdiction and coastal reconnaissance missions over Europe. Just a figurative handful of Allison-powered Mustangs served in combat in 1942.

The following year, 1943, definitely served to point out the fine qualities of the P-38, in spite of the overwhelming demands placed on its services, and – frequently ignored – the tactical doctrinal errors that penalized the P-38 and its pilots until the picture was totally distorted. (Who has ever acknowledged that the P-51Ds were committed to the fray just at a time when many of the bomber doctrines that had prevailed for years were discarded? ETO and MTO P-38s had been "handcuffed" in protecting bombers for 18 months by that time.) Even so, the P-38 was without a peer in the MTO. In the ETO, it was the only fighter – until the advent of the Mustang – in the Allied forces that could escort the suffering B-17s and B-24s deep into Europe. The battle of the Southwest Pacific was strictly a P-38 show, crowned by the Yamamoto Mission and the dominant role played out over New Guinea. Air control of the Aleutians was held by the P-38s. The CBI was a polygenetic collection of whatever was available, but the few P-38s that were there certainly did not take a back seat to any other type.

In 1944, the revamped Mustangs, by then in large-scale mass production, and the improved breed of Thunderbolts

*Although aircraft were no longer in short supply in the CBI by the middle of 1944, most Lockheed Lightnings were still photo-recon types. A Lockheed F-5E-10-LO (AC42-67877), "K" for Kilroy, prepares to take off at Tingkawk Sekan, Burma, with a Noorduyn Norseman, Douglas Dakota, Republic T-bolt and several Stinson L-5s parked in the background. On June 30, 1945, Maj. Gen. George E. Stratemeyer was placed in command of the new HQ, AAF, China Theater. It comprised Tenth and Fourteenth Air Forces, China Air Service Command, and one photo-recon group. By July 16, Brig. Gen. Thomas J. Hanley, Jr., assumed command of the India-Burma Theater. P-38L airplanes were usually identifiable from all other P-38s by the landing light in the left leading edge, although about 100 late J models had the same recognition feature. Limitations on P-38 producibility penalized the war theater commanders many times. Example: In December 1944 there were only 92 Lightnings in the entire CBI Theater, but there were 405 Thunderbolts, 417 Mustangs and 205 Curtiss Warhawks. By July 1945, the number of Lightnings rose to 231, while only 62 P-40s remained. The Thunderbolt count fell to 296, but P-51 ranks had swollen to 753. (Kenneth Sumney)*

overwhelmed the P-38s in the ETO by dint of mass availability, not to mention their greatly improved performances. On the other hand, the P-47D was no match for the demands of the Pacific Theater, while the P-38J and L types continued to pound and hound the Japanese.

Meanwhile, the magazine and newspaper writers of the day continued to gnaw on the premise that the meatball-marked fighters could outmaneuver the P-38 at every turn. (A review of most popular aviation journals and news stories issued during the war years would lead you to believe that everything the Japanese flew was a "Zero" type.) Messrs.

*Almost pterodactyl-like, a gleaming Lockheed P-38L with everything extended comes in for a landing. Among the most celebrated fighter aircraft of the war, the Lightning was unique in having tricycle landing gear, a predictor of something that would become common to nearly every fighter after World War II.*

Any serious attempt to cover the highlights of nearly four years of active warfare involving the Fifth, Seventh, Tenth, Eleventh, Thirteenth and Fourteenth Air Forces – just the episodes relating to Lightnings – would fill volumes. Furthermore, most of those would involve intriguing stories. With that in mind, it has been necessary to select just a few of those tales for this history, primarily to provide the flavor of what must have been at least representative of multitude of combat encounters. People who believe either the Mustang, Spitfire or Bf 109G was the best all around fighter of World War II are as unlikely to be swayed from their opinion as most of us might be should someone try to convince us that Russia was primarily responsible for the defeat of Japan or Germany.

Bong, McGuire, Westbrook, Lynch, Homer, MacDonald and a host of others continued to show the other side of the coin. Most of 1944 was also a period of dominance for the P-38 in the tremendous assault on the underside and eastern expanses of Europe. The type also proved equal to the job assignments in China and Burma, and it would be difficult to identify any totally superior type in service in India.

Even in 1945, the P-38 was in there striving for the crown in such diverse places as the ETO (Ninth Air Force), the CBI, the Western Pacific and the counterpoint war in the MTO. Like the P-38, the P-47D gave ground to the P-51D throughout Europe. Furthermore, the early Thunderbolt never earned a favorable reputation in the Pacific, but that was soon to be dispelled by the appearance of the P-47N with its greatly improved performance. Again, the P-51D was coming on strong, as well as it should have through sheer availability and improved performance, not unexpected in a much newer aircraft.

There can be little, if any, doubt that the F-4 and F-5 camera planes were hands down winners over all other reconnaissance types in every theater of war. In that respect, the Lightning "had it all."

One largely misunderstood and misinterpreted episode of the Pacific war involved an aviator who had nearly unlimited expertise but – because of political animosity generated before America became involved in the war – remained on civilian status. Charles Lindbergh, former colonel in the USAAC Reserve[1], was never invited to actively partake in any military activity because of his determined opposition to America's entry into the war in Europe.

However, he was employed as a special technical advisor by Henry Ford for the Ford Motor Co., where he was deeply involved with the B-24 production project at the Willow Run Bomber Plant, and with Pratt & Whitney engine production programs in Detroit and Chicago. He was also retained by United Aircraft Corporation, where, in 1944, he was granted permission by the United States Navy to survey Vought F4U Corsair operations and performance under combat conditions (primarily, of course, with U.S. Marine Corps aviation). There were many Corsair crashes and casualties at that time, with many of them probably attributable to the vicious stall characteristics of that type. Chance Vought was particularly anxious to design a new fighter as successor to the F4U/FG series, but they were having great difficulty trying to decide if it should be a small single-engine type, a pioneering jet fighter, or a powerful twin-engine machine.

Following some interesting and productive activity with the naval mission, Lindbergh proceeded on down to Vth Fighter Command Headquarters at Nadzab, New Guinea, from Henderson Field on Guadalcanal. He arrived at Nadzab Strip No. 5 on June 15, 1944, planning to contact Gen. Ennis Whitehead (who had left for another destination at that time).

**TABLE 17-1. FIGHTER AIRPLANE ACCEPTANCES 1945**

| Type | J | F | M | A | M | J | J | A | S | O | N | D | TOTALS |
|---|---|---|---|---|---|---|---|---|---|---|---|---|---|
| * Lockheed P-38L | 301 | 253 | 289 | 252 | 225 | 175 | 118 | 53 | - | - | - | - | 1666 |
| **Bell P-63C/RP-63G | 240 | 265 | 255 | 240 | 252 | 199 | 5 | - | 2 | 9 | 3 | 5 | 1475 |
| Republic P-47D/M/N | 480 | 544 | 539 | 591 | 528 | 415 | 305 | 157 | 67 | 25 | 1 | 5 | 3657 |
| North Amer. P-51D/K | 857 | 721 | 758 | 693 | 710 | 701 | 602 | 208 | 65 | 94 | 26 | - | 5435 |
| Lockheed P-80A | - | 1 | 3 | 6 | 11 | 20 | 36 | 31 | - | 15 | 47 | 66 | 236 |
| North Amer. F-6K | - | - | 44 | - | - | 37 | - | 2 | - | - | - | - | 83 |
| Bell P-59B | 5 | 5 | 5 | 8 | 6 | - | - | - | - | - | - | - | 29 |
| Northrop P-61 | 37 | 33 | 26 | 26 | 26 | 26 | 13 | 12 | 2 | 7 | 5 | 6 | 219 |
| North Amer. P-82 | - | - | - | - | - | - | - | - | - | 1 | - | - | 1 |

*\* No photographic versions of the P-38 show up in these official manufacturing records for 1945. All F-5E, F-5G and P-38M were converted from P-38s at Dallas, Texas.*

*\*\*Note that production of Bell P-63/RP-63 Kingcobras almost equalled P-38 production in 1945, although few P-63s reached USAAF combat groups. Most went to Russia and the Free French.*

---

*1. After a particularly vindictive attack (in the press) by his political adversary, President Franklin D. Roosevelt, Lindbergh reluctantly resigned his Air Corps commission – although he prized it highly – on April 28, 1941. That was the same day that the Wehrmacht entered Athens, Greece.*

RIGHT: Parked in front of the "Twin Dragons" Operations tent in the China-Burma-India Theater, a camouflaged P-38L-1-LO of the 459FS, 80FG, was seen to be at the "ready" for combat. The pilot and ground crew personnel relaxed under a hot sun in the basically humid climate. No location information was provided, but it was probably Chittagong, India. Awards to the outfit included two Distinguished Unit Citations. (Lockheed)

LOWER RIGHT: "Hammer's Destruction Co." emblazoned on the nose of this P-38L-5-LO appears to be given much credibility by five Rising Sun flags to indicate ace status. The 80th FG, 459th Fighter Squadron late-series fighter was normally piloted by Maj. Samuel E. Hunter. Unusual canvas structure was peculiar to India. (Tenth Air Force)

BOTTOM: At war's end, both the P-38 and the ever-present Marston mats, dating back to pre-war maneuvers, had reached the pinnacle of usefulness and remained there – untarnished in reputation. This P-38L-5-LO of the 475th Fighter Group remained dominant in the Pacific-Asiatic theaters until nearly unlimited supplies of P-51Ds and Ks replaced the Lightning. Top aces in the Pacific, e. g., Bong, McGuire, MacDonald, Johnson, Lynch, Robbins, Westbrook, Homer, and others had proven that the Lightning was, indeed, a "dogfighter" of the first magnitude. The highly organized and concentrated publicity emanating from the ETO was an avalanche compared to what came out of the far reaches of the Pacific in 1942-44. Farseeing Gen. George Kenney was never disappointed in his expectations regarding the P-38, unless it was with the numbers available. This P-38L was photographed at Lingayen airstrip, Luzon, P. I., in August 1945. Reflecting the difference in command attitudes, it became commonplace for P-38s in the FEAF to fly missions with one 300/310-gallon and one 165-gallon fuel tanks. Special techniques had to be developed to safely jettison the big tanks. (USAF)

In spite of Whitehead's absence, Lindbergh managed too obtain the necessary permission to visit an active P-38 fighter group "to observe the performance of the Lightning twin-engine fighter under combat conditions."

Although some preliminary arrangements had been completed with respect to his arrival at the forward base, it was all relatively understated. (Lindbergh's orders were evidently misplaced at Nadzab, which generated some serious problems a month or so later.) Col. Robert Morrissey, a senior flying officer at headquarters, arranged for Lindbergh to make his first flight in a P-38. "Slim" (a name he much preferred over "Lindy") had never flown any P-38 prior to June 16, contrary to the universal belief that his specific mission in the Southwest Pacific was to teach Lightning pilots good cruise control techniques.

Following a rather brief cockpit check, Lindbergh followed Morrissey off the strip, wanting to familiarize himself with the most powerful fighter he had ever flown.

After an hour or so of checking on stall characteristics, aircraft reaction to maneuvering, control operation, etc., he felt pretty comfortable in the P-38J. He headed in for his first landing on the strip. One wheel locked, either through brake malfunction or the possibility that the Lone Eagle had inadvertently applied brake pressure as soon as he touched down. The tire blew out immediately after contact, giving the civilian a few anxious moments. With good reaction, he had to apply full opposite rudder and brake to remain on the somewhat crude runway. The P-38 finally wound up about 20 feet to the right of the strip. (It would have been characteristic of him not to toss off illogical excuses.)

A few days later, Lindbergh ventured out with some of the most celebrated pilots from the 8th Fighter Group's 35FS. Flying out of Nadzab's Airstrip No. 4, he went on a mission lasting only 80 minutes. Some defensive fire came up to greet them, but it all came from Allied naval vessels when the fighters ventured too close to the beachhead area.

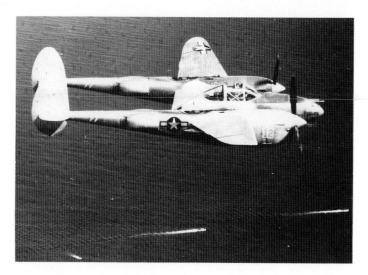

In spite of his little-known resignation from the Air Corps. Lindbergh was generally accorded the treatment of an active colonel by everyone. (His khakis bore no wings, rank badges or emblems, etc. He wore the identification patch supplied for technical representatives).

Taking off from Nadzab No.3 on June 26. Lindbergh flew his P-38J west along the coast and mountain ranges to Hollandia to join the 475th Fighter Group, composed of the 431FS (code: Hades), the 432FS (Clover), and the 433FS (Possum). The 475th was under command of one of the leading aces, Col. Charles MacDonald, who eventually wound up as the third-ranking ace from the Pacific Theater of Operations with 27 aircraft to his credit.

Not a bit constrained by his civilian status, "Slim" probably flew more active combat missions in World War II than the vast majority of pilots graduated from military flying schools in the 1940-45 era. He shot at the Japanese and they shot at him. By demonstration alone, Lindbergh was far from being a pacifist.

Less than 24 hours after arriving in Hollandia, he went on his first of many missions with the 475th. It was no milk-run operation either, and he was with some illustrious company. The first flight in which he was assigned as wingman in the No. 4 slot, consisted of Col. MacDonald as flight leader. Maj. Meryl M. Smith (Group Deputy C.O.) and Maj. Thomas McGuire, Jr.! Damned impressive company when you figure that the second and third ranking aces in the Pacific area were involved. Their target for the day included shipping in the vicinity of Jefman and Samate.

Lindbergh, in his forties, was right in the thick of it with the others, shooting up self-propelled barges and a small coastal freighter of the Fox Tare Charlie type (official code name). The mission duration was 6 hours and 24 minutes. A few days later it was a bombing mission, with each of seventeen P-38Js carrying a 1,000-pound bomb to Noemfoor Island. The next day they flew an intercept mission with Col. MacDonald that lasted nearly 7 hours. Even when Lindbergh had to maintain formation with P-38 pilots who were not using power settings which would permit him to use his own optimum "prescription," he still managed to return to base with 210 gallons of fuel on board after 7 hours. He led White Flight on a mission to Noemfoor Island on the following day and on a long bomber escort to Jefman after that.

By that time, Lindbergh had proven to his own satisfaction that combat radius limitations in effect in the Vth Fighter Command could be boosted by as much as 30 percent. That would foster a combat radius of action of 700 to 750 miles by using proper cruise control techniques.

Col. MacDonald listened to Lindbergh's proposal and OK'd

a lecture session for all pilots on July 3. Standard technique involved cruising at 2200-2400 rpm in auto-rich at low manifold pressures. Slim's recommendation was to cruise at 1600 rpm in auto-lean mixture at 185 mph IAS with higher manifold pressures. This reduced fuel consumption to about 70 gallons per hour.

Since the 475th FG was operating P-38Js from the batch of aircraft that had been modified by Lt. Col. Edward M. Gavin's 482nd Air Service Squadron in the early months of 1944, they had the benefit of about 110 gallons of fuel in the internal tanks above and beyond the 306 gallons carried in P-38H and P-38J-5-LO through P-38J-20-LO airplanes, unless those Js had been retrofitted. With the intercoolers removed from the wing leading edge on all J and L models, the wing leading edge structure had been revamped. This allowed the installation of a 55-gallon fuel cell in each wing. (Some documents listed the cells as having a capacity of 62 gallons each.) Although P-38Hs and early Js had enough range to get them to Berlin and back (and allowed for 30 minutes of combat), it was not uncommon to refer to them as being "short legged." (According to official AAF records, that additional fuel was supposed to increase their radius of action to 650 miles.) It should be recalled that the 54FS in the Aleutians was flying 600-mile-radius combat missions to Kiska in the summer of 1942 without benefit of the leading edge tanks. (With no cheating, Milo Burcham had demonstrated that a properly flown P-38E, F, G or H that was equipped with the 300/310 gallon external tanks could fly to a maximum ferry range of more than 3,000 miles.)

Aircrews in the Pacific Theater and in the MTO had conducted range extension tests. They soon learned that through the expedient of installing one 310-gallon external tank in place of one of the 165-gallon tanks, fuel capacity could be increased to nearly 900 gallons.* That gave a combat range of more than 11 hours and still provided for 10 to 15 minutes of aerial combat. (With judicious use of cruise control techniques, flights of that duration were actually commonplace in one or two theaters of operation, especially if the airplanes were P-38Ls.)

*(Maximum combat fuel capacity for a P-38L could easily exceed 1,030 gallons.)

On the Fourth of July, the 433FS went to Jefman at the western end of New Guinea on a heavy bomber escort mission involving B-24s. Although it was definitely not a maximum endurance mission, it lasted 6 hours and 40 minutes. This was in the same time frame when the 20FG and the 55FG in the ETO would fly a 5-hour and 48-minute mission where everybody would come home on the fumes. Col. Jack Jenkins had some of the lads pinching down to less than 1800 rpm and 23 inches on manifold pressure as he attempted to help them make the English coastline. Most of the 20FG airplanes were early P-38Js, but only a few had the 55-gallon leading edge tanks (one in each wing). There may have even been a few P-38Hs along.

Just for blatant comparison, the P-38Js of the 433FS that went far out to Jefman with Lindbergh had a radically different "end of mission" situation. Not one airplane returned with less than 160 gallons of fuel remaining in the tanks! Evidently there was not an engine failure on any aircraft in the squadron.

ABOVE: Passing over emerald-green jungles – probably in the Philippines – 15 Lockheed P-38Ls are seen on a two-tank mission. The four 475FG flights always seemed to be shy a "Tailend Charlie" for some reason. (Dennis G. Cooper)

RIGHT: A hero through and through, Lt. Col. Gerald R. Johnson of the 49th Fighter Group scored no fewer than 22 victories in the far reaches of the SWPA. He is frequently confused with Eighth Air Force ace (17 e.a.) Gerald W. Johnson. The Pacific P-38 ace had fought in the Aleutians in 1942 before moving thousands of miles to New Guinea to do what he did best. He was killed after the war while flying a B-17 that was caught in a typhoon, having given up his own parachute to a passenger who had none. (Col. Jack S. Jenkins)

BELOW: One of only eleven P-38L-1-LO fighters assigned to the 333FS at Kagman Field on Saipan for long-range missions, this airplane was employed for escort of heavy bombers and for interdiction of Japanese assaults. It bore a minimum of specialty markings. (Joseph Maita)

All of the youthful pilots were pretty well impressed with the results.

On the very next evening, Col, Morrissey informed Lindbergh that a message had been received to the effect that Lindy was being recalled to headquarters in Australia. As might be expected, at least somebody had become upset over a "rumor" that the famous New York-Paris flyer was involved in combat missions on P-38s. Morrissey and Lindbergh headed for Nadzab together. However, they encountered terrible weather, including what Lindbergh described as "the worst storm front I had ever seen." When the storm passed on by, Lindy flew to Australia the next day to face a problem that might, unhappily, bring his successful tour to an end. He did not relish the thought. Now there was a least one old, bold pilot in the SWPA.

While Gen. George Kenney seemed to be somewhat stern about the past events in their initial moments of discussion, he suddenly turned to Lindbergh's defense when discussing the matter over the telephone with Gen. R. K. Sutherland (Gen. MacArthur's Chief of Staff), and it wasn't long before they were in MacArthur's office talking about the matter in friendly terms. Not only did Lindbergh obtain permission to return to his previous base and activities, an enthusiastic MacArthur fully endorsed a plan that would permit him to instruct virtually all Fifth Air Force pilots about improved cruise control.

Leaving Australia on July 14, Lindbergh ferried a P-47D back to New Guinea, rejoining the 8th Fighter Group at Owi on the 16th. He then went back to the 475th, flying a mission with Col. MacDonald, Meryl Smith and Col. Morrissey 4 days later. Rather amazingly, no Japanese aircraft had been encountered in over one month of combat operations. He got back together with the 433FS at Mokmer Strip on Biak on July 24, and went on a major strike to Halmahera on the 27th. There were more than forty B-25s, escorted by several squadrons because they expected to encounter as many as 100 Japanese fighters. The fighters never accepted the challenge, allowing the B-25s to plaster the bases with machine gun fire and bombs.

The next day, he flew with Col. MacDonald in Blue Flight of Possum 1 (the 433rd), with Ceram as the target. It was to be a big day for the rather shy and retiring Lindbergh. Radio contact gave the first hint that the 8th Fighter Group was tangling with enemy fighters over Elpaputih Bay, but the "Headhunters" were being frustrated by a shortage of ammunition. Suddenly, Lindbergh spotted a Japanese fighter headed directly at him. The "Lone Eagle" jammed down on the trigger buttons, sending .50-caliber and 20-mm bursts directly into the enemy aircraft. But the aircraft did not explode, it kept on coming. Instinctively, Lindbergh hauled back on the yoke ... hard ... just as his adversary zoomed upward. They missed each other by less than 5 feet and the Japanese monoplane arched over in a long graceful curve and fell, out of control toward the water. Lt. Miller, Lindbergh's wingman, watched the fighter splash. He had witnessed the whole thing. Although the victory was confirmed, the score was never entered on the records of the 433FS.

By August 16, with many more missions under his belt, "Slim" was grounded on orders from Gen. Kenney. Knowing that he could not expect to gain permission to participate in the forthcoming Philippines invasion, he packed up and prepared to leave for the Zone of the Interior. After aiding some local P-47D outfits with some expert advice on cruise control, he was on his way home.

That is the way it happened. Not planned in advance at all, but the success of his contribution to P-38 effectiveness cannot be denied. Lindbergh was obviously a man far ahead of his time, and a man for all time.

The sometimes unpleasant tricks that fate can play on a man's life certainly affected the career potential of Charles Lindbergh. As his brilliant wife, Anne Morrow Lindbergh, once said, "Charles was a very stubborn man." His stand on isolationism was not universally palatable in America in 1941, albeit proponents of that idealistic nonsense caused President Roosevelt some lost hours of sleep. "Lindy" was 100 percent correct in warning Americans about the power of the new German air force. If he, like aviation magazine gadfly journalist Cy Caldwell, had limited his criticism of Roosevelt and his supporters to their mistake in underestimating the Hitler threat, who knows where he might have gone in the war. Starting as a vastly knowledgeable aviation specialist as a full colonel on December 17, 1941, he would have obviously paralleled the rise of Jimmy Doolittle, even perhaps outdoing him. Outside the realm of the political arena, Lindbergh's powers of persuasion and technical ability were top rung. He was a brilliant problem solver; what's more he was widely respected by American youth. As a politician, he was overmatched, even overzealous, in trying to outpoint Roosevelt (the master politician); but when it came to things aeronautical, he was a true champion.

There is a distinct possibility that it all worked out in favor of the average American anyway. Had he remained in reserve active military service, his analytical ability might not have ever had a chance to come into play.

Few commanders who flew fighters in the war enjoyed more personal popularity that Lt. Col. Robert B. Westbrook, a character straight out of the movie scripts and a real-life resident of Hollywood, California. He was handsome, had a good personality, flew P-38s with great skill and his leadership qualities were outstanding. But, like several of his contemporaries, he pushed his luck too far.

Most of the airmen and ground crew members had passed through the evening chow line by the time they learned that "Westy" Westbrook would not be returning to his Dutch New Guinea base at Middleburg Island off the northern coast of New Guinea. His 339th Fighter Squadron mates (347FG) were late in returning home from the 1,900-mile mission to Makassar Strait, vividly pointing out the fabulous range capabilities of the P-38Ls. By the next morning the death of "Westy" was known to thousands of Allied combat men as far north as Morotai and Leyte and southeast to Biak and Hollandia. Even pilots in Australian R&R camps knew about the loss by noon. There was a widespread feeling of almost personal loss among the fighting veterans of the sprawling Pacific battle zone. Men who had known the best – from "Buzz" Wagner and Tommy Lynch to Dick Bong and Tommy McGuire – looked upon Westbrook as one of the greatest combat fighter pilots of the war. Participating in aerial battles from Henderson Field at Guadalcanal to the wilds of Borneo, the 27-year-old from Los Angeles County had dispatched no less than 20 Japanese fighters. At the time of his death, he was the leading ace of the Thirteenth Air Force, and nobody in that command ever exceeded his score.

Not many pilots of the Thirteenth's jungle air force will forget Westbrook's inspired and aggressive leadership as commander of the "Vampires" squadron (44FS, 18FG) during the intensive attack on Rabaul. Those same men will recall his victory spree during Christmas week in 1943 when he nailed six Japanese aircraft in 3 days over New Britain. As might be expected of men like Westbrook and Robert DeHaven, "Westy" once took singer-actress Frances Langford (touring with the Bob Hope Troupe) for a piggy-back ride in a P-38.

While he was a "pilot's pilot," Westbrook was also a crew chief's pilot. He often worked for hours on his own airplane to make sure he didn't miss any missions. He had an intense interest in aircraft maintenance, which inspired many others in the "Vampire" squadron to work out the bugs in their own fighters on those hot and humid flight lines through the Solomons and New Guinea.

As his group commander, Lt. Col. Leo F. Dusard, said, "Westy knew everybody. Not just officers, but also the GIs, and not just in the Air Corps [sic] but also in the infantry and every other branch that we've worked with."

The 6-foot 2-inch Westbrook was a member of the California National Guard before the war, having been ROTC cadet captain at Hollywood High School. He went on active duty when President Roosevelt proclaimed a state of national emergency in 1940, going on to gain his commission at Infantry OCS before going to flight training.

Westbrook had completed *367* combat missions, totaling *554* combat hours, when he met his fate. Awards received included the DSC, Silver Star, DFC and Air Medal with 15 Oak Leaf Clusters. He was inclined to dislike glamorization and was adamant in pointing out the importance of teamwork and the fact that shooting down enemy aircraft was "partly luck in being at the right place at the right time."

His final mission involved a 950-mile-radius overwater flight to strafe an enemy airfield in the Celebes and enemy shipping in Makassar Strait on November 22, 1944. Such a mission would have been impossible a year earlier and certainly not possible without the P-38. It was "Westy's" first mission of his *eighth combat tour* of duty!

Leading a flight from the "Sunsetters" (39th) squadron, top outfit of the 13AF, he made two passes at Japanese freighters in Makassar Town harbor. Within seconds of the first pass, he came to realize that a 140-foot enemy gunboat was making the assault by the Lightnings very hazardous. Charging in at the vessel, he was scoring hits when flak hit his aircraft and his right engine virtually erupted in flames. The C.O. of the "Sunsetters" squadron, Maj. John Endress, yelled to him to feather his engine [sic]. "I think I'm OK," Westy called back calmly. Down to 700 feet, his plane was setting up for a wet landing (not really recommended in a P-38) when it suddenly dove straight into the sea, disintegrating on impact. Westbrook's parachute bobbed to the surface along with one aileron, but there was no sign of the fighter ace. The flak gunboat was left with only one battery in commission and the vessel was listing badly from Westbrook's assault. His wingman had also peppered the ship heavily. Thus ended the life and career of yet another top notch fighter ace.

ABOVE: Beautiful and Deadly! One of the best P-38 formation flight pictures to come out of the Pacific was this view of four P-38Ls from the 431st Fighter Squadron in flight over Leyte Gulf. Lt. T. M. Oxford was flying No. 122 named "Doots II." The picture was taken by the pilot of an F-5E. (475FG Association)

BELOW: Ingenious use of a Lockheed F-5E-3-LO of the 28th Photo-Reconnaissance Squadron permitted the U. S. Fleet Marine Force to obtain special motion picture and still photo coverage of an air strike against Kushi-Take on central Okinawa in June 1945. A drop tank was modified to hold photographer Lt. Duncan so that he could obtain the film coverage desired. The drop tank was fitted with a streamlined plexiglass nose cap that provided an excellent field of view. The F-5E made the target strike runs with the napalm-and-rocket-equipped Corsairs in their attempt to dislodge the Japanese defenders. (U. S. Marines)

Through some strange quirks of fate, remarkably aggressive attitudes while at the controls of a fighter aircraft, and possibly an unlucky turn of a card, several of the top-scoring aces who fought valiantly in the Pacific Theater of Operations failed to survive the war years. Bong and McGuire, of course, top the list, and it wasn't even an enemy combat that claimed Richard Bong.

Their first-hand accounts of aerial combat would have been prized by the general public, but even when they were still flying, some were definitely reluctant to talk about the subject in detail. And just as circumstances conspired to take the lives of some who had attained the pinnacles of success in aerial warfare, "Gremlins" and "Murphy's Law" or similar things frequently prevented some pilots with real potential from basking in glory as rewards for utmost achievement in battle.

One largely unknown Pacific ace – who might have become rather famous except for a few twists of fate and the effects of the sub-tropical climatic conditions – is Major Sammy Pierce, an exceptionally longtime member of the famed 49th Fighter Group's 8th Fighter Squadron. Maj. Pierce concluded his two combat tours with seven confirmed victories and five probables. In circumstances not unlike those of a number of his fellow pilots, all of the "probables" were, more than likely, really valid victories. Why couldn't they be confirmed?

First of all, gun camera film reaching the sub-tropical combat zones in 1943 and even in 1944 was frequently impossible to interpret after exposure because of effects of moisture (water spotting, fungus). That meant that either two fellow pilots had to confirm your victory, or surface-based personnel had to do it. That latter situation was subject to locating the people and having them confirm which aircraft were involved – a nearly impossible task. An outstanding example involved Sammy Pierce's air-to-air combat in a P-40E on October 13, 1943. Off the coast of New Guinea, near New Britain at dusk, with only PT boat crews as surface observers (while under attack), Pierce shot down two Aichi D3A Val dive bombers and a Kawasaki Tony fighter. The Navy crews reported no less than 17 separate "splashes" in the fading light, none of which could be counted as a confirmed victory for anyone. Pierce's camera film was impossible to decipher, so he was limited to claiming three probables.

However, we are primarily concerned with the P-38, so the specific encounter with which this story is concerned hinges on Sammy Pierce's second tour of duty with the 8th Fighter Squadron. The outfit could boast of having had some of the best fighter jockeys, including Bong, McGuire, Gerry Johnson, Jordan, "Duckbutt" Watson, DeHaven and Aschenbrener. As a matter of record, both Pierce and Aschenbrener were taking rest and relaxation in the U.S.A. when they received an urgent request to return to the group because of a critical shortage of experienced pilots in the Philippines. Pierce had been with the 8th from late 1942 until May 1944, flying P-40Es, P-40Fs, P-40Ks and P-40N-15-CUs. (In his early days with the Air Corps, he had logged time in P-36s, P-40Bs, plus some time in Allison-powered P-51s. He describes the P-39D as "a flying electrical system looking for a place to go haywire." He had also flown P-39Fs and a P-39Q.)

Sammy Pierce and Robert Aschenbrener rejoined the 49th Group at Tacloban on Leyte Island just after the group moved into that new base. They may have been "experienced" fighter pilots, but Pierce – for one – had not spent as much as 5 minutes even sitting in any P-38 type since his Army career began. To make matters somewhat more interesting, the 8th Squadron had received tired P-38J-15-LOs that had been thoroughly flogged by their former owners, the 8th Fighter Group and the 35th Fighter Group. (The latter groups had received new P-38L-1-LOs at Biak Island just before the invasion of the Philippines had gotten under way.

Pierce said that the initial 45 days in combat were absolute murder for the maintenance crews. Those P-38Js were relatively old and terribly war weary from battling the Japanese, long missions, bad weather and tropical rot in New Guinea. Replacement parts were nearly non-existent, and to make matters worse, it rained constantly. Enemy cooperation was lacking too, for the Japanese gleefully strafed and bombed the airfield at every opportunity. Although most of the crews did not leave the flight lines for days and nights on end, it was

*BELOW LEFT: Charisma! The Lightning had it. No doubt about that. These P-38L-1-LOs prove that the design did not grow ugly due to wartime exigencies. In the summer of 1944, the outside production lines were as commonplace as they had been in 1941. W. A. "Dick" Pulver was Chief Project Engineer during most of the growth and development years when the P-38 was mass produced. Although the camouflage paint had disappeared from the sleek fighters, huge nets still hung over Plant B-1 to disguise it from a no-longer-imminent danger of enemy attack. Lockheed performed a major miracle in achieving a production rate of 14 fighters a day. An airplane designed for production at a rate of one per week does not lend itself to a mass production concept. The rather hodgepodge factory setup that grew like a gold mining town at Burbank could hardly be equated with the massive unitized facilities constructed by Ford at Willow Run or by Boeing at Renton. (Lockheed)*

*BELOW RIGHT: It could get mighty cold at Ladd Field, Alaska, and heavy snow made maintenance and flight operations most difficult. Winterized P-38s had been rushed to Alaska in the early days of the war to counteract any Japanese invasion force. Mechanics work on the carburetor controls of this fairly colorful P-38L at the coming of spring in 1945. (Logan Coombs)*

rarely possible for the squadron to field a dozen operational fighters at a time.

Some of the younger replacement pilots remained firm in the belief that you could not bail out of a Lightning without fatal results, more than two full years after Lt. Harry C. Crim, Jr. (now Col., USAF, Ret.) had done it at Paine Field. First and 14th Fighter Group pilots had been the first to discover that it wasn't all that difficult even under the most severe combat conditions, sometimes at absurdly low altitudes in North Africa. The new replacements were so poorly indoctrinated in certain aspects of P-38 operation that they were unanimous in their opinion that the airplane would not glide. Pierce had an entirely different opinion.

"Basically, it was probably one of the easiest aircraft in the world to fly if all systems were working properly. Actually, it was a beautiful flying thing, even with things going wrong and some systems out."

Fortunately for Pierce, he had some twin-engine time in Lockheed C-40s, Beech C-45s and Curtiss AT-9 Jeeps when he was introduced to the P-38J at Tacloban. His transition flight No. 1 was an air cover flight to support a Navy operation. He was tremendously impressed with the P-38 as a gun platform and found the J-15 model very easy to fly except for turbo regulation.

Maj. Pierce's most memorable mission in a Lightning was flown on Christmas Day 1944, when the squadron flew cover for a number of B-24s dispatched to bomb Clark Field on Luzon. On that particular mission, he received credit for four confirmed victories and one probable victory over enemy aircraft, all against Japanese fighter types. One of the aircraft he encountered and dispatched that day was possibly the first Japanese Army Nakajima Ki.84-1a, an aircraft code named Frank, that had been encountered.

Maj. Pierce, who had not previously been interviewed about his personal exploits, enjoyed relating the mission events as if they had happened only in the past week.

Here is his story, based on confirmed wartime facts and his personal notes:

"Our squadron was the rear (tail end) squadron in the entire group (the 49th) flying mid-level cover at 20,000 feet. The 8th Fighter Group was flying top cover above a thin overcast, and the 475th Group was flying close support just above and off to one side of the '24s. Our group had eleven P-38s operational at takeoff, enough to make up a couple of four-ship flights and one three-ship flight that I was to lead at

237

the back of the bunch. One plane in the second flight aborted on takeoff and my No. 3 man dropped out shortly thereafter. My wingman stayed with me as I pulled up to form a rather loose second element of the second flight.

"As the B-24s approached the IP (Initial Point), the boys from the 8th Fighter Group started to call in Bogies (enemy aircraft). As the Libs turned off from the IP, I spotted several flights of enemy fighters – three to five planes in each flight – breaking out of the overcast at about 10 o'clock position. I called the Bogies into the 49th's lead flight and went through my tank jettison and switching procedures. Evidently the lead flight hadn't heard my warning call, so they were turning away from the attacking flights of Japs. Something had to be done, so I pushed on full power and zoomed up directly into the middle of the Jap flights. There just wasn't any alternative.

"As the enemy flight leader reached my altitude, he flattened his dive to meet me head on. We closed to firing range and I was surprised to see his nose drop and thought it rather odd to observe some flashes over the top of his canopy. Of course I fired about the same time and my first burst struck between the cowling and windshield near the left wing root. Pieces started to flake off his airplane, followed by smoke as we closed to pass.

*Even birds of a different feather flock together. These parallel assembly lines at Burbank were producing two of Kelly Johnson's best fighter types simultaneously as 1945 dawned. This photo, rather unique in history, shows P-38L Lightnings being built on side-by-side mechanized conveyor lines while the earliest production P-80A Shooting Stars proceed on a line formerly devoted to P-38 production. Although the P-80 nose shape approximated that of the P-38's, the relationship was no more than superficial. Finishing touches on both types were added in a building at the corner of Buena Vista Street and Empire Avenue. It was nicknamed "The Cottonshed." It is doubtful that any other factory in the world produced first-line piston-engine and jet-engine fighters on parallel assembly lines.*

*Consolidated-Vultee's plant at Nashville, Tennessee, had built P-38 sub-assemblies for months prior to D-Day. When the USAAF decided to cancel production of Republic P-47Ds shortly after the success of the invasion was assured, they also decided to open additional production lines for the P-38, a long overdue decision. P-47D and P47M Thunderbolt range was considered too limited for use in the Pacific, but development of the P-47N model saved the day for Republic. Convair's southern plant had built the major components of Lightnings shown here, so the changeover to production of complete aircraft was a relatively easy step. Up to that time, much valuable plant capacity had been squandered on building Vultee Vengeance dive bombers and efforts to build the Convair TBY-2 Seawolf, an ill-fated torpedo bomber for the Navy. (Lockheed)*

"I pulled up to go over him and he exploded at that moment. I swung into a maximum power climbing turn to gain an altitude advantage and try to pick up my wingman. When I couldn't locate him, I assumed that one of the attackers had hit him as we passed through them. During my search, I saw the other two flights from the 475th with two enemy fighters in pursuit. Using my altitude advantage, I dove down after the enemy while trying to call our flights to warm them, without success.

"By the time I came within range of the enemy aircraft, the leader was firing at the No. 3 man in the second flight of P-38s. (I couldn't help but wonder why nobody in the two flights were being alerted to attacks from the rear and above and I was frustrated because my shouted warning could not penetrate the chatter filling the air.) Just as I lined up in firing position, smoke puffed from the left engine of the No. 3 man's aircraft. He skidded left and rolled, so I assumed he had been hit. The attacking Jap aircraft was a type totally unfamiliar to me. As I started to fire, the pilot realized that I was behind him; he rolled to start a split-ess, but that merely exposed his belly. My fire was accurate and hits were seen all across the midsection. The aircraft blew up.

"While trying to locate that smoking No. 3 man, I pulled around only to see eight enemy aircraft in two flights firing at the B-24s. The three-plane flight was intercepted by a flight of P-38s from the 475FG, and the leader nailed two enemy aircraft on one pass as the third Jap broke away. I was in position to hit the five-plane Japanese flight from the rear, and one plane burst into flames. The other four broke off their attack on the formation just as a Jap fighter appeared in my mirror, so I nosed down and applied full power to gain speed.

"It was then that I saw my left oil temperature was well into the red and the coolant temp was right at the maximum. My good luck held because a flight from the 80th Fighter Squadron met me head on and the Jap chasing me broke off his pursuit as they charged at him. I set the manual switch for the oil and coolant shutters to full open position on the left engine. Almost immediately the temperatures started to move down, but I did have some trim problems to contend with.

"My eyes focused on a lone Jap fighter below me at the 11 o'clock position and on my same heading. I made a normal 'curve of pursuit' pass on him but goofed it up and wound up practically flying formation with him. He was sitting there staring straight ahead, so I slid out, pulled up and made another pass that I botched by overshooting. Expecting him to break rather abruptly, I pulled my nose slightly to the left and fired a second short burst. Slugs appeared to hit him between his cockpit and the tail section with no positive results. He reached a cloud bank and I fully expected him to dive down into it and get away. Instead, he remained only far enough into it that I could trace his shadowy im-

*Lockheed and the AAF quickly responded to changing combat conditions in the ETO and the Pacific by installing high-velocity air rockets (HVARs) on zero-length launchers. Although fourteen 5-inch HVARs provided the punch of a heavy cruiser, the installation was uncomfortably complex, and the non-retractable mounts proved to be aerodynamically unacceptable. Interrupted spacing on the starboard wing was required to match spacing on the port wing, where the pitot tube was located between the third and fourth rockets. Christmas-tree pylon mounts were developed for the P-38L-5-LO type later in 1944, providing a much simpler electrical installation, fewer aerodynamic problems, and a unit that was completely removable when required. The rocket "tree" was located outboard of the propeller arc and inboard of the pitot tube location. Few, if any, P-38Ls with rocket mounts like this reached the Ninth Air Force for attacks on Germany. (Lockheed)*

age. Suddenly he pulled up directly in front of me, so I fired a burst that was really just a reaction to his sudden move. Parts began to fly from the aircraft, it belched a lot of smoke and snaprolled back into the clouds. I didn't see any sign of him after that.

"Looking for a 'friendly,' I pulled up and observed several P-38s chasing a single Jap fighter, but in their enthusiasm and overeagerness, they were all overruning or overshooting him. When it looked like he might escape their attack by getting into the clouds, I cut power, rolled into a normal firing pass and fired a fairly long burst that caused him to start smoking and

*Flying at about 1,500 feet over Japan, this F-5G was probably representative of the most completely marked F-5 photo airplanes in service. It carried the colors of the 8th PR Squadron of the 6th PRG. Markings on the glycol coolant radiator scoops appear to be the banded Nipponese Rising Sun used on all Japanese planes. (C. Daniels)*

## TABLE 17-2

### TABLE 17-2 USAAF MAJOR P-38/F-4/F-5 SERVICE ASSIGNMENTS - OTHER THAN ETO AND MTO
1942-1945

Standard Group Strength (Fighters) was 75 Airplanes

NOTE: Table arranged by numerically sequenced Air Forces

**FOURTH AIR FORCE**
329th Fighter Group
  330th Fighter Sqdn.
  331st Fighter Sqdn.
  332nd Fighter Sqdn.
  337th Fighter Sqdn.
360th Fighter Group
  371st Fighter Sqdn.
  372nd Fighter Sqdn.
  373rd Fighter Sqdn.
  446th Fighter Sqdn.
473rd Fighter Group
  482nd Fighter Sqdn.

**FIFTH AIR FORCE**
8th Fighter Group
  35th Fighter Sqdn.
  36th Fighter Sqdn.
  80th Fighter Sqdn.
35th Fighter Group
  39th Fighter Sqdn.
49th Fighter Group
  7th Fighter Sqdn.
  8th Fighter Sqdn.
  9th Fighter Sqdn.
475th Fighter Group
  431st Fighter Sqdn.
  432nd Fighter Sqdn.
  433rd Fighter Sqdn.
Vth Fighter Command
  418th Night Fighter Sqdn.
  547th Night Fighter Sqdn.
(6th Night Fighter Sqdn., 15th Fighter Group, operated on detached service)
6th Photo-Recon Group
  8th Photo-Recon Sqdn.
  25th Photo-Recon Sqdn.
  26th Photo-Recon Sqdn.

**SIXTH AIR FORCE**
XXVI Fighter Command
  28th Fighter Sqdn.
  51st Fighter Sqdn.

**SEVENTH AIR FORCE**
15th Fighter Group
  6th Night Fighter Sqdn.
21st Fighter Group
  46th Fighter Sqdn.
  72nd Fighter Sqdn.
  531st Fighter Sqdn.
318th Fighter Group
  19th Fighter Sqdn.
  73rd Fighter Sqdn.
  333rd Fighter Sqdn.
7th Photo Group/9th Photo-Recon Group
  28th Photo-Recon Sqdn.

**TENTH AIR FORCE**
33rd Fighter Group
  58th Fighter Sqdn.
  (Later to Fourteenth Air Force)
  59th Fighter Sqdn.
  60th Fighter Sqdn.
80th Fighter Group
  459th Fighter Sqdn.
  (Also w/33rd Fighter Group)
  35th Photo-Recon Sqdn.
  (Also with Fourteenth Air Force)
  91st Photo-Recon Sqdn.

**ELEVENTH AIR FORCE**
343rd Fighter Group
  11th Fighter Sqdn.
  18th Fighter Sqdn.
  54th Fighter Sqdn.
  344th Fighter Sqdn.

**THIRTEENTH AIR FORCE**
18th Fighter Group*
  12th Fighter Sqdn.
  44th Fighter Sqdn.
  70th Fighter Sqdn
  419th Night Fighter Sqdn.
  36th Photo-Recon Sqdn.
(Also with Seventh Air Force)
*Apparently assigned/transferred to Fifth Air Force as part of FEAF.
347th Fighter Group
  67th Fighter Sqdn.
  68th Fighter Sqdn.
  339th Fighter Sqdn.
4th Photo-Recon Group
  17th Photo-Recon Sqdn.
  38th Photo-Recon Sqdn.

**FOURTEENTH AIR FORCE**
23rd Fighter Group/51st Fighter Group
  449th Fighter Sqdn.
(33rd Fighter Group w/58th, 59th and 60th Fighter Sqdns. assigned from Tenth Air Force.)
  51st Fighter Group
  25th Fighter Sqdn.
  8th Photo-Recon Group
  9th Photo-Recon Group
  40th Photo-Recon Group

Other photo-reconnaissance units working with the USAAF:
**FREE FRENCH AIR FORCE**
Group 2/33

**ITALIAN AIR FORCE**
3rd Aerobrigata RT
4th Aerobrigata

---

because I got a brand new (one of the first) P-38L-5-LO that arrived just a few days later at our base at Tacloban. My confirmed score for the day – December 25, 1944 – was four definites and one probable. All were confirmed on the basis of witnesses or camera film, and every one of the aircraft was a fighter. The first of these was a late-model Zeke that had a 20-mm cannon mounted in the aft fuselage and firing at an angle over the cockpit enclosure. The second victory was the Frank fighter that was totally unknown to us (in the 49th) prior to that mission."

Major Pierce's combat episode can be viewed as only slightly atypical of numerous air-to-air combat events that involved P-38s in the Pacific Theater of Operations in the last year or so of the war. He was having an exceptionally good day, it's true, because his old P-38J didn't let him down, his gunnery was 4.0 and he managed to get some very good breaks. But many other pilots had days that were nearly as successful, and some of those pilots had it happen more than one or two times. Until the advent of the P-51D in large numbers in 1945, there simply was no other AAF or Allied fighter in the area that was capable of performing in such an exceptional manner.

In summary, factual evidence is the only thing that really counts if any semblance of truth is to be maintained in documenting history. Men are still searching for specific truths in attempting to define exactly what occurred in shooting down Admiral Yamamoto over Bougainville in the Solomon Islands as his Mitsubishi G4M (Betty) bomber-transport headed for a landing at Kahili Air Field. Among the facts (or suppositions) that cannot be contested, the mission of the Thirteenth Air Force to "get Yamamoto" was a supreme success. Lockheed P-38s were the only aircraft in the Pacific (SWPA) arena that could be expected to do the job, and it was done at less that squadron strength. That April 1943 mission was accomplished with P-38G aircraft, most certainly not the definitive P-38L that was the contemporary of North American's revered P-51D. (For comparison purposes, the first P-51B Mustangs were being prepared for shipment to the ETO in August 1943.)

Another example of the difficulty in separating fable from fact is the case of the first *Luftwaffe* aircraft ever shot down in the ETO by an American AAF airplane. Most people believe that a Bell P-39F shot down – or shared the victory with a Curtiss P-40 – a Focke-Wulf Fw 200 Condor merchant raider over Icelandic territory. By eyewitness account, there was no P-39 involved at all. And the first one to intercept – the P-40 – had only damaged the Condor, which subsequently was found to be in 99 percent flying trim. Two P-38Fs attacked, scoring hits, but the main attacker was damaged and had to return to base. Lt. Elza Shahan, the P-38 wingman, decided that the Fw 200 was going to get away; he attacked it and shot it down. Officially the lead P-38 received no credit for the confirmed "kill," but Shahan had to share his victory with the P-40 pilot. "Willy" Weltman in the leading P-38 obviously did more damage to the Condor than the P-40 did; yet he received no credit at all.

When the Lockheed P-38s were returned to the scene of action in the ETO as Operation POINTBLANK brushed up against disaster, the new ETO CG was not known to be a devoted advocate of the Lightning, but pragmatism forced him to accede to the fact that it was the *only* weapon he had for the job. In "real time" if there had been an equal number of P-51Bs on line to do the job, they would have enjoyed little more success.

Neither the P-38 pilots, mechanics, facilities or logistics programs were prepared to operate efficiently in one

---

the plane began to break up. When I joined up with the flight that was chasing him, the leader turned out to be none other than Maj. Tom McGuire of the 475th Group – one of the ex-members of our own 49th FG.

"We all cruised around, collecting most of the stray 'friendlies' and then headed for home. My fuel was going at a pretty rapid rate because I was using extra power to compensate for the wide open cooler doors and oil cooler flaps. Low fuel reserves forced us to put down at the recently built San Jose Strip on Mindoro. My landing was OK until the nose-wheel hit. The gear collapsed. My main gear held up, so I cut the switches and skidded to a bumpy stop.

"Post-flight inspection indicated that when that first enemy aircraft exploded directly under me, skin panels from the fighter had lodged in my cooler scoops. Although I lost that airplane (written off), I wasn't bent too far out of shape

*Above Saipan, three of the Army Air Force's top fighters team up for a family photograph. The P-47D razorback was used primarily in the assault role in the Central Pacific area, helping to take the Marianas Island bases from which P-38s could strike at Iwo Jima. The Lightnings, kin to this P-38L, were the heavy duty fighters in the Pacific for most of the war, supported for a lengthy period by Curtiss P-40s. As P-51D and K production increased, the Mustang became the air superiority fighter for the Far East Air Forces. P-38s shot down the final enemy aircraft of the war on the day before orders came down to cease hostile aggressive action. The unlucky Japanese pilots were flying six Nakajima Franks, possibly the finest enemy fighter. In keeping with the high combat victory percentages that prevailed during the Leyte and Luzon battles, the Lightnings shot down all of the aircraft in that final encounter. (USAF)*

of the bitterest European winters on record. No other Allison-powered aircraft had ever operated at altitudes of more than 20,000 feet over the Continent for even a half hour. (In fact, it is doubtful that any P-38s in the Aleutians, Northwest Africa, the Southwest Pacific or any place had operated for any length of time at high altitude in a combat environment by autumn 1943.)

How was anyone to know the engine type – the ONLY inline engine type with turbosupercharging – would not respond happily under the command of youthful pilots who had never been subjected to even a few short periods of operation at 30,000 feet under optimized conditions, let alone under the worst possible conditions? That same group of pilots probably had never released a drop tank, may never have spent even 15 minutes shooting at a moving sleeve target and, in fact, may not ever have even fired the guns of a P-38. Suddenly they were being commanded to fly twice as far into *Festung Europa* territory as any P-47 pilot had been able to venture, after hearing all the stories from B-17 bomber crews and seeing the battered state in which most of them returned to England. What did they know about cruise control? Had any of them even heard of it?

Second Lt. Royal D. "Junior" Frey likes to tell about his early introduction to the Lightning, a type he flew with some success as a member of 20FG's 55th Fighter Squadron out of Kings Cliffe. At the tender age of 18, his informants would have had him believe that "the P-38 will not fly on one engine, it can't be rolled," and we presume they also added that "nobody can bail out of a P-38 and survive." Well, "Junior" Frey got in 35 hours of combat flying (pre-

combat in a P-38H, combat in an early J) and claimed two Messerschmitt Bf 110s shot down ... in somebody else's backyard. Unfortunately, he failed to return from a mission on February 10, 1944. He became a POW and very shortly thereafter got to meet Lt. Col. Mark Hubbard, a 20FG commander under whom he had not actually served. Hubbard became a POW on March 18. Royal Frey can be reported as being a man who loves the P-38.

If anyone wrote a fiction story suggesting that a thin olive drab line of not more than 75 fighters would be expected to fly protective cover for the most vulnerable of 600 to 750 heavy bombers at a distance of up to 450 miles deep inside enemy-controlled territory, it would hardly draw rave critical reviews.

*BELOW LEFT: Originally designed for best performance at very high altitudes (for that era), Lightnings in the guise of P-38Js and Ls came down to medium and low levels for most effective performances. Here a P-38J is flying at "weedtop" level during a practice strafing run in Panama. Sixth Air Force activity in the Caribbean/Canal Zone Theater has usually been ignored in coverage of World War II air operations. (AFM)*

*BELOW RIGHT: The production P-38M differed only in minor detail from this development night fighter. Flame dampeners were installed on all guns, and the Navy-type search radar "bomb" was located under the nosecap on a bomb-release mechanism. In an emergency, the radar bomb could be jettisoned. Relocation of the VHF radio mast to the left tail boom was required. Notice small antennas at both vertical fins, added as tests progressed. (USAAF)*

Add in the expectation that the same fighters, after a few hours of flight, would have to try and ward off attacks by hundreds of the best German fighters (in their own ballpark) over a period of hours and the critics would probably be joined by many others scoffing at "such a ridiculous impossibility." But that is exactly what happened in anything but a fictional environment.

Spitfire and Hurricane pilots defended the United Kingdom in a fight at odds during the July-October period of 1940, receiving the greatest possible accolades. And they were deserved. But USAAF P-38 pilots who operated at "arm's length" from their home bases and then had to fight against odds that were every bit as devastating were not often lauded; they were pitied for having to fly aircraft in which the cockpits were so cold and the engines so unreliable.

Who, may we be so bold as to ask, was able to or inclined to go out there and support them. The WPB was capable. It was just indifferent.

Roger A. Freeman, one of the most respected aviation writers of our time, wrote: "Probably the greatest single contribution of the Eighth Air Force to victory in Europe was the star part its fighters played in attaining combat superiority in continental air space. Originally furnished for bomber protection, the U.S. fighters came to be a potent offensive weapon." Amen.

Early versions of the P-38 – F, G, and H models – more than held their own in the ETO despite insufficient pilot training, application of unsuitable tactics in combat, and a total failure to commit adequate numbers of the type (or any equally capable type) to the fray. Nobody can blame it on lack of time; the P-38 was on the scene as early as January 1, 1939 ... all *one* of it. Just to put things in perspective, fighters and bombers provided to the military in the 1930s might be expected to have a first-line lifetime expectancy of perhaps 4 or 5 years, and that in a peacetime environment. The Lightning was just really getting into its best fighting trim 6 years after its initial flight.

Is it not noteworthy that three of the five top American aces ran up their scores against some of the most maneuverable fighters in the entire world, not Heinkel He 111 bombers or sitting duck B-17s and B-24s committed to a straight and level course from the IP? That was not pure dumb luck either. Maj. Richard Bong had confirmed that if he had been able to experience valid gunnery training before his first tour of duty in the Pacific, he *probably* could have doubled his score. Did anybody ever hear Bong "badmouth" the Lightning? I doubt it. In the case of ace Dick West, he was (fortunately, he says) asked if he wanted to go to a P-47 unit or a P-38 unit from P-40s. He specifically asked for ... and got ... P-38s.

Oh, the Lightning was far from perfection. C. L. "Kelly" Johnson absolutely delighted a vast audience at our P-38 symposium in 1977 by enumerating 15 things that were wrong about the P-38 ... after giving the listeners a rundown on 15 good things about his fabulous fighter. But, nobody can take away the fact that it was the first military aircraft in the world to attain – even exceed – 400 mph in level flight. And, of course, that was in full military trim.[2] Only a couple of purebred racing seaplanes had ever exceeded 400 mph as of February 1939.

Given the capability demonstrated by Packard Motors to manufacture adequate numbers of Rolls-Royce Merlin engines, it seems that one of the great errors of World War II

was the failure of the War Production Board to even consider Lockheed's plans to equip at least one model of the P-38 with a high-altitude version of the Merlin. Such proposals were on the drawing board in the early months of 1941, and it was generally conceded that the modification would be no more difficult than the revised Allison installation made in the definitive P-38J. There would have been no intercooler problems to contend with, and leading-edge fuel tanks could have been a bonus asset early in 1943. (It must be remembered that for all of Lt. Gen. William Knudsen's charm and ability, he had been the top executive at General Motors Corp. prior to formation of the Office of Production Management, earlier civilian counterpart of the WPB. Allison Engineering was a division of General Motors. Just having completed large new manufacturing facilities for the V-1710 in 1941, and with no precedent at all for utilizing foreign engines in American production military aircraft, U.S. officialdom was hardly inclined to endorse Lockheed's clairvoyant new proposal.)

G Lockheed's P-38 was not really one design, any more than the Spitfire Mk I was directly comparable to the Spitfire Mk 47; the P-47B Thunderbolt was quite unlike the P-47N; North American's P-51D had changed considerably in appearance since its NA-73 beginnings, but the wing and airframe were technically very close to the original.

However, hardly anyone would have remembered the Mustang with much more affection than they would the Bell Airacobra but for one important change: through a simple chain of unremarkable circumstances, the engine that Kelly Johnson had (at an earlier date) wanted for his P-38 was wedded to the Mustang airframe. A review of Lockheed's earlier drawings for such an installation reveals that it was no more complex than the North American arrangement. The Merlin installation not only improved the Mustang's appearance, but *voila*, it transformed the airplane. It was a wedding made in heaven.

The Lightning was remarkable, almost beyond compare, in that the wing, central fuselage, boom fuselages and empennage (except for one tiny percentage increase in horizontal stabilizer area) remained unchanged in shape between 1937 and 1945. Few aircraft other than the Hurricane, Hellcat and Wildcat can make such a claim, with most of the others undergoing considerable change in a shorter timespan.

About the British version of the Lightning, the Model 322-B. Lockheed never would have designed such an airplane for presentation to anybody. That is a fact. The airplane preferred design was there, but the British and French teams sent to the U.S.A. to make panic purchases – France was within days of collapse before the Nazi forces and the British forces in continental Europe were being threatened with annihilation – were insistent that Allison V-1710C series

---

2. Granted, no guns protruded from the nose of the XP-38 – calculated to increase speed by less than 2 mph – but it was fully ballasted to provide gun and ammunition weight.

Converted from one of the first ten P-38L-5-LOs built a Burbank, No. 5067 was most likely the first F-5G-6-LO to roll out of the Dallas Mod Center. The event also resulted in two of the best F-5G photographs produced during the war, suggesting that lensman Eric Miller went to Texas to record the event. With a nose like that on W. C. Fields, the F-5G was not a thing of beauty as it cruised over the city of Dallas.

Long-range capabilities of the P-38, stemming from its fabulous lifting powers, helped make it the best photo-recon airplane of World War II. It was durable, required only a one-man crew, was fast enough to avoid interception and carried an excellent assortment of cameras. The F-5G-6-LO, identified easily by its bulbous nose, was the final version in the long series that began with the F-4. This particular example was not equipped with an ADF loop antenna for extended-range missions. It was possible to stretch out the range to as much as 14 1/2 hours, or approximately 3,750 miles. (Lockheed)

engines be installed with all engines having the same direction of rotation. In 1940, before they learned the lessons of the Battle of Britain,, they expressed firm opposition to the idea of employing turbosuperchargers. Engines and propellers were to be virtually identical with those powering the Curtiss Tomahawk II (H81-A2), an airplane that the British (and, supposedly, the French) would be receiving in short order. With that engine and propeller combination and no superchargers, the two Allies would reduce their logistics and maintenance difficulties by a massive amount.

It had to be presumed that the British Air Purchasing Commission top officials (Sir Henry Self, Air Vice Marshal G. B. A. Baker and Mr. H. C. B. Thomas) were supported by a technical staff. No records uncovered to date give any clue about date and conditions under which the requirements were accepted, but Lockheed's Specification No. 1756 was first issued on March 21, 1940. Company contractual records contain a great deal of information, as well they should, but omissions and errors are plentiful.

(Some LAC records state that the reason the 322-Bs did not have turbosuperchargers was that they were "secret." But those records were compiled at a much later date – postwar – by employee Russ Peete. Much of that information came from the Lockheed Public Relations staff. As we have revealed, there was nothing secret about turbos which had been on dozens of airplanes dating back before 1925. If anything, the French Rateau firm developed them first in World War I.)

For unbelievers, it is well to look at the engines selected for the 322-F/-B Lightnings. Within days or weeks of the time

that the C-15 (-33) right-hand rotation engines were specified by the commission, they also ordered the North American NA-93 Mustang fighter into production with the Allison V-1710F3R (-39) engine. Spur reduction gearing replaced the weaker and less reliable epicyclic gearing utilized in C series engines and the F3R produced anywhere from 30 to 80 bhp more than the C-15 engine turned out. That would have been an additional 60 to 160 bhp for the 322 if Lord Self's staff had specified it. Lt. Kelsey and Kelly Johnson had already agreed to use the F-series powerplants in YP-38 and subsequent airplanes more than a year earlier. The AAF and Lockheed would never have specified any C-series Allison beyond the prototype XP-38.

No Lockheed contractual records list the date on which the British Contract No. A-242 was signed (no copy of the contract could be obtained from any file). What is far more interesting, though, is why Lockheed agreed to build 667 versions of an airplane that C. L. Johnson would never have proposed to anyone. He had proven that a thousand times by his decisions. Lacking a verbatim deposition, it has been necessary to make certain suppositions; hypotheses, if you prefer. Subsequent actions by Lockheed and British officials provide about all the circumstantial evidence needed for confirmation.

Jimmy Gerschler had a drinking problem. Faced with tremendous pressures at Burbank and in New York, he was known to have been arrested on a firearms charge in the "big" city. At a time when he could buy 2 pounds of seedless grapes in Los Angeles for 5 cents, he was negotiating a contract for about $70,000,000! The Frenchmen were virtually throwing money at him with both hands as the *Wehrmacht* headed for Paris. Lord Self had to know that RAF Home Defense forces possessed no more than 25 squadrons of first-line fighters to battle an invasion force that was certain to come. A "guaranteed" force of 400-mph fighters sounded great, and Gerschler was the guarantor.

*Ah that deceit should steal such gentle shapes –* Shakespeare.

The question is, who was flim-flamming who? The French were not likely to be able to pay, even if they got the airplanes. Gerschler may have never asked, but evidently nobody at Burbank asked later. Once the press got it into print, who was likely to back out of the contract? Look at the results. At least one RAF pilot flew a 322-B in California.[3] Was he happy with it? More than a year after the *Luftwaffe* quit throwing itself at the RAF over what was left of London's East End, the answer had to be a raucous NO! You can rest assured that the pilot had not been in NYC during the 1940 negotiations there.

Worse, Lockheed was virtually drowning in buffeting and compressibility problems in 1941, but nobody really knew that the latter problem could not possibly affect the Model 322-B type. It was hardly likely that one would ever see 30,000 feet.

3. A question remains: Exactly when did the flight(s) actually take place? That pilot may not have even been familiar with contract specifications for the 322-B. The RAF's requirements certainly had changed radically.

Critical altitude was 14,300 feet, or just where you might find some Curtiss Tomahawks cavorting.

The Ministry of Supply said (in 1941) they would refuse to take any of the Lightnings. Robert Gross evidently stared them in the eye and said, "I'll see you in court," or words to that effect. And he meant it. The 322s could meet the guarantees, said the engineers and test pilots. There was nothing in the contract about buffeting. Few people had ever heard of a thing called "compressibility tuck."

Circumstantial evidence: Three Lightning Is went to the United Kingdom; as noted elsewhere, no Lockheed Lightnings ever served with the RAF, and the British never bought the first three airplanes. Well, they really weren't the first three; just the only three to get across the ocean in British markings. They eventually were returned to the USAAF.

Camouflaged by the mists of time, hardly anybody noticed that after 1941 the British placed very few orders for any Lockheed airplanes during World War II. And they never flew P-80s and they also never trained people in T-33s. The same goes for F-104s. But, some old-time pragmatism finally set in much later, and the bought the Hercules years – decades – after the 322-B had become history.

One other distortion of the facts has to be brought to light; at least we raise the issue.

The issue of personal opinion (again), and how political expediency can be used to distort truth. It was not in the same category as the 1980s Iran-Contra Affair, but it amounts to the same sort of thing. On May 29, 1944, Maj. Gen. William Kepner issued a document entitled "Long Reach." In a nutshell, Kepner admitted that P-47 Thunderbolts, in what he referred to "as the early stage (?) of bomber escort", could only provide escort on short penetrations of "some 165 miles, roughly to Brussels, Cambrai, Paris, etc., and part way protection to the bombers ..." He did not qualify that by including the period prior to his assumption of command of VIIIFC in August 1943. (Lockheed P-38Hs were soon streaking to Kiel, at least 500 miles – in a direct line – from Nuthampstead! More importantly, they could have been doing that before Christmas 1942.)

What external tanks the P-47s had prior to development of the "paper" drop tanks were hardly successful in combat. In a subsequent paragraph, he stated that with the development of belly tanks, the Fortresses and Liberators were escorted by Thunderbolts to any point on an arc swung from Kiel through Hannover, Stuttgart, Vichy and ending at La Rochelle on the coast of France. And the general's document said that was a radius of 450 miles. As a sort of afterthought, he stated that the Lightnings (in 1943) could protect the bombers at their target areas, but *there were not enough of them to cover the bombers from the point where the Thunderbolts would finally have to leave them.* We are well versed on that. But nowhere does he say that those targets included Berlin or that it was about 600 miles (combat radius) from Kings Cliffe, for example. Then he brightly refers to the P-51s being added to his command in March 1944, and being able to go to Berlin, "by large measure longer in range than any other fighter on the battle fronts."

*O, what a tangled web we weave/When first we practice to deceive* – Scott

What were those 55FG P-38s doing over Berlin on so many days in March 1944? Now Kepner may have been the commanding general of the whole works over there, but facts seem to have been ignored. The official maximum *ferrying* (not combat) range of a P-51D with two 108-gallon drop tanks was 2,230 miles. Way, way back in 1942, it should be remembered,

Milo Burcham demonstrated a ferry range on an early model P-38 of more than 3,000 miles. It is really doubtful that anybody flew a P-51D on a combat mission of nine and a half hours, but that was almost routine with a P-38J and L models in the SWPA.

Well, Gen. Kepner loved the 4th and 56th Fighter Groups for their exploits, as well he should. Even his personal airplane was a P-47D. What was missing was a heated debate between Gen. George Kenney and Gen. Bill Kepner. Now that could have been interesting.

Just about two years more than a half century ago, America said "Hello!" to the first military aircraft in the world that could fly at a speed of more than 400 miles per hour. It was the Lockheed XP-38 that had been designed by Clarence (Kelly) Johnson, and with Lt. Ben Kelsey at the controls it had sped across the United States from California to New York in just 7 hours and 2 minutes flying time. It was not an official record flight because of the leisurely pace of refueling crews at stops in Texas and Ohio, extending the total elapsed time to 7 hours 43 minutes. Without "pushing" the engines, a speed of 400 mph was touched between Dayton and New York City. The date: February 11, 1939.

That brightly polished XP-38 was also the first real military fighter designed and built by Lockheed Aircraft Corporation.

On March 6, 1990, another Johnson-designed twin-engine airplane departed from California before dawn and just 68 minutes and 17 seconds later it flashed past the tower at Dulles International Airport in Virginia, not far from the final home of the late Brig. Gen. Benjamin S. Kelsey, USAF. This time, the aircraft was dead black in keeping with its stealthy spying mission. Lockheed's SR-71 had long since demonstrated (officially) that it could fly more than 2200 mph. That same basic airframe had flown for the first time – as the A-11 – just shy of 28 years earlier. SR-71s, all exteen of them (nobody really likes to discuss actual quantities of airplanes that come from Lockheed's famed "Skunk Works") have been reconnoitering strategic targets all over the globe for more than a quarter century.

Designed to fly at speeds approaching Mach 4 (estimated), four times the speed of sound or about 2760 miles per hour, the Blackbirds are able to fly at more than six times as fast as any P-38 ever flew in level flight. Kelly Johnson was awarded his second Collier Trophy in 1964 for the spectacularly fast and successful aircraft. No aircraft in history, including the newest designs by the world's premier designers, have ever been able to match the SR-71's performance. And no other person has ever been awarded two Collier Trophies.

Any man in the world would be proud just to have designed the P-38 Lightning. Or the P-80/F-80 jet fighter. Or the F-104 Starfighter. Or the U-2 spy plane and its improved clone, the TR-1. Or the A-11/YF-12/SR-71 Blackbird. Clarence Johnson is a warm, helpful, brilliant designer who has no peer. He was the designer of all those stupendously successful airplanes!

What was really remarkable about the March 6 flight of the Blackbird is that it – and several duplicates – are being put out to pasture. Retired with honors. Not many Ancient Eagles are still capable of flying across America at 2153.24 mph, establishing several new records in the process, just to reach the retirement home.

America produced two really honest-to-God heroes in the persons of Clarence L. Johnson (Kelly) and Benjamin S. Kelsey (Ben) who probably saved more lives than anybody will ever know. What more could one ask than to just stand in their shadows?

It was the Lockheed P-38 Lightning that had brought them together.

# COMPREHENSIVE TABLE OF

| CUSTOMER MODEL | LAC MODEL NO. | CONTRACT NUMBER | NO. DELIVERED | ENGINE MODEL | LAC C/N |
|---|---|---|---|---|---|
| XP-38 | 022-64-01 | AC-9974 | 1 | V-1710C-9 | 2201 – |
| YP-38 | 122-62-02 | AC-12523 | 13 | V-1710F-2 | 2202 – 2214 |
| P-38/RP-38 | 222-62-08 | AC-13205 | 18 | V-1710F-2 | 2215 – 2232 |
| " | " | " | 11 | " | 2234 – 2244 |
| P-38D/RP-38D | 222-62-08D | AC-13205 C.O.3377 | 36 | V-1710F-2 | 2245 – 2280 |
| XP-38A | 622-62-10 | AC-13205 C.O.8 | 1 | V-1710F-2 | 2233 – |
| XP-49 | 522-66-07 | AC-13476 | 1 | XIV-1430-13 &-15 | |
| P-38E/RP-38E | 222-62-09 | AC-15646 | 115 | V-1710F-4 | 5201 – 5315 |
| " | " | " | 21 | " | 5318 – 5338 |
| " | " | " | 1 | " | 5390 – |
| " | " | " | 1 | " | 5437 – |
| " | " | " | 72 | " | 5439-5510 |
| F-4-1-LO | 222-62-13 | AC-15646 C.O. 11 | 2 | V-1710F-4 | 5316-5317 |
| " | " | " | 36 | " | 5339-5374 |
| " | " | " | 14 | " | 5376-5389 |
| " | " | " | 46 | " | 5391-5436 |
| " | " | " | 1 | " | 5438 – |
| F-5A-2-LO | 222-62-16 | AC-15646 | 1 | V-1710F-4 | 5375 – |
| P-38F | 222-60-09 | AC-15646 | 29 | V-1710F-5 | 5511 – 5539 |
| " | " | " | 36 | " | 5541 – 5576 |
| " | " | " | 4 | " | 5601 – 5604 |
| " | " | " | 5 | " | 5606 – 5610 |
| " | " | " | 11 | " | 5613 – 5623 |
| " | " | " | 16 | " | 5625 – 5640 |
| " | " | " | 9 | " | 5643 – 5651 |
| " | " | " | 5 | " | 5653 – 5657 |
| " | " | " | 3 | " | 5659 – 5661 |
| " | " | " | 3 | " | 5663 – 5665 |
| " | " | " | 2 | " | 5669 – 5670 |
| " | " | " | 1 | " | 5672 – |
| " | " | " | 1 | " | 5674 – |
| " | " | " | 1 | " | 5678 – |
| F-4A-1-LO | 222-60-13 | AC-15646 | 20 | V-1710F-4 | 5580 – 5599 |
| P-38F-1-LO | 222-60-15 | AC-15646 | 1 | V-1710F-5 | 5540 – |
| " | " | " | 3 | " | 5577 – 5579 |
| " | " | " | 1 | " | 5612 – |
| " | " | " | 1 | " | 5624 – |
| " | " | " | 2 | " | 5641 – 5642 |

# LOCKHEED P-38 PRODUCTION

| CUSTOMER NO. FROM | (AC) THROUGH | DELIVERY DATES | NOTES |
|---|---|---|---|
| 37-457 | – | Feb. 1939 | |
| 39-689 | 39-701 | Sept. 1940 – May 1941 | Contract completed July 1941. |
| 40-744 | 40-761 | June 41 – July 41 | Did not incorporate changes of European |
| 40-763 | 40-773 | July 41 – Aug. 41 | combat experience.  7/39 contract. |
| 40-774 | 40-809 | June 41 – Sept. 41 | Built to AAF "combat" standards. |
| 40-762 | – | Dec. 42 | Pressure cabin.  Out of P-38 batch. |
| 40-3055 | – | Nov. 43 | Lockheed Model L-106. |
| 41-1983 | 41-2097 | Sept. 41 – April 42 | |
| 41-2100 | 41-2120 | Mar. 42 – April 42 | |
| 41-2172 | – | April 42 | |
| 41-2219 | – | Feb. 42 | |
| 41-2221 | 41-2292 | Feb. 42 – April 42 | Total P-38E = 210. |
| 41-2098 | 41-2099 | Mar. 42 | First high-performance photo-reconnaissance |
| 41-2121 | 42-2156 | Mar. 42 – May 42 | aircraft for USAAF to be mass produced. |
| 41-2158 | 41-2171 | April 42 – June 42 | Suggested by Lt. Col. George W. Goddard. |
| 41-2173 | 41-2218 | May 42 – Aug. 42 | Total F-4-1 = 99. |
| 41-2220 | – | Aug. 42 | |
| 41-2157 | – | July 42 | |
| 41-2293 | 41-2321 | Mar. 42 – April 42 | P-38F airplanes have one 2,000-pound |
| 41-2323 | 41-2358 | Mar. 42 – April 42 | external store pylon under each wing |
| 41-2383 | 41-2386 | April 42 | center section. |
| 41-2388 | 41-2392 | April 42 | |
| 41-7486 | 41-7496 | Mar. 42 – April 42 | World's first fighter aircraft to be delivered by air |
| 41-7498 | 417513 | April 42 | across a major ocean. |
| 41-7516 | 41-7524 | " | |
| 41-7526 | 41-7530 | " | |
| 41-7532 | 41-7534 | " | |
| 41-7536 | 41-7538 | " | |
| 41-7542 | 41-7543 | " | |
| 41-7545 | – | " | |
| 41-7547 | – | " | |
| 41-7551 | – | April 42 | Total P-38F = 126. |
| 41-2362 | 41-2381 | Aug. 42 | |
| 41-2322 | – | June 42 | Numerous a/c converted for Project |
| 41-2359 | 41-2361 | June 42 | BOLERO. |
| 41-7485 | – | May 42 | Certain a/c converted for Projects SUMAC |
| 41-7497 | – | May 42 | and BRONZE. |
| 41-7514 | 41-7515 | May 42 | |

# COMPREHENSIVE TABLE OF

| CUSTOMER MODEL | LAC MODEL NO. | CONTRACT NUMBER | NO. DELIVERED | ENGINE MODEL | LAC C/N |
|---|---|---|---|---|---|
| P-38F-1-LO | 222-60-15 | AC-15646 | 1 | V-1710F-5 | 5652 – |
| " | " | " | 1 | " | 5658 – |
| " | " | " | 1 | " | 5662 – |
| " | " | " | 3 | " | 5666 – 5668 |
| " | " | " | 1 | " | 5671 – |
| " | " | " | 1 | " | 5673 – |
| " | " | " | 3 | " | 5675 – 5677 |
| " | " | " | 129 | " | 5679 – 5807 |
| P-38F-1-LO | 222-60-12 | AC-15646 | 1 | V-1710F-5 | 5600 – |
| " | " | " | 1 | " | 5605 – |
| " | " | " | 1 | " | 5611 – |
| P-38F-5-LO | 222-60-12 | AC-21217 | 100 | " | 7001 – 7100 |
| P-38G-1-LO | 222-68-12 | AC-21217 | 80 | V-1710F-10 (-51/-55) | 7121 – 7200 |
| P-38G-3-LO | 222-68-12 | AC-21217 | 12 | V-1710F-10 (-51/-55) | 7221 – 7232 |
| P-38G-5-LO | 222-68-12 | AC-21217 | 68 | V-1710F-10 (-51/-55) | 7233 – 7300 |
| P-38G-10-LO | 222-68-12 | AC-21217 | 97 | V-1710F-10 (-51/-55) | 7304 – 7400 |
| " | " | " | 80 | " | 7421 – 7500 |
| " | " | " | 140 | " | 7561 – 7700 |
| " | " | " | 231 | " | 7761 – 7991 |
| F-5A-1-LO | 222-68-16 | AC-21217 | 20 | V-1710F-10 (-51/-55) | 7101 – 7120 |
| F-5A-3-LO | 222-68-16 | AC-21217 | 20 | V-1710F-10 (-51/-55) | 7201 – 7220 |
| F-5A-10-LO | 222-68-16 | AC-21217 | 20 | V-1710F-10 (-51/-55) | 7401 – 7420 |
| " | " | " | 60 | " | 7501 – 7560 |
| " | " | " | 60 | " | 7701 – 7760 |
| 322-F | 322-61-03 | A-242 | 0 | V-1710C-15 (-33) | |
| 322-B | 322-61-04 | BR-A-242/AC-31707 | 3 | V-1710C-15 (-33) | 3001 – 3003 |
| P-322-I | 322-61-04 | BR-A-242/AC-31707 | 19 | V-1710C-15 (-33) | 3004 – 3022 |
| P-322-II | 322-62-18 | BR-A-242/AC-31707 | 121 | V-1710C-15/V-1710F-2 (Conv.) | 3023 – 3143 |
| P-38F-13-LO | 322-60-19 | A-242/AC-31707 | 29 | V-1710F-5 | 3144 – 3172 |
| P-38F-15-LO | 322-60-19 | A-242/AC-31707 | 121 | V-1710F-5 | 3173 – 3293 |
| P-38G-13-LO | 322-68-19 | A-242/AC-31707 | 174 | V-1710F-10 | 3294 – 3467 |
| P-38G-15-LO | 322-68-19 | A-242/AC-31707 | 33 | V-1710F-10 | 3468 – 3500 |
| P-38G-15-LO | 322-68-19 | A-242/AC-31707 | 167 | V-1710F-10 | 3502 – 3668 |
| P-38H-1-LO | 422-81-20 | AC-21217 | 1 | V-1710F-17 | 1005 – |
| P-38J-1-LO | 422-81-14 | AC-21217 | 3 | V-1710F-17 | 1001 – 1003 |
| " | " | AC-21217 | 7 | V-1710F-17 | 1006 – 1012 |
| P-38H-1-LO | 422-81-20 | AC-24636 | 225 | V-1710F-17 | 1013 – 1237 |
| P-38H-5-LO | 422-81-20 | AC-24636 | 375 | V-1710F-17 | 1238 – 1612 |

# LOCKHEED P-38 PRODUCTION

| CUSTOMER NO. FROM | (AC) THROUGH | DELIVERY DATES | NOTES |
|---|---|---|---|
| 41-7525 | – | May 42 | |
| 41-7531 | – | " | |
| 41-7535 | – | " | |
| 41-7539 | 41-7541 | " | |
| 41-7544 | – | " | |
| 41-7546 | – | " | |
| 41-7548 | 41-7550 | " | |
| 41-7552 | 41-7680 | May 42 – June 42 | |
| 41-2382 | – | July 42 | |
| 41-2387 | – | April 42 | |
| 41-7484 | – | May 42 | Total P-38F-1-LO = 151. |
| 42-12567 | 42-12666 | June 42 – Mar. 43 | Delays for Projects BRONZE and SUMAC; |
| 42-12687 | 42-12766 | Aug. 42 – Oct. 42 | also prop and landing gear shortages. Many P-38G |
| 42-12787 | 42-12798 | Sept. 42 – Oct. 42 | a/c modified for Projects SNOWMAN and |
| 42-12799 | 42-12866 | Aug. 42 – Oct. 42 | WILDFLOWER. |
| 42-12870 | 42-12966 | Oct. 42 – Mar. 43 | Delayed deliveries. |
| 42-12987 | 42-13066 | Nov. 42 –Dec. 42 | |
| 42-13127 | 42-13266 | Jan. 43 – Mar. 43 | |
| 42-13327 | 42-13557 | Mar. 43 – May 43 | Total P-38G-10-LO deliveries = 548. |
| 42-12667 | 42-12686 | Aug. 42 – Dec. 42 | P-38G-1-LO configuration with camera nose. |
| 42-12767 | 42-12786 | Oct. 42 | |
| 42-12967 | 42-12986 | Nov. 42 – Jan. 43 | |
| 42-13067 | 42-13126 | Dec. 42 – Jan. 43 | |
| 42-13267 | 42-13326 | Mar. 43 | Total F-5A deliveries = 140. |
| | | | France collapsed in June 1940. |
| AE 978 | AE 980 (comingled in modification) | Mar. 42 | * No turbos. AE 978, AE 979 and others produced |
| AE 981 | AE 999 (comingled in modification) | Dec. 41 – July 42 | before 12/7/41.  * AAF records show 3 + 19 to P-322-I. |
| AF 100 | AF 220 (comingled in modification) | Jan. 42 – July 42 | * Engine change. No turbos. To Training Command. |
| 43-2035 | 43-2063 | Aug. 42 – Oct. 42 | Ordered by RAF as Lightning II. |
| 43-2064 | 43-2184 | Sept. 42 – Oct. 42 | "  "  "  "  "  " |
| 43-2185 | 43-2358 | Nov. 42 – Jan. 43 | (c/n 3144 was originally AF 221) |
| 43-2359 | 43-2391 | Jan. 43 | c/n 3501 is not accounted for! |
| 43-2392 | 43-2558 | Jan. 43 – Mar. 43 | |
| 42-13559 | – | Mar. 43 | Prototype. |
| 42-12867 | 42-12869 | Mar. 43 | Prototypes – new intercoolers and glycol |
| 42-13560 | 42-13566 | July 43 – Oct. 43 | coolers. |
| 42-66502 | 42-66726 | May 43 – Aug. 43 | |
| 42-66727 | 42-67101 | June 43 – Dec. 43 | |

* LAC P-38 Model Summary, LAC Production History and USAAF AFPI Form 41 Disagree on RAF/USAAF Deliveries and LAC Model Designations.

| CUSTOMER MODEL | LAC MODEL NO. | CONTRACT NUMBER | NO. DELIVERED | ENGINE MODEL | LAC C/N |
|---|---|---|---|---|---|
| P-38J-5-LO | 422-81-14 | AC-24636 | 210 | V-1710F-17 (-89&-91) | 1613 – 1822 |
| P-38J-10-LO | 422-81-14 | AC-24636 | 790 | " | 1913 – 2702 |
| F-5B-1-LO | 422-81-21 | AC-24636 | 90 | " | 1823 – 1912 |
| " | " | AC-24636 | 110 | " | 2703 – 2812 |
| P-38J-15-LO | 422-81-22 | AC 35374 | 450 | " | 2813 – 3262 |
| " | " | " | 800 | " | 3263 – 4062 |
| " | " | " | 150 | " | 4063 – 4212 |
| P-38J-20-LO | 422-81-22 | " | 350 | " | 4213 – 4562 |
| P-38J-25-LO | 422-81-22 | AC-40040 | 210 | V-1710F-17 | 4563 – 4772 |
| P-38K-1-LO | 422-85-14 | AC-21217 | 1 | V-1710F-15 | 1004 – |
| P-38L-1-LO | 422-87-23 | AC-40040 | 1290 | V-1710F-30 | 4773 – 6062 |
| P-38L-5-LO | 422-87-23 | AC-40040 | 2200 | V-1710F-30 | 6063 – 8262 |
| " | " | AC-40040 | 320 | V-1710F-30 | 8263 – 8582 △ |
| (See XP-49) | 522 | | | | |
| (See XP-38A) | 622 | | | | |
| P-38L-5-VN | | AC-760 | 113 | V-1710F–30 | |
| **MODIFICATION CENTER CONVERSIONS AND/OR SPECIAL MODIFICATIONS BY USAAF** | | | | | |
| F-5C-1-LO | 422-81-20 | AC-24636 | (123) | | |
| XF-5D | 222-68-16 | AC-21217 | (1) | V-1710F-10 | 7409 – |
| F-5E-2-LO | 422-81-22 | AC-35374 | (Unk.) | V-1710F-17 | |
| F-5E-3-LO | 422-87-23 | AC-40040 | (705) | V-1710F-30 | |
| F-5E-4-LO | 422-87-23 | AC-40040 | (Unk.) | V-1710F-30 | |
| F-5F | 422-81-22 | AC-35374 | (Unk.) | V-1710F-17 | |
| F-5F-3-LO | 422-87-23 | AC–40040 | (Unk.) | V-1710F–30 | |
| F-5G–6-LO | 422-87-23 | AC-40040 | (Unk.) | V-1710F-30 | |
| ☆ P-38M-6-LO | 422-87-23 | AC-40040 | (75) | V-1710F-30 | |
| P-322-I | 322-61-04 | AC-31707 | (22) | V-1710C-15 | |
| P-322-II | 322-62-18 | AC-31707 (C.O.) | (121) | V-1710F-2 | |

Lockheed Total: 9925

Total Production: 10038

Modified (XXX) : (904)   (Does not include mods accomplished at depots, Langford Lodge or Fresno. Dallas Modification Center aircraft only. There is evidence that some CBI fighters had complete photographic noses installed, or fighter noses were reworked at second or third echelon facilities. Does not include reworked 322-B airplanes, generally reworked at LAC.)

NOTES: **1**: △ Contracts for a/c through c/n 9962. c/n 8583 and subs cancelled at V-J Day.
**2**: Although P-38 Droop Snoot and Pathfinder mods were as extensive as F-5 modifications, no separate designations were allocated.
**3**: ☆ Does not include one "proofing" nightfighter conversion accomplished at Fresno, California (Hammer Field).
**4**: XP-49 is a "22" series aircraft (522). Includes near standard wings, tailplane, NLG, and central fuselage (gondola) from P-38 line.

# LOCKHEED P-38 PRODUCTION

| CUSTOMER NO. FROM | (AC) THROUGH | DELIVERY DATES | NOTES |
|---|---|---|---|
| 42-67102 | 42-67311 | Aug. 43 – April 44 | |
| 42-67402 | 42-68191 | Oct. 43 – Dec. 43 | |
| 42-67312 | 42-67401 | Sept. 43 – Oct. 43 | Last production F-5s. P-38Js with camera noses. |
| 42-68192 | 42-68301 | Dec. 43 – Jan. 44 | |
| 42-103979 | 42-104428 | Dec. 43 – Feb. 44 | |
| 43-28248 | 43-29047 | Jan. 44 – May 44 | |
| 44-23059 | 44-23208 | April 44 -- May 44 | Total P-38J-15-LO = 1400. |
| 44-23209 | 44-23558 | May 44 – June 44 | |
| 44-23559 | 44-23768 | June 44 – Nov. 44 | Interim L model configuration. |
| 42-13558 | – | Sept. 43 – | H-S Hydraulic props; hi-output engines. |
| 44-23769 | 44-25058 | June 44 – Nov. 44 | Boosted ailerons; dive flaps; increased fuel. |
| 44-25059 | 44-27258 | Oct. 44 – June 45 | Many to F-5G-6-LO and P-38M-6-LO. |
| 44-53008 | 44-53327 | May 45 – Aug. 45 | Total P-38L-5-LO = 2520. |
| | | | |
| | | | |
| 43-50226 | 43-50338 | | CVA Nashville, Tenn., production. |
| | | | |
| | | | From P-38J quantities. |
| 42-12975 | – | Sept. 43 | Apparent W-PAFB conversion from F-5A. |
| | | | |
| | | | |
| | | | |
| | | | |
| | | | |
| **Refer to separate P-38M-6-LO listing** | | | 2-seat nightfighter. |
| Not sequential | | Jan. 42 | Trainers. |
| Not sequential | | Jan. 42 – Dec. 42 | Trainers; engine change. |

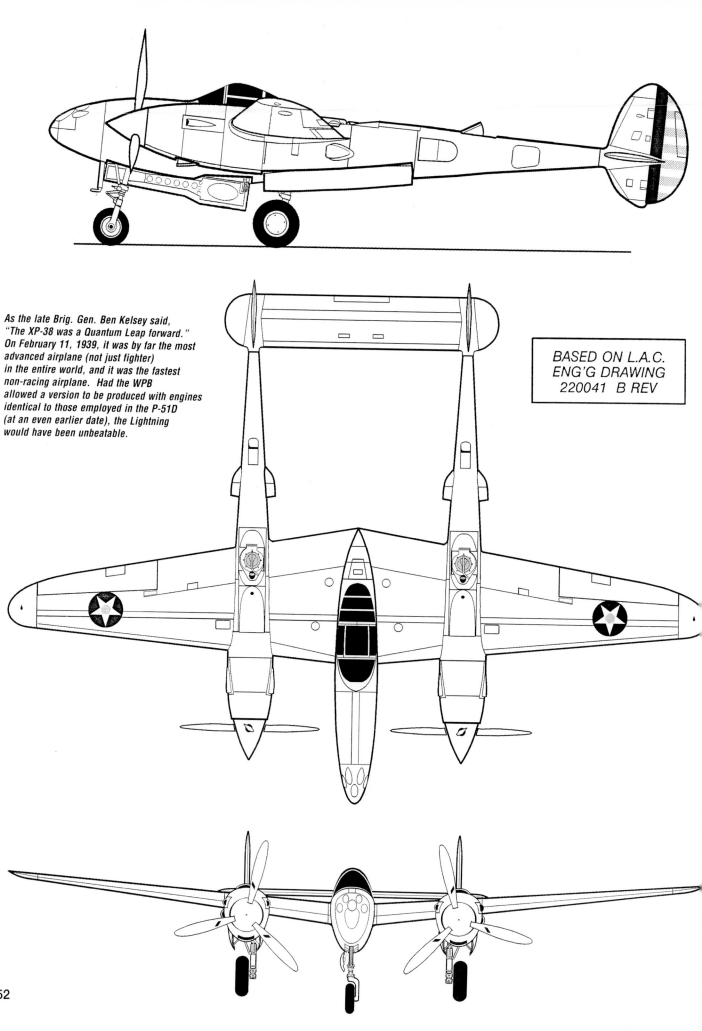

As the late Brig. Gen. Ben Kelsey said,
"The XP-38 was a Quantum Leap forward."
On February 11, 1939, it was by far the most
advanced airplane (not just fighter)
in the entire world, and it was the fastest
non-racing airplane. Had the WPB
allowed a version to be produced with engines
identical to those employed in the P-51D
(at an even earlier date), the Lightning
would have been unbeatable.

BASED ON L.A.C.
ENG'G DRAWING
220041  B REV

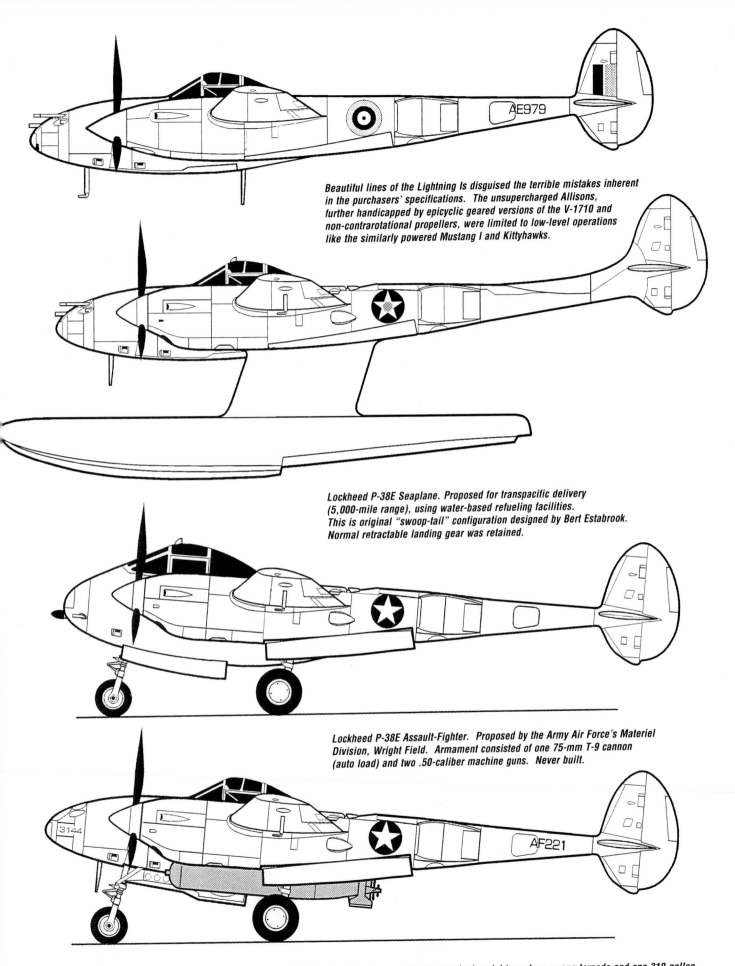

Beautiful lines of the Lightning Is disguised the terrible mistakes inherent in the purchasers' specifications. The unsupercharged Allisons, further handicapped by epicyclic geared versions of the V-1710 and non-contrarotational propellers, were limited to low-level operations like the similarly powered Mustang I and Kittyhawks.

Lockheed P-38E Seaplane. Proposed for transpacific delivery (5,000-mile range), using water-based refueling facilities. This is original "swoop-tail" configuration designed by Bert Estabrook. Normal retractable landing gear was retained.

Lockheed P-38E Assault-Fighter. Proposed by the Army Air Force's Materiel Division, Wright Field. Armament consisted of one 75-mm T-9 cannon (auto load) and two .50-caliber machine guns. Never built.

Lockheed P-38F-13-LO Lightning II, Model 322-60-19. Flight test vehicle for carrying two standard aerial torpedoes or one torpedo and one 310-gallon external drop tank. Successfully dropped a full-weight dummy torpedo.

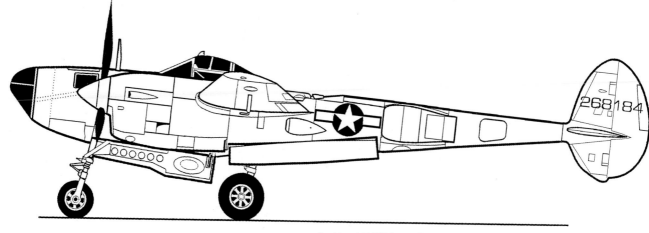

Lockheed P-38J Droop Snoot Lightning. Conceived by 8th AF Technical Operations Section, originally designed and built by LOC at Langford Lodge, North Ireland. Used for precision level bombing. Bomb-laden Lightnings dropped on signal from Droop Snoot leader. Norden bombsight used.

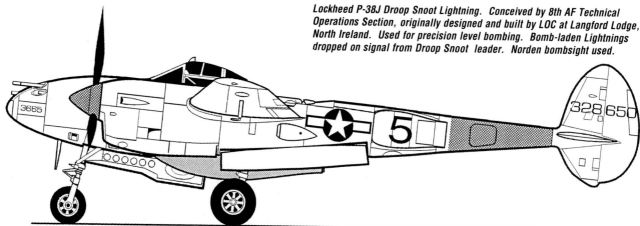

Lockheed P-38J-15-LO (AC43-28650) of the 27FS, 1FG, Fifteenth Air Force. Typical of the definitive Lightnings employed in combat squadrons of virtually all of the U. S. Army Air Forces deployed in every theater of operations. Shown with standard 165-gallon drop tanks.

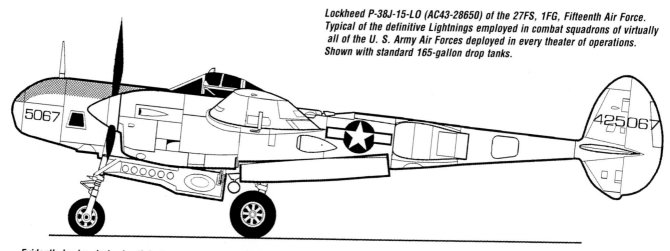

Evidently having derived satisfactory aerodynamic data from tests of the P-38J or L Pathfinder at Burbank, Lockheed offered the F-5G as a photo-recon derivative of the P-38L-5-LO design. None came from Plant B-1. All F-5G-6-LO versions were products of the Dallas Modification Center in Texas. A large selection of cameras could be carried in the bulbous nose. Most of the fast F-5Gs carried a DF loop or an ADF "bomb" for navigation. Maximum duration/range was 14.5 hours and approximately 3,750 miles. Some were based in Japan after VJ-Day.

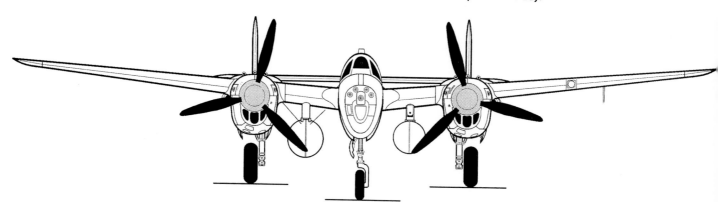

Front view of P-38L.

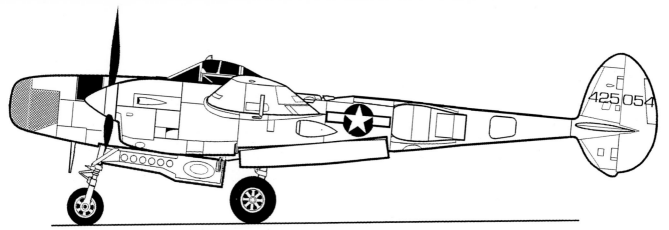

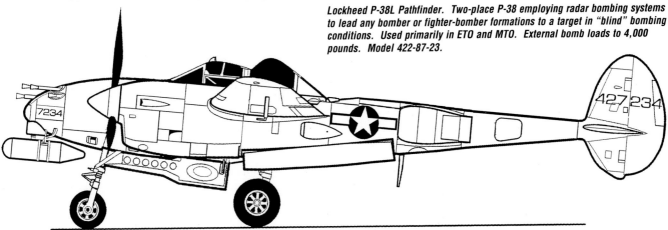

Lockheed P-38L Pathfinder. Two-place P-38 employing radar bombing systems to lead any bomber or fighter-bomber formations to a target in "blind" bombing conditions. Used primarily in ETO and MTO. External bomb loads to 4,000 pounds. Model 422-87-23.

Lockheed P-38M-6-LO Night Lightning. One prototype developed at Hammer Field, Fresno, California. Seventy-five P-38L-5-LO aircraft modified to P-38M-6-LO, probably at Dallas, Texas. Correct performance ratings for V-1710F-30 engines: 1500 bhp for takeoff; 1725 bhp WEP (5 minutes) power at critical altitude, 24,000 feet. Interception equipment: ASH (AN/APS-4) radar.

Note: XP-58 drawings are not to scale used for P-38.

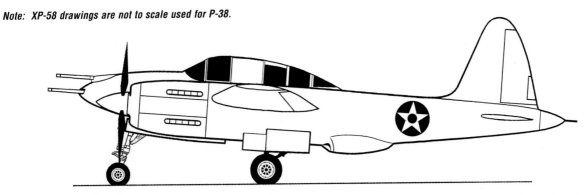

Lockheed XP-58 proposal of June 1940, to comply with Lightning Foreign Release Agreement. Powered by two Pratt & Whitney X-1800 (XH-2600) 24-cylinder liquid-cooled engines. Armament: Four 37-mm M-9 cannons and two tail-mounted .50-caliber machine guns. Not built in this configuration.

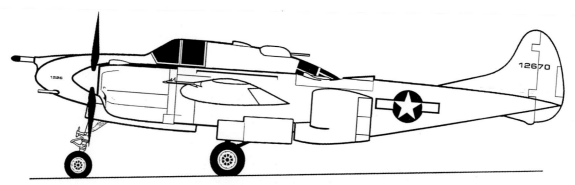

Lockheed XP-58, Model 20-86-04 Chain Lightning (AC41-2670). Two Allison V-3420 turbosupercharged engines rated at 3000 bhp each. Armed with one 75-mm T-9 cannon and six .50-caliber machine guns. Built and flown. Project engineer - Neil Harrison.

## LOCKHEED P-38 CONTRACT PRICES, WITH CONTEMPORARY AIRCRAFT

### PRICE COMPARISONS

| Make and Model | 1938 | 1939-41 | 1942 | 1943 | 1944 | 1945 |
|---|---|---|---|---|---|---|
| Lockheed P-38 | $163,000 | $134,280 | $120.407 | $105.567 | $97,147 | $95,150 |
| Boeing B-17 | | $301,221 | $258,949 | $204,270 | | $187,742 |
| North American B-25 | | $180,031 | $153,396 | $151,894 | $142,194 | $116,752 |
| Republic P-47 | | $113,246 | $105,594 | $104,258 | $85,578 | $83,001 |

SOURCE: Army Air Forces Statistical Digest

NOTE: Lockheed Aircraft Corp. delivered (according to their records) a total of 9,924 Lightning airplanes. An actual count of constructor's numbers and customer serial numbers (cross-checked against AFPI Form 41) indicates that 9,925 were actually delivered, excluding the XP-58 aircraft. Included are 9,425 fighters (P-38 type) and 500 reconnaissance (F-4/F-5 type) aircraft. Add 113 fighters delivered in 1945 by the Nashville Division of Consolidated-Vultee (LV) for a total of 10,038. Col. Cass Hough confirmed that three 322-B fighters were delivered to RAF establishments in the United Kingdom on loan; however, LAC totals for the 322-61-04 (23 aircraft) and the 322-62-18 (120 aircraft) do not match USAAF records exactly. All Lightning I models (143 airframes) are included in the AAF records, giving proof that the British never accepted even one 322-B.

The AAF accepted 22 unmodified airplanes as P-322-I trainers, apparently taking delivery of the three aircraft in the U.K., but no disposition is given in any known source. (Lockheed records indicate that 23 remained in unmodified form.) The AAF records show that there were 121 Lightning I airframes modified to P-322-II configuration (322-62-18), having been converted from V-1710C-15 engines to V-1710F-2 engines. (Supposedly, that was a Lockheed Aircraft Corp. factory rework.)

It should be noted that the actual cost to Lockheed (offset by the $163,000 provided by the contract) of the Model 22 (XP-38) airplane was $761,000. Without the Hudson contract, the company would have been bankrupted by the XP-38 program.

### BACKGROUND INFORMATION

U.S. dollar valuations in 1939-45 are in stark contrast to values some 50 years later. For example: Average hourly wage in the American aircraft industry was 75 cents per hour. The average civil service salary at Wright Field was $160 per month, based on a 44-hour week.

A new 1941 Packard 110 coupe was priced at $907 plus tax, F.O.B. Detroit. Including tax and fully equipped (radio, heater, whitewall tires), a new 1941 Ford Deluxe convertible was delivered at a dealership for $1,077 retail (Detroit).

A new 2-bedroom, 1-bath house in Inglewood, California, was generally priced less than $3,000, requiring a $50 down payment.

*Life* magazine was 10 cents per copy. Twelve subscription issues of *Flying & Popular Aviation* cost $2.50. In California, lemons cost 5 cents a dozen. Navel oranges were priced at 35 cents for two dozen.

## LOCKHEED DRAWING STRUCTURE BREAKDOWN FOR YP-38
(Selected Drawings Only)

| DRAWING NUMBER | DRAWING TITLE |
|---|---|
| 22025 | Final Assembly |
| 220047 | Body Assembly |
| 223000 | Empennage Assembly |
| 230002 | Wing Assembly – Complete |
| 220050 | Fuselage Structure Assembly |
| 230800 | Center Section Assembly – Complete* |
| 221006 | Removable Nose Assembly – Center Section |
| 225179 | Main Landing Gear Assembly |
| 225000 | Main Landing Gear Installation |
| 225034 | Nose Landing Gear Assembly |
| 225080 | Nose Landing Gear Installation |
| 224000 | Nacelle Installation |
| 224201 | Engine Installation |
| 224001 | Supercharger Installation |
| 224200 | Power Plant Installation |
| 230845 | Fixed Equipment Installation |
| 226000 | Surface Controls Installation |
| 227700 | Armament Installation |
| 227651 | .30- & .50-caliber Gun Charger Installation |
| 232882 | Army Insignia Diagram |

*Approved by C.L Johnson 9/30/39*

\* Includes "gondola" and wing center section.
*Once assembled, they are not separable.*
*(Total rebuild might be possible, with some jigs.)*

**Allison V-1710F-Series engine.**

**Service Test Lockheed YP-38, 1941.**

## LOCKHEED P-38M-6-LO NIGHT FIGHTERS

All P-38M-6-LOs, the only officially recognized night fighters in the Lightning line, were derived from P-38L-5-LO aircraft delivered at random to the Lockheed Modification Center. None of the P-38Ms was manufactured as such on the Burbank or Nashville assembly lines

One "Proofing" night fighter aircraft was created at Fresno, California, and served as a development prototype for all subsequent P-38Ms. It was officially a P-38L-5-LO, AC44-25237. As modified, it was actually a P-38M in every detail.

A total of 75 Lockheed P-38Ls received all necessaary modifications. All were aircraft with Fiscal year 1944 serial numbers, i.e., AC44-XXXXX. This constitutes the only known complete listing of P-38M type aircraft:

26831, 26863, 26865, 26892, 26951, 26997, 26999, 27000, 27108, 27233, 27234, 27236-27238, 27245, 27249-27252, 27254, 27256-27258, 53011, 53017, 53019, 53020, 53022, 53023, 53025, 53029-53032, 53034, 53035, 53042, 53050, 53052, 53056, 53062, 53063, 53066-53069, 53073, 53074, 53076, 53077, 53079, 53080, 53082-53090, 53092-53098, 53100, 53101, 53106, 53107, 53109, 53110, 53112.

Seventy-five aircraft would constitute a basic fighter group. It would be a logical quantity to produce via the modification route.

P-38L-5-LO AC44-25237 was not painted black during its proofing trials. It remained in its natural metal finish with black lettering/numbers.

*Lockheed P-38M-6-LO Night Lightning.*

## 15 GOOD POINTS OF THE LOCKHEED P-38*

1. Basic wing design – stall, lift, vol., etc.
2. Center line fire of guns – good armament
3. Good forward visibility
4. Counter-rotating propellers to counteract torque and improve stability.
5. Turbosupercharging.
6. Structural strength.
7. Low basic drag.
8. High lift wing and flap configuration.
9. Good tricycle landing gear with ample size tires.
10. Ease of hanging on external stores of all types.
11. Compressibility control flap.
12. Power boost ailerons.
13. Lack of any flutter characteristics.
14. Favorable slipstream effects.
15. Reasonable size cockpit.

*\* C. L. "Kelly" Johnson's comments, Split-S Society P-38 Symposium 9/23/77. (Warren Bodie, Chairman. Symposium co-produced with G. O. Glenn).*

## 15 BAD POINTS OF THE LOCKHEED P-38*

1. Engine problems.
   A. Back-firing – blew wing intercooler.
   B. Cooling – 3L – spark plugs
      (battle of San Fernando Valley – 9 engs.)
   C. Solid fuel!! – glass lines.
2. Wing intercooler – OK for 1000 hp, but not enough cooling for higher power – waited too long to go to conventional intercooler.
3. Compressibility limit Mach 0.68 to 0.7 – wing thickness shape, and induced fuselage nacelle flow field the cause.
4. Insufficient cockpit heat!!
5. High aileron forces until power boost used (Gp. Capt. Bulman – "What is it for?")
6. Tail clearance for pilot on parachute bail out – elevator counterweights in the way.
7. Accessibility to engine and equipment in booms poor – very crowded.
8. Sun heat effect on Curtiss propeller circuit breakers – difficulty in going around field with engines over-revving.
9. Turbosupercharger over-revving – use of a tachometer – metal deflector ring – special CLJ rigging of throttle.
10. Inability to use a turbine hood to get exhaust thrust – supercharger wouldn't take any back pressure.
11. Supply problems with two kinds of engine gear boxes and propellers to get counter rotation required.
12. Insufficient rear vision.
13. Difficult pilot entrance and exit provisions.
14. Hard to build – very tight tolerances and jigging required.
15. Sensitivity of wing fillet fits – difficult to maintain.

# GLOSSARY

| | |
|---|---|
| A&AEE | Aircraft & Armament Experimental Establishment |
| AAC | Army Air Corps |
| AAF | Army Air Force(s) |
| ACS | Army Chief of Staff |
| AEAF | Allied Expeditionary Air Force |
| AFPI | Air Force Production Inventory |
| AJAX | VIIIth Fighter Command HQ at Bushey Hall, England |
| ARGUMENT | Joint 8AF and 15AF Air Offensive against Germany |
| ATC | Air Transport Command |
| AVALANCHE | Invasion of Italy at Salerno, Sept. 1943 |
| BAYTOWN | British Invasion of Italy at Reggio, Sept. 1943 |
| BHP | Brake horsepower |
| BOLERO (Operation) | Transatlantic delivery of USAAF aircraft by air |
| BOLERO | Buildup of U.S. forces in U.K. to attack Europe |
| CBO | Combined Bomber Offensive |
| CG | Commanding General |
| CO | Commanding Officer |
| CORKSCREW | Allied Invasion of Pantelleria |
| C-B-I | China-Burma-India Theater |
| DFC | Distinguished Flying Cross |
| DSC | Distinguished Service Cross |
| DSM | Distinguished Service Medal |
| DUC | Distinguished Unit Citation |
| ETO | European Theater of Operations |
| FAD | Fairfield Air Depot |
| FEAF | Far East Air Force |
| FLAX | Operation to attack Axis transports shuttling between Europe and Tunisia |
| FRANTIC | Operation for shuttle bombing of Axis Europe from U.K., Italy and USSR |
| GHQ AF | General Headquarters Air Force |
| HUSKY | Invasion of Sicily |
| IAS | Indicated air speed |
| Jabo | *Jagdbomber* (Fighter-Bomber) |
| Jagd | Fighter/Pursuit |
| JG | *Jagdgeschwader* (Fighter Group) |
| L.A.T. | Lockheed Air Terminal (former Union Air Terminal) |
| MAAF | Mediterranean Allied Air Force |
| Mach's No. | Dr. Mach's relationship of a/c speed to the speed of sound (later, Mach No.) |
| MoS | Ministry of Supply |
| MTO | Mediterranean Theater of Operations |
| NAAF | Northwest African Air Force |
| NACA | National Advisory Committee for Aeronautics |
| NASAF | Northwest African Strategic Air Force |
| NRA | National Recovery Act |
| OPM | Office of Production Management |
| OVERLORD | Invasion of Occupied Western Europe |
| POINTBLANK | Combined Bomber Offensive against the *Luftwaffe* and German a/c industry |
| PINETREE | VIIIth Bomber Command Headquarters at High Wycombe, England |
| RAE | Royal Aeronautical Establishment |
| TAS | True airspeed |
| TDY | Temporary duty |
| TIAS | True indicted airspeed |
| TORCH | Invasion of North and Northwestern Africa, Nov. 1942 |
| USSAFE | United States Strategic Air Forces in Europe |
| USSTAF | Later designation for USSAFE |
| WEP | War Emergency Power (water injection) |
| WIDEWING | Eighth Air Force HQ at Bushy Park, England |
| WPA | Works Progress Administration |
| WPB | War Production Board |
| ZI | Zone of the Interior (United States) |
| ZG | *Zerstörergeschwader* (Destroyer/attack-fighter Group) |